William Carew Hazlitt

Third and final series of bibliographical collections and notes on early English literature,

1474-1700

William Carew Hazlitt

Third and final series of bibliographical collections and notes on early English literature, *1474-1700*

ISBN/EAN: 9783337718473

Printed in Europe, USA, Canada, Australia, Japan

Cover: Foto ©Lupo / pixelio.de

More available books at **www.hansebooks.com**

W. CAREW HAZLITT

THIRD AND FINAL SERIES

OF

BIBLIOGRAPHICAL

COLLECTIONS AND NOTES

ON

𝕰arly 𝕰nglish 𝕷iterature

1474—1700

LONDON

BERNARD QUARITCH, PICCADILLY

1887

The impression of this Book is strictly limited to 270 copies, of which 20 only are on Large Paper.

BALLANTYNE, HANSON & Co.

INTRODUCTION.

I VERY respectfully, yet with cordial pleasure, submit to such sections of the educated and reading English community in the United Queendom, the States of America, and elsewhere, as feel an interest in that early literature, which ought to be dear to the entire English-speaking race, a THIRD and FINAL Series of my BIBLIOGRAPHICAL COLLECTIONS AND NOTES, forming (with my *Handbook*), the fourth volume of my achievement in this province of research.

Charles Lamb says in one of his Letters that what a man could write, he ought to be able to read. So much the rather, then, what a man could write, I can at least describe.

The objection to the multiplication of alphabets by the sectional treatment, which I have adopted since the appearance of the *Handbook* in 1867, is a very valid objection indeed from the point of view of the consulter. But as this has been, and remains, a labour of love, and as the cost of production was a grave problem, I simply had no alternative ; and to the suggestion which I offered in a prior Introduction, that, after all, these serial volumes might be regarded in the same light as so many catalogues of public or private collections, I have now the gratifying announcement to add, that *a complete Index to the Handbook and the three Series of Collections and Notes* is in preparation by Mr. GRAY OF CAMBRIDGE, who has most generously volunteered to do the work, and will form a separate volume, to be published by Mr. Quaritch, when it is completed.

I have incorporated (generally with additions and corrections) in my volumes by degrees nearly the whole of the *Bibliotheca Anglo-Poetica*, Corser's *Collectanea* (excepting, of course, the lengthy and elaborate extracts and annotations), the British Museum Catalogue of *Early English Books to 1640*, the *Typographical Antiquities* of Ames, Herbert and Dibdin, the Chatsworth, Huth, Ashburnham, and other private cabinets, and the various publications of Haslewood, Park, Utterson, and Collier.

Since the Second Series came from the press in 1882, several large private libraries have been dispersed under the hammer, and all the articles previously overlooked by me have been duly taken up into my pages. I may enumerate, for example's sake, the celebrated collections of the Earl of Jersey, the Earl of Gosford, Mr. James Crossley of Manchester, Mr. Payne Collier, the Duke of Marlborough, Mr. Hartley, Mr. N. P. Simes of Horsham, Sir Richard Colt Hoare, Mr. Michael Wodhull, Sir Thomas Phillipps of Middle-Hill, the Rev. J. Fuller Russell, Mr Henry Pyne, and Professor Solly.

For kindness and help extended to me I have again to thank my friends at the British Museum, especially Mr. George Bullen and Mr. George Fortescue; and Messrs. Sotheby, Wilkinson, and Hodge, the eminent auctioneers, have continued to afford me every possible facility in examining, before the time of sale, the important properties which have passed through their hands during the last five or six years—since, indeed, the former volume was completed and published.

The leading topics under which the articles in these COLLECTIONS range themselves are :—

A. B. C.
Agriculture.
Ale.
Almanacks.
Americana.
Anatomy.
Angling.
Archæology.
Architecture.
Arithmetic.
Astrology.
Astronomy.
BALLADS.
Bee-culture.
Beer.
Bibliography.

Biography.
Botany.
Brewing.
Calligraphy.
Cambro-British literature.
Cartography.
Chemistry.
Chocolate.
Civil War in England, 1641-8.
Coal.
Coffee.
Coins and Coinage.
Colonization.
Cookery.
Courtesy and Deportment.
Currency.

Cyder.
Dancing.
Demonology.
Distillation.
Dictionaries.
Drama.
Drolleries.
East India Company.
Education.
Emigration and Settlement.
Enclosure.
English books printed abroad.
Engraving.
Essays.
Facetiæ.
Farriery.
Familism.
Fencing.
Finance.
Fine Arts.
Fishery.
Floriculture.
Folklore.
Fortification.
FRANCE.
Free thought.
Gardening.
Geography.
Germany.
Grammar.
Greek authors.
Herbals.
HISTORY, County.
———— English.
———— Family.
———— Foreign.
———— Local.
———— Natural.
Horsemanship.
Horticulture.
Hydrostatics.
IRELAND.
Italy.
Jest-books.
Jews.
Law and Jurisprudence.
Liturgies.
LONDON.
Love.
Marriage.
Maritime affairs.
Mathematics.
Medicine.

Memoirs.
Military science.
Mineral waters.
Mining.
Music.
Navy.
Netherlands.
Numismata.
Occult sciences.
Orthography.
Painting.
PARLIAMENT.
Phenomena (Fires, Floods, Earthquakes, &c.)
Philology.
Philosophy.
Poetry.
Popery.
Population.
Portugal.
Prayer, Forms of.
Primers.
Proverbs.
Psalms.
Puritanism.
Registration of land.
Roman authors.
Roman Catholic books.
Romances.
Russia.
School-books.
Scotland.
Scriptures.
Sculpture.
Sects.
Songs.
Spain.
Sports and Games.
Statutes.
Stuart Family.
Surgery.
Surveying.
Tea.
Tenures.
Topography.
Trade.
TYPOGRAPHY.
Universities.
Voyages and Travels.
Wales.
Wine.
Witchcraft.
Women.

The stress laid by Lord Macaulay on the value of pamphlets in illustrating history was of course only declaratory, as they say of statutes. Their importance had been recognised long before his time by the publication of the *Harleian Miscellany* and the *Somers Tracts*.

My pages abound with this fugitive literature, from the earliest period to the accession of the House of Orange; and I may add that I have had the advantage of recently going through the *original series* of volumes collected by Lord Chancellor Somers (30 folios), and selecting for my purpose a large number of rare broadsides and other small temporary pieces, besides the exceedingly rare and interesting *editio princeps* of the *Laws of New York*, 1694, and other examples of early New York typography. I am glad to have had this historical set of books under my own eyes; and it furnished me with the means of supplying many gaps.

The vast stores of which I have constituted myself the cataloguer and describer, are, of course, of various degrees of merit, just as they are of an endless variety of character. First-rate capacity and value are generally calculable by units. There is only one Shakespear (although the admirers of Mr. Browning imagine that there are two!), only one Raleigh, only one Cromwell.

But my COLLECTIONS, when they are attentively looked at, present more than a single aspect, in which they possess, or should possess, interest and worth for my countrymen and for English speakers throughout the world. For they are rich in historical, political, social, and literary illustrations of every kind. They are monumental records of the life of the past. They are the legacies of thousands of intelligent human beings, who were to their century what we try to be to ours—contributing factors to its improvement, instruction, and pleasure.

Among other noteworthy points, the extraordinary storehouse of proper and Christian names, which the present volume and its predecessors constitute, the biographical information, the extensive assemblage of broadsides relating to topographical and personal history, and the clues casually afforded by the prefaces or dedications to old ways of life and obsolete street nomenclature, are deserving of attention.

Notions concerning authors and other public men are apt to vary and fluctuate. The line of distinction between Shakespear and his contemporaries was not so broadly drawn a century ago; he has been an object of idolatry scarcely more than thirty years, when the writings of Schlegel, Tieck, Coleridge, Lamb, and Hazlitt had had their influence in directing the public attention to his unique power.

Yet in some respects the obscurer writers of other times have an even stronger claim on our attention than those who are, to say nothing more, too well known and too firmly established in favour to require bibliographical resuscitation or enshrinement. It adds little indeed to Spenser or Milton to accord them a place in these columns of mine; but they find themselves in the book as of right, and I am glad enough to see them here; for they brighten the gloom, and leaven the dough.

The strength of this and the three companion volumes lies, however, after all, not in the registration of first-rate works and standard authors of the past, but in the classified assortment of about five and twenty thousand articles belonging to all branches of literature, science, and art, under the names of the writers, or, where they are anonymous, under the subject or the locality with which they happen in each case to be connected. How striking becomes, under such conditions, the aphorism that Union is Power! In the most cursory and superficial study of the following pages, hundreds of items meet the eye which have possibly no individual significance or weight, but which, ranged under heads pursuantly to a given plan, acquire a clear aggregate utility and rank.

The sooner the widely-prevailing misapprehension as to our independence of the past is removed, assuredly the better. Between the transactions of prior ages and of this one, which is before our eyes, there are, on the contrary, an indissoluble link and uncountable points of touch and relationship, and by the light of what was done or thought by our progenitors, I conceive it possible, nay as much as probable, that the now extant Englishman may come to a readier and more true comprehension, amid the ever-recurrent incidents of political and social life, of the nature, bearings, and just treatment of questions of the day.

The England in which we dwell is one with the England which lies behind us. So far as the period which I comprehend goes, it is one country and one race; and I do not think that we should precipitately and unkindly spurn the literature, which our foregoers left to us and to our descendants for ever, because it may at first sight strike us as irrelevant to our present wants and feelings, because it may seem unpolished, or because we may be of opinion that sufficient and best for an age is the work of an age.

The considerer of modern opinions and customs is too little addicted to Retrospection. He seems to me too shy of profiting, on the one hand by the counsels or suggestions, on the other by the mistakes, of the men who have crossed the unrepassable line; who have already dealt with the topics and problems with which he has to deal; who have advised or resisted the Remedial Measures which he is perhaps at this very moment advising or resisting.

It appears as if each generation of us preferred to think, discover, err for itself, somewhat on the same principle as the little maiden in the story, who would rather see and suffer the folly of her conduct than listen to the maternal warning.

Let me exhort our public men henceforward, if they seek to preside with honour and influence over an educated Democracy, to lend closer attention to literature and its teachings; to have an eye to something higher and broader than mere Parliamentary effect; to hold it as part of the education of an English statesman to cultivate an intellectual reach and a philosophical outlook, and not to live, as it were, from hand to mouth, and set his watch to Greenwich time.

I should love to see our governing body calculating their speech and thought for something more solid and noble than a transient party meridian, and not ostensibly judging the treasures and lessons of bygone times to be as lumpish and inarticulate as the pillar of salt, which had been the wife of Lot the Just.

The politician, whose sentiments are as current as the coinage, forgets that the past and the present are a Federation in as large a degree as we and our colonies are. He can judge only by halves. Arithmetically speaking, he is not an integer, but a fraction. Let him take a new departure, and unite the reputation for culture with enlarged administrative sympathies and experience. It seems strange that our public men should not sometimes cast their eyes back and study questions which come before them by the light of their aspect or handling in former days. But the statesman aspires to be a creator of history; and, God-amercy, very odd history he often creates. Turning to IRELAND alone, what a number of books there are which would yield suggestive and profitable matter to the Executive! I annex the short titles of a few which readily present themselves. But there are many more in this and also in the other volumes, as a reference to the GENERAL INDEX will shew. They were chiefly written by men of experience and observation, in some cases by eye-witnesses or by practical politicians:—

Borlase (E.), The History of the Execrable Irish Rebellion, folio, 1680.

C. (J.), The State of the Papist and Protestant Proprietors in the Kingdom of Ireland, 1641-53, 4°, 1689.

Eachard (Laurence), An Exact Description of Ireland, 12°, 1691.

French (Nicholas), Narrative of the Earl of Clarendon's Settlement and Sale of Ireland. 4", 1676, 1704.

Story (George), True and Impartial History of the most Material Occurrences in Ireland during the Two last Years, 4°, 1690.

Walker (George), True Account of the Siege of Derry, 4°, 1689.

Walsh (Peter), A Prospect of the Estate of Ireland, 8°, 1682.

Ware (Sir James), Antiquities and History of Ireland, folio, 1705.

The truth is, that it was not my original intention to devote so considerable a space to Irish political and general literature; but the late Mr. Henry Bradshaw informed me, when I last saw him in London, that the project for publishing a new *Bibliotheca Hibernica* had been, as he understood, relinquished, and I therefore resumed my old practice of taking notes of such items as fell in my way, or were more or less readily accessible.

The extensive assemblage of tracts and broadsides on Irish affairs, which I have now registered, cannot be ignored by any future historian.

Macaulay employed that class of material to a certain extent in his book; but his researches were very imperfect and superficial.

It should be observed that I have made it enter into my scheme, in this as well as in the other divisions or instalments of my labours in this particular direction, to furnish the reader or consulter with something more than the bare title of a book in all instances where I perceived matter of special interest in the preface or the dedication, or the body of the volume; and even if the circumstances did not necessitate such a course, I have laid before the public the full particulars from the work itself, and not, as is generally done, an abbreviated text of it. The cogency of resorting to originals in all instances has grown upon me more and more; and the difference between a bibliographical account of any given production with that production lying before you, and an account borrowed, and perhaps spoiled in the loan, is wider than the difference between the Portland Vase and the cheapest *replica* of it, since in the former case the original lines, the *ipsissima verba*, are lost. It might be thought invidious if I were to set in parallel columns my own description of a book and that of Lowndes or Allibone; but the juxtaposition would generally prove edifying, and not seldom ludicrous. In my *Handbook*, 1867, which was my maiden essay in the present department, 1 inserted entries for which I was a debtor to others; and I have found it the rule, not the exception, that the discrepancy between the actual titles and those supplied by my authorities was only a question of degree. I have it in my power to adduce examples, where the two would be hardly identifiable.

Now, I must conclude that these men, who enjoyed the highest reputation for accuracy and scholarship, were not incompetent to transcribe what they had under their eyes, but were deficient in a sense of what they owed to their immediate readers, to posterity, and to themselves.

It is in turning over the pages of such works as the Grenville, Chatworth, Corser, and Huth Catalogues, that one becomes more thoroughly aware of the magnitude of an attempt to grasp the whole of our miscellaneous early printed literature in a small series of volumes like these of mine. A large private library is, after all, a mere handful—a book here and there; while the contents of the *Bibliotheca Anglo-Poetica* or the Rowfant gatherings may be held, as it were, between finger and thumb. Taking away the ordinary publications and works of reference, which are or may be common to every collection, all libraries, save the British Museum and the Bodleian, are individually unimportant in a broad and general sense, and are apt to be regarded by an experienced investigator with the eyes with which Mr. Gulliver saw the folk of Lilliput.

This feeling may sound disrespectful and ungracious, though I have no wish that it should be so construed; and it may prove to be at variance with that entertained by others. But it has forced itself upon me marvellously since I have had such unparalleled opportunities of gauging the most famous assemblages of ancient and curious literature formed in Great Britain in the course of the last and present century, as they have periodically migrated from their resting-places to the sale-room.

I imagine that of all the private collectors who ever lived, the one whose range was vastest, and whose familiarity with the innumerable volumes which he amassed together was most conspicuous, was RICHARD HEBER; and I will say that, had he made it part of his gigantic plan to reduce his acquisitions to some lucid order, the *Bibliotheca Heberiana* would have remained the grandest monument of the kind ever built up by an individual.

But with all his perseverance, enthusiasm, knowledge, and scholarship, Heber unhappily failed to unite judgment and method; and his incomparable library resembled the condition of the universe, as it is depicted in the opening lines of the *Metamorphoses* of Ovid.

I trust that it may not be considered that, in describing an insignificant and obscure publication, I have often erred in being too copious. But I desire it to be recollected in my defence, that (as I have said) the object which I have been all along proposing to myself was not one, but manifold; that I aimed at laying before my constituents in this and other countries a good deal more than a meagre summary of bibliographical particulars; and that, so far as considerations of space and cost might allow, I aspired to raise my Work to the dignity of a Catalogue Raisonné, or, at all events, of a Descriptive Calendar. In order, however, not to claim on my title-page more than appears to be my fair due, I have christened the Three Series now completed BIBLIOGRAPHICAL COLLECTIONS AND NOTES.

In honest truth, with this unexampled accumulation of faithful and laborious record before them for reference and judgment, my fellow-students will, I hope and believe, be brought round to the conclusion that the long space of time, and the large proportion of my maturer life, consumed in accomplishing the result which they see, piecemeal and volume by volume as I could, not only without any pecuniary requital, but at a very serious loss, have not from a literary and public point of view been uselessly expended.

I have only to add, that for the loan of the block of Wynkyn de Worde's device, which is on the title-page, I am indebted to the courtesy of Messrs. Wyman & Son. The other three woodcuts are from the originals in my own possession.　　　　　　　　　　　　　　W. C. H.

BARNES COMMON, SURREY,
January 1887.

BIBLIOGRAPHICAL

COLLECTIONS AND NOTES.

A. Th., *J.C.*
Catholiqve Traditions... London Printed by W. Stansby, for Henry Fetherstone, ... 1610. 4°, A—Ii 2 in fours. Dedicated by the author to Prince Henry.

A. T.
A Satyr against Vertue. *Aude aliquid* ... Juven. Sat. London : Printed in the Year, 1679. 4°, A—B in fours. In verse.

A. T.
A Letter of a Catholike Man beyond the seas, written to his friend in England : Inclvding Another of Peter Coton Priest, of the Society of Iesus, to the Queene Regent of France. Translated out of French into English. Tovching the imputation of the death of Henry IIII. late K. of France, to Priests, Jesuites, or Catholicke doctrine ... Permissu Superiorum. M.DC.X. 8°, A—C in eights. *B. M.*

A. W., *Barrister at Law, Author of the first Answer to the late Chief Justice Herbert's Defence of the Dispensing Power.*
An Apology for the East-India Company: With an Account of some large Prerogatives of the Crown of England, anciently exercised and allowed of in our Law, in relation to foreign Trade and foreign Parts. ... London, Printed for the Author, 1690. 4°, A—E in fours.

A. B. C.
The A. B. C. Or The Institution of a Christian. ... Dvblin, Printed by the Company of Stationers. 1631. 8°, A in eights. Engl. and Irish. *B. M.*

ABERCROMBY, DAVID.
A Discourse of Wit. *Qui velit ingenio cedere rarus erit.* London, Printed for John Wild ... 1686. 12°. A, 6 leaves: B—L 10 in twelves. With some verses at the end. Dedicated to Alexander Murray of Blackbarronie Esq.

ADAMS, EDWARD.
The Young Souldiers Desire Answered : Or, A Piece of Military Discipline, wherein is shewed, Distances, Facings, Doublings, Counter-Marches, and Wheelings. With some Firings both Offensive and Defensive against an Enemy. By Edward Adams. ... London : Printed for John Evans at the Marygold in Perpool Lane, and are to be sold by William Jacob, ... and by the Author in Shore-ditch. 1678. 4", A—E 2 in fours. Dedicated to Mr. John Evans captain of a trained Band under Lord Craven.

ADAMS, JOHN.
Proposals for the Actual Survey of all the Counties in England and Wales, by Mr. Adams of the Inner-Temple. [1690.], Folio, 2 leaves.

ADIS, HENRY.
A Fannaticks Testimony against Swearing ; Being an Answer to Four Books published by John Tombes, Jeremiah Ives, and Theophilus Brabourne : But more especially to that by Henry Den. By Henry Adis, a Baptized Believer, undergoing the Name of a Free-Willer ; and also most ignomineously by the tongue of infamy, called a Fannatick, or a mad man. ... London, Printed by S. Dover ... 1661. 4°, A—F in fours, and a leaf of G. *B. M.*

ADVICE.
A Timely Advice. Or, A Treatise of Play, and Gaming. Wherein is shewed how far forth it is lawfull to use such Play : And how dangerous and hurtfull by excesse to abuse it. ... London, Printed by Th. Harper for Richard Stevenson, and are to be sold at his shop in Princes street neare Lincolns Inne fields. 1640. 8°, A—I 6 in eights, I 6 with the *Imprimatur. B. M.* (*Bliss's copy.*)

A

ÆLIANUS.

The Tactiks of Ælian Or art of embattailing an army after ye Grecian manner Englished & illustrated wth figures throughout & notes vpon ye Chapters of ye ordinary motions of ye Phalange by I. B. The exercise military of ye English by ye order of that great Generall Maurice of Nassau Prince of Orange . . . is added. At London for Laurence Lisle & are to be sold at his shoppe . . . [1616.] Folio. Title engraved by Ægidius Gelius of Wondrichem in Holland, dated 1616, 1 leaf: dedication to Prince Charles by Jo. Bingham the translator, dated "From my Garrison at Woudrichem in Holland the 20 of September 1616," 2 leaves: A, 7 leaves: B—O 3 in sixes, besides plates at pp. 46, 64 (4), 80, 86, 92, 98 (2), 106 (3), 110 (2), 114 (2 one unmarked of an elephant caparisoned for war), 116 (4), 132 (2), 136 (4), 140, 142 (3), 144 (4), 146 (5), 148 (5), 154, 156 (2); nearly all of which are marked with the chapters, to which they refer.

ÆSOP.

[The Fables of Æsop. Colophon] Finis. Emprynted by Richard Pynson. Folio, [a—]s 5 in sixes, s 6 having been probably blank. With numerous fine large woodcuts. *B. M.*

> This copy begins on sign c i, and is otherwise complete. On the last leaf is the autograph of an early owner: "R. Johnson pro. xij^d. 1520." The last figure of the date has been altered so as to resemble 6.
>
> This is an altogether different impression from that described in the *Handbook*, 1867, and of later execution.

The Fables of Æsop . . . . The Third Edition, wherein are the Compleat Set of Cutts. London, Printed for T. Basset . . . 1683. 8°, A—R 2 in eights: The Annotations, (a)—(d 6) in eights: vol. 2, *B—*S 6 in eights, besides 3 leaves with title and Table: Annotations, (*a) —(*b) in eights. With a frontispiece to each volume and a plate to each Fable.

Æsop's Fables, In English and Latin, Interlineary, . . . The Second Edition with Sculptures. By John Locke, Gent. London: Printed for A. Bettesworth, . . . 1723. 8°. a, 4 leaves: A—Y 4 in eights. With 74 small engravings in compartments.

Æsop at Bathe, Or, A few Select Fables in Verse. By a Person of Quality. London, Printed for A. Baldwin in Warwicklane. MDCXCVIII. 8°. Title and preface, 3 leaves: B—E in fours.

Æsop at Tunbridge. Or, A few select Fables in Verse. By no Person of Quality. London: Printed, and are to be Sold by E. Whitlock, . . 1698. 8°, A—C 4 in eights.

Old Æsop at White-Hall, Giving Advice to the Young Æsops at Tunbridge and Bath: Or, some Fables relating to Government. By a Person of what Quality you please. London, Printed, and Sold by J. Nutt, . . . 1698. 8°. A, 3: B—E in fours. In verse.

Æsop at Paris, His Letters and Fables. Translated from the Original French. Printed in the Year 1701. 8°, A—E in fours. Chiefly in verse.

Æsop at Court. Or, State Fables. Vol. I. Vendidit hic auro patriam . . . Virg. Æn. London, Printed and Sold by J. Nut, . . . 1702. 8°, A—F 2 in fours, A 1 with half-title. In verse.

Æsop Return'd from Tunbridge: Or, Æsop out of his Wits. In a Few Select Fables, in Verse. London, Printed for J. F. in Bedlam. [1702.] 8°. A, 4: B, 8: C, 7: D, 4.

Æsop at Oxford: Or, A few select Fables in Verse, ... London: Printed in the Year 1709, . . . 8°. A, 2 leaves with title and dedication to Thomas Lewis Esqr. M.P. for Whitchurch, Hants: B—L 2 in fours.

Æsop at Utrecht. London, Printed in the Year 1712, and Sold by the Booksellers. Price 1d. 8°, 4 leaves. In verse.

AFRICA.

The Discription of the Countrey of Aphrique, the fyrst part of the worlde, with the cituation of the countreys together with the perticuler maners, lawes, and ceremonies, of dyuers people inhabetyng in the same part Translated out of French into Englyshe by Wyllyam Prat of London, the fyrst daye of the newe yere, M. CCCCC L. IIII. Rede it dylygently. Marke it perfectly. Reuolue it thorowly. Beare it equally Beholde the auctours simplicitie. And prayse God almyghty. [Col.] Imprinted at Londō in Fletestrete at the signe of the George next to saynt Dunstones Churche by Wyllyam Powel. 8°, black letter, A—L in eights, L 8 blank. Dedicated by Prat to William Courtney, Earl of Devonshire. *Grenv. Coll.*

> The Epistle to Courtenay is of some biographical interest.

Act for a Company Tradeing to Affrica,

and the Indies. June 26, 1695. [Col.] Edinburgh, Printed by the Heirs and Successors of Andrew Anderson, ... 1695. Folio, 4 leaves.

AGA, ZARAIN.

A Relation of the Late Siedge and taking of the City of Babylon by the Turke. As it was written from thence by Zarain Aga, one of his Captaines to Caymaran (his Brother) Vice-Roy in Constantinople. . . . Englished by W. H. London, Printed by I. Raworth, for N. Butter, and N. Bourne. 1639. 4°, A—E in fours, A 1 blank.

The translator, William Holloway, subscribes " The Coppy of a letter sent to a private merchant of London, from Ragouza."

AGER, THOMAS.

A Paraphrase on the Canticles, Or, Song of Solomon, By the late Learned, and Pious Protestant, Thomas Ager. London, Printed by A. Godbid and J. Playford, . . . 1680. 8°, A—Bb in eights.

AGIATIS.

Agiatis, Queen of Sparta, Or, The Civil Wars of the Lacedemonians, in the Reigns of the Kings Agis and Leonidas. In Two Parts. Translated out of French. . . . London, Printed by R. E. for R. Bentley. 1686. 8°, B—Q 6 in eights, and the title.

AGLIONBY, WILLIAM.

Painting Illustrated in Three Dialogues, Containing some Choice Observations upon the Art Together with the Lives of the Most Eminent Painters, from Cimabue, to the time of Raphael, and Michael Angelo. With an Explanation of the Difficult Terms. London, Printed by John Gain, for the Author, . . . MDCLXXXV. 4°. Title and *Imprimatur*, 2 leaves : dedication with the name of the dedicatee left unsupplied, 2 leaves : a—d 2 in fours : A—3 C 2 in fours.

AGRIPPA, H. C.

Three Books of Occult Philosophy, Written by Henry Cornelius Agrippa, of Nettesheim, Counsellor to Charles the Fifth, Emperor of Germany : And Iudge of the Prerogative Court. Translated out of the Latin into the English Tongue, By J. F. London, Printed by R. W. for Gregory Moule, . . . 1651. 4°. Portrait. Encomium in verse by Eugenius Philalethes, 1 leaf : title, 1 leaf : Life, 1 leaf : translator's Dedication to Dr. Child, M.D., 2 leaves : A—Qq 2 in eights.

AHUDERNUS, JOSEPHUS.

The True History of the Jacobites of Ægypt, Lybia, Nubia, &c. Their Origine, Religion, Ceremonies, Laws, and Customs. Whereby you may see how they differ from the Jacobites of Great Britain. Translated by a Person of Quality from the Latin of Josephus Ahudernus, a Man of Integrity, and born in Cairo in Ægypt. London, Printed for Eliphal Jaye. . . . MDCXCII. 4°, A—E in fours. *B. M.*

AINSWORTH, R.

The Most Natural and Easie Way of Institution : Containing Proposals for making a Domestic Education less Chargeable to Parents and more Easie and Beneficial to Children. By which Method, Youth may not only make a very considerable Progress in Languages, but also in Arts and Sciences, in Two Parts. . . . The Second Edition, with Additions. London, Printed for Christopher Hussey, . . . 1699. 4°, A—D in fours. Dedicated to Sir William Hustler, M.P.

ALBAN OR ALBON, ST., *Protomartyr*.

Cest la vie de monseigneur sainct albain. roy de hongrie et martir. [Col.] Cy finit la vie du glorieux martir möseigneur sainct albain roy de de [*sic*] hongrie. translate na gueres de latin en fräcoys. Imprime a lyon sur le rone. Le xviij. iour dauril. L'an de grace. Mcccclxxxiij. 4°, a—c in eights : d, 6, d 6 blank.

Syston Park Sale, Dec. 1884, No. 2040.

ALBERTUS MAGNUS.

Liber aggregationis seu liber secretor? Alberti magni de virtutibus herbar? lapidum & animalium quorumd? ℂ Liber primus de viribus quarund? herbar? [Col.] Albertus Magnus de Secretis nature Explicit Necnon per me Wilhelmum de Mechlinia Impressus In opulentissima Ciuitate Londoniarū Juxta pontem qui vulgariter dicitur Flete brigge. [About 1480.] 4°, a—f 4 in eights, text commencing with a headline on a ij and colophon occurring on f ij, the remaining half-sheet occupied by observations on the zodiac, feasts, &c.

Syston Park Sale, Dec. 1884, No. 53. W. Herbert's copy with his autograph. In the conclusion the date 1476 is mentioned as an incidental illustration.

Incipiunt Secreta mulierum et virorum ab Alberto magno composita. [This is on the *verso* on the second leaf, the first and the *recto* of the second being occupied by a proemium. At the end occurs :] Finis huius tractatuli venerabilis Alberti magni. secreta expliciunt mulierum. [London, W. de Machlinia, about 1480.] 4°, a—g in eights=56 leaves. of which the first and last were apparently blank.

See Herbert's *Ames*, p. 1773.

ALCOCK, JOHN, *Bishop of Ely.*
Mons perfectionis. [A cut of a bishop.
On a ii *recto*, col. 1, occurs : Exortatio
facta Cartusiensibus & aliis religiosis p
reuerendū in cristo patrem & dūm domi-
nuȝ Johannē Alkok Eliens. episcopum.
The colophon reads :] Here endeth the
treatyse called Mons perfectionis. Emprynted by Rycharde Pynson in the . xiii.
yere of our souerayne lorde Kynge Henry
the . vii. [1497-8.] 4°, a — b in sixes :
c, 4 : d, 6 : e, 4, the last leaf with Pynson's
device only. *B. M.* (a i wanting.)
Compare Herbert's *Ames*, p. 244.
Mons perfectionis / otherwyse in Englysshe the hylle of perfeccyon. [Col.]
Enprynted at London in fletestrete at the
sygne of yᵉ sonne by Wynkin de worde/
the yere of our lorde . ᴍ. ᴄᴄᴄᴄ. & . i. & in
the yere of yᵉ reygne of yᵉ moost vyc-
toryous prynce our moost naturell souvo-
rayne lorde Henry the seuenth / at the
Instaunce of the reuerende relygyous fader
Thomas Pryour of the house of saynt
Anne yᵉ order of yᵉ Chartrouse. And
fynysshed the . xxvij. daye of yᵉ moneth of
Maye in the yere aboue sayd. 4°, A—D
in sixes : E, 3. In two columns.
Sothebys, June 26, 1885, No. 14. The
title is beneath a woodcut of a bishop or
prior holding a crozier, and there are others
at the back of the leaf and at the end. This
is the earliest book, which I have yet seen,
printed by De Worde in Fleet Street. The
Ortus Vocabulorum of 1500 has Westminster
in the imprint.

ALEHOUSES.
Articles of direction touching Alehouses.
. . . Imprinted at London by Robert
Barker . . . 1609. 4°, A—B in fours,
B 4 blank.

ALGIERS.
A Letter Written by the Governour of Algiers, to the States-General of the United
Provinces of the Low-Countreys, &c. In
relation to the Signing the Peace concluded between them. London, Printed
for Thomas Burrel, . . . 1679. Folio, 2
leaves.

ALMANAC.
Almanach Ephemerides In anno domini.
M.d.vii. in latitudo Oxonia . . . [London,
Richard Pynson, 1506-7.] 8°. With
woodcuts. *B. M.* (very imperfect).
The first page is occupied by the printer's
mark, beneath which occurs, perhaps in his
own hand : *Rychardus pynson huius scriptor.*

ALPHABETUM.
Alphabetvm Latino-Anglievm. [The rest
of the page is occupied by a series of Alphabets. Coloph.] : Londini in officina
Thomæ Bertheleti typis impress : Cum

priuilegio ad imprimendum solum. Anno·
ᴍ.ᴅ.xʟɪɪɪ. 4°, 4 leaves. *B. M.*
This copy is printed on vellum.

AMBOYNA.
A True Relation of the Unjust, Cruel,
and Barbarous Proceedings against the
English at Amboyna . . . London, Printed
for Will. Bentley, . . . Anno Domini 1651.
12°. *,* 6 leaves : A—H in twelves, H 12
blank, and a frontispiece.

AMERICA
[A Proclamation respecting Kidnapping
for the American Plantations.] December
the Thirtieth, 1682. London, Printed by
the Assigns of John Bill deceas'd : . . .
1682. A broadside.
Treaty of Peace, Good Correspondence &
Neutrality in America, Between the most
Serene and Mighty Prince James II. . . .
And . . . Lewis XIV. . . . Concluded the
16ᵗʰ Day of Novemb. 1686. . . In the Savoy : Printed by Thomas Newcomb, . . .
ᴍᴅᴄʟxxxvɪ. 4°, A—C 2 in fours.

[AMES, RICHARD.]
A Dialogue between Claret & Darby-
Ale, A Poem. Considered in an accidental
Conversation between two Gentlemen.
London : Printed for E. Richardson, 1692.
4°, A—C, 2 leaves each. *B. M.*
The Bacchanalian Sessions ; Or The Con-
tention of Liquors : With A Farewel to
Wine. By the Author of the Search after
Claret, &c. To which is added, A Satyrical
Poem on one who had injur'd his Memory.
London. Printed for E. Hawkins. 1693.
4°, A—E, 2 leaves each. In verse.

AMYRALDUS, MOSES.
A Discourse concerning the Divine Dreams
Mentioned in Scripture. . . . Translated
out of French, by Ja. Lowde, Fellow of
Clare-Hall in Cambridge. London, Printed
by A. C. for Walter Kettilby, . . . 1676.
8°. A—K 3 in eights, and a—e 4 in eights.
Dedicated by the translator to John Earl
of Bridgewater.

ANDERSON ALEXANDER.
Alexandri Andersoni Scoti Exercitationvm
Mathematicarvm Decas Prima . . . .
Parisiis, Apud Oliuerivm de Varenes
. . . . Anno 1619. 4°, ã, 2 leaves : A
—D 2 in fours. With diagrams. Dedi-
cated to Cardinal de Retz.

ANDREWS, EUSEBIUS.
The Last Speech of Col Eusebius Andrews,
Sometimes A Lawyer of Lincolns-Inne,
at the time of his Execution on the
Scaffold at Tower-hill, Thursday the 22
of August, 1650 : With Several questions
propounded to him by Doctor Stradling,

and his answer thereunto . . . London, Printed by John Clowes, 1650. 4°, 4 leaves.

ANDREWS, WILLIAM, *Student in Astrology.*

The Yearly Intelligencer, Or A Perfect Chronology : of all the Battailes, Sieges, Conflicts, Actions . . . which have happened in the World. From September the 29th 1671. to September the 29th 1672. With Allowance. London, Printed by E. Crowch, for T. Vere, . . . 1673. 4°, A—C in fours, C 4 blank.

The preface is dated from Radwinter, near Saffron-Walden.

ANNE OF CLEVES, *Queen Consort of England.*

Repvdio della Reina Maria [Anna] D'Inghilterra, Sorella del Duca di Cleues, & difesa sua con molta eloquentia inuerso il Re, tradotto di Franzese in Toscano dal Cap. Gio : Battista del Grillandari, Fiorentino. In Bologna . . 1558. 4°, A—G 2 in fours.

ANNE OF DENMARK, *Queen Consort of Great Britain.*

L'Ordre des Ceremonies Observees, a L'Enterrement de la Royne d'Angleterre. Depuis sa maison iusques en l'Eglise d'Ouestmest a Londres. Le 23. May. 1619. A Paris, Chez Abraham Savgrain, . . . M.DC.XIX. 8°, 4 leaves. *B. M.*

Academiæ Oxoniensis Fvnebria Sacra, Æternæ Memoriæ Serenissimae Reginae Annæ . . . Iacobi . . . Sponsæ, Dicata. Oxoniæ, Excudebant Joannes Lichfield, & Jacobvs Short, . . . Anno Dom. 1619. 4°, A—S in fours, S 4 blank.

ANNESLEY, ARTHUR, *Earl of Anglesey.*

Memoirs of the Right Honourable Arthur Earl of Anglesey, Late Lord Privy Seal. . . . Published by Sir Peter Pett Knight, Advocate General for the Kingdom of Ireland. London, Printed for John Dunton, . . . 1693. 8°. A, 8 leaves : a, 8 leaves : B—Z in eights. Dedicated by Pett to Lord Altham, after which is printed a letter from the Earl of Anglesey to Pett, dated from Totteridge, July 18, 1683.

ANSTRUTHER, SIR WILLIAM, OF ANSTRUTHER, *one of the Senators of the College of Justice.*

Essays, Moral and Divine ; In Five Discourses : . . . Edinburgh, Printed by George Mosman, Anno Dom. 1701. 4°. Title and three following leaves : ** and ***, 6 leaves : A—Gg in fours, Gg 4 blank. Dedicated to John Earl of Tillibardine.

One of these Essays is on Trifling Subjects, Stage-Plays, and Romances.

ANSWER.

A iust and moderate Answer To a most iniurious, and seditious Pamphlet, Intituled, An exact Discovery of Romish doctrine . . . With licence of Superior. 4°. A—P, 2 leaves each, P 2 with the *Errata,* and a, 2 leaves.

A witty Answer, And Vindication to a foolish Pamphlet, intituled New Orders New, Agreed upon by a Parliament of Round-heads. Or, Old Orders Old, newly vampt by a Parliament of Rattle-heads. . . . . London, Printed for Nat : Morton. 4°, 4 leaves.

ANTHONY, FRANCIS, *M.D.*

Medicinae Chymicæ, et veri Potabilis Auri assertio, ex lucubrationibus Fra. Antonii Londinensis, in Medicina Doctoris : . . . Cantabrigiæ, Ex officina Cantrelli Legge, . . . 1610. 4°. ¶, 4 leaves, first blank : A—H 2 in fours.

The Apologie, Or Defence of a Verity heretofore Pvblished concerning A Medicine called Avrvm Potabile, that is, the pure substance of Gold, prepared, and made Potable and Medicinable without corrosiues, . . . As an Vniversall Medicine. Together with the plaine, and true Reasons, manifold and irrefragable Testimonies of Fact, confirming the Vniuersalitie thereof. And lastly, the manner and order of administration or vse of this Medicine in sundrie Infirmities . . . London Printed by Iohn Legatt, 1616. 4°. ¶, 4 leaves, first blank : A—Q in fours, Q 4 blank.

The volume includes a very curious series of testimonials from persons who had tried this specific.

ANTHONY OF PADUA, ST.

The Life of St. Anthony of Padona, With the Miracles He wrought Both before, and after his Death. Written Originally in Italian, and Now done into English [by John Burbury.] Printed at Paris, 1660. Cum Privilegio. 8°. Title and dedication to Elizabeth Countess of Arundel and Surrey, 3 leaves : A—K 4 in twelves.

ANTIDOTE.

A Book of Directions And Cures done by that Safe and Succesful Medicine Called, An Herculean Antidote, Or The German Golden Elixir . . . . [London, about 1695.] 4°, 4 leaves. *B. M.*

It may be remarked that there is a very rich assortment of quack advertisements, &c., in the Museum under the Old House mark 8 N h 12, 2 vols. folio, and 1 vol. 8vo.

ANTROBUS, BENJAMIN.

Some Buds and Blossoms of Piety Also, Some Fruit of the Spirit of Love, which directs to the Divine Wisdom, Being A Collection of Papers, written by a Young Man, some of them in the time of his Apprenticeship, . . . Also, some Lines written by J. C. London, Printed and Sold by Andrew Sowle, 1684. 4°, A—K in fours, K 3–4 blank, and 5 leaves in A. With a metrical address to the Reader by the Editor, N. B.

Crossley, part 2, No. 307.

APOTHECARIES.

Lex Talionis ; Sive Vindiciæ Pharmaco-pœorum ; Or A Short Reply to Dr. Merrett's Book ; And Others, written against the Apothecaries : Wherein may be discovered The Frauds and Abuses committed by Doctors Professing and Practising Pharmacy. . . . London, Printed,and are to be Sold by Moses Pitt . . . 1670. 4°, A—E in fours.

APPIAN OF ALEXANDRIA.

The History of Appian of Alexandria, In Two Parts. . . . Made English by J. D. London, Printed for John Amery . . . 1679. Folio, A—4 L in fours, a leaf of 4 M, and a, 3 leaves between A and B. Dedicated by J. D. to the Earl of Ossory.

ARISTOTLE.

Incipit præfacio leonardi arretini in libros ethicorum. [Col.] Explicit textus ethicorum Aristotelis per leonardū arretinū lucidissime translatus correctissimeq̃ Impressus Oxoniis Anno dñi M.cccc.lxxix. 4°, a—x in eights ; y, 6. *B. M.* (a i wanting.)

The second book known to have been printed at Oxford.

Here begynneth the Nature, and Dysposycyon of the dayes in the weke, and sheweth what the Thondre in euery Moneth in the yere, chaunsyng. doth protend & sygnyfye / with the Course and dysposycyon, of the dayes of the Month : whiche be good, and whiche be bad : after the influences of y⁰ Moone, drawen out of a laten boke of Aristotiles de Astronomis. [Col.] Imprynted by me Robert Wyer, dwellynge at y⁰ sygne of saynt John euangelyst, in saynt Martyns parysshe, at charyuge crosse. 8°, a—b in eights. In verse.

ARMY.

The Argument against a Standing Army Rectified,and the Reflections and Remarks upon it in Several Pamphlets, Considered. In a Letter to a Friend. . . . *Pro Rege &*

Patria. London : Printed in the Year 1697. 4°, A—D in fours, A 1 with half-title, and D 4 blank.

The Second Part of an Argument, Shewing, that a Standing Army is inconsistent . . . London, Printed in the Year 1697. 4°, A—D 2 in fours.

A Letter to A. B. C. D. E. F. &c. Concerning their Argument about a Standing Army ; Examining their Notions of the supposed Gothick, or other Ballance, by the Constitution and Interest of the English Monarchy. . . . London, Printed for D. Brown . . . 1698. 4°, A—E in fours.

A Letter, ballancing the Necessity of keeping a Land-Force in time of Peace : With the Dangers that may follow on it. Printed in the Year 1697. 4°. Title preceded by a blank, 2 leaves : A, 4 : B, 2.

A Confutation of a late Pamphlet Intituled, A Letter Ballancing the Necessity . . . London, Printed for A. Baldwin, MDCXCVIII. 4°. A, 2 leaves : B—F 2 in fours.

A Letter from the Author of the Argument against a Standing Army, To the Author of the Ballancing Letter. . . . London, Printed in the Year, 1697. 4°, A—B in fours.

A Brief Reply to the History of Standing Armies in England. With some Account of the Authors. London : Printed in the Year 1698. 4°, A—D in fours.

A View of the Short History of Standing Armies in England. London : Printed in the Year MDCXCVIII. 4°. A—G, 2 leaves each.

The Case of Disbanding the Army at present, Briefly and Impartially Consider'd. Published by John Nutt, . . . 1698. 4°, A—B 2 in fours.

An Argument, Proving, that a small Number of Regulated Forces Established during the Pleasure of Parliament, cannot damage our Present Happy Establishment. . . . London : Printed for A. Baldwin, . . . MDCXCVIII. 4°. Title and Introduction. 2 leaves : B—C in fours : D—E, 2 leaves each.

The Case of a Standing Army Fairly and Impartially Stated. In Answer to the late History of Standing Armies in England : And other Pamphlets writ on that subject. London : Printed in the Year, 1698. 4°. Title and Preface, 3 leaves : D—E 2 in fours.

Reflections on the Short History of Standing Armies in England. In Vindication of His Majesty and Government. . . . London, Printed in the Year 1699. 4°. Title and Preface, 2 leaves : B—G, 2 leaves each : a, with Postscript, 2 leaves.

The Seaman's Opinion of a Standing Army in England, In Opposition to a Fleet at Sea, As the best Security of this Kingdom. In a Letter to a Merchant, Written by a Sailor. London, Printed for A. Baldwin, . . . 1699. 4°. A, 4 : B—E in twos.

A Letter to a Member of Parliament Concerning The Four Regiments commonly called Mariners. London, Printed for A. Baldwin . . . 1699. 4°, A—B in fours, B 4 blank.

A Short Vindication of Marine Regiments. In Answer to a Pamphlet, Entituled, A Letter to a Member of Parliament, concerning the Four Marine Regiments. London, Printed for A. Baldwin, . . . 1699. 4°, 6 leaves.

A True Account of Land Forces in England : And Provisions for them, from before the Reputed Conquest downwards : And of the regard had to Foreigners. In a Letter to A. B. C. T. T. T. &c. . . . London, Printed and are to be sold by J. Nutt, . . . 1699. 4°, B—K in fours, and the title.

ARNAULD, ANTOINE.
Le franc Discours. A Discourse, presented of late to the French King, in aunswer of sundry requests made vnto him, for the restoring of the Iesuits into Fraunce, as well by theyr freinds abroad, & at home, as by themselues in diuers Petitionarie Bookes. Written in French this present yeere, 1602. and faithfully Englished. Printed Anno. Domini. 1602. 8°, A—I 7 in eights, I 8 blank, and ¶, 3 leaves, with the Epistle to the Reader.

ARWAKER, EDMUND, *M.A.*
The Second Part of the Vision, A Pindarick Ode: Occasioned by Their Majesties Happy Coronation . . . . London, Printed by J. Playford for Henry Playford, . . . 1685. Folio, 5 leaves.

ASCENSIUS, JODOCUS BADIUS, *Parisiensis.*
Ascensius declynsyons with the playne exposition. [This is a head-line on A 1. No place, printer's name, or date, but printed abroad about 1520.] 4°, A—D in sixes.
    Herbert's *Ames,* p. 301, from a copy belonging to himself. Compare Dibdin, ii.

203. Extracts from this remarkable tract are given in my small volume on *School-Books.*

ASCHAM, ANTHONY, *Political Writer.*
Of the Confusions and Revolutions of Governments . . . Three parts, with several Additions. By Ant: Ascham, Gent. London, Printed by W. Wilson, . . . 1649. 8°. A, 4 leaves : B—O 4 in eights.

À SCHURMAN, ANNA MARIA, *of Utrecht.*
The Learned Maid ; Or, Whether a Maid may be a Scholar ? A Logick Exercise written in Latine by that incomparable Virgin Anna Maria à Schurman of Vtrecht. With some Epistles to the famous Gassendus and others. [Quot. from Ignatius.] London, Printed by John Redmayne. 1659. 8°, A—D in eights, A 1 blank. With a portrait. Dedicated by the translator, C[lement] B[arksdale] to the Honourable Lady, the Lady A. H.

ASGILL, JOHN.
An Essay on a Registry, for Titles of Lands. By John Asgill, of Lincolns-Inn, Esq ; London, Printed in the Year 1698. 8°, A—F in fours.

An Argument Proving, That according to the Covenant of Eternal Life revealed in the Scriptures, Man may be translated from hence into that Eternal Life, without passing through Death, altho the Human Nature of Christ himself could not be thus translated till he had passed through Death. . . . Anno Dom. 1700. 8°, A—K 2 in fours.

ASH, SIMEON, AND GOODE, WILLIAM.
A Continuation of True Intelligence from the English and Scottish Forces, in the North, for the service of King and Parliament, and now beleaguring York, from the eighth of this instant June to the 17th thereof . . . . By Sim. Ash and William Goode, Preachers to the Earle of Manchesters Armie. Allowed of by Authoritie, and entered according to Order. London, Printed for Thomas Underhill, ... 1644. 4°, 4 leaves.

A Continuation . . . from the 16th of June, to Wednesday the 10th of July, 1644. Wherein is given a full and particular Accompt of the Battaile with Prince Rupert, and the Marquesse New-Castle, together with the successe thereof. By Sim. Ash, Chaplaine to the Earle of Manchester, and one of the Ministers of the Assembly. Allowed . . . London, Printed

*

for Thomas Underhill, . . . 1644. 4",
4 leaves.

ASHE, THOMAS, *of Gray's Inn.*
Fasciculus Florum. Or A Handfvll of
Flowers, Gathered out of the seueral
Bookes of . . . Sir Edward Coke Knight.
. . . At London Printed by G. Eld. 1618.
8", A—O 6 in eights, A 1 blank.

ASHURST, SIR H., *Bart.*
Some Remarks vpon the Life of . . . M^r
Nathanael Heywood, Minister of the Gos-
pel of Christ at Ormeskirk in Lancashire.
Who died in the 44th Year of his Age.
London: Printed for Tho. Cockerill . . .
MDCXCV. 8", A—H 4 in eights. Dedi-
cated to Lord Willoughby of Parham.

ASSIZE OF BREAD.
Artachthos Or A New Booke declaring
The Assise or Weight of Bread not onely
by Troy weight, according to the Law,
but by Avoirdupois weight the Common
weight of England. . . . London Printed
by E. G. and R. B. and are to be sold
according to the direction in the Frontis
piece, 1638. 4". Title and Composer's
Premonition, &c., 2 leaves : Frontispiece,
1 leaf : B—H in fours. Dedicated to Sir
Richard Fen, Lord Mayor, by John Penke-
thman.

The Assize of Bread, With sundry good
and needful Ordinances . . . Newly
Corrected & Enlarged . . . London :
Printed for And. Crook, . . . 1671. 4",
A—G in fours. With cuts.

The Assize of Bread : . . . London,
Printed for R. Scot, T. Basset, J. Wright,
. . . 1684. 4", A—G in fours. With
cuts.

The Assize of Bread : . . . London :
Printed for R. Chiswell [and Others] 1698.
4", A—G in fours. With cuts.

ATLAS.
The New Atlas : Or, Travels and Voyages
in Europe, Asia, Africa and America, Thro'
the most Renowned Parts of the World,
. . . Performed by an English Gentleman,
in Nine Years Travel and Voyages, more
exact than Ever. London, Printed for J.
Cleave . . . and A. Roper . . . 1698. 8",
A—R 2 in eights.

AUGUSTINE, ST.
The twelfe steppes of abuses writē by the
Famus Doctor S. Augustine translated
out of laten by Nicolas Lesse. [Col.]
Imprinted at London by Jhon Daie,
dwelling ouer Aldersgate, and Wylliam
Seres dwelling in Peter Colledge. The
yere of our Lorde God M. D. L. the fourth
daye of Maye . . . 8", A—F in eights,

F 8 blank. Dedicated by Lesse to Queen
Mary.

A worke of the predestination of saints
wrytten by the famous doctor S. Augustine byshop of Carthage, and translated
out of Latin into Englysshe, by Nycolas
Lesse, Londoner. Item, another worke
of the sayde Augustyne, entytuled, Of the
vertue of perseueraunce to thend, translated by the sayd. N. L. Londini. Anno.
1,5,50. Cum priuilegio. . . . [Col.]
Imprinted at London in Aldersgate strete
by the wyddow of Jhon Herforde, for
Gwalter Lynne, and are to be soulde, at
the sygne of the Spred Eagle in Poules
church yarde by the schole. . . . 8", black
letter. A, 6 leaues, the 6th blank : B—z
in eights, and two sheets beyond of 8 and
4. Dedicated to Ann, Duchess of Somerset.

Certaine select Prayers gathered out of S.
Augustines Meditations . . . At London
Printed by John Daye . . . 1574. Cum
gratia . . . 8", A—T 4 in eights. Printed
within borders.

Certaine select Prayers gathered out of S.
Augustines Meditations, whiche he call-
eth his selfe Talke with God. At London
Printed by Iohn Day dwelling ouer
Aldersgate. 1575. Cum gratia & Priui-
legio . . . 8", printed within borders,
A—T 4 in eights.

A Pretiovs Booke of Heauenlie Meditations, called. A priuate talke of the soule
with God : Which who so zealvslie will
vse and peruse, shal feele in his mind an
vnspeakeable sweetenes of the euerlasting
happines : Written (as some thinke) by
that reuerend, and religious Father, S.
Avgvstine ; and not translated onlie, but
purified also, . . . by Thomas Rogers.
. . . Printed at London by H. Denham,
. . . 1581. Cum priuilegio . . . 12",
A—K in twelves, title on A 4, and K
10–12 blank, K 9 with the printer's
mark.

A Pretiovs Booke of Heauenlie Meditations, Called, a priuate talke of the soule
with God. . . . Written (as some thinke)
by that reuerend, and religious Father S.
Avgvstine ; and not translated onelie,
but purified also . . . by Thomas Rogers.
. . . Printed at London by Peter Short,
. . . 1600. Sm. 8". a—i in eights : k, 12,
last two leaues blank : *St. Augustine's
Prayers,* A—L 6 in twelves. L 3 blank on
recto : St. Augustine's *Manual,* A—E 10
in twelves. Dedicated to Dr. Wilson.

These three portions seem to have been

published together. The separate titles are dated 1600.

S. Avgvstines Manvel . . . Corrected, translated, and adorned, by Thomas Rogers . . . Imprinted at London, by Richard Yardley and Peter Short . . . 1591. 12°, A—E 10 in twelves.

The Confessions of S. Avgvstine Bishop of Hippon and D. of the Church. Translated into English by S. T. M. The second Edition. Printed at Paris M.DC.XXXVIII. 12° or sm. 8°. â, 4 leaves, including a frontispiece : A—Bb in twelves : Cc, 8.

Saint Augustines Confessions translated : And With some marginall notes illustrated. Wherein, Diuers Antiquities are explayned : And the marginall Notes of a former Popish Translation, answered, By William Watts, Rector of St. Albanes. Woodstreete. London, Printed by Iohn Norton, for Iohn Partridge, . . . 1631. 12°. A, 6 leaves, besides the engraved title or frontispiece : B—Vv in twelves : Xx, 6, Xx 6 with the *Errata*. Dedicated to Lady Elizabeth Hare, wife of Sir John Hare, of Stow, co. Norfolk.

El Alma del incomparable San Avgvstin Sacada Del Cverpo de svs Confessiones, Collegida por la Ilustrissima Señora Doña Anna Condessa de Argyl. . . . En Amberes . . . M.DC.XXII. 4°. Title and dedication to Isabella Clara Eugenia, Princess of the Netherlands, from Brussels, August, 1622, 3 leaves : A—V 3 in fours.

Sothebys, June 30, 1882, No. 378.

AUSTEN, RALPH.

Observations upon some part of Sʳ Francis Bacon's Naturall History as it concerns, Fruit-trees, Fruits, and Flowers : especially the Fifth, Sixth, and Seventh Centuries, Improving the Experiments mentioned, to the best Advantage. By Ra : Austen Practiser in the Art of Planting. . . . Oxford, Printed by Hen : Hall, for Thomas Robinson, 1658. 4°, A—G in fours.

Dedicated to the honourable Robert Boyle Esq ; son to the Lord Boyle, Earl of Cork.

AUSTRIA.

The Supplication : That the nobles and comons of Osteryke made lately by their messaungers vnto kyng Ferdinandus, in the cause of the Christen Religion Item. The kynges answere to the same. Wvherpon foloweth the wordes that the mes-

saungers spake vnto the kyng agayne at their departing. [London, 1543.] 8°. black letter. Title and Myles C[overdale] to the Reader, 4 leaves : A—C 4 in eights, C 4 blank.

Translated by Coverdale from the German.

Newes from Vienna the . 5. day of August . 1566. of the strong Towne and Castell of Jula in Hungary, XL : myles beyond the riuer Danubius, which was cruelly assaulted by the great Turke, but now by Gods mighty working relieued, & the sayd Turke marueylously discomfited and ouerthrowen. Translated out of hye Almaine into English, and printed in Augspurge by Hans Zimmerman. Imprinted at London by John Awdeley, dwelling in litle Britaine streete without Aldersgate . The . 21. of September . 1566. 4°, black letter, 4 leaves, the fourth containing a Prayer. With a rough romance cut on the title. *B. M.*

AVENAR, JOHN.

The Enimie of Securitie. . . . At London, Printed by Humfrey Lownes, for the Company of the Stationers. 1611. 12°, A—R in twelves, A 1 blank.

AVRIL, FATHER, *of the Society of Jesus.* Travels into divers Parts of Europe and Asia, undertaken by the French King's Order to discover a new Way by Land into China . . . . Done out of French. To which is added, A Supplement extracted from Hakluyt and Purchas . . . London : Printed for Tim. Goodwin, . . . MDCXCIII. 12°. A, 6 leaves : B—H in twelves : I, 6 leaves.

AYMON.

The right pleasaunt and goodly Historie of the foure sonnes of Aimon . the which for the excellent endytyng of it, and for the notable Prowes and great vertues that were in them : is no les pleasaunt to rede, then worthy to be knowen of all estates bothe hyghe and lowe. [Col.] . . . Imprinted at London, by Wynkyn de Worde, the .viii. daye of Maye, and yᵉ yere of our lorde . M.CCCCC.iiii. at the request and commaundement of the noble and puissaunt erle, the Erle of Oxenforde, And now Emprinted in the yere of our Lorde. M.CCCCC.liiii. the vi. daye of Maye, By Wylliam Copland, for Thomas Petet. Folio, black letter, printed in two columns. A—z in sizes : ĩ, 6 leaves : a or A—f 5 in sizes. With woodcuts.

Osterley Park Sale, 1885, No. 125.

B.

B. A., *Novice*.
Mutatus Polemo. The Horrible Stratagems of the Jesuits, lately practised in England, during the Civil-Wars, and now discovered by a Reclaimed Romanist : imployed before as a Workman of the Mission from his Holiness. . . . Also A discovery of a Plot laid for a speedy Invasion. By A. B. Novice. . . . Published by special Command. London, Printed for Robert White. 1650. 4°, A—G in fours, the last 4 leaves occupied by an Epilogue by M. P.

Dedicated to Lord President Bradshaw.

B. C., *Gentleman*.
A Short Method of Physick : Shewing the Cure of Fourty-five severall Diseases, . . . To the which is Annexed the Portrature of a Man, . . . Very necessary for young Practitioners, or Chyrurgions that goe to Sea ; . . . London : Printed by M. S. for Thomas Jenner . . . 1659. 4°, A—F 2 in fours.

B. E.
A Faithful Testimony for God & my Country : Or, A Retro-spective Glass for the Legislators, and the rest of the Sons of the Church of England, (So called) who are found persecuting the Innocent. London, Printed for the Author, in the Year, 1664. 4°, A—B 2 in fours.

B. F., *Gent*.
Vercingetorixa : Or, The Germane Princess Reduc'd to An English Habit. By F. B. Gent. . . . London : Printed in the Year MDCLXIII. 4°, A—F in fours, and a leaf of G. In verse.

B. I.
A Brife and Faythfull declaration of the true fayth of Christ, made by certeyne men suspected of heresye in these articles following. . . . Anno. M. D. xlvii. Per me I. B. Sm. 8°, black letter, A—B in eights.

A Position maintained by I. B. before the Late Earle of Huntingdon : viz. Priests are executed not for Religion, but for Treason. Newly imprinted. 1600. 8°, 8 leaves, the first blank.

B. I.
Herefordshire Orchards, A Pattern for all England. Written in an Epistolary Address to Samuel Hartlib Esq. By I. B. London, Printed by Roger Daniel, Anno CIƆ. IƆC. LVII. 8°, A—D in eights.

B. I. of *London, Merchant*.
The Merchants Remonstrance. Wherein is set forth the inevitable miseries which may suddenly befall this Kingdom by want of Trade, and decay of Manufactures. This is licensed and entered into the Hall-Booke according to Order. London, Printed by R. H. February 12. 1644. 4°, A—B in fours.

B. I. D.
Eclogve, ov Chant Pastoral Svr les Nopces des Serenissime Princes Charles Roy de la Grand' Bretagne, . . . & de Henriette Marie, fille de Henry Le Grand, Roy de France, & de Nauarre. A Londres, M.DC.XXVII. 4°, A—E, 2 leaves each : F, 4, the last blank. In verse.

B. J.
The Poets Knavery Discouered, in all their lying Pamphlets : Wittily and very Ingenuously Composed, laying open the Names of every lying Lybel that was Printed last yeare, and the Author who made them, being above three hundred Lyes. Shewing how impudently the Poets have not onely presumed to make extreame and incredible Lyes, but dare also feigne false Orders and Proceedings from the Parliament, with many fictitious Speeches. Well worth the Reading and Knowing of every one, that they may learn how to distinguish betwixt the Lyes and reall Books. Written by J. B. London, Printed for T. H. [1642.] 4°, 4 leaves.

Many popular tracts of the day are here denounced as false or supposititious.

B. J., *M.A*.
A Serious Item to secure Sinners : Or, God discovered to be as well a Burning as a Shining Light. By J. B. M. A. . . . London, Printed in the year 1666. 8°, B—R in eights, and the title.

B. J., *A.M*.
The Amoret, Or, Love Poems. *Tristia quo possum* . . . . Ovid. . . . . London, Printed for George Sawbridge, at the Three Golden Flower D'Luces in Little-Britain [About 1690.] 8°, A—E in fours.

The author speaks of these poems as written thirteen years before in his youth. They appear to be only a residue of a larger collection. I see no clue to date.

B. N., *M. D.*

A Discourse of Trade. London, Printed by Tho. Millbourn for the Author, 1690. 12°, A—G 4 in eights.

A New Discourse of Trade . . . The second Edition. London Printed, and Sold by Sam. Crouch, Tho. Horn, & Jos. Hindmarsh in Cornhill. 1694. 8°, A—S in eights, S 8 blank.

B. R.

Adagia Scotica Or A Collection of Scotch Proverbs and Proverbial Phrases. Very Usefull, and Delightfull. . . . London, Printed for Nath. Brooke, . . . 1668. 12°, A—C 6 in twelves.

B. W.

The Covrt of good Counsell. Wherein is set downe the true rules how a man should choose a good Wife from a bad, and a woman a good Husband from a bad. Wherein is also expressed, the great care that Parents should haue, for the bestowing of their Children in Mariage : And likewise how Children ought to behaue themselues towardes their Parents : And how Maisters ought to gouerne their Seruants, . . . At London printed by Ralph Blower, and are to be solde by William Barley at his shop in Gratious Streete. 1607. 4°, black letter. A—I in fours. Dedicated to Sir John Joles, Knight, Alderman of London.

A Helpe to Discovrse : . . . The Twelfth Edition. . . . London, Printed by N. and I. O. for Nicolas Vavasour, . . . 1636. 12°, A—R 6 in twelves.

B. W.

The Non-Entity of Protestancy. Or, A Discourse, wherein is demonstrated, that Protestancy is not any Reall thing, but in it selfe a Platonicall Idea ; a wast of all Positive fayth ; and a meere Nothing. Written by a Catholike Priest of the Society of Iesvs. . . . Permissu Superiorum 1633. 8°. *, 8 leaves : A—R 4 in eights.

B. W.

The Yellow Book, Or A Serious Letter sent by a Private Christian to the Lady Consideration, The first day of May, 1659. Which she is desired to communicate in Hide-Park to the Gallants of the Times a little after Sun-set. Also, A brief Account of the Names of some vain persons that intend to be there, whose company the new Ladies are desired to forbear. London. Printed, and are to be sold by Tho. Butler in Lincoln-Inn-fields. . . . 1659. 4°, A—C in fours.

A New Trial of the Ladies, Hide-Park, May-Day. Or, The Yellow Books Partner. London, Printed, and are to be sold by Thomas Butler, . . . May 1. 1659. 4°, A—G 2 in fours, and the title.

B. W. *of London, Goldsmith.*

A Touchstone for Gold and Silver Wares. Or, A Manual for Goldsmiths, and all other Persons, whether Buyers, Sellers, or Wearers of any manner of Goldsmiths Work. . . . London, Printed for John Bellinger in Cliffords-Inn Lane, . . . 1677. 8°. A, 8 leaves, including the frontispiece : (*), 4 ll : (**), 2 ll : B—I 2 in eights. Dedicated to Sir Joseph Williamson, Knight and Baronet.

Br. J.

The Jesuite Countermin'd. Or, An Account of a New Plot carrying on by the Jesuites : Manifested by their present Endeavours (under all Shapes) to raise Commotions in the Land, . . . London, Printed in the Year 1679. 4°, B—F 2 in fours, besides title and Preface.

BACON, FRANCIS, *Viscount St. Alban.*

OEvres Morales et Politiqves de Messire François Bacon grand Chancellier d'Angleterre. De la version de L. Baudvin. M. DC. XXXIII. A Paris. . . . 8°. a, 8 leaves, the last with the portrait : A—3 G in eights. The title is engraved.

Certaine Considerations touching the better pacification, and Edification of the Church of England : Dedicated to his most Excellent Maiestie. Printed for Henry Tomes. [1604.] 4°, A—F in fours, A 1 and F 4 blank.

Putticks, June 24, 1885, in lot 212.

True Peace : Or A Moderate Discourse to compose the unsettled Consciences, and Greatest Differences in Ecclesiastical Affaires. Written long since by the no less famous than Learned Sir Francis Bacon, Lord Verulam, Viscount St. Alban, London, Printed for A. C. 1663. 4°, B—G in fours, and the title.

Francisci Baronis de Vervlamio, Vicecomitis Sancti Albani, Historia Vitæ & Mortis. Sive, Titvlvs Secvndvs in Historiâ Naturali & Experimentali ad condendam Philosophiam : Quæ est Instavrationis Magnæ Pars Tertia. Londini, in Officina Io. Haviland, impensis Matthaei Lownes. 1623. 8°, A—Fi 6 in eights. *B. M.*

The only prefatory matter is a Latin address headed *Virentibus et Posteris Salutem.*

Sylva Sylvarvm : Or, A Naturall Historie. In Ten Centvries. Written by the Right Honourable Francis Lo. Verulam Viscount St Alban. Published after the Authors death, By William Rawley, Doctor of Diuinitie, late his Lordships Chaplaine. London, ¶ Printed by J. H. for William Lee . . . 1627. Folio, A—Nn 2 in fours, besides the portrait of Bacon by Cecill, an. æt. 66, the frontispiece, the title-page, and Rawley's dedication to the King, 4 leaves : the *New Atlantis*, a—g in fours, g 4 blank. Mm 1 is also blank. *B. M.*

Sylva Sylvarvm : Or, A Naturall Historie. . . . . London, Printed by John Haviland for William Lee . . . 1635. Folio. Portrait and engraved title. 2 leaves : A —bb in sixes : cc, 4 leaves : *New Atlantis*, a—g in fours, g 4 blank.

BAGSHAW, HENRY, *M.A., Chaplain to the Embassy at Madrid.*
A Sermon Preacht in Madrid, July 4. 1666. S.N. Occasioned By the Sad and much Lamented Death of his late Excellency Sir Richard Fanshaw, Knight and Baronet, of his Maiesties most Honourable Privy Council, and his Embassador in Ordinary to that Court. Where falling Sick of a Violent Feaver, June 14th —66. He ended his Life the 26th day of that Moneth ; in the Third Year of his Negociation in that place, and the 59th Year of his Age. . . . London, Printed for G. Beadle and T. Collins, . . . 1667. 4⁰, A —F 2 in fours, A 1 blank. Dedicated to Lady Fanshawe.

BAGSHAW, W.
De Spiritualibus Pecci. Notes (or Notices) Concerning the work of God, And some of those who have been Workers together with God, in the Hundred of the High Peak in Derbyshire. . . . London, Printed for Nevill Simmons, Bookseller in Sheffield, 1702. Sold by A. Baldwin in Warwick Lane. 8⁰, A—G 4 in eights.

BAKER, THOMAS.
Hampstead Heath. A Comedy. As it was Acted at the Theatre Royal in Drury Lane. By the Author of The Yeoman of Kent. London, Printed for Bernard Lintott, . . . 1706. 4⁰. A, 2 leaves : B —I in fours.

BALAAM.
The Open Movth of Balaams Asse. First, To his Master Balaam. Secondly, To his Masters Chaplins. . . . . And this is all that Balaams Asse will speak for this Term. Printed in the yeer, 1642. 4⁰, 4 leaves.

BALDWIN, WILLIAM, *Printer.*
A treatise of Morall Phylosophye, ...

Imprinted at Londō, in Fletestrete, at the signe of the Sunne, . . . by Edwarde Whitchurche, the fyrst day of Februarye, in the yeare of oure Lorde. M.D.L. Cum priuilegio . . . 8⁰. Title, &c., 7 leaves : A—R in eights, R 8 blank.

A Treatise of Morrall Philosophie : . . . . London, Printed by Thomas Snodham. 1610. 8⁰, A—Bb in eights. Black letter.

With the introductory matter by Thomas Palfreyman still retained.

BANK.
Remarks on the Proceedings of the Commissioners for putting in Execution the Act past last Session, for Establishing of a Land-Bank. London, Printed, . . . 1696. 8⁰, A—B in eights : C, 4 : D, 3.

A Reply in Defence of the Bank : Setting forth the Unreasonableness of their Slow Payments. . . , In a Letter to his Friend in the Country. By a true Lover of his Countrey and the present Government. London, Printed for E. Whitlock, . . . 1696. 8⁰, A—C 2 in fours.

BARBA, ALBARO ALONSO.
The Art of Metals ; In which is Declared the manner of their Generation, and the Concomitants of Them. In Two Books. . . . Translated in the Year, 1669. By the R. H. Edward Earl of Sandwich. London : Printed for S. Mearne, . . . 1674. 8⁰, A—K in eights, and A—F in eights. With cuts.

BARBADOES.
A Short Account of the Manifest Hand of God That hath fallen upon several Marshals and their Deputies, Who have made Great Spoil and Havock of the Goods of the People of God called Quakers, in the Island of Barbadoes, For their Testimony against Going or Sending to the Militia. With a Remarkable Account of some others of the Persecutors of the same People in the same Island. Together with an Abstract of their Sufferings. London, Printed and Sold by T. Sowle, . . . 1696. 4⁰, A—C in fours, besides a folded leaf with the Abstract of the Losses.

BARBARY.
A Dolorous discourse, of a most terrible and blovdy Battel, fought in Barbarie, the fowrth day of August, last past. 1578. Wherein were slaine two Kings, but (as most men say) three, besyde many other famous personages : with a great number of Captains, . . . Whereunto is also annexed, a note of the names of diuerse

that were taken prisoners at the same time. [Col.] Imprinted at London by Iohn Charlewood, and Thomas Man. 8°, A—B in eights. *B. M.*

This was the famous battle of Alcazar, August 4, 1578, in which Sebastian, King of Portugal, perished.

BARBETTE, PAUL, *M.D.*
The Practice of the Most Successful Physitian Paul Barbette, Doctor of Physick. With the Notes and Observations of Frederick Deckers, Doctor of Physick. Faithfully rendered into English. London, Printed by T. R. for Henry Brome, . . . 1675. 8°, A—S in eights, including a frontispiece by Van Hove.

BARCLAY, JOHN.
Ioannis Barclaii Argenis. Parisiis, . . . M.DC.XXI. . . . 8°. ã, 8 leaves : A—4 G 4 in eights. Dedicated to Louis XIII. from Rome, July 1, 1621.

The Mirrovr of Mindes, Or Barclay's Icon animorum, Englished by T. M. London, Printed by Iohn Norton for Thomas Walkley, . . . 1631. 12°. A, 6 leaves : B—Ii in twelves : Kk, 4. Dedicated to Lord Treasurer Weston.

BARLOW, WILLIAM, *D.D.*
A Sermon preached at Paules Crosse, on the first Sunday in Lent ; Martij 1. 1600. With a short discourse of the late Earle of Essex his confession, and penitence, before and at the time of his death. By William Barlow Doctor of Diuinite. At London Printed for Mathew Law, dwelling in Paules Church-Yard neere Watling-streete. 1601. 8°, A—E 6 in eights.

BARNES, BARNABE.
Fovre Bookes of Offices : Enabling Priuat persons for the speciall seruice of all good Princes and Policies. Made and deuised by Barnabe Barnes. London Printed at the charges of George Bishop, T. Adams, and C. Burbie. 1606. Folio. Title. 1 leaf : dedication by the author to James I., 4 leaves : verses by W. Percy, John Ford, &c. 2 leaves : Preface, 2 leaves : the work, B—Cc, in fours : Dd, 5 leaves. At the end occurs : Imprinted at London by Adam Islip. 1606. Wholly in prose.

The Divils Charter : A Tragædie Conteining the Life and Death of Pope Alexander the sixt. As it was plaide before the Kings Maiestie, vpon Candlemasse night last : by his Maiesties Seruants. But more exactly renewed, corrected and augmented since by the Author, for the more pleasure and profit of the Reader.

At London Printed by G. E. for Iohn Wright, and are to be sold at his Shop in New-gate market, neere Christ church gate. 1607. 4°, A—M in fours, M 4 blank. Dedicated to Sir William Herbert and Sir William Pope, Knights.

BARNES, ROBERT.
A supplicacion vnto the most gracyous prynce H. the . viii. [Col.] Imprinted at London in Fletestrete By Iohã Byddell, at the signe of our lady of Pitie, nexte to Flete brydge. The yere of our lorde God. 1534. In the moneth of Nouember. 4°, B—X 2 in fours. *B. M.*

There is no signature A, nor any regular title, the work commencing on B 1 with a head-line as above. On F 1 occurs a second head-line : *The cause of my condempnacion,* which is also addressed to the King, and which ends on Q 1, but between F and H the sheet is wrongly marked B. On Q 2 occurs a third head-line : "By Gods wordo it is lawfull to prestes, that hath not the gyfte of chastite, to mary wyues." On Q 1 *rerso* is a woodcut head of Barnes.

BARNETT, H.
The Crafts-mens Craft. Or The Wiles of the Discoverers. In abusing and incensing Authority and the People against innocent and harmlesse Men, by false Accusations, and Sophistical Suggestions. . . By H. B. London Printed by J. and J. M. for W. L. . . . 1649. 4°, A—B in fours.

The Charity of Church-Men : Or, A Vindication of Mr. William Walwyn Merchant, from the aspersions plentifully cast upon him in a Pamphlet, Intituled, Walwyns Wiles. By H. B. a friend to Truth, his Country and Mr. Walwyn. . . . London, Printed by H. Hils, . . . M.DC.XLIX. 4°, A—B in fours.

[BARON, WILLIAM, *of Enborn, near Newbury, Co. Berks.*]
A Just Defence of the Royal Martyr K. Charles I. From the many false and malicious Aspersions in Ludlow's Memoirs, and some other virulent Libels of that Kind. . . . London, Printed for A. Roper . . . and R. Basset . . . 1699. 8°. A—O 4 in eights: Part 2, A—P in eights.

The name of the author is added on the title of this copy in coeval MS.

BARONETS.
His Maiesties Commission to all the Lords, and others of the Priuie Counsell, touching the Creation of Baronets. . . . Imprinted at London by Robert Barker . . . 1611. 4°, A—G 2 in fours, A 1, F 2, and G 2 blank.

A Catalogue of the Baronets of the Kingdom of England ; From the first erection
of that Dignity until this time. London : Printed by E. Cotes for A. Seile,
MDCLXVII. 8°, A — I 2 in fours, A 1
with *Imprimatur.*

BARON'S COURT.
The Copie of a Barons Court : Newly
translated by Whats-you-call-Ilim, Clerk
to the same. Printed at Helicon, beside
Parnassus. and are to be sold in Caledonia.
[About 1700.] 4°. A—D, 2 leaves each.
In verse.

BARROUGH, PHILIP.
The Method of Phisick, Conteining the
Cavses, Signes, and Cvres of Inward
diseases in mans bodie from the head to
the foote. Whereunto is added, the forme
and rule of making remedies and medicines, . . . Imprinted at London by
Richard Field, dwelling in the Blacke-
friers by Lud-gate. 1590. 4°, A — Ce
4 in eights. Dedicated to Lord Burleigh.

The Method of Phisick, . . . The third
Edition corrected and augmented, with
two other bookes newly added by the
Author. Imprinted at London by Richard
Field, . . . 1596. 4°, A—Ii 6 in eights.

The Method of Physick, Contaning the
Cavses, Signes, And Cvres of Inward
Diseases in Mans Body, . . . Whereunto
is added, the forme and rule of making
remedies and medicines, . . . The sixth
Edition. London, Imprinted by Richard
Field, . . . 1624. 4°, A—Ii 2 in eights.

BARRY, GERRAT, *Irishman.*
The Siege of Breda by the Armes of Phillip the Fovrt vnder the Government of
Isabella Atchived by the Condvct of
Ambr. Spinola. Louanii ex officina Hastenii M. DC. XXVII. [Col.] Lovanii, Ex
Officina Henrici Hastenii, . . . M. DC.
XXVIII. Folio. Engraved title, 1 leaf :
dedication subscribed *Captaine Gerrat
Barry, Irish*, to Spinola, 2 leaves : A—V
in fours, V 4 with the colophon. With
plates (including one of siege-pieces) at pp.
6, 10, 15, 28, 31, 38, 47–8, 66, 80, 85, 93,
118, 123, 125. *B. M.*

> To the numismatist the author's account
> of the numerous pieces of money of neces-
> sity which passed current during the siege
> should be interesting, and is probably little
> known. The coins figured are three dia-
> mond - shaped tokens similar to some of
> those struck during the Civil War in Eng-
> land, particularly the Newark money.

Militarie Discipline Composed by Captaine Gerat Barry. Dedicated to the
right honorable Dauid Barry Earle of
Barri Moar, Vicoute of Buteuant, . . .
1634. [A printed title follows :] A Discourse of Military Discipline, Devided into
Three Boockes, Declaringe the partes and
sufficiencie ordained in a private Souldier, and in each Officer ; . . . Composed
by Captaine Gerat Barry Irish. At Brux-
ells, By the Widowe of Jhon Moumart.
M. DC. XXXIV. Folio. Engraved and
printed titles, 2 leaves : dedication and
to the Reader, 3 leaves : A—Dd in fours :
Ee, 6 leaves. With diagrams, woodcuts,
and plates separate from the letterpress at
pp. 104, 112, 120, 122, 144, 154, 198,
200, 202 (2), 204. and 206 (2). *B. M.*

BARTHOLOMEUS DE GLANVILLE,
of the Order of Minorites.
Incipit prohemiū de proprietatibus rerū
fratris bartholomei anglici de ordine fratrū
minorum. [Col.] Explicit tractatꝑ de
proprietatibus rerum edittꝙ a Frē bartolo-
meo āglico ordīs fratrum minorum. [Col-
ogne, no date, but about 1470.] Large
folio, 247 unnumbered leaves, without
signatures, catchwords, &c. *B. M.*

> First edition of a highly popular and
> successful book, which passed through
> many impressions in Germany before the
> close of the XVth century. That so many
> should have been demanded is a powerful
> evidence of the different notions and tastes
> in literary matters which formerly pre-
> vailed. Wynkyn de Worde, in the English
> edition printed at Westminster before 1501,
> states that Caxton executed an impression
> of the work at Cologne in Latin. Probably
> he refers to this ; but Caxton, perhaps, did
> little more, if he was actually concerned in
> its production, than assist in setting up the
> text as a journeyman.

Incipiūt tituli librorū et capitulorꝙ venerabilis bartholomei anglici de proprietatibus rerum. [Col.] Impressus per me
Johānem Koelhoff de lubeck Colonie
ciuem. Anno natiuitatis domini.
Mccccclxxxi. Thick folio, long lines,
without title, signatures, and paging, but
with catchwords. *B. M.*

> The Prohemium begins on the 11th leaf,
> the Table occupying the preceding leaves.

Incipiunt tituli . . . [On the 11th leaf
occurs :] Prohemiū in opus . . . [Col.]
Impressus et completus per me Johānē
koelhoff de Lubeck Colonie ciuē. Anno
grē Mccccclxxxiij. in vigilia Sebastiani
martyris. Folio, printed in two columns,
with signatures, but without foliation
and catchwords. Table, 10 leaves : a—z
in eights, a i blank : A—Mm in eights,
except that in Mm there is a 9th leaf.
There is no Z in the second alphabet.
B. M. (a i wanting.)

Bartholomeu° de proprietatibȝ reruȝ [This is in large white letters on a black ground, and is the whole of the title.] Wynkyn de Worde, [at Westminster before 1500.] folio, black letter, printed in two columns. A, 5 leaves : B, 8 leaves : b, 6 leaves : c—z in eights : two sheets of six and eight under irregular signatures, the *recto* of the last having Wynkyn de Worde's device, and the reverse blank : Book xii. with a new set of signatures—A—V in eights : X—Z in sixes : aa—cc in eights : dd—gg in sixes : hh—mm in eights : nn—oo in sixes, oo 6 having a duplicate of the title on the *recto*, and on the reverse the printer's large device. With numerous line cuts. *B. M.* (the Banks copy.)

This English version, the earliest known to survive, of a writer whom Warton styles the Gothic Pliny, but who seems to have borrowed much of his material from the *Speculum Historiale* of Vincent of Beauvais, was executed by John Trevisa, Canon of Westbury in Gloucestershire. His conclusion or envoy occurs on oo iij *verso*, and states that the translation, made at the request of Thomas Lord Berkeley, was ended the 6th of February, 1398-9, in the 47th year of his lordship's age. See Hazlitt's *Warton*, 1871, ii. 297. Bibliographers have usually ascribed this noble old volume to 1494 ; but I see no authority for that date. Herbert thought that Ames might have had some reason for his statement to this effect, because his own copy wanted the concluding leaf, which might have had a note of the year of printing ; but that leaf is in the Museum copy, and does not bear any evidence of the kind. Nor do I observe any exact internal clue.

BATES, GEORGE, AND SKINNER, THOMAS.

Elenchus Motuum Nuperorum in Anglia : Or, A short Historical Account of the Rise and Progress of the Late Troubles in England. In Two Parts. Written in Latin by Dr. George Bates. . . . Motus Compositi : Or, The History of the Composing the Affairs of England . . . written in Latin by Tho. Skinner, M.D. Made English. To which is added a Preface by a Person of Quality, . . . London : Printed for Abel Swalle, . . . and are to be sold by Samuel Eddowes . . . 1685. 8°, A in eights : [a] 4 leaves : B—M in eights : Part 2, +A—+R 2 in eights : Part 3, +A—+H 2 in eights.

BAXTER, RICHARD.

Poetical Fragments: Heart-Imployment with God and It Self. . . . The Second Edition. London, Printed for J. Dunton . . . 1689. 12°, A—G in twelves. With a portrait by Van Hove.

BAYLIE, ROBERT, *Minister at Glasgow*.

An Historicall Vindication of the Government of the Church of Scotland, From the manifold base calumnies which the most Malignant of the Prelats did invent of old, . . . London, Printed for Samuel Gellibrand . . . 1646. 4°, A—K in fours : *An Answer*, A—G in fours, without a regular title.

BAYNE, PAUL.

Christian Letters, of Mr. Pavl Bayne. Replenished with divers Consolations, Exhortations, Directions, tending to promote the honour of godlinesse. [Quot. from Heb. 3, 13.] Imprinted at London by T. O. for Nath. Newbery . . . . 1620. 12°. Title and other prefixes, 4 leaves : A—X in twelves : Y, 8.

Dedicated by Ez. Ch. to Lady Weld and Lady Lennard.

BEALE, THOMAS.

A Trve Discovery of A Bloody Plott intended to have been put in practice on Thursday the 18 of this present November, against some of the chiefe of the Lords and Commons in Parliament assembled by bloody-minded Papists. As also a relation of intended insurrections in six severall parts of this Land. . . . London Printed for the Author, to bee presented to the high Court of Parliament, and are to be sold by Henry Walker. 1641. 4°, 4 leaves.

BEAUMONT, FRANCIS.

Poems. The Golden Remains of those so much admired Dramatick Poets, Francis Beaumont & John Fletcher Gent. . . . The second Edition enriched with the addition of other Drolleries by severall Wits of these present Times. London Printed for William Hope . . . 1660. 8°, A—K in eights.

BEAUMONT, JOHN, *Gentlemen*.

An Historical, Physiological and Theological Treatise of Spirits, Apparitions, Witchcrafts, and other Tragical Practices. Containing An Account of the Genii or Familiar Spirits, . . . Also of Appearances after Death, . . . Likewise the Power of Witches, . . . With a Refutation of Dr. Bekker's World bewitch'd . . . London : . . . 1705. 8°, A — Cc in eights. With a frontispiece in two compartments. Dedicated to John Earl of Carbery.

BEAUMONT, JOHN, *Junior*.

The Present State of the Universe, . . . To which are added some other Curious Remarks ; . . . London : Printed, and

are to be Sold by Randal Taylor, . . .
1694. 4°. A. 2 : B—O 2 in fours. Dedicated to his kinsman, Charles Cottington,
Esquire.

BEAUMONT, SIR JOHN.

Bosworth-Field : A Poem. . . . London :
Printed and Sold by H. Hills . . . 1710.
8°, A—C 4 in eights.

BECANUS, MARTINUS.

The Confvtation of Tortvra Torti : Or,
Against the King of Englands Chaplaine :
for that he hath negligently defended the
Kinges Cause. By the R. F. Martinvs
Becanvs, of the Society of Iesvs : And
Professour in Diuinity. Translated out of
Latin into English by W. I. P[riest.] Per-
nissu Superiorum. M.DC.X. 4°, A—I in
fours.

The English Iarre. Or Disagreement
amongst the Ministers of Great Brittaine,
concerning the Kinges Supremacy . . .
translated into English by I. W. P[riest.]
Imprinted Anno M.DC.XII. 4°, A—H in
fours.

BECKET, THOMAS, *Archbishop of Can-terbury.*

A Letter Written to a Friend in Wilts,
Upon occasion of a late Ridiculous Pamphlet, Wherein was inserted a pretended
Prophesie of Thomas Becket's. &c. London, Printed by R. D. Anno Dom. 1666.
4°, A—C 2 in fours.

BEDFORDSHIRE.

The Case in Law and Equity of Tristram
Woodward Esq; for the Mannors of Tud-
dington, Hartington, and Tyngrith, and
other Lands in the County of Bedford,
Reported to the Commissioners of Ob-
structions, by Mr. St. Nichlas the Councell for the Common-wealth. [1652.]
4°, A—C in fours, and a leaf of D.

A true and Impartial Narrative of Some
Illegal and Arbitrary proceedings by certain Justices of the Peace and others,
against several innocent and peaceable
Nonconformists in and near the Town of
Bedford, upon pretence of putting in
execution the late Act against Conventicles. Together with a brief Account of
the late sudden and strange Death of the
Grand Informer, . . . Printed in the
year, 1670. 4°, A—B in fours.

BEDLOE, WILLIAM.

The Examination of Captain William
Bedlow Deceased, Relating to the Popish
Plot, taken in his last Sickness, by Sir
Francis North, Chief Justice of the
Court of Common Pleas . . . . London.
. . . 1680. Folio. A—D, 2 leaves each.

BEER.

Reasons Most Humbly Submitted to the
Wisdom of Parliament for the taking off
the present Duty of Excise upon Beer and
Ale, and laying the Duty upon the Original Malt : Which is designed by a Lover
of his Country, for the equal Service,
Benefit, and Advantage both of the Crown
and of the Subject. London, Printed for
Tho. Parkhurst, . . . 1695. 4°. A—G, 2
leaves each.

BEHAVIOUR.

The Rule of Behaviour, Touching Spiritual Matters & Temporal. In Respect
of the Laity and Clergy, Government and
Country. . . . London, Printed for Tho.
Chapman, . . . MDCXCII. 12°, A—Eg
in twelves.

BEHN, APHRA.

A Pindarick Poem on the Happy Coronation of His most Sacred Majesty James
II. and his Illustrious Consort Queen
Mary. By Mrs. Behn. London, Printed
by J. Playford for Henry Playford, near
the Temple-Church : 1685. Folio. A—
F, 2 leaves each, F 2 blank.

BEKKER, BALTHAZAR, *D.D., Pastor at Amsterdam.*

The World Bewitched : Or, An Examination of the Common Opinions concerning Spirits : Their Nature, Power, Administration, and Operations. As also,
The Effects Men are able to produce by
their Communication. Divided into IV.
Parts. . . . Vol. I. Translated from a
French Copy, approved of and subscribed
by the Author's own Hand. Printed
for R. Baldwin in Warwick-Lane, 1695.
12°. A, 6 leaves, including a blank and
half-title : b—d in twelves : B—M in
twelves.

I have not yet seen more than the first
volume in English.

[BELHAVEN, JOHN, *Lord.*]

The Countrey-Mans Rudiments : Or, An
Advice to the Farmers in East-Lothian
how to labour and improve their Ground.
Edinburgh, Printed by the Heirs and
Successors of Andrew Anderson, . . .
1699. 8°, A—C in eights, A repeated.

BELLENDEN, WILLIAM.

Ciceronis Consvl, Senator, Senatusq;
Romanus. Illustratus publici obserua-
tione iuris, grauissimi vsus disciplina, . . .
De statu rerum Romanarum vnde iam
manauit Ciceronis Princeps, . . . Editio
Prima. Ad Inclytum. . . . Henricvm
Principem Scotiæ, et Walliæ. Per G.
Bellendenvm magistrum Supplicum libel-

lorum Avgvstv Regis Magnæ Brittanniæ, &c. Parisii, . . . M.DC.XII. . . . 8⁰. ã, 8 leaves : A—Aa 4 in eights, Aa 4 with the *Errata.*

Gvlielmi Bellendeni Magistri Svpplievm . . . De Statv Libri Tres. I. De Statu prisci orbis in Religione, Re Politica, & literis. II. Ciceronis Princeps, sine de Statu Principis & Imperij. III. Ciceronis Consul, Senator, Senatúsque Romanus, sine de Statu Reip. & vrbis imperantis Orbi. Primus, nunc primùm editus : cæteri, cum tractatu de Processu & Scriptoribus Rei Politicæ, ab autore aucti & illustrati. Parisiis, . . . M. DC. XVI. . . . 8⁰, A—F in eights : The *Princeps,* A—F 3 in eights : the Consul, ã, 8 leaves : A—Aa 4 in eights, Aa 4 with *Errata.* The last portion is dedicated to Henry, Charles, and Elizabeth, children of Charles I., with an emblematical engraving superscribed *In Tribus Vnum,* and representing three heads surmounted by a crown.

BELLERS, JOHN.
An Essay towards the Improvement of Physick. In Twelve Proposals . . . With an Essay for Imploying the Able Poor ; . . . By John Bellers. . . . London : Printed by the Assigns of J. Sowle, . . . 1714. 4⁰, B—II in fours, a leaf of 1, and the title.

BELMAN.
The British Bell-man. Printed in the Year Of the Sainte Fear. Anno Domini, 1648. 4⁰, A—C in fours, A 1 with a mock *Imprimatur.*

BELVALETUS, F. MONDONUS, *Professor of Theology.*
Catechismvs Ordinis Eqvitvm Periscelidis Anglicanæ ; seu Specvlvm Anglorvm. . . . [Edited from an ancient MS. by Philippus Bosquierus, and addressed to the King of England.] Coloniae Agrippinae . . . Anno M. DC. XXXI. 8⁰, A—F 2 in eights.

> An elaborate treatise on the Order of the Garter. At the end occurs : Explicit tractatus vulgariter dictus, La Garretiere, alias, Specvlvm Anglorvm. In the Approbation the writer is described as Fellondonus Belvaleti.

BENGALA.
A Relation of an Unfortunate-Voyage to the Kingdom of Bengala Describing the deplorable condition, and dismal accidents, attending those therein concerned. . . . By Mr. Glanius. London, Printed for Henry Bonwick . . . 1682. 8⁰. A, 3 leaves, besides the engraved title : B—N 4 in eights.

An English version by Glanius, probably a teacher in London, of a Dutch narrative printed at Amsterdam in 1681.

BERKLEY, GEORGE, *Earl of.*
Historical Applications and Occasional Meditations upon Several Subjects. *Vis a dubio* . . . S. Angus. Written by a Person of Honour. London, Printed by J. Macock, for R. Royston . . . MDCLXX. 8⁰, A—L in eights.

BERKSHIRE.
A Rehearsall both straung and true, of hainous and horrible actes committed by Elizabeth Stile, Alias Rockingham, Mother Dutten, Mother Deuell, Mother Margaret, Fower notorious Witches, apprehended at winsore in the Countie of Barks, and at Addington arraigned, condemned, and executed, on the 26 daye of Februarie laste. Anno. 1579. Imprinted at London for Edward White at the little Northdoore of Paules, at the signe of the Gun, and are there to be sold. 8⁰, black letter, with cuts. A, 8 leaves : B, 2. *B. M.*

BERNARD, NICHOLAS, *Dean of Ardagh.*
The Whole Proceedings of the Siege of Drogheda in Ireland, With a thankfull Remembrance for its wonderfull delivery. Raised with Gods speciall assistance by the Prayers, and sole valour of the besieged. . . . London, Printed by A. N. for William Bladen, 1642. 4⁰, A—N 2 in fours.

BERNARD, RICHARD), *of Batcombe.*
The Isle of Man : . . . The eighth Edition. London, Printed by G. M. for Edward Blackmore . . . 1632. 8⁰, A—N in twelves.

BEWICK, JOHN, *Minister of Bengeo, near Hertford.*
Confiding England vnder Conflicts triumphing in the middest of her terrors . . . London, Printed by I. D. for Andrew Crooke, . . . 1644. 4⁰, A—G in fours.

BIBLE.
The true and lyuely historyke Pvrtreatvres of the vvoll Bible. At Lyons, By Iean of Tovrnes. M. D. LIII. 8⁰, A—N in eights, N 8 with a type ornament only. Dedicated by Peter Derendel to Master Pikeling, ambassador of the King of England.

BIDDLE, JOHN, *M.A.*
An Humble Advise to the Right Honorable the Lord Mayor, The Recorder, And the rest of the Iustices of the Honorable Bench. To the good men of the Jury, and at the Sessions House in the Old-

Bayley, London, in behalf of M². John Bidle, Prisoner in Newgate. [London, 1653–4.] 4º, A—B in fours. Without a regular title.

To the Officers and Souldiers of the Army, more especially to those Officers that sit in Councill at White-Hall, a sober admonition from some sighing Souls. [1655.] 4º, 4 leaves.

> An appeal from the Scilly Islands on behalf of Biddle.

Two Letters of M². Iohn Biddle, Late Prisoner in Newgate, But now hurried away to some remote Island. One to the Lord Protector. The other to the Lord President Laurence. Wherein you have an account of his Judgement concerning those opinions whereof he is accused. London, Printed in the Yeer 1655. 4º. 4 leaves.

The True State of the Case of Liberty of Conscience in the Common-wealth of England. Together with a true Narrative of the Cause, and Manner. of M². John Biddle's Sufferings. London, Printed in the year, 1655. [Col.] London : Printed for Richard Moone, . . . 1655. 4º, 8 leaves.

The Spirit of Persecution again broken loose, By an Attempt to put in Execution against M². John Biddle Master of Arts, an abrogated Ordinance of the Lords and Commons for punishing Blasphemies and Heresies. Together with a full Narrative of the whole Proceedings upon that Ordinance against the said M². John Biddle and M². William Kiffen Pastor of a baptised Congregation in the City of London. Printed at London for Richard Moone . . . 1655. 4", A—C in fours.

BILBERY, JOHN.

A Voyage of the Late King of Sweden, And another of Mathematicians, sent by Him : In which are discovered, The Retraction of the Sun, which sets not in the Northern Parts, . . . By Command of the Most Serene, . . . Charles X . . . Faithfully Render'd into English. London, Printed for Edward Castle, next Scotland-Yard-Gate, by Whitehall, 1698. 8º, A—H in eights. With diagrams.

BINNING, THOMAS.

A Light to the Art of Gunnery. Wherein is laid down the True Weight of Powder both for Proof and Action, of all sorts of Great Ordnance. Also the true Ball, and allowance for Wind. . . . By Capt Thomas Binning. London ; Printed by J. D. for W. Fisher and R. Mount, . . .

1689. 4º, A—Z in fours. With diagrams, folding plates at pp. 56, 104, 123, 163, three other plates at pp. 117, 156, and after Z 4, and an engraved title or frontispiece.

BIONDI, GIO. FRANCISCO.

Eromena, Or, Love and Revenge. Written originally in the Thyscan tongue. By Gio. Francisco Biondi . . . Divided into six Books. And now faithfully Englished, by Ia. Hayward, of Graies-Inne Gent. London, Printed by Richard Badger, for Robert Allot, . . . 1632. Folio. A, 4 leaves, the first blank : [a], 4 leaves, with verses by Sir T. Salusbury, James Howell, &c. : B—Cc 2 in fours. Dedicated to Frances, Duchess Dowager of Richmond and Lenox.

BIRCH, DR.

A Birchen Rod for D². Birch : Or Some Animadversions upon his Sermon Preached before the Honourable House of Commons, . . . January 30, 1694. In a Letter to Sir T. D. and M². H. Printed in the Year, 1694. 4º, A—D in fours, D 4 blank.

BIRKENHEAD, SIR JOHN.

Bibliotheca Parliamenti . . . Classis secunda. Done into English for the Assembly of Divines. Anno Domini, 1653. 8º, A in eights, A 7–8 occupied by the ballad of the Four-Legged Elder.

> The last-named piece opens with a headline on A 7 : The Four-Legg'd Elder, Or, A Horrible Relation of a Dog and an Elder's Maid. The Tune of *The Ladies Fall.*

BIRMINGHAM.

The Brimigham Ballad on Their Royal Highnesses Return from Scotland. To the Tune of, Monk's *March.* London : Printed for Nath. Thompson, MDCLXXXII. A leaf of verses.

BIRNIE, WILLIAM.

The Blame of Kirk-Bvriall, tending to perswade Cemiteriall Civilitie. First Preached, then Penned, and now at last propyned to the Lords inheritance in the Presbyterie of Lanerk, by M. William Birnie, the Lord his Minister in that llk, as a pledge of his zeale, and care of that reformation. Matt. 8. 22 . . . Edinbvrgh Printed by Robert Charteris . . . 1606. 4º. A, 2 leaves : B—F in fours. Dedicated to the Marquis of Hamilton. *B. M.*

Reprinted by Mr. Turnbull, 8vo, 1833.

BISHOPE, GEORGE.

An Appendix to the Book, Entituled, New England Judged : Being Certaine Writings (never yet Printed) of those Persons which were there Executed. Together with a Short Relation, of the 'Tryal, Sentence, and Execution, of William Leddra. Written by them in the time of their Imprisonment, in the Bloody Town of Boston. London, Printed for Robert Wilson, . . . 1661. 4°, Z—Cc in fours (continued from former portion).

BISHOPS.
Lord Bishops None of the Lords Bishops. Or A Short Discovrse, wherein is proved that Prelaticall Jurisdiction, is not of Divine Institution, . . . Printed in the Moneth of November, 1640. 4°, A—L in fours, L 4 blank.

An Humble Examination of a Printed Abstract of the Answers to Nine Reasons of the House of Commons, against the Votes of Bishops in Parliament. Printed by order of a Committee of the Honourable House of Commons, now assembled in Parliament. London, Printed for P. Stephens and C. Meredith. 1641. 4°, A—K in fours.

BISPHAM, THOMAS.
Iter Australe, A Reginensibus Oxon. Anno 1658. Expeditum. 4°, A—D in fours, A 1 blank. Dedicated to Thomas Barlow, Master of Queen's College, Oxford.

BLACKWOOD, ADAM.
Adami Blackvodæi in Cvria Præsidiali Pictonvm Et Vrbis in decurionum Collegio Regis Consiliarij. Opera Omnia. Parisiis, . . . M. DC. XCIV. 4°. ã—ŏ, 4 leaves each : ŭ, 8 leaves : A—5 E 2 in fours. With a portrait of the Author on ã 3.

BLAEU, W.
A Tutor to Astronomy and Geography ; Or, An Easie and Speedy way to Understand the Use of both the Globes, . . . Translated from the first Part of Gulielmus Blaeu, Institutio Astronomica. Published by J. M. London, Printed for Ioseph Moxon, . . . 1654. 8°. A, 4 : B—Aa 6 in eights.
The translator does not appear.

BLAGRAVE, JOHN.
The Evil Spirit Cast-out. Being a True Relation of the Manner of Performing the Famous Operation or Cure, on the Maiden Gentlewoman, whose Body was Possessed with an Evil Spirit. . . . London, Printed by E. Golding. 1691. 8°, 4 leaves.

BLANCKEN, GERRARD.
A Catalogue of all the chiefest Rarities in the Publick Theater and Anatomie-

Hall of the University of Leyden. . . . Printed in Leyden, By Hubert vander Boxe, 1697. 4°, 6 leaves.
Perhaps the copy described wanted something at the end.

BLANDE, JOHN.
To the Kings most Excellent Majesty, The humble Remonstrance of John Blande of London Merchant, on the behalf of the Inhabitants and Planters in Virginia and Mariland. [About 1665.] Folio, 2 leaves. *B. M.*
Sotheby, June 1, 1882, £2.6.0. On the last page Blande refers to a previous publication presented to the King, called *Trade reviv'd*.

BLITH, WALTER.
The English Improver, Or a New Survey of Husbandry. Discovering to the Kingdome, That some Land, both Arable and Pasture, may be Advanced Double or Treble ; Other Land to a Five or Tenfold : And some to a Twenty fold Improvement : . . . Held forth under six Pieces of Improvement . . . By Walter Blith a Lover of Ingenuity. London, printed for J. Wright . . . 1649. 4°, A—Z in fours, besides title and following leaf.

BLONDEAU, PIERRE, *Engraver.*
A most humble Remonstrance of Peter Blondeau, Concerning the offers made by him to this Commonwealth, for the coyning of the monie by a new Invention, not yet practised in any State ; . . . Septemb. 9, 1653. 8°, A—B 4 in eights, B 4 occupied by a statement of the essay of Blondeau's scheme at Goldsmiths' Hall.

BLOUNT OR BLUNT, SIR HENRY.
A Voyage into the Levant : . . . The fourth Edition. London, Printed by R. C. for Andrew Crooke, . . . 1650. 12°, A—K 6 in twelves.

BLOUNT, THOMAS.
The Academie of Eloquence. Containing a Compleat English Rhetoriqve, Exemplified. With Common-Places, and Formes, digested into an easie and Methodical way . . . Together with Letters both Amorovs and Moral, upon emergent occasions. By Tho. Blount Gent. . . . London, Printed by T. N. for Humphrey Moseley, . . . 1654. 12°. Frontispiece with portraits of Sydney, Bacon, &c., 1 leaf : A, 4 leaves : B—K in twelves : L, 6.

BLOUNT, SIR THOMAS POPE.
Censura Celebriorum Authorum : Sive Tractatus in quo Varia Virorum Doctorum

de Clarissimis cujusque Seculi Scriptoribus judicia traduntur. . . Omnia in Studiosorum gratiam collegit, . . . Thomas-Pope Blount, Anglo - Britannus Barouettus. Cum Iudice locupletissimo. Londini, Impensis Richardi Chiswel, . . . MDCXC. Folio, A—5 C in fours, including a half-title with the *Imprimatur*.

Sir Tho. Pope Blount's Essays on Several Subjects. . . . The Third Impression, with very Large Additions. Besides a New Essay of Religion . . . London, Printed for Richard Bently, . . . MDCXCVII. 8º. A, 4 leaves : B—S in eights.

BOCCACCIO, GIOVANNI.
The Decameron . . . The last Fiue Dayes. London, Printed by Isaac Iaggard. 1620. Folio. Title, 1 leaf : ¶—3 ¶ 2 in fours : B—Zz in fours : 3 A, 6. With the title engraved and cuts.

BOCCALINI, TRAJANO, *of Rome*.
The New-found Politicke. Disclosing the Secret Natvres and dispositions as well of priuate persons as of Statesmen and Courtiers . . . translated into English for the benefit of this Kingdome. London, Printed for Francis Williams, neere the Royall Exchange. 1626. 4º, A—Ii 2 in fours, Ii 2 blank, besides the title and an interesting dedication by [Sir] William Vaughan, the translator, to James I., in which he mentions Florio.

BODENHAM, JOHN, [AND LING, NICHOLAS?].
Politeuphuia. Wits Common wealth.
Si tibi difficilis formam natura negauit,
Ingenio formæ damna repende tuæ.
At London, Printed by I. R. for Nicholas Ling, . . . 1597. 8º. A, 4 leaves : B—Mm 4 in eights. *B. M.*

Dedicated by Ling to Master J[ohn] B[odenham], who, it appears, began the work long since, and left it to be completed either by Ling or by some one else.

BOECE, HECTOR.
Scotorvm Historiæ a prima gentis origine, cum aliarum & rerum & gentium illustratione non vulgari : præmissa epistola nûcupatoria, tabellisque amplissimis, & non pœnitenda Isagoge quæ ab huius tergo explicabuntur diffusius. Quæ omnia impressa quidem sunt Iodoci Badii Ascensii typis & opera : impensis autem Nobilis & prædocti viri Hectoris Boethii Deidonani : a quo sunt & condita & edita. [1527.] Folio. ā, 8 : ĕ, 8 : ī, 8 : ŏ, 8 : ū, 10 : AA—CC 6 in eights : a – z in eights : A—Z in eights. Dedicated to James V. from Aberdeen, April 1, 1526.

Heir beginnis the hystory and croniklis of Scotland. [Col.] Heir endis the hystory and Croniklis of Scotland, with the Cosmography & dyscription thairof. Compilit be the noble clerk maister Hector Boece channon of Aberdene. Translatit laitly in our vulgar and commeon langage, be maister Johne Bellenden Archedene of Murray. And Imprentit in Edinburgh, be me Thomas Danidson, prenter to the kyngis nobyll grace ∴ Cvm Privilegio. Folio, A—E in sixes, A ii apparently misprinted A i : E (repeated for F), 6 leaves : A—Yy in sixes and fours : Zz, 6 leaves : then two sheets of six and eight, the last page occupied by a cut of the Crucifixion. In two columns. On the back of the title occurs "The excusation of the prentar" in 5 7-line stanzas, and after the Contents comes "The proheme of the Cosmographe" in 9-line stanzas, which fills seven pages.

Hamilton Sale, May 1884, No. 301, a copy on vellum, said to have been the one dedicated and presented to James V., with *J. R.* on the top of the title, supposed to be in the King's autograph. The book was in the old oak boards covered with calf, and richly tooled, and bore on the obverse of the cover *Iacobvs Quintvs*, and on the reverse *Rex Scotorvm*. Other copies on vellum are in Edinburgh University Library and at Ham House.

BOETHIUS.
Boetivs De Consolatione philosophiæ. The boke of Boecius, called the comforte of philosophye, or wysedome, moche necessary for all men to reade and know, . . . Translated out of latin into the Englishe tounge by George Coluile, *alias* Coldewel to thintent that such as be ignorant in' the Latin tounge, and can rede Englysshe, maye vnderstande the same. Anno. M. D. LVI. [Col.] Imprynted at London in Paules churche yarde at the sygne of the holy Ghost, by Jhon Cawoode, Prynter to the kynge and Queenes Maiesties . . . 4º, A—Ff in fours, Ff 4 blank. Dedicated to the Queen. With the Latin in the margin.

BOHEMIA.
Bohemiæ Regnum Electinum. That is, A Plaine and Trve Relation of the proceeding of the States of Bohemia, from the first foundation of that Prouince, by Free Election of Princes and Kings vnto Ferdinand the eighteenth King of the House of Austria. . . . MDCXX. 4º, A — B in fours.

The History of the Bohemian Persecution, From the beginning of their conversion to Christianity in the year 894 to the year 1632. Ferdinand the 2 of Austria, Reigning. In which the unheard of secrets of policy, Counsells, Arts, and dreadfull Judgements are exhibited. London Printed by B. A. for John Walker. . . . MDCL. 8°. A, 4 leaves : B—Bb 4 in eights. *B. M.*

> The preface to the Godly Reader is subscribed *N. N. N. &c.* "In our banishment in the year, 1632."

BOLNEST, EDWARD.

Aurora Chymica : Or A Rational Way of preparing Animals, Vegetables, and Minerals, for A Physical Use ; By which Preparations they are made most efficacious, . . . London, Printed by Tho. Ratcliffe, and Nat. Thompson, . . . 1672. 8°, A—K in eights. Dedicated to George, Duke of Buckingham.

BOLTON, ROBERT.

Certaine Devout Prayers of Mr. Bolton upon solemne occasions. Published by E. B. by Mr. Boltons owne Coppy. London, Printed by George Miller dwelling in Black-Fryers. 1638. 12°, A—N in twelves, with a preface by W. Gouge.

BONAVENTURA.

Here begynneth the lyfe of the gloryous confessoure of oure lorde Jhesu criste seynt Francis. [Col] Here endeth the lyfe of the gloryous confessoure of our lorde Jhesu criste / seynte Francis. Imprynted at London in Fletestret at the sygne of the George by Rycharde Pynson / prynter vnto the Kynges noble grace . *.* 4°, A—N in eights and fours, N 8 *verso* with the printer's mark.

> Sothebys (Fuller Russell), June 26, 1885, No. 138. At Tutet's sale in 1786, No. 319, a copy sold for 14s. 6d.

BOND, HENRY, *Senior.*

The Art of Apparelling and fitting of any Ship with Masts, Yards, and Cordage. . . . With Rules for the Sizes and Lengths of all sorts of Cordage . . . The second Impression, Newly corrected, . . . Printed for the Widow Seyle in the Bulwark by the Tower, 1663. 4°, A—E in fours, first and last leaves blank.

BONDE, W.

Here begynneth a denout treatyse in Englysshe / called the Pylgrimage of perfection : very plitable for all christen people to rede : and in especiall / to all relygious psons muche necessary. [Col.] Thus endeth the seuenth and last day of the pylgrimage of perfection. Imprinted at London in Fletestrete / besyde saynt Dunstans churche by Richarde Pynson /

priter to the kynges noble grace. Cū priuilegio. Anno domini. 1526. 4°. A, 6 leaves : a, 6 : A (repeated)—E in fours and eights : F, 6 : G—T in fours and eights : AA, 6 leaves : AAA — BBB, 6 leaves each : Table of Book iii. 3 leaves : a, 8 leaves : AA—RR in fours and eights : AAA—ZZZ in fours and eights : Table of the 3rd Book of the 7th day, 3 leaves : d—h in fours and eights : h, 6 leaves, h 6 blank except the mark on the *verso.*

BOOK.

The contētes of this boke. A Werke of preparacion / or of ordinaunce vnto cōmunion / or howselyng. The werke for housholders with the golden pistle and alphabete or a crosrowe called an A. B. C. all duely corrected and newly prynted. [Col.] Imprynted by Robert Redman. Cum priuilegio. [A second title :] A Werke for housholders. . . . [Col.] Imprynted at London in Flete strete / at the sygne of the George / by me Roberte Redman. The yere of our lorde god. M.D.xxxi. The . xix . day of Auguste. 8°, black letter. The first portion, A—L in eights : the second, A—G 4 in eights, G 4 with the mark and a page woodcut on the *recto.*

The Boke of Knowledge / Whether a sycke person beynge in perylle shall lyue or dye. &c. [Col.] Imprynted by me Robert Wyer : . . . 8°, black letter, A—B 2 in fours, B 2 having the colophon and mark. *B. M.*

BOOKER, JOHN.

Mercurius Cœlicus : Or, A Caveat to all People of the Kingdome, That now have, or shall hereafter happen to reade the counterfeit, and most pernicious Pamphlet written under the name of Naworth : Or, A New Almanacke, And Prognostication For . . . 1644. (Said in the Title Page thereof to be) Printed at Oxford by His Majesties Command. London, Printed by J. Raworth, for John Partridge. [1644.] 4°, A—C in fours.

> On B occurs a new title : Mercurio-Cœlico-Mastix. Or An Anti-caveat to all such, as have (heretofore) had the Misfortune to be Cheated, and Deluded, by that Grand and Traiterous Impostor of this Rebellious Age, Iohn Booker. In Answer to . . . Mercvrivs-Cœlicvs. . . . By G. Naworth. Printed Anno Dom. 1644.

The Bloudy Almanack, For this present Jubilee. To which England is directed, to fore-know what shall come to passe, by that famous Astrologer, Mr. John Booker. . . . London : Printed by John Clowes, 1647. 4°, 4 leaves. *B. M.*

BOREMAN, THOMAS, *Astrologer.*
Love's True Oracle. Or, A most New
and Curious Fortune Book : Both for
Men and Maids, Wives and Widows, . . .
To which is Added The Signification of
Dreams and Moles ; . . . Printed for T.
Norris at the Looking-glass on London-
Bridge. 4⁰, A—C in fours. With cuts.
Partly in verse.

Crossley, part 2, No. 326.

BORRI, CRISTOFORO.
Cochin-China : Containing many admir-
able Rarities and Singularities of that
Country. Extracted out of an Italian
Relation, lately presented to the Pope, by
Christophoro Borri, that lived certaine
yeeres there. And published by Robert
Ashley. *Cum hac persuasione* . . . Seneca.
London. Printed by Robert Raworth,
for Richard Clutterbuck, . . . 1633. 4⁰,
A—I in fours, I 4 blank, and the title-
page. Dedicated by Ashley to Sir Maurice
Abbot, Governor of the East India Com-
pany.

BOYD, ZACHARY.
The Balme of Gilead prepared for the
Sicke. The whole is divided into Three
Parts . . . Published by M*. Zacharie
Boyd, Preacher of God's Word in Glasgow.
. . . Edinbvrgh Printed by Iohn Wreit-
tovn. 1629. 8⁰, ¶, 4 leaves : A—Q 4
in eights. Dedicated to the Archbishop
of Glasgow.

Two Sermons, For those who are to come
to the Table of the Lord. With diverse
prayers . . . Carefully digested by M*.
Zacharie Boyd . . . Edinbvrgh Printed
by Iohn Wreittovn. Anno Dom. 1629.
8⁰. Dedicated to the In-dwellers of the
Burgh and Barony of Glasgow.

Sothebys, July 7, 1885, No. 180, imperfect.

BOYER, PIERRE, *Minister of the Gospel.*
The History of the Vaudois. Wherein is
shewn their Original ; how God has preserved the Christian Religion among them
in its Purity, from the time of the Apostles, to our days ; The Wonders he has
done for their preservation, . . . newly
translated out of French by a Person of
Quality. London, Printed for Edward
Mory, at the Three Bibles in St. Paul's
Church-Yard. MDCXCII. 12⁰. A. 6 leaves:
B—M 6 in twelves, M 6 blank. Dedicated
to William III.

BOYLE, ROBERT, *F.R.S.*
Hydrostatical Paradoxes, made out by
New Experiments, (For the most part
Physical and Easie.) By the Honourable
Robert Boyle, . . . Oxford, Printed by

William Hall, for Richard Davis, Anno
Dom. M.DC.LXVI. 8⁰, A—R 4 in eights :
a—b 2 in eights ; and three folded leaves.

Tracts Consisting of Observations about
the Saltness of the Sea : An Account of
a Statical Hygloscope and its Uses : Together with an Appendix about the Force
of the Air's Moisture : A Fragment about
the Natural and Præternatural State of
Bodies. . . . London, Printed by E.
Flesher for R. Davis . . . MDCLXXIV.
Sm. 8⁰. A, 4 leaves : B—N in eights.

This volume comprises A Dialogue about
the Positive or Privative Natures of Cold,
by a Fellow of the Royal Society.

Tracts : Containing 1. Suspicions about
some Hidden Qualities of the Air ; . . .
II. Animadversions upon M*. Hobbes's
Problemata de Vacuo. III. A Discourse
of the Cause of Attraction by Suction.
By the Honourable Robert Boyle, Esq ;
. . . London, Printed by W. G. and are
to be sold by M. Pitt, . . . 1674. 8⁰.
Title and first Preface, 3 leaves : Second
Preface, 2 leaves : 3rd Preface, 2 leaves :
Advertisement to the Binder, followed
by a blank, 2 leaves : B—F 4 in eights :
Observations about the Growth of Metals,
A—B 6 : *Some Additional Experiments*
. . . A in eights : *Animadversions,* title
and preface, 5 leaves ; and A 2—F 8 in
eights : *On the Cause of Attraction by
Suction,* A—E 4 in eights, E 4 blank :
New Experiments . . . A, 8 : B, 2.

New [Experiments and Observations
touching Cold, Or, An Experimental
History of Cold, begun. To which are
added An Examen of Antiperistasis, . . .
By the Honourable Robert Boyle . . .
London, Printed for Richard Davis,
Bookseller in Oxford, 1683. 4⁰. Title,
1 leaf : Publisher to the Reader, 4 leaves :
A—3 B 2 in fours. With two plates at
pp. 4 and 160.

This book includes an examen of Hobbes
upon Cold, an Account of Freezing by Dr.
Merret, and an Appendix containing some
experiments and observations on the precedent history of Cold.

The General History of the Air, Designed
and Begun by the Honᵇˡᵉ Robert Boyle
Esq. . . . London, Printed for Awnsham
and John Churchill, . . . MDCXCII. 4⁰,
A—Ll 2 in fours, and a, 2 leaves.

BOYLE, ROGER, *Earl of Orrery.*
Parthenissa, That most Fam'd Romance.
The Six Volumes Compleat. Composed
by the Right Honourable The Earl of
Orrery. London, Printed by T. N. for
Henry Herringman, . . . MDCLXXVI. Folio.

A, 2 leaves : B—5 K in fours, last leaf blank.

Parthenissa, A Romance. In Four Parts. Dedicated to the Lady Northvmberland, And the Lady Svnderland. The First Part. London, Printed for Henry Herringman, . . . 1655. 4°. Title, 1 leaf : Dedication, 2 leaves : The Preface, 4 leaves : B—3 G in fours, besides a leaf before B 1.

Parthenissa, A Romance . . . The Second Part. London, Printed for Henry Herringman, . . . 1655. 4°, A—3 M in fours. and an extra leaf in 3 M.

Parthenissa, A Romance . . . The Third Part. London, Printed for Henry Herringman, . . . 1655. 4°, A—3 H 2 in fours, besides title and 2 leaves of Dedication to Lady Sunderland.

Parthenissa, . . . The Fourth Part. London, Printed for Henry Herringman, . . . 1655. 4°, A—3 A in fours, and the title.

Parthenissa . . . The Last Part. The fifth Tome. London, Printed by T. R. & E. M. for Henry Herringman . . . 1656. 4°, B—Rr 2 in fours, Rr 2 blank, and the title.

Parthenissa : . . . The Last Part. The Sixth Tome. London, Printed for Henry Herringman, . . . 1669. 4°, A—Qq in fours. Dedicated by the Earl of Orrery to Henrietta Maria, Duchess of Orleans.

BOYSE, J.
Some Remarkable Passages in the Holy Life and Death of Mr. Edmund Trench ; Most of them drawn out of his own Diary. . . . London, Printed by Tho. Warren, for Tho. Parkhurst, . . . and Jonathan Robinson, . . . 1693. 8°, A—H in eights, A 1 and H 8 blank. With a portrait by R. White.

BRADY, ROBERT, M.D.
A Complete History of England, From the First Entrance of the Romans . . . Unto the End of the Reign of King Henry III. . . . By Robert Brady, Doctor in Physic. In the Savoy, Printed by Tho. Newcomb for Samuel Lowndes, . . . MDCLXXXV. Folio. With a portrait of James II. The Continuation, dated 1700. With a frontispiece. 2 vols.

BRATHWAITE, RICHARD.
The English Gentleman ; And the English Gentlewoman. Both in one Volvme couched, and in one Modell portrayed : to the living glory of their Sexe, the lasting story of their Worth. Being presented to present times for ornaments, commended to posterity for Presidents. With a Ladies Love-Lectvre And a Svpplement lately annexed, and Entituled The Tvrtles Trivmph. The third Edition revised, corrected, and enlarged. By Richard Brathwait Esq. *Turture sic Turtur jungit amanda suo.* London, Printed by Iohn Dawson. 1641. Folio. Frontispiece by W. Marshall and folded metrical explanation, 2 leaves : printed general title and title to *English Gentleman,* 2 leaves : dedication to Philip Earl of Pembroke and Montgomery, 3 leaves : To the Reader, &c., 1 leaf : B—3 N 2 in fours : a folded leaf with "the Contents, &c., of this Ladies Love-Lectvre :" the *Turtles Triumph,* Aaa—Ggg 2 in fours.

BRECKNOCK.
A Declaration of the Gentlemen and Inhabitants of the County of Brecknock, Concerning their firm Resolutions for the Parliament, . . . London, Printed for Edw. Husbands, . . . December 6. 1645. 4°, 4 leaves.

BREREWOOD, EDWARD.
De Ponderibvs, et Pretiis vetervm Nvmmorum, eorumq ; cum recentioribus collatione. Liber vnvs. Authore Edovardo Brerewood : nuper in Collegio Gressamensi Londini, Astronomiæ Professore. Londini, Apud Ioannem Billium. 1614. 4°, A—H in fours. Dedicated to Sir Thomas Egerton, Lord Ellesmere.

BRETHREN.
Brethren in Iniquity : Or A Beardless Pair : Held forth in a Dialogue betwixt Titchburn and Ireton, Prisoners in the Tower of London. Printed for Daniel Webb, in the year 1660. 4°, 4 leaves.

BRETNOR, THOMAS.
Bretnor. 1616. A Newe Almanacke and Prognostication, ... Cum priuilegio. [No place, &c. 1616.] 8°, A—C in eights.
The last page is occupied by six stanzas, "A Prognostication M. Astromastigas."

BRETON, NICHOLAS.
Characters vpon Essaies Morall, and Diuine, Written For those good Spirits, that will take them in good part, And Make vse of them to good purpose. London Printed by Edw. Griffin, for Iohn Gwillim, and are to be sold at his shop in Britaines-Burse. 1615. 8°, A—D in eights, A 1 and D 7-8 blank. Dedicated to Sir Francis Bacon, Attorney-General. With verses by W. D., R. B., &c., and a short preface signed N. B.
The work is in prose.

Crossing of Proverbs. Crosse-Answeres. And Crosse-Humours. By E. N. Gent. At London, Printed for Iohn Wright, and are to be solde at his Shop without Newgate, at the signe of the Bible. 1616. 8°.

    Collier's Sale, August 7, 1884, No. 47, title and 5 following leaves; but as the title makes A 2, there was probably a blank before it, so that this fragment contained the whole of sign. A except A 8.

BREVAL, D.
Caroli Secundi, Magnæ Britanniæ Regis, Epitaphium. Excudebat Thomas Newcombe . . . MDCLXXXV. A broadside in verse.

BREVIA.
[Natura Brevium. The Colophon :] Here endeth the boke of Natura breuium Emprynted by Richard Pynson. [About 1500.] Folio. a, 8 leaves, a 1 blank on *recto* and occupied on the reverse by a shield : a (repeated)—e in eights, a 1 blank : d—e in sixes : f, 8 : g, 6 : h, 6 : i, 4, the last leaf with the mark only.

    At the foot of (a 8 *verso*) of the first gathering occurs : "This Booke with the Natura Breuium was Empryntyd by me Rychard Pynson at the Instaunce of my maysters of the còpany of Stronde Inne with oute tempyll Barre, off londoñ."
    A copy, wanting a leaf, was sold among the Addington books, and I know no other.

La Vievx Natura breuium, dernierment corrigee. . . . Londini. In ædibus Richardi Tottelli. 1584. . . . 8°, A—Z in eights.

BREVIARIUM.
Breviarium ad usum tocius congregationis sancti Albani. [St. Albans, about 1534.] 4°, 488 leaves. Printed in red and black. *Marquis of Bute.*
    Communicated by Mr. Jacobus Weale.

BREWSTER, SIR FRANCIS, *Knight.*
New Essays of Trade. . . . London, Printed for H. Walwyn, . . . 1702. 8°, A—I in eights and a folded table.

BRIDGES, THOMAS.
A String of Pearles : Or, The best things reserved at last. Discovered, in a Sermon preached in London, June 8. 1657. at the Funeral of (that Triumphant Saint) Mris Mary Blake, late Wife to (his Worthy Friend) Mr Nicholas Blake Merchant. with an Elegy on her Death. . . . London, Printed by R. I. for John Hancock, . . . 1657. 8°, B—N 4 in eights, N 4 with the label, no A.

BRIDGMAN, SIR ORLANDO.
A Congratulatory Poem on the Right Honourable Sr. Orlando Bridgman, Lord

Keeper of the great Seal of England. Printed for William Cadman . . . A poetical broadside.

BRIGHT, TIMOTHY, *M.D.*
A Treatise of Melancholy. . . . Imprinted at London by Iohn Windet. 1586. 8°. *, 8 leaves : A—S 2 in eights.
    A totally different edition from that printed the same year by Vautrollier.

BRINKLOW, HENRY.
The complaint of Roderyck Mors, sometime a gray Fryre, vnto the parliament-house of Englande his natuturall [*sic*] countrye : . . . Imprinted at Geneue in Sanoye by Myghell bors. Sm. 8°, A—Q in fours, Q 4 blank.
    Sothebys, June 30, 1885, No. 799.

BRISCOE, JOHN.
A Discourse of the late Funds of the Million-Act, Lottery-Act, and Bank of England. . . . The Third Edition, with an Appendix. London, Printed by J. D. for Andrew Bell . . . 1696. 8°. A, 2 leaves : B—N 6 in eights.

BROWN, EDWARD.
An Account of Seviral Travels through a great part of Germany : In Four Journeys I. From Norwich to Colen. II. From Colen to Vienna, . . . III. From Vienna to Hamburg. IV. From Hamburg to London. Wherein the Mines, Baths, and other Curiosities of those Parts are Treated of. Illustrated with Sculptures. By Edward Brown . . . London. Printed for Benj. Tooke, . . . 1677. 4°. A, 2 leaves : B—Aa 2 in fours. With plates at pp. 68, 76, 80, 110, 132, 136.

[BROWN, THOMAS.]
The Life of the Late Famous Comedian, Jo. Haynes. Containing, His Comical Exploits and Adventures, both at Home and Abroad.
Quæ Regio in terris nostri non plena Laboris?
London, Printed for J. Nutt, . . . 1701. 8°, A—I in fours. Dedicated to William Mann, Esq; of Chartham, under the name of Tobyas Thomas.

BROWNE, HUMPHREY.
A Map of the Microcosme, Or, A Morall Description of Man. Newly compiled into Essayes : By H. Browne. . . . London, Printed by T. Harper, for John Williams, . . . 1642. 12°, A—I 6 in twelves. Dedicated to the Marquis of Hertford.

BROWNE, JOHN.
Admochoiradelogia : Or, An Anatomick-Chirurgical Treatise of Glandules & Stru-

maes, Or Kings - Evil - Swellings. To-
gether with the Royal gift of Healing,
. . . . By John Browne, one of His
Majesties Chirurgeons in Ordinary, and
Chirurgeon of His Majesties Hospital . . .
London : Printed by Tho. Newcomb for
Sam. Lowndes, . . . 1684. 8⁰. Frontis-
piece, portrait, and leaf of verses : A, 8
leaves : (a)—(d) in eights : B—Aa 4 in
eights : Bb—Rr 4 in eights. Dedicated
(1) to the King and (2) to the Duke of
Ormond.

BROWNE, ROBERT, *Founder of the*
Brownists.
A Booke which sheweth the life and
manners of all true Christians, and howe
vnlike they are vnto Turkes and Papistes,
and Heathen folke. . . . By me, Robert
Browne. Middelbvrgh, Imprinted by
Richard Painter. 1582. 4⁰, A—B in
fours : C, 2 leaves : D—O in fours.

BROWNISTS.
An Apologie or Defence of svch trve
Christians as are commonly (but uniustly)
called Brownists. Against such imputations as are layd vpon them by the Heads
and Doctors of the Vniversity of Oxford,
in their Answer to the humble Petition
of the Ministers of the Church of England, . . . 1604. 4⁰. * and **, 4 leaves
each : A—P in fours, P 4 blank. Dedicated to the King.
    Attributed to Francis Johnson and Henry
    Ainsworth.

BRUCE, ROBERT.
Sermons Preached in the Kirk of Edin-
burgh be M. Robert Bruce, Minister of
Christs Euangel there, as they wer re-
ceived from his mouth : Meet, &c. Edin-
bvrgh Printed be Robert Walde-graue,
Printer to the Kings Majestie. 1591.
Cum priuilegio Regali. 8⁰. A, 4 leaves,
A 1-2 blank : B—Bb 4 in eights. Dedi-
cated to the Provost, Baillies, &c., of
Edinburgh.
    Compare Herbert, p. 1509.

BUCHANAN, GEORGE.
Ane Detectiovn of the duinges of Marie
Quene of Scottes . . . [1572.]
    The account found here will now have to
    undergo collation with the Hatfield Papers
    and the other information published since
    1880 on this subject.

Historia Animæ Hvmanæ, Avctore Davide
Bvchanano Scoto. M.DC.XXXVI. 8⁰. ă,
8 leaves : č, 4 leaves : A—Rr in eights :
Ss—Tt in fours.

BUGG, FRANCIS.
The Painted - Harlot both Stript and

Whipt, Or the Second Part of the Naked
Truth, Containing A further Discovery of
the Mischief of Imposition, among the
People called Quakers, . . . London,
Printed by J. Gain, for the Author, Anno,
1683 . . . 4⁰, A—B 2 in fours, and A—I
in fours.

BULTEEL, JOHN.
The Apothegmes of the Ancients ; Taken
out of Plutarch, Diogenes Laertius, . . .
Collected into one Volume for the Benefit
and Pleasure of the Ingenious. London,
Printed for William Cademan . . . 1683.
8⁰, A—Y 4 in eights, A 1 blank. Dedi-
cated by Bulteel from York Garden, 20
Jan. 1683, to Mᵐ Esther Woodward,
Relict of Richard Woodward Esq.

BUNYAN, JOHN.
Profitable Meditations, Fitted to Mans
Different Condition. In a Conference
between Christ and a Sinner. In Nine
Particulars. By John Bunyan, Servant
to the Lord Jesus. London, Printed for
Francis Smith, at the sign of the Elephant
and Castle, without Temple-Bar. [in coeval MS. is added] 1661. 4⁰, A—D in
fours. In verse. *B. M.*
    This tract was obtained from Cornwall
    by a former owner in a volume with others.

Differences in Judgment about Water-
Baptism, No Bar to Communion : Or To
Communicate with Saints, as Saints,
proved lawful . . . By John Bunyan . . .
London, Printed for John Wilkins . . .
1673. 8⁰, A—H in eights.

The Pilgrim's Progress From this World,
to that which is to come : Delivered under
the Similitude of a Dream Wherein is
Discovered, The manner of his setting
out, His Dangerous Journey, And Safe
Arrival at the Desired Countrey. *I have*
used Similitudes, Hos. 12. 10. By John
Bunyan. Licensed and Entered according
to Order. London, Printed for Nath.
Ponder at the Peacock in the Poultry
near Cornhil, 1678. 8⁰, A—Q 4 in eights,
A 1 and Q 4 blank. *B. M.*
    First edition. This copy was lately pur-
    chased ; others are in the possession of Mr.
    Holford and Mr. Elliot Stock. Doubtless,
    yet more copies will be brought to light
    from time to time.

Voyage d'Un Chrestien vers l'Eternité
Ecrit en Anglois, Par Monsieur Bunjan,
F. M. de Bedfort ; Et nouvellement traduit
en François. Avec Figures. à Amsterdam, . . . 1685. 12⁰. *, 12 leaves : A
—N 10 in twelves. With eight plates
and a frontispiece.

The Greatness of the Soul, And vnspeakableness of the Loss thereof ; with the Causes of the Losing it. First Preached at Pinners Hall, and now enlarged, and Published for Good. By John Bunyan. London, Printed for Benj. Alsop . . . MDCLXXXIII. 12⁰, A—K 6 in twelves.

Seasonable Counsel : Or, Advice to Sufferers. By John Bunyan. London, Printed for Benjamin Alsop,... MDCLXXXIV. 12⁰, A—L in twelves, A 1 and L 12 blank.

A Holy Life the Beauty of Christianity : Or, An Exhortation to Christians to be Holy. By John Bunyan . . . London, Printed by B. W. for Benj. Alsop, . . . 1684. 12⁰, A—K 6 in twelves.

A Discourse upon the Pharisee and the Publicane. By John Bunyan. London : Printed for Joh. Harris, . . . 1685. 12⁰, Frontispiece containing portrait, title, and to the Reader, 3 leaves : B—K 5 in twelves.

The Work of Jesus Christ, as an Advocate, Clearly Explained, and Largely Improved, . . . By John Bunyan, Author of the *Pilgrims Progress*. London, Printed for Dorman Newman, . . . 1688. 12⁰, A—K in twelves. With a portrait.

BURNET, GILBERT, *Bishop of Salisbury.*
Reflections on Mr Varillas's History of the Revolutions that have happened in Europe in matter of Religion. And more particularly on his Ninth Book that relates to England. By G. Burnet, D.D. Amsterdam, Printed for W. Savonret in the Warmoes-street near the Dam, 1686. 12⁰. A, 6 : B—P in twelves : Q 6.

A Continuation of Reflections on Mr Varillas's History of Heresies . . . By G. Burnet, D.D. Amsterdam, Printed for J. S. 1687. 12⁰. A, 2 : B—G in twelves : H, 4.

A Defence of the Reflections on the Ninth Book of the First Volume of Mr Varillas's History of Heresies. Being a Reply to his Answer. By G. Burnet, D.D. Amsterdam, Printed for J. S. 1687. 12⁰. A, 6 : B—G in twelves.

A Letter to Mr Thevenot. Concerning A Censure of M^r Le Grand's History of King Henry the Eighth's Divorce. To which is Added, A Censure of M^r. de Meaux's History of the Variation of the Protestant Churches . . . London, Printed for John Starkey and Richard Chiswell. MDCLXXXIX. 4⁰. B—l in fours, besides title and half-title.

BURTON, RICHARD.
The Strange and Prodigious Religions, Customs, and Manners, of Sundry Nations . . . Faithfully collected from ancient and modern Authors ; and adorned with divers Pictures of several remarkable Passages therein. By R. B. London, Printed for and sold by Hen. Rodes . . . 1683. 12⁰. A, 2 leaves : B—L 6 in twelves. With plates numbered A to T.

England's Monarchs : Or, A Compendious Relation of the most Remarkable Transactions, . . . from the Invasion of the Romans to this present. Adorned with Poems, and the Pictures of every Monarch, from William the Conqueror, to His present Majesty, . . . By R. B. . . . London, Printed for Nath. Crouch . . . 1685. 12⁰, A—K in twelves, besides a frontispiece containing a portrait of Charles II.

The History of Oliver Cromwel : Being an Impartial Account of all the Battles, Sieges, . . . And Likewise, of his Civil Administrations . . . Relating only Matters of Fact, without Reflection or Observation. By R. B. London, Printed for Nath. Crouch, . . . 1693. 12⁰, A—H in twelves, including a portrait of Cromwell.

The History of the House of Orange ; Or, A Brief Relation of the Glorious and Magnanimous Atchievements of His Majesties Predecessors, and likewise of His own Heroick Actions till the Late Wonderful Revolution. Together with the History of William and Mary . . . By R. B. London, Printed for Nath. Crouch . . . 1693. 12⁰, B—l in twelves, A omitted, and a frontispiece.

The History of the Two Late Kings, Charles the Second and James the Second . . . Together with a Relation of the Happy Revolution, and the Accession of their present Majesties . . . By R. B. London, Printed for Nath. Crouch . . . 1693. 12⁰, A—H in twelves, besides a frontispiece.

The Kingdom of Darkness : Or The History of Dæmons, Spectres, Witches, Apparitions, Possessions, Disturbances, . . . Collected from Authentick Records . . . Together with a Preface . . . By R. B. London, Printed for Nath. Crouch . . . 1695. 12⁰, A—H in twelves, besides the frontispiece.

BUSHELL, THOMAS.
The First Part of Youths Errors. Written by Thomas Byshel, the Superlative Prodigall. Luke 15, 18. *I will arise* . . .

Imprinted at London. 1628. 8°, A—M in eights, A 1 with a portrait. Dedicated by Bushel "To the Honourable and right vertuous, Thomas, Lord Windsor, my very good Lord."

Sothebys, June 26, 1885, No. 199.

An Extract by Mr Bushell of his Late Abridgment of the Lord Chancellor Bacons Philosophical Theory in Mineral Prosecutions. Published for the Satisfaction of his Noble Friends, that importunately desired it. London, Printed by Tho. Leach, in the Year, 1660. 4°, A—G in fours : ****, 4 leaves : leaf with parliamentary license, Aug. 14, 1641, followed by a blank : †, 2 leaves : ‡, 4 leaves : The Impression of Mr. Bushel's Golden Medal, 1 leaf : then G 3–4 repeated with a Postscript, and H—K 2 in fours, with verses. With a portrait by Faithorne of Charles II., to whom the volume is dedicated.

Putticks, June 28, 1886, No. 248, Charles the Second's copy.

BUTLER, SAMUEL.

To the Memory of the Most Renowned Du - Vall : A Pindarick Ode. By the Author of *Hudibras.* London : Printed for H. Brome, . . . 1671 . . . 4°, A—B in fours.

BYFIELD, NATHANIEL.

An Account of the Late Revolution in New-England. Together with the Declaration of the Gentlemen, Merchants, and Inhabitants of Boston and the Country adjacent. April 18. 1689. Written by Mr Nathanael Byfield, a Merchant of Bristol in New-England, to his Friends in London. . . . London : Printed for Ric. Chiswell, . . . MDCLXXXIX. 4°, A—C 2 in fours.

BYFIELD, T., M.D.

Two Discourses : One of Consumptions, With their Cure by a New Method. The other contains some Rules of Health. London : Printed for Dorman Newman, . . . MDCLXXXV. 4°, A—E in fours, A 1 blank.

The Preface is dated from the author's house in New Street, by Fetter Lane, near the Five Bells.

BYRD, WILLIAM.

Songs of sundry natures, . . . Lately made and composed into Musicke of 3. 4. 5. and 6. parts : . . . By William Byrd, . . . Imprinted at London by Lucretia East, the assigne of William Barley, . . . 1610. 4°. Superius, A—G 2 in fours : Bassus, the same.

C.

C. A.

An Answer to a Pamphlet Intitvled : The Fisher Catched in his owne Net . . . By A. C. . . . M.D.C.XXIII. 4°, A—M in fours.

Trve Relations of Svndry Conferences had betweene certaine Protestant Doctours, and a Iesvite called M. Fisher (then Prisoner in London for the Catholique Fayth) togeather with Defences of the same. . . . By A. C. . . . Permissu Superiorum. M.DC.XXVI. 4°. *, 4 leaves : **, 4 leaves : A—K 2 in fours, K 2 blank.

The Preface of the Publisher has the initials *W. I.*

C. A.

The English Oracle : Or, A Late Prophecy of the Miseries that will happen this Next Year, 1679. . . . London, Printed for W. M. . . . 1679. . . . 4°, 4 leaves.

C. J.

The new Parlement of Ladies. Being a very Merry Dialogue, Between Gyll-Flirt a Chamber-maid, and Skip-kennell a Lackquey. . . . By J. C. a lover of the Vertuous, and hater of the Vicious of their Sex. Printed in the Year, 1655. 4°, 4 leaves. In prose.

C. J.

The State of the Papist and Protestant Proprietors in the Kingdom of Ireland, In the Year 1641. . . . and how disposed in 1653, when the War and Rebellion was declared at an End, . . . London, Printed for Richard Baldwin . . . 1689. 4°, A—E in fours. Dedicated to the King.

C. P.

A Short and Impartial View of the Manner and Occasion of the Scot's Colony's coming away from Darien. In a Letter to a Person of Quality. *Quia Veritas* . . . Tacit. Printed in the year, M.DC.XC.IX. 4°, A—E in fours.

C. R.

. . . . Regulation of the Coyn of England, and how the East India Trade may be preserved and encreased. London. Printed for Roger Clavel . . . 1696. 4°, A—F in fours.

> The top of the title in this copy is mutilated.

C. RO.

A True Historicall discourse of Muley Hamets rising to the three Kingdomes of Morocco, Fes and Sus. The dis-vision of the three Kingdomes, by ciuill warre, . . . The Religion and Policie of the More, or Barbarian. The aduentures of Sir Anthony Sherley, and diuers other English Gentlemen, in those Countries. With other Nouelties. At London, Printed by Thomas Purfoot for Clement Knight, . . . An. Dom. 1609. 4°, A—L 2 in fours.

> Dedicated to Sir Robert Cotton of Connington, Knight.

C. S.

The Famous and Delectable History of Cleocreton & Cloryana, Wherein is set forth The Noble and Heroick Actions of Cleocreton Prince of Hungary, His Wonderful and Warlike Atchievements in sundry Kingdoms. Herein is also declared, His constant love to the most beautiful Princess Cloryana, the onely Daughter of the Emperor of Persia. London, Printed by J. B. for Charles Tyus at the three Bibles on London - Bridge. [about 1670.] 4°, black letter, A—O 2 in fours. With a large cut on the last page. *B. M.*

> Dedicated by S. C. "To her Discerning and most Knowing Brother, Mr E. C." This book is advertised at the end of the *Destruction of Troy*, 1684.

C. T., *a friend to truth.*

A Glasse for the Times by which according to the Scriptures, you may behold the true Ministers of Christ, how farre differing from false Teachers. . . . London, Printed by Robert Ibbitson. 1648. 4°, 6 leaves, including a frontispiece.

> Among the false teachers appear Milton and John Williams, writer of the *Bloody Tenent.*

C. T., *Med.*

[Instructions for persons attacked by the Plague, or enabling them to avoid it.] London, Printed for Joseph Leigh, 1665. A broadside.

C. W., *M.D.*

Hydro-Sideron : Or, A Treatise of Ferruginous Waters, Especially the Ipswich Spaw, . . . London : Printed by W. P. . . . 1717. 8°, A—K in eights. Dedicated to Dr. John Bateman, President of the College of Physicians.

C. W.

The Siege of Vienna, A Poem. By W. C. London, Printed for H. Hills Jun. 1685. 4°, A—F in fours. Dedicated to the Earl of Plymouth, Lord Lieutenant of Worcester.

CABALA.

The Count of Gabalis : Or, The Extravagant Mysteries of the Cabalists, Exposed in Five Pleasant Discourses on the Secret Sciences. . . . Done into English, By P. A. Gent. With Short Animadversions. London, Printed for B. M. Printer to the Cabalisticall Society of the Sages, at the Sign of the Rosy-Crusian. CIƆIƆC.LXXX. 12°. A, 4 : B—I in twelves : K, 2.

CALDERWOOD, DAVID.

Perth Assembly, Containing 1. The Proceedings thereof. 2. The Proofe of the Nullitie thereof. 3. Reasons presented thereto against the receiving the fiue new Articles imposed. . . . MDCXIX. 4°, A—O 2 in fours.

CALDWELL, JAMES, *sometimes preacher at Fawkirke.*

The Countesse of Marres Arcadia, or Sanctuarie. Containing Morning, and Evening Meditations for the whole Weeke. Edinburgh, Printed by Iohn Wreittoun, and are to bee sold at his Shop, at the Nether Bow. 1625. 12°. 7 preliminary leaves with title and dedication to Lady Mary Stewart, Countess of Mar, by the Editor, M. P. Anderson : A — V in twelves. *B. M.*

CALVERT, PHILIP.

A Letter from the Chancellour of Maryland to Col. Henry Meese Merchant in London : Concerning the late Troubles in Mary-Land. [Col.] London : Printed for A. Banks, 1684. A broadside. *B. M.*

CALVIN, JOHN.

The Institvtion of Christian Religion, written in Latine By maister Iohn Caluine, and translated into English according to the Authors last edition. by T. N. . . . Seen and allowed. . . . Imprinted at London in White Crosse strete by Richarde Harrison. Anno. 1562. Cum priuilegio. . . . Folio. Title, 1 leaf : A, 9 leaves : A (repeated)—3 X in eights.

The Catechisme, or maner to teache Children . . . Imprinted at London, by the Widdow Orwin. 1594. 8°, black letter, A—K in eights.

An Admonicion against Astrology Ivdiciall and other curiosities, that raigne now in the world : written in the french tonge by Ihon Calvine and translated into Englishe, by G[oddred] G[ilby.] . . . Imprinted at London by Roulande Hall, dwellyng in Goldyng lane, at the signe of the thre arrowes. [About 1560.] 8°, A—E in eights.

Sermons of Mr Iohn Caluine Vpon the X. Commandementes of the Lawe . . . Translated out of Frenche into English by I[ohn] H[armar.] Imprinted at London for Thomas Woodcocke. 1579. [Col.] Imprinted at London, at the three Cranes of the Vine-tree, by Thomas Dawson, for Thomas Woodcocke, Anno. 1579. 4°, chiefly black letter. Title, &c., 4 leaves, first blank : A—Ii 2 in fours. Dedicated to Dudley, Earl of Leicester.

CAMBRIDGESHIRE.
A sad Relation of a Dreadful Fire at Cottenham, Four miles distant from Cambridge . . . Written by an Eyewitness, . . . Printed for Thomas Pierce. 1676. 4°, 4 leaves.

CAMDEN, WILLIAM.
V. Cl. Gulielmi Camdeni Elogia Anglorum. Hi Majores Tui sunt, si Te illis dignum præstes. *Sen.* Londini, Excudebat T. W. . . 1653. 8°, A—B in eights, A 1 and B 8 blank. *B. M.*

CAMPANELLA, TOMMASO.
Thomas Campanella An Italian Friar and Second Machiavel. His Advice to the King of Spain for attaining the universal Monarchy of the World. Particularly concerning England, Scotland and Ireland, how to raise Division between King and Parliament, to alter the Government from a Kingdome to a Commonwealth. . . . Translated into English by Ed. Chilmead, and published for awakening the English to prevent the approaching ruine of the Nation. With an admonitorie Preface by William Prynne of Lincolnes-Inne Esquire. London, Printed for Philemon Stephens. . . . [1660.] 4°, A—Gg in fours, besides Pryme's Preface, 3 leaves, dated from Lincoln's Inn, Dec. 16, 1659.

CAMPBELL, ARCHIBALD, *Marquis of Argyll.*
The Speech and Plea of Archibald Mar-

quesse of Argyle to the Parliament of Scotland at Edinburgh on the 5. of this instant March. In answer to the Charge of High Treason against him. London, Printed by H. Lloyd, and R. Vaughan, for Thomas Johnson, at the Golden Key in St. Paul's Church-yard 1661. 4°, A—B 2 in fours, B 2 blank.

CAMPION, THOMAS, *Mus. Doc.*
Thomæ Campiani Epigrammatvm libri II. Vmbra. Elegiarum liber vnus. Londini Excudebat E. Griffin, Anno Domini. 1619. 8° or 12°, A—F in twelves. *B. M.* There is no preliminary matter.

CARDAN, JEROME.
Cardan His Three Books of Consolation English'd. Of great Vse in these Times. London : Printed for B. Aylmer, . . . and S. Crouch, . . . 1683. 8°. A, 2 : B—L in eights.

CARE, HENRY.
The Grandeur and Glory of France, Drawn in the Triumphant Portraicture of her present Victorious Monarch. And most Illustrious Nobility. *Toto quid Augustius Orbe ?* London, Printed in the Year, 1673. 8°. A, 4 leaves : B—I 4 in eights, besides a duplicate title called *Galliæ Speculum,* &c., and a portrait of Louis XIV. Dedicated to the Duke of Monmouth.

Draconica : . . . By Henry Care. The Third Edition with Considerable Additions. . . . London : Printed by George Larkin, . . . 1688. 4°, A—C in fours. Printed in two columns.

CARLETON, SIR DUDLEY.
The Speech of Sir Dvdly Carlton Lord Ambassadovr for the King of Great Britaine, made in the Assembly of the Lords the Estates Generall of the vnited Prouinces of the Low Countries : Being assembled at the Hague. Tovching the Discord and Trovbles of the Church and Policie, caused by the Schismaticall Doctrine of Arminivs. Exhibited the 6. of October. 1617. Set forth by Authoritie London, Printed by William Iones, for Nathaniel Browne, . . . 1618. 4°, A—B in fours, A 1 and B 4 blank.

Oratie Ghedaen door den Doorluchtigen eerentveiten welgeborenen Heere Dudley Carleton Ridder Ambassavieur van syne konincklijcke Maiesteyt van groot Britannien &c. Aende Grootmoghende Heeren Staten Generael . . . Ghedruct . . . M DC.XVII. 4°, black letter, 4 leaves.

CARLETON, GEORGE, *Bishop of Chichester.*
A Thankfvll Remembrance of Gods

Mercy. . . . The second Edition, revised, and enlarged . . . London Printed by I. D. for Robert Mylbourne, . . . 1625. 4°, A—Mm 2 in fours, besides the frontispiece.

CARLETON, JOHN, *of the Middle Temple.* The Replication, Or Certain Vindicatory Depositions, Occasioned by way of Answer, to the Various Aspersions, . . . Concerning the Late Acted Cheat. Written by John Carleton of the Middle Temple London, Gent. Printed by the Authors Appointment in the Year, 1663. 4°, 4 leaves.

CARLETON, MARY, *the German Princess.* The Arraignment, Tryal and Examination of Mary Moders, Otherwise Stedman, now Carleton, (Stiled, The German Princess) . . . for having two Husbands ; viz. Tho. Stedman of Canterbury Shooemaker, and John Carleton of London, Gent . . . London: Printed for N. Brook, . . . 1663. 4°, pp. 16 and the title.

An Historicall Narrative of the German Princess, Containing All material Passages, from her first Arrivall at Gravesend, the 30th of March last past, . . . Wherein also is mentioned, Sundry private Matters, between Mr John Carlton, and others, and the said Princess, Not yet Published. Together with a brief and notable Story, of Billing the Brick-Layer, . . . Written by her Self, for the Satisfaction of the World, at the Request of Divers Persons of Honour. London, Printed for Charles Moulton, 1663. 4°, A—C in fours.

The Case of Madam Mary Carleton, Lately stiled The German Princess, Truely Stated: With an Historical Relation of Her Birth, Education, and Fortunes; In an Appeal to His Illustrious Highness Prince Rupert. By the said Mary Carleton. . . . London, Printed for Sam: Speed . . . and Hen: Marsh . . . MDCLXIII. 12°. A, 6 leaves: B—G 10 in twelves, besides the title and portrait.

The Articles And Charge of Impeachment against the German Lady, Prisoner in the Gate-house, to be exhibited according to the Records of the City of Canterbury, in order to her Trial at the Sessions-house in the Old-Bailey. . . . As also a true Narrative of her Proceedings since 25th day of March last, . . . London, Printed for G. Winnam, 1663. 4°, 4 leaves.

The Tryall of Mis. Mary Carleton, (formerly the German Lady, Henereta Maria de Woolva) at the Old Baily, Thursday morning Inne the 4: Between Eight and Eleven of the clock: Wherein you have the substance of all that was said . . . With the Verdict given thereupon. London, Printed in the Year, 1663. 4°, 4 leaves.

A True Account of the Tryal of Mrs Mary Carlton, at the Sessions in the Old-Bayly, Thursday the 4th of June, 1663. She being Indicted by the Name of Mary Mauders alias Stedman. Sometime supposed by Mr Carlton and others, to be a Princess of Germany. Published for her Vindication, at her own Request. London. Printed for Charls Moulton, 1663. 4°, 4 leaves.

News from Jamaica In a Letter from Port Royal Written by the Germane Princess to her fellow Collegiates and Friends in New-Gate. London, Printed by Peter Lillicrap, for Philip Brigs, living in Mer-maid Court near Amen corner in Pater Noster Row, 1671. 4°, 4 leaves, the 4th with the Imprimatur only.

An Exact and True Relation of the Examination, Tryal, and Condemnation of the German Princesse, . . . London, Printed for R. O. 1672. 4°, 4 leaves. Black letter.

The Deportment and Carriage of the German Princess, Immediately before her Execution : And Her last Speech at Tyburn : Being on Wednesday the 22th of January, 1672. London, Printed for Nath. Brooke . . . 1672. 4°, 4 leaves.

Memories of the Life of the Famous Madame Charlton ; Commonly Stiled the German Princess . . . London, Printed for Phillip Brooksby, . . . 1672. 4°, A, 2 leaves : B—C in fours. With a rough cut on the title.

The Life and Character of Mrs Mary Moders, alias Mary Stedman, alias Mary Carleton, alias Mary —— The Famous German Princess. . . . The Second Edition. London : Printed for J. Cooke. . . . [about 1720.] 8°, B—L 3 in eights, and the title.

CARLSTADT.

Strange Neves. [A large woodcut of atmospheric and physical phenomena.] At London printed for G. Vincent and W. Blackwal and are to be sold at Guildhall gate. [Then follow two leaves to the Reader from the translator Edward Gresham, dated Feb. 11, 1605-6, and then a second title:] Strange fearfull & true newes, which hapned at Carlstadt, in the kingdom of Croatia. Declaring how the Sonne did shine like Blonde nine dayes together, and how Armies were seene in the Ayre, . . . And how also a Woman was deliuered of three prodigious sonnes, . . . All which happened the twelfth of Iune. last, 1605. . . . Translated out of the Dutch Coppie, Printed at Vienna in Austria. London. Printed by R. B. for G. Vincent and W. Blackwall, & are to be solde ouer against Guild-hall Gate. [1606.] 4°, A—B in fours, A 1 and B 4 blank. *B. M.*

CARMINA.
Carminvm Proverbialivm, Totius humanæ vitæ statum breuiter deliniantium, necnon de moribus doctrinam iucunde proponentium, Loci Communes. . . . Impressum Londini. 1577. [Col.] Londini. Excudebat Christopherus Barkar. 8°. ¶, 4 leaves: A—O 4 in eights. *B. M.*

CAROLINA.
Party-Tyranny Or An Occasional Bill in Miniature: Being An Abridgement of the Shortest Way with the Dissenters. As now Practised in Carolina. Humbly offered to the Consideration of both Houses of Parliament . . London: Printed in the Year 1705. 4°, A—D, 2 leaves each: E—F in fours.

CARON, R., *Professor Jubilate of Divinity.*
Loyalty Asserted, And the late Remonstrance or Allegiance of the Irish Clergy and Layty Confirmed and Proved. . . . London, Printed by T. Mabb, . . . 1662. 4°, A—I in fours. Dedicated to Charles II.

CARPENTER, NATHANIEL.
Achitophel, Or The Picture of a Wicked Polititian . . . By Nath. Carpenter B.D. & Fellow of Excet. Coll. in Oxford. Oxford, Printed by Leonard Lichfield for Mathew Hunt. 1640. 12°. A, 4: B—H in twelves: I, 6.

CARPENTER, RICHARD, *Pastor of Sherwill, in Devon.*
A Pastoral Charge. Faithfully giuen and discharged, at the Trienniall Visitation of the Lord Bishop of Exon: Holden in Barnstaple the seventh of September. 1616. . . . London, Printed by Edward Griffin for Francis Constable. . . . 1616. 8°, A—K 4 in eights.

CARTIGNY, JEAN.
The Voyage of the Wandring Knight . . . London, Printed by John Cadwell, for Andrew Crooke, . . . 1661, 4°, black letter, A—P in fours.

CARTWRIGHT, THOMAS.
To the godly Readers, Grace, and peace from God, &c. [This is a head-line on A, and occupies the whole of that leaf and the top of A 2. Then follows a second head-line :] An Admonition to the Parliament. [Zurich, 1567–8], small 8°, A—D 4 in eights.

This small piece includes other matter at the end—Letters to the Bishops from Beza and Rodolph Gualter, the Admonition itself occupying only 16 leaves.

A Second Admonition to the Parliament. [Wandsworth ? 1570.] Sm. 8°, A—H in fours, and * with 4 leaves of introduction.

Certaine Articles, collected and taken (as it is thought) by the Byshops out of a lytle boke entituled an Admonition to the Parliament / wyth an Answere to the same. Containing a confirmation of the sayde Booke in shorte notes. [Quot. from Esay. 5, 10. and *The Prynter to the Reader*, 8 lines of verse.] Imprinted we know where / and whan. Judge you the place and you can. J. T. J. S. Sm. 8°, A—B in fours. In prose, except seven 4-line stanzas *To the Prefacie* on the back of the title.

J. T. may be the initials of Job Throckmorton.

CARTWRIGHT, WILLIAM.
Comedies, Tragi-comedies . . . 1651.

I have before me Dr. Bliss's copy of this book, bought of Thorpe, with the bookplate of "Thomas Cartwright of Aynho in the County of Northampton Esqr 1698." It is in the original calf binding, and on the fly-leaf Bliss notes: "A fair copy in the original state, with the cancelled leaves pp. 301, 2, 3, 4, 5, 6, but those leaves not in their first state, *i.e.*, with the blanks filled up, of which there is a copy in Christ Church Library. In general the duplicate or cancelled leaves are wanting. A duplicate copy in this copy sign. C 2, the marginal notes having been cut away in the original leaf. Since writing the above I have been able to make this Copy one of the most perfect known, having added the original leaves pp. 301-6 in the first state, *& with the blanks filled in the letterpress:* together with a variation in one of the leaves containing the commendatory verses by Lord Monmouth and T. P. baronet, the initials in the added leaf being replaced with a rose and crown and a harp and crown." At the end of the commendatory verses the publisher has this note: "We shall not trouble you with an *Index*, for already the Book is bigger than we meant, although we chose this Volume and Character purposely to bring down its bulk. . . . " Nevertheless, it is said that in a copy in the Bodleian are fragments of an Index.

The duplicate pages 301-6 contain: 1. *On the Queen's Return from the Low-Countries;* 2. *Vpon the death of the Right valiant Sir Bevill Grenvill Knight ;* 3. *On a vertuous young Gentleman that dyed suddenly.* The verses on Grenvill are printed entire in the Oxford verses on his death, 1643 and 1684.

The Royall Slave. . . . The second Edition. Oxford, Printed by William Turner for Thomas Robinson. 1640. 4°, A—H in fours.

CARVE, THOMAS, *of Tipperary.*
Rervm Germanicarvm Ab Anno M.DC.XVII. Ad Annum. M.DC.XLI. Gestarvm Epitome Avctore Thoma Carvæo Hyberno. Anno Christi M.DC.XLI. 12°, A—F in twelves : G, 1 leaf.

CARVER, MARMADUKE.
A Discourse of the Terrestrial Paradise. Aiming at a more probable Discovery of the true Situation of that happy place of our First Parents Habitation. [Quotations from Ovid, &c.] London, Printed by James Flesher, 1666. 8°. A—M 4 in eights, and a, 8 leaves. Dedicated to Gilbert Sheldon, Archbishop of Canterbury. With a large folding map. *B. M.*

It appears that this work was written about 1640.

CARY, JOHN, *of Bristol.*
A Discourse concerning the East-India Trade. . . . Written by Mr John Cary . . . Reprinted at London, 1696. 4°, A—B 2 in fours.

CARY, WALTER.
A boke of the propreties of Herbes called an herball, whervnto is added the tyme ye herbes, Floures and Sedes shoulde be gathered to be kept the whole yere, with the vertue of ye Herbes whē they are stylled Also a generall rule of al manner of Herbes drawen out of auncient bokes of Physycke by W. C. [Col.] Imprinted at London by Wyllyam Copland. 8°, black letter, A - K 4 in eights, besides title and 3 following leaves with the "general rule."

Caries Farewell to Physicke. First published in the yeare 1587 . . . At London printed for the Companie of Stationers, 1611. 8°, A—F in eights, F 8 blank.

The *Hammer for the Stone* commences with a new title on E 5.

CASTAMORE, *pseud.*
Conjugium Languens : Or, The Natural, Civil, and Religious Mischiefs arising from Conjugal Infidelity and Impunity.

Tu quoque suscepti curam dimittis amici ;
Officiique pium tam cito ponis onus?
Ov. Trist.

London : Printed by R. Roberts. 1700. 4°, A—D in fours, D 4 blank.

CASTANIZA, JOHN.
The Christian Pilgrime in his Spirituall Conflict and Conquest. At Paris M.DC.LII. 8°. Title-page, *Approbatio* in Latin and English, and frontispiece to Part 1, 4 leaves : [a new title :] The Spiritual Conflict : Or The Arraignment of the Spirit of Self-love and Sensuality at the Barre of Truth and Reason. First published in Spanish, by the Reverend Father John Castaniza a Benedictine Monk of Oña. Afterwards, put into the Latine, Italian, German, French, and now lastly into the English Tongue, according to the Originall Copy. With many profitable Additions and Explications. The Second Edition . . . At Paris. M.DC.LII. a—b in twelves : B—O in twelves : [a third title :] The Spiritvall Conqvest, In Five Treatises, Enabling all Christian Warriors, to Conquer themselves, and come to a vicinity with God. . . . At Paris, M.DC.LI. A—S, 12 leaves each : T, 4 leaves : U, 2. including the *Errata.* With numerous engravings, including a frontispiece on A 1.

CASTELL, EDMUND.
Sol Angliæ Oriens Auspiciis Caroli II Regum Gloriosissimi. Londini, Typis Tho. Roycroft. Impensis Jo. Martyn, Ja. Allestry, & Tho. Dicas, . . . MDCLX. 4°, A—D in fours. *B. M.*

A Collection of verses in the several languages employed in the Polyglot.

Oratio in Scholis Theologicis Habita ab Edmvndo Castello S. T. D. Et Linguæ Arabicæ in Academia Cantabrigiensi Professore . . . Londini, Typis Thomæ Roycroft, . . . MDCLXVII. 4°, A—F 2 in fours.

The speech was on the Second Book of the Canon of Avicenna.

CASTELL, WILLIAM.
A Petition of W. C. Exhibited to the High Covrt of Parliament now assembled, for the propagating of the Gospel in America, and the West Indies ; and for the setling of our Plantations there, which Petition is approved by 70. able English Divines. Also by Master Alexander Henderson, and some other worthy Ministers of Scotland. Printed in the yeare, 1641. 4°, A—C 2 in fours, A 1 blank.

CATALOGUE.
A Catalogve of the Dvkes, Marqvesses

Earles, . . . With the Knights of the Garter . . . Collected by T. W. Printed at London by T. Dawson, for Thomas Walkley, . . . 1642. 8°. Title and the names of the Royal Family, 4 leaves : B—M 2 in eights.

> In this copy the names of Oliver Cromwell's Privy Council, &c., are added at the end in a hand of the time.

A New Catalogue of the Dukés, Marquesses, Earls, . . . With the Knights of the Garter . . . Collected by T. W. London, Printed for Thomas Walkley, 1652. 8°, A—K 4 in eights : A Catalogue of the Dukes, ... Made by the late King since the Fourth of January, 1641. With the day of the Moneth they were Created in, *with a new title*, A—B in eights, B 8 blank, B 7 with those of uncertain dates.

> On K 4 *verso* the title-page to the first portion is repeated by mistake.

A Catalogue of the Names of the Dvkes, Marqvsses, Earles and Lords, that have absented themselves from the Parliament, and are now with His Maiesty. . . . As also, a List of the Army of his Excellency, Robert, Earle of Essex : With the Names of the Troops of Horse under the Command of William Earle of Bedford, . . . A List of the Navie Royall, and Merchants Ships : . . . Lastly, The Field Officers chosen for the Irish Expedition, for the Regiments of 5000. Foote and 500. Horse. Printed 1642. 4°, A—C in fours.

Catalogus Variorum . . . Viz. D. Hen. Stubb Nuperrime Londinensis D. Dillinghami de Oundle Northamptoniensis . . . Cui accessit Bibliotheca non minus Elegans Doctissimi Viri Johannis Duntoni. Quorum Auctio habebitur . . . in vico vulgo dicto Warwick-lane, 29 Nov. 1680. 4°, pp. 44 + 150.

> A very curious collection.

CATECHISM.

A Satyrical Catechisme betwixt a Newter and a Rovnd-Head. Also how the Newter converted the Round-head, and promised him an Excise Office. Very pleasing to reade to all those which love God, honour their King, and are their own wel-wishers. With a Song. . . . London, Printed in the Year, 1648. 4°, 4 leaves.

CATERPILLARS.

The Caterpillers of this Nation Anatomized, In a Brief yet Notable Discovery of House-breakers, Pick-pockets, &c. Together with the Life of a penitent Highway-man, discovering the Mystery of that Infernal Society. To which is added, the manner of Hectoring & Trapanning, as it is acted in and about the City of London. London, Printed for M. H. at the Princes Armes in Chancery-lane. 1659. 4°, A—F in fours, F 4 blank. *B. M.*

CATHOLICS.

Histoire Mervellevse Advenves [*sic*] Par Feu du Ciel en trois villes d'Angleterre, à l'encontre de douze Iuges heretiques, & de deux Ministres qui voulloient persecuté [*sic*] les Catholiques. Ensemble les noms des Iuges & des deux Ministres à qui le Diable tordict le col dadans leur temples. A Paris Iouxte la copie imprimee à Rouen . . . [1578.] 8°, A—B in fours.

> Part of this tract is an extract from a book printed at London by William Bartel [Bartlet ?] giving an account of the deaths of certain persons at the Oxford assizes in 1577; the rest is a second extract from Abraham Fleming's book, published in 1577, respecting an incident at Bungay.
> Sunderland Sale, 1882, No. 4974.

Advertissement Des Catholiqves Anglois avx François Catholiques, du danger où ils sont de perdre leur Religion, & d'experimenter, comme en Angleterre, la cruauté des Ministres s'ils recoyvent à la Couronne vn Roy qui soit Heretique. Ezekiel. 33. . . . . 1586. 8°. A, 4 leaves : B—I in eights.

Repliqve Povr le Catholiqve Anglois, contre le Catholique associé des Huguenots. M.D.LXXXVIII. 8°, A—F in fours, F 4 blank.

Responce Des Vrays Catholiqves François, À L'Avertissement des Catholiques Anglois, pour l'exclusion du Roy de Navarre de la Couronne de France . . . Traduict du Latin. M.D.LXXXVIII. 8°, A—Pp in eights, Pp 7–8 blank.

A Petition Apologeticall, Presented to the Kinges Most Excellent Maiesty, By the Lay Catholikes of England, in Iuly last. Printed at Doway by Iohn Mogar . . . 1604. 4°, A—E in fours, E 4 with the Copy of the Banished Priests' Letter.

An Answere to Certaine scandalous Papers, Scattered abroad vnder colour of a Catholicke Admonition. *Qui facit viuere, decet orare.* Imprinted at London by Robert Barker . . . 1606. 4°, A—F 2 in fours, A 1 blank.

A Relation of Two Free Conferences between Father L' Chese, and Four Considerable Jesuits, Touching the Present S[t]ate of the Romanists in England. In order to the Carrying on their Great Design. Sent in a Letter from Paris, to a Considerable Popish Lord in England.

Printed, in the Year, 1680. 4°. A, 2 leaves : B—C in fours : D, 2 : E—F in fours, F 4 blank.

CAUSE.

Causæ veteris Epitaphii Editio Altera . . . Neapoli sive Augustæ Trinobantum : . . . MDCLXXXV. 4°, a, 2 leaves, and A—C 2 in fours.

CAUSTON, PETER.

Carmina Tria Petri Causton Merc Lond. 1. De Conflagratione Londini. 2. In Laudem Holandiæ nunquam antehac editum. 3. Tunbrigialia. Editio Tertia. Londini, Typis J. Richardson, . . . MDCLXXXIX. 4°, A—B in fours, and the *Tunbrigialia*, 5 leaves from a collection.

Tunbrigialia. Authore P. Causton. Londini : Anno M. DCCIX. 8°, 6 leaves. In verse.

CAVALIERS.

The Speech of a Cavalcere to his Comrades, in answer to the Wardens Speech. Written by Agamemnon Shaglock Van Dammee, Clerke of the Regiment. London, Printed Anno Domini 1642. 4°, 4 leaves.

The Wicked Resolution of the Cavaliers ; Shewing their malice and hatred to the Parliament the Commonwealth, and especially the City of London. . . . London, Novemb. 22. Printed for Jo. Smith. 1642. 4°, 4 leaves.

The Image of the Malignants Peace : Or A Representation of the seditious Carriages of the London Cavaliers, in their first endeavours for the Saccage and plunder of the City, under the specious Vizor of a Petition for Peace and Accommodation. [Without any regular title, 1643.] 4°, 4 leaves.

CAVENDISH, GEORGE.

The Negotiations of Thomas Woolsey, . . . London : Printed for the good of the Commonwealth. 4°, A—O in fours, including the portrait.

CAVENDISH, WILLIAM, *Duke of Newcastle.*

La Methode Nouvelle & Invention extraordinaire de dresser les Chevaux les travailler selon la nature et parfaire la nature par la subtilité de l'art la quelle n'a jamais eté treuvée que Par Le tresnoble haut et tres-puissant Prince Guillaume Marquis et Comte de Newcastle . . . . Traduit de l'Anglois de l'Auteur en Francois par son Commandement. A Anvers Chez Iacques Van Meurs. l'an M.DC. LVIII. Large folio. a—g, 2 leaves each : *Additions*, a—f, 2 leaves each : A

—4 A, 2 leaves each, besides engraved title and plates numbered 1–42.

CHAMBER, JOHN.

A Treatise against Ivdicial Astrologie. Dedicated to the right Honorable Sir Thomas Egerton Knight, . . . Written by Iohn Chamber, one of the Prebendaries of her Maiesties free Chappell of Windsor, and Fellow of Eaton College. Printed at London by John Harison . . . 1601. 4°, A—T 3 in fours : *Astronomiæ Encomium*, A—F 2 in fours.

CHAMBERLAYNE, EDWARD.

The Rise & Fall of the Late Eminent and powerful Favorite of Spain, The Count Olivares. The Unparallel'd Imposture of Michael de Molina Executed at Madrid in the Year, 1641. The Right and Title of the present King of Portugall Don John the fourth ; With the most memorable Passages of his Reign unto the year 1644. Translated out of the Italian, Spanish, and Portughez, by Edw. Chamberlayne, Gent . . . London, Printed by T. N. for Thomas Heath . . . 1652. 8°. A, 4 leaves, including *Errata :* B—M in eights.

Angliæ Notitia ; . . . The Fourth Edition, Corrected, and newly Augmented . . . In the Savoy, Printed by T. N. for John Martyn . . . MDCLXX. 12°. A, 6, besides the frontispiece : B – Z 2 in twelves.

An Academy or Colledge : Wherein Young Ladies and Gentlewomen may at a very moderate Expence be duly instructed in the True Protestant Religion, and in all Vertuous Qualities that may adorn that Sex : . . . London, Printed by T. N. MDCLXXI. 4°, A—B 2 in fours.

This was one of the pieces which Chamberlayne ordered to be buried with him. It appeared anonymously.

CHAMPNEY, ANTHONY, *Priest and Doctor of the Sorbonne.*

A Treatise of the Vocation of Bishops, and other Ecclesiasticall Ministers . . . And in particuler the pretended Bishops in England, to be no true Bishops. Against Mr Mason . . . At Dovay, By Iohn Heigham, . . . 1616. 4°. ¶, 4 leaves : A—Tt 2 in fours. Dedicated "To Mr George Abbat called Arch-Bishop of Canterbvry."

CHARACTER.

The Character of a Bawd : Or, A Description of their ways and means how they get Money, by Impoverishing others, to enrich themselves.

Farewell all Whores, and Bawds, and such as do By any means live with such Hellish Crew.

London, Printed for J. Hose, over-against Staples-Inn, in Houlbourne, near Gray's-Inn Gate. 1674. Sm. 8º, A in eights, with three small cuts on the title.

CHARLES STUART THE FIRST, *King of Great Britain* (1625–48).

A Trve Relation and Iovrnall . . . London, Printed by Iohn Haviland for William Barret. M. DC. XXIII. 4º, A—E in fours, A 1 blank.

> In this copy the *ninth* of March is mentioned, instead of the *seventh*. Sothebys, March 10, 1882, No. 318, Bandinel's copy.

The Ioyfull Returne, Of the Most Illvstriovs Prince, Charles, Prince of great Brittaine, from the Court of Spaine. Together, with a Relation of his Magnificent Entertainment in Madrid, . . . The Royall and Princely Gifts interchangeably giuen. Translated out of the Spanish Copie. His wonderfull dangers on the Seas, . . . and most happy-safe Landing at Portsmovth on the 5. of October, . . . London : Printed by Edward All-de for Nathaniell Butter and Henry Seile. 1623. 4º, A—F in fours.

The Popes Letter to the Prince : In Latine, Spanish, and English. Done according to the Latine and Spanish Coppies Printed at Madrid. A Iesuites Oration to the Prince in Latine and Englishe. London : Printed for Nathaniell Butter. 1623. 4º, D 2—H 3 in fours.

> It is readily apparent that this tract either forms part of some other publication (at present unknown to me), or was intended to do so.

Cantabrigiensium Dolor & Solamen : Sev Decessio Beatissimi Regis Jacobi Pacifici : Et Svccessio Avgvstissimi Regis Caroli . . . Excudebat Cantrellvs Legge, . . . MDCXXV. 4º, A—H 2 in fours, besides 2 leaves with title and Preface.

Instrvctions directed from the Kings most Excellent Maiestie, Vnto all the Bishops of his Kingdome, and fit to be put in execution, agreeable to the necessitie of the Times. London, Printed by Bonham Norton and Iohn Bill, . . . 1626. 4º, A—B in fours.

> This is in the form of a letter from the Primate, and is dated from Croydon, 26 Sept. 1626.

A Iovrnall, And Relation of the Action which by his Maiesties commandement, Edward Lord Cecil, Baron of Putney, and Vicount of Wimbledon, Admirall, and Lieuetenant Generall of his Maiesties Forces, did vndertake vpon the Coast of Spaine, 1625. *Veritas premitur, sed non*

opprimitur. Printed in the yeere 1627. 4º, A—D in fours.

Three severall Treatises concerning the Trvce at this present proponument. The first, laying open divers Considerations and Reasons, why a Trvce ought not to be Contracted, . . . The second, discusseth this question very pithily and at large, whether or no it bee lawfull to make Truce with the King of Spaine, . . . Lastly, here is added a Remonstrance, represented to the States theyr Excellencies, In the behalfe of the King of Bohemia, . . . All truly and faithfully Translated out of the Low Dutch Copie. London, Printed for Nathaniel Butter and Nicholas Bourne. 1630. 4º, A—D in fours, A 1 blank.

Articles of Peace, Entercovrse, and Commerce, Concluded in the names of . . . Charles . . . King of Great Britaine, . . . And Philip the fourth King of Spaine, &c. . . . Translated out of Latine into English. Imprinted at London by Robert Barker . . . 1630. 4º, A—I in fours, A 1 and I 4 blank.

Academiæ Glasguensis Charisterion, Ad augustissimum Monarcham Carolum. . . . Edinbvrgi Excudebat R. Junius, 1633. 4º, A—H in fours, besides the title and 8 leaves between C and C 2.

The Heads of Severall Petitions and complaints made against 1. Sir Iohn Conyars Lievtenant Generall of the Horse in the Northerne expedition. 2. Dr Heywood of St. Gyles in the Fields. 3. The Parishioners of St. Mary - Woolchurch. 4. Dr Fuller of St. Giles Cripple-gate. 5. Mr Booth of St. Botolphs Aldersgate. . . . London, Printed for Iohn Thomas. 1641. 4º, 4 leaves.

> These, except the first, are in reference to ritualistic practices, &c.

Matters of note made known to all true Protestants. First, the plot against the City of London, . . . London, Printed for Fr. Coles, 1641. 4º, 4 leaves.

> The title of this small tract occupies nearly the whole of a 4º page.

A most true Relation of the great and bloody Battel : fought vpon Monday last neer the Coast of England, by three of the Earl of Warwicks ships ; Namely, the James, George, and Grey-hound, Against Col. Goring with 7. ships, . . . Also how the States of Holland hath taken 30. Sail of ships that were comming to England, . . . Decemb. 8, Printed for I. Wright, 1641. 4º, 4 leaves.

Horrible News from Yorke : Hull, and Newcastle. Concerning the Kings Maiesties intent to take up Arms against the Parliament. . . . With His Majesties threatening to imprison the Lord Fairfax, . . . Also the Lord Stamfords Report . . . May 24. Printed for Iohn Greensmith. An. Cov. 1642. 4°, 4 leaves.

Horrible Newes from Yorke, Hull, and Newcastle, Concerning the Kings Maiesties intent to take up Armes against the Parliament. With His Majesties threatnings to imprison the Lord Fairefax, Sir Phillip Stapleton, and the rest of the Committee, . . . London, Printed for T. Ryder, 1642. May 25. 4°, 4 leaves.

Five speciall Passages: vizt. Two Petitions of the Covntie of Yorke. . . . The Petition of the Kingdom of Scotland, . . . Also His Majesties Letter to the Lords of his Privie Counsell of the Kingdome of Scotland. And a Letter from Sir Io. Bourchier to Sir Thomas Barrington. . . . London, Printed for Edward Blackmore, Iune 8. 1642. 4°, 4 leaves.

Matters of High Consequence concerning the Great Affaires of the Kingdome ; . . . London, Printed by T. P. & M. S. for W. Gaye, the 21. of June, 1642. in Goldsmiths Alley. 4°, 4 leaves.

This piece comprises the Lancashire Petition to the King, with his Auswer, the King's Proclamation, June 9, a Letter from Lord Essex to the Speaker, &c.

Delightfull Newes for all Loyall Subiects. Being his Majesties Royall Assent to the Scotch Commissioners, for assistance to our Brethren in Ireland. . . . Printed at London for Iohn Howell, 1642. 4°, 4 leaves.

His Maiesties Answer to the Declaration of both Houses of Parliament. Concerning the Commission of Array. Of the first of July, 1642. . . . reprinted at London, 1642. 4°, A—E in fours.

The Petition . . . delivered . . . the 16. day of Ivly : . . . With the Votes Die Martis. 12. Julii, 1642. London, Printed by A. Norton, for Mathew Walbancke, and Richard Lownds. Anno. 1642. 4°, 4 leaves.

By the King. To Our trusty and well beloved Our Colonells, . . . and all other Our Officers of Our Army. From Our Court at Oxford, this Twentieth of January, 1642. [(ii.)] An Agreement of the great Inquest made at the last Sessions for the County of Worcester, for the raising of three Thousand pound Monethly,

towards the payment of His Majesties Forces, sent and raised for defence of the said County and City of Worcester. Printed at Oxford by Leonard Lichfield . . . 1642. A broadside.

Sundry Observations of severall Passages and Proceedings in the North, There taken by a Subject well-affected to the Protestant Religion, . . . Sent unto a faithfull and intimate Friend of his in London. Containing a Description of the Qualities, Conditions, Aims, and Intents of such as intend to act this fearfull Tragedie, The Destruction of His Majesty, and His Kingdoms. . . . London, Printed for F. C. July 29. 1642. 4°, 4 leaves.

Exceeding Good Newes from Beverley, Yorke, Hull, and Newcastle. With the valliant Acts of Sir John Hotham over the walls of Hull . . . And how Sir John Hotham gave command to pull the Mayors Gowne of Hull off from his backe, and fix a guard about his House. . . . London, Printed for I. T. Iuly 20. 1642. 4°, 4 leaves.

The Petitions of Northampton-Shire and Oxford-Shire. Presented vnto the High Covrt of Parliament. London, Printed by R. Olton, and G. Dexter . . . MDCXLII. 4°, 4 leaves.

A Soveraign Antidote to prevent appease, and determine Our unnaturall and destructive Civill-Wars and Dissentions. [1642–43.] 4°, A—D in fours.

A Soverayne Antidote . . . The second Impression much enlarged. . . . London, Printed in the Yeare 1642. 4°, A—D in fours, besides title and Preface.

A Short Discourse, tending to the Pacification of all unhappy differences, betwene His Majesty and His Parliament. Shewing the meanes, whereby the same may speedily be done, and that it rests in His Majesties sole power to effect it. Presented for the Consideration of all those that love the Truth and Peace : By a friend and Servant to both. Sine ullâ notâ. [About 1643.] 4°, 4 leaves.

There is no title-page.

Lord have mercie upon us : Or, A Plaine Discovrse Declaring that the Plagve of Warre, which now wasts this Nation, tooke its beginning in and from the Citie of London, . . . Written vpon occasion of his Majesties Proclamation of the seventeenth of Iuly, . . . Printed in the Yeare, M.DC.XL.III. 4°, A—F 2 in fours.

A Letter to the Earle of Pembroke from Sir Edward Baynton in Glocester. Shewing the true manner how himselfe and Captaine Edward Eyre were surprised at Malmsbury . . . With the reasons inducing him formerly to seize upon Sir Edward Hungerford. London, Printed for Thomas Creake, January 22. 1643. 4°, 4 leaves.

An Ordinance for the better raysing and levying of Marinors, Saylors, and others, for the present guarding of the Sea, and necessary defence of the Realme and other his Majesties Dominions. London, Printed for I. Wright in the Old baily, February 4. 1642. A broadside.

His Maiesties Gracious Message to both his Houses of Parliament, February the 20th. [1642-3.] A broadside.

A Briefe Relation of the siege at Newark, As it was delivered to the Covncel of State at Derby-house, by Lievetenant Col. Bury, whom the Earl of Manchester sent to Report. Together with Articles of Agreement betwixt Prince Rupert and Sir Iohn Meldrum . . . London, Printed for Peter Cole, March 26. 1644. 4°, 4 leaves.

A Paradox. That Designe upon Religion, Was not the cause of State Misgovernment : But an effect of it. London, Printed for T. W. 1644. 4°, A—B in fours.

Letters by which it is certified, that Sir Samuell Luke tooke at Islip Fiftie Horse, and fiftie pound in Money, Twentie Seaven Prisoners : Sir —— Fortescue being one ; three were taken prisoners at New-Castle under line : By Collonell Ridgley. . . . And how a Cavalier Priest preaching, that those English, and Irish, that are slaine in Arms against the Parliament, are Marters, and their soules shall be saved, was strooke dumb in his Pulpit at Bvrton. Testified by Collonell Chadwick. Printed according to Order. London printed by F. L. May 28. 1644. 4°, 4 leaves.

The Kings Answer to the Propositions for Peace, as was pretended in the Clubmens petition to his Majestie. With the copie of a Letter from Sir Lewis Dives, and another from Colonell Butler Governour of Wareham . . . Imprinted at London by R. A. and I. C. 1645. 4°, 8 leaves.

A Word to the Wise. Displaying great augmented grievances, and heavie pressures of dangerous consequence. Appearing, By certain materiall, weighty passages of speciall concernment. Remonstrating the great danger which the

Counties of Cumberland and Westmoreland are in (though now in the hands of the Parliament) but like to be possessed by the Enemy . . . [London, 1645-6.] 4°, A—C 2 in fours.

The Kings Letter to the Marquesse of Ormond : And the Marquesse of Ormonds Letter to Monroe. Relating the Kings whole Design, concerning all the three Kingdoms. London : Printed, by I. C. Iune 8. 1646. 4°, 4 leaves.

The Reasons of the War, With the Progress and Accidents thereof. Written by an English Subject. Wherein also the most materiall Passages of the Two Books printed at Oxford (in which His Majesties party do undertake to justifie their proceedings) are briefly examined ; . . . London : Printed for Iohn Field, and are to be sold by Stationers. 1646. 4°. A, 2 leaves : B—V in fours.

Looke about You : Or, A word in Season to a Divided Nation. *Cavete ab Esauitis, Take heed of the Iesuit. Abundans cautela non nocet.*

  Never was yet a Nation
  Vndone by too much caution.

. . . London : Printed for Robert Bostock, . . . 1647. 4°, 6 leaves.

Papers of the Treatie, At a great Meeting of the Generall Officers of the Army, at the Head-quarters at Putney, on behalf of the whole Kingdome of England, . . . Die 20. Septemb. 1647. Printed for R. V. and are to be sold neer Temple Barre, 1647. 4°, 4 leaves. With a woodcut head on title.

 The account of the meeting at Putney is subscribed *Peter Cradock*, who perhaps wrote the whole.

The Mad Dog Rebellion, worm'd and muzzl'd. With some Reasons why a Personall Treaty with his Majesty is delayed. . . . [1647.] 4°, 4 leaves.

The Four Bills Sent to the King to the Isle of Wight to be passed. Together with the Propositions sent unto Him at the same time, which upon the passing of those Bills were to be treated upon . . . . London : Printed for Edward Husband, . . . March 20. 1647. 4°, A —F in fours, A 1 and F 4 blank.

A true Abstract of a List, In which is set down the severall entertainments allowed by His Majesty to the Officers and other souldiers of His Army. . . . London, Printed for Iohn Mathewes. [About 1647.] 4°, 4 leaves.

 A curious tract, giving a minute account of the pay of the troops.

A Narrative of the Great Victory Obtained by the Lord Generall in Kent : With the names of the Knights, and Collonels slaine, and taken prisoners. . . . Also The new besieging of Dover by the Kentishmen, and the fight at Bow in Essex. . . . Printed at London by Robert Ibbitson . . . 1648. 4°, 4 leaves.

A True Relation of the Fight between Major Gen. Lambert, and the Scots Army neer Appleby, July 24. 1648. With a Letter written from Colonell Charles Fairfax, touching the Surrender of Thornhill House in Yorkshire, ... London, Printed for Robert White, 1648. 4°, 4 leaves.

Colonel Rich's Letter to the House of Commons of a great Victory Obtained against Eight hundred of the Princes Forces, Lately landed in Kent by Sandown Castle . . . London, Printed for Edward Husband, . . . August 16. 1648. 4°, 4 leaves.

The Faerie Leveller : Or, King Charles his Leveller described and deciphered in Queene Elizabeth's dayes. By her Poet Laureat Edmond Spenser, in his unparaleld Poeme, entituled, The Faerie Qveene. A lively representation of our times. Anagram : Parliaments Army. Paritie mar's al men. Printed just levell anent the Saints Army : in the yeare of their Saintships ungodly Revelling for a godly Levelling. 1648. 4°, 6 leaves.

A New-yeers Gift for the Kings most excellent Maiesty now at Windsore, from his loyall and faithfull Subjects residing in and about the Cities of London and Westminster, and a Declaration of the Kings Majesties coming to London. London : Printed for T. G. 1649. 4°, 4 leaves. With a large print of the King occupying great part of the title.

Manifeste Dv Roy de la Grand Bretagne, à ses Sujets du Royaume d'Angleterre. A Paris, . . . M.DC.XLIX. 4°, 4 leaves.

The ghost of K. Charls and Serieant Bradsha. Being A Discourse Betwixt Charles late King of England, The ArchBishop of Canterburie and Serjeant John Bradshaw. . . . London : Printed in the Year 1649. 4°, 4 leaves. With a cut on the title.

Les Memoires dv fev Roy de la Grand Bretagne Charles Primier, . . . Traduit de l'Anglais en nostre langue, Par le sieur de Mareys. Et enrichis d'Annotations, . . . A Paris, . . . M.DC.XLIX. 4°. Frontispiece, 1 leaf : à and ô, 4 leaves each : Table, 1 leaf, A—S 2 in fours.

The head-line on A is : Les Memoires dv fev Roy . . . Escrits de sa propre main dans sa Prison.

Les Ivstes Sovpirs et Pitovables Regrets des Bons Anglois, Svr la Mort de Tres-Avgvste . . . Charles Roy de la grande Bretagne, . . . Composez premiereuent en vers Latins, & depuis traduits en François par I. R. A Paris, . . . M.DC.XXXXIX. 4°, A—C, 2 leaves each. In verse.

CHARLES [STUART] THE SECOND, *King of Great Britain* (1660-85).

The Princes first Fruits : Or, A Full and Perfect Relation of Two Victories Obtained by Col. Rich's Brigade, together with the Forces under the Command of Sir Michael Levesey, over some forces landed out of the Revolted ships neer Sandown Castle, in the County of Kent, August 10. & 14. . . . To the three Sons of their Father the D. [here follow some satirical verses.] Printed in the yeer 1648 4°, 4 leaves.

The Princes Standard set up in the Vice-Admirall on the Downes neere Sandown Castle. His Highnesse Demand of twenty thousand pounds from the City of London : the Declaration, and heads of two Letters . . . Also his Highnesse Message to Sir Michael Lycusay of Kent. sent by a Trumpeter : the burning of the towne of Deale : . . . London : Printed for B. A. 1648. 4°, 4 leaves. Cut on title.

His Majesties Declaration to all His Loving subjects in His Kingdome of England and Dominion of Wales. Published with the advice of his Privie Councell. Dated in Castle-Elizabeth in the Isle of Jersey, the 31. day of October 1649. Hage, Printed by Samuel Broun English Bookeseller, . . . Anno M DC XLIX. 4°, 4 leaves.

Iter Australe Attempting something upon the happy Return of our most Gracious Soveraign Lord, Charls II. from Banishment to His Throne. By a Loyal Pen. —— *Virum non Arma Cano.* London, Printed by Tho. Leach, in the Year, 1660. 4°, A—C 2 in fours, C 2 blank. In verse.

The Landing of His Sacred Maiesty King Charles at Dover, With His Highness Prince James Duke of York, . . . Printed for H. Seamer, near the Inner-Temple-Gate, 1660. 4°, 4 leaves.

The Tryal of the Pretended Judges, That signed the Warrant for the Murther of King Charles the 1. of Ever Blessed Memory, At the Sessions-House in the Old-

Baily October 10. 1660 . . . London Printed in the year 1660. 4°, A—B in fours, B 4 blank.

This is a report of the first day only.

By the King. A Proclamation To Summon the Persons therein named, who sate, gave Judgment, and assisted in that horrid and detestable Murder of His Majesties Royal Father of blessed memory, to appear and render themselves within Fourteen days, under pain of being excepted from Pardon. London, Printed by John Bill and Christopher Barker . . . 1660. A broadside.

A Letter from the King to F. M. Bruxels, 10. April. 1660. Your Loving Friend, C. R. A broadside.

[A Letter and Declaration from Charles II. delivered by Viscount Mordaunt and Sir John Greenville Knight. April, 1660.] Printed by James Flesher, Printer to the Honorable City of London, 1660. 4°, A—B in fours, A 1 blank.

B 4 contains the answer of the City, dated May 1, 1660. Charles dates from Breda.

A True Narrative and Relation of His Most Sacred Majesties Miraculous Escape from Worcester on the Third of September, 1650. Till His Arrival at Paris. London, Printed for G. Colborn. 1660. 4°, 4 leaves.

Vox Populi, The Voice of the People, Congratulating His Majesty, King Charles . . . in thirty Heroick Stanzas : with a brief Panegyrick, in Praise of his Illustrious Majesty. London, Printed for H. Brome, . . . 1660. 4°, 4 leaves.

Britains Glory : Being A Relation of the Solemnity wherewith the English Nation Residing in Livorne, Entertained the Joyful Tidings of His Sacred Majesties Happy Return to His Royal Throne. July 13. Stilo Novo. London : Printed for Edw. Farnham in Popes-head Alley, 1660. 4°, 4 leaves.

Domidnea Oxoniensis : Sive Musæ Academicæ Gratulatio ob Auspicatissimum Serenissimæ Principis Catharinæ Lusitanæ, Regi suo Desponsatæ, In Angliam appulsum. Oxoniæ, Exudebant A. & L. Lichfield, . . . M.DC.LX.II. 4°, A—M in fours, and A—C in fours, the last set of signatures with English verses Upon the Queen's Landing.

His Majesties Most Gracious and Royal Commission, For the Relief of Poor

Distressed Prisoners. Published by Authority. London, Printed for M. D. and are to be sold by Nathaniel Webb, . . . M.DC.LX.IV. 4°, A—C 2 in fours, black letter, C 2 having only a cut of the Royal Oak.

Bellum Belgicum Secundum, Or, A Poem Attempting something on his Majesties Proceedings against the Dutch. [Quot. from Claudian.] Cambridge, Printed by J. Field, and are to be sold by Robert Nicholson, Bookseller in Cambridge, 1665. 4°, A—B in fours, A 1 and B 4 blank.

Omnia Comesta a Bello. Or, An Answer out of the West to a Question out of the North. Wherein the Earth is opened, and the Napkin found, in which the Trading Talent of the Nation hath bene tyed up, and lyen hid for some Years last passed ; for want of which, all persons in England, from the Tenant to the Landlord, from the Weaver to the Merchant, have languished of a deep Consumption. . . . Printed in the Year, 1667. 4°, A—B in fours.

The Peoples Ancient and Just Liberties Asserted, In the Tryal of William Penn, and William Mead, At the Sessions held at the Old-Baily in London, the first, third, fourth, and fifth of Sept. 70. against the most arbitrary procedure of that Court. . . . Printed in the Year, 1670. 4°, A—H in fours.

The Second Part . . . . Asserted in the Proceedings against, and Tryals of Tho. Rudyard, Francis Moor, Rich. Mew, Rich. Mayfield, ... in the year 1670. . . . Printed in the Year, 1670. 4°, A—I 2 in fours.

Appel de l'Angleterre touchant la secrete Cabale ou l'Assemblée a Withael à & envers Le Grand Conseil de la Nation . . . à Amsterdam, 1673. 4°, (A)—(G) in fours.

England's Independency upon the Papal Power Historically and Judicially Stated, By Sr. John Davis, Attorney Generall in Ireland, and by Sr. Edward Coke, Lord Chief Justice in England. In Two Reports, Selected from their greater Volumes ; . . . With a Preface written by Sir John Pettus, Knight. London, Printed by E. Flesher, ... MDCLXXIV. . . . 4°, A—M 2 in fours, and a, 4 leaves. Dedicated by Pettus to James, Earl of Suffolk.

By the King: A Proclamation for the Apprehending certain Offenders therein named, and for the better Security of His Majesty and His Government, from Dangers arising from Popish Recusants. [17 Nov. 1678.] London, Printed by John Bill, . . . 1678. A broadside, printed on two leaves for the purpose of being pasted together.

> The persons named in this document are George Couniers, Charles Walsh, —— Symonds, —— Le Phaire, —— Biston or Beeston, late servant to Lady Bellasis, and —— Prichard.

A Paradox against Liberty Written by the Lords, During their Imprisonment in the Tower. A Poem ... London. Printed in the Year. 1679. Folio, 2 leaves.

An Antidote against the Present Fears and Jealousies of the Nation. By an Impartial Hand. With Approbation, London, Printed by R. E . . . 1679. 4°, A—D 2 in fours.

The Execution of William Ireland, And John Grove who were Drawn, Hang'd, and Quartered at Tyburn, on Friday the 14ᵗ of January 167⁸₉ for High-Treason . . . . London : Printed for R. G. 167⁸₉. 4°, 4 leaves.

The Several Informations of Simeon Wright, Thomas Saunders and Richard Perkin. Concerning the Horrid Popish Plot . . . London, Printed for Thomas Simmons, . . . 1681. Folio, A—E, 2 leaves each, and b, 2 leaves.

The Character of a Rebellion, and what England may expect from one. Or, The Designs of Dissenters Examined by Reason, Experience, and the Laws and Statutes of the Realm. London, Printed for Benj. Tooke, 1681. Folio, A—F, 2 leaves each.

An Excellent New Ballad, To the Tune of, *How Unhappy is Phillis in Love.* Printed for Benjamin Harris at the Stationers Arms at the Royal Exchange, and are to be sold by Langley Curtis in Goatham Court on Ludgate-hill, 1681. A leaf of verses.

Ignoramus : An Excellent New Song. To the Tune of, *Lay by your Pleading, Love lies a bleeding.* London : Printed in the year MDCLXXXI. A leaf of verses.

A New Ignoramus : Being the second New Song. To the same Old Tune, *Love lyes a Bleeding.* London, Printed for Charles Leigh, 1681. A leaf of verses.

Ignoramus Justice : Or,

> The English Law, turn'd into a Gin,
> To let Knaves out, and keep Honest Men In.

An Excellent New Song, To the Tune of, *Sir Egledemore.* London : Printed for Allen Banks. 1682. A broadside in verse.

A New Song. A broadside in verse, with the music. [1688.]

> The refrain is *Lilliburlero.*

The Old Pack. A broadside in verse.

An Account of the Principal Officers Civil and Military of England. May 1684. London, Printed for Christopher Wilkinson . . . 1684. A large broadside.

State Tracts: Being a Collection of Several Treatises Relating to the Government. Privately Printed in the Reign of K. Charles II. London : Printed in the Year, 1689. Folio, A—6 C, 2 leaves each.

Memoirs of what past in Christendom, from the War Begun 1672. To the Peace Concluded 1679. London : Printed by R. R. for Ric. Chiswell, . . . MDCXCII. 8°. A, 4 leaves : B—Cc 4 in eights.

> Dedicated by the anonymous author to his son under date of 1683 (April). The publisher seems to speak of this as the second part only out of three, the first and third not having come to his hands. On the title of the present copy is written : "By Sir John Couentree."

CHARLETON, WALTER, *M.D.*
Natural History of Nutrition, Life, and Voluntary Motion. Containing all the New Discoveries of Anatomists, and most probable Opinions of Physicians. Concerning the Œconomie of Human Nature. Methodically delivered in Exercitations Physico-Anatomical. By Walt. Charlton: MD. London, Printed for Henry Herringman, . . . 1659. 4°, A—Ff in fours, and a, 4 leaves. Dedicated by the author to Thomas, Viscount Fauconberg and (in Latin) to his friend Dr. George Ent.

A Character of His most Sacred Majesty Charles the Second, . . . Written by Dʳ Charleton, Physician in Ordinary to His Maiestie. Who most Religiously affirms, *Se non diversas spes, sed incolumitatem Cæsaris simpliciter spectare.* London, Printed for Henry Herringman . . . 1661. 4°, A—C in fours, A 1 blank.

Chorea Gigantum ; Or, The most Famous Antiquity of Great-Britain, vulgarly called Stone-Heng, Standing on Salisbury Plain, Restored to the Danes ; By Walter Charleton. Dʳ in Physic, and Physician in Ordinary to His Majesty. . . . London, Printed for Henry Herringman, . . . 1663. 4°. A, 4 leaves, including *Imprimatur :* a—b,

2 leaves each : B—I in fours. With two plans, one folded. Dedicated to the King. With verses by John Dryden and Robert Howard.

Matrona Ephesia. Sive Lusus Serius, In Petronii Arbitri Matronam Ephesiam Huic adjiciuntur Dissertatiunculæ Quatuor Philosophicæ . . . Opera B. Harrisii, M.A. traduct. Ejusq ; sumptibus excus . . . Londini, Impensis Authoris. 1665. 12°, A—D in twelves, D 12 with a varying title : Matrona Ephesia sive Lusus Serius de Amore a Gualt. Charletono ante decennium Anglice conscriptum et nunc demum Latinitati donatus a Barth. Harrisio, A.M. . . .

CHARNOCK, STEPHEN, *S.T.B.*
Bibliotheca Charnockiana Sive Catalogus Librorum . . . Domini Steph. Charnock, S.T.B. Nuperrime Defuncti. Quorum Auctio habebitur Londini Apud Insigne Agni in vico vulgo dicto Cornhill, Quarto die Octobris, 1680. These Catalogues are Distributed Gratis at the above-mentioned Sign of the Lamb in Cornhill an Upholsterers Shop, and at the Sign of the Three Legs in the Poultrey, a Booksellers Shop. 1680. 4°. Title and to the Reader, 2 leaves, and pp. 32.

CHAUCER, GEOFFREY.
The Workes of Geffray Chau/cer newly printed / with dyuers workes whi/che were neuer in / print before : As in the table more playnly / dothe appere. / Cum priuilegio./ [Col.] Thus endeth the workes of Geffray / Chaucer. Printed at Lōdon / by Thomas Godfray. / The yere of our lorde. M.D.xxxii. / Cum prinilegio a rege indulto./ Folio, black letter, in two columns. With cuts of a peculiar character. A, 4 leaves, with first title, Dedication by the Editor, Table, and Ballads : B—Z in sixes : Romaunt of the Rose, &c., with new title, Aa—3 V in sixes. The title is within a rich woodent border.

> Sign. Qq has three extra leaves, in consequence of the insertion in that sheet by an after-thought of Henryson's *Testament of Cresseid.*
> This is the earliest collected edition, and was superintended by William Thynne, chief clerk of the kitchen to Henry VIII., to whom he dedicated it.

Chaucer's Whims : Being some Select Fables and Tales in Verse, very Applicable to the Present Time s; . . . London, Printed by D. Edwards, 1701. 8°, A—F 2 in fours. *B. M.*

CHEKE, SIR JOHN.
The Trve Subiect to the Rebell. Or The Hvrt of Sedition . . . Oxford, Printed by Leonard Lichfield, . . . 1641. 4°, a—c in fours, and A—H in fours.

CHESHIRE.
Magnalia Dei. A Relation of some of the many Remarkable Passages in Cheshire before the Siege of Namptwich, during the Continuance of it : And at the happy raising of it by the victorious Gentlemen Sir Tho. Fairfax and Sir William Brereton. Together with the Deliverance and Victory by the Garrison at Nottingham. . . . London : Printed for Robert Bostock 1644. 4°, A—C in fours, besides title and a preface "To the Well-Affected Reader."

The Speech of the Right Honourable Henry Earl of Warrington, Lord Delamere, to the Grand Jury at Chester. April 13. 1692. London, Printed for Richard Baldwin . . . 1692. 4°, A—D in fours, A 1 blank.

CHIDLEY, CATHERINE.
The Ivstification of the Independant Chvrches of Christ. Being an Answer to Mr Edwards his Booke, which hee hath written against the Government of Christ's Chvrch, . . . London, Printed for William Larnar, . . . 164[9.] 4°. *, 4 leaves : A—K in fours : L, 1 leaf.

CHILD, JOHN.
The Mischief of Persecution Exemplified : Or A True Narrative of the Life and Deplorable End of Mr John Child, who miserably destroy'd himself, Octob. 13, 1684. Giving an Account of his Despair ; And divers Conferences had with him by several of his Friends. . . . London, Printed for Tho. Fabian, . . . 1688. 4°, A—G 2 in fours.

CHILD, SIR JOSIAH.
The East-India-Trade a most Profitable Trade to the Kingdom. And best secured and improved in a Company, and a Joint-Stock. Represented in a Letter written upon the Occasion of two Letters lately published, insinuating the Contrary. London, Printed in the Year 1677. 4°, A—D in fours, D 4 blank.

> On the title in an old hand occurs : "Supposed to be written by Mr. Joseph [Josiah] Child."

A New Discourse of Trade, Wherein is Recommended several weighty Points relating to Companies of Merchants. The Act of Navigation, Naturalization of Strangers, And our Woollen Manufactures. The Ballance of Trade. . . . By Sir Josiah Child. London, Printed, and Sold

by John Everingham. . . . 1693. 8°,
Title and Imprimatur, 2 leaves : (A)—(C)
in eights : (d), 4 leaves : (D)—(E) in
eights : A—P in eights.

A New Discourse of Trade, . . . London,
Printed and Sold by T. Sowle . . . 1698.
8°, A—S in eights, S 8 blank.

CHIRURGEONS.
The practyse of Cyrurgeons of Mountpyller : and of other that neuer came
there. [Col.] Finis pro tempore. Imprynted by me Rycharde Banckes. Cum
prinilegio Regali. Ad imprimendum
solum. 4°, 4 leaves. Large black letter.
With a woodcut on title of two doctors
conversing. *B. M.*

CHRIST'S HOSPITAL.
The Present State and List of the Children
of His Late Majesty King Charles II.
His New Royal Foundation in Christ's-
Hospital, Presented in all Humility and
Duty to their Most Sacred Majesties, K.
William and Q. Mary, by the Lord Mayor
. . . January, 16⅞⅜. Folio, 6 leaves, the
last blank.

CHRISTIANITY.
The summe of Christianitie, reduced into
eight propositions, briefly and plainly
confirmed out of the holy worde of God
. . . London, Owen Rogers [about 1560.]
8°, black letter, A—C in eights. Without
any place and printer's name, but with
O. R. at the foot of the compartment
which encloses the title.
> Sothebys, Bedford's sale, March, 1884,
> No. 1376.

A Declaration of the Principall Pointes
of Christian Doctrine, Gathered ovt of
diuerse Catechismes, and Set forth by
the English Priests dwelling in Tournay
Colledge. At Paris, By Sebastian Cra-
moisy, Printer to the King. M.DC.XLVII.
12°. ⅔, 4 leaves : A—Bb 6 in twelves.

CHURCH.
An humble supplicacion vnto God / for
the restoringe of hys holye woorde / vnto
the churche of Englande / mooste mete
to be sayde in these oure dayes / euen
with teares of euery true & faythfull
English harte. Esa. 59. Beholde / the
Lordes hāde . . . . Imprynted at Stras-
burgh in Elsas / at the signe of the goldē
•Bibell / In the moneth of Auguste. The
yeare of our Lord. 1554. 8°, black
letter, A—E 3 in eights, but E 4 was
probably blank.

Consilivm Delectorvm Cardinalivm et
Aliorvm Prælatorvm, de emendanda

Ecclesia . . . Libellus verè aureus . . .
Ex Bibliotheca W. Crashaui . . . Londini,
Excudebat Felix Kingston, . . . 1609. 4°,
A—C in fours. Dedicated to Matthew,
Archbishop of York.

Ecclesiæ Gemitvs sub Anabaptisticâ Ty-
rannide. . . . . Anno Dom. 1649.
Æræ Martyrii Caroli I. Britanniarum
Regis, Anno primo. 8°, A—D in eights.
In verse.

The History of the Persecutions of the
Reformed Churches in France, Orange,
and Piedmont. From the year 1655. to
this time. Shewing by what steps . . .
they were destroyed. . . . With A Short
Account of the Present Condition of the
Protestants of France, and elsewhere.
Wherein are many remarkable passages
never before printed. London, Printed
for Tho. Newborough . . . and John
Nicholson . . . 1699. 4°, B—K 2 in
fours, and the title.

CHURCH, NATHANAEL.
Cheap Riches, Or A Pocket Companion,
Made of Five hundred Proverbial Apho-
rismes, &c. . . . London, Printed for S. G.
. . . 1657. 12°, A—F in twelves. Dedicated to the Honourable William Pen,
Vice-Admiral to the English Navy.

CHURCHILL, SIR WINSTON.
Divi Britannici . . . 1675.
> *Revised collation :* Title, 1 leaf : dedica-
> tion to Charles II., 2 leaves : b—l, 2 leaves
> each, with an Essay on Government : A—
> Tt in fours, A 1 with half-title. With
> engravings.

CIBBER, C.
Love's Last Shift ; Or, The Fool in
Fashion. A Comedy. As it is Acted at
the Theatre Royal, By His Majesty's
Servants. Written by C. Cibber . . .
London, Printed by H. Rhodes . . . 1696.
4°, A—N in fours. Dedicated to Richard
Norton of Southwick Esquire.

Love makes a Man : Or, The Fop's Fortune. A Comedy. Acted at the Theatre
Royal in Drury Lane, By His Majesty's
Servants. Written by C. Cibber. *Inter-
dum tollit Comœdia Vocem.* Hor. London, Printed for Richard Parker . . .
1701. 4°, A—H in fours. Dedicated to
Sir William Brownlow, Bar.

The Rival Fools. A Comedy. As it is
Acted at the Theatre-Royal in Drury
Lane By His Majesty's Sworn Comedians.
Written by Mr Cibber. London : Printed
for Bernard Lintott . . . 4°. A, 3 leaves :
B—K in fours.

CICERO, M. T.

The First Book of Tullies Offices Translated Grammatically, and also according to the propriety of our English Tongue; For the more speedy and certain attaining of the singular Learning contained in the same, . . . Done chiefly for the good of Schools, . . . At London, Printed by H. Lownes, for Thomas Man, . . . 1616. 8°. A, 6 leaves : B—X in eights. Dedicated by John Brinsley to Dr. Hunton, M.D., his reverend and worthily respected friend.

CIPRIANO, GIO.

A Most Strange and Wonderfvll Prophesie vpon this Trovblesome world. Calculated by the famous Doctor in Astrologie, Maister Iohn Cipriano, . . . Whereunto is annexed Torquatus Vandermers seauen yeres study in the arte of Magick, vpon the twelue moneths of the yeare, . . . Translated out of Italian by Anth. Hollaway Gent. Imprinted at London [by A. I. 1596.] 4°, A—B in fours, A 1 and B 4 blank. *B. M.*

> The large cut on the title has led to the line of imprint being mutilated. It is repeated on sign. B. The second portion is dated January, 1569.

CLAPHAM, JOHN.

Narcissvs. Sive Amoris Ivvenilis et Præcipve Philavtiæ Brevis atqve Moralis Descriptio. Londini. Excudebat Thomas Scarlet. 1591. 4°, A—B in fours. In Latin verse. Dedicated to Henry, Earl of Southampton. *B. M.*

The Historie of England. The first Booke. Declaring the estate of the Ile of Britannie vnder the Roman Empire. London Printed by Valentine Simmes, for Iohn Barnes, . . . 1602. 4°, A—Q 2 in fours, A 1 and Q 2 blank.

> An epitome selected from a variety of sources for the convenience of ordinary readers.

The Historie of Great Britannie Declaring the successe of times and affaires in that Iland, from the Romans first entrance, vntill the raigne of Egbert, the West-Saxon Prince ; . . . At London, Printed by Valentine Simmes. 1606. 4°. A, 4 leaves, A 1 blank : Table of the Roman Emperors and British Princes, 2 leaves : B—V in eights, V 8 with the *Errata*.

CLARE, JOHN, *of the Society of Jesus.*

The Converted Iew Or Certaine Dialogves betweene Michaeas a Learned Iew, and others, touching diuers points of Religion, controverted betweene the Catholicks and Protestants. . . . Dedicated to the two Vniuersities of Oxford and Cambridge. Permissv Svperiorvm. Anno. M. DC. XXX. 4°. . . . å and ĕ, 4 leaves each : A—Q in fours, Q 4 blank : *Second Part*, A—V 2 in fours: *The Arraignment of the Converted Jew*, A—S in fours. *B. M.*

CLARK, EDWARD, *B.D.*

The Protestant School-Master, Containing Plain and Easie Directions for Spelling and Reading English, with all necessary Rules for the True Reading of the English Tongue. . . . London, Printed by T. B. and are to be sold by John How . . . 1680. 12°. A, 10 leaves, including a double frontispiece on 2 leaves : B—I in twelves ; K, 5.

CLARK, R., *Chymist.*

Vermiculars Destroyed with an Historical Account of Worms. . . . The Eighth Impression. London : Printed for the Author, 1698. 4°, A—F in fours.

CLARKE, SAMUEL, *D.D.*

A Martyrologie, Containing A Collection of all the Persecutions which have befallen the Church of England since the first Plantation of the Gospel to the End of Queen Maries Reign . . . London, Printed by T. Ratcliffe and E. Mottershed, and are to be sold by John Browne . . . 1652. Folio. A, 4 leaves : a, 4 : c, 4 : B—Qq 3 in fours : the Supplementary Lives of Coligny, &c., A—T in fours. With a portrait of Clarke and of the persons whose lives are given, verses by Thomas Dugard, and a dedication to John Corbet, M.P. for Bishop's-Castle, Salop.

A Mirrour or Looking-Glasse both for Saints, and Sinners, Held forth in about two thousand Examples : . . . Collected out of the most Classique Authors both Ancient and Modern . . . By Sa. Clark, Minister in Bennet Fink, London. . . . London, Printed for Tho. Newbery, . . . 1654. 8°, A—Ss in eights, and a, 8 leaves, besides a frontispiece and portrait by Gaywood, the latter dated 1654.

CLARKE, THOMAS.

The Recantation of Thomas Clarke (sometime a Seminarie Priest of the English Colledge in Rhemes ; and nowe by the great mercy of God conuerted vnto the profession of the Gospell of Iesvs Christ) made at Paules Crosse after the Sermon made by Master Bvckridge Preacher, the 15. of April, 1593 . . . . Imprinted at London by the Deputies of Christopher Barker . . . 1594. 8°, A—C in eights.

CLAUDE, M.

The Life and Death of Monsieur Claude The famous Minister of Charenton in France. Done out of French by G. P. . . . London, Printed for Thomas Dring, ... 1688. 4°, A—I 2 in fours, and 3 leaves of a between A and B.

CLAVELL, ROBERT, *Bookseller and Publisher.*

A Catalogue of all the Books Printed in England since the Dreadful Fire of London, in 1666. To the End of Michaelmas Term, 1672 . . . Collected by Robert Clavel. London, Printed by S. Simmons, . . . M.DC.LXXIII. Folio, A—Y, 2 leaves each.

The present copy contains a supplement of 7 leaves with the books printed to Michaelmas Term, 1674.

CLAY, MARY.

The High-Way Woman : Or, A True and Perfect Narrative of the Wicked Life, and Deplorable Death of Mary Clay, Otherwise called Jenny Fox. Who being Condemned to be Hanged, with other Malefactors, at Tyburn, on Wednesday, the 12ᵗʰ of April, Instant, did on the Tuesday fore-going, Poyson her self, to avoid the Shame of that kind of Death . . . London, Printed by T. L. MDCLXV. 4°, A—B in fours.

With a cut on the title, a small full-length, supposed to represent the heroine.

CLELAND, JAMES.

The Instruction of a young Noble-man. By Iames Cleland. At Oxford, Printed by Ioseph Barnes. 1612. 4°. ¶ and ¶¶, 4 leaves each : A—Ll in fours, Ll 4 blank.

CLEOMBROTUS.

Most Strange and Wonderful Predictions of Cleombrotus an Heathen Jew, Prophesied in the Year One thousand Two hundred Seventy and two ; upon the Reigns of Twenty Nine Kings of England, from Edward the First to Charles the Fifth, One thousand Seven hundred Ninety nine. Found in the Colledge of Wittenburgh in Germany. London, Printed for Langley Curtis, ... MDCLXXIX. 4°, 4 leaves.

CLERGY.

A Reasonable Motion In the behalfe of the Clergie, As are now questioned in Parliament for their places . . . Printed [abroad] in the vnfortunate yeare to Preists, 1641. 4°. In verse. With a curious cut on title.

The copy used (Sothebys, March 14, 1882, No. 1349) ended on the second leaf, apparently leaving something incomplete.

CLERIO.

The Loves and Adventures of Clerio & Logia. A Romance. Written Originally in French, and Translated into English By Fra. Kirkman, Gent. London Printed by J. M. and are to be sold by William Ley at his shop at Pauls Chain 1652. 12°. A, 4 : B—M in eights : N, 4. Dedicated to William Beeston Esq. by F. Kirkman Jun.

CLEVELAND, JOHN.

Poems. By John Cleaveland. With Additions, never before Printed. London, Printed by J. R. for John Williams, 1669. 8°, A—P in eights, A 1 and P 8 blank.

The Rustick Rampant, Or Rurall Anarchy Affronting Monarchy : In the Insurrection of Wat Tiler. By J. C. London, Printed for F. C . . . 1658. 8°, A—L 4 in eights, L 4 blank.

CLEVES, DUCHY OF.

Newes out of Cleaue-land ; Being the true relation of the taking in of the town and castle of Gulicke in Germanie, with the articles of peace there concluded and agreed vpon. As also the seruices and fights, performed while the siege lasted. London, Printed by T. H. for Iohn Budge, . . . 1610. 4°, A—D in fours, A 1, C 2, and D 4 blank. *B. M.*

Newes out of Cleaue-land. . . . London, Printed by T. H. for Iohn Budge, . . . 1611. 4°, A—D in fours, A 1, C 2, and (probably) D 4 blank. *B. M.*

CLINTON, ELIZABETH, *Countess of Lincoln.*

The Covntesse of Lincolnes Nvrserie. At Oxford, Printed by Iohn Lichfield, and Iames Short . . . 1622. 4°, A—D in fours, D 4 blank. With a short address by Thomas Lodge and a dedication by Lady Lincoln to Bridget Countess [dowager ?] of Lincoln. *B. M.*

CLORIA.

The Princess Cloria : Or, The Royal Romance. In Five Parts. Imbellished with divers Political Notions, and singular Remarks of Modern Transactions. Containing the Story of most part of Europe, for many Years last past. Written by a Person of Honour. London, Printed by Ralph Wood, and are to be sold by William Brooke, . . . 1661. Folio, A—4 I in fours, besides the title and a curious frontispiece.

CLOWES, WILLIAM.

A Frvtefvll and Approoved Treatise, for

the Artificiall Cure of the Malady called in Latin *Strenna*, and in English, the Evill, cured by Kinges and Queenes of England. Very necessary for all young Practizers of Chyrurgery. Written by William Clowes, one of her Maiesties Chyrurgions, in the yeare of our Lord. 1602. Imprinted at London by Edward Allde 1602. 4°, black letter, A—K 3 in fours.

At the end it is stated that this book had been examined, and was to be sold at Master Laybourne's, a barber-chirurgeon's, on St. Mary's Hill, near Billingsgate.

CLUB.
The Country Club. A Poem. London : Printed for Walter Kettilby . . . 1679. 4°, A—E 2 in fours, and the title.

COACHES.
A Copy of a Printed Letter from J. C. to a Post-Master in the Country, with Directions about the Management of his Designe for putting down Stage-Coaches. . . . Together with a Copy of a Letter to J. C. from a Post-Master in the Country, in Answer . . . [1672.] Folio, 2 leaves.
Stage-Coaches Vindicated : Or, Certain Animadversions and Reflections upon several Papers writ by J. C. of the Inner Temple, Gent. against Stage-Coaches. [1672.] Folio, 3 leaves.

COAL.
The Mischief of the Five Shillings Tax upon Coal, Here is humbly Represented, by [Robert Bell, Advocate for the Corporation of Sandgate and Prolocutor to the Infernal Society of Pitrats.] That this Tax is inconsistent with the Safety of England, . . . London, Printed by H. Hills, for Edward Poole, . . . 1699. 4°, B—E 2 in fours, and the title.

The portion between brackets is inserted in MS., a blank space having been left for that purpose, and each copy being filled up, doubtless, with a different name.

COBBLER.
The Cobler of Canterburie. Or An Inuectiue against Tarltons Newes out of Purgatorie. A merrier Iest then a Clownes Iigge, and fitter for Gentlemens humors. Published with the cost of a Dickar of Cow-hides. London, Printed by Nicholas Okes for Nathaniel Butter, and are to be sold at the signe of the pide Bull neere to Saint Austins gate. 1608. 4°, black letter, A—K in fours.

COCKER, EDWARD.
The Pen's Triumph : Containing Variety of Examples of all Hands practised in this Nation, . . . Also an excellent Receipt

for Ink, and to write with Gold. Invented, Written and Engraven by Edward Cocker, dwelling on the South side of St. Pauls Church, over against Pauls Chain. . . . Are to be sold, with [Fair Writings Storehouse] by Robert Walton Printer and Stationer at the Globe and Compasses on the North-side of St. Pauls Church London, 1660. Obl. 8°, pp. 16 of letterpress, 1 leaf of advertisements of books, and 28 plates.

COFFEE.
The Vertues of Coffee. Set forth in the Works of the Lord Bacon his *Natural Hist.* Mr Parkinson his *Herbel*, Sir George Sandys his *Travails*, James Howel Esq; his Epistles. Collected and Published for the Satisfaction of the Drinkers thereof. . . . London, Printed by W. G. 1663. 4°, 4 leaves. *B. M.*

The School of Politicks : Or, The Humours of a Coffee-House. A Poem.

Tantumne ab re tua otii est, aliena ut cures ?
—Terent.

. . . London, Printed for Richard Baldwin, . . . 1690. 4°. A, 2 leaves : B—D in fours.

COGAN, THOMAS.
The Haven of Health : Chiefly made for the comfort of Students, and consequently for all those that haue a care of their health, . . . Hereunto is added a Preseruation from the Pestilence : With a short Censure of the late sicknesse at Oxford. . . . Imprinted at London by Thomas Orwin, for William Norton. 1589. 4°. ¶ and ¶¶, 4 leaves each : A—Nn in fours. Dedicated to Sir Edward Seymor, Knight.

COLBATCH, JOHN, *M.D.*
A Relation of a very Sudden and Extraordinary Cure of a Person Bitten by a Viper. By the means of Acids. . . . London, Printed for Dan. Brown . . . 1698. 8°. Title and list of books by the same Author, 2 leaves : A, 4 leaves : B—H in eights : I, 2.

COLBERT, JEAN BAPTISTE.
The Life of the Famous John Baptist Colbert, Late Minister and Secretary of State to Lewis XIV. the Present French King. Done into English from a French Copy printed at Cologne this present Year 1695. London, Printed for R. Bentley, . . . 1695. 8°, A—R in eights. A 1 with a frontispiece and R 8 blank.

COLCHESTER.
The Siege of Colchester by the Lord Fairfax as it was with ye Line & Outworks.

1648. An engraved map in obl. folio.
B. M.

An Elegie, On the most { Barbarous, Vnparallel'd, Vnsouldiery } Murder, Committed at Colchester, upon the persons of the two most incomparable, Sir Charles Lucas, and Sir George Lisle. London. Printed in the Year, 1648. 4°, 4 leaves.

The Colchester Spie. Truly informing the Kingdome of the estate of that gallant Town, and the attempts of Fairfax against it : with some other remarkable passages from the English and Scots Army, also from Westminster and London. Printed in the Yeere. 1648. 4°, 4 leaves.

COLCLOUGH, GEORGE.

The Spectacle to Repentance. *Mathew.* xviii. *Wo to the World* . . . Imprynted at London in Fletstreete, at the signe of S. John Euangelist by Thomas Colwell. 1571. 8°, A—E 2 in eights. Black letter. In stanzas of 4 lines. *B. M.*

> Dedicated by the author to his uncle, Anthony Colclough, Esquire, whom, in the subscription to the epistolary Address, he terms, as was then not unusual, his *cousin*, that word being employed in a generic sense.

COLE, WILLIAM, *A Lover of his Country.*
A Rod for the Lawyers ; Who are hereby declared to be the grand Robbers & Deceivers of the Nation : . . . London, Printed in the year, 1659. 4°, A—C 2 in fours.

COLLIER, JEREMY, *M.A.*
Essays upon Several Moral Subjects. In Two Parts . . . By Jeremy Collier, M.A. The Third Edition. London : Printed for R. Sare . . . 1698. 8°. Part I. B—R 4 in eights, besides prel. 3 leaves : Part II. A—N in eights.

A Defence of the Short View . . . Being a Reply to Mr Congreve's Amendments, &c. And to the Vindication of the Author of the Relapse. By Jeremy Collier, M.A. . . . London : Printed for S. Keble . . . 1699. 8", B—K 6 in eights, besides two leaves with title and Preface.

COLMENERO, ANTHONIO, *Doctor in Physic and Chirurgery.*
A Curious Treatise of the Nature and Quality of Chocolate. Written in Spanish . . . And put into English by Don Diego de Vadesforte [James Wadsworth.] Imprinted at London by J. Okes, dwelling in Little St. Bartholmewes. 1640. 4°, A—D 2 in fours. Dedicated by Wads-worth to Edward Viscount Conway. *B. M.*

COLVIL, SAMUEL.
A Mock Poem. Or, Whiggs Supplication. Part 1. London, Printed in the Year, 1681. 8°, A—H 4 in eights. H 4 blank : Part 2, with a new title, A—E 4 in eights, E 4 blank.

The Scotch Hudibras : Or, A Mock Poem. The First Part. Corrected and Amended, with Additions and Alterations. London, Printed by T. B. and are to be Sold by Randal Taylor. 1692. 8°, A—M in eights.

COMPLAINTS.
The Lamentable Complaints of Nick Froth the Tapster, and Rvlerost the Cooke Concerning the restraint lately set forth, against drinking, potting, and piping on the Sabbath day, and against selling meats. Printed in the yeare, 1642. 4°, 4 leaves. With a large cut on the title.

CONFORMITY.
The Course of Conformitie, As it hath proceeded, Is concluded, Snould be refused . . . Printed in the yeare 1622. 4°. A, 4 leaves : a, 4 leaves : *₊*, 4 leaves : B —Zz in fours.

The Grounds of Unity in Religion : Or An Expedient for a general Conformity and Pacification. By a Gentleman of the Middle Temple. Printed in the Year 1679. 4°, 4 leaves.

CONGREVE, WILLIAM.
The Birth of the Muse. A Poem. To the Right Honourable Charles Montague, Chancellour of the Exchequer, &c. By Mr Congreve . . . London, Printed for Jacob Tonson . . . 1698. Folio, A—C, 2 leaves each.

CONSOLATION.
A Consolation for troubled Consciences. [Col.] Imprynted at London in Fletestrete next to saynt Dunstones churche at the sygne of the George . . . Small 8°, A—E 4 in eights.

> Without a regular title. This was perhaps printed to accompany the *Creed*, the *Prayers of Holy Fathers,* and the *Paternoster, &c.,* all printed by Robert Redman in or about 1527.

CONSTABLE, HENRY.
Diana . . . 1592.

> This collection of Sonnets appears to have belonged on the 6th November, 1598, to William Wood. See Arber, iii. 44.

CONSTITUTIONS.
Constitvtions and Canons Ecclesiasticall,

Treated vpon by the Bishop of London President of the Conuocation for the Prouince of Canterbury; and the rest of the Bishop and Clergie of the said Prouince: . . . Imprinted at London by Robert Barker, . . . Anno 1604. 4°, A—Y in fours, A 1 and Y 4 blank.

Constitvtions and Canons Ecclesiasticall . . . now published for the due observation of them, by his Majesties authority under the Great Seale of England. London, Printed by Iohn Norton, for Ioyce Norton, and Richard Whitaker, . . . 1633. 4°, A—P in fours.

> Apparently a reprint of the edition of 1604.

CONTRARIES.

The Defence of Contraries. Paradoxes against common opinion, debated in forme of declamations in place of publike censure: only to exercise young wittes in difficult matters. Wherein as no offence to Gods honour, . . . Translated out of French by A. M. one of the Messengers of her Maiesties Chamber. . . . Imprinted at London by Iohn Windet for Simon Waterson. 1593. 4°, A—O in fours, title on A 2.

> This is only Book I. At the end Munday the translator says that he broke off here to spare the reader—a singular instance of moderation.

COOK.

The Compleat Cook: . . . . . London, Printed for Nath. Brooke, at the Angel in Cornhill, 1662. 8°, A—F 5 in twelves. *B. M.*

COOKERY.

A Booke of Cookerie. otherwise called: The good Huswiues Handmaid for the Kitchen. . . . . Wherunto are annexed sundry necessary Conceites for the preseruation of health. London Printed by E. Allde dwelling in Aldersgate streete ouer against the Pump. 1597. 8°, A—H 3 in eights. *B. M.*

COOPER, ANTHONY ASHLEY, *Earl of Shaftesbury.*

A Dialogue between the Earl of Sh——y, E. Settle and Dr Oats at parting. London, Printed for J. S. 1682. A broadside.

Toney's Soliloquies. To the Tune of Dagons Fall, Or the Lamentation of a Bad Market. London, Printed Anno Domini 1682. A leaf of verses.

COOPER, JOSEPH.

The Art of Cookery Refin'd and Augmented. Containing an Abstract of some rare and rich unpublished Receipts of Cookery: Collected from the practise of that incomparable Master of these Arts, Mr Jos. Cooper, chiefe Cook to the Late King; . . . London, Printed by J. G. for R. Lowndes . . . 1654. 12°. A, 6 leaves: B—I in twelves.

COOPER, WILLIAM.

A Philosophicall Epitaph in Hieroglyphicall Figures. With Explanations. A Briefe of yr Golden Calfe the Worlds Idoll / Glaubers golden Ass well managed Gehor the three Principles or Originall of all things. Published by W. C. Esq. With a Catalogue of Chymicall Bookes. London Printed for William Cooper at the Pellican in Litle Britain. 1675. 8°, A—O in eights: the Catalogue, separate title, &c., 4 leaves: p, 4: Q—R in fours: A—G in fours. With an engraved title and plates at pp. 1, 16, of first paging, and 40 of second. Dedicated to Elias Ashmole and the Honourable Robert Boyle by W. C. in two epistles.

COOTE, EDWARD.

[The English Schoolmaster. At the end occurs:] At London. Printed by the Widow Orwin, for Ralph Jackson, and Robert Dexter. 1596. 4°, A—N in fours.

> The only copy at present known begins on sign. B with the series of alphabets.
> After the Grammar itself follows *A Short Catechisme*, then graces, prayers, versions of Psalms, 1, 51, 104, 112-13, 119-20, 148, and some quaint verses headed *The Schoolemaister to his Scholers.* We next have a general Chronology, preceded by some remarks on Arithmetic and *Directions to the Ignorant*, and the work concludes with a rather long Vocabulary, introduced by some remarks on Greek, Latin, and French terminations.

COPLAND, ROBERT, *the Younger.*

The seuen sorowes that women haue when theyr husbandes be deade. Compyled by Robert Copland. [Col.] Imprented at London in Lothburi ouer agaynste Sainct Margarytes church by me Wyllyam Copland. 4°, black letter, A—C in fours. In verse. With cuts. *B. M.*

> On the back of the title is *The excuse of the Authour*, 8 lines of verse, followed by a Prologue in the form of a Dialogue between Copland and Quidam. The series of *Sorrows* commence on A 3 verso.

COPLEY, JOHN, *Seminary Priest.*

Doctrinall And Morall Observations concerning Religion: Wherein the Avthor declareth the Reasons of his late vn-enforced departure from the Church of

*

Rome: and of his incorporation to the present Church of England . . . London, Imprinted by W. S. for Richard Moore, . . . 1612. 4°. ¶, 4 leaves: A—Ii 2 in fours. *B. M.*

COPPIN, RICHARD.
Michael opposing the Dragon: Or, A Fiery Dart struck through the Heart of the Kingdome of the Serpent. . . . By Richard Coppin . . . London, Printed, and are to be sold at the Black-Spread Eagle neer the west-end of Pauls; and at the Blackamore neer Fleet-bridge, 1659. 4°, B—Oo in fours, and the title. Without prefixes.

CORDEMOY.
A Philosophicall Discourse concerning Speech, Conformable to the Cartesian Principles, Dedicated to the most Christian King. Englished out of French. In the Savoy, Printed for John Martin, . . . 1668. 12°, A—G 6 in twelves, G 6 blank.

CORDEROY, JEREMY, *Student in Oxford.*
A Warning for Worldlings. Or a comfort to the godly, and a terror to the wicked. Set forth Dialogue wise, betweene a Scholler and a Trauailer . . . At London, Printed by Thomas Purfoot, for Lawrence Lisle . . . 1608. 12°, A—D 4 in twelves, A 1 and D 4 blank. Dedicated to Lord Chancellor Ellesmere. *B. M.*

CORNEILLE, PIERRE.
The Cid, A Tragicomedy, out of French made English: And acted before their Majesties at Court, and on the Cock-pit Stage in Drury-lane, by the servants of both their Majesties. London, Printed by John Haviland for Thomas Walkley . . . 1637. 12°, A—D 6 in twelves, D 5 with Imprimatur, and D 6 presumably blank. Dedicated by the translator, Joseph Rutter, to Edward, Earl of Dorset, Lord Chamberlain. *B. M.*

Pompey. A Tragedy. Acted with Great Applause. London, Printed for John Crooke, at the Sign of the Ship in St. Paul's Church-yard. 1663. 4°, A—I 2 in fours.

CORNWALL.
The Voice of the Lord in the Temple. Or, A most strange and wonderfull Relation of Gods great Power, Providence, and Mercy, in sending very strange sounds, fire, and a Fiery Ball into the Church of Anthony in Cornwall neere Plimmouth, on Whitsunday last. 1640. to the scorch-

ing and astonishing of 14. severall persons who were smitten. . . . Imprinted at London by T. Paine for Francis Eglesfield . . . 1640. 4°, A—C in fours, C 4 blank. *B. M.* (imprint mutilated.)

CORNWALLIS, SIR WILLIAM, *the Younger.*
Discovrses vpon Seneca the Tragedian. By Sir William Cornwalleys, Knight. Imprinted at London for Edmund Mattes, at the hand and plough in Fleetstreet. 1601. 8°. Title and dedication to Sir John Popham, Lord Chief Justice of England, 2 leaves: ¶, 2 leaves: A—H 6 in eights, H 6 blank. *B. M.*

The Miracvlovs And Happie Vnion of England and Scotland; by how admirable meanes it is effected; how profitable to both Nations, and how free of any inconuenience either past, present, or to come. London Imprinted for Edward Blount. 1604. 4°, A—E in fours, A 1 blank. *B. M.*

Essayes of Certaine Paradoxes. The second Impression, inlarged. London: Printed for Richard Hawkins, . . . 1617. 4°. A, 2 leaves: B—H 2 in fours.

CORROZET, GILLES, *Libraire.*
Memorable Conceits of Divers Noble and famous personages of Christendome, of this our moderne time. London, Printed for Iames Shaw, 1602. Sm. 8°, A—S in eights. Dedicated to the towardly young gentleman Master Walter Raleigh, son to Sir Walter Raleigh, by I. S. probably the publisher.
A translation of the *Divers Propos Memorables*, 12°, 1557.

COTTA, JOHN, *of Northampton, M.D.*
A Short Discoverie of the Vnobserved Dangers of seuerall sorts of ignorant and vnconsiderate Practisers of Physicke in England. . . . By Iohn Cotta of Northampton Doctor in Physicke. London, Imprinted for William Iones, and Richard Boyle dwelling in the Blacke-Friars. 1612. 4°, A—S in fours. Dedicated to his friends and patients in Northamptonshire.

The Triall of Witch-craft, Shewing the Trve and Right Methode of the Discouery: With A Confutation of erroneous wayes. By Iohn Cotta, Doctor in Physicke. London, Printed by George Pvrslowe for Samvel Rand, . . . 1616. 4°, A—R in fours. Dedicated to Sir Edward Coke.

COTTON, CHARLES.
The Wonders of the Peak. . . . Notting-

ham : Printed by John Collyer, and sold by H. Contrel and H. Allestres in Derby, J. Bradley and S. Gunter in Chesterfield, and M' Whitworth in Manchester, Booksellers. 1725. 12", B—K in fours, and the title.

COTTON, JOHN.

The Bloudy Tenent, Washed, And made White in the bloud of the Lambe : . . . Whereunto is added a Reply to M' Williams Answer, to M' Cottons Letter. By John Cotton . . . London, Printed by Matthew Symmons for Hannah Allen, . . . 1647. 4°, B—Ss in fours and the title.

COURTENAY.

Reqveste Presentee au Roy par Messienrs de Courtenay le xv. Juin mil six cens dixhuit. [Paris, 1618.] 8°, 6 leaves.

COURTS.

Diuersite de courtzt et lour iurisdictions / et alia necessaria & vtilia. [Col.] Thomas Bertheletus regius impressor excudebat. Anno dñi. M.D.XXX. 8°, A—C 4 in eights.

COVERDALE, MILES

The Christian State of Matrimony . . . . Imprinted at London by John Awdeley. 1575. 8°, black letter, A—N in eights, N 8 blank.

Translated from the Latin of Henry Bullinger.

A christē exhortacion vnto customable swearers. What a righte & lawfull othe is : when, and before whom it ought to be. Item. The maner of saying grace, & genyng thākes vnto God . . . [Col.] Imprinted at London by Nicholas Hyll, for Rycharde Kele. 8°, black letter, A—E 4 in eights, E 4 blank.

Sothebys, March 31, 1882, No. 330.

COWLEY, ABRAHAM.

The Works of M' Abraham Cowley . . . . The Eighth Edition. London, Printed for Henry Herringman, . . . MDCXCIII. Folio. Title, 1 leaf : a—c in fours : B—C in fours : C*, 4 leaves : Table, 4 leaves : D—3 Z 2 in fours : The Cutter of Coleman Street, A—E in fours. With the same portrait.

The Works of M' Abraham Cowley : . . . The Ninth Edition. To which are added, some Verses by the Author, Never before Printed. London, Printed for Henry Herringman, . . . 1700. Folio. Title and portrait : a—d in fours : A—T in fours : V, 1 leaf : C*—R* in fours : a (with *Davideis*)—q in fours : Table, &c., on **, 4 leaves : B—I, 2 ll. each : Second

and Third Parts of Works, with title and frontispiece, 2 ll. : Separate title to *Juvenile Poems*, 1 leaf : Verses and Contents, 4 ll. : A, 2 leaves : B—X in fours.

COWPER, WILLIAM, *Bishop of Galloway.*

The Life and Death of the Reverend Father, and faithfull Seruant of God, M' William Cowper, Bishop of Galloway, who departed this life at Edenburgh, the 25. of February. 1619. Wherevnto is added a Resolvtion penned by himselfe, some few dayes before his death, touching the Articles concluded in the late generall Assemblie holden at Perth. 1618. London, Printed by George Purslowe, for Iohn Budge, . . . 1619. 4°, A—D in fours.

COX, NICHOLAS.

The Gentleman's Recreation : In Four Parts. . . . The Fourth Edition . . . London : Printed by J. Dawks, for N. Rolls, in Petty-Canons-Hall, in St. Paul's Church-yard, 1697. 8°, A—3 G 4 in eights, 3 G (4 leaves) repeated with the Table, besides the plate of *Blowing the Horn* and three others.

This edition embraces the Laws of the Forest, &c.

COX, NICHOLAS, AND RICHARD BLOME.

The Gentlemans Recreation. In Two Parts. The First being an Encyclopedy of the Arts and Sciences. To wit, An Abridgment thereof, . . . being a Translation from the most Authentick Authors, by Persons well Experienced therein. To which Divers Sculptures, and Schemes, are added . . . The Second Part, Treats of Horsmanship, Hawking, Hunting, Fowling, Fishing, and Agriculture. With a Short Treatiso of Cock-Fighting, . . . All which are collected from the most Authentick Authors. London, Printed by T. Roycroft, for Richard Blome, Dwelling at the Upper End of Dutchy-Lane, near Somerset-House in the Strand, MDCLXXXVI. Folio. Royal Privilege, frontispiece, title, and dedication to the King, 4 leaves : armorial bearings, badges, &c., 10 leaves numbered : Preface and Table of Arts and Sciences, followed by two engraved leaves, together 4 leaves : B—3 O, 2 leaves each, besides an engraved Scheme or Illustration to each section (2 to *Navigation, Heraldry,* and *Architecture,* 3 to

D

Fortification, 4 to *Painting*, and none to *Natural Philosophy, History, Perspective,* and *Astronomy* in this copy) : THE SECOND PART, A—Zzz, 2 leaves each : 4 A, 3 leaves. With plates at pp. 1 (2), 8, 10, 26, 32, 34, 38, 42, 44, 66, 70, 80 (2), 82 (9), 86 (2), 88 (2), 90, 94, 96, 100 (2), 118, 124, 126. 134, 142, 170, 177, 180, 190, 206, 212, 234. 246, besides numerous woodcuts accompanying the letterpress.

CRAB, ROGER.
The English Hermite, or, Wonder of this Age. Being a relation of the life of Roger Crab, living neer Uxbridg, taken from his own mouth, Shewing his strange reserved and unparallel'd kind of life, who counteth it a sin against his body and soule to eate any sort of Flesh, Fish, or living Creature, or to drinke any Wine, Ale, or Beere. He can line with three farthings a week. . . . London, Printed, and are to be sold in Popes-head Alley, and at the Exchange, 1655. 4°, A—C in fours, including a woodcut frontispiece. C 4 is occupied by some religious verses.

Dedicated by Crab from his poor cottage near Uxbridge, January 1654.

CRAIG, SIR THOMAS, *of Riccarton.*
The Right of Succession to the Kingdom of England, In Two Books ; Against the Sophisms of Parsons the Jesuite, . . . Written Originally in Latin . . . and now Faithfully Translated into English, . . . London, Printed by M. Bennet, . . . 1703. Folio. a—g, 2 leaves each : h, 1 leaf : B—5 Y, 2 leaves each, besides title and following leaf. Dedicated by J. G. to the Dean and Faculty of Advocates of Scotland.

CRAKANTHORP, RICHARD.
Iustinian the Emperor defended against Cardinal Baronivs. London Printed by George Eld, and are to be sold by Nathaniel Newbery . . . 1616. 4°, A—H 2 in fours, H 2 blank, and the title. Dedicated to Sir John Bennet, Knight, and others, Professors of the Civil Laws.

CRANLEY, THOMAS.
Amanda : Or, The Reformed Whore. Composed, and made by Thomas Cranley, Gent. now a Prisoner in the Kings-Bench, Anno Dom. 1635.

Admiranda canunt, credenda aliquando Poetæ.
Poets doe tell of strange things not a few,
Yet often times those things, though strange, are true.

Printed at London, and are to be sold at the golden Key, over against the middle

[Temple, 1635.] 4°. A, 3 leaves : B—M in fours : N, 1 leaf. In verse.

Dedicated by the Author to his brother-in-law, Thomas Gilbourne, Esquire.

CRAVEN, WILLIAM, *Lord Craven.*
The Lord Craven's Case, Briefly Stated. London, Printed by Tho. Newcomb, 1654. 4°, A—B 2 in fours.

CREECH, THOMAS.
Daphnis : Or, A Pastoral Elegy upon the Unfortunate Death of M[r] Thomas Creech. With a Poem on the Despairing Lover, and The Despairing Shepherd. London : Printed and Sold by H. Hills, . . . 1709. 8°, 8 leaves.

CREED.
The Crede or Beleue. [Col.] Imprynted at London in Fletestrete next to saynt Dunstones churche at the sygne of the George. Cum priuilegio Regali. Sm. 8°, A—B 6 in eights.

From Robert Redman's press. Without a regular title.

CRESSY, S.
An Epistle Apologetical of S. C. To a Person of Honour : Touching his Vindication of D[r] Stillingfleet . . . Permissu Superiorum, An. Dom. MDCLXXIV. 8°, A—I 6 in eights.

This is dated by Cressy "From my Cell the 21 of March 1674. being the Anniversary day of S[t] Benedict."

CRICHTON, JAMES.
In. Appvlsv Ad. Celeberrimam Vrbem. Venetam De Proprio. Statv Iacobi. Critonii Scoti Carmen Ad Aldnm Mannucium [Col.] Venetijs, Ex Typographia Guerraea. CIƆ.IƆ.XXC. 4°, italic letter, 4 leaves.

Syston Park Sale, December 1884, No. 643.

CROKE, RICHARD.
Orationes Richardi Croci duæ, altera a cura, qua vtilitatem laudemq; Græcæ linguæ tractat, altera a tempore, qua hortatus est Cantabrigienses, ne desertores essent eiusdem. [Col.] Lutetiæ Parisiorum cura Simonis Colinæi. . . . M.D.XX, 4°, a—c in eights : d, 3.

CROMER, MARTIN.
A notable example of Gods vengeance, vppon a murdering King. Written in Latine by Martine Cromer the writer of the historie of Polonia, and is to be founde in the xxxvii. page of the sayde historie. . . . Truely translated according to the Latine. Imprinted at London by John Daye ouer Aldersgate. And are to be

solde ready stitched for a penny. 8°, A in eights. *B. M.*

The case of Popiel the Younger, King of Poland. There is no introductory matter.

A notable example . . . Imprinted at London by Iohn Daye ouer Aldersgate. 8°, A in eights. *B. M.*

This is a different edition, and does not name the selling price.

CROMMELIN, LOUIS.
An Essay towards the Improving of the Hempen and Flaxen Manufactures in the Kingdom of Ireland. By Louis Crommelin, Overseer of the Royal Linnen-Manufacture of that Kingdom. Dublin : Printed in the Year, 1705. And Re-Printed [at Dublin] M,DCC,XXXIV. 4°, B—G 2 in fours, the title, and 9 leaves with engravings and description.

CROMWELL, ELIZABETH, *Lady Protectress* (1653-8).
The Court & Kitchen of Elizabeth, Commonly called Joan Cromwel, the Wife of the late Usurper, Truly Described and Represented, And now Made Publick for general Satisfaction. London, Printed by Tho. Milbourn for Randal Taylor in St. Martins Le Grand, 1664. 12°. A, 8 leaves, including a frontispiece : B—H in twelves : I, 4 leaves. *B. M.* (no frontispiece.)

This is a book of receipts, alleged to have been used in the Protectress's kitchen, and an account of her public life, both perhaps equally veracious.

CROMWELL, OLIVER, *Lord Protector* (1653-8).
A Coppie of a Letter, To be sent to Lieutenant Generall Crumwel from the Well-affected Partie in the City. Printed in the Yeare 1647. 4°, 4 leaves.

A Word to Lieut. Gen. Cromwel : And Two Words for the selling of the King, Parliament, and Kingdom. Written by a Friend to them, the Peace, the Ministry, and Fundamental Laws of the Land ; . . . . Printed in the Year, MDCXLVII. 4°, A—G in fours. Dedicated to Sir Thomas Fairfax.

A Case for Nol Cromwells Nose, And The Cure of Tom Fairfax's Gout. Both which Rebells are dead, and their deaths kept close, by the policy of our new States . . . [Here follow four 4-line stanzas.] Printed in the Yeare 1648. 4°, 4 leaves.

A Declaration and Order of his Excellency the Lord Generall Cromwell, and His Councill of Officers : For the Continuance of the Assessment for six moneths, from the 24th of June 1653. to the 25th of December following, at the rate of one hundred and twenty thousand pounds by the moneth, towards the maintenance of the Armies and Navies of this Commonwealth. . . . London : Printed by and for H. Hills, G. Calvert and T. Brewster, . . . 1653. Folio, 4 leaves, concluding with Cromwell's warrant appointing Hills and the two others printers of the Monthly Assessments.

The Lord General Cromwel's Speech Delivered in the Council-Chamber, Upon the 4. of July, 1653. To the persons then assembled, and intrusted with the Supreme Authority of the Nation. This is a true Copie : . . . Printed in the yeer 1654. 4°, A—D 2 in fours.

By the Council [A Proclamation declaring Oliver Cromwell, Captain-General of all the Forces of the Commonwealth, Lord Protector ; Whitehall, December 16, 1653]. London, Printed by Henry Hills, Printer to the Council, MDCLIII. A small broadside printed lengthwise, surmounted by the arms of the Commonwealth.

Mosarvm Oxoniensivm Elaiophoria. Sive, Oh Fœdera, Auspiciis Serenissimi Oliveri Reipub. Ang. Scot. & Hiber. Domini Protectoris, Inter Rempub. Britannicam & Ordines Fœderatos Belgii Fæliciter Stabilita, Gentis Togatæ ad vada Isidis Celeusma Metricum. Oxoniæ, Excudebat Leonardus Lichfield . . . 1654. 4°, A—L in fours, besides a folded leaf of Address by John Harmar to the Protector as Chancellor of the University.

King Richard the Third Revived. Containing a Memorable Petition and Declaration contrived by himself and his Instruments, whiles Protector, in the name of the three Estates of England, . . . London, Printed for William Leak, . . . 1657. 4°, A—B 2 in fours.

Musarum Cantabrigiensium Luctus & Gratulatio : Ille In Funere Oliveri Angliæ, Scotiæ, & Hiberniæ Protectoris ; Hæc de Ricardi Successione Felicissima, Ad Eundem. Cantabrigiæ : Excudebat Joannes Field, . . . 1658. . . . 4°. Title and dedication to Richard Cromwell, 2 leaves : *, 4 leaves : B—H in fours.

Margery Good-Cow, that gave a Gallon of Milk, and kickt down the Pail, and beraid the Milk-Maid, what did she merit? speak, Gentlemen. Or, A Short Discourse, Shewing that there is not a Farthing due from this Nation to old Oliver for all his pretended services : and if any thing be given his Son, it must be in respect to his own personal Virtues, and modest behaviours, during his being Protector; and not out of any respect to his ill deserving Father. London, Printed in the Year 1659. 4⁰, 4 leaves.

A Most Learned, Conscientious, and Devout Exercise, Or Sermon, Held forth the last Lords-day of April, In the Year 1649. At Sir P. T.'s house in Lincolns-Inne Fields. By Lieutenant-General O. Cromwel. As it was faithfully taken in Characters By Aaron Guerdon. London : Printed in the Year 1680. 4⁰, A—C 2 in fours.

The Case is Altered. Or, Dreadful news from Hell. In a discourse between the Ghost of this grand Traytor and Tyrant Oliver Cromwel, and Sir reverence my Lady Joan his wife, at their late meeting neer the Scaffold on Tower-hill. With an Epitaph written in hell, on all the grand Traytors, now in the Tower. London Printed, for John Andrews at the White Lyon near Pie-Corner. [Aug. 6, 1660.] 8⁰, A in eights, including the frontispiece with rough woodcut heads of Cromwell and his consort. B. M.

CROMWELL, RICHARD, Lord Protector (1658-9).

The Speech of His Highness the Lord Protector, Made to both Houses of Parliament at their first meeting, on Thursday the 27th of January 1658. As also the Speech of the Right Honorable Nathaniel Fiennes, one of the Lords Keepers of the Great Seal of England, made at the same time. London, Printed by Henry Hills and John Field, . . [1659.] 4⁰, 6 leaves: A, 2 : B, 4 : the *Chancellor's Speech*, A—D 3.

This is a very rare and interesting tract, and contains some very remarkable references by Richard Cromwell to his departed father. The Chancellor's Speech is printed "for Henry Twyford, in Vine Court, Middle Temple, 1659," and was annexed to the Protector's address.

CROSS.

The Resolvtion of those Contemnors that will have no Crosses. Being ingeniously expressed in exhortation to those that will admit of no Crosse, unlesse it be their crosse-Wives ; or some crosse Street where their Conventicles are. . . . London, Printed by T. Reinor. 1641. 4⁰, 4 leaves.

CROWNE, JOHN.

A Poem on the Lamented Death of our Late Gratious Soveraign, King Charles the II. of ever Blessed Memory. With a Congratulation to the Happy Succession of King James the II. By Mr Crown. London, Printed for John Smith . . . 1685. 4⁰, A—B in fours, A 1 blank.

CRUSO, J.

Militarie Instructions for the Cavallrie : Or Rules and Directions for the Service of Horse, Collected out of Divers Forrain Authors Ancient and Modern, and Rectified and Supplied, according to the present Practise of the Low-Countrey Warres. . . . Printed by the Printers to the Universitie of Cambridge. MDCXXXII. Folio, A—O in fours, besides plates at B 2, D 2, F 3, K 2, O 1, O 2-3 (8). Dedicated by J. Cruso to Thomas, Earl of Arundel and Surrey.

CRYMES, *alias* GRAHAM, GEORGE, *of Peckham.*

Parliamentum Imperatorium : Seu Carmina Progymnastica ; In Centum quinquaginta quatuor omnium Romanorum, Græcorum, & Germanicorum Cæsarum. . . . Symbola, & dicta imperatoria. Opera Ludi-literaria Thomæ Crymes, D. Georgii Crymes (alias Graham) de Peckham in Com. Surr. Equitis filii natu maximi. Ætatis suæ decimo quarto. . . . Londoni, Excudebat G. Dawson, venundat. L. Chapman. . . . 1654. 8⁰. A, 3 leaves : B 2 (no B 1)—M in eights. With a portrait by T. Cross.

CUCKOLDOM.

The Law against Cuckoldom : Or, The Tryal of Adultery. London : Printed in the Year 1700. Folio, 6 leaves. In verse.

CULPEPPER, N.

The English Physician Or An Astrologo-physical Discourse of the vulgar Herbs of this Nation . . . By N. Culpeper, Student in Physick and Astrology. London, Printed for the benefit of the Common-wealth of England. 1652. 12⁰. A, 6 : [a*], 6 : B—Bb in sixes. With a small three-quarter portrait.

Culpepers Semeiotica Vranica : Or, An Astrological Judgement of Diseases from the Decumbiture of the sick much Enlarged. 1. From Aven Ezra by way of Introduction. 2. From Noel Duret by way of Direction. . . The third Edition. London, Printed for Nath. Brooke . . . 1658. 8⁰, A—R 4 in eights, R 4 blank, and A 1 with a portrait.

CUTLERS.

Worke for Cvtlers. Or, A Merry Dialogve betweene Sword, Rapier, and Dagger.

Acted in a Shew in the famous Vniuer-sitie of Cambridge. London Printed by Thomas Creede, for Richard Meighen and Thomas Iones, . . . 1615. 4°, A—B in fours, A 1 blank. *B. M.*

CURTIUS RUFUS, QUINTUS.
The Ten Books of Quintus Curtius Rufus : Containing the Life and Death of Alexander the Great. Exactly conferred with the Original, and purged from many gross Errours and Absurdities, with which it before abounded. By the same hand

which translated the last Volume of the Holy Court. London, Printed by Bernard Alsop, . . . 1652. 4°, A—Rr in fours. Dedicated by Robert Codrington to Baptist, Viscount Campden.

CYRIL, *Patriarch of Constantinople.*
The Confession of Faith of the most Reverend Father in God Cyrill, Patriarch of Constantinople. Written at Constantinople, 1629. . . . London, Printed for Nicolas Bourne, . . . 1629. 4°, A—B in fours.

D.

D. E.
A Vindication of the Historiographer of the University of Oxford, and his Works, from the Reproaches of the Lord Bishop of Salisbury, in his Letter to the Lord Bishop of Coventry and Litchfield, . . . London, Printed and Sold by Randal Taylor, MDCXCIII. 4°, A—D in fours, A 1 with half-title and D 4 blank.

D. G.
A Briefe Discoverie of Doctor Allens seditious drifts, contriued in a Pamphlet written by him, Concerning the yeelding vp of the towne of Deuenter, (in Ouerissel) vnto the King of Spain, by Sir William Stanley. . . . London Imprinted by I. W. for Francis Coldock. 1588. 4°, A—R in fours, A 1 blank.

D. P.
The Lives & Deaths of the Holy Apostles of Our Lord and Saviour Jesus Christ. Together with the Two Evangelists, St Mark and St Luke. As Also, Some other of our Saviours Disciples : Containing An Account of Their Travels, Sayings, Miracles, Sufferings, and Martyrdoms. All Collected from the Best Authors, for Publick Use and Benefit. London, Printed for Dorman Newman, . . . 1685. 8°, A—K in eights, A 1 blank, and A 2 with a frontispiece. Black letter, with cuts.

D. T.
Massachusetts Or The first Planters of New-England, The End & Manner of their coming thither, And Abode there : In several Epistles. [Quotations.] Boston in New England, Printed by B. Green, and J. Allen. Sold by Richard Wilkins, at his Shop near the Old-Meeting-House.

1696. 8°, A—D 4 in eights, and the title. Dedicated by T. D. to Bridget, Countess of Lincoln.

DAINES, SIMON.
Orthoepia . . . 1640. 4°, B—O in fours, no sign. A. *B. M.* (Bright's copy.)
This copy opens, after the title, with some sets of commendatory verses, and may want a dedication, occupying A.

D. R.
A Satyr against Satyrs : Or, St. Peter's Vision Transubstantiated, . . . By R. D. London, Printed, and are to be sold by Richard Janeway . . . 1680. 4°. Title and *Advertisement*, 2 leaves : A—D 2 in fours. In verse.

D'ACRES, R.
The Art of Water-Drawing, Or A Compendious Abstract of all Sorts of Water-Machins, or Gins, practised in the World : . . . London, Printed for Henry Brome, . . . 1660. 4°, A—E in fours, an extra leaf after E 4, and title and preface.

DALGARNO, GEORGE.
Ars Signorum, Vulgo Character Universalis et Lingua Philosophica. . . . Authore Geo. Dalgarno. —— *hoc ultra.* Londini, Excudebat J. Hayes, Sumptibus Authoris, Anno reparatæ salutis, 1661. 8°, A—I in eights.

Didascalocophus Or The Deaf and Dumb mans Tutor, To which is added A Discourse of the Nature and number of Double Consonants. . . . Printed at the Theater in Oxford. 1680. 8°. A, 6. including a woodcut : B—H in eights : 1 2.

DAMON, WILLIAM.
The Psalmes of David . . . 1579.

Collation: A—L in fours to each of the four parts, Triplex or Treble, Tenor, Contratenor, and Bassus. The book has a Preface by Edward Hake "Vpon the Edition of these Psalmes in meter, to the Reader." Quaritch's Catalogue, 1882, No. 343, lot 85991, imperfect in Contratenor.

The Booke of the Musicke . . . . 1591.
Collation: Cantus, Altus, Tenor, and Bassus, A, 2*leaves, with title and dedication to Sir W. Cecil, B—G in fours, each. Sothebys, Nov. 28, 1882, No. 739, title and dedication to Cantus wanting.

DAMPIER, WILLIAM.
A New Voyage round the World. Describing particularly, The Isthmus of America, several Coasts and Islands in the West Indies. the Isles of Cape Verd, ... Their Soil, Rivers, Harbours, Plants, Fruits, Animals, and Inhabitants. . . . Illustrated with Particular Maps and Draughts. The Second Edition Corrected. London, Printed for James Knapton, . . . MDCXCVII. 8°, A—Nn 4 in eights. With a map of the world and others of N. America (p. 1), S. America (p. 27), E. Indies (p. 284) and the Bashee Islands (p. 385), the last counting in the sheets. Dedicated to the Right Honourable Charles Montague, a Commissioner of the Treasury.

Voyages and Descriptions. Vol: II. In Three Parts, viz. 1. A Supplement of the Voyage round the World, . . . 2. Two Voyages to Campeachy ; . . . 3. A Discourse of Trade-Winds, Breezes, ... With an Account of Natal in Africk, . . To which is Added, A General Index to both Volumes. London, Printed for James Knapton, . . . MDCXCIX. 8°. Part I, A, 4 leaves : B—N 4 in eights : Part II. Aa—Ii 4 in eights : Part III. Aaa—Ggg in eights : Index, [A]—[D] in fours, a sheet of lower-case [a] following each sheet of capitals, and [c] 2 leaves after [E]. With maps of Malacca, Campeachy, and the Coasting and Trade Winds. Dedicated to the Earl of Oxford.

A Voyage to New Holland. &c. In the Year, 1699. Wherein are described, The Canary-Islands, the Isles of Mayo and St. Jago. . . . Their Inhabitants, Manners, Customs, . . . Illustrated with several Maps and Draughts ; . . . Vol. III. By Captain William Dampier. London : Printed for James Knapton. . . . 1703. 8°, A—M in eights, and a, 4 leaves. With a folded map of the Voyage and other plans and engravings at pp. 4, 14, 96, 117, 123, 140 (3), and 160 (5). Dedicated to the Earl of Pembroke.

DANCING.
A Satyr against Dancing. By a Person of Honour. London, Printed for A. Baldwin . . . . . MDCCII. Folio, A—C, 2 leaves each. In verse.

DANCING-MASTER.
The English Dancing Master : Or, Plaine and easie Rules for the Dancing of Country Dances, with the Tune to each Dance. London, Printed by Thomas Harper, and are to be sold by John Playford, . . . 1651. 4°, A—O in fours. With an engraving on the title. Oblong.

The Dancing-Master : Vol. the First [and Second.] Or, Directions . . . The 18th Edition, containing 358 of the Choicest Old and New Tunes . . . London, Printed by W. Pearson, . . . 1728. Obl. 8°. With an engraving on the title of each volume. Vol. I. A, 4 leaves : B—Hh 5 in sixes. Vol. II. A—Hh in sixes.
The date is on the title to vol. ii., which is described as the 4th edition.

DANGERFIELD, THOMAS.
Mr Tho. Dangerfeilds Particular Narrative of the Popish Design, . . . Written by Himself. London, Printed for Henry Hills, . . . 1679. Folio. A—U, 2 leaves each, besides title and preceding leaf.

The Information of Thomas Dangerfield, Gent. Delivered at the Bar of the House of Commons [Tuesday, Oct. 6, 1680.] London, . . . 1680. Folio, A—D, 2 leaves each.

D'ANVERS, ALICIA.
Academia Or, The Humours of the University of Oxford, In Burlesque Verse. London, Printed and Sold by Randal Taylor . . . 1691. 4°. A, 2 leaves : B —I 2 in fours.

D'ARANDA, EMANUEL.
The History of Algiers and it's Slavery. With Many Remarkable Particularities of Africk. Written by the Sieur Emanuel D'Aranda, Sometime a Slave there. English'd by John Davies of Kidwelly. London, Printed for John Starkey, . . . M.DC.LXVI. 8°, A—S in eights, besides a folded frontispiece. Dedicated by Davies to the Honourable Sir Philip Howard.

DARE, JOSIAH.
Counsellor Manners His Last Legacy to his Son. . . . London : Printed for J. & B. Sprint, . . . 1710. Price 1/. 8°, A —H in eights. With a preface by Sir R. L'Estrange.

DARELL, JOHN.
Strange News from the Indies : Or East-

India Passages further discovered. August in Jubile, 1650. *A Jove Principium* . . . The Manner and Tenour of East-India-Trade hitherto : . . . The wofull, and sad sufferings of William Courten Esquire, &c. . . . London, Printed for Stephen Bowtel, . . . 1652. 4°, A—F in fours.

DARIEN.

An Ode made on the Welcome News of the safe Arrival and kind Reception of the Scottish Collony at Darien in America. Edinburgh, Printed by James Watson in Craig's Closs 1699. A sheet.

A Congratulatory Poem, On the safe Arrival of the Scots African and Indian Fleet in Caledonia, and their kind Reception by the Natives, with an Amicable advice to all concerned. [1699.] A sheet subscribed *R. A.*

An Health to Caledonia, To the Tune of *Marin's* Trumpet Air. Two stanzas. [1699.] A sheet.

A Short Vindication of Phil. Scot's Defence of the Scots Abdicating Darien : Being in Answer to the Challenge of the Author of the Defence of that Settlement, . . . With a Prefatory Reply, to the False and Scurrilous Aspersions, of the New Author of, The Just and Modest Vindication . . . London : Printed in the Year, 1700. 8°, A—F in fours.

A Full and Exact Collection of all the Considerable Addresses, Memorials, . . . relating to the Company of Scotland, trading to Africa and the Indies, . . . Printed in the Year 1700. 8°. Title and preface, 2 leaves : Act, 4 leaves : B—U in fours.

DARLEY, JOHN, *B.D., Rector of Northill, co. of Cornwall.*

The Glory of Chelsey Colledge Revived. Wherein is declared ; I. Its Original, Progress, and Design, for preserving, and establishing the Church of Christ, . . . II. How this design was by the Renowned King James, . . . highly applauded ; . . . III. By what means this excellent work . . . hath been impeded and obstructed. London, Printed for J. Bourn at the South entrance of the Royal Exchange, 1662. 4°, A—G 2 in fours, and the title. Dedicated to Charles II.

DARRELL, JOHN.

A Trve Narration of the Strange and Grevovs vexation by the Devil, of 7. Persons in Lancashire, and William Somers of Nottingham. Wherein the Doctrine of Possession and Dispossession of Demoniakes ovt of the word of God is par-

ticularly applyed vnto Somers, and the rest of the persons controuerted togeather with the vse we are to make of these workes of God. By Iohn Darrel Minister of the word of God. [Quot. from Matth. 12. 30.] Printed 1600. 4°. Title and following leaf unmarked : **, 2 leaves : A—C in fours : A (repeated)—I in fours : K—S, 2 leaves each, S 2 with the *Errata.*

A Detection of that Sinnfvl Shamfvl Lying, and Ridicvlovs Discovrs, of Samvel Harsnet, Entitvled : A Discoverie of the Fravdvlent Practises of Iohn Darrell. Wherein is manifestly and apparantly shewed in the eyes of the World not only the vnlikelihode, but the flate impossibilitie of the pretended counterfayting of William Somers, Thomas Darling, Kath. Wright, and Mary Couper, togeather with the other 7 in Lancashire, and the supposed teaching of them by the saide Iohn Darrell . . . Imprinted 1600. 4°. Title, 1 leaf : Preface by Darrell, 4 leaves : A 1, A 3, A 4, 3 leaves : B, 4 : C—Y, 2 leaves each : A—Z, 2 leaves each : A—II, 2 leaves each, the second leaf only marked, and with 3 for 2 : an extra leaf after II 3.

A Svrvey of Certaine Dialogical Discovrses written by Iohn Deacon, and Iohn Walker, concerning the doctrine of Possession and Dispossession of Diuels. . . . Published by Iohn Darrell minister of the gospell. . . . Imprinted 1602. 4°, A—L in fours.

The Replie of Iohn Darrell, to the Answer of Iohn Deacon, and Iohn Walker, . . . Imprinted 1602. 4°. A—R, 2 leaves each.

DAVID.

The Psalmes of Dauid, Trvely Opened and explaned by Paraphrasis, according to the right sence of euery Psalme. . . . Set fovrth in Latine by . . . Theodore Beza. And faithfully translated into English by Anthonie Gilbie . . . At London, Printed by Iohn Harison and Henrie Middleton. 1580. 8°. ¶, 8 leaves : A—Bb in eights. Dedicated by Gilbey from Ashby to the Countess of Huntingdon.

Paraphrasis Poetica Psalmorvm Davidis. Auctore Artvro Ionstono, Scoto. Accesserunt ejusdem Cantica Evangelica. Symbolvm Apostolicvm. Oratio Dominica. Decalogvs. Aberdoniæ, Imprimebat Edwardus Rabanus, Anno 1637. 8°. Title, dedication, and to the Reader (both in verse), 3 leaves : A—M in eights, M 8 blank.

Psalterium Davidis Latino-Saxonicum-vetus. A Johanne Spelmanno D. Hen. fil. editum . . . . Londini, Exendebat R. Badger, . . . 1640. 4°, A—Zz 2 in fours. Dedicated to Archbishop Laud.

The MS. was the property of Sir H. Spelman. The text is interlinear.

The Psalms of David . . . By William Barton, M.A. And Set to the best Psalm-Tunes, In Two Parts, Viz. Treble and Bass : . . . The Second Edition, Corrected and Amended. With the Basses. By Thomas Smith . . . Dublin : Printed by J. Brocas, . . . 1706. Price Bound 2s. 6d. 12°, A—R 4 in twelves, besides the title and Gamut.

The Psalms of David in Metre : Fitted to the Tunes used in Parish-Churches. By John Patrick, D.D. Preacher to the Charterhouse, London. Imprimatur. Sept. 30. 1691. Ra. Barker. London, Printed for John Churchill, at the Black Swan in Paternoster-Row ; . . . [1691.] 12°. A, 12 leaves : A 2—O in twelves. Without prefixes, but with the music.

The Psalms of David in English Metre : Translated from the Original And Suited to all the Tunes now Sung in Churches : With the Additions of several New. By Luke Milbourne, A Presbyter of the Church of England. . . . London, Printed for W. Rogers, . . . 1698. 8°. A, 8 leaves : a, 6 : b, 6 : B—P 6 in twelves. Dedicated to His Highness the Duke of Gloucester.

DAVILA, H. C.
The Historie of the Civill Warres of France, Written in Italian by H. C. Davila. Translated out of the Original. London, Printed by R. Raworth, . . . M.DC.XLVII. Folio. Title and Imprimatur, 2 leaves : B—9 B in fours.

DAVISON, FRANCIS.
Anagrammata In Nomina Illvstrissimo-rvm Herovm, Thomae Egertoni, Sigilli magni Custodis. . . . Londini, ex officina Simonis Stafford. 1603. A large broadside.

Among the other personages celebrated are the Earls of Oxford, Southampton, Northumberland, &c., Sir G. Carew, Sir Julius Cæsar, &c. Collier's Sale, August 1884, No. 712.

DAVY, MICHAEL.
Davy's Miscellanies : Being, for the most part, A Brief Collection of Mathematical Theorems, From divers Authors upon these Subjects following. . . . By Michael Davy. London, Printed by W. G. and

sold by Moses Pitt . . . 1669. 8°, A—D in eights.

DAWSON, RICHARD.
The Humble Addresse and Remonstrance of Richard Dawson Gentleman, now Prisoner in the Fleet. To the Right Honourable the Lords & Commons in Parliament Assembled. With all possible Submission, representing the sad Oppressures under which he groans, his Estate being pluckt away from him by Injustice, . . . By the Confederacy of Roger Portington Gentleman, Philip Read Attorney of the Kings Bench, Edward, and Francis Luttrel, Sollicitour, and Counsellor of Law, Sir John Lenthall Knight Marshall of the Kings Bench, and others . . . London, Printed for the Author 1661. 4°, A—D in fours.

DAY, JOHN.
The Ile of Gvls. As it hath been often playd in the blacke Fryars, by the Children of the Reuels. Written by Iohn Day. Printed for Iohn Trundle, and are to be sold by Iohn Hodgets in Paules Church-yard. 1606. 4°, A—H in fours. Without prefixes.

The imprint in this copy varies from that given by Mr. Bullen in his reprint. Sothebys, May 13, 1882, No. 672.

DE ARGENSOLA, BARTHOLOMEO LEONARDO, *Chaplain to the Empress, and Vicar of Villahermosa.*
The Discovery and Conquest of the Molucco and Philippine Islands Containing their History, Ancient and Modern, Natural and Political : Their Description, Product, . . . With an Account of many other Adjacent Islands, and several remarkable Voyages through the Streights of Magellan, and in other Parts . . . Now Translated into English [by Captain John Stevens] : And Illustrated with a Map and several Cuts. London, Printed in the Year, 1708. 4°, A—Ll in fours, A 1 blank : Index, 4 leaves. With a map and three plates.

DE BENESE, SIR RICHARD, *Canon of Merton Abbey.*
This boke sheweth the maner of measurynge of all maner of lande, as well of woodlande, as of lande in the felde, and comptynge the true nombre of acres of the same. Newlye inuented and compyled by Syr Rycharde Benese Chanon of Marton Abbay besyde London. Prynted in Southwarke in Saynt Thomas hospitall, by me James Nicolson. [About 1536.] 4°. *, 4 leaves : A—Y in fours :

AA—CC in fours, CC 4 with *Errata*. *B. M.*

> This appears to be the impression inaccurately described by Collier, *Bibl. Cat.* ii. 135. But it would seem that the Bagford fragment noticed in my *Bibl. Coll.* 1876, p. 476, is a different one.
>
> On the back of the title occur "The contentes of thys boke," and on * 2 we have "The preface of Thomas paynell Chanon of Marton to the gentle reader." Paynell calls De Benese "a fryode and louer of myne," and says that he was not willing "to hyde the treasure, that God hath euryched hym wyth all."

The Hidden Treasure Discovered by the Surveyors Schoolmaster. Teaching and setting the most exact and readiest way that is practised in that Art or Science. With the true measuring of Woodland, . . . Written by Sir Ric. Benet [*sic*], and now renised and enlarged by Tho. Norton, Professor of the Art. Printed at London by T. B. 1651. 8°, A—M in eights, M 7-8 blank, and (b), 2 leaves.

DEATH.

A most frutefull / piththie and learned treatyse, how a Christō mā ought to behaue him selfe in the danger of death : . . . . [London, about 1550.] 8°, A—Q 7 in eights, black letter.

> The running title is : *The Boke of deathe.* Perhaps Q 8 had the colophon.

DE CAUS, ISAAC.

Hortvs Penbrochianvs. Le jardin de Vuilton Construict Par Tres noble et tres puissant Seigneur Philippe Comte de Penbrooke et Mongomeri . . . . [About 1645.] Folio, 22 leaves, the whole engraved, and inclusively of the frontispiece.

> Osterley Park Sale, 1885, No. 396. I conclude that the Earl here mentioned was the first Earl of Pembroke and Montgomery, who died in 1650.

Novvelle Invention de Lever l'eav plvs havlt que sa source auec quelques machines mouantes par le moyen de l'eau et vn discours de la conduite d'ycelle. Par Isaac de Cavs Ingenyeur et Architecte Natif de dieppe. Imprime a londre l'an 1644. Folio. Printed and engraved titles, 2 leaves : A—H, 2 leaves each. 26 plates numbered, besides some cuts on the text.

> Osterley Park Sale, 1885, No. 397.

DECKER, THOMAS.

Canaan's Calamitie, Jerusalem's Misery; and Englands Mirror . . . . London. Printed by Tho. James for Edward Thomas at the Adam and Eve in little Brittain. 1677. 4°, A—H in fours. Printed within head and tail pieces. *B. M.*

Londons Tempe ; Or, The Feild of Happines. In which Feild are planted seuerall Trees of Magnificence, State and Beauty, to celebrate the Solemnity of the Right Honorable Iames Campebell, at his Inauguration into the Honorable Office of Praetorship, or Maioralty of London, on Thursday the 29. of October, 1629. All the particular Inuentions, . . . At the sole Cost, and liberall Charges of the Right worshipfull Society of Ironmongers. Written by Thomas Dekker. *Quando magis Dignos licuit spectare Triumphos ?* [London, Nicholas Okes ?] 4°, A —C 2 in fours. *Duke of Devonshire* (imprint cut off).

> Collier's Sale, August 1884, No. 556, Imprint cut off, and imperfect at end.

The Second Part of the Honest Whore, With the Hvmors of the Patient Man, the Impatient Wife : the Honest Whore, perswaded by strong Arguments to turne Curtizan againe : her braue refuting those Arguments. And lastly, the Comicall Passages of an Italian Bridewell, where the Scene ends. Written by Thomas Dekker. London, Printed by Elizabeth Ali-de, for Nathaniel Butter. An. Dom. 1630. 4°, A—L 2 in fours.

DE CASTELNAU, MICHEL, *Seigneur de Mauvissiere.*

Les Memoires . . . Illvstrez et Avgmentez de plvsievrs Commentaires & Manuscrits, tant Lettres, Instructions, Traittez, qu'autres Pieces Secrettes & Originalles seruants à donner la verité de l'Histoire des Regnes de François II. Charles IX. & Henry II. & de la Regence & du Gouuernement de Catherine de Medicis. . . . A Paris . . . M.DC.LIX-LX. Folio. 2 vols. With a portrait of Jacques, Marquis de Castelnau.

> Edited by J. Le Laboureur, Councillor and Alumoner to the King, and Prior of Juvigné.
>
> "The Memoirs of Castlenau were written during his second Embassy in England, and are important for British History, especially that of Mary, Queen of Scots, whom he accompanied after the death of her husband, Francis II., to Scotland. He is the only historian who has noticed Mary and Bothwell's daughter, who died a nun in the convent of Soissons."—Note in Sothebys' Catalogue, July 23, 1886, No. 332.

DE DOMINIS, MARCVS ANTONIVS.

A Manifestation of the Motiues, Wherevpon the most Reuerend Father, Marcvs Antonivs De Dominis, Archbishop of Spalato, (in the Territorie of Venice) Vndertooke his departure thence. Englished out of his Latine Copy. At London Printed by Iohn Bill. Anno 1616. 4º, A—M in fours, A 1 and M 4 blank.

A Sermon Preached in Italian, By the most Reuerend father, Marc Antony de Dominis, Archb. of Spalato, the first Sunday in Aduent, Anno 1617. In the Mercers Chappel in London . . . London. Printed by Iohn Bill. M.DC.XVII. 4º, A—L in fours, A 1 and L 4 blank.

A Svrvey of the Apostasy of Marcvs Antonivs De Dominis. Sometyme Archbishop of Spalato. Drawne out of his owne Booke, and written in Latin, by Fidelis Aunosús, Verementanus Druinus, De-nine: And Translated into English by A. M. Permissu Superiorum. M.DC.XVII. 4º, A—T 2 in fours, T 2 blank, besides title and to the Reader.

The Rockes of Christian Shipwracke, Discouered by the holy Church of Christ to her beloued Children, . . . written in Italian by the Most Reuerend Father, Marc. Ant. De Dominis, Archb. of Spalato, And thereout translated into English. London, Printed by Iohn Bill. M.DC.XVIII. 4º, a—b in fours, a 1 blank: A—Y 2 in fours. With an engraving on the title.

Marcvs Antonivs De Dominis Archiep. Spalaten. Sui reditus ex Anglia Consilium exponit. Romae, . . . M.DC.XXIII. 4º. A, 8: B, 6.

The Second Manifesto of Marcvs Antonivs De Dominis, Archbishop of Spalato: wherein for his better satisfaction, and the satisfaction of others, he publikely repenteth, and recanteth his former errors, . . . Liege: By Guilliaume Honins, with permission of Superiours. 1623. 4º, A—G 2 in fours.

M. Ant. de Dñis Arch-Bishop of Spalato, his Shiftings in Religion A Man for many Masters. . . . London, Printed by Iohn Bill. MDCXXIV. 4º. A, 2 leaves: B—N 2 in fours.

A Relation Sent from Rome, Of the Processe, Sentence, and Execvtion, Done Vpon the Body, Picture, and Bookes, of Marcvs Antonivs de Dominis, Archbishop of Spalato, after his Death. Published by Command. London, Printed by John Bill, . . . 1624. 4º, A—B in fours, A 1 occupied by a woodcut of the process.

DE DUILLIER, NICOLAS FACIO.

Fruit-Walls Improved, By inclining them to the Horizon: Or, A Way to Build Walls for Fruit-Trees, whereby they may receive more Sun Shine, and Heat, than ordinary. By a Member of the Royal Society. London: Printed by R. Everingham ; and are to be sold by John Taylor . . . MDCXCIX. 4º. Title, 1 leaf: a, 4 leaves: b, 2 leaves: c—d in fours, d 4 with Errata: A. 4 leaves: no B: C—R 3 in fours. With two folded plates. Dedicated to the Marquis of Tavistock.

DEE, JOHN.

Propædegmeta Aphoristica Ioannis Dee, . . . Londini. Anno. M.D.LX.VIII. [Col.] Excusum Londini apud Reginaldum Vuolfium, . . . Anno Domini M.D.LXVIII. Iannarij 9. 4º. Title and preface, 4 leaves: A—G in fours: colophon followed by a blank, 2 leaves. With a few diagrams.

DE FLORES, JUAN.

Seconda Editione De L'Historia di Aurelio e Issabella, ... A Paris Ou vend les semblables au Palais, en la botique de Gilles Corrozet. 1547. 8º, A—Q in eights. Ital. and Fr.

L'Histoire D'Avrelio et Isabelle en Italien et Francoys: . . . A Lyon, Par Guillaume Rouille. 1555. 8º, a—s in eights.

DE GHEŸN, JACOBUS.

Maniement D'Armes D'Arquebuses. Mousquetz, & Piques. . . . Representé par Figures . . . . Gedrvckt zv Franckfvrt am Main . . . 1619. 4º. Title and Dedication, 4 ll., the 4th blank: A—L in fours, the plates counting with the text: Briefs Enseignementz svr les Povrtraicts et Figvres, tovchant le Maniement du Mousquet, A—L in fours: The portion for the Pike, A—I in fours, I 4 blank.

This edition, in French and German, was intended for more general and popular use than the folio of 1608.

DE GREY, OR DE LA GREY, THOMAS.

The Compleat Horse-Man, and Expert Ferrier. In Two Books. . . . By Thomas de Grey, Esquire. The Fourth Edition corrected with some Additions. London, Printed by E. C. and A. C. for Samuel Lowndes, . . . 1670. 4º, A—4 M in fours, and (a)—(d 2) in fours.

In the dedication to the Marquis Hamilton the author calls himself Thomas de la Grey.

DE GUEVARA, ANTHONIO.

A looking Glasse for the Court. Composed in the Castalian tongue by the Lorde Anthony of Gueuara . . . . And out of Castalian drawne into Frenche by Anthony Alaygre. And out of the French tongue into Englishe by Sir Franncis

Briant Knight one of the priuy Chamber, . . . and now newly printed, corrected and set forth wyth sundry apt notes in the margent by T. Tymme Minister. Imprinted at London for William Norton. An. 1575. 8°. A, 4: B—L 4 in eights.

> Dedicated by Tymme to John, Lord Russell. There are some lines by him in verse to the reader. The original "Dispraise of the Life of a Courtier" under a new title.

The Familiar Epistles of Sir Antony of Guevara, Preacher, Chronicler, and Chancellour to the Emperour Charles the fifth. Translated out of the Spanish toung, by Edward Hellowes. Groome of the Leash. . . . Printed at London for Raufe Newbery, . . . [Col.] Imprinted at London by Henrie Middelton, for Rafe Newbery: . . . 1574. 4°. ¶, 4 leaves: A—3 X in fours, 3 X 4 with the colophon. Dedicated to Sir Henry Lee, Knight, Master of the Leash, by the translator.

The Familiar Epistles . . . At London, Printed by Ralph Newberie anno salutis. 1584. Cum priuilegio . . . 4°. A, 4 leaves: A (repeated)—Dd 4 in eights.

Golden Epistles, Contayning varietie of discourse both Morall, Philosophicall, and Diuine : gathered as well out of the remaynder of Guenaraes workes, as other Authors, Latine, French, and Italian. By Geffray Fenton. Mon heur vieudra. Imprinted at London by Henry Middelton, for Rafe Newbery . . . 1575. 4°. ¶ and 2 ¶, 4 leaves each : A—Dd 6 in eights. Dedicated by Fenton to Anne, Countess of Oxford, from his Chamber in the Blackfriars, Feb. 4, 1575-6.

DE LA LOUBERE, M.

A New Historical Relation of the Kingdom of Siam. By Monsieur De La Loubere, Envoy Extraordinary from the French King, to the King of Siam, in the years 1687 and 1688. Wherein a full and curious Account is given of the Chinese Way of Arithmetick, and Mathematick Learning. In Two Tomes Illustrated with Sculptures. Done out of French by A. P. Gen. R. SS. London, Printed by F. L. for Tho. Horne . . . MDCXCIII. Folio, A—3 U, 2 leaves each.

> The second tome begins after Oo 2 with a new title. With maps and plates separate from the text at pp. 2, 4, 6, 12, 24, 40, 72, 112, 170, 176, and 182.

DELAMERE, HENRY, LORD.

The Late Lord Russels Case, With Observations upon it. Written by the Right

Honourable Henry Lord De la Mere. London, Printed for Awnsham Churchill . . . MDCLXXXIX. 4°, A—B in fours.

> See the tract described under Cheshire above.

DE LA QUINTINYE, M.

The Compleat Gard'ner : Or, Directions for Cultivating and Right Ordering of Fruit-Gardens and Kitchen-Gardens. Now compendiously Abridg'd, and made of more Use, with very Considerable Improvements. By George London, and Henry Wise. London, Printed for M. Gillyflower, . . . MDCXCIX. 8°. Frontispiece and title, 2 leaves: a, 8 leaves: A—U in eights: X, 4 leaves: Y, 2 leaves. With folded plates at pp. 24, 86, 98, 100, 102, 106 (2). 114, and 138 (2).

DE LA RAMÉE, PIERRE.

The Art of Arithmeticke in Whole Numbers and Fractions. In a more readie and easie method then hitherto hath bene published. Written in Latin by P. Ramvs : And translated into English by William Kempe. Imprinted at London by Richard Field for Robert Dexter dwelling in Paules Church yard at the signe of the brazen serpent. 1592. 8°, A—F 6 in eights, chiefly black letter, besides a folded leaf. B. M.

> Dedicated by Kempe, the Plymouth schoolmaster, to Sir Francis Drake. There are verses by Kempe to Drake on bringing the Reservoir to Plymouth, and by W. A. complimenting him on his naval achievements.

DE LA SALLE, M.

An Account of Monsieur de la Salle's Last Expedition and Discoveries in North-America. Presented to the French King, and Published by the Chevalier Tonti, Governour of Fort St. Louis, in the Province of the Islinois. Made English from the Paris Original. Also The Adventures of the Sieur de Montalban, Captain of the French Buccaneers on the Coast of Guinea, in the Year 1695. London, Printed for J. Tonson . . . 1698. 8°, B—R in eights and the title.

DELAUNE, THOMAS.

De Laune's Plea for the Non-Conformists : . . . Printed Twenty Years ago ; . . . London : Printed, . . . 1704. 4°, A—I in fours.

A Narrative of the Sufferings of Thomas Delaune, For Writing, Printing and Publishing a late Book, Called, A Plea for the Nonconformists, . . . By Thomas Delaune. . . . Printed for the Author. 1684. 4°, A—C in fours.

DE LA VEGA, LUIS GUTIERRES, of Medina del Campo

A Compendious Treatise entitled, De re militari, containing principall orders to be observed in Martiall affaires Newlie Translated into English, by Nicholas Lichefild . . . January primus 1582 . . Imprinted at London by Thomas East   4°, A—Z 2 in fours. Dedicated to Master Philip Sydney.

DE LOS SANTOS, FRANCISCO, Friar of St Jerome

The Escurial; Or, A Description of that Wonder of the world For Architecture and Magnificence of Structure : Built by K. Philip the II°. of Spain, and lately consumed by Fire . . . Translated into English by a Servant of the Earl of Sandwich in his Extraordinary Embassie thither. London, Printed for T. Collins and J. Ford, at the Middle Temple Gate in Fleet street, 1671.   4°, A—D in fours.

DE L'EPY, HELIOGENES, Doctor in Philosophy

A Voyage into Tartary. Containing A Curious Description of that Country, with part of Greece and Turky . . . London, Printed by T. Hodgkin, and are to be sold by Randal Taylor . . . 1689. 12°, A—I in twelves and the title. Dedicated by De l'Epy to the Earl of Clanricarde.

DE LUCINGE, RENÉ, Seigneur des Uymes et de Montrozet.

The Beginning, Continuance, and Decay of Estates : Wherein are handled many notable Questions concerning the establishment of Empires and Monarchies . . . Translated into English by I. F. London, Printed for John Bill. 1606. 4°. A, 2 : a, 1 : B—N 2 in fours. Dedicated by John Finett to the Primate.

DE L'HOPITAL, M.

In Franciscæ Illustriss. Franciæ Delphini, Et Mariæ Sereniss. Scotorvm Reginæ Nvptias. Ampliss. viri M. H. Carmen. Parisiis, Apud Federicum Morellum, . . . 1560 . . . 4°, 4 leaves.

> This piece forms part of a volume containing several of De l'Hopital's productions, without any general title. Sunderland Sale, part 3, No. 6541.

DE MALYNES, GERARD.

The Maintenance of Free Trade according to the Three Essential Parts of Traffique: Namely, Commodities, Money, and Exchange of Moneys, by Bills of Exchanges for other Countries . . . By Gerard Malynes Merchant. London. Printed by I.

L. for William Shefford, .   1622. 8°, A—H in eights, first two and last three leaves blank

DE MARSOLIER, M, Chanoine de l'Eglise d'Uzes.

Histoire de Henry VII Roy D'Angleterre, Surnommé Le Sage, & Le Salomon d'Angleterre. A Paris, . . . M.DCC. 8°, 2 vols.

DE MEDICIS, KATHERINE.

A Mervaylous discourse vpon the lyfe, deedes, and behaviour of Katherine de Medicis, Queene mother : wherin are displayed the meanes which she hath practised to atteyne vnto the vsurping of the Kingdome of France, and to the bringing of the estate of the same vnto vtter ruine and destruction. At Heydelberge, 1575. 8°, A—N 2 in eights.

DE MENDOÇA, DIEGO HURTADO.

Lazarillo : Or the Excellent History of Lazarillo de Tormes, The witty Spaniard. Both Parts. . . . London, Printed by R. Hodgkinsonne 1655. 8°. A, 4 leaves: B—Y 4 in eights, Y 4 occupied by verses addressed to the Publisher by T. P. Inscribed in this edition by James Blakeston to Lord Chandos of Sudeley.

DEMPSTER, THOMAS.

Apparatvs ad Historiam Scoticam Lib. II. Accesservnt Martyrologivm Scoticvm Sanctorvm DCLXXIX. Scriptorvm Scotorvm MDCIII. Nomenclatura. Avctore Thoma Dempstero Barone de Muresk, . . . Bononiæ, Typis Nicolai Tebaldini. M.DCXXII. 4°, a—b in fours: A—L in fours : Liber II. with a separate title, M—T in fours, besides the separate title and dedication.

De Ivramento Lib. III. Locus ex Antiq. Rom. retractatus : Satisfactvm Famæ Ill^{mi} B. M. Cardinalis Bellarmini . . . Thomas Dempstervs I. C. Scotvs . . . Bononiae, Apud Nicolaum Tebaldinum. 1623. . . . 8°, A—Aa in eights.

DE MORNAY, PHILIPPE.

A Discovrse of Life and Death. Written in French by Philip Mornay. Done in English by the Countesse of Pembroke. At London, Printed for William Ponsonby. 1600. Sm. 8°, A—F 6 in eights. Printed within borders.

A Discovrse of Life and Death : Written in French by Phil. Mornay. Done in English by the Countesse of Pembroke. At London, Printed by H. L. for Mathew Lownes, . . . 1606. 12°, A—G 6 in twelves, G 5-6 blank.

Animalium quadrupedum Auium . . . A Booke of Beasts, Birds, Flowers, Fruits, Flies, and Wormes exactly drawne with their Liuely Colours truly described. Ar to be sould by Thomas Johnson in Brittaynes Burse. 1630. Obl. 4°, 20 leaves, including the engraved title. *B. M.*

DE PONTIS, SIEUR.
Memoirs of the Sieur de Pontis ; who served in the Army Six and fifty Years, under King Henry IV. Lewis the XIII. and Lewis the XIV. . . . Faithfully Englished by Charles Cotton, Esq; . . . London, Printed by F. Leach, for James Knapton, . . . MDCXCIV. Folio. Title and dedication by Beresford Cotton to the Duke of Ormond, 2 leaves: a, 2 leaves : B—5 D, 2 leaves each.

DE QUEVEDO, FRANCISCO.
Hell Reformed Or A Glasse for Favorits. Their Falls and complaints. Also the Complaints of Princes against their Favorits. . . . Discovered in a vision, By D : F : Q : V : A Spanish Knight, . . . Published by E: M: Gent. London, Printed by E: Griffin for Simon Burton, . . . 1641. 8°, A—H in eights, and a, 4 leaves. Dedicated by Edward Messervy to Henry Jermyn Esq ; Master of the Horse to the Queen.

The Visions of Dom Francisco de Quevedo Villegas, Knight of the Order of S¹ James. Made English by R. L. London, Printed for R. Herringman. . . . 1667. 8°. A, 4 leaves : B—Z 4 in eights. A 1 has only the Imprimatur.

DERBY.
The Paradice of Pleasure: Or, An Encomium upon Darby Ale. In Answer to a Scurrilous Lampoon, call'd Sott's Paradice : Or, A Satyr against Darby-Ale. . . . London, Printed for A. Baldwin, . . . 1700. Folio, A—D, 2 leaves each. In verse.

DE RIBADENEYRA, PEDRO.
The Lives of Saints with other Feasts of the Year according to the Roman Calendar Written in Spanish by the Reverend Father Peter Ribadeneyra Priest of the Society of Jesus and Translated into English [with Additional Lives] by W. P. Esqvire. Printed with Licence. At S. Omers by Ioachim Carlier. At the signe of the name of Iesvs. In the year M.DC.LXIX. Folio. Frontispiece and plates. 2 vols. Vol. 1.—Frontispiece, title, and plate of *Jesv Admirabilis*, 3 leaves : To the Reader, &c., 6 leaves : A—5 U, 2 leaves each : *Additional Life* (St. Francis of Sales), A—G, 2 leaves each : Vol. II.—

A—7 G, 2 leaves each : Table, 3 leaves. Without any separate title to vol. 2.

The engravings consist of full-page plates of Jesus and his Mother, and plates in compartments illustrative of the months.

DE ROCOLES, J. B., *Historiographer of France and Brandenburgh.*
The History of Infamous Impostors. Or, The Lives & Actions of Several Notorious Counterfeits, . . . now Done into English. London, Printed for William Cademan . . . MDCLXXXIII. 8°, A—N 4 in eights.

DE ROHAN, HENRI, *Duc de Rohan.*
A Declaration of the Dvke of Rohan Peere of France, &c. Containing the instnes of Reasons and Motiues which haue obliged him to implore the Assistance of the King of Great Britaine, and to take armes for the defence of the Reformed Churches. Translated according to the French Copie. London, Printed for Nathanael Butter, 1628. 4°, A—D in fours, A 1 and D 4 blank.

DE SALAS BARBADILLO, DON ALONSO GERONIMO, *of Madrid.*
The Fortunate Fool. Written in Spanish. . . . Translated into English by Philip Ayres, Gent. London. Printed, and are to be sold by Moses Pitt at the White Hart in Little Britain, 1670. 8°, A—Bb in eights, Bb 8 blank. Dedicated to John Turnor, Esq., son and heir of Sir Edmond Turnor of Stoake, co. Lincoln, one of the Farmers of the Customs.

Inserted in this copy, formerly Brand's and Heber's, occurs a memorandum, communicated by Edmund Turnor, Esq., May 8, 1802: "Philip Ayres Esq¹ of St. Martins in the Fields died 1713. His effects were administered to by his brother and next of kin. [Signed] DALLINGTON AYRES."

DE SAINT EVREMOND, SIEUR.
Mixt Essays upon Tragedies, Comedies, Italian Comedies, English Comedies, and Opera's. Written Originally in French, By the Sieur de Saint Evremont. London : Printed for Timothy Goodwin at the Maidenhead, over against St. Dunstan's Church in Fleetstreet. 1685. 4°, A—E 2 in fours.

DESAINLIENS, CLAUDE, alias HOLYBAND.
A Treatise for declining of Verbes, which may be called the Second Chiefest worke of the frenche tongue. Set foorth by Clavdivs Hollyband. Imprinted at London by Richard Field dwelling in the Blacke-Friers. 1590. 8°.

Sothebys, Jan. 13, 1886. No. 816, ending imperfectly on K 3. Dedicated to Mademoiselle Anne Harington, from London, 15 November 1580.

DE SAUMAISE. CLAUDE.

Salmasius His Dissection and Confutation of the Diabolical Rebel Milton, in his Impious Doctrines of Falshood, Maxims of Policies, and destructive Principles of Hypocrisie, Insolences, Invectives, Injustice, Cruelties, and Calumnies against his Gracious Soveraign King Charles 1. . . . *Regi qui perfidus, nulli fidus.* London, Printed for J. G. B. Anno 1660. 4º, A—Ll 2 in fours, A 2 in duplicate. Dedicated to Charles II.

DESCARTES, M.

The Life of Monsieur Des Cartes, Containing the History of His Philosophy and Works : As Also, The most Remarkable Things that befell him during the whole Course of his Life. Translated from the French, By S. R. London, Printed for R. Simpson, . . . MDCXCIII. 8º, B—T in eights, T 8 with advertisements. Without any introductory matter.

DE SCUDERY, GEORGES.

Ibrahim. Or The Illvstrivos Bassa. An Excellent New Romance. The Whole Work, In Foure Parts. Written in French by Monsieur de Scudery, And now Engglished by Henry Cogan, Gent. London, Printed for Humphrey Moseley, . . . M.DC.LII. Folio. A, 6 leaves, besides a frontispiece : B—4 F in fours : 4 G, 1 leaf. Dedicated to the Duchess of Richmond and Lenox.

DESMARETS DE SAINT SORLIN, JEAN.

Ariana. In Two Parts. As it was Transslated out of the French, and presented to my Lord Chamberlaine. London : Printed by John Haviland, for Thomas Walkley. 1636. Folio. A, 2 leaves : B—Tt in fours, besides the frontispiece. In prose and verse. *B. M.*

DE SOLLEYSELL, JACQUES, *Equerry to the King of France.*

The Compleat Horseman : Discovering the Surest Marks of the Beauty, Goodness, Faults and Imperfections of Horses : . . . To which is added, A most excellent Supplement of Riding . . . By Sir William Hope, Kt Deputy-Lieutenant of the Castle of Edinburgh. Made English from the Eighth Edition of the Original, and Adorn'd with Figures. London, Printed for M. Gillflower, . . . MDCXCVI. Folio.

*—9 *, two leaves each : A—3 Z, 2 leaves each : Sir W. Hope of Kirklistoun's *Supplement*, with a new title, title and preface, 2 leaves : A—Y, 2 leaves each : *Second Part* — Advertisement, 1 leaf : a—c, 2 leaves each, d, 1 leaf : engraved title and portrait of De Solleysell, 2 leaves : B—Pp in fours : Qq—Rr, 2 leaves each. With six folded plates. Dedicated to the King by Hope.

Hope's Supplement appears to have been printed at Edinburgh.

D'ESPENCE, CLAUDE.

Oraison Fvnebre es Obseqves de tres Haute, tres Puissante, & tres Vertueuse Princesse, Marie par la grace de Dieu Royne donairiere d'Escoce. Prononcee à nostre Dame de Paris, le douzieme d'Aoust, mil cinq cens soixante. A Paris, . . . M.D.LXI. 8º, A—F in eights, F 8 blank.

DE QUEROUAILLE, LOUISE, *Duchess of Portsmouth.*

The Secret History of the Dutchess of Portsmouth : Giving an Account of the Court, during her Ministry. And of the Death of K. C. II. London, Printed for Richard Baldwin, . . . 1690. 12º. A, 6 leaves : B—G in twelves, G 12 blank.

DETHICKE, HENRY.

The Gardeners Labyrinth, Or, A New Art of Gardening : . . . London, Printed by Jane Bell, . . . 1652. 4º, A—Ll in fours. With cuts.

DE VALDES, FRANCISCO, *Master of the Camp.*

The Serieant Maior. A Dialogve of the Office of a Sergeant Maior . . . Translated into Englishe, by Iohn Thorius. London. Printed by John Wolfe. 1590. 4º, A—H in fours, and a leaf of I. Dedicated by Thorius to Sir John Norris, President of Munster.

DE VEITIA LINAGE, DON JOSEF, *Treasurer and Commissioner of the India House.*

The Spanish Rule of Trade to the West-Indies : Containing An Account of the Casa de Contratacion, or India-House, its Government, Laws, Ordinances, Officers, and Jurisdiction : . . . Made English by Capt. John Stevens. To which is added, Two Compleat Lists : One of the Goods transported out of Europe to the Spanish West-Indies ; the other of Commodities brought from those Parts into Europe. London : Printed for Samuel Cronch, . . . 1702. 8º. A, 8 : a, 4 : B—Aa in eights :

Bb, 4. Dedicated by the translator to Sir William Hodges, Bart.

DEVIL.

The Devils Last Legacy : Or, A Round-headed Ironmonger, made Executor to Pluto. Wherein is shewed, the Discent of the Round-heads . . . Composed by W. K. first a Turke, and now turned Roundhead. London, Printed Anno Domini, 1642. 4º, 4 leaves. Partly in verse.

The Devils Cabinet Broke Open : Or A New Discovery of the High-Way Thieves. Being A Seasonable Advice of a Gentleman lately converted from them, to Gentlemen and Travellers to avoyd their Villanies. Together with a Relation of the Laws, Customes, and Subtilities, of Hovse-Breakers, Pick-Pockets, and other Mecanick Caterpillars of this Nation. As also, The Apprehension and Imprisonment of the Hang-Man of the City of London . . . London : Printed for Henry Marsh. . . . 1658. 4º, A—F in fours.
The Epistle of the anonymous author to the Reader is dated " From on Ship-board in the Downs, September 20, 1657."

The Infernal Wanderer, Or, The Devil Ranging upon Earth. London : Printed in the Year MDCCII. Folio. A—D, 2 leaves each. In prose and verse.

DE VILLA CASTIN, THOMAS, *S.J.*

A Manval of Devovt Meditations and Exercises, Instructing how to pray mentally. Drawn for the most part out of the Spirituall Exercises of S. Ignatius. Translated into English by H. M. . . . Permissu Superiorum. Anno 1624. 12º. *, 6 leaves : A—Z in twelves : Aa, 6 leaves. Dedicated by I. W. to the Religious Brothers of the Society of Jesus in the English Noviciate at Watten.

DEVONSHIRE.

A Trve Relation of those Sad and Lamentable Accidents, which happened in and about the Parish Church of Withycombe in the Dartmoors, in Devonshire, on Sunday the 21. of October last, 1638. [Quot. from Psal. 46. 8.] London, Printed by G. M. for R. Harford, . . . 1638. 4º, A —C 2 in fours, A 1 blank. *B. M.*

A Trve Relation . . . London, Printed by G. M. for R. Harford, . . . 1638. 4º, A—C 2 in fours, A 1 blank, C 2 with the *Imprimatur* only. *B. M.*

A Second and Most Exact Relation of those Sad and Lamentable Accidents, which happened in and about the Parish Church of Wydecombe neere the Dart-

moores, in Devonshire, on Sunday the 21. of October last, 1638. . . . London, Printed by G. M. for R : Harford, and are to be sold at his shop in Queenes-head-alley in Pater-noster-row at the guilt Bible. 1638. 4º, A—F 2 in fours, A 1 blank.

Fovrtie Articles in the High Covrt of Parliament, against William Lang, who was Vicar in the Parish of Bradworthy, in the County of Devon, but now prisoner in the City of London. With a Petition to the Right Honourable House of Commons, Shewing the odiousnesse of his life and actions, . . . London, Printed for Tho. Bates in the Old Bayley. 1641. 4º, 4 leaves.

Good Newes from Plymouth : Being a true Relation of the death of Sir Ralph Hopton, and many of his Commanders, who by treachery sought to surprise the good Towne of Plymouth. London, Printed for Francis Wright, Febr. [*sic*] 20. 1643. A broadside.

A Full and Exact Relation of the Storming and Taking of Dartmouth, With above Five hundred Prisoners, Sixty peece of Ordnance, great store of Ammunition and Ships belonging to the said Town. . . . London, Printed for Edw. Husband, . . . January, 23. 1645. 4º, 4 leaves.

D'EWES, SIR SIMONDS.

The Primitive Practise of preserving Truth. Or An Historical Narration, shewing what course the Primitive Church anciently, and the best Reformed Churches since have taken to suppresse Heresie and Schisme. . . . By Sir Simonds D'Ewes. London, Printed by M. S. for Henry Overton, . . . 1645. 4º, A—F in fours, A 1 occupied by a certificate as to the book from John Bachiler.

DEY, RICHARD, *Minister of the Gospel.*
The Right and Legall Chvrch-Warden. Declaring and expressing their lawfull admittance into the said office by the choice and appointment of the Lord Major and Aldermen of London, the Majors, and Bailiffs of Cities and Corporations, and by the Justices of peace. . . . London, Printed for Thomas Vnderhill . . . 1643. 4º, 4 leaves.

DE YEPES, DIEGO, *of the Order of St. Jerome, Confessor of Philip II. and Bishop of Tarragona.*
Historia Particvlare de la persecution de Inglaterra de los martirios masinsignes

desde el año del Señor. 1570. . . . Con Privilegio. En Madrid. Por Luis Sanchez. Año M.D.XC.IX 4°. ¶, 8 leaves : A—3 K 4 in eights, the last leaf with the colophon.

DIALOGUE.

A Dialogve or Familiar talke betwene two neighbours, côcernyng the chyefest ceremonyes, that Were. by the mighti power of Gods most holie pure Worde. suppressed in Englande, and nowe for our vnworthines. set vp agayne by the Bishoppes. the impes of Antichrist : right learned, profitable, and pleasaunt to be read. for the comfort of weake côsciences in these troublous daies. Read first, and then iudge. From Roane. by Michael Wodde, the . xx. of February. Anno Domi. M.D.L.IIII. 8°, A—E 6 in eights.

A Short Dialogve Proving that the Ceremonies, and some other Corruptions now in question, are defended, by none other Arguments then such as the Papists haue here tofore vsed, And our Protestant writers haue long since answered. . . . Printed 1605. 4°, A—K 2 in fours.

> A tract of considerable importance. At p. 36 the writer ascribes to Dr. Fulke the tract called *Newes from Spaine and Holland*. 8°, 1593, usually, but erroneously, no doubt, assigned to Father Parsons.

A Merrie Dialogve, Betwene Band, Cvffe, and Rvffe : Done by an Excellent Wit, And Lately acted in a shew in the famous Vniversitie of Cambridge. London, Printed by William Stansby for Miles Partrich, and are to be sold at his shop in Fleet-street, neare vnto Chancerielane. 1615. 4°, A—B in fours, title on A 2 and B 4 apparently blank. *B. M.*

Collier's Sale, August 1884, No. 704.

A Dialogue between a Brownist and a Schismatick. Wherein is discovered the Schismatick's endeavour to bring to Confusion the Government of Church and State in this our Kingdom of England. London, Printed for J. Franklin. 1642. 4°, 4 leaves.

DICK, SIR WILLIAM.

Unto his Grace, Her Majesty's High Commissioner, and the Right Honourable Estates of Parliament, The Petition of William Dick, Heir to the deceast Sir William Dick of Braid, and of William Viscount of Kilsyth, Sir Robert Sibbald of Kipps D' of Medicine, John Spottiswood of that Ilk Advocat, Walter Lockhart of Kirktown, M' James Colvil Advocat, and M' Thomas Ackman Writer to the Signet, for themselves, and in name and

behalf of the remanent Creditors of the said deceast Sir William Dick of Braid and his Sons. A folio leaf.

The State of Sir William Dick his businesse concerning monie due unto him at Goldsmiths - Hall. 4°, A—B in fours. Without a general title.

DICKENSON, JONATHAN.

Gods Protecting Providence Man's Surest Help and Defence In the times Of the greatest difficulty and most Imminent danger ; Evidenced in the Remarkable Deliverance of divers Persons, From the devouring Waves of the Sea, amongst which they Suffered Shipwrack. And also From the more cruelly devouring jawes of the inhumane Canibals of Florida. Faithfully related by one of the persons concerned therein ; . . . Printed in Philadelphia by Reinier Jansen. 1699. 4°. *, 2 leaves : **, 4 leaves : A—M in fours.

Sothebys, Feb. 22, 1882, No. 829.

DIGBY, EVERARD.

Everard Digbie his Disuasiue From taking away the lyuings and goods of the Church . . . Hereunto is annexed Celsus of Verona, his Disuasiue translated into English . . . Printed by Robert Robinson, and Thomas Newman. 4°, A—Hh 2 in fours, and a. 1 leaf. Dedicated to Sir Christopher Hatton.

DIGBY, SIR KENELM.

Discovrs fait en vne Celebre Assemblee, par le Chevalier Digby, . . . Tovchant la Gverison des Playes, . . . Iouxte la copie Imprimee, A Paris, . . . 1666. 12°, A—G 8 in twelves.

Bibliotheca Digbeiana, Sive Catalogus Librorum in variis Linguis Editorum, Quos post Kenelmum Digbeium eruditiss. Virum possedit Illustri-simus Georgius Comes Bristol, nuper defunctus. . . . Quorum Auctio. . . . Aprilis 9. 1680. . . . 4°, pp. 135 + 2 leaves of title and Preface, where the 19th April is named as the first day of sale.

DION CASSIUS.

The Emperor Augustus His Two Speeches, In the Senate-House at Rome ; The First addressed to the Married Romans, The other to the Unmarried. Translated out of Dion Cassius, . . . London, Printed for J. B. . . . 1673. 4°, 4 leaves.

DIONYSIUS OF ALEXANDRIA.

The Surveye of the World, or Situation of the Earth, so much as is inhabited. Comprysing bryefely the generall partes thereof, with the names both new and

E

olde, of the principal Countries, . . . Also of Seas, with their Clyffes, Reaches, Turnings, Elbows, . . . First written in Greeke by Dionise Alexandrine, and now englished by Thomas Twine, Gentl. Imprinted at London, by Henrie Bynneman. Anno. 1572. 8°, black letter. Title, dedication from London, 15 May, 1572, to Serjeant Lovelace, and Preface, 4 leaves : A—F 2 in eights. *B. M.*

DIRECTORY.

[The Dyrectory of Conscience a pr]ofytable [Treatyse to suche] that he Tymorous or ferfull in Conseyence / copyed by one of the fathers of Syon & now put in Impressyō at the instāt request of an other deuout religyous man. &c. [Col.] Enprynted be my Laurence Andrewe Cum gratia et preuilegio. Goddys graeye shall euer endure. [Below is the mark.] 4°, a or A—G in fours. With a woodcut of the Virgin and Child on back of the title and the common one of the *Scriptorium* on the *recto* beneath the title.

> The only preliminary matter is a prologue by the printer : on a iii occurs on a head-line : Here begynneth the Dyrectory of the conseyence. Mr. Fuller Russell's copy wanted the portions of the title which I have supplied from Herbert between brackets. But I own that I am not quite satisfied that the latter did not use the same copy, and trust to conjecture.

DISCOURSE.

A Brieff discours off the troubles begonne at Franckford in Germany Anno Domini 1554. Abowte the Booke off common prayer and Ceremonies / and continued by the Englishe men theyre / to thend off Q. Maries Raigne / . . . M.D.LXXV. 4°, A—Cc in fours : Dd, 5 leaves.

A Trve Coppie of a Discourse written by a Gentleman, employed in the late Voyage of Spaine and Portingale : Sent to his particular friend, and by him published, for the better satisfaction of all such, as hauing been seduced by particular report, haue entred into conceipts tending to the discredit of the enterprise, and Actors of the same. At London Printed for Thomas Woodcock dwelling in Paules Churchyard, at the signe of the blacke Beare. 1589. 4°, black letter, A—H 2 in fours, H 2 blank. *B. M.*

A Discovrse vpon the Meanes of Wel Governing and Maintaining in good Peace, a Kingdome, or other Principalitie. Divided into three parts, . . . Against Nicholas Machiavell the Florentine. Translated into English by Simon Patericke. London, Printed by Adam Islip.

1602. Folio. ¶, 4 leaves, the first blank : A, 4 leaves : B—Kk 4 in sixes, Kk 4 blank. Dedicated by the translator to Francis Hastings and Edward Bacon, whom he describes as youths of great promise, under date of August, 1577.

An Honest Discourse between Three Neighbours, Touching the Present Government in these three Nations : Viz. Between Goodman Past, Goodman Present, & Goodman Future. London, Printed for Thomas Brewster, . . . 1655. 4°, A—C in fours. *B. M.*

> Written shortly after the commencement of the Protectoral government.

A Brief Discourse of the Most assured Ways and Means to ruine and pull down the vast Monarchy of the Ottoman Princes. Written by a Judicious Gentleman, who for above twenty years resided at the Turkish Port, being there Employ'd by a great Prince, as his Ambassador. Also An Historical and Political Discourse of the War in Hungary. . . . London, Printed by J. H. for B. Aylmer . . . 1687. 12°, B—K 6 in twelves, K 6 with Advertisements, besides title and *Imprimatur*.

A Seasonable Discourse Wherein is Examined What is Lawful during the Confusions and Revolutions of Government ; Especially in the Case of a King deserting his Kingdoms : and how far a Man may lawfully conform to the Power and Commands of those, who with Various Successes hold Kingdoms. . . . As also, Whether the Nature of War be Inconsistent with the Nature of the Christian Religion. London, printed, and are to be sold by Rich. Janway, . . . 1689. 4°, B—K in fours, besides the title and an advertisement, stating that the tract had been written some years since by an eminent and learned gentleman.

DISSENTER.

A New Ballad, Or, The Trew-Blew Protestant Dissenter : With their sad Lamentation for their late Loss in Aldergate-Street. To the Tune of the *Down-fall of Anthony*. Printed for W. Davis, in Amen-Corner. 1682. A leaf of verses.

A True and Impartial Narrative of the Dissenters New Plot : With A large and exact Relation of their old Ones. . . . London, Printed for Richard Newcome. . . . 1691. 4°. Title and Index, 2 leaves : B, 2 leaves : C—E in fours.

DIXON, ROBERT, *D.D.*

The Degrees of Consanguinity, and Allinity. Described, and Delineated. London, Printed by T. R. and N. T. for Benjamin Took. . . . 1674. 8°, A—D 2 in eights, besides 6 leaves of tables.

DOBSON, EDWARD.
XIV Articles of Treason and High Misdemeanors, Exhibited to Isaac Pennington, by Master Chamfield, alias Captain Cloak-Bag, against Edward Dobson, the Malignant Stationer without Newgate. Oxford. Printed by Leonard Lichfield, for Edward Dobson. 1643. 4°, 4 leaves.

DOCTORS' COMMONS.
The Last Will And Testament of Doctors Commons : Wherein is exprest the Legacies bequeathed to her best Benefactors and Friends,

> As Advocates, Officials, Delegates and Doctors,
> Messengers, Sumners, Promoters, and Proctors,
> And others, which here in my Will is made knowne,
> Repaire to the Commons, and there take your owne.

Printed in the yeare, of Doctors Commons feare. 1641. 4°, 4 leaves.

DODDRIDGE, SIR JOHN.
The Compleat Parson : Or, A Description of Advowsons, or Church-lining. Wherein is set forth, the intrest of the Parson, Patron, and Ordinarie, &c. With many other things . . . By I. Dodderidge, Anno, 1602, 1603. And now Published for a Common good, by W. J. London. Printed by B. A. and T. F. for Iohn Grone, . . . 1630. 4°, A—N in fours, A 1 blank.

DODSON, COLONEL WILLIAM.
The Designe for the perfect Draining of the Great Level of the Fens, (called Bedford Level) Lying in Norfolk, Suffolk, Cambridgeshire, Huntingtonshire, Northamptonshire, Lincolnshire, and the Isle of Ely. As it was delivered to the Honourable Corporation for the Draining of the said Great Level, the 4th of June. 1664. As Also, Several Objections answered . . . London, Printed by R. Wood, and are to be sold by Henry Twiford . . . and Rich. Marriot . . . 1665. 4°, A—F in fours, A 1 blank, and the folded map.

DONALDSON, JAMES.
Husbandry Anatomized, Or, An Enquiry into the Present Manner of Tilling and Manuring the Ground in Scotland for most Part ; . . . . By Ja: Donaldson. Edinburgh. Printed by John Reid, in the Year, M.DC.XC.VII. 8°, A—S in fours, and ¶, 4 leaves : *Postscript*, A—F in fours. Dedicated to Patrick, Earl of Marchmount.

The Undoubted Art of Thriving; Wherein is shewed, 1. That a Million L. Sterling Money, or more if need be may be raised for Propagating the Trade of the Nation, &c. . . . 2. How the Indian and African Company may Propagate their Trade, . . . 3. How every one according to his quality, may Live Comfortably and Happily, . . . Edinburgh, Printed by John Reid, 1700. 12°, A—R in fours, and preface, 4 leaves. Dedicated to John, Duke of Queensberry.

Overture Regulating the Length and Breadth of Linnen. To His Grace James Duke of Queensberry . . . Edinburgh, Printed by John Reid, 1700. 8°, A—C in fours.

An Essay upon Agriculture, With a Proposal for Reprinting *Husbandry Anatomized* with Amendments and considerable Enlargements. By Ja. Donaldson. Edinburgh, Printed by John Moncur, . . . 1714. Price 6 pence. 8°, 8 leaves. In verse.

DOWNAME, GEORGE, *D.D.*
A Replye Answering a Defence of the Sermon, preached at the Consecration of the Bishop of Bathe and Welles, by George Downame, Doctor of Diuinitye. In defence of an Answere to the foresayd Sermon Imprinted Anno 1609 . . . Imprinted Anno 1613. 4°. 6 preliminary leaves and A—Oo in fours.

DRAKE, SIR FRANCIS.
The Voyages of the Ever Renowned Sr. Francis Drake into the West Indies. . . . Collected out of the Notes of the most Aproved Authors. To which is added, An Account of his Valorous Exploits in the Spanish Invasion. London, Printed for Thomas Malthus, ... 1682. 8°. Title, Preface, and List of Books, 3 leaves : B—M 4 in eights. *B. M.*

The Life and Most Dangerous Voyages of Sir Francis Drake, With the Surprising of Nombre de Dios, and the manner of his gaining large Quantities of Gold and Silver. And a large Account of that Voyage wherein he encompassed the whole World . . . . With the last Voyage in which he died. London : Printed for H. Dean, . . . 12°, A—G in twelves, including a woodcut frontispiece.

DRAYTON, MICHAEL.
The Works of Michael Drayton, Esq'; A Celebrated Poet in the Reigns of Queen Elizabeth, King James 1. and Charles I., . . . London : Printed by J. Hughs, near Lincoln's-Inn-Fields, . . . MDCCXLVIII. Folio. Title, Account of the Author, &c.

a—d, 2 leaves each : B—G H, 2 leaves each : G 1, 1 leaf.

> The edition of 1753, 4 vols. 8vo, is said to be identical with this, and to have been printed from the same forms.

Englands Heroicall Epistles. Newly Corrected. With Idea. By Michaell Draiton. At London, Printed by I. R. for N. L. and are to be sold at his shop, in Paules Churchyard at the signe of the Crane. 1600. 8°, A—Q in eights, except A, which has only 4 leaves.

DREAMS.

A Most Briefe and pleasant Treatise of the Interpretation of sundrie Dreames intituled to be Iosephs, and sundry other Dreames out of the worke of the wise Salomon. Being in all 140. Written first in the Hebrue tongue. . . . Imprinted at London by Simon Stafford : And are to be sold by Roger Iackson . . . 1601. 8", black letter, A—C 2 in eights. *B. M.* (Bliss's copy.)

DRUMMOND, WILLIAM, *of Hawthornden.*

The History of Scotland, . . . The Second Edition, with a Brief Account of the Author's life. London, Printed for Tho. Fabian . . . 1681. 8", A—C 4 in eights : D—Hh 2 in eights. With a portrait of the author by Gaywood, and prints of James I.—V. by the same.

> This edition includes *Memorials of State, Familiar Letters,* and *A Cypress Grove.*

Polemo-Medinia inter Vitarnam et Nebernam. [Edinburgh, about 1650.] 4°, 3 leaves.

DRUMMOND, WILLIAM, *son of the preceding.*

Anagram Of his Excellency the Lord Generall George Monck, King Come Ore. For M' William Clark, Sec. W. Drummond, Gent. [1660.] A broadside, containing 26 lines.

DRUNKARDS.

A Looking Glasse for Drunkards : Or, The Hynting of drunkennesse. Wherein drunkards are vnmasked to the view of the world. Very connenient and vsefull for all people to ruminate on in this drunken Age. [Quot. from Esay. 5. 22.] Printed at London for F. C. 1627. 8°, A—B 4 in eights. *B. M.* (Bliss's copy.)

DRYDEN, JOHN.

The Friendly Vindication of M' Dryden From the Censure of the Rota By His Cabal of Wits.

> Danda est hellebori nostro pars magna Poetæ, Nescio an Anticyram ratio illi destinet omnem.

Cambridge Printed in the Year M.DC.LXXIII. 4°. B, 4 leaves : C, 5, and the title.

> At the end occurs : Finis or not Finis As M'. Dryden pleaseth.

Notes and Observations on the Empress of Morocco Revised. With some few Errata's to be Printed instead of the Postscript, with the next edition of the *Conquest of Granada.* . . . London, Printed for William Cademan . . . 1674. 4°. A—Bb, 2 leaves each.

Troilus and Cressida, Or, Truth Found too late. A Tragedy As it is Acted at the Dukes Theatre. To which is Prefix'd. A Preface Containing the Grounds of Criticism in Tragedy. Written by John Dryden Servant to his Majesty. . . . London, Printed for Abel Swall, . . . and Jacob Tonson . . . 1679. 4". A, 4 leaves : a, 4 : b, 5 : B—K in fours. Dedicated to Robert, Earl of Sunderland.

Threnodia Augustalis : . . . The Second Edition. London, Printed for Jacob Tonson . . . 1685. 4", A—D 2 in fours.

King Arthur : Or, The British Worthy. A Dramatick Opera. Perform'd at the Queens Theatre By their Majesties Servants. Written by M' Dryden. . . . London, Printed for Jacob Tonson, . . . 1691. 4°, A—H 2 in fours, and the title. Dedicated to the Marquis of Halifax.

The Medall. A Satyre . . . Edinbvrgh, Re-Printed Anno Dom. 1682. 4", A—C 2 in fours.

MacFlecknoe, Or A Satyr upon the True-Blew-Protestant Poet, T. S. By the Author of Absalom & Achitophel. London, Printed for D. Green, 1682. 4°, A —B in fours, B 4 blank.

An Evening's Love : Or, The Mock-Astrologer. As it is Acted By Their Majesties Servants. By M' Dryden. *Mallem Convivis quàm placuisse Cocis.* Mart. London, Printed for Henry Herringman, . . . 1691. 4". A—K in fours. Dedicated to William, Duke of Newcastle.

Alexander's Feast ; Or the Power of Musique. An Ode, in Honour of St. Cecilia's Day. By M' Dryden. London, Printed for Jacob Tonson . . . 1697. Folio. A—C, 2 leaves each, including title and half-title.

Homer and Virgil not to be Compar'd with the Two Arthurs. . . . London, Printed by W. B. for Luke Meredith . . . 1700. 12". A, 6 leaves : B—H in twelves.

DU CLOS, M., *Physician to the King.*
Observations on the Mineral Waters of
France, Made in the Royal Academy of
the Sciences. Now made English. Lon-
don, Printed for Henry Faithorne, and
John Kersey . . . 1684. 12°. Title
and preface, 2 leaves : B—F in twelves :
G, 5.

DUFFETT, THOMAS.
An Amorous Old-woman : Or, Tis Well
if it Take. A Comedy. Acted By His
Majesties Servants. Written by a Person
of Honour. London, Printed for Simon
Neale . . . and B. Tooth . . . MDCLXXIV.
4°. Title, Prologue spoken by Major
Mohun, and *Personæ*, 3 leaves : B—K in
fours : L, 1 leaf.

The Mock-Tempest : Or The Enchanted
Castle. Acted at the Theatre Royal.
Written by T. Duffett. *Hic totus volo
rideat libellus.* Mart. London, Printed
for William Cademan . . . 1675. 4°.
Title, Introduction, and Prologue, 3
leaves : B—H in fours.

Psyche Debauch'd, A Comedy, As it was
Acted at the Theatre-Royal. By T. D.
London, Printed for J. Smith Bookseller
in Great Queen-street, 1678. 4°. A, 2
leaves : B—M 2 in fours.

Beauties Triumph ; A Masque. Presented
by the Scholars of Mr Jellery Banister,
and Mr James Hart, at their New Boarding-School for Young Ladies and Gentlewomen, kept in that House which was
formerly Sir Arthur Gorges, at Chelsey.
Written by T. Duffett. . . . London,
Printed in the year MDCLXXVI. 4°. A,
2 leaves : B—D in fours.

DU FRESNOY, C. A.
De Arte Graphica. The Art of Painting,
By C. A. Du Fresnoy. With Remarks.
Translated into English, Together with
an Original Preface containing A Parallel
betwixt Painting and Poetry. By Mr
Dryden. As also a Short Account of the
most Eminent Painters both Ancient and
Modern, . . . By another Hand. . . .
London, Printed by J. Heptinstall for
W. Rogers, . . . MDCXCV. 4°. Title and
frontispiece by Gribelin, 2 leaves : (a)—
(h) in fours : B—Zz 2 in fours.
  Ellis, 1885, large paper, with notes in the
  autographs of Dryden and Pope, £15, 15s.

DU GARD, WILLIAM.
An humble Remonstrance Presented to
the Right Worshipfull Company of Mer-
chant-Tailors Maii 15. 1661. By William
Du-Gard. [Quotations from Cicero and
Plautus.] London, Printed in the Year
of our Lord. 1661. 4°, A—B 2 in fours.

This tract relates to Du-Gard's dismissal
from the head-mastership. He is known as
the Editor of Lucian's *Dialogues*, and many
other Greek and Roman books for the use
of schools.

DUNNIDGE, JAMES, *Notary.*
The Case of J[ames] W[histon.] 4°, A—
C in fours.
        Privately printed about 1704.

DU MOULIN, PIERRE.
A Wittie Encounter betweene Monsieur
du Moulin, and Monsieur de Balzac. . . .
Wherein they deliver things weighty,
and important both in Religion and State.
Faithfully translated out of the French
coppy by A. S. Gent. Imprinted at London for B. Fisher . . . 1636. 8°, A—I
4 in eights, A 1 and I 4 blank. Dedicated by the translator to his much honoured friend Sir William Howard, son of
the Earl of Suffolk.

Brevis et Fidelis Narratio motuum in
Regno & Ecclesia Scotica, Excerpta . . .
Per Irenævm Philalethen . . . Dantisci,
Anno 1640. 4°, A—I in fours, 1 4 blank.

The Great Loyalty of the Papists to K.
Charles I. (of Blessed Memory.) Dis-
covered, By Peter Du Moulin, D.D. In
His Vindication of the Protestant Reli-
gion. London, Printed in the Year
MDCLXXIII. 4°, A—B 2 in fours.

DUNCON, JOHN.
The Holy Life and Death of the Lady
Letice, Vi-Countess Falkland. With the
Returns of Spiritual Comfort. . . . The
third Edition, Enlarged. London, Printed
for Rich: Royston, . . . 1653. 8°. A—
L in twelves. With the same frontis-
piece as in the two former editions.

DUNTON, JOHN.
Heavenly Pastime, Or, Pleasant Observations on all the most remarkable Passages
throughout the Holy Bible, of the Old
and New Testament. Newly Allegoriz'd,
in several Delightful Dialogues, Poems,
Similitudes, and Divine Fancies. By
John Dunton, Author of the Sickmans
Passing-Bell. The Second Edition. London, Printed for John Dunton, . . . 1685.
12°, A—G in twelves : Aa—Ff in twelves.
In verse and prose.

The Dublin Scuffle : Being a Challenge
sent by John Dunton, Citizen of London,
to Patrick Campbel, Bookseller in Dublin.
Together with the small Skirmishes of
Bills and Advertisements. To which is
Added, The Billet Doux, sent him by a
Citizens Wife in Dublin, tempting him to
Lewdness, with His Answers to Her . . .

In several Letters . . . with a Poem on the whole Encounter. . . . London, Printed for the Author, . . . 1699. 8°. a, 4 : b, 8 : B—4 B in eights : 4 C, 6 leaves. Dedicated to Colonel Butler, a member of the Irish Parliament.

DU PLESSIS, JEAN ARMAND, *Duc de Richelieu.*
Emblema Animæ . . . London Printed by Nic: and Joh: Okes 1635. 12°. A, 5 leaves : B—M in twelves : N, 6. The title is engraved as in the issue of 1633.

DUQUESNE, M.
A New Voyage to the East-Indies in the Years 1690 and 1691. Being a full Description of the Isles of Mandives, Cocos, Andamans, [Andema ?] and the Isle of Ascension ; and all the Forts and Garrisons now in possession of the French, with an Account of the Customs, Manners, and Habits of the Indians. By Monsieur Duquesne. To which is added, A New Description [by Le Maire] of the Canary Islands, Cape Verd, Senegal and Gambia, &c. Illustrated with Sculptures. . . . London, Printed for Daniel Dring . . . 1696. 8°, A—M in eights : B—I in eights. With maps of the Indies and Canaries, and plates in the second part at pp. 16, 32, 36, 52, and 70.
This is said to be translated from the last Paris edition.

DURER, ALBERT.
Albert Durer Revived : Or, a Book of Drawing, Limning, Washing, . . London, Printed for John Garrett . . . Folio, B—L, 2 leaves each, besides the title and frontispiece.

DURFEY, THOMAS.
The Siege of Memphis, Or The Ambitious Queen. A Tragedy, Acted at the Theater-Royal. Written by Tho. Durfey, Gent. . . . London, Printed for W. Cademan . . . 1676. 4°. Title, dedication to the truly generous Henry Chevers, Esq; and Prologue, 3 leaves : B—K 2 in fours.

Madam Fickle : Or The Witty False One. A Comedy. As it is Acted at his Royal Highness the Duke's Theatre. Written by Tho: Durfey Gent. . . . London, Printed by T. N. for James Magnes . . . M.DC.LXXVII. 4°. A—K 2 in fours. Dedicated to the Duke of Ormond.

The Fond Husband : Or, The Plotting Sisters. A Comedy : As it is Acted at His Royal Highness the Duke's Theatre . . . Written by Tho. Durfey Gent . . . London : Printed by R. E. for James

Magnes and Rich. Bentley, . . . 1678. 4°, A—H in fours. Dedicated to the Duke of Ormond.

The Fool Turn'd Critick : A Comedy : As it was Acted at the Theatre-Royall. By His Majesties Servants. By T. D. Gent. London, Printed for James Magnes and Richard Bentley, . . . 1678. 4°. A, 2 leaves : B—I 2 in fours.

Squire Oldsapp : Or, The Night-Adventurers. A Comedy : As it is Acted at His Royal Highness the Duke's Theatre. *Incidit in Scyllam* . . . London : Printed for James Magnes and Richard Bentley, . . . 1679. 4°. A, 2 leaves : B—K 2 in fours.

Sir Barnaby Whigg : Or, No Wit like a Womans. A Comedy. As it is Acted by Their Majesties Servants at the Theatre-Royal. Written by Thomas Durfey, Gent. . . . London, Printed by A. G. and J. P. for Joseph Hindmarsh, . . . 1681. 4°, A—I in fours. Dedicated to George, Earl of Berkeley.

The Royalist. A Comedy ; As it is Acted at the Duke's Theatre. By Thomas Durfey, Gent. London, Printed for Jos. Hindmarsh . . . 1682. 4°, A—I in fours.

A New Collection of Songs and Poems. By Thomas D'urfey. Gent. London : Printed for Joseph Hindmarsh, at the Black Bull in Cornhill : 1683. 8°. Title, 1 leaf : B—G in eights, G 8 blank, and G 6-7 with Advertisements. With the music. *B. M.*

The Common-Wealth of Women. A Play : As it is Acted at the Theatre Royal, By their Majesties Servants. By M^r D'urfey . . . London, Printed for R. Bentley . . . and J. Hindmarsh . . . 1686. 4°, A—H in fours. Dedicated to Christopher, Duke of Albemarle.

A Compleat Collection of M^r D'vrfeys Songs and Odes, Whereof the first Part never before Published . . . London, Printed for Joseph Hindmarsh, . . . 1687. 8°, (a)—(c 2) in eights : A—K in eights. Dedicated to the Earl of Carlisle.

The Fool's Preferment, Or, The Three Dukes of Dunstable. A Comedy. As it was Acted at the Queens Theatre in Dorset-Garden, by Their Majesties Servants. Written by M^r D'urfey. Together with all the Songs and Notes to 'em, Excellently Compos'd by Mr Henry Purcell. 1688. . . . Printed for Jos. Knight, and Fra. Saunders . . . 1688.

4°, A—N in fours. Dedicated to Charles, Lord Morpeth.

The *Songs* have a separate title.

Bussy D'Ambois, Or The Husbands Revenge. As it is Acted at the Theatre Royal. Newly Revised by Mʳ D'urfey. . . . London, Printed for R. Bently, . . . 1691. 4°, A—H 2 in fours. Dedicated to Edward, Earl of Carlisle.

Love for Money : Or, The Boarding School. A Comedy. Written by Mʳ D'vrfey. London : Printed for Abel Roper . . . 1691. 4°, A—I in fours : K, 1 leaf : *Dramatis Personæ*, 1 leaf after A 4. Dedicated to Charles, Lord Lansdowne.

Love for Money : Or, The Boarding School. A Comedy. As it is Acted at the Theatre Royal. Written by Mʳ D'vrfey. London : Printed for A. Roper, and E. Wilkinson, . . . 1696. 4°, A—H in fours. Dedicated to Charles, Viscount Lansdowne.

Wit for Money : Or, Poet Stutter : A Dialogue between Smith. Johnson, and Poet Stutter. Containing Reflections on some late Plays ; and particularly on *Love for Money*, or, *The Boarding-School* . . . London : Printed for S. Burgis. 1691. 4°. Title, 1 leaf : Dedication by Sr. Critick-Catcall to Mʳ T. D., 2 leaves : B—H 3 in fours.

The Richmond Heiress : Or, A Woman once in the Right. A Comedy, Acted at the Theatre Royal, By Their Majesties Servants. Written by Mʳ D'vrfey. London, Printed for Samuel Briscoe, over against Will's Coffee-House in Covent-Garden. 1693. 4°, A—I in fours. Dedicated by Durfey to his very much esteemed friend Sir Nicholas Garrard, Bart.

The Marriage-Hater Match'd : A Comedy. Acted at the Theatre Royal by Their Majesties Servants. Written by Tho. D'urfey, Gent. London, Printed for R. Bentley, . . . 1693. 4°. Title and Dedi-

cation to the Duke of Ormond, 2 leaves : B—H in fours, H 4 with a Prologue in a Dialogue between Mr. Monford and Mrs. Bracegirdle.

The Comical History of Don Quixote. As it was Acted at the Queen's Theatre in Dorset-Garden, By Their Majesties Servants. Part I. [-II.-III.] Written by Mʳ D'urfey. London, Printed for Samuel Briscoe, . . . 1694. The Comical History . . . Part the Second . . . London . . . 1694. The Third Part . . . London, . . . 1696. 4°. Part I. dedicated to the Duchess of Ormond, A, 2 leaves : B—G in fours : H, 1 leaf : Part II. dedicated in verse to the Earl of Dorset and Middlesex, A—I in fours : Part III. dedicated to Charles Montague, Esq., A—I 2 in fours, and a, 4 leaves.

A New Opera, Call'd, Cinthia and Endimion : Or, The Loves of the Deities. As it was designed to be Acted at Court, before the late Queen ; and now Acted at the Theatre Royal, by His Majesty's Servants. Written by Mʳ D'vrfey. London : Printed by W. Onley, . . . 1697. 4°, A—G in fours. Dedicated to Henry, Earl of Romney, Master-General of the Ordnance.

DU VERGER, S.

Dv Vergers Hvmble Reflections vpon some Passages of the Right Honorable the Lady Marchionesse of Newcastles Olio. Or An Appeale from her mesinformed, to her owne better informed iudgement. Printed at London. M.DC.LVII. 8°, A—L 4 in eights.

DYMOCK, JAMES, *a Clergyman.*

The Great Sacrifice of the New Law, . . . The Eighth Edition, Corrected. Permissu Superiorum. London, Printed for Matthew Turner . . . 1687. [A new title :] Vespers : Or Even-Songs for all the Sundays and Holy-Days in the Year, In Latin and English. Permissu Superiorum. London, . . . 1688. 12°. A, 4 : B—K in twelves : L, 8 : the *Second Part*, A—D in twelves.

E.

E. N.
Information for the Ignorant Or The Applicatory Part of a Late Printed Book, called, A Light for the Ignorant . . . Also a Postscript containing a Challenge (layd down in 9. Propositions) to all the Non-Conformists in Old and New England, and Holland. Made by N. E. . . . Printed in the Year of God, 1640. 4°, A—C in fours.

EACHARD, LAURENCE.
An Exact Description of Ireland: Chorographically Surveying all its Provinces & Counties after a more Accurate, Plain, Easie, and Particular Manner than any before done in this kind . . . With an Index of all the Provinces . . . By Lavrence Eachard of Christ-College in Cambridge. London: Printed for Tho. Salusbury . . . 1691. 12°. A, 6 leaves: B—G in twelves, besides a general map and four others of the Provinces.

EARLE, JOHN, *Bishop of Salisbury.*
Micro-Cosmographie . . . London, Printed by William Stansby for Edward Blount. 1628. 12°. A, 6 leaves: B—I in twelves: K, 5.
　This is the second edition with 55 Characters.

Micro-cosmographie: Or, A Piece of the World Discovered. . . . London, Printed for Samuel Crouch, . . . 1676. 12°, A—M in twelves, title on A 2.
　The unsold copies of 1669 with a new title.

ECLOGUES.
Eclogs and Pastorals on several Arguments.
　Nec non erubuit silvis habitare Thalcia.
London: Printed for Joseph Collier at the Bible on London Bridg. 1682. 4°, A, 2 leaves: B—E in fours.

EDINBURGH.
Scholæ Edinensis in Caroli II. . . . Restitutionem. Ode Eucharistica: Unâ cum Cygnea Caroli I. . . . Et Henrici filii tertii Glocestriæ Ducis . . . Edinbvrgi, Excudebat Gideon Lithgo, . . . 1661. 4°.
　The copy used ended imperfectly on the fourth leaf.

EDOUARD.
Histoire D'Angleterre . . . Suivant la Copie. A Paris . . . M.DC.XCVI. 12°. 2 vols.

EDWARDES, ROGER.
A Boke of very Godly Psalmes and prayers, dedicated to the Lady Letice Vicountesse of Hereforde. Imprinted at London, in Fletestreate, at the signe of the Faucon, by Wylliam Griffith. 1570. 8°, black letter. Title and dedication, 2 leaves: B 2—I 5 in eights. *B. M.*
　This was Bliss's copy; it is probably imperfect.

EGLISHAM, GEORGE. *M.D.*
Prodromvs Vindictæ In Ducem Bvckinghamiæ, pro virulenta cæde potentissimi Magnæ Britanniæ Regis Iacobi; necnon Marchionis Hamiltonij, ac aliorum virorum Principum. Iudice Georgio Eglisham Scoto . . . Francofvrti. 1626. 4°, A—F in fours.

EGERTON, SIR THOMAS, *Baron Ellesmere.*
The Speech of the Lord Chancellor of England, in the Eschequer Chamber, touching the *Post-nati.* London. Printed for the Societie of Stationers. An. 1609. 4°. A, 6 leaves, A 1 blank: B—Q in fours, Q 4 blank.

Certaine Observations Concerning the Office of the Lord Chancellor. Composed by the Right Honorable, and most Learned, Thomas Lord Ellesmere, late Lord Chancellor of England. Whereunto is annexed a perfect Table, and a Methodicall Analysis of the whole Treatise. London, Printed for Matthew Walbanck . . . for Henry Twyford . . . and Iohn Place . . . 1651. 12°. Title, 1 leaf: To the Reader, 2 leaves: Advertisements, 1 leaf: A—G in twelves: H, 6.

ELIOT, JOHN.
Tears of Repentance: Or, A further Narrative of the Progress of the Gospel Amongst the Indians in New-England: . . . Edited by Mr Eliot and Mr Mayhew, two Faithful Laborers in that Work of the Lord. Published by the Corporation for propagating the Gospel there, ... London: Printed by Peter Cole in Leaden-Hall, . . . 1653. 4°. Dedicated to the Protector Cromwell by the president of the Corporation from Cooper's Hall, London, March 26, 1653.
　Collation: Title and dedication, 2 leaves: Mr. Mayhew's Letter. 7 leaves: Eliot's Dedication to Cromwell, 1 leaf: his dedi-

cation to the Reader, 2 leaves : To the Christian Reader, 6 leaves : A True Relation, &c., E—K in fours.

A Late and Further Manifestation of the Progress of the Gospel amongst the Indians in New-England. . . . Being a Narrative of the Examination of the Indians, about their Knowledge in Religion, by the Elders of the Churches. Related by Mr John Eliot . . . London: Printed by M. S. 1655. 4°. A—D in fours, with a preface or epistle by Joseph Caryl.

The Indian Primer Or The First Book. By which Children may know truely to read the Indian Language. And Milk for Babes. Boston : Printed by B. Green. 1720. 12°. A—O in sixes, first title on A 2. Engl. and Indian.

ELISE.

Elise, Or Innocencie Guilty. A New Romance, Translated into English by Jo: Jennings, Gent. London, Printed by T. Newcomb for Humphrey Moseley, . . . 1655. Folio. A, 2 leaves : B—U in fours. Dedicated by Jennings to Frances, Countess of Dorset.

ELIZABETH TUDOR, *Queen of England.*

A Decree of the Priuye Counsell at westminster. Anno. 1.5.5.9. xx. October. Articles agreed vppon by the Lordes and other of the Quenes Maiesties pryuy Counsayle, for a reformation of their seruauntes in certayne abuses of apparell thereby to gyue example to al other Lordes, noble men and Gentlemen. God saue the Quene. Imprinted at London in Povvles Churchyarde bi Richard Iugge, and Iohn Cavvood, printers to the Quenes Maiestie. Cum priuilegio. . . . Black letter. A large broadside.

A petition directed to her most excellent Maiestie, wherein is deliuered
1. A meane howe to compound the ciuill dissention in the church of England.
2. A proofe that they who write for Reformation, doe not offend against the stat. of 23. Eliz. c. and therefore till matters bee compounded, deserue more fauour. . . . [No place, &c.] 4°, A—L 2 in fours.

A particular declaration or testimony, of the vndutifull and traiterous affection borne against her Maiestie by Edmond Campion Iesuite, and other condemned Priestes, witnessed by their owne confessions : in reproofe of those slaunderous bookes & libels deliuered out to the contrary by such as are malitiously affected towards her Maiestie and the state. Published by Authoritie. Imprinted at London by Christopher Barker, . . . An. Do. 1582. 4°, A—D in fours, A 1 blank and D 4 with colophon only.

Aduertisements partely for the order in the publique administration of Common prayers, and vsing the holy Sacraments : And partely for the apparell of all persons Ecclesiasticall, by vertue of the Queens Maiesties letters, . . . Imprinted at London . . . by Thomas Dawson. 1584. 4°, A—B in fours.

Unseen by Herbert.

An Order of Praier and Thankes-Giving, for the preseruation of the Queenes Maiesties life and Salfetie : to be vsed of the Preachers and Ministers of the Dioces of winchester. With a short extract of William Parries voluntarie confession, written with his owne hand. Imprinted at London by Ralfe Newberie. [1585.] 4°, 4 leaues.

Coppie de la Reqveste presentee au Turc par l'Agent de la Royne d'Angleterre, le 9. de Nouember 1587. . . . A Verdun. Pour Iacques Eldreton. 1589. 8°, 8 leaues.

A translation from the German copy printed at Ingolstadt in 1588. At the end, with some other verses, occur "Les vertus de Iezabel Angloise."

The Speeches and Honorable Entertainment giuen to the Queenes Maiestie in Progresse at Cowdrey in Sussex, by the right Honorable the Lord Montacute. 1591. London Printed by Thomas Scarlet, and are to bee solde by William Wright dwelling in Paules Churchyard neere to the French Schoole. 1591. 4°, A—B in fours, A 1 and B 4 blank. *B. M.* (Jolley's copy.)

Speeches Delivered to Her Majestie this Last Progresse at the Right Honorable the Lady Russels at Bissam ; the Right Honorable the Lord Chandos, at Sudeley ; at the Right Honorable the Lord Norris, at Ricote. Printed at Oxford by Ioseph Barnes. 1592. 4°, A—C in fours. In prose and in verse.

Oxoniensis Academiae Funebre Officium In Memoriam Honoratissimam . . . Elisabethae, . . . Oxoniae, Excudebat Iosephus Barnesius, . . . 1603. 4°, A—Z in fours, Z 4 blank, besides title and dedication to James I.

Threno-thriambeuticon. Academiae Cantabrigiensis ob damnum lucrosum, & infaelicitatem faelicissimam, luctuosus triumphus. Cantabrigiae, Ex officina Ioannis Legat. 1603. 4°, A—I in fours.

ELLIS, HUMPHREY, *Minister at Winchester.*

Psevdo Christvs : Or, A true and faithful Relation of the Grand Impostures, Horrid Blasphemies, Abominable Practises, Gross Deceits ; Lately spread abroad and acted in the County of Southampton, by William Frankelin and Mary Gadbury, and their Companions. . . . London, Printed by John Macock, for Luke Fawn, . . . 1650. 4°, A—H in fours, H 4 with *Imprimatur.*

ELLIS, TOBIAS, *Minister of the Gospel.*

The True English School, For their Majesties Three Kingdoms. Being A Catalogue of all the Words in the Bible, together with a Praxis in Prose and Verse ; . . . London, Printed for the Author, and are to be sold by W. Freeman, . . . 1691. 4°. Title and to the Reader from the author's house at Great Milton in Oxfordshire, 3 leaves : 3 engraved leaves : B—S in fours.

ELTON, RICHARD, *Serjeant-Major.*

The Compleat Body of the Art Military : Exactly compiled, and gradually composed for the Foot, in the best refined manner, . . . Divided into Three Books. . . . Illustrated with Varieties of Figures of Battail, very profitable and delightfull for all Noble and Heroick Spirits, . . . London : Printed by Robert Leybourn, in Monkswell Street neer Creeplegate. M DC L. Folio. Title, 1 leaf : Dedication to Lord Fairfax, and two other dedications, 3 leaves : verses to the author, 6 leaves : B—Bb in fours : no Cc : Dd, 2 leaves. With a portrait of the author by Droeshout, and plates at pp. 160, 162, 164, 172, and 174.

The Compleat Body of the Art Military. . . . London, Printed for W. L. and are to be sold by Henry Brome . . . 1668. Folio. Frontispiece, title, and dedication, 3 leaves : B—Ll 2 in fours. With plates at pp. 164, 166, 170, 172, 230, 232.

> With a Supplement by Thomas Rudd, Chief Engineer to Charles I.

EMILIA.

Emilia. London : Printed for the Author. 1672. 8°, A—N in fours.

> Dedicated " To the Onely Few," before its performance, to make it, according to the anonymous writer, more legible on production.

ENGLAND.

The Lamentacion of England. Esay . . . Joel . . . [At the end:] Soli Deo honor & gloria. 1558. 8°, A—B 4 in eights, the text concluding at the foot of B 4. *Grenv. Coll.*

Rervm Britannicarvm, Id est Angliae, Scotiae, Vicinarvmqve Insvlarvm ac Regionvm: Scriptores Vetvstiores ac Praecipvi. . . . Heidelbergæ. CIꓛ Iꓛ. lxxxvii. Folio. Title, dedication to Frederic, Count Palatine, and Catalogue, 4 leaves, the 4th blank: A—Z in sixes: a—z in sixes: Aa—Cc in sixes: *, 4 leaves.

> Geoffrey of Monmouth, Ponticus Virunnius, Gildas, Bede and his Continuator, William of Newbury, and Epitome of Froissart.

Manifeste Anglois. Adressé aux Reformez de France. Sur les troubles & diuision de ce temps. Sur la copie imprimée à Londre par George Bichops. M.DC.XXII. 8°, A—D in fours, D 4 blank.

A Remonstrance of the State of the Kingdome . . . Imprinted first at London, and reprinted at Edinburgh . . . 1641. 4°. A, 2 : B—D in fours.

Englands Ioy and Sorrow : Expressing their sorrow for the Kings going into Scotland, and their ioy for the Queene Mothers Farewell. London, Printed for F. Coules, 1641. 4°. 4 leaves. In verse. With rough woodcut three-quarter portraits on title of Charles and Mary de Medicis.

Considerations Upon the present State of the Affairs of this Kingdome. In relation to the three severall Petitions which have lately been in agitation in the Honorable City of London. And a Project for a fourth Petition. . . . Written upon the perusing of the Speciall Passages of the two Weeks, from the 29 of November, to the 13 of December, 1642 . . . By a Countryman, a Well-willer of the City, and a Lover of Truth and Peace . . . London, Printed Anno 1642. 4°, A—B in fours.

Englands Apology for Its late Change: Or, A Sober Persuasive, Of all Disaffected or Dissenting persons, to a Seasonable Engagement, for the Settlement of this Common-Wealth. . . . London, Printed by M. S. for Livevel Chapman, . . . 1651. 4°. A, 2 leaves : B—F in fours, F 4 blank.

Some Farther Intelligence of the Affairs of England. The death of the Renowned Oliver Lord Protector . . . With an Exact relation how Somerset-House was prepared for his Effigies. The Proclaiming according to the humble Petition of Advice, the Lord Richard, . . . A Parliament called Jan. 7. 1659. . . . A List of the English Fleet designed for the Sound,

. . . London, Printed by M. S. for Tho. Jenner . . . 1659. 4''. A—F in fours. With engravings, including the lying in state of Oliver and a full-page portrait of Richard.

England's Universal Distraction in the Years 1643, 1644, 1645. Left to the World by a judicious and conscientious Author, for the use of his Friends, Children, and Grand-Children, when they come to years of discretion. . . . Printed in the Year of our Lord, M.DC.LIX. 4'', A—C in fours.

Englands Safety in the Laws Supremacy. London, Printed in the Year 1659. 4'', A—C in fours, C 4 blank.

England's Guide to Industry : Or, Improvement of Trade, for the good of all People in general. London, Printed by R. Holt for T. Passinger . . . 1683. 12'', A, 6 : B—Dd in twelves : Ee, 2.

The faithful Analist : Or, The Epitome of the English History : . . . London, Printed for W. Gilbertson in Giltspur-street. 12''. Frontispiece, title, and dedication by W. G. to Matthew Giliff, Esquire, 5 leaves : A—O in twelves.

A Collection of Papers Relating to the Present Juncture of Affairs in England. . . . Printed in the Year, 1688. 4'', A—E in fours, and a leaf of F.

> Of this Series there were twelve parts, each with separate title and signatures, printed in 1688-9. Crossley, 1885, part 2, No. 298. The sixth collection contains an account of the missions to New England.

A New History of the Succession of the Crown of England. And more particularly, From the Time of King Egbert, till King Henry the Eighth. . . . London, Printed for Ric. Chiswell. . . . MDCXC. 4'', A—I in fours.

Anglia Sacra, Sive Collectio Historiarum Partim antiquitus, partim recenter scriptarum de Archiepiscopis & Episcopis Angliæ, A prima Fidei Christianae susceptione ad Annum MDXL. Nunc primum in Lucem editarum. Pars Prima [et Secunda.] . . . Londini : . . . . MDCXCI. Folio. 2 vols.
> Edited by Henry Wharton.

ENOS, WALTER, *of Dublin, D.D., Treasurer of Ferres.*
The Second Part of the Survey of the Articles of the late Reiected Peace Wherin the Invaliditie and Nvllitie of the Said Peace is Proved. . . . Printed at Kilkenny, by permission of Superiors, and approbation of Schoolemen in the yeare, 1646. 4'', A—V in fours.

ENQUIRIES.
Curious Enquiries. Being Six Brief Discourses, Viz. 1. Of the Longitude. II. The Tricks of Astrological Quacks. III. Of the Depth of the Sea. IV. Of Tobacco. V. Of Europe being too full of People. VI. The various Opinions concerning the Time of Keeping the Sabbath. . . . London : Printed, and are to be sold by Randal Taylor, . . . 1688. 4'', A—D in fours, A 1 with *Imprimatur.*

EPISTLE.
An Epistell exhortatorye, admonishing ãd warning all faithful Christiãs to beware of the false fained God of the aulter, and only to trust in the onelye lyuing God. [About 1560.] 8'', 4 leaves. Black letter. Without title-page and signatures.

EPULARIO.
Epulario, Or, The Italian Banquet : Wherein is shewed the maner how to dresse and prepare all kind of Flesh, Foules or Fishes. As also how to make Sauces, Tartes, Pies, &c. After the maner of all Countries. With an addition of many other profitable and necessary things. Translated out of Italian into English. London, Printed by A. I. for William Barley, and are to bee sold at his shop in Grativus Street, neere Leaden - hall. 1598. 4''. B—L 3 in fours, and the title. Black letter. *B. M.*
> There is an edition of the original Italian in the British Museum, 8'', Venetia, 1549.

ERASMUS, DESIDERIUS.
Bellvm Erasmi. translated into englyshe. Londini in Aedibvs Tho. Bertheleti. An. M.D.XXXIII. Cvm Privilegio. 8'', A—E in eights.
> The date in the colophon is 1534.

A sermon of the chylde Jesus made by Erasmus to be pronounced and preached of a chylde vnto chyldren. [This is a head-line on A 2 of a volume wanting the title. At the end occurs :] Impryuted at London in Flete-strete at the sygne of y[e] George by me Robert Redman. 8'', A—C in eights.

An exhortation to the diligent studye of scripture / made by Erasmus Roterodamus. And translated into englissh. An exposition in to the seuenth chaptre of the first pistle to the Corinthians. [Col.] At Marlborow in the londe of Hesse. M.D.xxix. xx daye Junii. By my Hans Luft. 8''. Title and 7 following leaves : A, 6 : B—I in eights. With the title within the border of naked women.

Enchiridion Militis Christiani, . . . Cum

priuilegio ad imprimendum solum. [Col.] Impryuted at London in Flete strete at the Sygne of the George next to saynt Dunstons church by Wyllyam Powel. In the yere of our lord God. M.D.xlviii. The xxv. daye of October. . . . 8°, black letter, A—Q 4 in eights.

Enchiridion militis Christiani . . . Cum priuilegio . . . [Col.] Imprinted at London in Poules Churchyard at the syne of the Labe by Abraham Veale. Cum priuilegio. . . . 8°, black letter, A—U in eights, U 8 blank.

A mery Dialogue, declaringe the propertyes of shrowde shrewes, and honest wyues. Ann. M.CCCCC.LVIJ. [Col.] Imprynted at London in Paules churche yearde, at the sygne of the Sunne, by Antony kytson. 8°, black letter, A—C 4 in eights. *B. M.*

This appears to be the same impression as that with A. Vele's name as the printer.

The Colloquies. Or Familiar Discourses of Desiderius Erasmus of Rotterdam, Rendered into English. . . . By H. M. Gent. London, Printed by E. T. and R. H. for H. Brome . . . 1671. 8°, A—Nn 7 in eights, except A, which has four leaves.

The Pope Shut out of Heaven Gates: Or, A Dialogue between Pope Julius the 2ᵈ. His Genius, and Saint Peter. . . . Exactly from the Original of the Famous and Learned Erasmus Roterodamus. *Lector, Risum exhibe.* London, Printed for Roger Vaughan, . . . 1673. 4°, A—F in fours.

ERBERY, WILLIAM.
The Bishop of London, The Welsh Curate, And Common Prayers. With Apocrypha in the End. . . . Printed at London, 1652. 4°, A—F in fours, and G, 1 leaf.

Perianma Epidemion : Or, Vulgar Errours in Practice Censured. Also The Art of Oratory, Composed for the benefit of young Students. London, Printed for Richard Royston, . . . 1659. 8°, A—H in eights : *Art of Oratory,* B—I in eights, besides title and *Parts of Rhetoric,* altogether 3 leaves.

EROTOPOLIS.
Erotopolis. The Present State of Betty-Land. London, Printed for Tho. Fox, at the White Hart, over against St. Dunstan's Church . . . 1684. 12°, A—H in twelves.

EASSYS.
Two Essays. The Former Ovid. *De Arte Amandi,* Or, The Art of Love. The First

Book. The later Hero and Leander of Musaeus. From the Greek. By a Well-wisher to the Mathematicks. . . . London, Printed by T. James for Richard Northcott . . . 1682. 4°. A, 2 leaves: B—K in fours : L, 2.

ESSEX.
Forresta de Waltham alias Forresta de Essex. The Meers, Meets, Limits, and Bounds of the Forrest of Waltham, otherwise called the Forrest of Essex, in the County of Essex, as the same are found, set out, limited and bounded by Inquisition ; Taken by vertue of his Majesties Commission . . . London, Printed for L. Chapman. 1642. 4°, A—C in fours, C 4 blank.

A True Relation of a cruel Robbery and Bloody Murther, Committed on the Body of Mr John Talbot, late Curate of Lainedone in Essex, in a Garden by Anna St. Clare near Shoreditch on Friday the 2. of July 1669 . . . London, Printed for Thomas Vere . . . and John Clarke . . . 1669. 4°, 4 leaves.

A Perfect Narrative of the Robbery and Murder Committed near Dame Annis so Cleer, on Friday night, the second of July, 1669. Upon the Person of Mr John Talbot: Quondam, Preacher to a Regiment of His Majesties Forces in Portugal, and lately, since his returne, Curate of Laindon in Essex. . . . London, Printed by William Godbid. MDCLXIX. 4°. A, 3 : B—E in fours.

Treason and Murther : Or, The Bloody Father-in-Law. Being a True and Perfect Relation of a Horrible Murther. Committed at Ham, neer Stratford in Essex, on the Wife of James Alsop, ... London, Printed by E. Miles. [1674.] 4°, 4 leaves, with 2 rough cuts at the end.

Crossley, part 2, No. 325.

Treason and Murther Discovered. Being a True and Perfect Relation of the Tryal & Condemnation of James Alsop the Father, and William Alsop his Son for Treason and Murder ; At the Assizes held at Chelmsford in the County of Essex, on Wednesday the 25th of March, 1674. Also The wonderfull Discovery both of the Treason and Murder, . . . London, Printed in the Year 1674. 4°, 4 leaves. *B. M.*

The charge of treason was founded on coin-clipping. It is a curious narrative. The elder Alsop was hanged before his own house at West Ham.

Notable News from Essex, Or, A True Account of the Most Remarkable Tryal of the Person for Robbing the Famous Tinker of Tilbury. . . . To which is added A Narrative of a most lamentable Robbery in Suffolk . . . London, Printed for L. C. 1679. 4°, 4 leaves.

A full and true Account of the Penitence of John Marketman, during his Imprisonment in Chelmsford Gaol for Murthering his Wife . . . London, Printed for Samuel Walsall, . . . 1680. 4°, A—C 3 in fours : b—c in fours.

EUGENIUS PHILALETHES.
Evphrates, Or The Waters of the East ; Being a short Discourse of that Secret Fountain, whose Water flows from Fire ; and carries in it the Beams of the Sun and Moon . . . London printed for Humphrey Moseley . . . 1655. 8°, A—I 4 in eights.

EVANS, ARISE.
The Voice of Michael the Archangel, To his Highness The Lord Protector ; For the salvation of himself and the three Kingdoms. Presented by Arise Evans . . . Printed, 1653, or as the Vulgar think it, 1654. 8°, A—B in eights.

[EVERARD, JOHN, D.D.]
Somewhat written by occasion of three Suns seen at Tregnie [Tregony] in Cornwall, the twenty-second of December last ; with other memorable occurrants in other places. Imprinted [at London for Thomas Walkley.] MDCXXII. 4°, 6 leaves. B. M.

The names of the author and publisher are ascertained from the Stationers' Register.

EVERARD, MARGARET.
An Epistle of Margaret Everard to the People called Quakers, and the Ministry among them. [Col.] London, Printed for Brabazon Aylmer, at the Three Pigeons, against the Royal Exchange in Cornhill, 1699. 4°, 4 leaves.

EXPOSITIO.
Expositio Sequentiarum [ad usum Sarum. Col.] Sequentiarum seu Prosarum secundum vsum Sarum in ecclesia Anglicana per totum annum cantandarum: diligenter . . correctarum finiunt feliciter. Anno dñi Millessimo quingentessimo sexto decima die. Junii. 4°, a—k in sixes, k 6 occupied only with a repetition of the large cut on the title on the recto and the rebus and name of ANDRO MYLLAR OF EDINBURGH on the reverse. B. M.

This copy was discovered in 1869 at Paris. It was probably printed for Myllar at Rouen, prior to his commencement of business in Scotland, although these service-books were often executed abroad for well-established English typographers.

Expositio hymnorum Secūdum vsum Sarum. [Col.] Impresse Londoniis per me Richardon [sic] pynson (Impressorem nobilissime Regis gratie). . . . M. CCCCC. xv. Decima quinta die mēsis Septembris. (ii.) Expositio sequentiarum [Col.] . . Impresse Londonii per me Richardum Pynson . . . M. CCCCC. xv. Tertia die mensis Julii. 4°. The first portion, A—K, eights and fours: L, 5, including the title: the Sequences, A—I 3 in sixes.

EXPOSITIONES.
Expositiones terminorū legum anglorū. Et natura breuium cum diuersis casibus regulis & fundamentis legū tam de libris Magistri Litteltoni quā de alijs legum libris collectis et breuiter compilatis pro iuuinibus valde necessariis. [Col.] Impressum xv. die Julij. anno dñi M.V.C. xxvii. Cum priuilegio regali. 8°. *, 8 leaves: A—O in eights, O 8 with woodcuts only.

Probably from the press of John Rastell.

- - -

F.

The History of the Life, Reign, and Death of Edward II. King of England, and Lord of Ireland. With the Rise and Fall of his great Favourites, Gaveston and the Spencers. Written by E. F. in the year 1627. And Printed verbatim from the Original. Qui nescit dissimulare, nequit riuere, perire melius. London: Printed by J. C. for Charles Harper . . . 1680. Folio, A—Ss, 2 leaves each. With a portrait of Edward.

Following the title is "The Publisher to the Reader," in which he refers us to the author's Preface, which follows. It is very short, is dated 20 Feb. 1627, and is subscribed *E. F.*, initials which, in an eighteenth-century hand on the title, are explained to be *Edward Fannant.* E. F. does not throw any light on the circumstances of his authorship, save that he owns to having written the work in a month, and apologises for any errors.

The History of the most unfortunate Prince King Edward II. With Choice Political Observations on Him and his unhappy Favourites Gaveston & Spencer : Containing Several Rare Passages of those Times, not found in other Historians. Found among the Papers of, and (supposed to be) Writ by the Right Honourable Henry Viscount Faulkland, Sometime Lord Deputy of Ireland. London : Printed by A. G. and J. P. and are to be sold by John Playford . . . 1680. 8°. A, 4 : B—F in eights, F 8 blank. With a portrait of the King.

F. G.
Duell-Ease A worde with Valiant Spirrits Shewing the abuse of Duells that valour refuseth Challenges and Priuate Combates. . . . Sett foorth by G. F. a Defendour of Christian Valour. Imprinted by Anne Griffin London 1635. 4°. A, 4 : B. 1 : C—N in fours. Dedicated to Prince Charles. The title is engraved in compartments.

F. J., *a Well-wisher to Industry.*
The Golden Fleece : Or, Old England Restored to its old Honest Vocation . . . London : Printed for Langley Curtis . . . 1679. 4°, 4 leaves.

F. J.
The Merchant's Ware-house laid open : Or, The Plain Dealing Linnen-Draper. Shewing how to buy all sorts of Linnen and Indian Goods : . . . Dedicated to Her Royal Highness the Princess Anne of Denmark. London. Printed for John Sprint . . . and Geo. Conyers. . . . 1696. 12°, A—H in fours and twos alternately.

F. S.
The Female Advocate : Or, An Answer to a Late Satyr against the Pride, Lust and Inconstancy of Woman. Written by a Lady in Vindication of her Sex. London : Printed by H. C. for John Taylor, . . . 1687. 4°, A—D 2 in fours. In verse.

F., SIR T.
The Practice of the Exchequer Court, With its severall Offices and Officers. Being a short Narration of the Power and Duty of each single Person in his severall Place. Written at the request of the Lord Buckhurst, sometime Lord Treasurer of England. Whereunto are added

the Rules and Orders of Proceedings by English Bill. London, Printed by T. R. for Tho. Twyford and W. Place, . . . 1658. 8°. Title and to the Reader, 2 leaves : B—M 6 in eights.

F. T.
A Defence of the Catholyke Cavse, Contayning a Treatise in Confvtaton of Svndry Vntrvthes and Slanders, published by the heretykes, . . . With an Apology, or Defence, of his Innocency in a Fayned Conspiracy against hir Maiesties person, . . . Imprinted with licence 1602. 4°. Title and Table, 2 leaves : A—S in fours : the *Apology*, with a new title, A—O in fours.

This *Apology* has reference to the alleged conspiracy of Edward Squire.

FAGE, MARY, *Wife of Robert Fage the younger, Gentleman.*
Fames Royle : Or, The Names of our dread Soveraigne Lord King Charles, his Royall Queen Mary, and his most hopefull posterity : Together with, The names of the Dukes, Marquesses, Earles, Viscounts, Bishops, Barons, Privie Counsellors, Knights of the Garter, and Judges. Of his thrice renowned Kingdomes, England, Scotland, and Ireland : Anagrammatiz'd and expressed by acrosticke lines on their names. London, Printed by Richard Oulton, 1637. 4°. A, 3 leaves, title on A 2 : ¶, 2 leaves : B—Pp in fours, and after Pp 4 a leaf [p. 297] unsigned. Dedicated to the King, &c.

FAGE, ROBERT.
A Description of the whole World, With some General Rules touching the use of the Globe, Wherein is contained the situation of several Countries . . . Very delightful to be read in so small a Volume. By Robert Fage, Esq. . . . London, Printed by J. Owsley, and sold by Peter Stent, at the White-horse in Guilt-spur-street, between Newgate and Pye-corner, 1658. 8°, A—E 4 in eights, besides a frontispiece.

FAIRFAX, SIR THOMAS.
A Declaration from his Excellence Sir Thomas Fairfax, and the Generall Councel of the Army, Held at Putney, on Thursday Septemb. 16. 1647. Concerning the Delaies in raising Monies for supply of the Army, and other Forces of the Kingdome. . . . Printed at London, for George Whittington, at the Blew Anchor, in Cornhill, neere the Royall Exchange, 1647. 4°, A—B in fours, B 3—4 blank.

A Declaration of His Excellency the Lord Generall Fairfax. Concerning the Supply of Bedding Required from the City of London For the lodging of the Army in voyd houses to prevent the Quartering of Souldiers upon any the Inhabitants. . . . London, Printed by John Macock, for John Partridge. 1648. 4°, 4 leaves.

A Letter from His Excellency the Lord Fairfax to the House of Peers, upon Munday being the fifth of June, 1648. concerning all the proceedings in Kent: With Severall Papers found in the pockets of some that are now taken Prisoners, discovering the whole Designe . . . Imprinted at London for Iohn Wright, . . . 1648. 4°, A—B 2 in fours.

FANATICS.
Semper Iidem : Or A Parallel betwixt the Ancient and Modern Phanaticks. . . . London: Printe l for Richard Lownds, . . . 1662. 4°, A—C in fours.

FARTHING, JOHN.
The Excise Rectified : Or, A Plain Demonstration. That The Revenue now raised thereby, is capable of being Improved at least Four or Five Hundred Thousand Pounds *per Annum*. . . . London, Printed, 169⅝. 4°, A—B in fours.

To the Honourable the Knights, Citizens and Burgesses, in Parliament Assembled. [1703.] A folio leaf respecting his former tract, subscribed *John Farthing*.

FARTHING TOKENS.
A Remedie against the losse of the Subject, By Farthing-Tokens : Discovering the great abuses of them heretofore : and the Prevention of the like hereafter : . . . London, Printed for Thomas Bates, . . . 1644. 4°, 4 leaves.

FASCICULUS.
Fasciculus Chemicus ; Or Chymical Collections. Expressing The Ingress, Progress, and Egress, of the Secret Hermetick Science, out of the choicest and most Famous Authors. . . . Whereunto is added, The Arcanum or Grand Secret of Hermetick Philosophy. Both made English By James Hasolle, Esquire . . . London, Printed by J. Flesher for Richard Mynne . . . 1650. 8°. Title and frontispiece, 2 leaves : * *, 8 leaves : A—R in eights : S, 6 leaves.

FEATLEY, D.
La Malette de David, Ou sont encloses trente deux excellentes Prieres, . . . Recueillies des œuvres du Sr Featley, Docteur en Theologie, & mises en François par Guillaume Herbert. Quatriesme Edition reueuë & corrigée. Se vend a Charenton, par Samvel Petit, . . . M.DC.

XXXXIIII. 12", A—P in eights : Q, 12 leaves.

The Dippers dipt. Or, The Anabaptists Duck'd and Plung'd . . . . The Sixth Edition, augmented with 1. Severall Speeches delivered before this Assembly of Divines. 2. The famous History of the frantick Anabaptists . . . . London, Printed by Richard Cotes for N. B. and Richard Royston . . . 1651. 4°, A—Mm in fours. With a portrait by W. Marshall, 1645.

A 1 is occupied by an engraved title by Marshall, representing the Anabaptists being dipped, with small portraitures round it of various sects.

FELGHENERE, PAULUS.
Postilion. Or a New Almanacke and Astrologicke, prophetical, Prognostication calculated for the whole World, and all Creatures, and what the Issue or Event will be of the English Warres, . . . translated into English, in the year 1655. . . . London ; Printed by M. S. for H : Crips and Lodo : Lloyd, . . . 1655. 4°, A—H in fours : Advertisements, 2 leaves.

FELIBIEN, M.
The Tent of Darius Explain'd ; Or The Queens of Persia at the Feet of Alexander. Translated from the French of Mr Felibien. By Collonel Parsons. London, Printed by William Redmayne for the Author, in the Old Palace Westminster, MDCCIII. Folio. Title and half-title. 2 leaves : dedication by Col. William Parsons to the Nobility and Gentry, 2 leaves : *, 4 leaves : A—N, 2 leaves each. Fr. and Engl.

FELTHAM, OWEN.
Resolves A Duple Century y° 4th Edition. By Owen Feltham wth a large Alphabetical Table thervnto . . . London Imprinted for Henry Seile . . . 1631. 4°. A, 4 leaves : B—Ff in eights : Gg—Hh in fours. Dedicated to Thomas, Lord Coventry.

FENWICKE, JOHN. *Senior, Master of the Hospital of Sherburn House, near Durham.* Englands Deliverer. The Lord of Hosts Her strong God, none like to Him. . . . In some Exercises upon the Thanksgiving for that late Memorable Victory at Dunbar in Scotland, Sept. 3. 1650 . . . Newcastle, Printed by S. B. 1651. 4°, A—C in fours, C 3-4 occupied by a Song of Sion.

FESTIVAL.
Incipit liber qui vocatur festiualis de nouo correctus & ipressus rothom. [Colo-

phon at end of *Festival:*] Finitum et
completum extat hoc opusculū In celeberrima vrbe Rothomagensi / per Magistrum
Martinum Morin. Anno Domini Millesimo quadringentesimo nonagesimonono /
die vero vicesima secunda mensis Junii /
impensis Johannis Richardi. 4°, a—z
in eights, and (probably) 2½ sheets of
eight after z, including the *Quatuor Sermones*, which commence on x 7.

> Quaritch, June 1885, No. 73, last leaf
> deficient. In this edition of an English
> service-book the second leaf of each signature is unmarked, the third being signed ij.

[Liber Festivalis. Col.] Finitum & cōpletū p Julianū notarii cōmorantē Apud
Westmonasterium. Anno incarnationis
dñi. M. cccc. Nonagesimonono Secūdo
die mensis Januarii. 4°, printed in two
columns, a—s in eights: t, 6: v, 5.

> Osterley Park Sale, May 1885, No. 662.
> I have not yet seen a copy of this *quarto*
> London edition of 1499 with the title. It
> is quite distinct from the Rouen one of the
> same date and size.

FIALETTI, ODOARDO. *of Bologna.*

The Whole Art of Drawing, Painting,
Limning, and Etching. Collected out of
the Choicest Italian and German Authors.
To which is added Exact Rules of Proportion for Drawing the Heads of Men
Women and Children, of what Bigness
soever. . . . Published for the Benefit of
all Ingenuous Gentlemen and Artists, by
Alexander Brown Practitioner. London,
Printed for Peter Stent . . . and Simon
Miller . . . M.DC.LX. Obl. 8°. Frontispiece, 1 leaf : title, 1 leaf : dedication by
Brown to Sir William Paston, 1 leaf :
Contents, 1 leaf : the book, pp. 1-54,
not including a leaf with children's heads.
A—F are marked, and pp. 44-8 are misplaced or misprinted. With engravings
counting in the pagination, except the
last leaf.

FIELD, JOHN.

A godlie exhortation, by occasion of the
late iudgement of God, Shewed at Parisgarden, the thirteenth day of Ianuarie :
where were assembled by estimation
about a thousand persons, whereof some
were shaine ; & of that number, at the
least, as is crediblie reported, the thirde
person maimed and hurt. Giuen to all
estates for their instruction concerning
the keeping of the Sabbath day. By
Iohn Field, Minister of the word of God.
. . . At London ; Printed by Robert
Walde-graue, dwelling without Templebarre, for Henry Carre in Paules Church-

yard. [1584.] 8°, black letter, A—C 4
in eights.

> Sothebys, March 31, 1882, No. 402, the
> date partly cut off.

FIESCHI, OTTOBONE.

Incipiunt opera super cōstitutiones prouinciales et Othonis. [This is over a cut
of a bishop with a crozier, enclosed in a
border of small pieces. At the end :]
Explicinnt constitutiones . . . Impresse
London. per me wynandum de worde in
the fletestrete insigno solis commorantem.
Anno dñi. M.cccc.viii. 8°, A—M in
eights. With the printer's mark on M 8
verso. B. M.

FILMER, SIR ROBERT.

The Free-holders Grand Inquest, Touching Our Sovereign Lord the King and
His Parliament. To which are added
Observations upon Forms of Government.
. . . London, Printed in the Year
MDCLXXIX. 8°, A—Aa 4 in eights, A 1
and Aa 4 blank.

The Power of Kings : And in particular
of the Kings of England. Learnedly
Asserted by Sir Robert Filmer, Kt. With
a Preface of a Friend : Giving an Account
of the Author and his Works. *In Magnis
voluisse sat est.* London : Printed for
W. H. & T. F. and are to be sold by
Walter Davis 1680. Folio, A—D, 2 leaves
each.

Patriarcha : Or The Natural Power of
Kings. By the Learned Sir Robert Filmer, Baronet. . . . London, Printed, and
are to be sold by Walter Davis Bookbinder, in Amen-Corner, . . . 1680. 8°,
A—K in eights, first and last leaves
blank. With a prefatory letter from Peter
Heylin to the author's son, Sir Edward
Filmer. With a portrait by Van Hove.

FINCH, EDWARD.

An Answer to the Articles Prefer'd
against Edward Finch, Vicar of ChristChurch, by some of the Parishioners of
the same. Whereunto is added a just
and modest Reply, to a most Scurrilous,
Scandalous, and Malicious Pamphlet (as
by the Title may appeare) of an uncertaine Avthor. By Edward Finch, Vicar
aforesaid. Printed in the Yeare, 1641.
4°, A—D in fours.

FINCH, HENEAGE, *Earl of Winchelsea.*

A True and Exact Relation of the Late
Prodigious Earthquake & Eruption of
Mount Ætna, Or Monte-Gibello, As it
came in a Letter Written to His Majesty
from Naples. By the Right Honorable
The Earle of Winchilsea, . . . Printed by

T. Newcomb in the Savoy. 1669. 4°, A—D in fours, D 4 blank. With a plate.

FIRMIN, THOMAS.
Some Proposals for the imployment of the Poor, and for the prevention of Idleness and the Consequences thereof, Begging. . . . In a Letter to a Friend by T. F. . . . London, Printed by J. Grover, and are to be sold by Francis Smith . . . 1681. 4°, A—F in fours, besides the frontispiece representing a woman at a spinning-wheel.

FISH, SIMON.
Klagbrief oder supplication der arman dúrífrigen in Engenlandt / . . . M.D.XXIX. 4°, a—b in fours : c, 2 leaves : D, 4.
Without any place and printer's name.

FISHER, JOHN, *Bishop of Rochester.*
Reuerendi patris Joannis Fisscher Roffensis in Anglia Episcopi, necnon Cambrigieñ. academię Cancellarii Dignissimi, de vnica Magdalena, Libri tres. Venüdatur in ędibus Iodoci Badii Ascēsii eorũdem impressoris. . . . [Col.] Finis in ædibus Iodoci Badii Ascensii, Ad octauũ Calendas Martias. MDXIX. 4°, A—F in eights : G, 6.

FISHER, PAYNE.
Turenodia Triumphalis, In Obitum Serenissimi Nostri Principis Olivari. . . . Per Fitzpaynæum Piscatorem. Londini, Excudebat Ja: Cottrel. MDCLVIII. Folio. Leaf with dedication to Richard Cromwell, and A—D, 2 leaves each : E, 1 leaf.

FITTON, ALEXANDER.
A true Account of the Unreasonableness of Mʳ Fitton's Pretences against the Earl of Macclesfield. [1686 ?] Folio, A—B, 2 leaves each.

FIT JOHN, JOHN.
A Diamonde most Precious, worthy to be marked. Instructing all Maysters and Seruauntes, how they ought to leade their lyues, in that Vocation which is fruitfull, and necessary, as well for the Maysters, as also for the Seruants, agreeable vnto the holy Scriptures.

> Reade me ouer, and then iudge,
> If I be not well, then grudge :
> Thinke well of him that mee made,
> For Gods worde shall neuer fade.

[Quot. from Rom. 10.] Imprinted at London, in Fleetestreate, beneath the Conduite, at the Signe of S. John Euaungelist, by Hugh Iackson. 1577. 4°. black letter, A—O 2 in fours. Dedicated to the Masters and Wardens of the City Companies. *B. M.*

A very curious dialogue between CIVIS

and PUER, in which, amid a good deal of Scriptural quotation, there is much valuable and interesting matter connected with Elizabethan life and opinions.

FITZGEFFREY, CHARLES.
The Curse of Corne-horders : With the Blessing of seasonable Selling, in three Sermons, on Pro. 11. 16. Begun at the general Sessions For the County of Cornwall, held at Bodmyn, and continued at Fowy. By Charles Fitz-Geffrie. . . . Printed at London by I. B. for Michael Sparke. 1631. 4°, A—H in fours. Inscribed to Sir Reginald Mohun, Bart.

FITZGEFFREY, HENRY, *of Lincoln's Inn.*
Satyres : And Satyricall Epigrams : With Certaine Obseruations at Black-Fryers ? By H: F: of Lincolnes - Inne Gent : Horat: Serm: Lib. 1.——*Nil mi officit vnquam* . . . London Printed by Edw : All-de, for Miles Patrich, and are to be sold at his shop neare St. Dunstons-Church in Fleet-street. 1617. 8°, A—G in eights, A 1 and G 8 blank, and G 7 with the *Errata.*
Osterley Park Sale, 1885, in lot 703.

FITZHERBERT, A.
The Boke of Hvsbandry. [Col.] Imprynted at London in fletestrete in the house of Thomas Berthelet, nere to the condite at the sygne of Lucrece. Cum priuilegio. [Circâ 1535.] 8°. A, 6 leaves : B—N 2 in eights. The title is in the border with 1534 in the sell.

FLATMAN, THOMAS.
Montelion, 1661. Or, The Prophetical Almanack : Being, A true and exact Accompt of all the Revolutions, that are to happen in the World this present year, 1661. Till this time Twelve Moneth. By Montelion, Knight of the Oracle, a Well-wisher to the Mathematicks.—— *Sapiens Dominabitur Astris.* London, Sold by Henry Marsh, . . . 8°, A—C in eights, including a frontispiece. With cuts.

FLAVELL, JOHN.
Husbandry Spiritualized. Or The Heavenly Use of Earthly Things. Consisting of many Pleasant Observations, Pertinent Applications, . . . By John Flavel, late Minister of the Gospel in Devon. London, Printed in the Year, 1669. 4°. Title, 1 leaf : [*], 4 leaves : [**], 4 leaves : B—Mm in fours.

FLEMING, ABRAHAM.
The Diamond of Deuotion : Cut and squared into six seuerall points : . . . Printed at London for the Company of

Stationers. 1608. 12°, A—O 10 in twelves. Black letter, printed within borders.

> This volume comprises six tracts : *The Footpath to Felicity, A Guide to Godliness, The School of Skill, A Swarm of Bees. A Plant of pleasure, A Grove of Graces.* The whole is dedicated to Sir George Cary, Knight Marshal of the Queen's Household.

FLEMING, ROBERT.

The Mirrour of Divine Love Unvail'd, In a Poetical Paraphrase of the High and Mysterious Song of Solomon. Whereunto is added a Miscellany of several other Poems, Sacred and Moral. Together with some few Pindariques in the close. By Robert Fleming. jun. V.D.M. . . . London, Printed by J. A. for John Salusbury, at the Rising Sun in Cornhill. 1691. 8°, A—Hh in eights, Hh 8 blank, and a, 4 leaves. With a frontispiece.

> The Paraphrase of the Song of Solomon has a separate inscription to Mrs. Susanna Soame, Spouse to Bartholomew Soame of Thurlow, Esquire, to whom Fleming appears to have been at one time chaplain.

Three Elegies : The First, to the Memory of Lieutenant - Generall Mackay. The Second, to the Memory of My Lord Angus, Only Son of the Marquiss of Dowglas. The Third, to the Memory of Lieut. Collonel Fullerton. Who were all Three Slain, at the Attacque at Steenkerken near Enguise . . . Anno Dom. 1692. Written by Ro. Fleming. Edinburgh, Printed in the Year 1692. 4°, 6 leaves,

FLETCHER, GILES, *the Elder.*

The History of Russia, Or The Government of the Emperour of Muscovia. . . . By G. Fletcher, . . . London, Printed by Roger Daniel for William Hope and Edward Farnham near the Exchange. 1657. 12". Frontispiece by W. Marshall, dated 1643, printed title, and Table, 4 leaves : A—M 8 in twelves.

> This seems to be the edition of 1643, with a printed title dated 1657 added to the unsold stock.

FORBES, JOHN.

The Mariner's everlasting Almanack. Wherein is set down diverse Motions of the Moon, with Rules and Tables for finding her Age . . . And Lastly, A pleasant Dialogue, containing some Orthographicall and Steriographicall Questions, . . . Calculated for the Latitude of 57 Degrees 10 minuts. By John Forbes Printer to Bon-Accord. & Philomat. The Second Edition, much Corrected and Enlarged. Aberdeen, Printed by the Author, . . . Anno 1683. 8°, A—Il 2 in fours. Dedicated to Captain John Tyler of Leith.

FORD, EMANUEL.

The First Part of Parismvs, the Renowmed Prince of Bohemia. . . . London Printed by Thomas Creede. 1615. (ii.) Parismenos. The Second Part . . . The fourth time Imprinted and amended. London, Printed by Thomas Creede. 1615. 4°, black letter, A—P in eights, A 1 and P 8 blank, and A—R 4 in eights, A 1 blank. *B. M.*

> Sothebys, July 17, 1883, No. 315.

The Most Famovs, Delectable, and pleasant Historie of Parismvs, . . . London. Printed by B. Alsop and T. Fawcet, and are to be sold by T. Alchorne, . . . 1630. 4°, black letter. Part 1, A—P 4 in eights, A 1 with the frontispiece : Part 2, A—T 4 in eights, T 4 with the colophon.

FORD, SIMON.

Londini Renascentis Imago Poetica. Ad Serenissimum Britanniarum Monarcham Carolum II. Londini Excudebat A. M. pro Sa: Gellibrand, 1668. 4°, A—C in fours repeated. Lat. and Engl.

> The Latin portion is dated 1669. The two were printed together.

A Discourse Concerning God's Judgments : Resolving many weighty Questions and Cases relating to them. Preached (for the substance of it) at Old Swinford in Worcestershire. (And now Published to accompany the Annexed Narrative concerning the Man whose Hands and Legs lately Rotted off, in the neighbouring Parish of Kings-Swinford in Staffordshire, Penned by another Author. By Simon Ford, D.D. and Rector of Old Swinford. London, Printed for Hen. Brome, . . . 1678. 12°, A—F 6 in twelves.

> The *Narrative* by James Illingworth has a separate title. The volume is dedicated by Ford to his friends Thomas Foley of Kidderminster, and Philip Foley of Prestwood-Hall.

FORD, THOMAS, *Minister of the Gospel in Exeter.*

Singing of Psalmes the Duty of Christians under the New Testament . . . London, Printed by A. M. for Christopher Meredith, . . . 1653. 8°, A—L 4 in eights.

FOULIS, HENRY, *M.A. of Lincoln College, Oxford.*

The History of the Wicked Plots and Conspiracies of our Pretended Saints : Representing the Beginning, Constitution, and Designs of the Jesuite. . . . With the Conspiracies . . . of some Presbyterians :

... The second Edition. Oxford: Printed by Hen: Hall for Ric. Davis M.DCLXXIV. Folio. A, 4 leaves, besides one before title with a memoir of Foulis: (b) 3 leaves: B—Ii in fours.

> Dedicated to his brother, Sir David Foulis of Ingleby Manor in Cleveland, and the Lady Catharine, his wife.

FOULIS or FOLLIS, JAMES.

Jacobi follisii Edinburgensis calamitose pestis Elega deploratio. Eiusdem ad diceam Margaritam reginam sapphicum carmen . . . et alia quedam carmina. Venale inuenitur hoc opusculum apud Egidium gourmötium e regione collegij cameracēsis. 4°, A—E in fours.

[FOWLER, E.]

Dirt Wipt oft: or A manifest Discovery of the Gross Ignorance, Erroneousness and most Unchristian and Wicked Spirit of one John Bunyan, Lay-Preacher in Bedford, which he hath shewed in a Vile Pamphlet Publisht by him, against the Design of Christianity. . . . London, Printed by R. N. for Richard Royston . . . MDCLXXII. 4°, A—L 3 in fours.

FOWLER, J., *Secretary to Sir George Douglas.*

The History of the Troubles of Suethland and Poland, which occasioned the Expulsion of Sigismundus the Third, King of those Kingdomes, with his Heires for ever from the Suethish Crown. With a Continuation of those Troubles, untill the Truce, An. 1629. As also, a particular Narrative of the daily Passages at the last and great Treaty of Pacification . . . 1635. Concluding with a Breife Commemoration of the Life and Death of Sʳ George Dvglas Knight, Lord Ambassadour Extraordinary from the late King of Great Brittaine, for the Treaty above mentioned. London, Printed by Thomas Roycroft for Thomas Dring, . . . 1656. Folio. Title, 1 leaf: dedication to the Protector, 1 leaf: B—C, 2 leaves each: D—3 U, 2 leaves each. With eight portraits after Cecill, Gaywood, &c.

FOX, GEORGE.

The Priests Fruits Made manifest. And the Fashions of the world, And the Lust of Ignorance: Also, A few Words to the City of London. G. F. London, Printed for Thomas Simmons . . . 1657. 4°, 4 leaves.

FOX, JOHN.

Christ Iesvs Triumphant. A fruitefull Treatise, wherin is described the most glorious Triumph, and Conquest of Christ Iesus our Saniour, . . . Made to be read for spirituall comfort, by Iohn Foxe, and from Latin translated intoo English by the Printer. . . . At London, Printed by Iohn Daye, and Richard his Sonne, dwelling at Aldersgate. 1579. Cum Gratia . . . 8°, A—E in eights. With a dedication by Richard Day the translator to Mr. William Killigrew, Gentleman of her Majesty's Privy Chamber.

FOXHUNTING.

The Fox-Hunting. [London, about 1670.] A broadside in 4-line stanzas, with a burden and the musical stave. In three columns. *B. M.*

FRANCE.

The Edict or Proclamation set forthe by the Frenche Kinge vpon the pacifying of the troubles in Fraunce, with the Articles of the same Pacification Read and published in the presence of the sayd King, sitting in his Parliament, the xiiij. day of May, 1576. Translated out of Frenche by Arthvr Golding. Cvm Privilegio. Imprinted at London by Thomas Vautrollier dwelling in the Blacke Friers. [1576.] 8°, A—H in fours. *B. M.*

L'Histoire Et Discovrs av Vray Dv Siege qvi Fvt mis devant la Ville d'Orleans, par les Anglois, le Mardi 12. iour d'Octobre 1428. regnant alors Charles VII. de ce nom Roy de Fráce. . . . Imprime a Paris, . . . M.D.LXXVII. . . . 4°. ã, 4 leaves, with the Editor, Saturny Hotton's dedication: A—N 2 in fours.

> This purports to be faithfully printed from a vellum MS. found in a house at Orleans.

L'Histoire . . . A Orleans, . . . 1606 . . . 8°. *, 4 leaves: A—O 4 in eights, besides a frontispiece containing the conventional portrait of Joan of Arc.

A Briefe discourse of the merueylous victorie gotten by the King of Nauarre, against those of the holy League, on the twentieth of October. 1587. Both in English, and in French as it was printed in Fraunce. London Printed by Iohn Wolfe dwelling in Distaffe Lane neare the signe of the Castle. 1587. 8°, black letter, 8 leaves.

A necessary Discourse concerning the right which the house of Guyse pretendeth to the Crowne of France. Faithfully translated out of the French. At London, Imprinted for Edward Aggas. 1588. 8°, A—B 4 in eights. *B. M.*

The French Kinges Declaration vpon the Riot, Felonie, and Rebellion of the Dvke of Mayenne, & the Duke and Knight of

Aumalle, and all their assistantes. Wherunto is adioyned Another Declaration of the same King, against the townes of Paris, Orleance, Amyeus, and Abbenile and their adherentes. Faithfully translated out of the French. Printed at London, for Thomas Cadman, 1589. 4°, A—C in fours, first and last leaves blank.

Newes from France. Where Monsieur de Liguiers in the Kings behalfe, most brauely discomfited the Armie of the King of Spaine and the Pope, consisting of ten thousand strong, being Neapolitans, Spaniards, Sauoians and Burgonians. . . . With some notes and newes from Deruerne in Holland. London Printed by Thomas Scarlet for William Wright. 4°, 4 leaves.

This tract is in the shape of a letter from the writer to his kinsman, but no names appear.

Le Vray Discovrs de la victoire merueilleuse obtenue par le Roy de France et de Nauarre Henry 4. En la battaile donnée contre les rebelles ligués pres le bourg d'Yury en la plaine S. André, le 14. de Mars l'an 1590. Dressé et ennoyé par deça par vn des principaux Officiers de sa Maiesté. . . . A Londres Par Thomas Owrin [Orwin], pour Thomas Man, demourant a Pater noster-row. [1591.] 4°, A—E [?] in fours. B. M. (imperfect at end.)

Ordinances Set foorth by the King, for the rule and gouernement of his Maiesties men of warre. Read and published at Caen the 30. of March. 1591. Faithfully translated out of the French Coppie Printed at Caen by E. A. London Printed by John Wolfe, . . . 1591. 4°, 4 leaves. B. M.

Bref Advertissement de Monsievr L'Evesqve d Evrevx a ses diocesains, contre vn pretendu Arrest donné à Caen le 28. de Mars dernier, par lequel il appert de l'introduction & establissement en France, du schisme, heresie, & tyrannie d'Angleterre. . . . A Paris, . . . 1591. 8°, A—D in fours.

A Proposition of the Princes, Prelats, Officers, Officers of the Crowne, & others of his Maiesties Councell, propounded to the Duke of Mayenne, and other his adherents, assembled in the Cittie of Paris. With the Kings declaration against the sayd assembly and rebells, published at Caen in the parliament the three and twenteth of Februarie last. Both which were printed in Caen by the kings printer

in French. London Imprinted by Iohn Wolfe. 1593. 4°, A—E 2 in fours. B. M.

The Decree of the Court of Parliament against Iohn Chastel, Scholler, Student in the Colledge of the Iesuites, vpon the Parricide by him attempted against the Kings person. Also for the banishment of the whole societie of the said Iesuits out of France and al the Kings Dominions, Withal containing a prohibition, not to sende their children to any Colledge of the saide societie. Faithfullie translated out of the French Copy . . . London Printed by Thomas Creede, for Thomas Millington, . . . 1595. 4°, A—B 2 in fours, A 1 blank. B. M.

A Discovrse of the Conference holden before the French King at Fontainebleau, betweene the L. Bishop of Eureux, and Munsieur du Plessis L. of Mornay, the 4. of May 1600. Concerning certaine pretended corruptions of Authors, cyted by the sayd Munsieur du Plessis in his booke against the Masse. Faithfully translated out of the French. London, Printed by E. A. for Mathew Selman and William Ferbrand, and are to be solde in Flete-streete, next the Inner Temple gate. 1600. 4°, B—H in fours, and the title.

The Voluntarie Confession and Severall Recantations, of foure great learned men, professed Fryers in sundry Monasteries of Fraunce. from the Errovrs of Idolatrie and Poperie, to the true Religion established in the Reformed Church. . . . All conuerted this last year, 1603. as their seuerall discourses following at large doe testifie, vnder their owne hands. Truely translated out of the French printed Copies. Imprinted at London by Richard Bradocke, for W. Iones, . . . and are to be solde by W. Aspley in Paules Churchyard. 1604. 4°, A—G 2 in fours. Dedicated, probably by the translator, "To his Worthilie Respected Kinde Friend, Master George Gibson, Citizen and Marchant Taylor of London."

The names of the four Friars are John Le Vager, John Forent, Denis Boucher, and Daniel Dusert.

The View of Fraunce. London printed by Symon Stafford, 1604. 4°, B—Y 2 in fours, and the title, besides a folded pedigree of the descendants of St. Louis. B. M.

The Fvnerall Pompe and Obseqvies of the Most mighty and puissant Henry the fourth, . . . Together with the order and ceremonie of remouing the body of Henry, the third of that name, . . . Faithfully translated out of the French Coppy . . . . London, Printed by Nicholas Okes, . . . 1610. 4°, A—C 2 in fours. *B. M.*

A Trve Relation of the Conferences and Proceedings concerning the peace and mutuall agreements betweene the King of France, and the Prince of Conde . . . . London, Printed by Edward Griffin, for Nathaniel Butter, . . . 1616. 4°, A—E in fours. *B. M.*

The Association of the Princes of France, With the Protestations and Declarations of their Allegeance to the King. Also A Discovrse vpon the Svrrender of the Seales into the Kings hands by M. du Vaiz. [Translated from the French.] London Printed for William Barret. 1617. 4°, A—E in fours, E 4 blank.

The French Kings Declaration against the Dukes of Vendosme and Mayenne, The Marshall of Bouillon, the Marques of Coeuure, the President le Iay, and all who assist them. Verified in the Covrt of Parlement the 13. of February, 1617. Stilo Nouo. London Printed for William Barret. 1617. 4°, A—F in fours. *B. M.*

Newes out of France : Concerning great troubles likely to ensue, by occasion of the departure of the Queene Mother from Blois : And the causes thereof. Contayned in the Letters of the said Queene Mother, vnto her Sonne the French King, ... Faithfully translated . . . London : Printed by T. S. for Nathanael Newbery, . . . 1619. 4°, A—D 2 in fours, D 2 blank, and A 1-2 repeated. *B. M.*

Articles Conclvded and Agreed vpon by the Lords, the Cardinalls, de la Roche-Foucaud, and de Bethune, in the name of the King of France, to the Queene Mother. Together with certaine Letters . . . Translated out of the French Copie. Printed by G. E. for George Fairebeard, . . . 1619. 4°, B—C in fours, besides the title and portrait of Louis XIII., two leaves more. *B. M.*

The Remonstrance made by the Queene-mother of France, to the King her Sonne, for remedy of such disorders and abuses as She pretendeth to be in the present Gouernement and managing of affaires of State, in the Realme of France. . . . Faithfully translated out of French. London : Printed by T. S. for Nathanaell Newbery, . . . 1619. 4°, A—C 2 in fours, A 1 blank. *B. M.*

A Declaration Made and published by the King of France, Whereby the Princes, Dukes, and Barons therein named, are all proclaymed Traytors, if within one moneth after the publication thereof, they doe not ceasse from Armes, . . . Faithfully translated . . . 1620. 4°, A—B in fours, A 1 blank. *B. M.*

The Late Newes from France : Being an Important Remonstrance or admonition to the King of France, concerning the disordered affaires of that Estate at this present. Faithfully Translated . . . M. D. C. XX. 4°, A—B in fours. *B. M.*

Letters Patents made by the French King, declaring his intent touching those of the Reformed Religion . . . With two Letters of the Assembly at Rochell vnto the Duke de Lesdiguieres. Printed MDCXXI. 4°, A—C in fours. *B. M.*

Newes from France. A true Relation of the great losses which happened by the lamentable accident of fire in the Citie of Paris, the 24. day of October last past, 1621. Which burnt down the Merchants Bridge, the Changers Bridge, . . . [Translated from the French.] London, Printed for R. R. at the Golden Lyon in Paules Churchyard. 1621. 4°, A—B in fours. *B. M.*

A Declaration made by the Reformed Chvrches of France and the Principalitie of Bearn, concerning their vniust persecution by the Enemies of the Estate and of their Religion. Together with their lawfull and necessarie defence. According to the French Copie printed in Rochell. M.DC.XXI. 4°, A—E in fours.

The 4. of November. The Peace of France. Or, The Edict, with the Articles of Peace, granted by the French King vnto his Subiects of the Reformed Religion . . . the nineteenth day of October. 1622. Faithfully Translated out of the French Copie. London, Printed by I. D. for Nathaniel Newbery, . . . 1622. 4°, A—B in fours, A 1 blank : the French Proclamation, 4 leaves under sign. A without any title. *B. M.*

The Reqvests Presented vnto the French King, By the General Deputies of the Reformed Churches of France. Together with his Maiesties Answers thereunto. London, Printed for Nathaniel Butter and William Sheffard. 1623. 4°. A—C 2 in fours, A 1 blank.

The French Kings Edict vpon the Peace which it pleased his Majestie to grant vnto all those of the Reformed Religion within his seuerall Dominions, Including likewise those of Rochell. . . . . Printed for Mercurius Britannicus. 1626. 4°, A—B in fours.

The Apologie of the Reformed Chvrches of France. Wherein are expressed the Reasons, why they haue loyned their Armies ; to those of the King of Great Brittaine. Translated according to the French Coppie. London, Printed for Nathaniell Butter. 1628. 4°, A—H in fours. Dedicated by the translator John Reynolds to the English Parliament.

A Declaration of the Qveene, Mother of the most Christian King. Containing the reasons of her departure out of the Low-Countreys; And disadvowing a Manifest, set out in her Name vpon the same Argument. London, Printed by John Raworth, for Joshua Kirton and Thomas Warren, . . . 1639. 4°, A—C 2 in fours, A 1 blank and C 2 with the *Imprimatur*.

The Ecclesiasticall Discipline of the Reformed Churches in France Or, The Order whereby they are governed. Faithfully transcribed into English out of a French Copy. London : Printed by E. P. for Nicholas Bourne, . . . 1642. 4°. Title and Index, 2 leaves : A—F in fours.

A Warning peece for London Being A True Relation of the Bloody Massacre of the Protestants in Paris, by the Papists and Cavaleers : . . London, Printed for Joseph Hunscott, 1642. 4°, A—F in fours.

Articles Agreed by the Duke d'Angvjou, Lieutenant Generall of the Kings Army in Flanders, and Luxemburgh, to the Marquesse De Leden, for the rendition of Dunkirke . . . to the King of France. Also, A Letter from Chester, . . . And the last Newes from Ireland. London Printed by E. E. 1646. 4°, 4 leaves.

Remarqves Svr la Reddition de Dvnkerqve Entre les Mains Des Anglois. A Paris, . . . M.DC.LVIII. . . 4°, a—c 2 in fours.

Memoire Presenté av Serenissime Protecteur, par le Marquis de Leyde, & Dom Alonse de Cardenas, Ambassadeurs du Roy Catholique en Angleterre, le vingt-vniesme de May mil six cent cinquante-cinq. A Paris, . . . M.DC.LVIII. . . 4°, A—E 2 in fours.

Negotiations de Paix de Messievrs les Electevrs de Mayence et de Coloigne Faites à Francfort par leurs Altesses,

Entre M' Le Mareschal Dvc de Grandmont et M' de Lionne. Ambassadevrs Extraordinaires . . . de France Et M' Le Comte de Pegnaranda Ambassadevr . . . d'Espagne. En 1658. A Paris, . . . M.DC.LIX. 12°. A, 6: B—M in twelves: N, 6.

This also relates to the treaty for the surrender of Dunkirk to England.

An Answer to the French Declaration. London, Printed for the Author, 166⅜. A broadside in verse.

A Brief Relation of the Persecution and Sufferings of the Reformed Churches in France. Translated out of French, . . . London, Printed by A. Maxwell, 1668. 4°, A—C in fours.

Memoires of Henry D. of Guise, Relating his Passage to Naples, and heading there the Second Revolt of that People, Englished . . . . London, Printed by T. N. for H. Herringman, . . . 1669. 8°, A—Pp in eights, Pp 8 with the Errata, A 1 blank, and A 2 with the *Imprimatur*.

With a Preface and a Character of the Guise by a Person of Quality. But neither he nor the translator is named.

Popery and Tyranny: Or, The Present State of France : In relation to its Government, Trade, Manners of the People, and Nature of the Countrey . . . London, Printed in the Year 1679. 4°, A—C 2 in fours.

Actes of the General Assembly of the Clergy of France. Anno Domini. 1682. Concerning Religion. Translated into English for the satisfaction of Curious Inquisitors into the present French Persecution of Protestants. London, Printed By J. R. An. Dom. 1682. 4°, A—E 2 in fours.

Loves Empire ; Or, The Gallantries of the French Court. London, Printed for Dorman Newman. 1682. 8°. B—F 7 in eights : B—P in eights, and the title.

There is no preliminary matter.

French Intrigues ; Or, The History of their Delusory Promises since the Pyrenæan Treaty. Printed in French at Cologne, and now made English. London: Printed for W. Hensman, . . . 1685. 12°. Title and Preface, 2 leaves : B—H in twelves: I, 4 leaves.

The Politicks of the French King, Lewis the XIV. Discovered : With respect to Rome. Emperour, and Princes of the Empire, Spain. England. United Provinces. Northern Princes. Suisse Cantons: And of Savoy. With a Short Account of Religion. Translated from the French. . . . London, Printed for Mat. Wotton . . . 1689. 4º. Title and blank, 2 leaves: B—N in fours.

The History of the Famous and Passionate Love, between a Fair Noble Parisian Lady, and a Beautiful Young Singingman; A Chanter at the Quire of Nôtre-Dame at Paris, and a Singer in Operas. An Heroic Poem. In Two Cantos. Being in imitation of Virgil's Dido and Æneas, . . . London, Printed for R. T. near Stationers-Hall, 1692. 4º. A, 2 leaves: B—D in fours: E, 2.

The Present Condition of France, In Reference to Her Revenues, Comparing them with the Infinite Expences She is forc'd to be at. Demonstrating thereby, That it is impossible for Her to support Her Self, if the War with the Confederates continues. Done out of French. London, Printed for Henry Rhodes . . . and John Harris . . . 1692. 4º. A, 2 leaves: B—D in fours: E, 2.

An Answer to a Paper Written by Count d'Avant, The French King's Ambassador in Sweden, Concerning the Proposals of Peace made by France to the Confederates. London : Printed for Richard Baldwin, . . . MDCXCIV. 4º, A, 2 : B—D in fours : E, 2.

The French King's Declaration for Settling the General Poll-Tax : Together with His Edict, Ordering all Communities both Regular and Secular, and all particular Persons, (who have any Water from Rivers, Brooks, Springs and Fountains, or otherwise, whether for the Ornament of their Houses, or the Improving of their Estates) to pay such Sums as shall be impos'd . . . London : Printed for Richard Baldwin, . . . 1695. 4º, A—D in fours. *B. M.*

The French Spy : Or, The Memoirs of John Baptist De La Fontaine, Lord of Savoy and Fontenai, late Brigadier and Surveyor of the French Kings Army, now a Prisoner in the Bastile. . . . Translated from the French Original, . . . London : Printed for R. Basset, . . . 1700. 8º, A—Bb in eights. Dedicated by the translator, J. C., M.D., to Sir Charles Duncombe, Sheriff of London.

The French Rogue : Or, The Life of Monsieur Ragone de Versailles. Containing His Parentage, Monstrous Birth, Early Rogueries, . . . With large Additions not in any former Impression. Done from

the Original by J. S. London, Printed for N. Boddington . . . 1704. 12º, A—I 6 in twelves. With a frontispiece.

The Political Quack's Advice ; With Merry Andrew's Pacquet. Design'd for the Entertainment of the Grave and Merry, the Politick and Impertinent, the Scholar and Critick, the Witty and Dull, the Old and Young ; in short, for every Body that can Read, and no Body that cannot. *Quos pendere vult Jupiter hos dementat. Quos tueri vult suscitat.* London, Printed in the Year 1705. (Price One Shilling.) 4º. A, 2 : B—F in fours : G, 2 : H, 4.

This odd tract belongs to the French series, and relates to the schemes of the Grand Monarque. The *Pacquet* is in verse, and in two parts.

A Letter from A Minister of State at Turin, to a General-Officer, Relating to the Expedition into Provence, and Siege of Thoulon. Also the Motives that Engag'd his Royal Highness and Prince Eugene in that Stupendous Undertaking, . . . Done from a French Copy transmitted from the Hague. London : Sold by John Morphew. . . . 1707. 4º, A—D 2 in fours.

FRANCISCANS.
The Chronicle and Institvtion of the Order of the Seraphicall Father S. Francis. Conteyning His life, his death, and his miracles, and of all his holy disciples and companions. Set foorth first in the Portugall, next in the Spanish, then in the Italian, lastlie in the French, and now in the English tongue. The First Tome. At S. Omers. By Iohn Heigham, Anno 1618. With permission of Superiors. 4º, A—5 I in fours.

Apparently all that appeared.

FRANKE, WALTER, *Minister of God's Word.*
The Epitome of Divinity. Poetically compos'd by way of Dialogue, for the more easie, and pleasant learning and retaining of it in memory. . . . London, Printed by J. G. for Francis Eaglefield . . . 1655. Sm. 8º, A—II in fours, first and last leaves blank. Dedicated to the Lady Anne, and Mrs Jane and Mrs Elizabeth, Basset.

FRANKLAND, THOMAS, *LL.D.*
The Annals of King James and King Charles the First, . . . From the Tenth of King James, M.DC.XII. to the Eighteenth of King Charles M.DC.XLII. . . . London, Printed by Tho. Braddyll, for Robert Clavel, . . . 1681. Folio. Title and

Errata, 2 leaves : a—b, 2 leaves each : A—5 Z in fours : 6 A—B, 2 leaves each.

FREDERIC V., *Elector Palatine, &c.*

A Faithfvll Admonition of the Paltsgraves Churches, to all other Protestant Churches in Dutchland. That they world consider the great danger that hangeth ouer their heads as well as ours by the Popedome, ... Together with a Short Abstract of the warning about the Iesuites bloodthirsty plots published in print at Tubing. Published by Authoritie. According to the Originall Printed in the Electors Palsgraues Country . . . Englished by Iohn Rolte. Imprinted at London by Edward Griffin for George Gibbes, . . . 1614. 4°, A—F in fours, F 4 blank. Dedicated by Rolt to Oliver, Lord St John.

A Fvll Declaration of the Faith and Ceremonies Professed in the dominions of the most Illustrious and noble Prince Fredericke, 5. Prince, Elector Palatine. Translated into English by John Rolte. London, Printed for William Welby, . . . 1614. 4°, A—Cc 2 in fours. Dedicated to Sir Edward Coke. *B. M.*

A Declaration of the Pfaltzgraves : Concerning the Faith and Ceremonies professed in his Churches. According to the Originall printed in the High Dutch, translated by I. R. London, Printed for Thomas Iones, . . . 1637. 4°, A—F in fours.

An abridgment of the larger book.

A Declaration of the Cavses, for the which, Wee Frederick, by the Grace of God King of Bohemia, ... haue Accepted of the Crowne of Bohemia, and of the Covntryes therevnto annexed. Middlebvrg. Printed by Abraham Schilders. M.D.C.XX. 4°, A—C in fours, and the title.

Secretissima Instrvctio Gallo-Britanno-Batava, Friderico, V. Comiti Palatino, Electori data. Ex Gallico conversa, ac bono publico in lucem emulgata. Anno M.DC.XX. 4°, A—D in fours.

A Briefe Description of the reasons that make the Declaration of the Ban made against the King of Bohemia, as being Elector Palatine, Dated the 22. of Iannarie last past, of no value nor worth, and therefore not to be respected. Printed at the Hayf [Hague] by Arnold Meuris Booke seller, at the Signe of the Bible. 1621. 4°, A—B in fours. *B. M.*

FREDERIC OF JENNEN.

Here begynneth a propre treatyse of a marchauntes wyfe, that afterwards wente lyke a man, and became a grete lorde, and was called Frederyke of Jennen. [Col.] And thus endeth this lytell story of lorde Frederyke. Imprynted at London, in Paules churchyarde at the sygne of the Lambe, by Abraham Vele. 4°, black letter, A—E 2 in fours. *B. M.*

A reprint of the Antwerp edition, from which the blocks for the cuts were probably borrowed.

FREEMAN, SIR RALPH.

Imperiale, A Tragedie. Ovid. 2. Trist. ad Cæs. August. *Omne genus scripti gravitate Tragædia vincit.* London, ¶ Printed by Thomas Harper. M.DC.XXXIX. 4°, A—H in fours, A 1 blank. With no other prefixes but the Argument. *B. M.*

FREJUS, ROLAND, *of Marseilles.*

The Relation of a Voyage made into Mauritania, In Africa, . . . by the French King's Order, in the Year 1666. To Muley Arxid, King of Tafiletta, &c. For the Establishment of a Commerce in all the Kingdom of Fez, and all his other Conquests. . . . Englished out of French. London, Printed by W. Godbid, and are to be sold by Moses Pitt, . . . 1671. 8°. A, 4 leaves : B—I 4 in eights : A Letter in Answer to divers Curious Questions, A—E 4 in eights, and a separate title.

FREIRE DE ANDRADA, JACINTO.

The Life of Dom John De Castro, The Fourth Vice-Roy of India. Wherein are seen the Portuguese's Voyages to the East-Indies ; Their Discoveries and Conquests there ; . . . Written in Portuguese, and By Sr Peter Wyche Kt. Translated into English . . . London, Printed for Henry Herringman, . . . 1664. Folio. Title, dedication to the English Queen, and Author's dedication, 3 leaves : Preface, 7 leaves : B—4 E, 2 leaves each. With two plates at L and V.

The house of Dom John at Cintra is still in existence (1885).

FRENCH, NICHOLAS, *Bishop of Ferns.*

Recit Exact et Fidele de la Vente et Partage du Royaume d'Irlande, Faits sous Charles II. par le Comte de Clarendon Ecrit premièrement en Anglois, & ensuite traduit en François. . . . M.DC.XCVI. 8°, A—R in fours, and the title. *B. M.*

FRIARS.

The Alcaron of the Barefote Friers, that is to say, an heape or numbre of the blasphemous and trifling doctrines of the wounded Idole Saint Frances taken out of the boke of his rules, called in latin, *Liber conformitatum.* A. 1550. [Col.]

R. G. excudebat. 1550. Cum Priuilegio ad imprimendum solum. 8°, black letter, a—l in eights.

> On L 8 *recto* we have: "Here an ende, for I wyll trouble you no longer with this stuffe, though the booke out of which this is taken côteyneth much more."

The Friers Last Fare-well, Or, Saint Francis must Pack for France. Shewing, How the Mass-monging Fathers were by order of Parliament, brought from Somerset-House in the Strand, by many Officers, Watch-men, and others: And by them put into safe custody, till the next faire winde shall blow for Paris. On Saturday the 26. of February, An. Dom. 1642. Being a dolefull Dialogue between Pere Robert and Pere Cyprian, two lamenting Fathers. God send them good Shipping. London, Printed by Iohn Hammond. 1642. 4°, 4 leaves.

> Compare Ellis's *Original Letters*, 1st Series, iii. 210, 244.

FROISSART, SIR JOHN.

Here begynneth the fyrst volum of Syr Johan Froyssart: of the Cronycles of Englande | Fraunce / Spayne / Portyngale / Scotlande / Bretayne / Flaunders and other places adioynynge. Translated out of frenche into our mater[n]all Englysshe tonge / by Johan Bou[r]chier knyght lorde Berners. At the cōmaundement of our moste highe redoubted souerayne lorde kynge Henry the. viii. kynge of Englande and also of Irelande in earth the supreme heade [Col.] Thus endeth the firste volume of sir Johan Froissart . . . Imprinted at London in Fletestrete at the sygne of the George by Wyllyam Myddylton. Folio. A, 6 leaves : B, 4 leaves : a—v in sixes : aa—vv in sixes : aaa—ooo 4 in sixes.

> Putticks, April 16, 1886, No. 433, Thynne Sale, in the old calf binding, perfect and genuine. The second volume was of Pynson's printing.

FROZER, T.

A Relation of a Voyage Made in the Years 1695, 1696, 1697, on the Coasts of Africa, Streights of Magellan, Brasil, Cayenna, and the Antilles, by a Squadron of French Men of War, under the Command of M. de Gennes. By the Sieur Frozer, Voluntier-Engineer on board the English Falcon. Illustrated with divers strange Figures drawn to the Life. London, Printed for M. Gilliflower. . . . 1698. 8°. Engraved and printed titles, 2 leaves : A, 4 leaves : B—M in eights. With plates and maps at pp. 10, 14, 32 (2), 34, 42, 48, 64 (2), 74, 76, 88, 98, 120.

FRUITS.

Some Fruits of Solitude : In Reflections and Maxims Relating to the Conduct of Human Life. . . . London : Printed for Thomas Northcott, . . . 1693. 12°. A, 6 : B—F in twelves ; G, 7.

FRYER, JOHN, *M.D. and F.R.S.*

A New Account of East India and Persia, In Eight Letters. Being Nine Years Travels, Begun 1672. And Finished 1681. . . . Illustrated with Maps, Figures, and Useful Tables. London : Printed by R. R. for Ri. Chiswell, . . . MDCXCVIII. Folio. Title, dedication to John Holles, Duke of Newcastle, and Preface, 3 leaves : b—c in fours : B—3 M 2 in fours. With a portrait by R. White taken *ad vivum*, and plates, including a few separate from the text at pp. 7, 36, 40, 50, 111, 230, and 417.

FULBECKE, WILLIAM, *of Gray's Inn.*

A Direction or Preparatiue to the study of the Lawe : Wherein is shewed, what things ought to be obserued and vsed of those that are addicted to the study of the Law, . . . At London Printed by Thomas Wight. Anno Domini. 1600. 8°. A, 4 leaves : B—N in eights, N 8 blank.

> The Epistle is dated from Gray's Inn, September 1599.

FULKE, WILLIAM, *D.D.*

A goodly Gallery . . . . Imprinted at London in Fletestrete by Wylliam Gryffith. 1571. 8°.

> A new title-page only to the unsold stock of 1563.

Newes from Spayne and Holland conteyning an information of English Affayres in Spayne with a conference made thervpon in Amsterdame of Holland. Written by a Gentleman trauelour borne in the low countryes, and brought vp from a child in Ingland, vnto a Gentleman his frend and Oste in London. Anno. M.D.XCIII. 8°, A—F 4 in eights, A 1 and F 4 blank.

> This is erroneously ascribed on conjecture to Parsons the Jesuit in all former catalogues, but in a tract printed in 1605, and noticed *supra* under DIALOGUE, it is distinctly stated that it was written by Dr. Fulke.

FULLER, THOMAS, *D.D.*

Anthologia. The Speach of Flowers. Partly Morall Partly Misticall. Sould by Iohn Stafford neare Fleetebridge 1655. [This is an engraved title by R. Vaughan ; a printed one follows :] Anthologia Or the Speech of Flowers. London, Printed for John Stafford, . . . 1655. Title and engraved do., 2 leaves : dedication by the publisher to his much honoured friend, William Stafford, Esquire, Merchant of Bristol, 2 leaves : a leaf containing the words *The Speech of Flowers. The Speech of Birds. Triana*, apparently intended as a bastard title : then B—G 6 in eights, G 6 blank : [a new title :] Ornithologie, Or The Speech of Birds. London, Printed for John Stafford, . . . 1655. A—D 6 in eights. Dedicated to the Worshipful, Roger Le Strange, Esquire, by the publisher. Small 8°.

> I describe the Beckford copy ; but, although that copy possesses the bastard title, the latter may have been printed with the second part, so that the two pieces might form one volume, if so desired. Each is, no doubt, complete in itself.

FULLER, WILLIAM, *Grandson of the preceding.*
A Brief Discovery of the True Mother of the Pretended Prince of Wales Known by the Name of Mary Grey. To which is added, His further Discovery of the late Conspiracy against His Majesties Sacred Person, and Government, &c. . . . By William Fvller, Gent. sometime Page of Honour to the late Queen in France. London, Printed for the Author, Anno Dom. 1696. 8°. Title, dedication to the Duke of Gloucester, and two leaves (pp. 5-8) : C—G in fours.

> See *Current Notes* for February 1853.

A Brief Discovery . . . . Dublin, Re-Printed in the Year, 1696. 8°, A—D in fours.

A Further Confirmation that Mary Grey was the True Mother of the Pretended Prince of Wales. . . . Published by William Fuller, who was Privy to the whole Management. To which is added, The Author's Vindication of Himself, from the Male-Contents of this Kingdom. London, Printed for the Author, 1696. 8°, A—F in fours.

Mr Fuller's Appeal to Both Houses of Parliament, With Letters, relating to Sir John Fenwick, and Himself. By William Fuller, Gent. . . . London : Printed for the Author. 1697. 8°, A—F in fours, A 1 with the half-title.

A Plain Proof of the True Father and Mother of the Pretended Prince of Wales, By several Letters written by the late Queen in France ; the Earl of Tyrconel, Lord Deputy of Ireland, the Dutchess of Powis, Governess to the Pretended Prince, Mr Carrell, the Queen's Secretary, and Father Lewis Sabran, Chaplain and Tutor to the Prince. With the Informations

. . . Now Published by William Fuller, Gent. London : Printed for the Author, . . . 1700. 8°, a—b in fours : A—H in fours, A 1 with the Duke of Shrewsbury's certificate.

Mr Toland's Clito Dissected. And Fuller's Plain Proof . . . made out to be no Proof. In two Letters from a Gentleman in the Country to his Friend in London . . . London : Printed in the Year 1700. Price Sixpence. 8°, A—E in fours.

Mr Fuller's Letter to the Right Honourable the Lord Mayor : Being an Answer to a Late Scandalous Pamphlet, Intituled Fuller's Plain Proof . . . With that Part of His Majesty's Declaration, Relating to that Imposture, Publish'd in December, 1688. London : Printed for the Author, and to be Sold by Eliz. Harris, . . . 1700. 8°, A—C in fours.

Mr Fuller's Answer to the Jacobites. London : Printed for the Author ; and to be sold by Eliz. Harris, at the Harrow, in Little-Britain. 1700. 8°, A—C in fours.

The Life of William Fuller, Gent. Being A Full and True Account of his Birth, Education, Employs, and Intreagues, both of Publick and Private Concerns ; his Reconciliation to the Church of England, and the Occasion of his coming into the Service of the present Government. Written by his own Hand, and the Truth referred to the knowledge of several Gentlemen, &c. London : Printed and Published by A. Baldwin . . . 1701. 8°, A—G in fours, B repeated, and G 7-8 occupied by Advertisements, &c.

> Dedicated to the Earl of Romney.

The Life of Wm Fuller, alias Fullee, alias Fowler, alias Ellison, &c. By Original, a Butcher's Son ; by Education a Coney-Wool-Cutter ; by Inclination, an Evidence ; by Vote of Parliament, an Impostor ; by Title of his own making, a Colonel ; and by his own Demerits now a Prisoner at large belonging to the Fleet. The First and Second Part. . . . London, Printed to prevent his further imposing on the Publick, 1701. Price 1/. 8°, A—L and A—F in fours, A 1 with a copy of the vote of Parliament.

The Life of Mr William Fuller : Being an Impartial Account of his Birth, Education, Relations, and Introduction into the service of the late King James and his Queen. Together with a True Discovery of the Intrigues . . . Impartially writ by Himself, during his Confinement in the Queen's Bench. London : Printed

... MDCCIII. 8°, A—K in eights, K 8 blank.

M' William Fuller's Letter to M' John Tutchin, Author of the Observator. London : Printed for the Author, in the Year, 1703. 8°, 4 leaves.

The Sincere and Hearty Confession of M' William Fuller : Being a True Account of the Persons that assisted Him in the Design of Imposing M'' Mary Grey upon the World, as the Mother of the Pretended Prince of Wales ; . . . London, Printed, ... MDCCIV. 8°, A—E in fours.

In this Series of tracts, especially in those dealing with the biography of Fuller, there is much entertaining and curious anecdote and private history.

FULWOOD, WILLIAM.
The Enimie of Idlenesse : The whole diuided into foure Bookes : nowe newly published and augmented, by W. F. . . . Imprinted at London by Henrie Middleton, dwelling in Fleetstreate, at the signe of the Falcon. Anno. 1578. 8°, A—U in eights, concluding with a Table. *B. M.*

G.

I. I., *Gent.*
Little-Wits Protestation, to defend Popery : Since the decease of his Sister Svperstition. Anno Dom. 1642. London, Printed for F. Coules, in the little Old-Baily, 1642. 4°, 3 leaves.

I. R.
Virginias Cure : Or An Advisive Narrative concerning Virginia. Discovering the true Ground of that Churches Unhappiness, and the only true Remedy. As it was presented to the Right Reverend Father in God Gilbert Lord Bishop of London, September 2. 1661. Now publish'd to further the Welfare of that and the like Plantations. . . . London, Printed by W. Godbid for Henry Brome . . . 1662. 4°, A—D in fours, D 4 blank, A 1 with *Imprimatur.*

I. W., *Professor of Divinity.*
A Discovery of Certaine Notoriovs Shifts, Evasions, and Vntrvthes Vttered By M. Iohn White Minister, (and now made Doctour) in a Booke of his lately set forth, and intituled, *A Defence of the Way*, &c. . . . Permissu Superiorum. M.DC.XIV. 4°, A—C in fours : D, 1 leaf.

GADBURY, JOHN.
De Cometis : Or, A Discourse of the Natures and Effects of Comets, As they are { Philosophically, Historically, & Astrologically } Considered. With a brief (yet full) Account of the III. late Comets, Or Blazing Stars, Visible to all Europe. And what (in a natural way of judicature) they portend. Together with some Observations on the Nativity of the Grand Seignior. By John Gadbury, Philomathematikos. . . . London, Printed for L. Chapman in Exchange-Alley. 1665. 4°, A—L in fours, besides a frontispiece. Dedicated to Robert Payton, Esq., Serjeant-Major to Lord Craven.

Londons Deliverance predicted : In A Short Discourse shewing the Causes of Plagues in General ; And the probable time . . . when this present Pest may abate, &c. By John Gadbury . . . London, Printed by J. C. for E. Calvert, . . . 1665. 4°, A—F in fours.

Astrological Predictions for the Year, 1679. . . . By J. G. Student in Astrology. . . . London, Printed for R. G. 1679. 4°, 4 leaves.

GAGE, THOMAS.
Nouvelle Relation, Contenant les Voyages de Thomas Gage dans la nouvelle Espagne, . . . Ensemble une Description exacte des Terres & Provinces que possedent les Espagnols en toute l'Amerique, . . . Avec Figures. Quatrième Edition revüe & corrigée. A Amsterdam, . . . M.DCCXX. 12°. 2 vols. With frontispieces, maps, and plates.

GALE, THOMAS.
Certaine Workes of Chirurgerie newly compiled and published by Thomas Gale, Master in Chirurgerie. Prynted at London by Rouland Hall. [1563.] 8°. A, 8 leaves, with a portrait of the Author, æt. 56, on A 8 (repeated on the back of the second title, &c.) : *, 4 leaves, containing an Address to the Readers from

Gale's house in London, 12 Sept. 1563 : [a new title :] An Institution of a Chirurgion . . . Printed at London by Rouland Hall, for Thomas Gale. 1563. A—K 6 in eights, K 6 blank, K 3–4–5 with cuts only : [a third title :] An Enchiridion . . . 1563. A—ll 7 in eights : [a fourth title :] An excellent Treatise of wounds . . . 1563. Aa—Cc in eights, Cc 7–8 with cuts only : Aaa—Mmm 4 in eights, with *An Antidotarie*, which has also a separate title, and is introduced by a curious metrical dialogue between the *Antidotary* and a Surgeon, subscribed *W. Cunyngham*. With two folded leaves at II 3 and 5 of the *Institution*. B. M.

> Dedicated to Lord Robert Dudley, after which comes an Epistle by Dr. W. Cuningham to Gale, concluding with some verses : *The Enchiridion*. There are also verses by John Feild, *Chirurgion*, before the *Treatise of wounds*, and a Preface to Gale preceding the *Enchiridion*, by Richard Ferris, Barber-Surgeon to Queen Elizabeth, from the writer's house at Paddington, July 2, 1563.

GALENUS, CLAUDIUS.

Galeni Pergamensis De Temperamentis, et de inaeqvali intemperie Libri Tres Thoma Linacro Anglo Interprete.. ·. Opus non medicis modo. sed et philosophis oppido q; necessariū nunc primum prodit in lucem Cvm Gratia & Priuilegio. [Col.] Impressum apud praeclaram Cantabrigiam per Ioannem Siberch. Anno M. D. XXI. 4". Title within a border, dedication by Linacre to Pope Leo X. and Elenchus, 8 leaves : A—S in fours : Index, 2 leaves. B. M.

> The first book printed at Cambridge.

Claudii Galeni Pergameni de motu Musculorum Libri duo Nicolao Leoniceno interprete. [Col.] Impress. Londini in aedibus Pynsonianis. An. Christi. 1522. Cum priuilegio a rege indulto. With Pynson's large device on L 6 *verso*. The title is within a border with boys and an elephant. With a preface to the Reader by Thomas Linacre.

Certaine Workes of Galens, called Methodvs Medendi, with a briefe Declaration of the worthie Art of Medicine, the Office of a Chirurgion, and an Epitome of the third booke of Galen of Naturall Faculties : translated into English, by Thomas Gale Maister in Chirurgerie. At London Printed by Thomas East, . . . 1586. 4". A, 4 leaves : verses (6 4-line stanzas) to the book and preface to the Reader, 2 leaves : A—S 2 in eights. Dedicated to

Sir Henry Nevell, Lord a Burgavene [Abergavenny]. B. M.

GALMY or GALMIEN, *of Scotland.*

Ein schone Vnd Liebliche history / von dem edlen vnd theüren Ritter Galmien / vnd von seiner züchtigen liebe / So er zū einer hertzogin getragen hat / welche er in eines Münches gestalt /. . . mit schönen figuren angezeygt. [Col.] Getrucht zū Straszburghen . . . M.D.L. 4", A—Dd in fours, Dd 4 with the colophon. With numerous woodcuts, including one on the title of *Ritter Galmy vsz Schotterland*.

> Sothebys, June 24, 1886, No. 163, a leaf deficient.

GARDINER, RICHARD, *of Hereford.*

Richardi Gardiner ex Æde Christi Oxon. Specimen Oratorium. Londini, Impensis Humfredi Moseley. M.DC.LIII. 8", A—B 4 in eights.

GARDINER, RICHARD, *of Shrewsbury.*

Profitable Instrvctions for the Manvring, Sowing and Planting of Kitchin Gardens. Very profitable for the common wealth and greatly for the helpe and comfort of poore people. Imprinted at London by Edward Allde for Edward White . . . 1603. 4", black letter, A—D in fours. Dedicated to his loving neighbours in Shrewsbury. With commendatory verses by Edward Thorne (or Thornes) of Melverley. B. M.

GARDNER, THOMAS, *of Southwold.*

A Pocket-Guide to the English Traveller: Being a Compleat Survey and Admeasurement of all the Principal Roads and most Considerable Cross-Roads in England and Wales. In One Hundred Copper-Plates. London : . . . . MDCCXIX. 4". Title, Preface, and Table, 6 leaves : the work, 100 engraved folded leaves, each inscribed to a separate patron. B. M.

GARNET, HENRY.

A Trve and Perfect Relation of the whole proceedings against the late most barbarous Traitors, Garnet a Iesuite, and his Confederates: Contayning sundry Speeches deliuered by the Lords Commissioners . . . The Earle of Northamptons Speech hauing beene enlarged . . . And lastly all that passed at Garnets Execution. Imprinted at London by Robert Barker . . . 1606. 4", A—3 F in fours, 3 F 4 blank.

GARTER, BERNARD.

The Tragicall and Trve Historie which happened betwene two English louers 1563. Written by Ber. Gar. In aedibus Richardi Tottelli. Cum priuilegio. [Col.] Imprinted at London in Fletestrete within

Temple Barre at the signe of the hand and Starre by Rycharde Tottel 1568. 8°, A—K 7 in eights. Black letter. With a preface and a few introductory verses by the author.

Osterley Park Sale, 1885, No. 703. A different edition from that mentioned in my *Handbook*, 1867, in v.

GARZONI, T.
Hospital of Incurable Fooles . . . 1600.

In respect to the translation, or rather English paraphrase of this, it is interesting to find a coeval memorandum on the back of the title of a copy (Sothebys, April 1, 1882, No. 702) to the following effect: " Tho. Nashe had some hand in this translation and it was the last that he did as I heare. P. W."

GATAKER, THOMAS.
A Discours Apologetical. Wherein Lilies lewd and Lowd Lies in his Merlin or Pasquil for the Yeer 1654. are cleerly laid open ; . . . . And a Postscript concerning An Epistle Dedicatorie of one J. Gadburie. By Tho. Gataker, B.D. . . . London, Printed by R. Ibbitson for Thomas Newberry, ... 1654. 4°, A—O in fours.

GATRIKE, ——.
[The Paternoster, the Creed by the old and the new Law. An Exposition on the Ten Commandments. At the end :] Imprynted in Fletestrete by me Robert Redman. Cum priuilegio Regali. Sm. 8°, A—E 4 in eights. Without a regular title.

This appears to be the little volume, mentioned by Fox (*Martyrs*, 1563, 453), as having been compiled by a worshipful clerk named Gatrike for the use of the common people, among whom they were distributed "in small pagines."

GAYTON, EDMUND.
Upon the Meeting of the Sons of the Clergy, At a Sermon Preached before them in Saint Pauls Church the eighth of November, 1655. Specifying their several Capacities, as they stood in the time of the Law, and now under the Gospel. By E. G. London, Printed by Tho. Roycroft, 1655. 4°, 4 leaves. In verse.

Hymnus De Febribus Scriptus ab Edmundo Gaytono, Bacc. in Med. Oxon. Academiæ S. Joan. Bapt. Londini, Imprimitur à Thomâ Warreno propter usum Reipublicæ & Authoris. [1659.] 4°. A—H in fours, and a, 4 leaves with commendatory verses.

On the back of the title occurs in MS.: Liber Gulielmi Smart a Johane Bartlett bibliopola westmonasteriensi dono datus : Sept. 2. 1659. Dedicated to William, Marquis of Hertford.

GAZOPHYLACIUM.
Gazophylacium Anglicanum : Containing the Derivation of English Words, Proper and Common ; Each in an Alphabet distinct : . . . . London, Printed by E. H. and W. H. and are to be sold by Randall Taylor. . . . MDCLXXXIX. 8°, A—Kk in eights, and a leaf of Ll.

With a curious preface ; but the author's name does not appear.

GENEVA.
A Perticular and true Narration of that great and gratious Deliuerance, that it pleased God of late to vouchsafe vnto the Cittie of Geneua, namely vpon the . xij. of December last in the yeere 1602. At London Printed for George Potter and Richard Canter, dwelling in the Popeshead Alley neare the Exchange. 1603. 4°, black letter, A—B in fours, A 1 blank.

A Trve Discovrse of the Discouerie of the Plot of Monsieur du Ferrail, and his Confederates for the Surprising of Geneua. And of their Apprehension, Confessions, and Executions done in the same, The 19. of April. 1609. London Printed for R. Bonian and H. Walley, and are to be sold at the Signe of the Spread-Eagle, right ouer against the great North-doore of S. Pauls. 1609. 4°, A—C in fours, A 1 blank, and a leaf of D.

The Geneva Ballad. To the Tune of '48. London : Printed for H. Brome, at the Gun at the West - end of St. Pauls, M.DC.LXXVIII. A broadside in verse.

GENNINGS, EDMUND.
Strange and Miraculous News from St. Omers : Being an Account of the Wonderful Life and Death of a Popish Saint and Martyr, named M[r] Edmund Gennings, Priest, who was Executed for Treason some Years since : With a Relation of the Miracles at, and after his Death. [London, about 1680.] Folio, 2 leaves.

GENTLEMAN, TOBIAS, *Fisherman and Mariner.*
England's Way to Win Wealth, and to Employ Ships and Marriners. Or, A plaine description of what great profite it will bring vnto the Common-wealth of England by the Erecting, Building, and aduenturing of Busses to Sea, a fishing . . . London Printed for Nathaniel Butter. 1614. 4°, A—G in fours, G 4 blank, and only 3 leaves in A, A 4 having perhaps been blank. Dedicated to Henry, Earl of Northampton.

The Best Way to make England the Richest and Wealthiest Kingdome in

Europe, By advancing the Fishing-Trade and improving Ships and Mariners. . . . London, Printed for the good and benefit of all his Majesties Subjects in these his Dominions. [About 1660.] Folio, A—E. 2 leaves each, besides a frontispiece of arms.

GERILEON.

La Plaisante et Delectable histoire de Gerileon d'Angleterre . . . Nouuellement mis en François par Etienne de Maisonneufue Bordelois . . . A Lyon Par Benoist Rigavd. M.D.LXXXI. 12°, A—X in eights, X 7–8 occupied by woodcuts.

GERMANY.

Certaine Orations and Answeres made by Iohn Casimire Countie Palatine of Rhyne, Duke of Bauier &c. and his Embassadours, vnto the French King & his Embassadours in defence of ye maintenance of his Peace, and christian Religion. Translated out of French. 1579. Imprinted at London. 1579. 8°, A—C in eights, C 8 blank.

A notable and prodigious Historie of a Mayden, who for sundry yeeres neither eateth, drinketh, nor sleepeth, neyther anoydeth any excrements, and yet liueth. A matter sufficiently opened and auerred, by the proceedings, examination, and diligent informations thereof, . . . At London, Printed by John Woolfe. Anno. MDLXXXIX. 4°, black letter. 6 leaves. *B. M.*

This remarkable character belonged to the town of Schmidweiler, in the dominions of the Count Palatine of the Rhine, in the jurisdictiou of Colberberg.

The Trve Coppie of a Letter, written from the Leager by Arnham, the 27. day of Iuly, according to the Computation of the Church of Rome. Wherin is particularly set forth, the ouerthrowe of the Prince of Parmaes Forces, before Knodtsenburgh Sconce. Translated out of Dutch. Seene and allowed. At London Printed for Andrew White, and are to be sold at his Shop by the Royall Exchange ouer against the Conduct in Corne-hill. 1592. 4°, 4 leaues.

The Estate of the Germaine Empire, with the description of Germanie. 1. Declaring how the Empire was translated from the Romaines to the Germaines: with diuers and syndrie memorable accidents following there-vpon. Written certaine yeeres past as the state then stood. 2. Describing the scituation of euery Countrie, Prouince, Dukedome, . . . Newly set forth for the profite and pleasure of all Gentlemen and others, that are delighted in trauaile or knowledge of Countries. At London Printed for Raphe Blower, and are to be solde at his shop in Fleetstreet, near the Middle Temple Gate. An. Do. 1595. 4°, A—G 2 in fours.

Dedicated to Robert, Earl of Sussex, by William Fiston, who acknowledges his obligation to two originals, one Latin, the other Italian.

A Strange and Miraevlovs Accident happened in the Cittie of Purmerent, on New-yeeres-euen last past 1599. Of a yong child which was heard to cry in the Mothers wombe before it was borne, and about fourteene dayes of age, spake certaine sensible words, to the wonder of euery body. Imprinted at London by Iohn Wolfe, . . . 1599. 4°, black letter, 4 leaues. With a cut of the child anno ætatis 14 days on the title.

A Trve Relation of the taking of Alba-Regalis, in the German Tongue, called Sfullweissenburgh, the chiefe Cittie in Nether Hungarie, which was taken by the Christian Armie the Twentith of September last past. 1601. Truely translated out of the German Tongue. London, Printed by Ralph Blower, for C. B. 1601. 4°. Title, 1 leaf: B, 4 leaues: C, 1 leaf.

A Pvblike Declaration, Made by the Vnited Protestant Princes Electors and other Princes, States and Lords, of the Holie Empire, Thereby shewing for what causes and reasons, they are mooued to ioyne together in a straight Vnitie and Alliance, to Aide and Assist the Princes Electors of Brandenbvrgh and the Palsgrave. . . . Translated out of the Duch Copie, . . . London, Printed for Iohn Bvdge, . . . 1610. 4°, black letter, A—B in fours, A 1 and B 4 blank.

A most true Relation of a very dreadfull Earth-quake, with the Lamentable effectes thereof, Which began vpon the 8. of December 1612. and yet continueth most feerefull in Munster in Germanie. Translated out of Dutch by Charles Demetrius, Publike Notarie in London. And Printed at Rotterdame in Holland, at the Signe of the White Gray-hound. 4°, large black letter, A—D in fours, A 1 and D 4 blank. With a large cut on title. *B. M.*

Two very lamentable Relations : The one, The grieuances for Religion, of those of Stiria, Carinthia, and Crayne, vnder Ferdinand then Duke of Gratz, now Emperour. The other, The now present most humble Supplication, of certayne of the States of lower Austria, vnto the said Emperour. . . . Done out of the Dutch, and Printed. 1620, 4°, A—C 2 in fours, A 1 blank.

The 2. of September. Two Great Battailes very lately fovght, The one betweene Count Mansfeld and Don Cordua the Spanish Generall, since his arrivall in Brabant, . . . The other, betweene Spinola and Berghen op Zoom, . . . With Mansfeilds and the Duke of Brunswicks arrivall at Bredaw, . . . Lastly, the late Proceedings in the Palatinate, . . . London Printed by I. D. for Nicholas Bourne and Thomas Archer, . . . 1622. 4°, A—C in fours, A 1 blank. *B. M.*

Motives and Reasons Concerning His Highnesse the Prince Elector Palatines comming into England. . . . With two Letters that were formerly sent from the Hague. London, Printed by Jane Col, 1644. 4°, 4 leaves.

A Brief Representation of the Protestant Cause in Germany. In what case it hath been, since the Peace at Munster ; and how it now stands. London, Printed in the year 1658. 4°, 4 leaves.

A Letter to the Most Illustrious Lord, The Count of Hohenlo, one of the Imperial Generals. Written by a Gentleman in the Army of Count Serini before Canisia. Concerning the Renegades amongst the Turks. Put into English by a Person of Quality. . . . London, Printed by John Redmayne, 1664. 4°, 4 leaves.

The initials *N. R. D.* are at the end.

A Short History of the Anabaptists of High and Low Germany. *Tantùm Religio potuit suadere malorum.* London, Printed by Robert Austin, 1647. 4°, A —H in Fours, A 1 and H 3-4 blank.

A Letter Written in High-Dutch by a Danish Gentleman to his Friend in Germany, Concerning the Imprisonment of John Adolff Kielman of Kielmans-Eck, President of State to the Duke of Sleswig-Holstein-Gottorp ; and of his three Sons. Printed in the Year, 1676. 4°, A—E in fours.

A Particular Relation of the Battel, Fought on the 29th of July, 1693. Between the Confederate Army, Commanded by His Majesty of Great Britain, And the Elector of Bavaria, &c. And that of France, Commanded by the M. of Luxemburgh. . . . London : Printed for Abel Roper, . . . 1693. 4°, 6 leaves.

A General Prospect of the Royall House and Garding at Hernhausen. [About 1700.] Oblong 4°, 16 numbered plates and a general plan. Engl. and Fr.

This is the palace mentioned by Thackeray in his *Four Georges.*

Campagna Maravigliosa Or An Exact Journal of the Imperial Army's Advance into, and Incampment in Italy, under the Command of Prince Eugene of Savoy. With the several Actions and Rencounters betwixt them, and the French and Spaniards. By an Officer of the German Army. Made English from the Original at Venice, By William Barton, Gent. London, Printed for A. Bell. . . . 1702. 4°, A—H 2 in fours.

The German Lazarus, Being A Plain and Faithful Account of the extraordinary Events that happened to John Engelbracht of Brunswick : Relating to his apparent Death, and Return to Life : . . . All Written by Himself. And done from the Original High-Dutch, . . . London : . . . 1707. 8°. A, 4 : B, 2 : C, 4 : D, 2 : E, 4 : F, 2 : G, 4 : H, 2 : I, 4 : K, 2 : L, 4 : M, 2 : N, 4 : O, 2.

GERSON, JOHN.

The folowing of Christ, translated out of Latin into Englishe, newely corrected and amended. Wherevnto also is added the golden Epistle of Saint Barnarde. The . xviii. of September . Anno M.D.L.VJ. Cum priuilegio . . . [Col.] Printed at London in Paules Churche yarde at the signe of the holye Ghoste by John Cawood, Printer to the king and Queenes Maiesties. 8°, A—Y in eights, A 8 blank.

In the Preface it is stated that the former version of Books I.–III. by William Atkinson was considered imperfect and unsatisfactory, and that the translation of Book IV. by the Countess of Richmond and Derby having been taken from the French, it was thought better to make a new one from the original language. Of this the author is not named.

Thomas of Kempis His Soliloqvies Translated ovt of Latine by Thomas Carre Confessour to the English Nunnes of Saint Augustines Order, Established at Paris. Printed at Paris. By M. Blageart. M.DC.LIII. 12°. ã, 12 leaves, with dedication to " His most Honored Deare Lady Marie Tredway First Abbesse . . . " and Preface : A—L in twelves : M, 4.

The Following of Christ. In Four Books Written by John Gerson, Abbot of Vercelles, of the Holy Order of St Benedict : Drawn out of Ten Ancient Manuscripts, . . . Printed at London, Anno Dom. 1673. 12°. A, 12 leaves : a, 6 : B—Y in twelves.

The translator was Thomas Carre.

GERVAIS, *Bishop of Grasse.*

The Life of the Apostle S‘ Paul, Written in French by the Famous Bishop of Grasse, and now Englished by a Person of Honour. London, Printed by James Young for Henry Twyford, . . . 1653. 12⁰. A, 4 leaves : B—D in twelves, besides the frontispiece. Dedicated by F. D. to Edward, Lord Vaux of Harrowden.

GERARDE, JOHN.

Catalogus arborum, fruticum ac plantarum tam indigenarum quam exoticarum, in horto Iohannis Gerardi ciuis & Chirurgi Londinensis nascentium. Londini, Ex officina Roberti Robinson. 1596. 4⁰, A—C in fours. *B. M.*

GERY, WILLIAM, *of Gray's Inn.*

Proposals for Reformation of Abuses and Subtilties in Practice against the Law and in Scandall of it. London, Printed for William Shears, . . . 1659. 4⁰, 4 leaves.

GESNER, CONRAD.

The Treasure of Evonymvs, conteynynge the wonderfull hid secretes of nature, touching the most apte formes to prepare and destyl Medicines, for the conseruation of helth : as Quintessēce, Aurum Potabile, Hippocras, Aromatical wynes, Balmes, Oyles, Perfumes, garnishyng waters, and other manifold excellent confections. Wherunto are ioyned the formes of sondry apt Furnaces, and vessels, required in this art. Translated (with great diligence, & laboure) out of Latin, by Peter Morwyng felow of Magdaline Colleadge in Oxford. Imprinted at London by Iohn Daie, dwelling ouer Aldersgate, beneath Saint Martines . . . [1559.] 4⁰. With woodcuts.

GILBERT, WILLIAM, *of Colchester.*

Gvilielmi Gilberti Colcestrensis, Medici Regij, De Mundo nostro Sublimari Philosophia Nova. Opus posthumum, Ab Authoris fratre collectum pridem & dispositum. . . . Amstelodami, . . . 1651. 4⁰. *, 4 leaves : **, 3 leaves : A—Rr in fours. With a folded plate at p. 172.

    The dedication of the author to Henry Prince of Wales is printed at **2.

Tractatvs Siue Physiologia Nova De Magnete . . . nunc diligenter recognita . . . opera & studio Wolfgangi Lochmans, M.D. . . . Excvsvs Sedini . . . Anno M.DC.XXVIII. 4⁰. Title, Preface, and verses, 3 leaves : A—Mm in fours. With 12 plates between B 2 and 3 and others in the volume. The title is engraved.

Tractatus, . . . Sedini, Typis Gotzianis. Anno M.DC.XXXXII. 4⁰. Title, &c., 4 leaves : A—Mm in fours.

[GILBY, ANTHONY.]

To my louynge brethren that are troublyd about the popishe aparrell, two short and comfortable Epistels. *Be ye constant for the Lorde shall fyght for you, yours in Christ.* No place, &c. 8⁰, black letter, A—C in fours.

To my faythfull Brethren now afflycted, & to all those that vnfaynedly loue the Lorde Jesus, the Lorde guyde vs with his holy spret, . . . No place, &c. 8⁰, black letter, A in eights. Without any title-page.

To the Reader. [An Address or Epistle.] No place, &c. 8⁰, black letter, A—C in fours.

    On B 3 occurs a fresh head-line: An Answere to a question, that was mouyd, whi the godly men could not weare a surples.

    Sothebys, Feb. 21, 1882, the three pieces in a volume. Printed abroad.

GILDAS.

The Epistle of Gildas, The most Ancient British Author: Who flourished in the yeere of our Lord, 546. . . . Faithfully Translated out of the Originall Latine. London, Printed by T. Cotes, for William Cooke . . . . 1638. 12⁰. a, 4 leaves, including a portrait by W. Marshall : b—f 3 in twelves : B—O in twelves : P, 8 leaves, P 8 blank.

    This book was reissued in 1641 with a fresh title as follows : "The History of the Destrvction of the Brittaines. Written Anno Domino, 546. By Gildas Sapiens in an Epistolary way."

GILL, ALEXANDER, *the Younger.*

Gratvlatoria Dicata Sereniss. ac Potentiss. Carolo Regi, e Caledone ad Trinobantes Suos reverso. Authore Alex: Gil, Londinate. Virg.——*Nihil Illo triste recepto.* Excusa Londini sumptibus Ioh: Waterson. 1641. 4⁰, 4 leaves.

GILL, GEORGE, *Colonel.*

Innocency Cleared : Or The Case and Vindication of Col. George Gill ; Wherein is made apparent how the Sentence of Parliament was procured against him, and by what means the Re-hearing hath been delayed. Humbly Presented to the Parliament, with desires of speedy Justice . . . Printed 10 September, 1651. 4⁰. A, 2 leaves : B—D 2 in fours.

GIOLO.

Prince Giolo Son to the King of Moangis or Gilolo : lying under the Equator in the Long. of 152 Deg. 30 Min. a fruitful

ɪding with rich Spices and
ᴇ Commodities. [1694.] A
:ribing the Prince, &c. *B. M.*

JOSEPH, *M.A., F.R.S.*
is, Or An Enquiry into the
he Eastern Sages, concerning
ᴇnce of Souls. Being a Key
: Grand Mysteries of Provi-
tion to Mans sin and misery.
ɪted and are to be sold at
nd Oxford. 1662. 8°, A—

ɪtifica : Or, Confest Igno-
:y to Science ; In an Essay
᾽ of Dogmatizing, and Con-
ɪn. With A Reply to the
the Learned Thomas Albius.
Glanvill, M.A. London :
. Cotes, for Henry Eversden
. 4°. A, 4 leaves, A 1 with
2) in fours : B—Aa in fours.
the Royal Society.
ɪ to White follows with a sepa-
d signatures : A—N 2 in fours,
ɴves.

phical Considerations touch-
: of Witches and Witchcraft.
ᴇetter to the much Honour'd
; Esq; By J. G. a Member
Society. London, Printed
ɪames Collins . . . 1667. 8°,
, and the title.

Or, The Progress and Ad-
Knowledge since the Days
In an Account of some of
arkable Late Improvements
ᴜseful Learning : . . . . By
London, Printed for James
668. 8°, A—M 6 in eights,
ɴd *Imprimatur.*

Happiness : Represented in
; and Incouragements ; and
many Popular and Danger-
. By Jos. Glanvill, M.A.
ɴted by E. C. & A. C. for
s . . . M.DC.LXX. 8°, A—M
with *Imprimatur.* With a
ᴠilliam Allen and a short
To a Dear Friend" by the

ɪnswer to Mʳ Henry Stubbe,
of Warwick. Wherein the
. of his Temper, . . . And
.ency of his Arguing &
n his Animadversions on
ᴇ discovered. By Jos. Glan-
on, Printed by A. Clark for
. 1671. 8°, A—P 4 in eights.
:eral Important Subjects in

Philosophy and Religion. By Joseph
Glanvill, Chaplain in Ordinary to His
Majesty, and Fellow of the Royal Society.
. . . London, Printed by J. D. for John
Baker, . . . and Henry Mortlock . . . 1676.
4°, A—Tt in fours, and a, 4 leaves.
Dedicated to Henry, Marquis of Worcester
and Earl of Glamorgan.

Saducismus Triumphatus : Or, Full and
Plain Evidence Concerning Witches and
Apparitions. In Two Parts. The First
treating of their Possibility, The Second
of their Real Existence. By Joseph
Glanvil late Chaplain in Ordinary to his
Majesty, and Fellow of the Royal Society.
With a Letter of Dʳ Henry More on the
same Subject. And an Authentick, but
wonderful story of certain Swedish
Witches done into English by Anth.
Horneck Preacher at the Savoy. Lon-
don : Printed for J. Collins . . . 1681.
8°. Part 1, A, 4 : B—R in eights, R 8
blank : Part 2, Aa—Aaa 4 in eights.
With a frontispiece to each portion.

GLEMHAM, EDWARD, *of Benhall,
Suffolk.*
The Honorable Actions of that Most
Famovs and Valiant Englishman, Edward
Glemham Esqvire, Latelie obtained
against the Spaniards, and the Holy
Leavge, in Fovre Svndrie Fights. With
his landing on Saint Georges Ile, belonging to our enemie. . . . Pvblished for an
Encovragement to our English adventurers, (Gentlemen, Sailors, and Soldiers,)
that serves against the enemies of God
and our Comntrey. London Printed by
A. J. for William Barley, and are to be
sold at his shop in Newgatemarket. Anno.
1591. 4°, A—B in fours, black letter.
B. M.
At the end are two 7-line stanzas by
H. R. "in commendation of the right worshipfull and valiant Generall Edward Glemham, Esquire."

GLOUCESTERSHIRE.
The Bloody Innkeeper, Or Sad and Bar-
barous News from Glocester-Shire : Being
A True Relation how the Bodies of Seven
Men and Women were found Murthered
in a Garden belonging to a House in
Pealey near Glocester. . . . London,
Printed with Allowance, 1675. 4°, 4
leaves.
Crossley, part 2, No. 325.

GODDARD, JONATHAN, *M.D.*
A Discourse Setting forth the Unhappy
Condition of the Practice of Physick in
London, And Offering Some means to
put it into a better ; for the Interest of

Patients, no less, or rather much more, than of Physicians. . . . London, Printed for John Martyn and James Allestry, . . . MDCLXX. 4°, A—H in fours, A 1 and H 4 blank.

GODFRIDUS.
Here begynneth the Boke of knowledge of thynges vnknowen apperteynynge to Astronomye with certayne necessarye Rules, and certayne speres conteynyng herein Compyled by Godfridus super Palladium de agricultura Anglicatum. [Col.] Imprynted by me Robert Wyer. . . . 8°, A—K in fours. With a cut on the back of the title. *B. M.* (a leaf deficient).

The Knowledge of Thinges Vnknowne. Apperteyning to Astronomy, wyth necessary Rules, and certayne Sp[h]eares contayned in the same. Compyled by Godfridus super palladium de agricultura Anglicatum. Imprinted at London, in Fleetestreete, . . . by H. Iackson. 1585. 8°, A—G in eights, G 8 blank. With cuts. *B. M.*

GODSKALL, JAMES, *the Younger.*
The Kings Medicines for this Present yeere 1604. prescribed by the whole colledge of the spirituall physitions, . . . Given, As a New Yeers Gift, to the honorable city of London, ... At London printed for Edward White . . . . [1604.] 8°, A—N in eights.

[GODWIN, FRANCIS.]
The Man in the Moone : Or A Discovrse of a Voyage thither by Domingo Gonsales. The speedy Messenger. London, Printed by John Norton for Ioshua Kirton and Thomas Warren. 1638. Sm. 8°. Title and frontispiece, 2 leaves : Preface by E. M., 2 leaves : B—I in eights.

GODWYN, MORGAN, *some time of Christ Church, Oxford.*
The Negro's & Indians Advocate, Suing for their Admission into the Church : Or A Persuasive to the Instructing and Baptizing of the Negro's and Indians in our Plantations . . . London, Printed for the Author, . . . 1682. 8°, A—M in eights, first and last leaves blank.

GOLBORNE, J., *of Trinity College, Dublin.*
A Friendly Apology, In the behalf of the Womans Excellency : Together with some Examples of Women-Worthies. As also the Character of a Virtuous and Accomplished Woman. Wherein Ladies of Pleasure are taxed and admonished. Written in Verse . . . London, Printed for Henry Mortlock, . . . 1674. 12°, A—C in twelves,

A 1 blank. Dedicated to Mrs. Katharine Booth.

GOLD.
An Advice touching the Currancie in payment of our English Golde. As also A Table of the seuerall Worths of all Pieces, . . . London Printed for F. Constable, ... 1627. 8°, A—C in eights, A and C 8 blank.

GOLD AND SILVER.
The valuacyō of golde and syluer made ī yᵉ yere . M.CCCC.lxxxix. holde ī the marke unce englice quart troye . dewes and aes The maner for to weight with pēnes and graynes and herein is sett ȳ fygures of ȳ spanysh and Portingalysh docates whiche is now. [Antwerp, John of Doesborch, about 1520.] 8°, a—c in eights. With numerous engravings of Spanish, Portuguese, French, and other foreign coins. *B. M.* (Herbert's copy)

This appears to be the earliest publication of the kind in English.

GOODALL, CHARLES, *M.D.*
The Royal College of Physicians of London Founded and Established by Law ; As appears By Letters Patents, Acts of Parliament, ... London, Printed by M. Flesher, for Walter Kettilby, . . . 1684. 4°, A—3 Q 2 in fours, besides title and *Imprimatur.* Dedicated to Francis, Lord Guilford.

GOODCOLE, HENRY.
The wonderfull discouerie of Elizabeth Sawyer A Witch, late of Edmonton, her conuiction and condemnation and Death. Together with the relation of the Deuils accesse to her, and their conference together. Written by Henry Goodcole . . . Published by Authority. London, Printed for William Butler, and are to be sold at his Shop in Saint Dunstons Church-yard, Fleetstreet. 1621. 4°, A—D in fours, first and last leaves blank. With a cut on title. *B. M.*

Natures Cruell Step-Dames : Or, Matchlesse Monsters of the Female Sex ; Elizabeth Barnes, and Ann Willis. Who were executed the 26. day of Aprill, 1637. at Tyburne, for the vnnaturall murthering of their owne children. . . . Further, a Relation of the wicked Life and impenitent Death of Iohn Flood, who raped his own Child. Printed at London for Francis Coules, dwelling in the Old-Baily. 1637. 4°, A—C in fours, C 4 with a woodcut only. *B. M.*

The authorship is ascertained from the Stationers' Register.

GOOKEN, VINCENT, *Esquire.*

The Author and Case of Transplanting the Irish into Connaught Vindicated, from the unjust Aspersions of Col. Richard Lawrence. By Vincent Gooken, Esquire. London, Printed by A. M. for Simon Miller . . . 1653. 4°. A, 2 : B—I 2 in fours.

GORDON, PATRICK.

The Famous History of the Renown'd and Valiant Prince, Robert Sirnamed, The Bruce, ... Re-printed at Edinburgh, By James Watson, His Majesty's Printer, 1718. 12°, A—I in twelves : K, 8.

The leaf following the title is marked A 6, and is preceded by the title, a half-title, and (probably) 4 blanks. In the copy used was inserted an Imprimatur, apparently for an intended Scotish edition of the *Bruce* in 1613-14.

GORDON, SIR ROBERT, *of Lochinvar.*

Encovragements. For such as shall have intention to bee Vndertakers in the new plantation of Cape Breton, now New-Galloway in America. By mee Lochinvar. *Non nobis nati sumus, aliquid parentes, aliquid Patria, aliquid cognati postulant.* Edinbvrgh, Printed by Iohn Wreittoun. Anno Dom. 1625. 4°. Title and dedication to Sir William Alexander of Menstrie, 2 leaves : B—E in fours, E 4 blank. *B. M.*

This was apparently the copy presented to Sir W. Alexander, and is in the original calf binding, with W. A. impressed in gold on sides.

GORGE, DAVID, *Founder of the first Family of Love.*

Dauid Gorge / borne in Holland / a very Blasphemer of our Messias Iesu Christ / of his Lyfe / and damnable Heresi / nowe come to light / thre years after his death / in the Year of our Lorde M.D.LIX. Set forth by the Reverendt Father in God, Gouener of the Vniuersitie of the cytie of Basel, throwe the desyre of the honorable Counsell of the same cytie, . . . and now newly translated out of Latyne into Englische, Anno 1560. [Col.] Printed at Basel / by Conradus Meuse / In the year of our Lorde M.D.LX. In the moneth of Januari. 4°, A—F in fours.

Sothebys, June 27. 1885, No. 479.

GORGES, FERDINANDO, *Esquire.*

America Painted to the Life. The True History of The Spaniards Proceedings in the Conquests of the Indians, and of their Civil Wars among themselves, from Columbus his first Discovery, to these later Times. As also, Of the Original Under-takings of the Advancement of Plantations into those parts ; With a perfect Relation of our English Discoveries, shewing their Beginning, Progress and Continuance, from the Year 1628. to 1658. . . . More especially, an absolute Narrative of the North parts of America, and of the Discoveries and Plantations of our English in Virginia, New England, and Berbadoes. . . . London, Printed for Nath. Brook at the Angel in Cornhil. 1659. 4°, A—P in fours, besides an allegorical figure of America as a frontispiece, and a folded map, *Americae Descrip. :* Part 2 and 3, A, 2 leaves with title and preface, and B—Ii 2 in fours : Part 4, A, 2 leaves, and B—K in fours.

Part 2 commences with a new title after F 2. The 4th leaf is marked I, G—H having been omitted. Mr. Henry Stevens has pointed out that the third part of this book is merely the unsold stock of Edward Johnson's *Wonder-Working Providences,* interpolated by the publisher ; and Gorges issued a notice in the *Mercurius Publicus* for Sept. 13, 1660, disclaiming that portion of the volume.

GOSTELO, WALTER.

Charls Stuart and Oliver Cromwel United, Or, Glad tidings of Peace to all Christendom, to the Jews and Heathen Conversion, to the Church of Rome, certain downfall : The Irish not to be Transplanted. Extraordinarily declared by God Almighty to the Publisher, Walter Gostelow. . . . Printed for the Author, 1655. 8°, A—V in eights, title on A 2, and an extra leaf to the Reader after A 8.

GOULD, ROBERT.

The Corruption of the Times by Money. A Satyr. By Robert Gould. London : Printed for Matthew Wotton . . . 1693. 4°, A—E 2 in fours. Dedicated to Fleetwood Sheppard Esq; Gentleman Usher to the King.

A Satyr against Wooing : With a View of the Ill Consequences that attend it. Written by the Author of the Satyr against Woman . . . London, Printed in the Year, 1698. 4°, A—G, 2 leaves each. Dedicated to Sir Fleetwood Sheppard.

GOVERNAL OF HEALTH.

[The Gouernayle of helthe. W. Caxton, about 1489.] 4°, A—B in fours, and two unsigned leaves with Lydgate's *Medicina Stomachi,* in verse. Without title and catchwords. *Ham House* (the only copy known).

GOWRY.

De Execrabili Et Nefanda Fratrvm Rvvenorvm, . . . conjuratione, apud Perth-

um . . . 1600. . . . Hinc accessere ad
Regem Soteria, Carmine Heroico. . . .
Edinbvrgi Excudebat Robertvs Charteris.
Typographus. 1600. . . . 4°, a—e, 2
leaves each, e 2 blank: A—E, 2 leaves
each: F—H in fours: I, 2.

GRANTHAM, THOMAS.

The Brainbreakers - Breaker: Or, The
Apologie of Thomas Grantham, for his
Method in teaching, dwelling in Lothbury, London . . . . Printed at London,
1644. 4°, 4 leaves.

> This tract contains some encomiums on
> the author, and testimonials to his effici-
> ency as a preceptor.

GRATAROLUS, GULIELMUS *of Bergo-*
matis, Doctor of Arts and Physic.

The Castel of Memorie: wherein is conteined the restorying, augmentyng, and
conseruyng of the Memorye and Remembraunce / with the safest remedyes, and
best preceptes thereunto in any wise apperteyning: . . . Englished by Willyam
Fulwod. . . . Printed at Londō by Rouland Hall, dwelling in Gutter lane at the
signe of the halfe Egle and the Keye.
1563. 8°, black letter, A—H in eights.
Dedicated to the Lord Robert Dudley in
a long metrical epistle, followed by a
prose Preface and *the Bookes verdicte*, in
verse. *B. M.*

> The Preface is dated 20 Novr. 1562. The
> dedication occupies eight pages, and is in
> 4-line stanzas.

GRAUNT, JOHN.

Natural and Political Observations. . . .
The Third Edition, much Enlarged. Lon-
don, Printed by John Martyn, and James
Allestry, . . MDCLXV. 8°, A—O in eights,
A 1 and O 8 blank, a, 6 leaves, and a
folding table.

GREAVES, JOHN.

A Discovrse of the Romane Foot, And
Denarivs: From whence, as from two
principles, The Measvres, and Weights,
used by the Ancients, may be deduced.
By Iohn Greaves, Professor of Astronomy
in the Vniversity of Oxford . . . London,
Printed by M. F. for William Lee, . . .
1647. 8°. A, 4 leaves: B—K 4 in eights.
Dedicated to his friend John Selden, Esq.

GREEN, THOMAS.

The Case of Capt. Tho. Green, Commander of the Ship Worcester, and his
Crew, Tried and Condemned for Pyracy
& Murther, in the High Court of Admiralty of Scotland. London: Printed
in the Year 1705. 4°, A—D in fours.

GREENE, ROBERT.

The Spanish Masquerado . . . . 1589.

> The two editions of this tract printed in
> this year appear to vary only typographi-
> cally.

Greenes Groatsworth of Witte Bovght
with a million of Repentance: . . . London, Printed by N. O. for Henry Bell, and
are to be sold at his shop in Bethlem
at the signe of the Sun. 1621. 4°, A—I
in fours, I 4 blank. Black letter.

Pandosto. The Trivmph of Time . . . .
London, Printed by T. P. for Francis
Faulkner, . . . 1632. 4", black letter,
A—G in fours.

GREENHILL, THOMAS.

Nekrokedeia: Or, The Art of Embalm-
ing; Wherein is shewn The Right of
Burial, The Funeral Ceremonies, And the
several Ways of Preserving Dead Bodies
in Most Nations of the World. . . . In
Three Parts. The whole Work adorn'd
with variety of Sculptures. By Thomas
Greenhill, Surgeon. London: Printed
for the Author. MDCCV. 4°. Frontispiece with portrait, 1 leaf: two printed
titles, 2 leaves: dedication to Lord Pembroke, Preface, &c., 11 leaves: B—3 A in
fours: Catalogue of Authors and Table,
6 leaves. With a folded map of Egypt and
plates at pp. 200, 202, 204, 208 (2), 288,
300, 310, 312, 314, 318, 326, and 334.

GREW, NEHEMIAH, *F.R.S.*

Mvsævm Regalis Societatis. Or A Cata-
logue & Description of the Natural and
Artificial Rareties belonging to the Royal
Society And preserved at Gresham Col-
ledge. Made by Nehemiah Grew M.D.
Fellow of the Royal Society, . . . Lon-
don, Printed by W. Rawlins, for the
Author, 1681. Folio. A, 6 leaves: B—3
D 2 in fours: Anatomy of the Stomach,
by Grew, A—F 2 in fours, and the title.

GRIFFYTH, W., *Esquire.*

Villare Hibernicum: Being an Exact
Account of all the Provinces, Counties,
Cities, Arch-Bishopricks, . . . And most
considerable Villages and Places of
Strength, which have been Reduc'd by
His Majesties Arms since His first Land-
ing in Ireland: With an Impartial Jour-
nal of the Siege of Lymerick . . . London
Printed: And are to be Sold by Richard
Janeway . . . 1690. 4", A—G, 2 leaves
each.

GRIMALKIN.

Grimalkin, Or, The Rebel-Cat: A Novell,
Representing the Unwearied Attempts of
the Beasts of his Faction against Sove-
reignty and Succession since the Death of
the Lyons in the Tower. *Dic mihi, si*

fias tu Leo, qualis eris? London, Printed for the Author, 1681. Folio, A—D, 2 leaves each.

GRISELDA.
The Pleasant and sweet History of patient Grissell. Shewing how she from a poor mans Daughter, came to be a great Lady in France, being a patterne for all vertuous Women. Translated out of Italian. London: Printed by E. P. for John Wright, dwelling in Gilt-spurstreet at the signe of the Bible. 1640. 8°, black letter, 12 leaves, including one with a half-title and a cut. Collier's *Bibl. Cat.* 1865, i. 340.

> This appears to be the metrical broadside narrative printed as a tract, with supplementary matter in prose.

GROSSETESTE, ROBERT, *Bishop of Lincoln.*
The Testaments of the twelue patriarches, . . . Printed at London for the Company of the Stationers. 1610. 8°, black letter, A—L 4 in eights, L 4 with the colophon.

The Testament of the Twelve Patriarchs . . . London, Printed by Andrew Clark, for the Company of Stationers, 1674. 8°, A—K in eights. With cuts.

The Testament of the Twelve Patriarchs . . . London, Printed by Andrew Clark, for the Company of Stationers, 1677. 12°, A—K in eights. Black letter, with cuts.

GUALDI.
The Life of Donna Olimpia Maldachini, Who Governed the Church during the Time of Innocent the X. Which was from the Year 1644. to the Year 1655. Written in Italian by Abbot Gvaldi: And faithfully rendered into English. London, Printed by W. Godbid, and are to be sold by R. Littlebury at the Unicorn in Little Britain. M.DC.LXVII. 8°. A, 4 leaves : B—P 4 in eights, P 4 blank.

GUEZ, JEAN LOUIS, *Sieur de Balzac.*
The Letters of Monsievr de Balzac. Translated into English, according to the last Edition. By W. T. Esq. *Lege & Collige.* London, Printed by Nicholas Okes, for Richard Clotterbuck, . . . 1634. 4°. ¶, 4 leaves, with title, William Tirwhyt's dedication to Lord Craven, &c.: A, 4 leaves : a, 4 leaves : B—3 G 2 in fours. *B. M.*

The Letters . . . London. Printed by I. N. and are to be sold by W. Edmonds, and I. Colby, . . . 1638. 4°. *, 4 leaves: A, 4 leaves : a, 4 leaves: B—3 F in fours. *B. M.*

A New Collection of Epistles of Mons. de Balzac. Newly Translated. Oxford Printed for Francis Bowman Stationer. 1639. [This is on an engraved title by W. Marshall. The printed title follows :] New Epistles of Movnsievr de Balzac. Translated out of French into English, By Sʳ Richard Baker, Knight. London, Printed by T. Cotes for Fra. Eglesfield, John Crooke, and Rich. Serger, . . . 1638. 8°. Frontispiece, printed title, and Baker's dedication to Lord Newburgh, 3 leaves : B—Q 4 in eights : *A Svpply to the Second Part; Or The Third Part of the Letters,* with a new title, A—Rr in eights, Rr 7–8 blank.

A Collection of Some Modern Epistles of Monsievr de Balzac carefvlly Translated out of French. [Quot. from Mart. l. 10. Ep. 4.] Oxford, Printed by Leonard Lichfield for Francis Bowman. MD.C.XXXIX. 8°, A—T in eights.

> With a Preface by Bowman, the publisher, who does not name the translator.

GUIDOTT, THOMAS.
A Discourse of Bathe, and the Hot Waters There. Also, Some Enquiries into the Nature of the Water of St. Vincent's Rock, near Bristol; and that of Castle-Cary. To which is added, A Century of Observations, . . . With An Account of the Lives, and Character, of the Physicians of Bath. By Tho. Guidott, M.B. Physician there. *Virtute vincam Invidiam.* London, Printed for Henry Brome, . . . 1676. 8°, A—P 4 in eights, including the frontispiece and metrical explanation, besides four leaves of plates and a plan of Bath.

GWALTER, RUDOLPH.
Antichrist, That is to saye: A true reporte, that Antichriste is come / wher he was borne, of his Persone, miracles, what tooles he worketh withall, and what shalbe his ende : Translated out of Latine into Englishe. By J. O. . . . Imprinted in Sothwarke by Christopher Trutheall. Cum priuilegio Regali. 1556. 8°, A—B 6 in eights.

> Dedicated by the author, Rudolph Gwalter, to the Preachers of the Gospel in Zurich, where the tract was probably printed.

GUNTON, S., *late Preacher of the Word of God in the Cathedral Church of Peterburgh.*
Orthoiatreia : Or, A Brief Discourse concerning Bodily Worship: Proving it to be God's Due ; . . . London, Printed for Gabriel Bedell, M. M. and T. C. . . . 1650. 4°, A—H in fours.

tories of those times and offered to the service of these. London, Printed by A. Maxey, and are to be sold by J. Rothwel . . . 1658. 4°, B—L in fours, besides title and preface.

GUY OF WARWICK.

Cy commence Guy de vvarwich cheualier Dagleterre qui en sons temps fit plusieurs prouesses et conquestes en Allemaigne / ytalie et Dannemarche. Et aussi sur les infidelles ennemys de la chrestientè Comme pourrez veoir plus a plain en ce present liure. Imprime nouuellement a Paris. [Device of the Elephant and Castle.] Cum

Nursing of Children . . . Written in French by Iames Gvillimeav the French Kings Chirurgion. London, Printed by Anne Griffin, for Ioyce Norton, and Richard Whitaker, 1635. 4°. ¶ and ¶¶ 4 leaves each: A—3 B 2 in fours. With woodcuts.

GULIELMA, SANTA.

Legēda de Sāta Gulielma figliola del Re de Inghelterra: moglie del Re de Ungaria . . . [Col.] Stampata nella Inclita Citta di Milano . . . M.D.XXXX VIIII. 8vo, A—E in fours: F, 6.

H.

H. A.

A Speedy Post from Heaven, to the King of England. Never put out by any before. London, Printed in the yeare, 1642. 4°, 4 leaves.

H. I.

The Antipodes, Or Reformation with the Heeles upward. Being A compendious Narrative or Discovery, of the great hypocrisie of our pretending Reformers, . . . Oxford Printed and published for the information of the oppressed Commons of England. 1647. 4°, 6 leaves.

H. J., *Esquire*.

A Gagg to Love's Advocate: Or, An Assertion of the Justice of the Parliament in the execution of Mr Love. By J. H. Esq. London, Printed by William Du-Gard . . . [1651.] 4°. Title and dedication to the Council of State, 2 leaves : B—D in fours, D 4 blank. B 1 is misprinted A.

H. M.

The Young Cooks Monitor: Or, Directions for Cookery and Distilling. Being

A choice Compendium of Excellent Receipts. Made Publick for the Use and Benefit of my Schollars. By M. H. London, Printed for William Downing in Great St. Bartholomews-Close, 1683. 8°, A—L in eights, A 1 blank.

H. N.

An Elegy on Sir George Jeffereys, Late Lord Chancellor of England, who died Prisoner in the Tower of London, April the 18th 1689. London, Printed in the Year, 1689. A broadside.

H. P., *M.D.*

Gutta Podagrica : A Treatise of the Govt. The severall sorts thereof. What Diet is good for such as are troubled therewith. . . . London, Printed by Thomas Harper. 1633. 4°, A—G in fours, A 1 blank. With a preface by H. H., a near relative of the deceased writer.

H. R.

The Warr in New-England Wisely Ended. King Philip that barbarous Indian now Beheaded, and most of his Bloudy Adherents submitted to Mercy, the Rest fled far up into the Countrey, which hath given the Inhabitants Encouragement to prepare for their Settlement. Being a True and Perfect Account brought in by Caleb More Master of a Vessel newly Arrived from Rhode-Island. And Published for general Satisfaction . . . London, Printed by J. B. for Dorman Newman . . . 1677. Folio, 2 leaves subscribed *R. H.*

H. T.

A True Discourse of the Two infamous upstart Prophets, Richard Farnham Weaver of White-Chappell, and John Bull Weaver of Saint Butolphs Algate, now Prisoners, the one in Newgate, and the other in Bridewell : with their Examinations . . . April 16. 1636. As also of Margaret Tennis now Prisoner in Old Bridewell, . . . Written by T. H. Printed at London for Thomas Lambert . . . 1636. 4°. A, 2 leaves : B—C in fours : D, 2. With a cut on the title.

The Famovs and Remarkable History of Sir Richard Whittington, Three times Lord Major of London. Who lived in the time of King Henry the Fift, in the yeare 1419. With all the remarkable Passages, and things of Note, which happned in his time : with his Life and Death. Written by T. H. London, Printed by W. Wilson, and are to be sold by Francis Coles in the Ould [Baily.] 1656. Sm. 8°, black letter. A, 6 : B—E 7 in eights, E 8 having probably been blank. With a frontispiece and cuts. *B. M.*

Sothebys, May 22, 1882, No. 2987, title slightly imperfect.

H. W.

A Changling no Company for Lovers of Loyaltie Or The Subjects Lesson in Poynt of Sacred Submission to, and humble Complyance with God and the King ; . . . London, Printed by M. Simmons, for Thomas Parkhurst, . . . 1660. 4° A—G in fours.

H. W.

Remarks on the Affairs and Trade of England and Ireland . . . By a hearty Wellwisher to the Protestant Religion, and to the Prosperity of these Kingdoms. . . . London, Printed for Tho. Parkhurst . . . 1691. 4°. A, 2 : B—L 2 in fours.

HAINES, RICHARD.

A Breviat of some Proposals Prepared to be Offered to the Great Wisdom of the Nation, . . . For the speedy Restoring the Woollen Manufacture, by a Method practised in other Nations . . . London, Printed for Langley Curtis . . . 1679. 4°, 4 leaves.

Aphorisms upon the New Way of improving Cyder, or making Cyder-Royal, lately discovered for the good of those Kingdoms and Nations that are Beholden to Others, and Pay Dear for Wine . . . To which are Added, Certain Expedients concerning Raising and Planting of Appletrees, Gooseberry-trees, &c. . . . London : Printed by George Larkin for the Author, . . . 1684. Folio. B—F, 2 leaves each, and the title.

HAKEWILL, GEORGE.

An Apologie of the Power and Providence of God in the Government of the World. . . . By G. H. D.D. . . . Oxford, Printed by Iohn Lichfield and William Tvrner, . . . 1627. Folio. b, 4 : c. 6 : d—e, 4 each : A—3 O 2 in fours. Dedicated to the University of Oxford.

HALL, JOHN.

The True Cavalier Examined by his Principles ; And found Not Guilty of Schism or Sedition. London, Printed by Tho. Newcomb, ... 1656. 4°, A—S 2 in fours. Dedicated to Cromwell.

HALL, JOSEPH.

The Discovery of A New World or A Description of the South Indies Hetherto Vnknowne By an English Mercury. Imprinted for Ed. Blount and W. Barrett. [1608 ?] 8°. ¶, 7 leaves : A, 8 leaves : ¶, 4 leaves : B—R 2 in eights. The title is engraved.

Dedicated by John Healey, the translator, to " the Trve mirror of truest honor, William Earle of Penbroke."

An Humble Remonstrance to the High Covrt of Parliament, By A dutifull Sonne of the Chvrch. London, Printed for Nathaniel Butter . . . 1640. 4°, A—F in fours, A 1 blank.

HALE, SIR MATTHEW.

Magnetismus Magnus : Or, Metaphysical and Divine Contemplations on the Magnet, Or Loadstone. Written by Sir Matthew Hale, Knight, some time Lord Chief Justice of the King's-Bench. London, Printed for William Shrowsbury, . . . 1695. 8° A, 4 leaves : B—L in eights.

HALYWELL, HENRY.

An Account of Familism as it is Revived and Propagated by the Quakers . . . By Henry Hallywell. . . . London : Printed for Walter Kettilby . . . 1673. 8°, A—I in eights, I 8 blank. Dedicated to Sir John Covert of Slaugham in Sussex.

The Sacred Method of saving Humane Souls by Jesus Christ. By Henry Hallywell Minister of the Gospel at Hellu in Sussex . . . London, Printed for Walter Kettilby . . . 1677. 8°, A—H in eights.

Melampopronoea: Or A Discourse of the Polity of the Kingdom of Darkness . . . By Henry Hallywell, Master of Arts, and sometimes Fellow of Christs Colledge in Cambridge. . . . London, Printed for Walter Kettilby, . . . 1681. 8°, A—I 4 in eights, I 4 blank. Dedicated to Sir James Morton of Slaugham in Sussex.

The Excellency of Moral Vertue, . . . By Henry Hallywell, Vicar of Cowfold, in Sussex. London, Printed for James Adamson, . . . 1692. 8°. A, 4 leaves: B—M in eights.

HAMILTON, JAMES, *Duke of Hamilton*.
A New Declaration Set forth by the Lord Gen. Hamilton Wherein is declared, The full Resolution of the Officers and Souldiers in the Scottish Army, to the Presbyterians of England, and their Resolution to settle the Kings Majesty in His Royal Throne, . . . Printed at Edinburgh, And re-printed at London, . . . 1648. 4°, 4 leaves.

HAMILTONS.
The manifold Practises and Attempts of the Hamiltons, And particularly of the present Duke of Hamilton Now Generall of the Scottish Army to get the Crown of Scotland. Discovered in an intercepted Letter written from a Malignant here in London to his friend in Scotland. . . . Printed at London, in the year 1648. 4°, A—C in fours.

The Liar laid open in a Letter, First Written to a Friend in the Country, at his desire, for his private satisfaction: And now Printed for the Publick. Touching a late Pamphlet, Intituled, The manifold Practises . . . London, Printed in in the Yeer, 1648. 4°, A—B in fours.

HAMMOND, HENRY.
A Practicall Catechisme. [Two quotations.] By H. Hammond, Doctour of Divinity. Oxford, Printed in the yeare 1646. 4°. Frontispiece, 1 leaf: A, 4 leaves: Contents, 1 leaf: A—P 2 in fours: *Additions*, with the Author's Preface, title, and following leaf and (b)—(i) in fours: Table, 4 leaves.

HAMMOND, CHARLES, *Captain*.
Truth's Discovery; Or The Cavaliers Case Clearly Stated by Conscience and Plain-dealing, Presented to the Honorable Commissioners, and all the truly

Loyall, and Indigent Officers, and Souldiers . . . London, Printed by Edward Crowch, dwelling on Snow-Hill. 1664. 4°, A—C in fours.

HAMOR, RALPH, *late Secretary for Virginia*.
A Trve Discovrse of the Present Estate of Virginia, and the successe of the affaires there till the 18 of Iune. 1614. Together with a Relation of the seuerall English townes and forts, the assured hopes of that countrie, and the peace concluded with the Indians. The Christening of Powhatans daughter and her marriage with an English-man . . . Printed at London by Iohn Beale for William Welby . . . 1615. 4°, A—K 3 in fours.

HAMPSHIRE.
Don Quixot Redivivus Encountring a Barns-Door, Or an Exact Narrative of the Rare Exploits of Captain Brains in a Dangerous Expedition against a certain Barn in a Town on the other Side of the River ANNE in the Land of Little Ease, and Less Justice . . . Printed for the Company of Informers. [1673-4.] 4°, A—E in fours.

An account of a local ritualistic dispute at Andover.

HARCOURT, ROBERT, *of Stanton-Harcourt, Esquire*.
A Relation of a Voyage to Gviana. Describing the Climat, Scituation, fertilitie, prouisions and commodities of that Country, containing senen Prouinces, and other Signiories. . . . The Pattent for the Plantation of which Country, his Maiestie hath granted to the said Robert Harcovrt vnder the Great Seale . . . At London Printed by Iohn Beale, for W. Welby, . . . 1613. 4°, A—L in fours. Dedicated to Prince Charles.

The Relation of a Voyage to Gviana. Describing the Climate, Situation, Fertilitie, & Commodities of that Country. . . . Now newly reviewed, & enlarged, by addition of some necessary Notes, for the more ample explaining of some things mentioned in the said Relation: Together, with a larger declaration of the famous Riuer of the Amazones, and the Country thereabout. Gathered from the modern experience of our owne Country-men. The Patent for the Plantation of which Country. His Maiestie hath lately Granted to a Corporation. . . . London Printed by Edw. Allde, dwelling neere Christ-Church. 1626. 4°, A—N 2 in fours. Dedicated to Charles I. *B. M.*

HARMER, ANTHONY.

A Specimen of some Errors and Defects in the History of the Reformation of the Church of England; Wrote by Gilbert Burnet, D.D. now Lord Bishop of Sarum. London, Printed for Randall Taylor, . . . 1693. 8°. A, 4 leaves: B—O 4 in eights.

HARIOT, THOMAS.

Merveillevx et Estrange Rapport, tovtesfois Fidele, des Commoditez, qui se trouvent en Virginia, des Facons des Natvrels Habitans . . . Tradvit Novvellement d'Anglois ē Frācois. Francoforti ad Moenvm Tipis Ioannis Wecheli, Svmtibvs vero Theodori De Bry Anno cɪɔ ɪɔ xc. . . . Folio. a, 4 leaves: b, 6: c, 4: d, 6: Plate of Adam and Eve and map of Virginia, 2 leaves: Then folios i–xvi with plates and letterpress: folio xvii with plate, 2 leaves: folio xviii, 1 leaf: folios xix–xxiii., 2 leaves each, one with plate, the other with separate letterpress: *Povrtraicts des Pictes*, 5 leaves of letterpress and five plates: Table, 2 leaves: colophon, 1 leaf.

HARPSFELD, NICHOLAS, *Archdeacon of Canterbury.*

Historia Anglicana Ecclesiastica A Primis Gentis Svsceptae Fidei Incvnabilis ad nostra fere tempora dedvcta . . . Adiecta breui narratione, de Diuortio Henrici VIII. . . . Scripta ab Edmvndo Campiano. Nunc primum in lucem producta Studio & Opera R. P. Richardi Gibboni Angli Societatis Iesv Theologi.- Dvaci, . . . Anno M.DC.XIX. . . . Folio. ã—Y in fours: A—5 E in fours.

HARRIS, JOHN.

The Pvritanes Impvritie: Or the Anatomie of a Puritane or Seperatist, by Name and Profession. . . . By John Harris Gent. London. Printed by T. Fawcet. MDCXLI. 4°, 4 leaves.

HARRIS, WALTER, *M.D., Physician to the Prince of Orange.*

A Description of the Kings Royal Palace and Gardens at Loo. Together with a Short Account of Holland. In which there are some Observations relating to their Diseases. London: Printed by R. Roberts, and Sold by T. Nutt, . . . MDCXCIX. 4°, A—F in fours, E repeated, and no C. With a folding plan of the Gardens.

HARRISON, WILLIAM, AND WILLIAM LEYGH.

Deaths Advantage little regarded, and the soules solace against sorrow. Preached in two funerall Sermons at Childwal in Lancashire at the buriall of Mistris Katherin Brettergh the third of Iune. 1601. The one by William Harrison, one of the Preachers appointed by her Maiestie for the Countie Palatine of Lancaster, the other by William Leygh, Bachelor of Diuinitie, and Pastor of Standish. Whereunto is annexed, the Christian life and godly death of the said Gentlewoman. The second Edition, corrected and amended. . . . At London. Imprinted by Felix Kyngston. 1602. 8°. A, 4 leaves, the first blank: a folded leaf: B—P in eights, P 8 blank. *B. M.*

The *Soules Solace* has a separate title on G 3, and on M 4 the *Life* opens with a third title: A Brief Discovrse of the Christian Life and death, of Mistris Katherin Brettergh, late wife of Master William Brettergh, of Bretterghoult, in the Countie of Lancaster Gentleman; who departed this world the last of May. 1601. With the manner of a bitter conflict she had with Satan, . . . London, Imprinted by Felix Kyngston. 1602.

Deaths Advantage. . . . London Imprinted by Felix Kyngston. 1605. 8°, A—P in eights, A 1 blank. *B. M.* (imperfect)

The *Life* begins on M 4 with a separate title, dated 1606.

Deaths Advantage little regarded, and the soules solace against sorrow. Preached in two funerall Sermons at Childwall in Lancashire at the buriall of Mistris Katherin Brettergh the third of Iune. 1601. Whereunto is annexed, the Christian life and godly death of the said Gentlewoman. The second Edition, corrected and amended. . . . At London Imprinted by Felix Kyngston, and are to be sold by Arthur Iohnson. 1612. 8°, A—P in eights, first and last leaves blank.

The *Life* begins on M 4 with a separate title.

Deaths Advantage . . . At London Imprinted by Felix Kyngston. 1617. 8°. A, 3 leaves: B—P in eights. *B. M.*

HARRISS, CHARLES.

A Scriptural Chronicle of Satans Incendiaries Viz. Hard-hearted Persecutors, and Malitious Informers. With their Work, Wages, and Ends, who were Instruments of Cruelty against true Worshippers. . . . Printed in the Yeer, 1670. 4°, A—C 2 in fours.

HARTLIB, SAMUEL.

Samuel Hartlib His Legacy of Husbandry. Wherein are bequeathed to the Common-

The Reformed Virginian Silk-Worm. Containing Many Excellent and Choice Secrets, Experiments, and Discoveries for attaining of National and Private Profits and Riches. London, Printed for Giles Calvert . . . 1655. 4⁰. The first portion, A—I in fours: the second, A—F 2 in fours.

Panegyricus Carolo Gvstavo Magno Suecorum, Gothorum, Vandalorumque Regi, incruento Sarmatiæ Victori, ... Heroi Afflictis solatia, Regibus in exemplum, nato. Londini, Væneunt apud Richardum Wodenothe, ... MCD.L.VI. 4⁰. Title and Samuel Hartlib to the Reader, 2 leaves : B—D in fours.

Olbia. The New Iland Lately Discovered. With its Religion, and Rites of Worship; Laws, Customs, and Government; Characters and Language ; . . . The First Part. From the Original. For Samuel Hartlib, in Ax-yard Westminster, and John Bartlet at the Guilt-Cup near Austins-Gate London and in Westminster-Hall. 1660. 4⁰, A—3 A in fours.

HARVEY, CHRISTOPHER.
The Synagogve, Or, The Shadow of the Temple. Sacred Poems, and Private Ejaculations. In Imitation of Mr George Herbert. . . . London, Printed by I. L. for Phil. Stephens and Christopher Meredith, . . . 1640. Small 8⁰ or 12⁰, A—B 6 in twelves, A 1 blank. B. M.

HARVEY, GABRIEL.
Gabrielis Harveii Ciceronianvs. Vel Oratio post reditum . . . habita Cantabrigiæ ad suos Auditores. Quorum potissimùm causa, diuulgata est. Londini, Ex Officina Typographica Henrici Binneman. Anno. CIƆ.IƆ.LXXVII. [In the colophon is added :] mense Iunio. 4⁰, A—I 2 in fours, besides a leaf of Errata.

HARVEY, GIDEON, M.D.
Great Venus Unmasked : Or a more exact Discovery of the Venereal Evil, . . . The Second Edition. London, Printed by B. G. for Nath. Brook . . . 1672. 8⁰.

from divers free-men of the same City, their true and proper goods, . . . London, Printed, for the good of all free-men, . . . 1647. 4⁰, A—B 2 in fours.

A singular tract, full of curious allusions.

HARVEY, WILLIAM, of Folkestone, M.D.
Exercitationes De Generatione Animalium. . . . Autore Gvilielmo Harveo. . . . Londini, Typis Du-Gardianis, . . . M.DC.LI. 4⁰. Title and following leaf, 2 leaves : a, 4 leaves : B—Ss in fours. Ss 4 blank. Dedicated to the College of Physicians.

HASLERIGG, SIR ARTHUR.
Sir Arthur Hesilrigs Lamentation, and Confession. Upon his being voted from sitting in this long-expected Parliament, Feb. 21. 1660. London : Printed by Edw. Mason. 1660. 4⁰, 4 leaves.

The Hang-mans Lamentation for the losse of Sir Arthur Haslerigge : dying in the Tower. Being a Dialogue between Esquire Dun and Sir Arthur Haslerigg. With their last Conference in the Tower of London a little before Sir Arthurs Death. Printed for Tho. Vere and W. Gilbertson. 1660. 8⁰, A in eights. Cut on title. B. M.

HAVEN.
The Haven-Finding Art, Or, The Way to find any Hauen or place at sea, by the Latitude and variation, Lately published in the Dutch, French, and Latine tongues, . . . And now translated into English for the common benefite of the Seamen of England. Imprinted at London by G. B. R. N. and R. B. 1599. 4⁰, A—F 2 in fours. With diagrams. Dedicated by E. Wright to Charles, Earl of Nottingham, and (ii.) to Richard Poulter, Master, and the Brothers of the Trinity House.

HAWKINS, SIR JOHN.
A true declaration of the troublesome voyadge of M. John Hawkins to the parties of Guynea [Guiana] and the west Indies, in the yeares of our Lord 1567. and 1568. Imprinted at Londõ in Poules Church-yarde, by Thomas Purfoote for

Lucas Harrison, dwelling at the signe of the Crane. Anno. 1569. 8°, A—B in eights, B 8 blank. *B. M.*

HAWKINS, SIR RICHARD, *son of the above.*
The Observations of S^{ir} Richard Hawkins Knight, in his Voyage into the South Sea. Anno Domini. 1593. *Per varios Casus* . . . Manil. li. I. London Printed by I. D. for Iohn Iaggard, . . . 1622. Folio. Title, the author's dedication to Charles, Prince of Wales, and Preface, 3 leaves: A—Y in fours.

HAYNE, THOMAS.
Grammatices Latini Compendium, Anno 1637. E Grammaticis tum veteribus tum neotericis, . . . Here also the most necessary Rules are expressed in English opposite to the Latine, that the one may facilitate and give light to the other. . . . Londini, Excusum typis Ed. Griffini, Prostant . . . apud Joh. Rothwell. 1640. 8°, A—K in eights. Dedicated to William, Archbishop of Canterbury.

> Sothebys, Jan. 29, 1886, No. 17, a copy in old blue morocco, presented to Charles II. by the author, who has written an inscription on the page facing the title. An early MS. note on the fly-leaf says: "This booke was the Grammar of the then Prince of Wales now Charles D. G. King of Scotland &c. vsed by his Brother James Duke of Yorke."
> The words *James Duke of Yorke* are in a different hand, probably the Duke's when a boy.

HAYWARD, SIR JOHN.
A Treatise of Vnion of the two Realmes of England and Scotland. By I. H. At London Imprinted by F. K. for C. B. . . . 1604. 4°, A—H in fours, and a leaf of I.

HEAD, RICHARD.
The Western Wonder : Or, O Brazeel, An Inchanted Island discovered ; with a Relation of two Ship-wracks in a dreadful Sea-storm in that discovery. To which is added, A Description of a Place, Called, Montecapernia, Relating the Nature of the People, . . . London, Printed for N. C. M.DC.LXXIV. 4°, A—E in fours.

The English Rogue : Or, Witty Extravagant : Described in the Life of Meriton Latroon . . . The Four Parts. To which is added a Fifth Part, completing the whole History of his Life. . . . London, Printed for J. Back . . . 1688. 12°, A—K in twelves.
> An abridgment of the original book with a supplement.

HEATH, JAMES.
Flagellum : Or The Life and Death,

Birth and Burial of O. Cromwell The late Usurper : Faithfully Described. With An Exact Account of His Policies and Successes . . . The Fourth Edition with Additions . . . London, Printed by E. C. for Randall Taylor, . . . 1669. 8°, A—O in eights, besides the title and portrait.

HECTORS.
A notable and pleasant History of the famous renowned Knights of the Blade, commonly called Hectors, Or, St. Nicholas Clerkes. Wherein is shewed how they first came to that Name and Profession, . . . Printed at London, for Richard Harper, at the Bible and Harpe in Smithfield. 1651. 4°, A—B in fours.

HEINSIUS OR HEYNE, DANIEL.
Laus Pediculi : Or An Apologeticall Speech, Directed to the Worshipfull Masters and Wardens of Beggars Hall. Written in Latine by the learned Daniel Heinsius. And from thence translated into English by Iames Gvitard, Gentleman. London, Printed by Tho. Harper. 1634. 4°, A—D in fours, A 1 and D 4 blank. Dedicated to Henry Cary, Lord Leppington, by the translator.

HENNEPIN, LOUIS.
A New Discovery of a Vast Country in America, Extending above Four Thousand Miles, between New France and New Mexico. With a Description of the Great Lakes, Cataracts, Rivers, Plants, and Animals : Also, the Manners, Customs, and Languages. . . . With a Continuation : Giving an Account of the Attempts of the Sieur De la Salle upon the Mines of St. Barbe, &c. Both Parts Illustrated with Maps and Figures, and Dedicated to His Majesty K. William. By L. Hennepin, now Resident in Holland. To which is added, Several New Discoveries in North-America, not publish'd in the French Edition. London : Printed for M. Bentley, J. Tonson, . . . 1698. 8°. A, 8 leaves : a, 4 leaves : B —V 6 in eights : *Continuation*, Aa—Oo 4 in eights : *Account of New Discoveries*, with a half-title, V 6—Aa 2 in eights. With a frontispiece and map, and plates at pp. 28 and 114 in first Part, and a map and plates at pp. 8, 32, 89, and 157 in Part II.
> The *Account of New Discoveries* follows by signatures the first part ; but the Continuation has been interposed.

HENRIETTA MARIA, *Queen Consort of Great Britain* [1625-48].
Memoires of the Life and Death of the

matchless Mirrour of Magnanimity and Heroick Virtues Henrietta Maria De Bourbon, . . . London, Printed, and are to be sold at the Booksellers Shops, A. Dom. 1671. 12°. Title and dedication, 2 leaves : B 2—F 9 in twelves, F 10-12 occupied by advertisements.

HENRY III., *King of England.*
The Troublesome Life and Raigne of King Henry the Third. Wherein five Distempers and Maladies are set forth. 1. By the Pope and Church-mens extortions. 2. By the places of best trust bestowed upon unworthy Members. 3. By Patents and Monopolies for private Favourites. 4. By needlesse expenses and pawning of jewels. 5. By factious Lords and ambitious Peeres. Sutable to these unhappie times of ours; . . . Imprinted at London for George Lindsey. 1642. 4°, A—B in fours.

HENRY VIII., *King of England.*
A copy of the letters / wherin the most redouted & mighty price our soverayne lorde kyng Henry the eight kyng of Englande & of France / defesor of the faith / and lorde of Irlāde : made answere vnto a certayne letter of Martyn Luther sent vnto hym by the same / & also the copy of ye foresayd Luthers letter / in suche order as here after foloweth. [Col.] Imprinted at London in Flete-strete by Richarde Pynson / priter to the kynges most noble grace. Cum priuilegio a rege indulto. 8°. A, 12 leaves : B—E in eights : F, 5 leaves.

Novitates Qvaedam ex diversor. prae-stantiū epistolis desumptæ. De sanctor. in regno Angliæ perseqution. ac martyrii constan:ia . . . . Breue Apostolicum ad Regem Rhomano[rum] Ferdinandum contra hanc crudelitatem. . . . Anno. M.D. XXXVI. Octauo Kalendas Maij. 8°, A—C in fours. *B. M.*

This little historical tract includes an account of the executions of Fisher and More.

The History of the Life, Victorious Reign, and Death of K. Henry VIII. Containing an Account of his Wars and Victories . . . London Printed, and are to be sold by H. Rodes . . . 1682. 12°. a, 6 : B—Ll in twelves. With portraits of Henry VIII. and Edward VI. and two plates in three compartments.

HENRY II., *King of France.*
Epitaphivm in Mortem Gallorvm Regis . . . eius nominis secundi . . . duodecim linguis . . . A Paris, De l'Imprimerie de Robert Estienne. M.D.LX . . . 4°, A—G in fours.

This volume includes two epitaphs by H. Keir, one in English, the other in Scotish.

HERBAL.
The grete herball ; whiche gyueth parfyt knowlege and vnderstandyng of all maner of herbes & theyr graciovs vertues whiche god hath ordeyned for our prosperous welfare and helth / for they hele & cure all maner of dyseases and sekenesses that fall or mysfortune to all maner of creatures of god created practysed by many expert and wyse maysters as Auicenna & other, &c. Also it gyueth vnderstandynge of the booke lately prynted by me (Peter treueris) named the noble experiēce of vertuous handwarke of surgery. [Col.] Thus endeth the grete herbal with his tables which is translated out of Frensshe itō Euglysshe. [Southwark, Peter Treveris, 1525-6.] Folio. Title, Table, &c., 5 leaves : A—Dd in sixes. With the device of Treveris on the last page and woodcuts. In two columns.

In *Collections and Notes,* 2nd Series, p. 701, I describe the edition printed by Treveris, 27th July 1526, which seems to correspond pretty closely with that of 1529. The present of course must have followed the *Noble Experience of Surgery,* 1525, which it cites as already in print, and perhaps therefore it intervened between the latter and the issue of July 1526.

The alleged impression of the Herbal by Treveris, 20th June 1516, I have not seen, nor had Herbert, I think, ever done so, as his account of it has every appearance of having been borrowed from Ames. The copy which I here record was stated in the auctioneers' Catalogue to be of 1516 indeed; but on examination I found it to be no such matter.

At the same time, as the month of printing differs according to Herbert, there is room for expectation that the *editio princeps* of the work may occur, though I am not at present aware of any collection which possesses it.

HERBERT, THOMAS.
Stripping, Whipping, and Pumping, Or, The live mad Shavers of Drury-Lane ; strangely Acted, and truely Related. Done in the Period, latter end, Tayle, or Rumpe of the Dogged Dogge-dayes, last past, August. 1638. Together with the names of the severall parties which were Actors in this foule businesse. London : Printed by J. O. for T. Lambert, 1638. 8°, A—B 4 in eights, A 1 with a rough woodcut and B 4 blank. In prose.

Collier's Sale, August 1884, No. 426.

An Answer to the most Envious, Scandalous, and Libellous Pamphlet, Entituled, Mercvries Message . . . [London, 1641.] 4°, 4 leaves subscribed *Tho. Herbert.* With a cut of an arm holding a knife on title, and the print of Laud on the back. In verse.

HEREFORDSHIRE.

The Late Commotion of certaine Papists in Herefordshire. Occasioned by the death of one Alice Wellington, a Recusant, who was buried after the Popish maner, in the Towne of Allens-Moore, neere Hereford, vpon Tuesday in Whitsun weeke last past. 1605. With other excellent matter thereby occasioned. Truely set forth. Imprinted at London by S. S. for I. Chorlton, and F. Burton. 1605. 4°, A—F in fours, A 1 blank. With a preface by Thomas Hamond. *B. M.*

A Declaration, Or Resolution of the Countie of Hereford. Imprinted at London for Tho. Lewes. 1642. A broadside.

HERMES TRISMEGISTUS.

The Divine Pomander of Hermes Mercurius Trismegistus, in XVII. Books. Translated . . . into English by that Learned Divine Doctor Everard. London, Printed by Robert White, for Tho. Brewster, and Greg. Moule, . . . 1650. 8°, A—P 4 in eights.

HERODIAN *of Alexandria.*

Herodian's History of the Roman Emperors, . . . Done from the Greek, by a Gentleman at Oxford. London, Printed for John Hartley, . . . 1698. 8°, A—Ee 4 in eights.

HERRICK, ROBERT.

Hesperides . . . 1648.
Some copies after the publishers' names read: "And are to be sold by Tho. Hunt, Bookseller in Exon."

[HERRIES, W.]

A Defence of the Scots Abdicating Darien : Including An Answer to the Defence of the Scots Settlement there. Authore Britanno sed Dunensi. . . . Printed in the Year, 1700. 8°, A—N in fours.

HERRING, FRANCIS, *M.D.*

Certaine Rvles, Directions, Or Advertisements for this Time of Pestilentiall Contagion : . . . London, Printed by William Iones. 1625. 4°, A—C in fours, C 4 blank. *B. M.*

Popish Pietie, Or The first part of the Historie of that horrible and barbarous conspiracie, commonly called the Powder-treason : . . . Written first in Latin verse

by F. H. [Doctor] in Physicke : and translated into English by A. P. London, Printed for William Iones. 1610. 8°, A—C in eights. Printed between borders. *B. M.*
This copy is mutilated.

HERTFORDSHIRE.

The Most Crvell and Bloody Mvrther committed by an Inkeepers Wife, called Annis Dell, and her Sonne George Dell, Foure yeeres since. On the bodie of a Childe, called Anthonie Iames in Bishops Hatfeild in the Countie of Hartford, and now most miraculously reuealed by the Sister of the said Anthony, . . . With the seuerall Witch-crafts, and most damnable practises of one Iohane Harrison and her Daughter vpon seuerall persons, men and women at Royston, who were all executed at Hartford the 4 of August last past. 1606. London Printed for William Ferebrand and Iohn Wright. . . . 1606. 4°, A—C in fours, Black letter. *B. M.*

A True Relation of a Devilish Attempt to Fire the Town of Barnet, in the County of Hartford, on Thursday the 16th of this Instant October 1679. In a Letter to a Friend in London. London, Printed for Jonathan Robinson, . . . 1679. Folio, 4 leaves.

The Case of a Murther in Hertfordshire. Found amongst the Papers of that Eminent Lawyer, Sir John Maynard, . . . [Col.] London, Printed in the Year, 1699. A folio leaf.
This murder occurred in 4 Charles I. The victim was Joan Norcott, wife of Arthur Norcott.

Some Observations on the Tryal of Spencer Cowper, J. Marson, E. Stevens, W. Rogers, that were Tried at Hertford, about the Murder of Sarah Stout. Together with other things relating thereunto. London, Printed, . . . 1700. 4°, A—C 2 in fours.

A Full and Impartial Account of the Discovery of Sorcery and Witchcraft, Practis'd by Jane Wenham of Walkerne in Hertfordshire, upon the Bodies of Anne Thorn, Anne Strut, &c. . . . Also Her Tryal . . . The Fourth Edition. London : Printed for E. Curll, . . . 1712. 8°, A, with title and preface, 2 leaves : B—F 2 in fours.

A Full Confutation of Witchcraft : More particularly of the Depositions against Jane Wenham, Lately Condemned for a Witch at Hertford. In which the Modern Notions of Witches are overthrown, and logia studĕte Parisiense . . . London, Richard Pynson [1509.] 4°, A—E in sixes, but only 5 leaves in A.

Sotheby's, June 30, 1885, No. 1032, Heber's copy. There is no imprint ; but Pynson's device surrounded by a broad border occupies the whole of the first leaf of A beneath the title given above.

HIGFORD, WILLIAM.

The Institution of a Gentleman In III. Parts. By William Higford Esq; *Virtus verus Honos.* London, Printed by A. W. for William Lee . . . 1660. 8°, A—G in eights, G 8 blank, besides a leaf with the *Interpretation of Poetical Sentences.* Dedicated to Lord Scudamore by Clement Barksdale.

HIGHWAYMEN.

The Confession of the Four High-Way-Men. As it was Written by One of them, and Allowed by the Rest the 14th of this Instant April (being the Day before their Appointed Execution). Viz. John Williams, alias Tho. Matchet. Francis Jackson, alias Dixie. John White, alias Fowler. Walter Parkhurst. . . . With Allowance. London, Printed for D. M. 1674. 4°, 4 leaves.

HILDERSHAW, ARTHUR, *of Ashby de la Zouche.*

The Canticles Or Song of Solomon Paraphrased ; and Explained by divers other Texts of Scripture, very useful . . . As also the same, together with the two Songs of Moses, and the Song of Deborah, Collected into Meeter. London, Printed by T. Millbourn, for Robert Clavel . . . . 1672. 8°. Title and to the Reader, 3 leaves : B—L in eights, L 8 blank.

HILL, THOMAS.

The proffitable Arte of Gardening, now the third tyme set fourth : to whiche is added muche necessary matter, and a number of Secretes with the Physick helpes belonging vnto eche herbe, and that easie prepared. To this annexed, two proper treatises, the one entituled The maru.eilous Gouernment . . . of the Beas . . . and the other, The Yerely Coniectures, meete for the husbandmā to knowe : Englished by Thomas Hill Londiner . . . Imprinted at London by Thomas Marshe. [Col.] Imprinted at London in Fletestrete . . . by Thomas Marshe. 1568. 8°, A—dd in eights, besides a folded leaf in cc : the Treatise on Bees with a new title, title and following leaves, including dedication to Master M. Gentleman, 6 leaves : Aa—Ll 4 in eights. With a few cuts and a portrait of Hill An. æt. 28, on back of second title.

HILLIARD, JOHN, *Preacher of the Word of Life in Sopley.*

Fire from Heauen. Burning the body of one John Hitchell of Holne-hurst, within the parish of Christ-church in the County of South-hampton the 26. of Iune last 1613. who by the same was consumed to ashes, and no fire seene, . . . With the fearefull burning of the towne of Dorchester vpon friday last the 6. of August last 1613. Printed at London for Iohn Trundle, and are to be sold at his shop in Barbycan at the signe of Nobody. 1613. 4°, A—C in fours. Woodcut on title. *B. M.*

Dedicated by the writer to his cousin, Nicholas Hillyard, his Majesty's servant in ordinary. This was, of course, the eminent miniature-painter.

HINDE, WILLIAM, *of Queen's College, Oxford.*

A Faithfull Remonstrance of the Holy Life. and Happy Death, of Iohn Bruen of Bruen-Stapleford, in the County of Chester, Esquire. (Brother to the Mirrour of Piety, Mistris Katherine Brettergh). . . . London, Printed by R. B. for Philemon Stephens and Christopher Meredith . . . 1641. 8°, A—U in eights, besides 4 leaves of Table. Dedicated by Samuel Hinde to Sir James Stanley, Lord Stanley and Strange.

HISPANUS, PETRUS.

The treasury of healthe conteynyng many profitable medycines gathered out of Hypocrates, Galen and Auicen, by one Petrus Hyspanus & translated into Englysh by Humfre Lloyde who hath added therunto the causes and sygnes of euerye dysease . . . [Col.] Imprinted at London in saynt Martyns Paryshe in the vynetre, vppon the thre Crane wharfe by Willyam Coplande. 8°, black letter. A, 4 leaves : B—Y in eights : a—g in eights.

HISTORY.

Instructions for History : With A Character of the most Considerable Historians, Ancient and Modern. Out of the French, By J. Davies of Kidwelly. London, Printed by A. G. and J. P. dwelling near the Grate in Little Britain. M.DC.LXXX. 8°, A—K in eights, A 1 and K 8 blank. Dedicated to Sir George Wharton, Baronet.

The Natural History of Coffee, Thee, Chocolate, Tobacco. In four several Sections ; With a Tract of Elder and Juniper-Berries, Shewing how useful they may be in our Coffee-Houses : And also the way of making Mum, With some Remarks upon that Liquor. Collected from the Writings of the best Physicians, and Modern Travellers. London: Printed for Christopher Wilkinson, . . . 1682. 4°, A—E in fours.

HIUD, JOHN.
The Storie of Stories, Or The life of Christ, According to the foure holy Evangelists : . . . London, Printed by Miles Flesher. M.DC.XXXII. 8°, A—Aa in eights, Aa 7 with *Errata*, and Aa 8 blank. Dedicated to the Lady Anne Twisden, widow of Sir William Twisden, Knight, to whom Hiud expresses his obligations.

HOBBES, THOMAS, *of Malmesbury*.
Elementa Philosophica de Cive. Auctore Thom. Hobbes . . . Amsterodami . . . Anno 1647. 12°. *, 8: **, 10, A—R in twelves. With the title engraved and a portrait of Hobbes on * 2 *verso*.

Elements of Philosophy, The First Section, Concerning Body. Written in Latine . . . And now translated into English. To which are added Six Lessons to the Professors of Mathematicks of the Institution of Sir Henry Savile, in the University of Oxford. London, Printed by R. & W. Leybourn, for Andrew Crooke, . . . 1656. 4°. a, 4 leaves, a 1 blank : B (for A), 4 leaves : B—3 E 2 in fours, 3 E 2 blank : *Lessons*, A—I in fours. With numerous diagrams.

Stigmai . . . Or Markes of the Absurd Geometry Rural Language Scottish Church-Politicks And Barbarismes of John Wallis Professor of Geometry and Doctor of Divinity. By Thomas Hobbes of Malmesbury. London, Printed for Andrew Crooke, . . . 1657. 4°, A—D in fours, besides the title and a dedication to the Marquis of Dorchester.

The True Effigies of the Monster of Malmesbury : Or, Thomas Hobbes in His Proper Colours. London, Printed in the Year, 1680. 4°. Title and to the Reader, 4 leaves : a second title, Mr. Cowley's Verses in Praise of Mr. Hobbes, Oppos'd ; By a Lover of Truth and Virtue. London, Printed in the Year, 1680.—A (repeated) —B 2 in fours.

HOCUS POCUS JUNIOR.
Hocus Pocus Juinor [*sic*] . . . London, Printed by G. Dawson, and are to be sold by Thomas Vere, . . . 1658. 4°, A—H in fours, including the frontispiece. With cuts.

Hocus Pocus Junior . . . Printed by T. H. and are to be sold by J. Deacon . . .

1682. 4°, A—H in fours, A 1 with a frontispiece.

HODGE, WILLIAM.
Ad Augustissimum, Invictissimumque Magnae Britanniae, &c. Regem, Gulielmum III. De Pace . . . Carmen Triumphale. Londini, Typis F. Collins, 1697. 4°, A—C in fours.

HODGES, NATHANIEL, *M.D.*
Loimologia. Sive Pestis Nuperæ Apud Populum Londinensem Grassantis Narratio Historica . . . . Londini, Typis Gul. Godbid, . . . 1672. 8°. A, 8 leaves, besides a folded table : *, 4 leaves : B—R 4 in eights.

HOLKOT, ROBERT.
Incipit plogus in librū de amore libror. qui dicitur philobiblon. [Col.] Explicit philobiblon · sci · liber de amore librorū Colonie īpressus anno dni M cccc. lxxiij. &c. 4°, 48 leaves.
> Written at the request of Richard de Bury or Aungerville, Bishop of Durham and Chancellor of England.

HOLLAND, JOHN, *Porter, an eye and ear witness*.
The Smoke of the Bottomlesse Pit. Or, A More true and fuller Discovery of the Doctrine of those men which call themselves Ranters : Or, The Mad Crew. . . . London, Printed for John Wright, . . . 1651. 4°, 4 leaves.

HOLT, JOHN.
Lac pueror. M. holti Mylke for Chyldren. [This title is on a ribbon beneath the common cut of the *scriptorium*. At the end we have :] Enprynted at London. by Wynkyn de worde / in Fletestrete in the sygne of the sonne. 4°, A—H in eights and fours. With two large cuts illustrative of the declensions on A 3 and A 5 in the form of a hand.
> Sothebys, June 29, 1885, No. 575.

paruolorum institutio ex stanbrigiana collectione. [This is over the common cut of the *scriptorium*, on a label or ribbon. At the end is :] Enprynted at London in the Fletestrete / at the sygne of the sonne by Wynkyn de Worde. 4°. A, 8 : B, 4.
> Sothebys, July 1, 1885, No. 1117. This is a different issue from that cited in *Collections and Notes*, 1882, p. 576.

HOLY DAYS.
The Holy-Days, Or the Holy Feasts & Fasts, as they are observed in the Church of England, (throughout the Year) Explained. . . . With Cuts before each Day. London, Printed for Samuel Keble, . . .

H *

logia studĉte Parisiense . . . London, Richard Pynson [1509.] 4⁰, A—E in sixes, but only 5 leaves in A.

Sothebys, June 30, 1885, No. 1032, Heber's copy. There is no imprint; but Pynson's device surrounded by a broad border occupies the whole of the first leaf of A beneath the title given above.

HIGFORD, WILLIAM.

The Institution of a Gentleman In III. Parts. By William Higford Esq; *Virtus verus Honos.* London, Printed by A. W. for William Lee . . . 1660. 8⁰, A—G in eights, G 8 blank, besides a leaf with the *Interpretation of Poetical Sentences.* Dedicated to Lord Scudamore by Clement Barksdale.

HIGHWAYMEN.

The Confession of the Four High-Way-Men. As it was Written by One of them, and Allowed by the Rest the 14ᵗʰ of this Instant April (being the Day before their Appointed Execution). Viz. John Williams, alias Tho. Matchet. Francis Jackson, alias Dixie. John White, alias Fowler. Walter Parkhurst. . . . With Allowance. London, Printed for D. M. 1674. 4⁰, 4 leaves.

HILDERSHAW, ARTHUR, *of Ashby de la Zouche.*

The Canticles Or Song of Solomon Paraphrased ; and Explained by divers other Texts of Scripture, very useful . . . As also the same, together with the two Songs of Moses, and the Song of Deborah, Collected into Meeter. London, Printed by T. Millbonrn, for Robert Clavel . . . . 1672. 8⁰. Title and to the Reader, 3 leaves : B—L in eights, L 8 blank.

HILL, THOMAS.

The profitable Arte of Gardening, now the third tyme set fourth : to whiche is added muche necessary matter, and a number of Secretes with the Physick helpes belonging vnto eche herbe, and that easie prepared. To this annexed, two proper treatises, the one entituled The marucilous Gouernment . . . of the Beas . . . and the other, The Yerely Coniectures, meete for the husbandmā to knowe : Englished by Thomas Hill Londiner . . . Imprinted at London by Thomas Marshe. [Col.] Imprinted at London in Fletestrete . . . by Thomas Marshe. 1568. 8⁰, A—dd in eights, besides a folded leaf in cc : the Treatise on Bees with a new title, title and following leaves, including dedication to Master M. Gentleman, 6 leaves : Aa—Ll 4 in eights. With a few cuts and a portrait of Hill An. æt. 28, on back of second title.

HILLIARD, JOHN, *Preacher of the Word of Life in Sopley.*

Fire from Heauen. Burning the body of one John Hitchell of Holne-hurst, within the parish of Christ-church in the County of South-hampton the 26. of Iune last 1613. who by the same was consumed to ashes, and no fire seene, . . . With the fearefull burning of the towne of Dorchester vpon friday last the 6. of August last 1613. Printed at London for Iohn Trundle, and are to be sold at his shop in Barbycan at the signe of Nobody. 1613. 4⁰, A—C in fours. Woodcut on title. *B. M.*

Dedicated by the writer to his cousin, Nicholas Hillyard, his Majesty's servant in ordinary. This was, of course, the eminent miniature-painter.

HINDE, WILLIAM, *of Queen's College, Oxford.*

A Faithfull Remonstrance of the Holy Life. and Happy Death, of Iohn Bruen of Bruen-Stapleford, in the County of Chester, Esquire. (Brother to the Mirrour of Piety, Mistris Katherine Brettergh). . . . London, Printed by R. B. for Philemon Stephens and Christopher Meredith . . . 1641. 8⁰, A—U in eights, besides 4 leaves of Table. Dedicated by Samuel Hinde to Sir James Stanley, Lord Stanley and Strange.

HISPANUS, PETRUS.

The treasury of healthe conteynyng many profitable medycines gathered out of Hypocrates, Galen and Auicen, by one Petrus Hyspanus & translated into Englysh by Humfre Lloyde who hath added thervnto the causes and sygnes of euerye dysease . . . [Col.] Imprinted at London in saynt Martyns Paryshe in the vynetre, vppon the thre Crane wharfe by Willyam Coplande. 8⁰, black letter. A, 4 leaves : B—Y in eights : a—g in eights.

HISTORY.

Instructions for History : With A Character of the most Considerable Historians, Ancient and Modern. Out of the French, By J. Davies of Kidwelly. London, Printed by A. G. and J. P. dwelling near the Grate in Little Britain. M.DC.LXXX. 8⁰, A—K in eights, A 1 and K 8 blank. Dedicated to Sir George Wharton, Baronet.

The Natural History of Coffee, Thee, Chocolate, Tobacco. In four several Sections ; With a Tract of Elder and Juniper-Berries, Shewing how useful they may be in our Coffee-Houses : And also the way of making Mum, With some Remarks upon that Liquor. Collected from the Writings of the best Physicians, and Modern Travellers. London: Printed for Christopher Wilkinson, . . . 1682. 4°, A—E in fours.

HIUD, JOHN.

The Storie of Stories, Or The life of Christ, According to the foure holy Evangelists: . . . London, Printed by Miles Flesher. M.DC.XXXII. 8°, A—Aa in eights, Aa 7 with *Errata*, and Aa 8 blank. Dedicated to the Lady Anne Twisden, widow of Sir William Twisden, Knight, to whom Hiud expresses his obligations.

HOBBES, THOMAS, *of Malmesbury*.

Elementa Philosophica de Cive. Auctore Thom. Hobbes . . . Amsterodami . . . Anno 1647. 12°. *, 8 : **, 10, A—R in twelves. With the title engraved and a portrait of Hobbes on * 2 *verso*.

Elements of Philosophy, The First Section, Concerning Body. Written in Latine . . . And now translated into English. To which are added Six Lessons to the Professors of Mathematicks of the Institution of Sir Henry Savile, in the University of Oxford. London, Printed by R. & W. Leybourn, for Andrew Crooke, . . . 1656. 4°. a, 4 leaves, a 1 blank : B (for A), 4 leaves : B—3 E 2 in fours, 3 E 2 blank : *Lessons*, A—I in fours. With numerous diagrams.

Stigmai . . . Or Markes of the Absurd Geometry Rural Language Scottish Church-Politicks And Barbarismes of John Wallis Professor of Geometry and Doctor of Divinity. By Thomas Hobbes of Malmesbury. London, Printed for Andrew Crooke, . . . 1657. 4°, A—D in fours, besides the title and a dedication to the Marquis of Dorchester.

The True Effigies of the Monster of Malmesbury : Or, Thomas Hobbes in His Proper Colours. London, Printed in the Year, 1680. 4°. Title and to the Reader, 4 leaves: a second title, Mr. Cowley's Verses in Praise of Mr. Hobbes, Oppos'd ; By a Lover of Truth and Virtue. London, Printed in the Year, 1680.—A (repeated) —B 2 in fours.

HOCUS POCUS JUNIOR.

Hocus Pocus Juinor [*sic*] . . . London, Printed by G. Dawson, and are to be sold by Thomas Vere, . . . 1658. 4°, A—H in fours, including the frontispiece. With cuts.

Hocus Pocus Junior . . . Printed by T. H. and are to be sold by J. Deacon . . .

1682. 4°, A—H in fours, A 1 with a frontispiece.

HODGE, WILLIAM.

Ad Augustissimum, Invictissimumque Magnae Britanniae, &c. Regem, Gulielmum III. De Pace . . . Carmen Triumphale. Londini, Typis F. Collins, 1697. 4°, A—C in fours.

HODGES, NATHANIEL, *M.D.*

Loimologia. Sive Pestis Nuperae Apud Populum Londinensem Grassantis Narratio Historica . . . . Londini, Typis Gul. Godbid, . . . 1672. 8°. A, 8 leaves, besides a folded table : *, 4 leaves : B—R 4 in eights.

HOLKOT, ROBERT.

Incipit plogus in librū de amore libror. qui dicitur philobiblon. [Col.] Explicit philobiblon · sci · liber de amore librorū Colonie īpressus anno dni M cccc . lxxiij. &c. 4°, 48 leaves.

Written at the request of Richard de Bury or Aungerville, Bishop of Durham and Chancellor of England.

HOLLAND, JOHN, *Porter, an eye and ear witness.*

The Smoke of the Bottomlesse Pit. Or, A More true and fuller Discovery of the Doctrine of those men which call themselves Ranters : Or, The Mad Crew. . . London, Printed for John Wright, . . . 1651. 4°, 4 leaves.

HOLT, JOHN.

Lac pueror. M. holti Mylke for Chyldren. [This title is on a ribbon beneath the common cut of the *scriptorium*. At the end we have :] Enprynted at London. by Wynkyn de worde / in Fletestrete in the sygne of the sonne. 4", A—H in eights and fours. With two large cuts illustrative of the declensions on A 3 and A 5 in the form of a hand.

Sothebys, June 29, 1885, No. 575.

paruolorum institutio ex stambrigiana collectione. [This is over the common cut of the *scriptorium*, on a label or ribbon. At the end is :] Enprynted at London in the Fletestrete / at the sygne of the sonne by Wynkyn de Worde. 4°. A, 8 : B, 4.

Sothebys, July 1, 1885, No. 1117. This is a different issue from that cited in *Collections and Notes*, 1882, p. 576.

HOLY DAYS.

The Holy-Days, Or the Holy Feasts & Fasts, as they are observed in the Church of England, (throughout the Year) Explained. . . . With Cuts before each Day. London, Printed for Samuel Keble, . . .

H *

1706. 8°. A, 4 leaves, including the frontispiece: B—F in eights. *B. M.*

HOLY GHOST.

A deuout treatyse called the tree & xij. frutes of the holy goost. [Col.] Here endeth the tree of ẙ holy goost, Enprynted at London in the Flete-strete, at the sygne of the rose Garlande, by Robert Coplande. Anno dñi. M. cccccc. xxxiiij. [A new title:] The . xij. fruytes of the holy goost. [Col.] Here endeth an epystle made and sent to a relygyous woman, of the . xij. fruytes of the holy goost. 4", black letter. The *Tree*, A—F in fours, F 4 blank: the *Treatise*, a—s in fours: t, 6. With the mark of Copland on F 3 *verso*.

> Sothebys, July 1, 1885, No. 1201, the blank leaf F 4, which was in Herbert's copy, deficient.

HOMER.

The First [Second and Third] Booke of Homers Iliads. Translated by Thomas Grantham, M.A. of Peter-House in Cambridge, Professor of the speedy way of teaching the Hebrew, Greek, and Latine Tongues in London, in White-Bear-Court, Over against the golden Ball upon Adlin Hill. London Printed by T. Lock, for the Author. Anno Dom. 1660. 4°. A, 3 leaves, including one between title and A 2, with some verses: B, 4 leaves: C, 6: *The second Book of Homers Iliads*, on a headline, A—B in fours: *The Third Book*, with a new title, A—B in fours.

> Grantham dates in the third book from his study in Mermaid Court, Gutter Lane.

Batrakomiomachia: Or: The Wonderfvll and Bloody Battell betwene Frogs and Mice . . . Paraphrastically done into English Heroycall verse, by William Fowldes, . . . London: Printed by T. H. for Lawrence Chapman, . . . 1634. 8°. A, 6 leaves: B—D in eights: E, 2. *B. M.*

The Travels of Ulysses; As they were Related by Himself in Homer's Ninth, Tenth, Eleventh & Twelfth Books of his Odysses, to Alcinous King of Phæacia. [Translated by Mr Tho: Hobbs Malmesb:] London: Printed by J. C. for William Crook, . . . 1673. 12°, B—F 4 in twelves, F 4 blank, and the title. *B. M.*

> The matter between brackets is inserted in an early hand on the title of the Museum copy. There is no preliminary matter.

HOPE, SIR WILLIAM.

The Compleat Fencing-Master: In which is fully Described the whole Guards, Parades & Lessons, Belonging to the Small-Sword, . . . By Sir W. Hope, Kt. London, Printed for Dorman Newman . . .

1691. 8°. A, 8 leaves: *, 4 leaves: B —N 4 in eights. With 12 folded plates.

HORATIUS FLACCUS, QUINTUS.

Odes of Horace The best of Lyrick Poets. Contayning much morallity and sweetnesse. Selected, and Translated by St T: H: 1625. Imprinted at London by A. M. for Will: Lee, and are to be sold at his shoppe in Fleet-street, at the signe of the Goulden Bucke. 4°, A—K 2 in fours, besides the engraved title. With a preface and verses by F. L., Sir John Beaumont, George Fortescue, Hugh Holland, and J. Chapperlin. *B. M.*

Odes of Horace The best of Lyrick Poets. Contayning much morallity and sweetnesse. Selected, Translated and in this Edition reviewed, and enlarged with many more by St T: H: 1631. Imprinted at London by A. M. for Will: Lee, . . . 8°, A—G in eights, G 8 blank. The title is engraved as in the ed. of 1625. *B. M.*

The Odes and Epodon of Horace, In Five Books. Translated into English by J. H. Esq; London. Printed for W. Crooke . . . 1684. 8°, B—I 2 in eights, the title and a frontispiece.

HOTHAM, CHARLES, *of Peter House, Cambridge.*

An Introduction to the Tevtonick Philosophie . . . By C. Hotham, one of the Fellows of Peter-House. . . . London: Printed by T. M. & A. C. for Nath. Brooks. . . . 1650. 12°, A—D in twelves, but 2 extra leaves in A.

Corporations Vindicated in their Fundamental Liberties, from a Negative Voice, and other unjust Prerogatives of their chief Officer . . . . London, Printed for Giles Calvert, . . . 1652. 12°, A—C 6 in twelves.

The Petition and Argument of Mr Hotham . . . Printed in the Year, 1651. 12", A—F in twelves, F 12 blank.

A true State of the Case of Mr Hotham, Late Fellow of Peter-house. . . Printed in the Year 1651. 12, A—D in twelves, D 12 with *Errata*, and the title.

HOUGH, ROGER, *a Lover of the Truth.*

A Wonder of Wonders: Or, Gods People the Worlds Wonder; Or They are Men wondred at: . . . London, Printed for T. Passenger . . . 1666. 8", A—B in eights.

HOWARD, SIR ROBERT.

The History of the Reigns of Edward and Richard II. With Reflections, and Characters of their Chief Ministers and Favourites. As also, A Comparison between those Princes Edward and Richard the Second, with Edward the First, and Edward the Third. Written in the Year 1685. By the Honourable S: Robert Howard. Hor. Lib. III. Ode IV. *Hic dies* . . . London: Printed by F. Collins, for Thomas Fox, . . . 1690. 8°, A—N 4 in eights, and (a)—(b) in eights. Dedicated to the King.

IOWELL, JAMES.
St. Paul's Late Progres Vpon Earth, About a Divorce 'twixt Christ and the Church of Rome, by reason of her dissolutenes and excesses. With the Causes of these present Commotions 'twixt the Pope, and the Princes of Italy. A new way of Invention agreeable to the Times. Published by James Howell, Armig. London, Printed by Richard Heron for Matthew Walbancke . . . 1644. 8°, A—L in eights, A 1 and L 8 blank.

Howell's Preface is dated from the Fleet.

Epistolæ Ho-Elianæ . . . . The Sixth Edition . . . London: Printed for Thomas Guy, . . . 1688. 8°, A—Ll in eights, including a frontispiece.

IUARTE, JOHN.
Examen de Ingenios . . . London, Printed by Adam Islip. 1604. 4°, A—Y in eights.

Examen de Ingenios Or, The Tryal of Wits. Discovering the great Difference of Wits among Men, . . . made English from the most Correct Edition by Mr Bellamy. Useful for all Fathers, Masters, Tutors, &c. London, Printed for Richard Sare, . . . MDCXCVIII. 8°. A, 4 leaves: a—b in eights: B—Kk 3 in eights. Dedicated by Edward Bellamy to Charles Montague, Chancellor of the Exchequer.

IUBBARD, WILLIAM, *Minister of Ipswich.*
A Narrative of the Troubles with the Indians in New-England, from the first planting thereof in the year 1607. to this present year 1677. But chiefly of the late Troubles in the two last years, 1675 and 1676. To which is added a Discourse about the Warrs with the Pequods in the year 1637. . . . Published by Authority. Boston; Printed by John Foster, in the year 1677. 4°. Certificate as to work, title, and dedication to John Leverett, Josiah Winslow, and William Leet, Governors respectively of Massachusetts, Plymouth, and Connecticut, 4 leaves: To the Reader and Verses by B. T., 3

leaves: B—L in fours: M, 6 leaves: m, 2 leaves: no n: O—R in fours: S, 2 leaves; *Map of New England:* ¶, 4 leaves: n, 3 leaves with conclusion of *Postscript: A Narrative of the Troubles* . . . A—L in fours, with a head-line only as a title: *The Happiness of a People* [a Sermon] with a new title dated 1676, A—I in fours.

HUBBERTHORN, RICHARD.
Antichristianism Reproved, And the Doctrine of Christ and his Apostles justified against Swearing. In Answer to John Tombe's Six Propositions . . . London Printed, . . . 1660. 4°, A—C in fours.

HUDSON, MICHAEL.
The Divine Right of Government: 1. Naturall, And 2. Politique. . . . Printed in the year 1647. 4°, A—Bb in fours. Dedicated to Charles I. from the Tower.

HUET, PAUL DANIEL, *Bishop of Avranches.*
A Treatise of Romances and their Original. By Monsieur Huet. Translated out of French. London, Printed by R. Battersby, for S. Heyrick, . . . 1672. 8°, A—H in eights, A 1 blank.

HUGHES, WILLIAM.
The Compleat Vineyard: Or A most excellent Way for the Planting of Vines: Not only according to the German and French way, but also long experimented in England . . . By William Hughes. London, Printed by W. G. for W. Crooke, . . . 1665. 4°, A—E 2 in fours.

The American Physitian; Or, A Treatise of the Roots, Plants, Trees, Shrubs, Fruit, Herbs, &c. Growing in the English Plantations in America. Describing the Place, Time, Names, Kindes, Temperature, Vertues and Uses of them, either for Diet, Physick, &c. Whereunto is added A Discourse of the Cacao-Nvt Tree, And the use of its Fruits with all the ways of making of Chocolate. The like never extant before. By W. Hughes. London, Printed by J. C. for William Crook, . . . 1672. 12°, A—H in twelves, A 1 and H 12 blank.

HULOET, RICHARD.
ABCDEdarivm Anglico-Latinvm, Pro Tyrunculis Richardo Huloeto Exscriptore. Londini. Ex officina Gulielmi Riddel. Anno. M.D.LII. Cum priuilegio . . . Folio. Title, dedication, and List of Authors, 4 leaves: A—Mm in sixes: Nn, 4 leaves, Nn 4 occupied by a Peroration to the English Reader.

HUMBIE, A.

A Letter from Newcastle, To the Right Honourable the Lord High Chancellour of Scotland, and the rest of the Scotish Commissioners at London. Containing a Relation of the taking of the Town of Newcastle by Storm. Dated the 19. of October, 1644. London, Printed for Robert Bostock and Samuel Gellibrand, Octob. 26. 1644. 4°, 4 leaves subscribed *A. Humbie.*

HUME, ALEXANDER.

Grammatica nova in usum juventutis Scoticae ad methodum revocata . . . Edinbvrgi, Excudebat Thomas Finlason. 1612. Cum Privilegio . . . 8°. A, 4 leaves : B —II 4 in eights: A—II 4 in eights. *B. M.*

HUMFREY, J., *a Nonconformist.*

The Authority of the Magistrate, about Religion, Discussed, In a Rebuke to the Prefacer of a late Book of Bishop Bramhalls. Being A Confutation of that mishapen Tenent, Of the Magistrates Authority over the Conscience in the matter of Religion, . . . London, Printed for the Author. 1672. 8°, A—I 4 in eights.

> *By J. H.* is all that occurs on the title ; but those initials are explained in the copy described as above.

HUNGARY.

The Declaration Or Manifesto of George Racokzkie, Prince of Transylvania, to the States and Peeres of Hvngarie ; Together with the reasons added thereunto of his modern taking up of Armes the 17. of February, Anno 1644. . . . London Printed for Edward Blackmore, . . . May 28. 1644. 4°, 4 leaves.

A Declaration Or Manifesto, Wherein the Roman Imperiall Majesty makes known to the States & Peers of Hungarie, what reasons and motiues have compelled him to proceed in open Warre against the Prince of Transylvania. . . . Printed according to Order for E. Blackmore. MDCXLIV. 4°, 4 leaves.

Florus Hungaricus : Or The History of Hungaria and Transylvania Deduced from the Original of that Nation, and their setling in Europe in the Year of our Lord 461. To . . . Anno 1664. London, Printed by W. G. for Hen. Marsh . . . 1664. 8°, B—V in eights, no A. Dedicated by J. H. to John, Earl of Bath.

A Prospect of Hungary, and Transylvania, With a Catalogue of the Kings of the one, and the Princes of the other ; Together with an account of the qualities of the Inhabitants, the Commodities of the Countries, . . . An Historical Narration of the bloody Wars amongst themselves, and with the Turks ; continued to this present Year 1664. As also A brief Description of Bohemia . . . London, Printed for William Miller. 1664. 4°, A—G in fours, and the Map.

The Declaration of the Hungarians War, Newly Published by the Most Illustrious Michael Apati, Prince of Transilvania, against his Imperial Majesty, 1682. [Col.] London : Printed by J. Grantham. 1682. 4°, A—B in fours.

An Historical Description of the Glorious Conquest of the City of Buda, The Capital City of the Kingdom of Hungary, By the Victorious Arms of the Thrice Illustrious and Invincible Emperor Leopold I. Under the Conduct of his most Serene Highness, the Duke of Lorraine, and the Elector of Bavaria. London : Printed for Robert Clavell, . . . MDCLXXXVI. 4°, Title and bookseller's preface, 2 leaves : B—K 2 in fours.

HURTADO DE MENDOÇA, DIEGO.

Lazarillo, Or. The Excellent History of Lazarillo de Tormes, The Witty Spaniard. Both Parts. . . . London, Printed by B. G. for William Leake, . . . 1669. 8°, A—Y in eights, first leaf blank.

> The Second Part, dated 1670, commences with a fresh title on sign. L. Compare *De Mendoça*, p. 60 suprâ.

HUSBAND.

The Obliging Husband . . . London, Printed for Ann Gifford . . . 1722. . . . 12°, A—E in twelves, E 12 blank.

HUSSY, W.

The History of the Bible in Meeter. And an Explanation of some hard Texts. With Doctrinall observations. . . . In two volumes. [By W. Hussy.] 8°. MS.

> Puttick & Simpson, March 28, 1882, No. 550, in old blue morocco, with the author's initials on sides. The title was in a modern hand, and *By Wm Hussy* added in a different one, perhaps that of Dr. Lort, whose autograph was on a fly-leaf. The MS. appears to have been executed about 1650, and is in a very minute character.

HUYBERTS, ADRIAN, *Physician.*

A Corner-Stone laid towards the Building of a New Colledge (that is to say, a new Body of Physicians) in London. Upon Occasion of the vexations and oppressive proceedings acted in the name of the Society called the Colledge of Physicians, . . . London, Printed for the Author. 1675. 4°, A—E in fours.

HYDE, EDWARD, *Earl of Clarendon.*
A Brief View and Survey of the Dangerous and Pernicious Errors to Church and State, in Mr Hobbes's Book, Entitled Leviathan. By Edward Earl of Clarendon. Oxon: Printed at the Theater, 1676. 4°. *, 4 leaves: A—Ss 2 in fours, Ss 2 blank. Dedicated to the King.

> In the epistle to Charles, Clarendon says: "Mr. Hobbes consulted too few Authors, and made use of too few Books;" but Hobbes is said to have remarked that, had he read as much as others, he should have known as little.

HYDE, T.
An Account of the Famous Prince Giolo, Son of The King of Gilolo, now in England : With an Account of his Life, Parentage, and his strange and Wonderful Adventures ; The Manner of his being brought to England : With a Description of the Island of Gilolo, and the Adjacent Isle of Celebes : Their Religion and Manners. Written from his own Mouth. . . . London, Printed and Sold by R. Taylor. . . . 1692. 4°, A—D in fours, including a frontispiece. *B. M.*

HYMNI.
Sequuntur hymni totum annum dicendi in vesperis et matutinis secundū tempus cui competunt ordinati : vesperarum / matutine / & laudū / ordine relicto / ad vsum Sarum et Eboracen. 4°. Printed in red and black.

> The copy used contained A—D 6 in eights without any title, but evidently wanted the end. The title given above occurred on A i. This Hymnal appears to have been published as an adjunct to the *Diurnale.*

I.

IMPRISONMENT.}
Some Reasons Humbly Offered to the Consideration of the Parliament, For the Continuance of the Writs of Capias, and Process of Arrest. And against the Course or Way proposed of a Summons peremptory and judgement by default thereupon. London, Printed in the Year MDCLXXI. 4°.

INDEPENDENTS.
The Last Will and Testament of Sir James Independent, who lyeth now dangerously sick of a Disease, called by some, *The Resolution of the Parliament and Citie, to oppose their mutinous Army;* by others, *The Impossibilitie of Independencie.* With his Confession, Admonition, and Legacies left to his deare Children, in and about the Citie of London. With his Death, Buriall, and Epitaph. Printed in the yeare 1647. 4°, 4 leaves.

INDIA.
A Letter written to the Right Worshipfull the Governovrs and Assistants of the East Indian Marchants in London : Containing the Estate of the East Indian Fleete, with the Names of the Chiefe men of Note dead in the Voyage. At London Imprinted for Thomas Thorpe, and are to be sould by William Aspley. 1603. 4°, A—B in fours, B 4 blank and A 1 with a cut of a ship.

A Trve Relation withovt all Exception, of Strange and Admirable Accidents, which lately happened in the Kingdome of the great Magor, or Magvll, who is the greatest Monarch of the East Indies. As also with a true Report of the Manners of the Countrey : of the Commodities there found, With the like of sundry other Countreyes and Ilands, in the East-Indies. Written and certified by persons of good import, who were eye-witnesses of what is here reported. London Printed by I. D. for Thomas Archer, . . . 1622. 4°, A—B in fours. *B. M.*

A Covrante of Newes from the East India. A true Relation of the taking of the Ilands of Lantore and Polaroone in the parts of Banda in East Indies by the Hollanders, . . . [Col.] Printed according to the originall copie the eighth Febr. 1622. Stilo Novo. 4°, 3 leaves. *B. M.*

The Petition and Remonstrance of the Governor And Company of Merchants of London, Trading to the East Indies, Exhibited to the Honorable the House of Commons assembled in Parliament. Ann° 1628. Printed at London for Nicholas Bovrne. 1628. 4°, A—F 2 in fours.

The East-India Trade. A true Narration of divers Ports in East-India ; Of the Commodities, and Trade one Kingdome holdeth with another ; whereby it appeareth, how much profit this Nation is deprived by restraint of Trade to those parts, which is farre greater then all the trade of Europe. [1644.] 4°, A—B in fours. Printed without a title.

An Impartial Vindication of the English East-India-Company, From the Unjust and Slanderous Imputations Cast upon them in a Treatise Intituled, *A Justification of the Directors* . . . London, Printed by J. Richardson, for Samuel Tidmarsh, . . . MDCLXXXVIII. 8°. *Imprimatur*, title and preface, 3 leaves : B—H 4 in eights.

> The title states that the Justification, which purported to be printed at London, was really from an Amsterdam press.

Rules, Orders, and Directions appointed and Established by the Governour and Committee of the East-India Company, for the well Regulating and Managing their Affairs in the Parts of India. [About 1680.] Folio, 2 leaves.

A Supplement, 1689. to a former Treatise, concerning the East-India Trade, Printed 1681. 4°, A—B in fours, B 4 blank. Without a regular title.

A Letter to a Friend. Concerning the East-India Trade. London, Printed, and are to be sold by E. Whitlock . . . 1696. 4°, A—C 2 in fours.

Some Reflections on a Pamphlet, Intituled, England and East-India Inconsistent in their Manufactures. London, Printed Anno MDCXCVI. 8°, A—B in eights, B 8 blank.

Proposals for Setling the East-India Trade. London, Printed, and are to be Sold by E. Whitlock, near Stationers-Hall, 1696. 4°, A—C in fours.

A Letter from a Lawyer of the Inner Temple, to His Friend in the Country, Concerning the East-India Stock, and the Project of Uniting the New and Old Companies. London : Printed in the Year MDCXCVIII. 4°, A—C 2 in fours, C 2 blank.

An Elegy on the Death of the Old East-India Company ; Who Died of a Wound she receiv'd from a Patent, value Two Millions. London : Printed for the Author in the Year 1699. Folio, A—D, 2 leaves each. In verse. With the Arms of the Company on the title.

Considerations upon the East-Indian Trade . . . London, Printed for A. and J. Churchill, . . . MDCCI. 8°. A, 6 leaves, A 6 blank : B—I in eights.

A List of all the Adventurers in the Stock of the Governour and Company of Merchants of London, trading into the East-Indies, the 15th of April, 1708. Whereof those Mark'd with a + are capable (by their Adventure) to be chosen Governour or Deputy-Governour, and those with a * to be of the Committee. [1708.] Folio, 2 leaves.

The Case of the United East-India Company. [1708.] A folio leaf.

INFIDELITY.

Infidelity Vnmasked Or The Confvtation of a Booke Pvblished by Mr William Chillingworth vnder this Title *The Religion of Protestants* . . . Printed in Gant, By Maximilian Graet. A° Dni M.DC.LII. Permissu superiorum. 4°. *, 4 leaves : **, 4 leaves, last blank : A—6 D in fours : Index, 6 leaves.

INNOCENT III., *Pope of Rome.*

The Mirror of Mans Lyfe. Plainely describing, all that weake moulde we are made of : what miseries we are subiect vnto : howe uncertaine this life is : and what shal be our ende. Englished [from the *Speculum humanum*] by H. K. Imprinted at London, by Henry Bynneman. 1576. 8°. ¶, 8 leaves : A, 4 leaves : B—K in eights. Dedicated to Anne, Countess of Pembroke. *B. M.*

> The last two pages are occupied by six stanzas headed *Speculum humanum* by Stephen Gosson.

INSTRUCTIONS.

Moral Instructions of a Father to His Son, Upon his Departure for a long Voyage : With an Hundred Maximes, . . . London, Printed for W. Crook, . . . 1683. 12°. A, 6 : B—F in twelves. Dedicated to Sir Thomas Grantham Knt. by the translator, Peregrin Clifford Chamberlayne. *B. M.*

> With a good deal of interest in the dedication, where the destruction of James Town in Virginia in 1676 by Sir Thomas Grantham, and other matters, are mentioned.

INTEREST.

Interest of Money Mistaken. Or, A Treatise, Proving, that the Abatement of Interest is the Effect and not the Cause of the Riches of a Nation, and that Six per Cent. is a Proportionable Interest to the present condition of this Kingdom. London, Printed in the Year, 1668, 4°, A—C in fours.

INVENTION.

A New Invention ; Or, A paire of Cristall Spectacles By helpe whereof may be read so small a Print that what twenty sheetes of paper will hardly containe shall be discover'd in one ; . . . Printed according to Order for G. Bishop, June 7. 1644. 4°, 4 leaves.

IRELAND.
Declaratio De Tyronensis et Tirconelli Comitvm, sociorumque fuga. Londini Excudebat Robertvs Barkervs . . . Anno 1607. 4°, 4 leaves.

A Collection of Svch Orders and Conditions, as are to be obserued by the Vndertakers, Vpon the distribution and Plantation of the Eschaeted Lands in Vlster. Imprinted at London by Robert Barker, . . . 1608. 4°, A—C 2 in fours.

The Wonderfvll Battell of Starelings : Fought at the Citie of Corke in Ireland, the 12. and 14. of October last past, 1621. As it hath been credibly enformed by divers Noblemen and others of the said Kingdome, &c. London. Printed for N. B. 1622. 4°, A—B in fours, A 1 blank. With a large cut on title. *B. M.*

A Relation of the Most lamentable Burning of the Cittie of Corke, in the west of Ireland, in the Prouince of Monster, by Thunder and Lightning. With other most dolefull and miserable Accidents, which fell out the last of May 1622, after the prodigious battel of the birds called Stares, . . . Printed this 20. of June 1622. London Printed by I. D. for Nicholas Bourne, and Thomas Archer, 1622. 4″, A—B in fours, A 1 blank. Woodcut on title. *B. M.*

The Sentence of the Covncell of Warre, pronovnced against the Lord Movntmorris, In Ireland the Twelfth of December, 1635. With the Lord Mountmorris Petition to the Parliament concerning his Iniuries and wrongs sustayned by the Lord Depvty deceased. Printed in the yeare, 1641. 4°, A—B in fours, and C, 1 leaf.

A Trve Relation of the Passages of Gods Providence in a Voyage for Ireland. With the additionall Forces sent for reducing of that Kingdome by his Maies-[t]ie, and Parliament. . . . London, Printed by Lvke Norton, for Henry Overton . in the Yeare . MDCXLII. 4°, A—D 2 in fours.

A Remonstrance of the Barbarous Cruelties and Bloody Murders Committed by the Irish Rebels against the Protestants in Ireland Both before and since the Cessation. Collected out of the Records at Dublin, by Thomas Morley, Gent. . . .

London, Printed by E. G. 12 June. 1644. 4°, A—B in fours.

The Propositions of the Roman Catholicks of Ireland, Presented by their Commissioners to His Sacred Majestie, in April, M.DC.XLIV. . . . Printed at Waterford by Thomas Bourke, . . . M.DC.XLIV. 4°. A, 2 leaves : B—K in fours.

A Persvasive Letter Exhorting the Natives of Ireland to stand in Defence of their Faith, King, and Countrey, against Parliamentary intruders, their errors, and temeritie, directed to Sir N. Th. . . Printed at Waterford in the year, 1645. 4°, 4 leaves.

The last Speeches And Confession of the Lord Maguire : The Irish Rebell, that was Hanged at Tyburne, and Drawne, and Quartered on Thursday last, the 20th of February, 1644. With all the Questions that were put to him, and his severall Answers. And the Coppies of those Letters, and other Papers which he then had in his hands. . . . And his Directory from the Romish Priests that gave him notice by the said papers to know them, in passing to Tiburne with him ; . . . Imprinted at London, by Iane Coe. [1645.] 4°, A—B in fours.

The Whole Triall of Connor Lord Macguire, With the perfect Copies of the Indictment, and all the Evidences against him. Also The Copie of Sir Philome Oneales Commission, the Popes Bull to the confederate Catholikes in Ireland, with many remarkable Passages of the grand Rebellion there, . . . His Plea of Peerage, and severall Answers : With the severall Replies made to him, By The Kings Sergeant at Law, and Sergeant Roll. William Prynne, Esquire, and M. Nudigate. . . . London, Printed for Robert Austin, in the Old-Baily. 1645. 4°. Title, 1 leaf : a and aa in fours : B—D in fours.

A Remonstrance of Grievances Presented to his most Excellent Majestie, in the behalfe of the Catholicks of Ireland. Printed at Waterford by Thomas Bourke, Printer to the Confederate Catholicks of Ireland. Anno Dom. 1645. 4°, A—D in fours.

Articles of Peace Made Conclvded Accorded and Agreed upon, by and between His Excellencie Iames Lord Marques of Ormond. . . . And Donogh Lord Viscount Muskery, and others appointed and Authorized by His Majesties said Roman Catholique Subjects, . . . Imprinted at

Dublin, by William Bladen, . . . 1646. 4°, A—D in fours, D 4 blank.

An Ordinance of the Lords and Commons . . . for Raising of Twenty thousand pounds a Moneth for the Relief of Ireland. . . . London, Printed for Edward Husband, . . . Febr. 24. 1646. 4°, A—F in fours.

A Declaration of the Lord Lievtenant Generall of Ireland. Printed at Corek, in the yeare 1648. and are to be sold at Roches building. 4°, 4 leaves.

News from Ireland concerning the Proceedings of the Presbytery in the County of Antrim in Ireland, in several Sittings in that County, Against Mr James Ker, & Mr Jeremy O Queen. . . . London, Printed by Edward Husband and John Field, . . . 1650. 4°, A—E in fours.

The Horrid Conspiracie of such Impenitent Traytors as intended A New Rebellion in the Kingdom of Ireland. With A List of the Prisoners, and the Particular Manner of seizing Dublin-Castle by Ludlow, and his Accomplices. Verbatim out of the Expresses sent to His Majesty from the Duke of Ormond . . . London, Printed for Samuel Speed . . . 1663. 4°, A—B in fours. With a frontispiece of arms.

Murder will Out : Or, The King's Letter, Justifying the Marquess of Antrim, and declaring that what he did in the Irish Rebellion, was by direction from his Royal Father and Mother, and for the Service of the Crown. . . . Printed in the Year, 1663. 4°, 4 leaves.

The State of His Majesties Revenue in Ireland, As the same was Given in to the Right Honourable the Lords Commissioners of His Majesties Treasury in England, By Francis Lord Angier Vice-Treasurer of Ireland. . . . In the Savoy: Printed by Tho. Newcomb, 1673. Folio. Title, 1 leaf : State of the Revenue, 2 leaves : Lord Ranelagh's Proposals, 4 leaves : Index, 4 leaves : B—Hh, 2 leaves each.

A Letter from a Gentleman in Ireland to his Brother in England, Relating to the Concerns of Ireland in matter of Trade. London, Printed and are to be sold by Langley Curtiss, . . . 1677. 4°, A—C in fours.

An Account of the Publick Affairs in Ireland, since the discovery of the Late Plot. London, Printed in the Year, 1679. 4°, A—C in fours, and a leaf of D.

A true Account of Divers most strange

and prodigious Apparitions, Seen in the Air, at Poins-Town in the County of Tipperary in Ireland : March the second, 167⅞ . . . . London : Printed for L. C. 1679. 4°, 4 leaves.

A Full and Impartial Account of all the Secret Consults, Negotiations, Stratagems, and Intriegues of the Romish Party in Ireland, From 1660, to this present Year 1689. For the Settlement of Popery in that Kingdom. London, Printed for Richard Chiswell, . . . MDCCXXXIX. 4°, A—U in fours, including a half-title.

Ireland's Lamentation : Being A Short, but Perfect, Full, and True Account of the Scituation, Nature, Constitution and Product of Ireland. . . . To which is added, A Letter from a Lieutenant in the Irish Army, . . . Written by an English Protestant that lately narrowly escaped with his Life from them. London, Printed by J. D. and Sold by Rich. Janeway, . . . 1689. 4°, B—F 2 in fours, besides title and half-title.

An Account of the Taking of the Fort of Ballymore, within 10 Miles of Athlone. On Monday the Eighth of June, 1691. [Col.] Printed by Edw. Jones in the Savoy, 1691. A broadside.

A Draught of the Incampment of the Irish Army at the Battle near Aghrim in Ireland, and the manner of Their Majesties Forces attacking them. By Colonel Richards, First Engineer of Ireland, being present at the Engagement. Published by Authority. Printed by Edw. Jones in the Savoy, 1691. Folio, 2 leaves.

An Answer to Mr Molyneux His Case of Ireland's being bound by Acts of Parliament to England, Stated : And His Dangerous Notion of Ireland's being under no Subordination to the Parliamentary Authority of England Refuted ; By Reasoning from his own Arguments and Authorities . . . London, Printed for Richard Parker, . . . 1698. 8°. A, 8 leaves : b, 8 : c, 4 : B—M in eights.

A Vindication of Marriage, As Solemnized by Presbyterians, in the North of Ireland . . . By a Minister of the Gospel . . . Printed in the Year 1702. 4°, A—I in fours.

Proposals for Raising a Million of Money out of the Forfeited Estates in Ireland : . . . Dublin, Reprinted . . . 1704. 4°, A—D in fours.

Ireland Preserv'd, and the Protestant Interest Defended ; In the Year 1689.

How, and by Whom. London : Printed in the Year 1707. 4°. Title and Preface, 2 leaves : A—E in fours.

An Account how the Court House in Roscommon fell down, while the Court was sitting, . . . Dublin, Printed by C. C. 1718–19. A broadside.

The Statvtes of Ireland, beginning the Third yere of K. Edward the second, and continuing vntill the end of the Parliament, begunne in the eleuenth yeare of . . . . King Iames, . . . Newly Pervsed and Examined . . . Anno Dom. M.DC.XXI. Dvblin, Printed by the Societie of Stationers, . . . Folio. a—b in sixes : A, 4 leaves : B—Oo in sixes, Pp, 8 leaves, the last blank.

> To the Crossley copy were annexed the Acts 10 and 11 Charles I., 1635, the Subsidy Act, 1634, and General Pardon, 1635, all printed at Dublin, the titles enclosed within the same border.

Anno Regni Caroli . . . Decimo & Vndecimo. At the Parliament begun and holden at Dublin, the 14. day of Iuly, ... And there continued untill the 18. day of Aprill, 1635. . . . Imprinted at Dublin by the Society of Stationers, . . . M.DC.XXXV. Folio. ¶, 5 leaves, including two shields of arms : a—cc 2 in fours. Black letter.

IRENÆUS PHILALETHES, *Cosmopolita.*

Secrets Reveal'd : Or, An Open Entrance to the Shut-Palace of the King : Containing, The greatest Treasure in Chymistry, Never yet so plainly Discovered . . . Published for the benefit of all Englishmen, by W. C. Esq ; a true Lover of Art and Nature. London, Printed by W. Godbid for William Cooper . . . 1669. 8°, A—I in eights, A 1 and I 8 blank, and a, 8 leaves. Dedicated by W[illiam] C[ooper] to Lord Lucas, Baron of Shenfield in Essex.

> It is said on the title that the Author attained the knowledge of the Philosopher's Stone at the age of 23 in 1645.

The Fountain of Chymical Philosophy. Written in Latin by Eyrenæus Philalethes / Printed in the Year, 1694. 8°.

> Translated by Philomathes. The volume consists of Three Parts : *The Art of the Transmutation of Metals, Brevis Manuductio*, and the *Fons Chymica.*

ISLEWORTH.

The Petition of the Inhabitants of Isleworth in the Countie of Middlesex, against

William Grant, Minister of the said Parish . . . London printed. 1641. 4°, 4 leaves.

ITALY.

A Letter lately written from Rome, by an Italian Gentleman, to a freende of his in Lyons in Fraunce. Wherein is declared, the state of Rome : The suddaine death & sollemne buriall of Pope Gregory the thirteenth. The election of the newe Pope, and the race of life this newe Pope ranne before hee was aduaunced. Thereto are adioyned the accidentes that haue fallen owt, not onely in Rome, but in Naples & other parts of the worlde also. Newly translated out of Italian into English by I. F. Imprinted at London by Iohn Charlewoode dwelling in Barbican, at the halfe Eagle and the Key. 1585. 8°, A—E 4 in eights, besides the title and dedication by John Florio, the translator, to Henry, Earl of Derby. *B. M.*

A Trve Discovrse of a cruell fact committed by a Gentlewoman towardes her Husband, her Father, her Sister and two of her Nephewes. First printed in French at Roan : and now translated into English. London Imprinted by Iohn Wolfe, and are to bee sold at his shoppe within Popes head Alley in Lombard-street. 1599. 4°, A—B in fours, B 4 blank. *B. M.*

> This narrative refers to a tragedy which took place at Lucera, near Naples. The gentlewoman was Anna de Loyse, wife of the Chancellor of Naples, and her accomplice, a young man named Maurice Talleys, with whom she had intrigued in her husband's absence.

Italy, In its Original Glory, Ruine and Revival, Being an Exact Survey of the Whole Geography, and History of that Famous Country ; With the Adjacent Islands of Sicily, Malta, &c. And whatever is Remarkable in Rome . . . Translated out of the Original for General Satisfaction. By Edmund Warcupp, Esquire. London, Printed by S. Griffin, . . . 1660. Folio. Title, frontispiece, and dedication to William, Lord Lenthal, 3 leaves : A—4 O in fours. With two folded maps.

A Discourse of the Dukedom of Modena. Containing the Origine, Antiquity, . . . of the People. As also, The Temperature of the Climate, with the Nature and Fertility of the Soil. London : Printed by J. C. for William Crook, . . . 1674. 4°. A, 2 : B—E in fours.

A Description of a Wonderful Child

that was seen at Naples, 1681. A folio leaf with a cut at top. *B. M.*

The Neopolitan, Or The Defender of His Mistress. Done out of French : By Mr Ferrand Spence. London : Printed for R. Bentley, . . . 1683. 12°. A, 6 leaves : B—E 6 in twelves.

Dedicated by Spence to James, Earl of Arran, son of the Duke of Hamilton.

Three Letters Concerning the Present State of Italy, Written in the Year, 1687. . . . Being a Supplement to Dr Burnet's Letters. Printed in the Year 1688. 12°, A—H in twelves, A repeated.

The Institutions, of the Congregation of the Oratory, at St. Maries in Vallicella, within the City of Rome. Founded by St. Philip Nerius. Printed at Oxford, 1687. 8°, A—N in fours, and a leaf of O.

IVIE, JOHN, *the Elder, of New Sarum.*

A Declaration Written by John Ivie the elder, of the City of New Sarum in the County of Wilts, and one of the Aldermen. Where he hath done his true and faithfull Service for above forty years, for the good of the Poor, and the Inhabitants thereof. . . . London, Printed for the Author, 1661. 4°. A, 2 leaves : B—F 2 in fours.

A relation of his grievances.

IVIE, THOMAS, *Esquire.*

Alimony Arraign'd : Or The Remonstrance and Appeal of Thomas Ivie, Esq. From the High Court of Chancery, To His Highness the Lord Protector . . . Wherein are set forth the unheard-of Practices and Villanies of Lewd and Defamed Women, in order to separate Man and Wife. London, Printed in the Year, 1654. 4°, A—G in fours.

IZACKE, RICHARD, *Chamberlain, of Exeter.*

Remarkable Antiquities of the City of Exeter. Giving an Account of the Laws and Customs of the Place, the Officers, Court of Judicature, Gates, Walls, Rivers, Churches, and Privileges. Together, With a Catalogue of all the Bishops, Mayors, Sheriffs, from the Year 1049 to 1677. . . . London, Printed for Rowland Reynolds, . . . 1681. 8°. A, 4 leaves, including a frontispiece of Arms : *, 8 leaves : 1*, 8 leaves : 2*, 8 leaves : 3*, 8 leaves : Map : A—Q in eights, Q 8 blank.

J.

J. A.

A Compleat Account of the Portugueze Language. Being a Copious Dictionary of English with Portugueze, and Portugueze with English. Together with an Easie and Unerring Method of its Pronunciation, by a distinguishing Accent, . . . To which is added by way of Appendix their usual Manner of Correspondence by Writing, . . . By A. J. London : Printed by R. Janeway, for the Author, M.DCC.I. Folio. Title and half-title, 2 leaves : To the Reader, 2 leaves : A—4 K, 2 leaves each : ddd—fff[f], 2 leaves each.

This volume includes an Anglo-Portuguese Grammar.

J. P., *Minister.*

A Brief Relation of the Surprise of the Forts of Weymouth, The Siege of Melcombe, The Recovery of the Forts, and Raising of the Siege. By P. J. Minister to the Garrison. London, Printed for Luke Fawne, . . . 1644. 4°, 4 leaves.

JACOB, HENRY, *Founder of Puritanism in New England.*

A Triall of Svbscription, by way of a Preface, vnto certaine svbscribers ; And Reasons for lesse rigour against non-subscribers. Both modestly written ; that Neither should offend. [Quot. from Esay, 44. 5.] 1599. 8°, A—C 4 in eights.

Reasons Taken ovt of Gods Word and the Best Hvmane Testimonies Proving a Necessitie of Reforming ovr Chvrches in England. . . . 1604. 4°, A—M 2 in fours. Dedicated to James I.

A Petition against vainglorious, and that which is falsly called Learned Preaching. 1604. 8°, A in 8 and then in 6.

A Shorte Treatise, of the crosse in Baptisme . . . Amsterdam Printed by I. H. 1604. 8°, A—D in fours.

A Treatise of Divine Worship, tending to prove that the Ceremonies imposed vpon the Ministers of the Gospell in England,

ntroversie, are in their vse
604. 8°, A—C in eights.

he Natvre and Vse of Things
Tending to prove, that the
in present Controversie
ministers of the gospell in
of England, are neither in
e indifferent. [Quotations
8, 23, and Matthew 5, 11].
8°, A—B in eights.
d, on sign. B 7, occurs the date
h. April 12.

of the Kings Svpremacie.
e Name of the afflicted
l opposed to the shamefull
s of the Prelacie. . . . Printed
—B 4 in eights.

The maine opinions of the
f those that are called Puri-
Realme. of Englande. . . .
8°. A, 8 : B—C in fours:

all Arguments, Proving that
es imposed vpon the Mini-
gospell in England, by our
unlawfull . . . . 1605. 8°,
ghts.

eginning and Institution of
isible or Ministeriall Church
Ienry Iacob. Imprinted at
enry Hastings. 1610. 8°,
. A—G 4 in eights.
ce by Jacob to the Christian
ted from Leyden, December 20,
name of the printer seems to

l cleere Exposition of the
andement. By Henry Jacob.
8°, A—F 2 in eights, besides
b's Preface.

f Sundry matters; Tending
cessary for all persons, actu-
in the use and practise of
ial ordinances . . . Anno
VI. 8°, A—C in eights.

i 1616. A Confession and
of the Faith of certaine
England, holding it neces-
e & keepe all Christes true
Ordinances for his Church
liticall . . . [Leyden, 1616.]
eights.

EORGE.
its Almanack, Or, The
ide ; Being A Description
ys of the Kingdom of Scot-
and Wales : Containing the

Names of the Shires, and Principal Marcat
Towns . . . All very useful for Merchants
and others, who travel either in Scotland or
England. Edinburgh, Printed by George
Jaffrey, Author hereof, and are to be sold
at his Shop, at the Tron Church door,
1702. 8°. A, 6 : B, 4.

JAMAICA.
By the King. A Proclamation for the
encouraging of Planters in His Majesties
Island of Jamaica in the West-Indies.
London, Printed by John Bill and Chris-
topher Barker, . . . 1661. A broadside.

The Present State of Jamaica, with the
Life of the Great Columbus The first Discoverer : To which is Added An Exact
Account of Sir Hen. Morgan's Voyage to,
and famous Siege and taking of Panama
from the Spaniards. London, Printed by
Fr. Clark for Tho. Malthus . . . 1683.
12°. A, 6 leaves, A 5-6 with Advertisements, A 1 blank : B—F in twelves, F 12
blank.

The Laws of Jamaica, Passed by the Assembly, And Confirmed by His Majesty
in Council, April 17. 1684. To which is
added, The State of Jamaica, As it is
now under the Government of Sir Thomas
Lynch. With a large Mapp of the Island.
London, Printed by H. H. Jun. for Charles
Harper, . . . M.DC.LXXXIV. Folio, A—Qq,
2 leaves each (title and following leaf
counted as A) : a—c, 2 leaves each.

The Continuation of the Laws of Jamaica
. . . December 26th 1695. Being the
Second Volume of the said Laws. Lon-
don, Printed for Charles Harper, . . .
MDCXCVIII. Folio, B—O in fours, besides
title and Index.

The Truest and Largest Account of the
Late Earthquake in Jamaica, June the
7th 1692. Written by a Reverend Divine
there to his Friend in London. With
some Improvement thereof by another
Hand. . . . London, Printed for Tho.
Parkhurst, . . . 1693. 4°. A—E 2 in
fours.

JAMES [STUART] V., *King of Scotland*
(1513–42).
Ad Serenissimum Scotorum Regem Iaco-
bum Quintum de Suscepto Regni Regi-
mine à diis feliciter ominato. Strena.
[Col.] Impressum Ediburgi apud Thomam Dauidson. [1514.] 4°, 4 leaves,
with the title enclosed in a broad border
and the printer's device on the last page.
B. M.

In hexameters and pentameters.

JAMES [STUART] VI. *of Scotland and* I. *of Great Britain.*

A Svpplication to the Kings most excellent Maiestie, Wherein, seuerall reasons of State and Religion are briefely touched : . . . 1604. 4°, A—G 2 in fours.

Mvsa Hospitalis Ecclesiæ Christi Oxon. In adventum Fælicissimum Sereniss. Iacobi Regis, Annæ Reginæ, & Henrici Principis ad eandem Ecclesiam. Oxoniæ . Apud Iosephum Barnesium. 1605. 4°, 4 leaves.

A Declaration of the iust causes of his Maiesties proceeding against those Ministers Who are now lying in prison, attainted of high Treason. Set foorth by his Maiesties Counsell of his kingdome of Scotland. Imprinted at London by Robert Barker, ... Anno 1606. 4°, A—F in fours.

In Camera Scaccarij. Maij. 1608. Directions for Commissioners, with the Steward of each Mannour, As well for admitting of Tenants to Copy hold Estates, as for Assessing of Fines of the same. . . . Imprinted at London by Robert Barker . . . 1608. 4°, A—B in fours, A 1 and B 4 blank.

Orders Appointed by his Maiestie to be straightly obserued for the preuenting and remedying of the dearth of Graine and other Victuall. Dated the first day of Iune. 1608. Imprinted at London by Robert Barker . . . 1608. 4°, A—D in fours, A 1 and D 4 blank.

To the right High and mightie Prince, Iames by the Grace of God, ... An humble Supplication for Toleration and libertie to enioy and observe the ordinances of Christ Iesvs in th' administration of his Churches, in lieu of humane constitutions. . . . 1609. 4°, A—F in fours, A 1 and F 4 blank

> On a spare leaf at the end of this copy occurs: "John Pykering pret. 4ᵈ."

A Booke of Proclamations, published since the beginning of his Maiesties most happy Reigne ouer England, &c. Vntill this present Moneth of Febr. 3, Anno Dom. 1609. Imprinted at London by Robert Barker . . . Folio. Title and Table, 6 leaves : A—T in sixes.

A Proclamation Pvblished vnder the Name of Iames King of Great Britanny With a briefe & moderate Answere thervnto. Whereto are added the penall Statutes, made in the same Kingdome, against Catholikes . . . Translated out of Latin into English . . . Imprinted witl Licence. M.D.[C.]XL 4°, A—Z in fours With a Preface signed *B. D. de Clerimond*

His Maiesties Declaration concerning His Proceedings with the States generall of the Vnited Prouinces of the Low Conntreys, In the cause of D. Conradvs Vorstivs. Imprinted at London by Robert Barker . . . 1612. 4°, A—M in fours, A 1 and M 4 blank.

His Maiesties Speach in the Starre Chamber, The xx. Of Ivne. Anno 1616. Imprinted at London by Robert Barker, . . . [1616.] 4°, A—H in fours, first leaf blank.

A Proclamation declaring his Maiesties Pleasure concerning the dissolution of the present Conuention of Parliament. Imprinted at London by Bonham Norton and Iohn Bill . . . 1621. 4°, A—C in fours, C 4 blank, and the title.

His Maiesties Declaration, Touching his proceedings in the late Assemblie and Conuention of Parliament. Imprinted at London by Bonham Norton and Iohn Bill . . . 1621. 4°, A—I 2 in fours, A 1 blank.

A Petition to the Kings most excellent Maiestie, the Lords Spirituall and Temporall, and Commons of the Parliament now assembled. Wherein is declared the mischiefes and inconveniences, arising to the King and Common-wealth, by the Imprisoning of mens bodies for Debt. Printed at London. 1622. 4°, A—F in fours.

Oxoniensis Academiæ Parentalia. Sacratissimæ Memoriæ . . . Iacobi, . . . Dicata. Oxoniæ, Excudebant Ioannes Lichfield, & Guilielmus Turner. Anno Dom. 1625. 4°. ¶, 4 leaves, ¶¶, 2 leaves: A—L 2 in fours.

Cygnea Cantio: Or, Learned Decisions, and most Prvdent and Piovs Directions for Stvdents in Divinitie; Delivered by our late Soveraigne of Happie Memorie, King Iames, at White Hall a few weekes before his Death . . . London, Printed for Robert Mylbourne . . . 1629. 4°, A—G 2 in fours, A 1 blank. Dedicated by Daniel Featley to King Charles.

> At the end is a curious notice by the stationer as to the tract having been ready for the press in 1625 with a dedication to Charles I., then just crowned, and of a delay occurring in its appearance, partly by reason of a disastrous fire, by which Mylbourne lost about 900 books. There is also an interesting account of the prosecution

of **Mylbourne** through the agency of some informer, and of the suppression of *Pelagius Redivivus*, of which 300 copies were taken from the printer, though many of these were subsequently restored.

King Iames His Iudgement of a King and of a Tyrant. Extracted out of His own Speech at White-Hall, to the Lords and Commons in Parliament, 1609. With certaine Notations . . . No place, &c. [1642.] 4°, 4 leaves.

King James His Apothegmes, Or Table-Talke : As they were by Him delivered Occasionally : And by the publisher (His *quondam* Servant) carefully received ; And now humbly offered to publique view, as not impertinent to the present Times. By B. A. Gent. London printed by B. W. 1643. 4°, A—B in fours.

Two Broad-Sides Against Tobacco : . . . . London, Printed for John Hancock, . . . 1672. 4°, A—K in fours, A 1 with a portrait of James I. and K 4 blank. With a woodcut of smokers occupying I 4.

AMES [STUART] VII. *of Scotland and* II. *of Great Britain.*

The Case Put. Concerning the Succession of His Royal Highness the Duke of York. London : Printed by M. Clark, for Henry Brome . . . 1679. 4°, A—S in fours.

To His Royal Highnes the Duke, upon his Arrival. A leaf of verses.

York and Albany's Wellcome to England. Or, The Loyal Subjects Joy for his most Miraculous Deliverance. To a New Play-House Tune, much in request. Printed for I. Iordan at the Angel in Guiltspur-street. A leaf of verses.

Old Jemmy : An Excellent New Ballad. To an Excellent New Tune, called, *Young Jemmy.* London : *Printed by Nath. Thompson, 1681. A broadside in verse.

Scotlands Good Wishes to His Royal Highness : Or, The Whigs Malice Dis-covered and Defeated. Being a most plea-sant New Song, to a New Tune. Printed for P. Brooksby, at the Golden-Ball, in West-Smithfield, 1682. A broadside with verses and music.

By the King, A Proclamation Signifying His Majesties Pleasure, That all Men being in Office of Government at the Decease of the late King, His Majesties most Dear and most Entirely beloved Brother, shall so continue, till His Majes-ties further direction. [6 Feb. 1684-5.] London, Printed . . . 1684. A broad-side.

An Impartial Account of the Names of His Majesty's most Honourable Privy-Council, and Principal Officers of this Kingdom, now in Commission, &c. Un-der the Most Puissant and Renowned Prince King James II. London, Printed by J. Leake, for Arthur Jones, . . . 1686. A large broadside.

A Second Letter from a Gentleman in the Country, To his Friends in London, Upon the Subject of the Penal Laws and Tests . . . London, Printed for J. H. and T. S. . . . 1687. 4°. A, 2 : a, 2 : B, 2 : b, 2 : C, 1.

A Letter to the Author of the Vindication of the Proceedings of the Ecclesiastical Commissioners, Concerning the Legality of that Court. By Philonomus Anglicus. Printed Eleutheropolis. [About 1688.] 4°, A—C in fours.

A Letter from Lewis the Great to J—— the Less, His Lieutenant in Ireland. With Reflections by way of Answer to the said Letter. A broadside in verse. [1688.]

At the Council-Chamber in Whitehall, Monday the 22. of October, 1688. [An Account of the proceedings in connection with the birth of the Prince of Wales, including the King's address and the depositions of numerous witnesses. At the end occurs :] London, Printed by Charles Bill, Henry Hills, and Thomas Newcomb, Printers to the King's most Excellent Majesty. 1688. Folio, A—K, 2 leaves each. Without a regular title.

To the Kings Most Excellent Majesty, The Humble Petition of the Lords Spiri-tual and Temporal. Whose names are Subscribed. London, Printed for H. Jones. 1688. A broadside.
    An appeal to James by the two arch-bishops, five of the bishops, and twelve temporal peers, to call a regular and free parliament.

Some Reflections upon the Humble Peti-tion . . . Presented November 17. 1688. [Col.] London, Printed, and are to be sold by Randall Taylor : 1688. A broad-side.

To the Kings Most Excellent Majesty : The Most Humble and Faithful Advice of Your Majesties ever Dutiful Subject and Servant the Bishop of Durham. [1688.] A broadside.
    At the foot of the present copy occurs in a hand, apparently the King's : "The Kings answer. 'My Lord Why would you not give me this advice before the Prince landed?'"

An Answer to the Bishop of Rochester's First Letter to the Earl of Dorset, &c. Concerning the Late Ecclesiastical Commission. By an Englishman. *Lege Rex.* London, Printed for W. Haight in Bloomsberry. 1689. 4°, A—E 2 in fours, A 1 with half-title, and E 2 blank.

His Majesties Gracious Commission to All His Loving Subjects for Liberty of Conscience. By His Majesties special Command. London, Printed by Charles Bill, Henry Hills, and Thomas Newcomb, . . . 1688. Folio, 4 leaves.
> A declaratory repetition of the Commission of 1687.

His Majesties Letter to the House of Lords and Commons, Writ from St. Germains the 3d of February 1688. [London, 1689.] A folio leaf.

An Account of the Private League betwixt the Late King James the Second, and the French King. In a Letter from a Gentleman in London, to a Gentleman in the Countrey. London: Printed for Ric. Chiswell, . . . M.DC.LXXXIX. Folio. A—E, 2 leaves each, A 1 with the *Imprimatur.*

Qvadriennivm Jacobi, Or The History of the Reign of King James II. From his first Coming to the Crown to his Desertion. London, Printed for James Knapton, . . . 1689. 8° or 12°. A, 4 leaves : B—M in twelves.

A most Pleasant, but True Description, And no less Modest, than Just Comparison of the Old and New Jacobites, down to these Present Times : With an Account of two Famous Bastards, the French King, &c. London, Printed in the Year, 1691. 4°, A—B 2 in fours. *B. M.*

Reflections upon the Late King James's Declaration, Lately Dispersed by the Jacobites. London, Printed for Richard Baldwin, . . . 1692. 4°, B—E in fours. E 4 blank, and the title.

The Jacobites Lamentation for the Death of the late King James, who deceased at St. Germains, September the 4th, 1701. In a Dialogue between two Jacobites, meeting together at the Devils Tavern near T. B. in Fleet-street, . . . [Col.] London, Printed for Robert Johnson in Holborn, 1701. 4°, 2 leaves. In verse.

The Generous Muse. A Funeral Poem, in Memory of his late Majesty K. James the II. Humbly Dedicated to Her Royal Highness. . . . London, Printed for William Turner, . . . 1701. Folio, 8 leaves.

Sacra Exequalia in Funere Jacobi II. Magnæ Britanniæ Regis Exhibita ab Eminentiss. et Reverendiss. Principe Carolo Sanctæ Romanæ Ecclesiæ Cardinali Barberino in Templo sui Tituli Sancti Laurentii in Lucina, Descripta A Carolo de Aquino Societatis Jesu. Romae, . . . MDCCIL. Folio. Title and Imprimatur, 2 leaves : B—F, 2 leaves each : 19 plates : Oratio in Funere . . . G—L, 2 leaves each, G 1 with half-title, besides a large folded portrait.

A Funeral Oration upon the Late King James. Composed from Memoirs furnished by Mr Porter, his Great Chamberlain. Printed by the Consent of the late Queen. Dedicated to the French King, and published by his Authority . . . With Remarks upon the Whole. London, Printed, and Sold by A. Baldwin, . . . 1702. 4°, A—C in fours.

JAPAN.

A Briefe Relation of the Persecvtion lately made against the Catholike Christians, in the Kingdome of Iaponia. Deuided into two Bookes. Taken out of the Annuall Letters of the Fathers of the society of Iesvs, . . . Newly translated into English by W. W. Gent. The First Part. Permissu Superiorum, M.DC.XIX. 8°, A—Y in eights. *B. M.*

JEAN À LUXEMBOURG.

Loraison & Remonstrance de haulte & puissante Dame, Dame Marie [*sic*] de Cleues, Seur de treshault & puissant seigneur, le Duc de Iuilliers, de Cleues, & de Gueldres, Faicte au Roy d'Angleterre, & a son Conseil. [Col.] Ioannes A Lvxembvrg. Imprimé à la Riuou, par Maistre Nicole Paris, maistre es arts, tres-humble & tresobeissant Scruiteur & Imprimeur de hault & puissant Seigneur, Missire Iean de Luxembourg. [About 1540.] 4°, A—G in fours. Roman letter.
> Putticks, April 18, 1882, No. 3234. The mistake of *Marie* for *Anne* is corrected in coeval MS.

JEFFERIES, SIR GEORGE, *Lord Jefferies, Lord Chancellor of England.*

A full and true Account of the Death of George Lord Jeffries, Late Lord High Chancellor of England, Who Dyed in the Tower of London, April 18, 1689. London : Printed for R. Gifford. 1689. A broadside.

JEREMIAH.

Jeremy the Prophete / translated into Englisshe : by George Joye : some tyme

elowe of Peter College in Cantebridge.
The songe of Moses is added in the ende /
o magnifye our Lorde for the fall of our
Pharao / the Bisshop of Rome. Anno.
I. D. and . xxxiiii. in the moneth of Maye.
I°, A—P in eights.

Sothebys, June 29, 1885, in No. 636,
Baynton's copy, with the bookplate of G.
Chalmers.

JROME, ST.

ncipit exposicio sancti Jeronimi in sim-
olum apostoloru ad papaʒ laurētiū . . .
Col.] Explicit exposicio sancti Jeronimi
n simbolo apostolorum ad papam laurē-
ium Impressa Oxonie Et finita Anno
lomini. M. cccc. lxviij. xvij. die decem-
ris. 4°, a—e in eights. B. M.

The first book printed at Oxford ; 1468 is
an error for 1478. A similar slip occurs in
an early Italian book, the Livio Volgariz-
zato, printed at Rome in 1476, of which the
second volume is misdated 1466.

As Jheronimus, sheweth In this begyn-
ynge, so wyll I wryte of the . iiij. Tokens,
he whiche shall be shewed afore the
redefull daye of Dome of our lorde
hesu Christe. For there shall We shewe
ur self yonge and olde. &c. [Col.] This
ranslated out of Duche into Englysshe,
y Johñ Dousbrugh. Imprinted by me
Robert Wyer. 8°, A—B in fours = 8
eaves, B 4 with the printer's device and
. second illustration on the back of the
itle in the form of a border of pieces,
nclosing a small cut and Jheronimus.
3. M.

JROME OF FERRARA, called SAVO-
NAROLA.

Sermo Fratris Hieronymi de Ferraria
n vigilia Natiuitatis domini / corā Fra-
ribus suis recitatus. [London, Richard
Pynson, 1509.] 4°, 4 leaves. With Pyn-
on's mark at the end, but no imprint.

Sothebys, June 30, 1885. No. 1038. The
date of the discourse is September 8, 1509.

JROME, STEPHEN, Domestic Chaplain
to the Earl of Cork.

relands Ivbilee. Or Ioyes Io-Pæan. For
Prince Charles his welcome home. With
he Blessings of great Brittaine, her Dan-
ʒers, Deliverances, Dignities from God,
nd Duties to God, pressed and expressed.
More particularly, Talloughs Triumphals,
vith the Congratulations of the adioyning
English Plantations in the Province of
Munster in Ireland, . . . Dvblin, Printed
or the Societie of Stationers. Anno
Domini. M.DC.XXIV. 4°. (·), 4 leaves,
rst blank : A—Dd 2 in fours. Dedi-
ated to Henry Wright, Esquire, Sove-

reign of the Borough and Corporation of
Tallough, &c. B. M.

JESUITS.

The Iesuites Gospel By W. Crashawe, B.
of Dininity and Preacher at the Temple.
London, Printed by E. A. for Leonard
Becket . . . 1610. 4°, B—P 2 in fours,
and the title.

This tract purports to be a translation by
Crashawe of a piece by Justus Lipsius, De
Virgine Hallensi, and of the reply to it by
Carolus Scribanius of Antwerp, writing
under the name of Clarus Bonarschius.
The translator furnishes a metrical version
of the lines by Lipsius to Our Lady of Halle
and the Child Jesus.

A Discouerie of the most secret and subtile
practises of the Iesvites. Translated out
of French. At London Printed for Robert
Boulton, and are to be sold at his shop in
Smith-field, neare to Long-lane end. 1610.
4°, A—C in fours, C 3-4 blank.

The Iesuites Pater Noster Giuen to Phillip
III King of Spaine for his new yeares
gift this present yeare : 1611. Together
with the Ave Maria. Written first in
French : Englished by W. I. Printed at
Oxford by Ioseph Barnes. 1611. 8°, 4
leaves. In verse. B. M.

The State-Mysteries of the Iesvites, By
way of Questions and Answers. Faith-
fully extracted out of their owne Writings
. . . Written for a Premonition in these
times both to the Publike and Particular.
Translated out of French. . . . London,
Printed by G. E. for Nicholas Bourne.
1623. 4°, A—H in fours, H 4 blank.
Dedicated by the translator to Sir Thomas
Penystone, Kt. and Bart.

A Letter from a Jesuite : Or, The Mysterie of Equivocation. Being The Copy of
a Letter of Recommendation, seeming
much in favour of the Bearer, but by
different Reading, rendered of quite contrary signification . . . London, Printed
for W. W. 1679. 4°, 4 leaves.

The Jesuits Letter of Thanks to the
Covenanters of Scotland : For their Com-
pliance in divers Material Points of Roman Catholick Doctrine and Practice.
The Second Edition. London, Printed
in the Year, 1679. 4°, A—I in fours.

This tract is dated at the end from the
writer's study at Basileopolis [Kingston],
January 1, 1640.

The Jesuites Ghostly Wayes to draw
other Persons over to their Damnable
Principle, of the Meritoriousness of de-
stroying Princes ; Made clear in the two
barbarous Attempts of William Parry,

and Edward Squire on our late Gracious
Soveraign Elizabeth of ever blessed Memory. London, Printed for Will. Bowtel,
... 1679. 4°, A—D in fours, A 1 and
D 4 blank.

JESUS CHRIST.

Here begynneth a Contemplacyon or
medytacyon of the shedynge of the blood
of our lorde Jhesu Cryste at seuen tymes.
[Col.] Here endeth a medytacyon of the
. vij. shedyng? of the blood of our lorde
Jhesu cryste. Enprynted at Westmynster
by Wynken de Worde. 4°. A. 6 : B. 4 :
but the first leaf apparently blank, and
deficient in the copy employed.

Sothebys, June 26, 1885, No. 1277.

A Proclamatyon of the hygh emperour
Jesu Christe, vnto all his faithfull Christen. Concerninge the castell of fayth . . . .
[Col.] Imprinted at London by Rycharde
Kele, dwellyng at the longe shoppe in
the Poultry vnder saynt Mildredes church.
8°, black letter, A—B in eights.

A reprint of Redman's edition.

JEWS.

A Narrative of the late Proceeds at White-
Hall, Concerning the Jews: Who had
desired by R. Manasses an Agent for them,
that they might return into England, and
Worship the God of their Fathers here in
their Synagogue, &c. . . . London :
Printed for L : Chapman . . . 1656. 4°,
A—B in fours.

In the Postscript there is an account of
the Progress of the Gospel among the Indians in New-England.

News from the Jews, Or a True Relation
of a Great Prophet, in the Southern parts
of Tartaria ; . . . Faithfully translated
into English, By Josephus Philo-Judæus,
Gent. London, Printed for A. G. Anno
Domini, 1671. 4°, 4 leaves.

JOB.

A Paraphrase upon Job ; Written in
French by J. F. Senault, Father of the
Oratory : And Dedicated to the Cardinal
of Richlieu. [Translated by Henry, Earl
of Monmouth.] London, Printed for
Robert Bostock, . . . 1648. 8°, A—T 6
in twelves, A 1 blank and A 2 with *Imprimatur.*

JOCELINE, ELIZABETH.

The Mothers Legacie, To her vnborne
Childe. By Elizabeth Iocelin. London,
! Printed by Iohn Hauiland, for William
Barret. 1624. Small 8°, A—G in eights,
A 1 blank. Dedicated to the writer's
husband, Tourell Jocelin.

The Mothers Legac
By Elizabeth Joce
at the Theater . .
fours : B—Q in fou

JOHANNES DE (

Synonima magistr
positione magistri
prime correcta &
[Col.] Explicit lil
nouiter Londonii:
winandum de wo
signo solis in vie
strete. Anno dñi
mensis Nouembris.
the last page with

Multoꝝ vocabuloꝛ ⸾
magistri Johannis
tico & latini cupido
incipit. [Col.] Lib
vocabulor scibus ⸾
cum interpretatiõe
cit. Adiuncto car
ristia / et de virgi
gremio suo defler
doniis per winandı
M. cccc. v. xiii. ⸾
4°. aa, 8 leaves :
leaf with the devic

This book, the
date, seems from
been intended to :

JOHN OF WERS'

Le Voyage de Croɪɪ
Et son Retour su
Nouveaux Dessein
trigues, pour co
Esprits : Represen
sieur John of W
Gentilhomme ordɪ
de Sa Majesté Br
Noir. Interprete d
. . . Seconde Editi
augmenteé de la
second . . . A Lou
Daniel pour Iean
raire dans Cheap-sɪ
3 preliminary le:
eights.

JOHNSON, EDWɪ

A History of Nev
English planting iɪ
the Yeere 1652.
their Government
Ecclesiastique. T
dians, their Troub
and other Heretiɑ
gathering of Chur
of the Country, ≀
principall Towns
great encouragemɪ

betwixt them and Old England. With the names of all their Governours, Magistrates, and eminent Ministers. London, Printed for Nath: Brooke at the Angel in Corn-hill. 1654. 4⁰. Title and to the Reader, 2 leaves: B—Hh in fours, Hh 3-4 with a Catalogue of Books on sale by N. Brooke.

JOHNSON, RICHARD.

The Most Famovs History of the seuen Champions of Christendome: Saint George of England, ... Shewing their Honorable battailes by Sea and Land: their Tilts, Iousts and Tournaments for Ladies: their Combats with Giants, Monsters, and Dragons: their aduentures in forraine Nations : ... London Printed for Elizabeth Burbie, and are to be sold at her shop in Pauls Church-yard. 1608. 4⁰, black letter, A—Ee 3 in fours.

> Sothebys, April 3, 1882. No. 969, bound up with Part II.

The second part of the famous Historie of the seauen Champions of Christendome. Likewise shewing the Princely prowes of Saint Georges three Sonnes, the liuely Sparke of Nobilitie. With many other memorable atchiuements worthy the golden spurres of Knighthood. London, Printed for Elizabeth Burbie, ... 1608. 4⁰, A—Bb 3 in fours. Black letter. Dedicated to the Lord William Howard.

The Crown Garland of Golden Roses. ... Divided into two parts by R. Johnson. London, Printed for W. Gilbertson at the sign of the Bible in Gilt-spur-street. 1659. 8⁰, A—H in eights. Black letter.

> Sothebys, April 3, 1882, No. 830.

JOHNSON, RICHARD, *M.A., Master of the Free School, Nottingham.*

Noctes Nottinghamicæ Or, Cursory Objections against the Syntax of the Common-Grammar, in order to obtain a Better: Design'd in the mean time for the Use of Schools. By Richard Johnson, M.A. Author of the *Grammatical Commentaries*, and Aristarchus *Anti-Bentlianus* . . . Nottingham: Printed for Henry Clements at the Half-Moon in St. Paul's Church-Yard, London. 1718. 8⁰, A—L in fours, M, 6, besides *⁎*, 4 leaves after the title.

JOHNSON, SAMUEL.

Julian's Arts to Undermine and Extirpate Christianity. Together with Answers to Constantius the Apostate, and Jovian. By Samuel Johnson. Licensed and Entered according to Order. London, Printed by J. D. for the Author, ... MDCLXXXIX. 8⁰. A. 8, A 1 with

half-title, A 2 with Notice as to the book not having been allowed to appear before, though printed in 1683: (a), 4: B—P 4 in eights.

JOHNSON, THOMAS, *of Selby, M.D.*

Iter Plantarum Investigationis ergo susceptum a decem sociis in agrum Cantianum Anno Domini 1629 Iulii 13. Ericetum Hamstedianum sive Plantarum ibi crescentium observatio habita Anno eodem 1. Augusti Descripta Studio et Operâ Thomæ Johnsoni. 8⁰.

> Unpublished MS. of 19 leaves, inserted in a copy of Johnson's *Mercurius*, 1634, sold at Sothebys', March 14, 1883, No. 827.

JONES, ANDREW, *a Lover of Sobriety.*

The Dreadful Character of a Drunkard .... The fourth Edition . . . London, Printed for John Andrews, at the White Lion near Pye-Corner. 1660. Sm. 8⁰, black letter, A—B 4 in eights. With a curious cut on the title.

[JONES, ROGER.]

Mene Tekel ; Or, The Downfal of Tyranny. A Treatise, wherein Liberty and Equity are Vindicated, and Tyranny Condemned, by the Law of God and Right Reason: And the Peoples Power, and Duty, to execute Justice, without, and upon, Wicked Governors Asserted. By Laophilus Misotyrannus. Printed in the Year, 1663. 4⁰, B—M 1 in fours, and the title.

> Attributed to Jones in a coeval hand, which has added other matter on the title-page.

JONES, THOMAS, *some time Domestic and Naval Chaplain to the Duke of York.*

Elymas the Sorcerer : Or, A Memorial towards the Discovery of the Bottom of this Popish-Plot, ... London : Printed for H. Jones, MDCLXXXII. Folio. A—K, 2 leaves each.

JONSTON, ARTHUR.

Musæ Querulæ, De Regis in Scotiam Profectione. The Muses Complaint of the Kings iourney to Scotland. London, Printed by Thomas Harper for Nathaniel Butter, . . . 1633. 8⁰, 10 leaves, the last with the colophon. Engl. and Latin.

> The translator into English was Sir F. Kinaston.

JONSTON, JOHN, *M.D.*

Enchiridion Ethicvm . . . Lugd. Batavorum ... cɪɔ.ɪɔ.c.xxxiv. 12⁰, A—P 2 in eights, and *. 2 leaves.

> A very diminutive volume, printed by Elzevir.

JONSTONUS, JOHANNES, *of Poland.*

An History of the Constancy of Nature.

Wherein, by comparing the latter Age with the former, it is maintained that the World doth not decay universally, in respect of it Self, or the Heavens, ... By John Jonston of Poland. Printed for John Streater, and are to be sold by the Booksellers of London. 1657. 8", A—N 4 in eights, A 1 and N 4 blank. Dedicated by John Rouland to George Pit, Esquire.

JORDAN, THOMAS.

Tricks of Youth, Or, The Walks of Islington and Hogsdon, With the Humours of Woodstreet-Compter. A Comedy, As it was pu[b]lickly Acted nineteen dayes together, with Extraordinary Applause. Never Printed before. Written by Tho. Jordan, Gent. *Carpere vel noli nostra, vel œde tua.* Mart. Epig. London, Printed by Authority for the use of the Author. 4", A—H in fours.

> Crossley, part 2, No. 1728. With a dedication, in which the name is left to be supplied by a stamp or some other process. It is headed "To the Succour and Security of all Civil Wit and Learning : The justly honored," which is addressed in this copy to M. Loman.

A Speech Made to the Lord General Monck, at Clotheworkers Hall in London The 13. of March, 1659. at which time he was there entertained by the Worthie Companie. [1660.] A broadside in verse.

A Dialogue Betwixt Tom and Dick. The former a Covntry-man, The other a Citizen, Presented to his Excellency and the Council of State, at Drapers-Hall in London, March 28. 1660. (To the Tune of *I'le never love thee more.*) [1660.] A broadside in verse.

A Speech Made to his Excellency the Lord General Monck, And the Councell of State, at Drapers-Hall in London : The 28ᵗʰ of March, 1660. At which time they were entertained by that honourable Company. Spoken by Walter Yeokney. ... London : Printed for Henry Broome at the Gun in Ivy-lane, 1660. A broadside in verse.

> Yeokney here disavows a spurious edition, doubtless the previous entry.

A Speech Made to his Excellency The Lord General Monck, And the Council of State, at Goldsmiths Hall in London, The tenth day of April, 1660. At which time they were entertained by that honourable Company. After a Song, in four parts, at the conclusion of a Chorus, Enter a Sea-Captain. London, Printed for H. B. ... 1660. A broadside in verse.

A Speech Made to his Excellency George Monck General, & on The Twelfth day of April, M.DC.LX. At a Solemn Entertainment at Vinteners Hal. Wherein His Illustrious Virtues are shaddowed forth under the Emblem of a Vine. [By Thomas Jordan, 1660.] A broadside in verse.

A Speech Made to His Excellency The Lord General Monck And the Council of State At Fishmongers-Hall in London The Thirteenth of April, 1660. ... Written by Tho. Jordan. Also a Song of difference betwixt the Lawyer, the Soldier, the Citizen and the Country-man. The Chorus being ended. Enter the Ghost of Massaniello Fisherman of Naples... Spoken by Walter Young. London, Printed by W. Godbid .... 1660. A broadside in verse.

A Nursery of Novelties in Variety of Poetry. Planted for the delightful leisures of Nobility and Ingenuity. Composed by Tho. Jordan——*Mediocribus esse Poetis* . . . Horace, . . . London, Printed for the Author. 8⁰. A, 4 leaves : B—F in eights.

> The dedication in this begging production is left blank. The volume is the same as the *Royal Arbor* to sign. F 8, which ends imperfectly in the latter, but is made ostensibly complete here by the erasure of a catchword *Single* and the addition of *Finis.*

A Royal Arbor of Loyal Poesie, Consisting of Poems and Songs. Digested into Triumph, Elegy, Satyr, Love, Droll. Composed by Tho. J.

——*Mediocribus*
Non Homines, non Dii, non concessere Col[umn]i
Horace, De Arte.

London, Printed by R. Wood for Eliz. Andrews at the white Lion near Pye-Corner, 1664. 8⁰. A, 4 leaves : B—F in eights : Aa—Ee 4 in eights. Dedicated to John Adams, Gent. *B. M.*

> Sothebys, April 3, 1882, No. 836, Collier's copy, bought for the B. M.

JORDEN, EDWARD, *M.D.*

A Briefe Discovrse of a Disease called the Suffocation of the Mother ... By Edward Iorden Doctor in Physicke. London, Printed by Iohn Windet, ... 1603. 4⁰, A—H 2 in fours, H 2 blank.

JOSEPH BEN GORION.

A compendious and most marueilons Historie . . . And nowe newely corrected and amended by the sayde translatour. 1575. [Col.] Imprinted at London by William Seres. 1579. Cvm Privilegio. 8⁰. A—Kk in eights, last leaf blank and Kk 7 with the colophon only.

JOURDAN, SILAS.

A Discovery of the Barmvdas, Otherwise called the Ile of Divels : By Sir Thomas Gates, Sir George Sommers, and Captayne Newport, with diuers others. Set forth for the loue of my Country, and also for the good of the Plantation in Virginia. London, Printed by Iohn Windet, and are to be sold by Roger Barnes, . . . 1610. 4°, black letter. Title and dedication to Master John Fitzjames, Esquire, a Justice of the Peace for Dorset: the Narrative, 11 leaves, or B—D 2 in fours, besides title and two following leaves unsigned. *B. M.*

JOYE, GEORGE.

A present consolacion for the sufferers of persecucion for ryghtwysenes. [Col.] 1544 in September. 8°, black letter, A—G in eights, G 8 blank.

JUNIUS ADRIANUS, *M.D.*

The Nomenclator, or Remembrancer of Adrianus Iunius Physician, diuided in two Tomes, conteining proper names and apt termes for all thinges vnder their conuenient Titles : which within a few leaues doe follow : . . . Imprinted at London for Ralph Newberie, and Henrie Denham. 1585. 8°, A—Tt in eights.

> Dedicated by John Higins to Dr. Dale. The translator from Junius was Higins ; but large additions were made by Abraham Fleming.

K.

K. C.

Some Seasonable and Modest Thoughts Partly occasioned by, and partly concerning the Scots East-India Company. Humbly offered to R. H. Esq ; a Member of the present Parliament. By an unfeigned and hearty Lover of England. Printed in the Year 1696. 4°, A—E 2 in fours.

KAYE, WILLIAM, *Minister of Stokesley, co. York.*

God's Gracious Presence, with his Highness Richard Lord Protector of Great Britain and Ireland, &c. With the Means to retain the same, whereby Church-Government, with tolleration or no tolleration of Conscience, is Remonstrated . . . London, Printed by J. Bell for Thomas Parkhurst . . . 1658. 4°, A—C 2 in fours.

KEACH, BENJAMIN.

Spiritual Melody, Containing near Three Hundred Sacred Hymns. By Benjamin Keach, Author of Tropologia, Pastor of the Church of Christ meeting on Horslydown, Southwark. . . . London, Printed for John Hancock . . . 1691. 12°, A—R in twelves.

Light broke forth in Wales, Expelling Darkness ; Or The Englishman's Love to the Ancient Britains. . . . By Benjamin Keach. . . . London, Printed, and sold by William Marshal . . . 1696. 8°, A—Y in eights, and a, eight leaves.

KEMP, W., *M.A.*

A Brief Treatise of the Nature, Causes, Signes, Preservation from, and Cure of the Pestilence. London, Printed for, and are to be sold by D. Kemp, at his Shop at the Salutation near Hatton-Garden in Holborn. M DC LXV. 4°, A—N 2 in fours. Dedicated to the King.

KEMPE, WILLIAM, *Schoolmaster at Plymouth.*

The Education of children in learning : Declared by the Dignitie, Vtilitie, and Method thereof. Meete to be Knowne, and practised aswell of Parents as Schoolemaisters. . . . Imprinted at London by Thomas Orwin, for Iohn Porter and Thomas Gubbin. 1588. 4°, A—H 2 in fours. Black letter. *B. M.* (Bright's copy.)

> Dedicated to William Hawkins, Esq., Mayor of Plymouth. With verses by Jo. Sw., Abraham Wislake, &c.

KENT.

A most true and Lamentable Report, of a great Tempest of haile which fell vpon a Village in Kent, called Stockbery, about three myles from Cittingborne, the niutenth day of Iune last past. 1590. Whereby was destroyed great abundance of corne and fruite, to the impouerishing and vndoing of diuers men inhabiting within the same Village. London Printed for the widow of Thomas Butter. 1590. 4°, black letter, 4 leaves.

The Lamentable and Trve Tragedie of M. Arden of Feversham in Kent. Who was most wickedlye murdered, by the meanes of his disloyall and wanton wyfe, who for the loue she bore to one Mosbie, hyred two desperat ruffins Black will and Shakbag, to kill him. Wherin is shewed the great malice and discimulation of a wicked woman, the vnsatiable desire of filthie lust and the shamefull end of all murderers. Jmprinted at London for Edward White, dwelling at the lyttle North dore of Paules Church at the signe of the Gun. 1592. 4°, black letter, A—I in fours, and a leaf of K. Without any introduction. *Bodleian* and *Dyce Coll.* (imperfect at end).

The Lamentable and Trve Tragedy of Master Arden of Feversham in Kent. . . . . London, Printed by Eliz. Allde dwelling neere Christs-Church. 1633. 4°, A—I in fours. With a cut on the back of the title representing the murder. *B. M.* and *Dyce Coll.*

The Groans of Kent: Or, An Humble Remonstrance from divers well-affected in the County of Kent. To His Excellency the Lord Generall Fairfax, and the Army under his Command. London, Printed for G. W. neer the Exchange. [1647-8.] 4°, A—B in fours.

A Vindication of a Distressed Lady. In Answer to a pernitious, scandalous, libellous Pamphlet, Intituled, The Lawyers Clarke . . . London, Printed 1663. 4°, 4 leaves.

Commission for Greenwich Hospital. [Col.] London, Printed by Charles Bill, and the Executrix of Thomas Newcomb, deceased; . . . 1695. Folio. A—D, 2 leaves each, and a leaf of E. Black letter.

English Sampson, His Strength Prov'd before the King: Being an Account of the Wonderful Exploits of Mr William Joyce perform'd before his Majestie at Kensington on Wednesday last, being the 15th of this Instant November, 1699. . . . London, Printed for J. W. near Fleet street, 1699. A folio leaf. *B. M.*

KER, PATRICK.

The Map of Man's Misery: Or, The Poor Man's Pocket-Book: Being a Perpetual Almanack of Spiritual Meditations or Compleat Directory for our Endless Week . . . . To which is added a Poem, Entituled, The Glass of Vain Glory . . . London, Printed for John Lawrence at the Angel in the Poultry, 1690. 12°. A, 4 leaves, including a frontispiece: B—G

in twelves: H, 8. Dedicated to Rachel, Lady Russell.

KETEL, RICHARDUS.

Elegia in Obitum Luctuosissimum Serenissimæ . . . Mariæ Stuart, . . . Quam Piæ Æternæque ejus Memoriæ dicat Richardus Ketel. Goudæ, Ex Officina Theodori Bockhovii, MDCXCV. 4°, 6 leaves. *B. M.*

KEYMOR, JOHN.

John Keymors Observations made upon the Dutch Fishing, About the year 1601. Demonstrating that there is more Wealth Raised out of Herrings and other Fish in his Majesties Seas, by the Neighbouring Nations in one Year, then the King of Spain hath from the Indies in four . . . London, Printed from the Original Manuscript, for Sir Edward Ford in the year, 1664. 4°, A—B 3 in fours.

KIDD, WILLIAM.

A Full Account of the Proceedings in Relation to Capt. Kidd. In Two Letters. Written by a Person of Quality to a Kinsman of the Earl of Bellomont in Ireland. London, Printed and Sold by the Booksellers of London and Westminster. MDCCI. 4°, A—H 2 in fours.

Articles of Agreement, made this 10th day of October in the Year of our Lord 1695. between the Right Honourable Richard Earl of Bellomont of the one part, and Robert Levingston Esq; and Capt. William Kid of the other part. London: Printed in the Year MDCCI. A broadside.

The Arraignment, Tryal, and Condemnation of Captain William Kidd, For Murther and Piracy, upon Six several Indictments, At the Admiralty-Sessions, . . . on Thursday the 8th and Friday the 9th of May, 1700, who, upon full evidence, was found Guilty, receiv'd Sentence, and was accordingly executed at Execution-Dock, May the 23d . . . . To which is added, Captain Kidd's Two Commissions: One under the Great Seal of England, and the Other under the Great Seal of the Court of Admiralty. London: Printed for J. Nutt . . . 1701. Folio, A—P, 2 leaves each.

The volume includes other tracts.

[KILLIGREW, H.]

A Book of New Epigrams. By the same Hand that translated Martial. *Epigrammatarius Omnium Scenarum Homo.* London, Printed for Henry Bonwicke . . . 1695. 8°, A—K in eights, K 8 with Advertisements: *New Epigrams*, Part 2, with a head-line only, A—G 4 in eights.

On the fly-leaf of the copy used, which belonged to Lord Coleraine, and has his book-plate, occurs: " H. Coleraue Ex Dono Authoris Killegrewe D.D." Sothebys, April 3, 1882, No. 849.

The book-plate reads: "The Right Hon^{bl.} Henry Lord Coleraue of Colerane in ye Kingdom of Ireland. 1702."

A Court of Judicature, In Imitation of Libanius. With New Epigrams. By the Hand that translated Martial . . . . London: Printed for Henry Bonwicke . . . 1697. 8°, A—G 2 in eights, and title.

KILLIGREW, SIR WILLIAM.

Fovr New Plays, viz.

{ The Seege of Vrbin. } Tragy-
{ Selindra. } Comedies.
{ Love and Frienship. }
{ Pandora. A Comedy.

Written by Sr William Killigrew, Vice-Chamberlaine to Her Majesty. Oxford, Printed by Hen: Hall, Printer to the University, for Ric: Davis, 1666. Folio. Title, 1 leaf: verses, 5 leaves: The Author to the Reader and Prologue, 2 leaves: Title to *The Siege of Urbin,* 1 leaf: A, 2 leaves: B—G in fours: H, 1 leaf: *Selindra,* B—H in fours, including a separate title: *Love and Friendship,* A—G in fours: *Pandora,* A—G 2 in fours: *Imperial Tragedy,* without title, Names of players, preceded by a blank, 2 leaves: B—O, 2 leaves each.

Sothebys, March 13, 1884, No. 1237, a copy presented by the author to Lord Anglesey, with additions and corrections in Killigrew's writing. On the first title occurs: " Anglesey. Giuen me by the worthy author Sept. 17, 1670 ; " and he has altered *Fovr* into *Five,* adding the *Imperial Tragedy* at the end, and subscribing it with his autograph signature.

Midnight and Daily Thoughts. In Prose and Verse. By Sir William Killigrew. London, Printed for Randal Taylor, near Stationers-Hall. MDCXCIV. 8°. A, 2 leaves: B—G 6 in eights.

KINASTON, SIR FRANCIS, *of Oteley, Salop.*

Corona Minervæ. Or A Masqve Presented before Prince Charles His Highnesse, The Duke of Yorke, his Brother, and the Lady Mary his Sister, the 27th of February, at the Colledge of the Mvseum Minervæ. London, Printed for William Sheares. 1635. 4°, A—D 2 in fours, besides an extra leaf *To the Reader.*

KING, JOHN, *Bishop of London.*

The Bishop of London His Legacy Or Certaine Motiues of D. King, late Bishop of London, for his change of Religion, and dying in the Catholike, and Roman Church. With a Conclusion to his Brethren, the LL. Bishops of England. . . . Permissu Superiorum, M.DC.XXIII. 4°. Title, 1 leaf: Advertisement of the Publisher, A. B., 3 leaves: Epistle to the Reader and Contents, 6 leaves : A—X 3 in fours, X 3 blank.

KIRBY, RICHARD, *Philo-Astrologus et Medicus.*

Catastrophe Galliæ, & Hiberniæ Restitutio. An Impartial Judgement, Denoting the Reduction of Ireland, This Revolution, 90. ending March 10th 1691. Also the Conquering of proud Lewis, and Abasing France. By Their present Majesties William and Mary. . . . London, Printed for Tho. Hawkins, in George Yard, in Lombard street, 1690. 4°, A—F in fours.

KIRKWOOD, JAMES, *of Dunbar.*

Rhetoricæ Compendium ; Cui subjecta est de Analysi Tractatiuncula . . . Edinbvrgi, ... MDCLXXVIII. 12°. 8 prel. leaves : A—B, 12 each : C, 4. Dedicated to the Duke of Lauderdale.

KIRKWOOD, JAMES, *Rector of Astwick, co. Bedford.*

A New Family-Book ; Or, The True Interest of Families. Being Directions to Parents and Children, . . . With a Preface, by Dr. Horneck. The Second Edition Corrected and much Enlarged. London : Printed for J. Taylor . . . and J. Everingham . . . 1693. 12°, A—M 6 in twelves: *Advice to Children,* A—G 10 in twelves. With a frontispiece to the First Part. Dedicated to Thomas Brown of Arlsey and his wife Mary by the Author.

KNEWSTUB, JOHN.

A Confutation of monstrous and horrible heresies, taught by H. N. and embraced of a number, who call themselues the Familie of Loue . . . . Imprinted in London at the three Cranes in the Vine-tree, by Thomas Dawson, for Richard Sergier. 1579. 4°, black letter. *—**, 8 leaves each, including a letter from W. C. to Knewstub: A—S in fours.

KNIGHT OF THE SUN.

The Second part of the first Booke of the Myrrour of Knighthood: In which is prosecvted the Illvstriovs deedes of the Knight of the Sunne, and his brother Rosiclere, Sonnes vnto the Emperour Trebatio of Greece: . . Now newly Translated out of Spanish into our vulgar tongue by R. P. Imprinted at London by Thomas Este. 1585. 4°, black letter.

Title and dedication by the printer to Master Thomas Powle, Esquire, Clerk in Chancery, 2 leaves : B—Ll 4 in eights.

KNOWLES, JOHN, *Preacher of the Gospel, formerly in and near Gloucester, now to the Life Guard of his Excellency Sir Thomas Fairfax.*

A modest Plea for Private Mens Preaching. Or An Answer to a Booke intituled, Private men no pulpit-men, composed by Master Giles Warkman. . . . London. Printed in the Yeare 1648. 4°, A—E in fours.

KNOX, JOHN.

A Faythfull admonition made by Iohn Knox, vnto the professours of Gods truth in England, Wherby thou mayest learne howe God wyll haue his Churche exercised with troubles, and how he defendeth it in the same. [Two quotations from Esaie ix. At the end occurs :] Imprynted at Kalykow the 20. daye of Julij. 1554. Cum gratia . . . 8°. A, 4 leaves : B—I 3 in eights.

A confession & declaratiō of praiers added therunto by Jhon knox / minister of christes most sacred Euangely / vpon the death of that moste verteous and moste famous king Edward the VI. kynge of Englande / Fraunce and Ireland / In whiche confession / the saide Jhon doth accuse no lesse hys owne offences / then the offences of others / to be the cause of the awaye takinge / of that moste godly prince / . . . . Imprinted in Rome, before the Castel of S. Aungel / at the signe of sainct Peter. In the moneth of July / in the yeare of our Lorde. 1554. 8°, A—C 3 in eights.

The Appellation of Iohn Knox from the cruell and most iniust sentence pronounced against him by the false bishoppes and clergie of Scotland, with his supplication and exhortation to the nobilitie, estates, and cōmunaltie of the same realme. Printed at Geneva, M.D.LVIII. 8°, A—K in eights.

At the end is a translation of the 94th Psalm by W. Kethe in 4-line stanzas.

A Sermon preached by Iohn Knox . . . in the Publique audience of the Church of Edenbrough, within the Realme of Scotland, vpon Sonday, the 19. of August. 1565. For the which the said Iohn Knox was inhibite preaching for a season . . . Imprinted Anno. 1566. 8°. A, 4 leaves : B, 2 : A (repeated), 6 leaves : B—H 4 in eights.

KYD, THOMAS.

The Spanish Tragedie : . . . [Col.] At London printed for Thomas Panier. 1611. 4°, A—M 2 in fours.

Sothebys, March 14, 1883, No. 1029, imprint cut off.

L.

L. W.

The Wood-Mongers Remonstrance, Or, The Carmens Controversie rightly stated : 1. Wherein The present Jurisdiction and Corporation of the Wood-mongers is vindicated. 2. The Original and Nature of Cars, and Car-rooms, . . . 3. The inconveniences attending the erroneous conceit of accounting them Goods and Chattels, . . . 4. The mistake concerning Sea-coal sacks rectified . . . By W. L. . . . London, Printed in the Yeer, MDCXLIX. 4°. A, 4 : B, 2 : C—D, 4 each : E, 2.

Proposalls for an Act for speedy setting at large all Prisoners both for damages and debt, (those in Prison for Damages, being many not provided for by the last Act) As well for the benefit of their Creditors as of Themselves. Offered to the consideration of all the People of this Nation, who desire the Common Good. . . . Lon[d]on, Printed by F. Leach, Anno Dom. 1649. 4°, 4 leaves, subscribed W. L.

LACTANTIUS.

A Relation of the Death of the Primitive Persecutors. Written Originally in Latin by L. C. F. Lactantius. Englished by Gilbert Burnet, D.D. . . . Amsterdam, Printed for J. S. 1687. 12°, A—G in twelves.

LADY.

The Ladyes Losse at the Adventures of Five Hours : Or, The Shifting of the Vaile. Printed in the Year, 1663. 4°, A—B 2 in fours, title on A 2. In verse.

The Ladies Catechism Useful for all Eminent Females, and necessary to be learnt by all Young Gentlewomen, that would attain to the Dignity of the Mode. Edinburgh Printed in the Year 1707. 8°, 4 leaves.

The Challenge sent by a Young Lady to Sir Thomas —— &c. Or, The Female War. Wherein the Present Dresses and Humours, &c. of the Fair Sex are Vigorously attackt by Men of Quality, and as Bravely defended by Madam Godfrey, . . . London, Printed, and Sold by E. Whitlock, . . . 1697. 12°. A, 6 leaves: B—Ee in twelves: Ff, 6 leaves.

LA FOUNTAINE, M.

A Precious Treasury of Twenty Rare Secrets. Most Necessary, Pleasant, and Profitable for all sorts of People. Published by La Fountaine an Expert Operator. London, Printed Anno Dom. 1649. 4°, 4 leaves.

LANCASHIRE.

A perfect Relation of the taking of the Towne of Preston in Lancashire By the Parliaments Forces under the Command of Colonell Sir John Seaton on Thursday the ninth day of February, 1642 . . . Together, with very good news from Cheshire . . . . London, Printed for Edward Husbands, Feb. 16. 1642. 4°, 4 leaves.

Lancashires Valley of Achor . . . . London: Printed for Luke Fawne, and are to be sold by Thomas Smith at his Shop in Manchester. 1643. 4°.
A different title only.

The Lancashire Levite Rebuk'd : Or, A Vindication of the Dissenters from Popery, Superstition, Ignorance, and Knavery, unjustly Charged on them by Mr Zachary Taylor, in his Book, Entituled, The Surey Impostor. In a Letter to Himself. By an Impartial Hand. With an Abstract of the Surey Demoniack. London, Printed by Rich. Janeway, Jun. . . 1698. 4°. A, 2 leaves: B—E in fours.

The Lancashire Levite Rebuk'd : Or, A Farther Vindication . . . In a Second Letter to Himself. London: Printed by R. J. and Sold by A. Baldwin . . . 1698. 4°, A—D in fours.

LANGHORNE, DANIEL, B.D.

An Introduction to the History of England : Comprising The Principal Affairs of this Land, From its First Planting, to the coming of the English Saxons. Together with a Catalogue of the British and Pictish Kings. By Daniel Langhorne, B.D. London, Printed for Charles Harper, and John Amery, . . . 1676. 8°.

Title and to the Reader, 2 leaves : B—O in eights.

LAS CASAS, B.

The Tears of the Indians : Being An Historical and True Account of the Cruel Massacres and Slaughters of above Twenty Millions of innocent People ; Committed by the Spaniards in the Islands of Hispaniola, Cuba, Jamaica, &c. As also, in the Continent of Mexico, Peru, & other Places of the West-Indies, to their total destruction of those Countries. Written in Spanish by Casaus, an Eye-witness of those things ; And made English by J. P. . . . London, Printed by J. C. for Nath. Brook, . . . 1656. 8°. A, 8, A 1 blank : b, 7 leaves : B—K 3 in eights. Dedicated to the Protector. With a frontispiece.

An Account of the First Voyages and Discoveries Made by the Spaniards in America. Containing the most Exact Relation hitherto publish'd, of their unparallel'd Cruelties on the Indians, in the destruction of above Forty Millions of People. . . . Illustrated with Cuts. To which is added, The Art of Travelling. London, Printed . . . . MDC.XC.IX. 8°. A, 4 : B—T in eights. With a folding plate.

LATIMER, HUGH, *Bishop of Worcester.*

Certayn Godly Sermons, made vppon the lords Prayer, preached by the right reuerende Father, and constant martyr of Christ, Master Hughe Latymer, before the ryght honorable, and vertuous Lady Katherine, Duches of Suffolke, in the yeare of our Lorde. 1553. Whereunto are annexed certaine other sermons, preached by the sayde reuerende Father, in Lincolneshire, which were gathered, and collected by Augustine Bernher, a seruaunt of his, though not so perfectly as they were vttered : yet faythfully & truly . . . Imprinted at Lōdon by John Day, dwelling ouer Aldersgate . . . An. 1562. 4°, black letter. A, 4 leaves : a, 2 leaves : B—T in eights: U, 4 leaves: 27 *Sermons Preached* [a new title]: A—Q in eights.
The first edition in quarto.

Fruitfull Sermons Preached by the right reuerend Father, and constant Martyr of Iesus Christ M. Hvgh Latimer, newly Imprinted . . . At London Printed by Iohn Daye, dwelling ouer Alders gate. 1584. Cum Priuilegio . . . 4°, black letter. *, 7 leaves : A—Tt in eights : Vv, 2 leaves.

LATIN LANGUAGE.

A Comfortable ayde for Schollers, full of variety of sentences, gathered out of an Italian Authour by Dauid Rouland *Bonis omnia in bonum.* Imprinted at London by Thomas Marshe. Anno. 1578. Cum Priuilegio. 8°. A, 4 leaves : B—L in eights. Dedicated to the Earl of Lennox. *B. M.*

> Taken from a book called *Speccio della lingua Latina.* This is the earliest and only edition known ; but the work was licensed to Henry Wykes in 1567-8 as "The myrror of the Laten touge."

A new and easie Institution. In which the Labour of many yeares, usually spent in learning the Latine Tongue, is shortened and made easie. In usum Juventutis Cambro-Britanniae . . . London, Printed by J. Young, for R. Royston, . . . 1647. 8°. A, 8 leaves, besides the frontispiece : (a), 3 leaves : B—H in eights, H 8 blank.

The Way of teaching the Latin Tongue by Use, to those that have already Learn'd their Mother-Tongue. In way of Dialogue. London, Printed for Nath. Ponder . . . 1685. 8°, B—F 3 in eights, and the title. *B. M.*

A clever and amusing tract.

LAUD, WILLIAM, *Archbishop of Canterbury.*

Articles Exhibited in Parliament against William Archbishop of Canterbury, 1640. Printed in the yeare 1640. 4°, 4 leaves.

The Charge of the Scottish Commissioners against Canterburie and the Lievetenant of Ireland. . . . London, Printed for Nath. Butter. 1641. 4°, A—G in fours.

M'Grymstons Speech in Parliament Upon the Accusation and Impeachment of William Lord Arch-bishop of Canterbury, upon high Treason. . . . Printed in the yeare, 1641. 4°, 4 leaves.

A Letter sent by William Layd, Archbishop of Canterburie. With divers Manuscripts to the Vniversity of Oxford . . . . Together with the Answer . . . Printed in the Yeare. 1641. 4°, 4 leaves.

A Briefe Recitall of the unreasonable proceedings of D' Laud, against T. W. Minister of the Word of God: which he conveyed into his hands in a Letter very lately sent to him in the Tower. Together with his absurd answer to the same. Published to the World for the honour of his Grace. London, Printed by E. G. for Henry Overton, and are to be sold at his shop in Popes-head-alley,

going into Lombard-street. 1641. 4°, 4 leaves.

The Bishops Potion Or, A Dialogue betweene the Bishop of Canterbury, and his phisitian, wherein He desireth the Doctor to have a care of his Bodie, and to preserve him from being let blood in the neck, when the signe is in *Taurus.* Printed in the Yeer, 1641. 4°, A in fours, A 4 blank. With two common cuts on the title.

The Recantation of the Prelate of Canterbury : Being his last Advice to his Brethren the Bishops of England : To consider his Fall, observe the Times, forsake their Wayes, and to joyne in this good work of Reformation. . . . London, Printed, 1641. 4°, A—F in fours, F 4 blank, and the title.

A Second Message to M' William Lavd Late Archbishop of Canterbury, now prisoner in the Tower : In the behalfe of Mercurie. Together with a Postscript to the Author of that foolish and ridiculous Answer to Mercury. [London, 1641.] 4°, 4 leaves. In verse. With the common woodent print of Laud.

Romes A B C, Being a Short Perambvlation, Or Rather Articvlar Accvsation of a late tyranicall Oppressour. With a Petition to the Archbishop of Canterbury, now prisoner in the Tower. Printed in the yeare 1641. 4°, 4 leaves. With the common cut of Laud.

A Discovery of the Notorious Proceedings of William Lavd, Archbishop of Canterbury, in bringing Innovations into the Church, and raising up troubles in the State, his pride in riding in his Coach when the King himselfe went along on foot, and being reproved, would not alight. . . . Confessed by John Browne a Prisoner in the Gatehouse, . . . London, Printed, and are to be sold by Henry Walker. 1641. 4°, 4 leaves.

Lambeth Faires Ended, Or A Description of the Bishops Holy Ghost lately set to sale at Lambeth Faire.

> The Faire is ended, all their trinkets sold,
> The Holy Ghost remaines, for that no Gold,
> Could buy 't, at which Dame Fortune shee,
> Spurnes downe the Prelates climing vp her Tree.

Printed in the yeare, 1641. 4°, 4 leaves. In verse. With a cut on the title.

Canterburies Tooles : Or, Instruments wherewith he hath effected many rare feats, and egregious exploits, as is very well known, . . . Printed in the yeere, when Prelates fall is neere, 1641. 4°, 4 leaves. With a common cut on the title.

The Lordly Prelate. Being, Diverse experimentall receits, how to recover a Bishop, if he were lost. Written for the satisfaction of after times, should they desire to recall, what we labour to reject. Printed in the yeare 1641. 4°, 4 leaves. With the common print of Laud.

Canterbvries Dreame : In which The Apparition of Cardinall Wolsey did present himselfe unto him on the fourteenth of May last past : It being the third night after my Lord of Strafford had taken his fare-well to the World. Printed in the yeare 1641. 4°, 4 leaves. With a cut on the title.

> This and many other tracts relating to Laud, Strafford, Suckling, &c., are denounced by the author of the *Poets Knavery Discovered* (1642) as fictitious.

Canterburies Potion : Wherein is shewed the great Art of his Doctor in finding out the nature of his Disease : Together with the Medicines hee applied, and the strange effects they wrought in him, To the great ease of his surcharged Body. Collected from the Doctors owne hand. Printed in the yeare 1641. 4°, 4 leaves. With the common cut on the title.

A Copie of a Letter Written from his Holinesse Court at Rome, to his Grace of Canterburie Palace now in the Tower. Deploring his Sequestration from his Liberty, but commending him for his late care in performing his Holinesse desires. London, Printed 1642. 4°, 4 leaves.

An Ordinance of the Lords and Commons . . . Concerning the Arch-Bishop of Canterbury, who by reason of many great and weighty businesses, cannot as yet be brought to his Tryall. London, May 19. Printed for John Wright, in the Old-Bailey. 1643. 4°, 2 leaves.

An Ordinance . . . That all the Temporal Livings, Dignities, and Ecclesiasticall Promotions belonging vnto William Lord Arch-bishoppe of Canterbury, be forthwith Sequestered by and unto the Parliament, . . . June 13. Printed for John Wright in the Old-Bailey. 1643. 4°, 4 leaves.

A Prophecie of the Life, Reigne, and Death of William Laud, Archbishop of Canterbury : By an Exposition on part of the 13. and 15. Chapters of the Revelation of John . . . . Perused and Allowed. Printed for R. A. 1644. 4°, 4 leaves. With a large cut on title.

A Briefe Relation of the Death and Svfferings of the Most Reverend and Renowned Prelate the L. Archbishop of Canterbvry : With A more perfect Copy of his Speech . . . Oxford ; Printed in the Yeare. 1644. 4°, A—D in fours. With some verses at the end.

The Bishop of Canterbury His Confession, Wherein is declared his constant Resolution, his Plots, and indeavours, to introduce Popery into England, . . . London, Printed in the Yeare, 1644. 4°, 4 leaves.

The Archbishop of Canterbury's Speech : Or His Funerall Sermon, Preacht by himself on the Scaffold, on Tower-Hill, on Friday the 10. of January, 1644. Upon Hebrews 12. 1, 2. Also, the Prayers which he used at the same time and place before his execution. All faithfully Written by John Hinde, whom the Archbishop beseeched that he would not let any wrong be done him by any phrase in false copies. Licensed and Entred . . . London, Printed by Peter Cole, . . . 1644. 4°, B—C in fours, and the title.

A Charme for Canterburian Spirits, Which (since the death of this Arch-Prelate) have appeared in sundry shapes, and haunted divers houses in the City of London. With his Graces waftage over the Red Sea of Cocitus in Charons Ferry-boat ; And his magnificent entertainment into the Dæmoniack Court. Printed for J. C. February the 15. 1645. 4°, 4 leaves. With a curious cut on title.

A Commemoration of King Charles His Inauguration. Or, A Sermon Preached at Pauls Crosse By William Laud then Bishop of London . . . London, Printed by M. B. 1645. 4°, B—E in fours, besides the title and a frontispiece of the Royal arms.

LAWRENCE, THOMAS, A.M.

Mercurius Centralis : Or, A Discourse of Subterraneal Cockle, Muscle, and Oyster-shels, Found in the digging of a Well at Sir William Doylies in Norfolk many foot under ground, and at considerable distance from the Sea. Sent in a Letter to Thomas Brown, M.D. London : Printed by J. G. for J. Collins, . . . 1664. 12°, A—E 6 in twelves, E 5-6 blank.

LAWSON, WILLIAM.

A new Orchard, and Garden ; . . . . . Whereunto is newly added the Art of Propagating Plants ; . . . . London, Printed by W. Wilson for John Harrison, . . . 1648. 4°. A, 4 : B—H in eights :

I, 7 : K, 4, the last leaf blank. With cuts.

LE BOVIER DE FONTENELLE, B.

New Dialogues of the Dead. In Three Parts. I. Dialogues of the Ancient with the Ancient. II. Dialogues of the Ancient with the Modern. III. Dialogues of the Modern with the Modern. Dedicated to Lusian in Elysium. Made English by J. D. London, Printed for D. Y. at the Foot of Parnassus-Hill. MDCLXXXIII. 12°. First title, &c., 6 leaves : A, 2 leaves: B—G 10 in twelves : *Second Part*, dated 1685—title preceded by a blank, 2 leaves: B—G in twelves, including advertisements.

This is the prototype of Landor's *Imaginary Conversations*.

LE CLERC, M.

Reflections upon what the World commonly call Good-Luck and Ill-Luck, with regard to Lotteries. And of the Good Use which may be made of them. Done into English. London, Printed for Matth. Gillyflower . . . 1699. 8°, A—K 6 in twelves.

The translator does not appear.

LEDERER, JOHN.

The Discoveries of John Lederer, In Three several Marches from Virginia, to the West of Carolina, And other parts of the Continent : Begun in March 1669, and ended in September 1670. Together with A General Map of the whole Territory which he traversed. Collected and Translated out of Latine from his Discourse and Writings, By Sir William Talbot Baronet . . . London, Printed by J. C. for Samuel Heyrick. . . . 1672. 4°, A—E 2 in fours, A 1 blank, besides the map.

LEE, WILLIAM, *D.D.*

Vox clamantis. Mark. 1, 3. A Stil Voice, to the three Thrice-honourable Estates of Parliament : And in them, to all the Soules of this our Nation, ... Printed by T. S. for John Teage, ... 1621. 4°. Title, dedication, and blank leaf before title, 4 leaves : A—K in fours.

LEECH, DAVID.

Philosophia Illachrymans, Hoc est, Querela Philosophiæ, Ei Philosophorvm Scotorvm, (præsertim vero Borealium) oratorie expressa : Publicè habita in Auditorio Maximo Collegii Regii Aberdonensis 26 die Iulii, 1637 . . . . Perorante Davide Leochæo, Philosophiæ Professore, . . . Aberdoniæ, Imprimebat Edwardus Rabanus . . . 1637. 4°, A—H. 2 leaves each. Dedicated to the Marquis of Huntly.

LEECH, JOHN.

Ioannis Leochæi Epigrammatum Libri Qvatvor. Editio Tertia, prioribus multo emendatior. Londini, Excudebat Bernardvs Alsopus, Anno Dom. M.DC.XXIII. 4°, A—K in fours. Dedicated to James Hay, Viscount Doncaster. *B. M.*

LEEDS, DANIEL.

A Trumpet sounded out of the Wilderness of America ; which may serve as a Warning to the Government and People of England to Beware of Quakerisme . . . Printed by William Bradford at the Bible in New York ; . . . 1699. 8°. Title, Preface, Contents, &c., 8 leaves : A—L 4 in eights.

LE FEBURE, N.

A Discourse Upon Sr Walter Rawleigh's Great Cordial ; By N. le Febvre, Royal Professor in Chymistry, and Apothecary in Ordinary to his Majesty's most Honourable Houshold. Rendred into English by Peter Belon, Student in Chymistry. London, Printed by J. F. for Octavian Pulleyn Junior, . . . 1664. 8°, A—H in eights, A 1 and H 8 blank, and a, 2 leaves.

LE FEVRE, RAOUL.

The Destruction of Troy . . . The Twelfth Edition . . . London, Printed for Eben. Tracey, . . . 1702. 4°, B—3 D 2 in fours, besides title and preface.

LE GRAND, JACQUES.

Here begynneth a lytell boke called good maners. [Col.] Here endeth and fynysshed the boke named and Intytled good maners. Enprynted at Westmynster by Wynken de worde. Laus deo. 4°, A—P in sixes : Q, 7, with the printer's mark on Q 7 *recto*, the reverse occupied by a repetition of the page-cut found on the back of the title.

Puttick & Simpson, Aug. 18, 1882, No. 673, Q 1 wanting.

The boke of good maners [This title is on a black ground in white letters over a cut occupying the rest of the page. At the end occurs :] Here endeth and fynysshed the boke named and Intytled good maners. Enprynted at London in ye Flete-strete at the sygne of the Sonne by Wynken de Worde In ye yere of our lorde. M.CCCCC. and . vii. The . x. daye of December. The xxiii. yere of the reygne of our soverayne lorde kynge Hary the seuenth. 4°. Title, preface, and Table, 4 leaves : A—N in eights, except that N has only 4 leaves.

Sothebys, June 26, 1885, No. 136.

LEICESTER, SIR PETER.
An Answer to Sir Thomas Mainwaring's
Book, Intituled,—An Admonition . . . .
Written by the same Sir Peter Leicester.
Printed in the Year, 1677. 8", A—C in
eights, C 8 blank.

LEICESTERSHIRE.
Strange and wonderfull Witch - crafts.
Discouering the damnable practises of
seauen Witches, against the liues of certaine Noble Personages, and others of
this Kingdome, as shall appeare in this
lamentable History. With an approued
triall how to find out either Witch, or any
Apprentise to Witch-craft. Imprinted
at London by G. Eld, dwelling in Little-
Brittaine. 1621. 4°, B—D in fours, and
the title, on which is a cut of a witch and
her cat.

> A reissue of the edition of 1619 of the
> Flower case, with a different title and omis-
> sions. Sothebys, Nov. 29, 1883, No. 544.

LEIGH, EDWARD.
Three Diatribes Or Discourses.
First of Travel, Or a Guide for Travellers
into Forein Parts.
Secondly, Of Money or Coyns.
Thirdly, Of Measuring of the Distance
betwixt Place and Place.
By Edward Leigh Esq; and Mr of Arts
of Magdalene-Hall in Oxford . . . London, Printed for William Whitwood, . . .
1671. 8°, A—G 4 in eights. Dedicated
to his friend Francis Willoughby, Esq.

LEIGH or LEA, RICHARD.
The Copie of a Letter sent ovt of England
to Don Bernardin Mendoza Ambassadour
in France for the King of Spaine, declaring the state of England, contrary to the
opinion of Don Bernardin, and of all his
partizans Spaniardes and others. This
Letter, although it was sent to Don Bernardin Mendoza, yet by good hap, the
Copies therof aswell in English as in
French were found in the Chamber of
one Richard Leigh a Seminarie Priest,
who was lately executed for high treason
committed in the time that the Spanish
Armada was on the seas. Whereunto
are adioyned certaine late Aduertisements, concerning the losses and dis-
tresses happened to the Spanish Nauie,
. . . [as in the other issue.] Imprinted
at London by T. Vautrollier for Richard
Field. 1588. 4°, A—F 2 in fours.

> The Advertisements are contained on the
> two leaves F and F 2 in an address from
> the Printer to the Reader.

The Copie of a Letter sent ovt of England . . . . Wherunto are adioyned cer-

tain Advertisements, . . . London, Printed
by George Miller . . . 1641. 4°, A—E
in fours.

LEITH.
A New and Easy Project of making the
Water of Leith Navigable; whereby Ships
may pass, and enter into the North-Lough.
[About 1700.] 4°, 4 leaves.

LEIUS, MATTHIAS.
Certamen Elegiacum Novem Mvsarum,
Apolline duce, contra Barbariem susceptum : & . . . D. Elizabethæ, Angliæ . . .
D.D.D. Matthias Leius, Germanus. Impressum Londini per Simonem Staf-
fordum. 1600. 4°, 8 leaves. *B. M.*

Matthiæ Leij, Aruillarijvbij Germani,
Liber De Triumphata Barbarie. [Lon-
dini.] Anno Domini. 1621. 4°, A—C in
fours. With a large cut on the title.
B. M.

LELAND, JOHN.
Genethliacon . . . 1543.

> *Corrected Collation :* a—f in fours: g, 6
> leaves, the sixth occupied by a device
> having the motto *Charitas.*

ΚΥΚΝΕΙΟΝ ΑΣΜΑ Cygnea cantio. Av-
tore Ioanne Lelando Antiqvario. Lon-
dini. [Apud Reginaldum vel Reynerum
Vuolfium.] M.D.XLV. 4°. A, 6 leaves :
B—E in fours : *Commentarii in Cygneam
Cantionem,* A—P in fours.

Cygnea cantio. Autore Joanne Lelando
Antiquario. Londini, Typis & Expensis
Johannis Streater. MDCLVIII. 8°, B—O
2 in eights, besides title and leaf with
woodcut and verses.

LEMERY, LOUIS, *Regent-Doctor of the
Faculty of Physic at Paris.*
A Treatise of Foods, in General : . . . .
Written in French . . . . Now done into
English. London, Printed for John
Taylor, ... MDCCIV. 8°. A, 8 leaves :
a, 8 : b, 6 : B—Y 4 in eights.

LEMINIUS, LEVINUS.
The Touchstone of Complexions. Gene-
rallye applicable, expedient, and profitable for all such, as be desirous & care-
full of their bodylye health. . . . englished
by Thomas Newton. Nosce teipsum.
Imprinted at London, in Fleete-streete,
by Thomas Marsh, Anno. 1576. Cum
Priuilegio. 8°, A—X in eights. Dedicated from Butley in Cheshire, Sept. 2,
1576, to Sir William Brooke, Lord Cobham.

The Touchstone of Complexions. . . .
Imprinted at London, in Fleete-streete,
by Thomas Marsh. Anno. 1581. Cum

Priuilegio. 8°, A—X in eights, A 1 blank.

An Herbal for the Bible. Containing a Plaine and Familiar Exposition of such Similitudes, Parables, and Metaphors, ... as are borrowed and taken from Herbs, Plants, ... Drawen into English by Thomas Newton. Imprinted at London by Edmund Bollifant. 1587. 8". Title and dedication to Robert, Earl of Essex, 3 leaves : B—V 4 in eights.

LE NOBLE, M.
Abra Mulé : Or. A True History of the Dethronement of Mahomet IV. Written in French by M. Le Noble. Made English by J. P. London, Printed for R. Clavel, ... 1696. 8°. A, 4 : B—I in eights : K, 2.

LENTON, FRANCIS.
The Muses Oblation / Expressed in Anagrammes Acrostickes and an Encomiastick Gratulation Reflecting on the Name Hono' and Dignity newly Conferred by king Charles his fauo' On the Honourable Nobly Mynded Affable & Ingenuous S' James Stonehouse knight and Baronett . . . . By Francis Lenton Gent . . . 1641. 4°, 12 leaves.

Sothebys, June 4, 1884, No. 155, the original unpublished MS.

LEON, JACOB JEHUDAH, *Hebrew, Author of the " Model of Solomon's Temple."*
A Relation of the most memorable thinges in the Tabernacle of Moses, and the Temple of Salomon, According to Text of Scripture. At Amsterdam, Printed by Peter Messchaert, in the Stoof-steech, 1675. 4°. *, 4 leaves : A—D 2 in fours.

LESLEY, JOHN, *Bishop of Ross.*
Dv Droict et Tiltre de la Serenissime Princesse Marie Royne d'Escosse, . . . A Roven, De l'Imprimerie de George l'Oyselet. [1587.] 8". A, 4 leaves : B —K in eights. With the genealogical tree.

LESLY, GEORGE, *Rector of Wittering, co. Northampton, afterward of Olney, co. Bucks.*
Divine Dialogues. Viz. Dives's Doom. Sodom's Flames, and Abraham's Faith. Containing the Histories of Dives and Lazarus, the Destruction of Sodom, and Abraham's Sacrificing his Son. To which is Added Joseph Reviv'd. . . . The Second Edition. London : Printed for Nicholas Woolfe . . . 1684. 8". A, 4 leaves : B —E in eights, E 8 blank. Dedicated to Charles, Earl of Westmoreland.

An Answer to a Book, Intituled, The State of the Protestants in Ireland Under the Late King James's Government ; In which their Carriage towards him is Justified, . . . London, Printed in the Year 1692. 4°, A—S in fours, and [aa] 1 leaf, besides a—c, 2 leaves each between A and A 2.

Israel's Troubles and Triumph. Or, The History of their dangers in, and deliverance out of Egypt. As it is recorded by Moses in Exod. and Turned into English Verse. . . . London, Printed for the Author, and sold by Nicholas Woolf, . . . 1699. 8". Title and Preface, 3 leaves : B—G in eights, G 8 blank.

LE STRANGE, SIR ROGER.
L'Estrange His Apology : With A Short View, of some Late and Remarkable Transactions, Leading to the happy Settlement of these Nations under the Government of our Lawfull and Gracious Soveraign Charls the II. whom God Preserve. By R. L. S. . . London, London, Printed for Henry Brome, . . . 1660. 4", A—X in fours, title on A 2.

The Recantation of a Penitent Proteus, Or The Changeling : As it was Acted with good Applause at St. Maries in Cambridge, and St. Pauls in London, 1663. To the Tune of *Doctor Faustus.* In verse. A broadside.

A Discourse of the Fishery. Briefly laying open, not only the Advantages, and Facility of the Undertaking, but likewise the Absolute Necessity of it ; in Order to the Well-Being, both of King, and People. Asserted, and Vindicated from all Material Objections. By R. L'Estrange. London, Printed for Henry Brome . . . 1674. 4", A—B 2 in fours.

The History of the Plot : Or a Brief and Historical Account of the Charge and Defence of Edward Coleman, Esq; William Ireland, [and 13 others, including five Jesuits and three Benedictines] . . . Not omitting any one Material Passage in the whole Proceeding. By Authority. London, Printed for Richard Tonson . . . 1679. Folio, A—Z, 2 leaves each, G 1 repeated.

On the title of this copy, in what appears likely to be his own handwriting, occurs : *Roger L'Estraunge author.*

The Observator Defended, By The Author of the Observators. In A Full Answer to Several Scandalls Cast upon him, in Matters of Religion, Government, and Good Manners. London, Printed for

Charles Brome, . . . 1685. 4°, A—E in fours. Dedicated to the Bishop of London.

LETI, GREGORIO.

Historia, E Memorie recondite sopra alla Viza di Oliviero Cromvele, Detto il Tiranno senza Vizi ; Il Prencipe senza Virtu . . . Amsterdamo, . . . 1692. 8°. *—***, 8 leaves each, * 1 blank : A—Ll in eights : Part II., A—Pp in eights. With a small map of Great Britain, portrait of Cromwell, and other portraits and plates.

Historia o vero Vita di Elizabetta, Regina d'Inghilterra detta per Sopra-nome la Comediante Politica . . . Amsterdamo, . . . 1693. 12°. 2 vols. With frontispieces, portraits, and other plates. Vol. I., *, 12 : A—Aa in twelves : Vol. II., A—Bb in twelves.

LETTER.

A Letter sent out of Holland from Hans Hue-&-Cry, Van Hang-&-draw, the Executioner ; To his trusty and ill-beloved friend, Gregory the second son of the Destinies, . . . With his Letter sent in answer, . . . September 28. and October 4. London, Printed for Thomas Iohnson. 1642. 4°, 4 leaves.

A Letter to Father Lewis Sabran Jesuite, In Answer to his Letter to a Peer of the Church of England. Wherein the Postscript to the Answer to Nubes Testium is vindicated. And F. Sabran's Mistakes further discovered. London, Printed for Henry Mortlock . . . 1688. 4°, 4 leaves.

A Letter of Advice to a Friend, Upon the Modern Argument of the Lawfulness of Simple Fornication, Half-Adultery, and Polygamy. London : Printed for William Keblewhite, . . . 1696. 4°, A—B in fours.

Certain most godly, fruitful, and comfortable letters of such true Saintes and holy Martyrs of God, as in the late bloodye persecution here within this Realme, gaue their lyues for the defence of Christes holy gospel : written in the tyme of theyr affliction and cruell imprysonment. *Though they suffer* . . . . Sap. 3. Imprinted at London by Iohn Day, . . . 1564. Cum gratia . . . 4°, black letter. A, 4 leaves : B—Yy in eights : Additional Letters, 4 leaves. With a Preface by Miles Coverdale and a large cut on back of title.

Certayne Letters / translated into English / being first written in Latine. Two, by the reverend and learned M' Francis Iunius, Divinitie Reader at Leyden in Holland. The other, by the exiled English Church, abiding for the present at Amsterdam in Holland. Together with the Confession of faith prefixed : where vpon the said letters were first written. . . . Printed in the yeare. 1602. 4°, A—H 2 in fours, B 4 blank.

The Copies of Certaine Letters which have passed betweene Spaine and England in matter of Religion, Concerning the generall Motiues to the Romane obedience. Betweene Master Iames Wadsworth, a late Pensioner of the Holy Inquisition at Siuill, and W. Bedell a Minister of the Gospell of Iesus Christ in Suffolke. London Printed by William Stansby for William Barret and Robert Milbourne. 1624. 4°. *, 4 leaves, the first blank, the others with the title and Bedell's dedication to Prince Charles : A—Y in fours, Y 4 with the *Errata.*

Three Letters Concerning the Surrender of many Scotish Lords to the High Sheriffe of the County of Chester, and the Condition of Duke Hamilton, Sir Marmaduke Langdale, Middleton, and others of note. . . . Imprinted at London for John Wright . . . 28. Aug. 1648. 4°, 4 leaves.

Three Letters of Thanks to the Protestant Reconciler. 1. From the Anabaptists at Munster. 2. From the Congregation in New-England. 3. From the Quakers in Pensilvania. London, Printed for Benj. Took, 1683. 4°, A—D 2 in fours.

LEY, JOHN, *Vicar of Great Budworth, and Prebendary of Chester.*

A patterne of Pietie. Or The Religious life and death of that Graue and gracious Matron, M'' Jane Ratcliffe Widow and Citizen of Chester . . . London. Printed by Felix Kingston for Robert Bostocke . . . . 1640. 8°, A—O 4 in eights, A 1 and O 4 blank. Dedicated to the Lady Brilliana Harley and the Lady Alice Lucy.

A Letter (Against the erection of an Altar.) Written Iune 29. 1635. to the Reverend Father Iohn L. Bishop of Chester. By Iohn Ley, Pastour of Great Budworth in Cheshire. London, Printed for George Lathum, . . . 1641. 4°. The copy ended imperfectly on D 4.

LEVENS OR LEVINS, PETER.

Manipvlvs Vocabvlorvm. A Dictionarie of English and Latine Wordes, set forthe in suche order, as none heretofore hath ben, the Englishe going before the Latine, necessary not onely for Scholers that wāt varietie of words, but also for such as vse

to write in English Meetre. Gathered
and set forth by P. Leuins. Anno 1570.
For the better vnderstanding of the order
of this present Dictionarie, read ouer the
Preface . . . Imprinted at London by
Henrie Byuneman, for John Waley.
[1570.] 4°. ¶, 4 leaves: *Errata*, 1 leaf:
A—S in fours. *B. M.*

Reprinted for the Early English Text
Society, 8°.

LHUYD, EDWARD, *M.A., of Jesus College, Keeper of the Ashmolean Museum
at Oxford.*
Archæologia Britannica, Giving some
Account Additional to what has been
hitherto Publish'd, of the Languages,
Histories and Customs of the Original
Inhabitants of Great Britain: From Collections and Observations in Travels
through Wales, Cornwal, Bas-Bretagne,
Ireland and Scotland. Vol. I. Glosso-
graphy. Oxford, Printed at the Theater
for the Author, MDCCVII. . . . Folio.
a—e, 2 leaves each: A—Ii, 2 leaves each.

No more was published.

LIBRARY.
The Compleat Library: Or, News for the
Ingenious. Containing Several Original
Pieces . . . As also, The State of Learn-
ing in the World. To be Published
Monthly. May, 1692. By a London
Divine [Rev. Mr. Wolley] &c. London,
Printed for John Dunton . . . 1692. 4°,
A—3 S 3 in fours, except that A has only
2 leaves.

The copy used extended from May to
November 1692.

LIGON, RICHARD.
A Trve & Exact History of the Island
of Barbados. Illustrated with a Mapp of
the Island, as also the Principall Trees
and Plants there, set forth in their due
Proportions and Shapes, drawne out by
their severall and respective Scales. Together with the Ingenio that makes the
Sugar, with the Plots of the severall
Houses, . . . London, Printed for Humphrey Moseley, . . . 1657. Folio. Title,
1 leaf: dedication from the Upper Bench
Prison, July 12, 1653, to Dr. Brian Duppa,
Bishop of Salisbury, 2 leaves: Bishop
Duppa's letter to the author in prison,
and verses to Ligon by George Walshe, 2
leaves: map: B—Ii 3 in twos. With
plates at pp. 70, 76, 78, 80, 82, 84 (5, of
which 4 are indexes, &c.), and 88.

Bishop Duppa's letter, subscribed "Your
most affectionate Friend, Br. Sar.," is dated
from Richmond, Septemb. 5, 1653, and
makes some allusions to Ligon's earlier
pursuits.

LILBURN. JOHN.
The out-cryes of oppressed Commons.
Directed to all the Rationall and understanding men in the Kingdome of England, and Dominion of Wales; (that have
not resolved with themselves to be Vas-
sells and Slaves, unto the lusts and wills
of Tyrants) from Lieut. Col. John Lilburne, prerogative prisoner in the Tower
of London, and Richard Overton, prerogative prisoner in the Infamous Gaole of
Newgate. Febr. 1647. [Privately printed
without a title-page.] 4°, A—C 2 in
fours.

A Whip for the present House of Lords,
Or The Levellers Levelled. In an Epistle
writ to Mr Frost, Secretary to the Committee of State, that sits at Darby House,
in answer to a lying book said to be
his called a declaratio [sic] &c. By L.
C. Io. Lilburne, Prerogative Prisoner in
the Tower of London, Feb. 27. 1647.
[Secretly printed without a title-page.]
4°, A—C in fours: D—E, 2 leaves each.

An Impeachment of High Treason. . . .
1649.
At p. 58 there is a curious reference to
the perusal by Cromwell and Ireton in a
garden-house at Putney of the King's Answer to certain Propositions, and on the
following page Ireton is pictured standing
at the fireside in his quarters at Kingston.
I am told that the spot near the church at
Putney, where the Parliamentarians piled
their pikes, still preserves the name of
Pike Lane.

A Just Reproof to Haberdashers-Hall:
Or, An Epistle writ by Lieut Colonel
John Lilburn, July 30, 1651, to four of
the Commissioners at Haberdashers-Hall,
. . . [1651-2.] 4°, A—E in fours. Without any title-page.

LILLY, WILLIAM, *Astrologer.*
Merlini Anglici Ephemeris, . . . 1671.
By William Lilly . . . London, Printed
by J. Macock for the Company of Stationers. 1671. 8°, A—F in eights. Portrait on title.

Anima Astrologiæ: Or, A Guide for
Astrologers. Being the considerations
of the Famous Guido Bonatus Faithfully
rendered into English. As also The
Choicest Aphorisms of Cardans Seaven
Segments. Translated, . . . With a New
Table of the fixed Stars, . . . By William
Lilly, Student in Astrology. London,
Printed for B. Harris at the Stationers
Arms in Sweethings Rents near the Royal
Exchange, 1676. 8°. Portrait of Lilly,
Cardan, &c., title, and prefaces, 4 leaves:
B—I 3 in eights: folded leaf with Cata-

logue of Stars : Aphorisms of Cardan, A—D in eights.

Lilly's Preface is dated from Walton-on-Thames, 2d August 1675.

Merlini Anglici Ephemeris : Or, Astrological Judgments for the year 1681. . . . London, Printed by J. Macock for the Company of Stationers. 1681. 8", A—B in eights. Portrait of Lilly on title.

LILY, GEORGE, *son of the Grammarian, and Master of St. Paul's School.*
Chronicon Sive Brevis Envmeratio Rervm et Principvm, in qvos variante fortuna, Britanniæ Imperium diuersis temporibus translatus est. Georgio Lilio Britanno Autore. Cum Cæsareæ Maiestatis Priuilegio in annos octo. Francoforti. M. D. LXV. [Col.] Francoforti Apud Ioannem Vuolfium, Anno M.D.LXV. 4°. aa in fours : A—X 2 in fours. *B. M.*

LILY, WILLIAM, *Grammarian.*
Gvlielmi Lilii, Olim Scholae Pavlinae apud Londinum moderatoris, de Latinorū nominum generibus, de uerborū præteritis & supinis, regulæ non minus utiles, quàm compendiosæ : cum annotationibus Thomae Robertsoni Eboracensis. Qvibvs accessit de nominibus heteroclitis, de uerbis defectiuis, ac demum de uersibus pangendis, auctariū neutiquā poenitendum, per eundem Thomam Robertsonvm, . . . Basileæ, Anno M.D.XXXII. 4°. A, 6 : B—R in fours. [Col.] Basiliae, Per Io. Bebelivm, . . . Mense Avgvsto, Anno M.D.XXXII.

A Shorte Introdvction of Grammar generally to be vsed : . . . . Excusum Londini apud Reginaldum Vuolfium, Regiæ Maiest. in Latinis Typographum. Anno domini M.D.LXVII. 4°. In two parts. Part 1, A—D in eights : *Brevissima Institutio,* A—L 6 in eights.

A Short Introduction of Grammar . . . London, Printed by Roger Norton, . . . 1670. 8", A—O in eights, O 8 and A 1 blank.

A Short Introduction of Grammar . . . To which are added useful Observations by way of Comment out of Ancient and late Grammarians. Oxford, At the Theater: An. Dom. M.DC.LXXIII. 8° or 12°. Frontispiece of the *Tree of Knowledge,* title, preface, and a blank, 5 leaves altogether : A 2—C 12 in twelves : *Brevissima Institutio,* A—H in twelves : I, 8.

LINACER, THOMAS.
Thomae Linacri Britanni De Emendata Strvctvra Latini Sermonis Libri Sex.

[Col.] Londini Apvd Richardum Pynsonum mense Decembri, M.D.XXIIII. Cum priuilegio regio. 4°. Title and To the Reader, 2 leaves : A—S in fours : T, 6.

Thomae Linacri Britanni de Emendata Strvctvra Latini Sermonis Libri Sex. Emendatiores. Index copiosissimus in eosdem. Lvtetiae, Ex officina Roberti Stephani typographi Regii. M. D. L. 8°, a—z in eights : A—E in eights, E 7 blank, and E 8 with colophon.

LINCOLN.
An Abridgment of that Booke which the Ministers of Lincoln Diocess deliuered to his Maiestie upon the first of December last. Being the First Part of an Apologye for themselves and their brethren that refuse the subscription, and conformitie which is required. . . . Printed 1605. 4", A—L in fours.

LINDEWOOD, WILLIAM.
Constituciones prouinciales ecclesie anglicae. per. do. Wilhelmū Lyndewode vtrinsqu; iuris doctorem edite. Incipiunt feoliciter. [Col.] Opus Presens fabricatum est. Et diligenter correctum per wynandum de worde. Apud westmonasteriū In domo caxston. Anno Incarnacionis Millesimo quadragetesimo nonagesimo sexto Vltima die May acabatūq; Gloria deo. Sm. 8°, A—X in eights. With the printer's small mark on U 8 and X 8.

Only the first leaf of each sheet is signed.

LISTER, MARTIN.
Martini Lister Historia Conchylorum Liber Primus Qui est de Cochleis Terrestribus. Londini. Ære incisus, Sumptibus authoris. 1685. Susanna et Anna Lister figuras pin. 4°. Six prel. leaves : 376 leaves, concluding with the Fourth Book, dated 1691.

Each of the parts has a separate title. Two differing titles seem to have been given to the volume. The other reads : Martini Lister. Historiæ sive Synopsis Methodicæ Conchyliorum quorum omnium Picturam, ad vivum delineatæ, exhibetur Liber Primus, qui est de Cochleis Terrestribus. Londini. ære incisus, Sumptibus authoris.

A Journey to Paris in the Year 1698. By Dr Martin Lister. The Second Edition. London, Printed for Jacob Tonson . . . 1699. 8". Title and dedication, 3 leaves : plates of shells and portraits, 6 leaves : B—R 4 in eights.

LITHUANIA.
A True Reporte of three straunge and wonderfull Accidents, lately hapened at

Pernaw, a Cittie in Liſflande. Wherein is conteyned a Prophesie of the great Dearth & Famine, which (by reason of the warres in those partes) hath there come to passe in the yeare last past, 1602. And also of the great Victorie lately atchiued by the great Sophy, . . . Truly translated out of the Dutch printed Coppie, printed at Nimmegen. At London printed by R. B. 1603. 4º, black letter. ¶, 4 leaves, first title on ¶ 2 : A—B in fours, A 4 blank. *B. M.*

Sheets A—B are transposed in this copy.

LIVONIA.

An Account of Livonia ; With a Relation of the Rise, Progress, and Decay of the Marian Teutonick Order, . . . With the Wars of Poland, Sweden and Muscovy, . . . To which is added The Author's Journey from Livonia to Holland, in 1698, . . . Sent in Letters to his Friend in London. London : Printed for Peter Buck, . . . 1701. 8º. A, 4 : B—Y in eights. With a portrait of Frederic William, Duke of Courland.

LITHGOW, WILLIAM.

Lithgow's Nineteen Years Travels . . . The Tenth Edition. London, Printed by J. Millet, for M. Wotton . . . and T. Passinger . . . 1692. 8º, A—Hh in eights, besides the frontispiece and folded cuts at pp. 252-3, 276-7, 354-5, 392-3, 426-7, and 434-5.

LLOYD, LODOWICK.

The pilgrimage of Princes. . . . W. Jones [1573.] 4º.

Collation :—*, 4 leaves : **, 4 leaves : A—3 K in fours. The title-page is followed by an acrostic on *Christophors Hattonrs*, occupying * 2 ; the five following leaves have the dedication to Hatton and verses by T. Drant, Christopher Carlile, Thomas Churchyard, &c.

On the title-page of a very fine copy before me occurs the autograph signature of RICHARD HOBY, with the motto : *Bonis et mors et vita dulcia sunt.*

The Consent of Time, Disciphering the errors of the Grecians in their Olympiads, . . . By Lodowick Lloid Esquire . . . Imprinted at London by George Bishop, and Ralph Newberie. Anno 1590. 4º. A, 8 leaves : A—3 A in eights, and a leaf of 3 B.

LOARTE, JASPER.

The Exercise of a Christian Life. Written in Italian by the Reuerend Father Laspar Loarte . . . Newly perused and corrected by the Translatour. With certaine very denout exercises . . . With Priuilege. 1584. 8º. Title and follow-ing leaf : A—Oo in eights : Pp—Qq in fours.

LOCKE, JOHN.

The Common-place Book to the Holy Bible : . . . London, Printed by Edw. Jones, for Awnsham and John Churchill, . . . 1697. 4º, A—Ss in fours, and a, 4 leaves.

LONDON.

An admonition to be redde in the churches of the citie and subburbes of London, by the pastours and ministers of the same. Imprinted at London by Wyllyam Seres dwellynge at the West ende of Paules church at the Sygne of the Hedgehogge. [1562.] A broadside.

Sothebys, June 29, 1885, No. 710.

A Collection of Certain Letters and Conferences lately passed betwixt certaine Preachers and two Prisoners in the Fleet. 1590. 4º, A—K 2 in fours.

The Valiant and most laudable fight performed in the Straights, by the Centurion of London, against fine Spanish Gallies. Who is safely returned this present Moneth of May. Anno. D. 1591. [London, 1591.] 4º, 4 leaves, the last blank. Black letter. With a large cut on title.

Sothebys, March 30, 1882, No. 217, the imprint cut off.

His Maiesties Commission giuing power to enquire of the Decayes of the Cathedral Church of St. Pavl in London, and for the repairing of the same. London Printed by Robert Barker, . . . and by the Assignes of John Bill. Anno Dom. 1631. 4º, A—G in fours, G 4 with the colophon, and A 1 blank.

His Majesties Commission concerning the Reparation of the Cathedral Church of St. Paul in London. London : Printed by John Bill and Christopher Barker . . . 1663. Folio, A—I, 2 leaves each, besides a frontispiece of the royal arms.

His Majesties Commission for the Rebuilding of the Cathedral Church of S. Paul in London. London, . . . 1674. Folio, A—K, 2 leaves each.

His Majesties Commission . . . London, Printed . . . 1685. Folio, A—G, 2 leaves each, G 2 blank.

Their Majesties Commission for the Rebuilding of the Cathedral Church of S. Paul in London. London : Printed by Benj. Motte. MDCXCII. Folio, A—C, 2 leaves each, and D, 3 leaves.

A Warrant sent from the Lord Maior and Aldermen, to all the trained Bands in

London, and the Liberties thereof. Also A true Platforme of Captaine Gifford, shewing how to plant Ordinance and batter by night. Likewise, The Quality of a Serjeant-Major, . . . London, Septemb. 23. Printed for Francis Coules. 1642. 4°, 4 leaves.

A Complaint to the House of Commons, And Resolution taken up by the free Protestant Subjects of the Cities of London and Westminster, and the Counties adjacent. Oxford, Printed by Leonard Lichfield, . . . 1642. 4°, A—C in fours.

A Trve Relation of two Merchants of London, who were taken Prisoners by the Cavaliers, and of the barbarous cruelty inflicted on them, . . . Also The maner of their examination before Prince Robert, together with the great familiarity of D' Soames, Vicar of Staynes, with the Cavaliers, and of their familiarity with his daughters . . . Printed for Humphrey Watson, 1642. 4°, 4 leaves.

To the Right Hon'ble the Commons of England Assembled in Parliament, The humble Petition of the auntient Hackney-Coachmen of London and Westminster. [About 1645.] A broadside.

A True Relation of the Cruell and un-parallel'd Oppression which hath been illegally imposed upon the Gentlemen, Prisoners in the Tower of London . . . . Printed in the Yeare, 1647. 4°, A—C in fours, C 4 blank.

Motives Grounded upon the Word of God, and upon Honour, Profit, and Pleasure for the present Founding an University in the Metropolis London : With Answers to such Objections as might be made by any (in their incogitancy) against the same. Humbly presented (in stead of Heathenish and Superstitious New-Yeares Gifts) to the Right Honourable the Lord Major . . . By a true Lover of his Nation, and specially of the said City. Printed at London. 1647. 4°, A—B in fours, A 1 blank.

London's Account : Or, A Calculation of the Arbytrary and Tyrannicall Exactions, Taxations, Impositions, Excises, Contributions, Subsidies, Twentieth Parts, and other Assessements, within the Lines of Communication, during the foure yeers of this Unnaturall Warre. . . . Imprinted in the Yeere, 1647. 4°, A—B in fours, A 4 blank.

A Speedy Cvre to open the eyes of the Biinde, and the Eares of the Deafe

Citizens of London. And may serve to recover the Sight and Hearing of all Englishmen, that are not past Cure, or wilfully Incurable. Printed in the Yeare 1648. 4", 4 leaves.

A Cittie-Dog in A Saints Doublet : A Missive to the Sage Common-Councell-men of London, . . . Printed in the Yeare, 1648. 4", 4 leaves.

Newes from Powles, Or the New Reformation of the Army : A true Relation of a Covlt that was foaled in the Cathedrall Church of St. Paul in London, and how it was Publiquely Baptized by Paul Hobsons souldiers, one of them pissing in his Helmet. and sprinkling it in the Name of the Father, Son, and holy Ghost ; and the Name (because a bald Coult) was called *Baal-Rex*. With a Catalogue of the Blasphemies, Murders, Cheats, Lies and Jugling of some of the Independent Party. Printed in the Yeer 1649. 4", 4 leaves.

A briefe and true Relation of the great disorders and riot attempted and committed upon the House and Goods of Thomas Hubbert Esquire, (one of His Maiesties Justices of the Peace for the County of Middlesex) in Moore-fields on the 21. day of March last, (being the Lords day.) . . . And vindicating the City Apprentices from the scandalous aspersion cast upon them, . . . London, Printed by I. C. and are to be sold by Henry Overton, . . . 4°, 4 leaves.

The honest Cryer of London. Printed for George Thompson, 1660. A broadside in three columns.

The 22. of April, 1660. A true Report of the President and Governours of the Corporation for the poor of the City of London, and Liberties thereof, . . . [London, 1660.] A broadside within an engraved border.

The Last Words and Actions of John James, At his Execution at Tyburne, the 27ᵗʰ of Novem. 1661. Wherein you have his confession and Prayer under the Gallowes, immediately before his Execution. London, Printed by R. Vaughan, in S. Martins le Grand. 1661. 4°, 4 leaves.

The Trve Speeches and Confession, of Ralph Taylor, Thomas Dey, Benj. Childerson, and Thomas Man, on Munday last near Kings-Gate in Holborn, the Place of Execution . . . London, Printed by R. Wood, 1662. 4°, 4 leaves.

The case was an assault on a person of honour in Lincoln's Inn Fields.

K

A True Relation of the manner of the dangerous Dispute, and bloody Conflict, betwixt the Spaniards and the French, at Tower-Wharfe and Tower Hill, on Munday September the 30ᵗʰ 1663. Upon the landing of the Lord Ambassador from the Crown of Sweden. . . . London, Printed in the Year, 1663. 4°, 4 leaves.

The Tryal of Captain Langston, Mʳ Comes, and Mʳ Wise, at the Sessions-House in the Old-Bayly, on Wednesday the 15. of this instant July, 1663. With the Evidence given in, to the Honourable Bench, touching Mʳ Davis, that was kil'd near Pankridge Church, and Sir William Coneyes Coach-man in Holborn ; . . . London, Printed for William Sanders, 1663. 4°, 4 leaves.

Londons-Nonsuch ; Or, The Glory of the Royal Exchange. Being A Short Prediction of the Great Trade that shall happen therein (according to the present auspicious Influence of the Superiour Planets, (viz.) The Intellectual Faculties, . . . Wherein is plainly fore-told the several Shop-keepers, both in the Walks above and below stairs, as may there very commodiously be provided for : Calculated for the Meridian of Gresham Colledge, . . . By a real well-wisher to the Trade, Peace, and prosperity of this Honourable City of London, . . . London, Printed by S. S. and are to be Sold at several Book-sellers Shops near Gresham Colledge ; And in Westminster-Hall, and in Little Brittain, 1668. Folio, A—E, 2 leaves each, A 1 with an engraved view of the Exchange. With a ground-plan. Dedicated to the Rebuilding Committee. In verse, except the explanation of the plan.

A Declaration of the Maids of the City of London, &c. [*Circâ* 1670.] A broadside in prose.

The Order of my Lord Major, The Aldermen, and the Sheriffs : For their Meetings and wearing of their Apparel throughout the whole Year. Printed by Andrew Clark, . . . 1673. 8°, black letter, A—C in eights, A 1 with a cut of the City Arms.

A True Relation of the Horrible Bloody Murther and Robbery, Committed in Holbourn, Next door to the Cross-keys-Tavern, in the House of Esq; Black, one of the six Clarks ; The Murther committed on the Body of one Widdow Brown, . . . Printed for Nathaniel Savedg. 1674. 4°, 4 leaves.

Strange and Terrible News from Shorditch, Of a Woman that hath sold her self to the Divel : Living in Badger-Alley ; And lying at this present in a sad and miserable Condition, . . . With Allowance. London, Printed for D. M. in the Year, 1674. 4°, 4 leaves.

News from the Exchange: Or, The Papist Acting the Quaker. Being a true Account of a Fanatical Pennance enjoyned by a Priest of the Church of Rome, and performed by one of her Obedient Sons at the Royal Exchange London, the 14ᵗʰ of this Instant January, 1674. Where pulling off his Shooes and Stockings in Change-Time, he march'd from thence with much Solemnity, Bare-Headed, Bare-Foot, and Bare-Legg'd through the City into the Strand. London, Printed for P. D. in Little-Brittain, 1674. 4°, 4 leaves.

News from Newgate : Or, An Exact and true Accompt of the most Remarkable, Tryals of Several Notorious Malefactors : At the Gaol delivery of Newgate, . . . the 29ᵗʰ and 30ᵗʰ, of April, and on Friday and Saturday the 1ˢᵗ and 2d. of May, 1674. . . . London, Printed for R. V. 1674. 4°, 4 leaves.

A Dialogue betwixt Jack and Will. Concerning the Lord Mayor's Going to Meeting-Houses with the Sword carried before him, &c. London, Printed in the Year 1675, 4°, A—B in fours.

News from the Sessions-house in the Old-Bayly. Being a full and true Relation of the Tryal and Condemnation of John Smith, John Darkin, and Geo. Marshal, for stealing the Plate out of the Parish church of St. Giles's in the Fields. . . . London : Printed for D. M. 1676. 4°, 4 leaves.

News from Newgate : Or, a true Relation of the manner of taking Seven persons, very notorious for Highway-men, in the Strand ; Upon Munday the 13 of this instant November, 1677. And of another apprehended on Friday the 16ᵗʰ: . . . London : Printed for D. M. 1677. 4°, 4 leaves.

A true Relation of all the Bloody Murders that have been committed in and about the Citie and Suburbs of London, since the 4ᵗʰ of this instant June 1677. . . . London : Printed for D. M. 1677. 4°, 4 leaves.

An Act for Preventing and Suppressing of Fires within the City of London, and

Liberties thereof. Printed by Andrew Clark, ... M.DC.LXXVII. 4°, 4 leaves.

Venn and His Mermydons : Or, The Linen-Draper Capotted : Being a Serious and Seasonable Advice to the Citizens of London, Occasioned by the Indirect Practices used in the late Election of Sheriffs. Written by a Citizen of London. London, Printed in the Year 1679. 4°, A—B in fours, B 4 blank.

Lex Londinensis : Or, The City Law. Shewing the Powers, Custom and Practice of all the several Courts Belonging to the Famous City of London : ... London, Printed by S. Roycroft for Henry Playford ... 1680. 8°. A, 4 leaves : B—G in eights.

A New Ballad, Of Londons Loyalty. To a Pleasant New Tune, Call'd *Burton-Hall*. London, Printed for Richard Sanders in the Year. 1681. A leaf of verses.

The Loyal Sherifs of London and Middlesex. Upon their Election. To the Tune of, *Now at last the Riddle is Expounded*. London, Printed for M. Thompson, 1682. A leaf of verses, with the music.

The German Princess Revived : Or The London Jilt : Being a True Account of the Life and Death of Jenney Voss ... [Col.] London, Printed by George Croom, ... 1684. 4°, 4 leaves.

The Dying Speech of Robert Frances of Grays-Inn, Esq ; July 24, 1685. Delivered by his own Hand to the Ordinary, at the Place of Execution, desiring the same might be published. [Col.] London, Printed by George Croom, ... 1685. Folio, 2 leaves.

A True Account of that Dreadful Fire, Which happened at the House of Mr Samuel Seaton, a Pewterer, at the corner of White-Cross-Street, ... London, Printed by William Downing, ... 1687. 4°, 4 leaves.

The Last Words of a Dying Penitent : Being An Exact Account of the Passages, Proceedings, and Reasons, on which was grounded the first Suspicion of his being concerned in the Bloody inhumane Murder of Dr Clinch, on the 4th of January 1691. between the hours of Nine and Eleven : For which he was Executed on the 15th of April 1692. ... Written with his own Hand after Condemnation, Hen. Harrison. London, Printed, and are to be sold by Randal Taylor ... 1692. 4°, A—D in fours, and the title.

A Just and True Account of the Malt Lottery Tickets, drawn in Guild-Hall, London. From the 10th of August, 1697, to the 27th inclusive, wherein the Prizes, with the Course & Manner of Payment of each several Thousand, are Numerically set down and Described. Printed by Order of the Managers. London : Printed and Sold by Freeman Collins ... 1697. Folio, A—F, 2 leaves each.

The Humble Petition of the Right Honourable the Lord Mayor ... on the Thirteenth of January, 1680. To the King's most Excellent Majesty, for the Sitting of this present Parliament Prorogu'd to the Twentieth Instant. ... London, Printed by Samuel Roycroft, ... 1680. Folio, A—D, 2 leaves each.

London Lampoon'd Formerly in the Jacobites' Songs ; And at present in a Scandalous Paper, call'd Heraclitus Ridens. With Reflections on Both. Dedicated to the Citizens of London. London, Printed in the Year 1703. 4°, A—D in fours.

Hell upon Earth : Or The most Pleasant and Delectable History of Whittington's Colledge, Otherwise (vulgarly) called Newgate : Giving an Account of the Humours of those Collegians who are strictly examin'd at the Old-Baily, and take their highest Degrees near Hyde-Park Corner. ... London, Printed in the Year, 1703. Folio, 8 leaves, or A—D, 2 leaves each. Dedicated to Richard P——ce, alias, Catch, Esquire by *Tuus Inimicus*.

LOPERUS, CHRISTOPHORUS, *of Paswalk*.

Laniena Paswakensis : That is, A Tragicall Relation of the Plundring, Butchering, Ravishing of the Women, and Fyreing of the Towne of Paswalke in Pomerland, situated vpon the riuer called the Vaker, written by one which escaped out of the Towne to his Friend in Penkum, living not farre from that place, dated the 12. of September 1630. ... First Translated out of high Dutch into Nether dutch .... and now Translated into English. ... Imprinted, Anno 1631. 4°, A—B in fours.

LOPE DE MENDOÇA, IAGO, *Marquis of Santillana.*

The Prouerbes of the noble and woorthy souldier Sir Iames Lopez de Mendoza Marques of Santillana, with the Paraphrase of D. Peter Diaz of Toledo : Wherin is contained whatsoeuer is necessarie to the leading of an honest and vertuous life. Translated out of Spanishe by Barnabe Googe. Imprinted at London by Richarde Watkyns. 1579. 8°. *, 8 leaves, and A—P 4 in eights. Dedicated by Googe to Sir W. Cecil. *B. M.*

LOREDANO, GIO. FRANCESCO.
The Novells of Gio. Francesco Loredano, A Nobleman of Venice. Translated for diversion into English. London, Printed for Thomas Fox at the Star, and Henry Lord at the Duke of Monmouth in Westminster-Hall. 1682. 12°, A—G 5 in twelves.

> On the title of this copy (from Harrison Ainsworth's sale) occurs: " E Libris I. Newton."

LORRAINE.
On the Ever to be Lamented Death of the Most Magnanimous and Illustrious Prince, Charles Leopold Duke of Lorraine, General of the Imperial Army; who died suddenly, April the Eighth 1690. London, Printed for Richard Baldwin . . . 1690. A broadside.

LOSA, FRANCISCO.
The Holy Life of Gregory Lopez. A Spanish Hermite in the West-Indies. Done out of Spanish. The Second Edition. . . . Printed in the Year, 1675. 8°. A, 8: (a)—(c 4) in eights: B—Q 4 in eights.

LOUIS OF BOURBON.
The Life of Lewis of Bourbon, Late Prince of Conde. Digested into Annals. With many Curious Remarks on the Transactions of Europe for these last Sixty Years. Done out of French. London: Printed for Tim. Goodwin. . . . MDCXCIII. 8°, A—T 4 in eights; the second Tome, B—P 7 in eights. With a portrait of Condé, and a dedication by N. Tate, the translator, to William, Earl of Devonshire.

LOVE.
The Character of Love, Guided by Inclination. Instanced in Two true Histories. Translated out of French. London: Printed for R. Bentley, . . 1686. 12°, A—F 6 in twelves.

LOVEDAY, ROBERT.
Loveday's Letters Domestick and Foreign . . . London : Printed by J. G. for Nath. Brook, . . . 1662. 8°, A—T in eights. With the portrait by Faithorne.

LOVER.
The Holy Practises of a Devine Lover: Or The Sainctly Idiots Deuotions. . . .

Printed at Paris by Lewis De La Fosse at the signe of the lookinge Glasse in the Caremes Strecte. 1657. With Approbation. 12°, A ij—N in twelves: O, 9 leaves, besides the frontispiece, title, and two leaves of dedication to Madame Catherine Gascoigne, Abbess of the English Monastery at Cambray.

LOWNDES, WILLIAM.
A Report Containing an Essay For the Amendment of the Silver Coins. London, Printed by Charles Bill, and the Executrix of Thomas Newcomb . . . 1695. 8°, A—K in eights.

LUCANUS, M. A.
Lucans Pharsalia : Or The Civill Warres of Rome, betweene Pompey the great, and Ivlivs Cæsar. The three first Bookes. Translated into English by T[homas] M[ay.] London. Printed by I. N. & A. M. and are to be sold by Math: Law at the signe of the Fox nere Saint Austens gate. 1626. 8°, A—E in eights. *B. M.*

> There is no preliminary matter.

LUCIAN.
The Religious Impostor: Or The Life of Alexander. A Sham-Prophet, Doctor and Fortune-Teller. Out of Lucian. Dedicated to Doctor Salmon, and the rest of the new Religious Fraternity of Free-Thinkers near Leather-Sellers-Hall. By Sebastian Smith, Esq; Amsterdam, Printed for the Company of the New Stamp, in the First Year of Grace, and Free-Thinking, and Sold next door to the Devil. 4°, A—D in fours. With a copy of verses at the end " To the Unknown Translator, by a Young Married Woman."

LUCRETIUS.
Lucretius: A Poem against the Fear of Death. With an Ode in Memory of the Accomplish'd Young Lady M" Ann Killigrew, Excellent in the Two Sister Arts of Poetry and Painting. London: Printed and Sold by H. Hills . . . . 1709. Price One Penny. 8°, 8 leaves.

LUDOLPHUS, JOB.
A New History of Ethiopia. Being a Full and Accurate Description of the Kingdom of Abessinia, Vulgarly, though Erroneously called the Empire of Prester John. In Four Books . . . Illustrated with Copper Plates . . . Made English by J. P. Gent. London, Printed for Samuel Smith Bookseller, . . . 1682. Folio, A— 3 H in fours, besides title, preface, and Table. With plates at pp. 7 (an

Æthiopic Alphabet), 38, 48, 52, 58 (2), 60, 192, 296, and 368.

LUPSET, THOMAS.

A Compendiovs and a very Frvtefvl Treatyse teachinge the waye of Dyeinge well, writen to a frende, by the flowre of lerned men of his tyme, Thomas Lupsete Londoner, late deceased on whose sowle Jesu haue mercy. [Col.] Londini in ȩdibus Thomæ Bertheleti . . . Anno M.D.XLI. 8°, A—D in eights : E, 9.

An Exhortation to Yonge men, . . . [Col.] Londini in ædibus Thomæ Bertheleti typis impress. . . . Anno M.D.XLIIII. 8°, A—D 4 in eights.

LUPTON, D.

London and the Covntrey Carbonadoed and Quartred into seuerall Characters. By D. Lupton. Hor. de Art. Poet. *Breuis esse Laboro.* London, Printed by Nicholas Okes, 1632. 8°, A—K in eights, A 1 blank. Dedicated to George, Lord Goring of Hurster-Point, Master of Horse to the Queen. Wholly in prose. *B. M.*

A Warre-like Treatise of the Pike. Or, Some Experimentall Resolves for lessening the number, and disabling the use of the Pike in Warre. With the praise of the Musquet and Halfe-Pike. . . . Penn'd for the generall good of our Nation, by a well wisher to the complete Musquetier. London : Printed by Richard Hodgkinsonne in Little-Britaine. 1642. 12°. A, 6 leaves, A 1–2 blank : B—H 6 in twelves. Dedicated to Robert, Earl of Essex and Ewe by D. Lupton. *B. M.*

The Quacking Mountebanck Or The Iesuite turn'd Quaker. In a witty and full Discovery of their Production and Rise, their Language, Doctrine, Discipline, Policy, Presumption, Ignorance, Prophanes, . . . With their Behaviours, Gestures, Aimes and Ends. . . . By one who was an Eye and Ear Witnesse of their Words and Gestures. . . . London. Printed for E. B. . . . 1655. [May 24.] 4°, A—C 2 in fours. *B. M.*

Flanders. Or, An Exact and Compendious Description of that fair, great, and far Countrey of Flanders. Wherein the Inhabitants, Bounds, Length, Breadth, Division, Riches, Rivers, Forests, . . . with the chief Estates are observed. As also a Distinct Relation of some Battels fought, and Towns won, unto the now victorious Proceedings of the English and French Armies therein, . . . London, Printed by Thomas Ratcliffe on Saint Bennets Hill neare the Church. 1658.

4°, A—B in fours. Dedicated to Richard Cromwell, Chancellor of the University of Oxford, and Gilbert, Lord Pickering, Lord Chamberlain to the Protector. *B. M.*

LUPTON, THOMAS.

A Thousand Notable Things. . . . Whereunto is now added one hundred Excellent conceits never before Printed, very witty, useful, and delightfull. . . . London, Printed for M. Wright . . . 1660. 8°, A—Cc in eights.

LYLY, JOHN.

¶ Euphves. The Anatomy of Wit. Very pleasant for all Gentlemen to reade, and most necessary to remember. Wherin are conteined the delights that Wit followeth in his youth, by the pleasautnesse of loue, and the happinesse he reapeth in age, by the perfectnesse of Wisedome. ¶ By Iohn Lylly Master of Art. Corrected and augmented ¶ Imprinted at London for Gabriell Cawood, dwelling in Paules Chnrch yard. [Col.] ¶ Imprinted at London, by Thomas East, for Gabriel Cawood, dwelling in Paules Church-yard. 1579. 4°, black letter. A to Z in fours : Aa in two : ¶ in two. *Bodleian.*

> The Colophon is on the *verso* of Aa ij, and is followed by the address "To my very good friends the Gentlemen Scholers of Oxford."

Evphves The Anatomie of Wit. Very pleasant for all Gentlemen to read, . . . Corrected and augmented. London, Printed by I. H. and are to be sold by Iames Boler. 1631. 4°, black letter, A—Aa in eights, *Euphues and his England* commencing with a new title on L 1.

> The title-page to the Second Part is dated 1630.

[Second Edition, revised.] ¶ Euphues and his England. Containing his voyage and aduentures, myxed with sundry pretie discourses of honest Loue, the discription of the countrey, the Court, and the manners of that Isle. Delightful to be read, and nothing hurtfull to be regarded : wher-in there is small offence by lightnesse giuen to the wise, and lesse occasion of loose-nes proffered to the wanton. ¶ By Iohn Lyly, Maister of Arte. Commend it, or amend it. ⬥ Imprinted at London for Gabriell Cawood, dwelling in Paules Church-yard. 1580. [Colophon :] ¶ Imprinted at London, by Thomas East, for Gabriell Cawood dwelling in Paules Churchyard. [1580.] A in four : ¶ in four : B to Z in fours : Aa to

Ll in fours. *Bodleian* (title slightly imperfect).

LYNDE, SIR HUMPHREY.

Via tuta : The Safe Way. Leading all Christians, by the testimonies, and confessions of our best learned Aduersaries, to the true, ancient, and Catholique faith, now professed in the Church of England. By Hvmfrey Lynde Knight. . . . London, Printed by G. M. for Robert Milbourne, . . . 1628. 12°, A—P 6 in twelves. Dedicated to the Religious and well-affected Gentry of this Kingdom.

Via Tvta : The Safe Way. . . . The fourth Edition reuised by the Author. London, Printed by Aug. M. for Robert Milbovrne, . . . 1630. 12°, A—Q in twelves, Q 12 with the *Errata.*

Via Tvta . . . The fifth Edition reuised and corrected by the Author. London, Printed by A. Math. for Rob. Milbovrne, . . . 1632. 12°, A—Q in twelves, Q 12 blank.

Via Devia : The By-Way : Misleading the weake and vnstable into dangerous paths of Error, by colourable shewes of Apocryphall Scriptures. . . . Discouered by Hvmfrey Lynde, Knight. . . . London, Printed by Aug. M. for Robert Milbovrne . . . 1630. 12°, A—Gg 6 in twelves, and a—b in twelves between A—B. Dedicated to the Ingenuous and moderate Romanish of the Kingdom.

LYNDESAY, DAVID, *Bishop of Brechin.* A Trve Narration of all the Passages of the Proceedings in the generall Assembly of the Church of Scotland, Holden at Perth the 25. of August, Anno Dom. 1618. Wherein is set downe the Copy of his Maiesties Letters to the said Assembly : Together with a iust defence of the Articles therein concluded, against a seditious Pamphlet. . . . London Printed by William Stansby for Ralph Rounthwait . . . 1621 4°, A—C in fours : D—L in eights : Mm in fours : Aa, 8 leaves : Bb —Ff in fours : Gg—Ii in eights : Kk, 4 leaves : 3 A—3 H in eights, 3 H 8 blank.

LYSTER, THOMAS.

The Blessings of Eighty-Eight : Or, A Short Narrative of the Auspicious Protection of our Reform'd Protestant Church, under the Number of Eight. . . . With Divine Poems and Meditations. . . . London, Printed by J. Matthews, for George Huddleston, . . . 1698. 8°, A—M in eights. A 1 and M 8 blank. With a portrait of the author by R. White.

LYTTELTON, SIR THOMAS, *K.B., Judge of the Palace to Henry V., afterward Chief Justice of the Common Pleas, ob.* 1481.

[Tenores Novelli.] Incipit Tabula h³ libri. [This is a leaf preceding a i with the commencement of the text. The colophon at the end is :] Expliciŭt Tenores nouelli Impſsi p nos Johes lettou & Willș de machlinia ī Citate Londoniarș iuxta ecclaȝ oīm ſcōrȝ. Folio. a, 8 leaves, including that of Table : b—h in eights : i, 4.

Putticks, April 7, 1884, No. 692, the whole inlaid and damaged.

M.

M. A.

Queen Elizabeths Closset of Physical Secrets, With certain approved Medicines taken out of a Manuscript found at the dessolution of our English Abbies : and supplied with the *Child-Bearers Cabinet,* and *Preservative against the Plague and Small Pox.* Collected by the Elaborate, paines of four famous Physitians, and presented to Queen Elizabeths own hands. London, Printed for Will. Sheares Junior . . . 1656. 4°, A—F in fours : the *Treatise against the Plague, &c.* (added from another work), 3 D—3 V in fours.

The *Choise and Select Medicines,* which commence on F, are printed on a different paper, and seem to have been subsequently added.

M. E.

The Present Danger of Tangier : Or, An Account of its being attempted by a great Army of the Moors by Land, and under some Apprehension of the French at Sea. In a Letter from Cadiz to a Friend in England [29 July, 1679.] Folio, 2 leaves.

M. G.

A Relation of Three Embassies from his Sacred Majesty Charles II to the Great Duke of Muscovie. The King of Sweden, and the King of Denmark. Performed by the Right Hoᵇˡᵉ the Earle of Carlisle in the Years 1663 & 1664. Written by an Attendant on the Embassies, and published with his Lᵈˢ Approbation. London, Printed for John Starkey . . . 1669. 8°, A—Gg in eights. Dedicated by the writer to Lord Carlisle.

M. J.
An Argument Or, Debate in Law: of the Great Qvestion Concerning the Militia ; And it is now settled by Ordinance of both the Houses of Parliament . . . By J. M. C. L. London : Printed by Tho. Paine, and M. Simmons, for Tho. Vnderhill, . . . 1642. 4°, A, 2 : B—G 2 in fours.

I. T.
Father Hubbards Tales : Or The Ant and the Nightingale. London Printed by T. C. for William Cotton, and are to be solde at his Shop neare adioyning to Ludgate. 1604. 4°. A—F in fours. In prose and verse. With a facetious dedication to Sir Christopher Clutch-fist by Oliver Hubburd, and a Preface to the Reader by T. M.

Sothebys, April 1, 1882, No. 696.

I. T.
Certaine Observations upon Some Texts of Scripture, Gathered together for the Setting forth the Kings Authority, and the Peoples Dvty. . . . Printed in the year, 1648. 4°, A, 2 : B—D in fours.

MACKENZIE, SIR GEORGE, *of Rosehaugh.*
Reason. An Essay. By Sir George Mackenzie. London, Printed for Jacob Tonson . . . 1690. 12°, A—G 7 in twelves, besides 4 leaves with dedication to Robert Boyle.

The Moral History of Frugality. With its opposite Vices, Covetousness, Niggardliness, and Prodigality, Luxury. Written by the Honourable Sir George Mackenzie, Late Lord Advocate of Scotland. London : Printed for J. Hindmarsh, . . . 1691. 8°, Title, preceded by *Imprimatur*, and Dedication to the University of Oxford, 4 leaves : B—G in eights.

The dedication appears to have been handed to the Publisher by Arch. Cockburn, whose letter to the publisher, describing this as a posthumous book, follows that.

MAGIC.
The Magick of Kurani King of Persia, And of Hippocration ; Comprising the Magical and Medicinal Vertues of Stones, Herbs, Fishes, Beasts, and Birds . . . Now Published and Translated into English from a Copy found in a private Hand. Printed in the Year MDCLXXXV. 8°, A—M in eights, and a leaf of N.

MAGNA CHARTA.
The great Charter called ī latyn Magna Carta with diuers olde statutes. . . . . Newly correctyd. Cvm Privilegio . . . [Col.] Thus endeth the boke called Magna Carta, trãslated out of latyn and frenshe into Englysh by George ferrerɏ. And Imprynted at London in Fletestrete by Elisabeth Wydow of Robert Redmã dwellyng at the sygne of the George next to saynte Dunstones churche . . . 8°, black letter. ✠, 4 leaves: A—Dd in eights, Dd 8 blank.

The great Charter called in latyn Magna Carta, with diuers olde statutes whose titles appere in the next leafe Newly corrected. Cum priuilegio ad imprimendum solum. [Col.] Thus endeth the boke called Magna Carta / translated out of Latyn and Frenshe into Englysshe By George Ferrerɏ. Imprynted at London in Paules church yerde at the signe of the Maydens heed by Thomas Petyt. M.D.XL.ij. Cum priuilegio . . . 8°, black letter. ✠, 4 leaves : A—Dd 7 in eights.

MAID.
The Unfortunate Maids Complaint, being Fifteen years of age, and never a Suitor yet. [About 1660.] A small broadside, containing 16. 6-line stanzas, besides the burden, in two columns.

There is no imprint.

MAIDWELL, LAURENCE.
The Loving Enemies : A Comedy, As it was Acted at His Highness the Duke of York's Theatre. [Quot. from Claudian.] London, Printed for John Guy at the Sign of the Flying Horse between St. Dunstan's Church and Chancery Lane. 1680. 4°, A—K in fours, and a leaf of L. Dedicated to the much honoured Charles Fox, Esquire.

MAINWARING, E., *M.D.*
Vita Sana & Longa, The Preservation of Life. Proposed and proved. In the due observance of Remarkable Precautions. And daily practicable Rules . . . London, Printed by J. D. Sold by the Booksellers, 1670. 8°. A, 4 leaves : B—Hh in eights, Hh 5-8 with advertisements or blank.

The Preface is dated from the author's house in Clerkenwell Close.

MAINWARING, ROGER, *D.D.*
Religion and Alegiance : In Two Sermons Preached before the Kings Maiestie: The one on the fourth of Iuly, Anno 1627. At Oatlands. The other on the 29. of Iuly the same yeere, At Alderton. By

Roger Maynwaring, Doctor in Diuinitie, one of his Majesties Chaplaines in Ordinarie: and then, in his Month of Attendance. By His Maiesties Speciall Command. London, Printed by I. H. for Richard Badger. 1627. 4°, B—E in fours, the title, and a leaf of F : the second Sermon, B—H in fours.

MAINWARING, SIR THOMAS, *of Peover. .*
An Admonition to the Reader of Sir Peter Leicester's Books. Written by Sir T. M. Printed in the Year 1676. 8°, A—B 4 in eights.

A Reply to Sir Peter Leicester's Answer to Sir Thomas Mainwaring's Admonition to the Reader of Sr Peter Leicesters Books. Written by the sayd Sir Thomas Mainwaring. But never yet Printed. 8°, pp. 107.

> Crossley, part 2, in No. 1644.

MAJOR, ELIZABETH.
Honey on the Rod: Or a comfortable Contemplation for one in Affliction ; With sundry Poems on several Subjects. By the unworthiest of the servants of the Lord Jesus Christ, Elizabeth Major. . . . London, Printed by Tho. Maxey, . . . 1656. 8°, A—I in eights, title on A 2: a new title with the Poems, *Sin and Mercy briefly discovered*, . . . [b], 8 leaves : K (no K 1) in twelves, K 12 blank.

MALBY, NICHOLAS.
Remedies for diseases in Horses. Approued and allowed by diuers very auncient learned Mareschalles. Imprinted at London in Paules Churchyarde, at the signe of the Lucrece, by Tho. Purfoote. 1576. 4°, black letter, A—C 2 in fours, besides the title and a poetical dedication to Lord Robert Dudley by the Printer in 8 7-line stanzas.

MALEBRANCHE, FATHER.
Father Malebranche's Treatise Concerning The Search after Truth. The Whole Work Compleat. To which is added The Author's Treatise of Nature, and Grace. Being A Consequence of the Principles contain'd in the *Search*. Together with His Answer to the Animadversions. . . . All Translated by T. Taylor, M.A. of Magd. Coll. in Oxford. Oxford, Printed by L. Lichfield, for Thomas Bennet, . . . London. M.DC.XCIV. Folio. Title and dedication to Sir William Glynn, Bart., 2 leaves : a—b, 2 leaves each : ¶, 2 leaves : A—3 E in twos, and A—L in twos.

MAN.
The Pilgrimage of Man, Wandering in a wildernes of Woe. Wherein is shewed the Calamities of the new World, and how all the principall Estates thereof are crossed with Miserie.

> *A gorgious Iemme for Gentilitie,*
> *That line in golden Felicitie.*

London, Printed for W. Barlie, and are to be sold at his Shoppe in Gracious streete. 1606. 4°, A—D in fours. *B. M.*

The Whole Dvty of Man. Necessary for all Families. With Private Devotions for seuerall Occasions. London. Printed for Timothy Garthwait. 8°. a, 8 leaves: B—Bb in eights, besides leaf with Arms, the engraved title, and A, 4 leaves, with H. Hammond's Epistle to the Publisher, dated March 7, 1657-8.

> The proof-sheets were read by Hammond, who does not, however, refer to the author.

MAN, STEPHEN, *one of the Yeomen of His Majesty's Chamber.*
A Relation of certaine things in Spaine, worthy of Obseruation : Imprinted for Iohn Browne, and are to be sold in S. Dunstanes Church-yard in Fleet-streete, 1619. 8°. *B. M.*

> Dedicated to the Marquis of Buckingham. This copy ends on the first leaf of C imperfectly, and contains 17 leaves.

MANDEVILLE, SIR JOHN.
Ce liure est appelle mandeuille et fust fait & compose par messiere Jehan de mandeuille cheualier natif dãgleterre . . . [Col.] Cy finist ce tresplaisant liure. . . . Folio, black letter, with cuts. a—b, 8 each; c—k in sixes : l, 7. Long lines. a i has only a page-woodcut.

> Sothebys, December 21, 1882, No. 2124. Attributed to the Lyons press.

MANLEY, THOMAS, *Gentleman.*
Usury at Six per Cent. examined, and Found unjustly charged by Sir Tho. Culpepper and I. C. with many Crimes and Oppressions, whereof 'tis altogether innocent. Wherein is shewed, The necessity of retrenching our Luxury, . . . Also The reducing the Wages of Servants, . . . London, Printed by Thomas Ratcliffe, and Thomas Daniel, . . . MDCLXIX. 4°, A—L in fours, K 3 blank.

MANLOVE, EDWARD, *Esquire.*
The Liberties and Cystomes of the Lead-Mines within the Wapentake of Wirksworth in the County of Derby, Part thereof appearing by extracts from the Bundels of the Exchequer. . . . Composed in Meeter by Edward Manlove Esq; heretofore Steward of the Barghmoot Court for the Lead-mines . . . London,

Printed, Anno Dom. 1653. 4°, A—B 2 in fours.

MANORS.
Reasons Humbly submitted to the Consideration of Both Houses of Parliament, for Passing an Act for Preservation of Manors, and of Copyhold-Estates and Tenures. *Sic utere tuo ut alieno non lædas.* Anno Domini 1677. 8°, 8 leaves.

MANUALE.
Ad laudem dei et honore tuã non immerito flos virgo maria ecce manuale quoddam secundu; vsũ matris eccl'ie Eboracēsis. nouis tandē ex repetita pelectione bonaque maturitate climatũ est. A mendis penitus (mea sentēcia) alienũ vigiliis lugubrationibus; & industria bona ita nũc redactũ Ut ĩ cymbalis inbatiõis . . . [Col.] Manuale insignis ecclē Eboracen. Impressum Per Wynandũ de Worde . . . Anno dñi millessimo quigētessimo nono quarto ydus Februarij. Sane hoc volumen digessit arte magister, Wynandus de Worde incola londonij. 4°, A—N 7 in eights. With the music. *Bodleian.*

Manuale ad vsum insignis ecclesie Sarum. Jam denuo Antwerpie impressum : et a multis erratis et mediis quibus scabebat repurgatum ac emunctissime vindicatum. Anno dñi. M. CCCC. XLij. [Col.] Explicit Manuale . . . Excusum Antwerpie in officina Vidue Christophori Ruremundensis. Anno domini. M. CCCCC. XL. JJJ. Mense Janua. 4°, finely printed in red and black, A—Z in eights, and A—B in eights. With the musical notation.

MANUEL, DOM FRANCISCO.
The Government of a Wife ; Or Wholsom and Pleasant Advice for Married Men : In a Letter to a Friend. Written in Portuguese, By Don Francisco Manuel. With some Additions of the Translator, distinguished from the Translation. There is also Added, A Letter upon the same Subject, written in Spanish by Don Antonio de Guevara, . . . Translated into English, By Capt. John Stevens. London, Printed for Jacob Tonson . . . 1697. 8°. A, 8 leaves : a, 4 : B—Q in eights.

MANUTIUS, ALDUS.
Phrases Lingvæ Latinæ ab Aldo Manvtio P. F. Conscriptæ, Nvnc Primvm in ordinem Abecedarium adductæ, & in Anglicum sermonem conuersæ . . . Londini, Ex officina Thomæ Vautrollerij. M.D. LXXIX. Cvm Privilegio. 8°, A—T in eights.
   The dedication of the printer to Robert Cecil is dated the Calends of July, 1573.

MANWOOD, PETER.
A Treatise of the Laws of the Forest, . . . The Third Edition Corrected, and much Inlarged. London, Printed for the Company of Stationers, 1665. 4°, a—b in eights : A—Ll in eights : Mm, 4.

MAPLETOFT, J.
Select Proverbs, Italian, Spanish, French, English, Scotish. British, &c. Chiefly moral. The Foreign Languages done into English. . . . London, Printed by J. H. for Philip Monckton . . . M DCC VII. 8°, A—I in eights, A 1 and I 8 blank.

MARBECKE, OR MERBECKE, JOHN.
The booke of Common praier noted. 1550. [Col.] Imprinted by Richard Grafton Printer to the Kinges Maiestie. 1550. Cum priuilegio . . . 4°, printed in black and red, with the music. A, 2 leaves : B—S 2 in fours.

MARGUERITE D'ANGOULEME, *Queen of Navarre.*
A Godly Meditation of the Soule, concernyng a Loue towards Christ our Lord, aptly translated out of French into English, by the right, high, and most vertuous Princesse Elizabeth, by the grace of God, of England, . . . Queene, &c. Wherevnto is added godly Meditations, set forth after the Alphabet of the Queenes Maiesties name. . . . Imprinted at London, by Henrie Denham. An. 1568. 8°, A—G 4 in eights. Dedicated to the Queen by James Canceller.

The Grand Cabinet-Counsels Unlocked : Or The most faithful transaction of the Court-affairs, and Growth and Continuation of the Civil Wars in France . . . Written in the French Tongue by Margaret de Valois, . . . And Faithfully translated into English, by Robert Codrington, Master of Arts. London, Printed by R. H. 1658. 8°. A, 4 leaves : B—Q 3 in eights.

MARIANUS.
Marianvs, Or, Loves Heroick Champion. Describing His Honorable Travailes and haughty attempts in Armes, with his successe in Love. Intermixed with many pleasant Discourses. wherein the Graver sort may take delight, and the Youthfull bee encouraged by Honourable and Worthy adventures to gaine Fame. London. Printed by B. Alsop and T. Fawcet, and are to be sold by Iames Becket at his shop at the Inner Temple-Gate. 1641. 12°. A, 6 leaves : B—R in twelves, besides a frontispiece in compartments by W. Marshall.

Dedicated by the publisher to the Inns of Court.

MARKHAM, GERVASE.

Cavalarice, Or The English Horseman : Contayning all the Arte of Horse-manship, as much as is necessary for any man to vnderstand, whether he be Horse-breeder, horse-ryder, horse-hunter, ... Together, with . . . an explanatiō of the excellency of a horses vnderstāding, or how to teach them to doe trickes like Bankes his Curtall : . . . . [On the title to Book 2 occurs:] London Printed for Edward White, and are to be solde at his shop neare the little north doore of Saint Paules Church . . . 1607. 4°. First title without imprint, dedication to Prince Henry, a second to the Nobility, &c., and Table, 8 leaves : B—4 H in fours : A ¶—T ¶ in fours : K—L in fours : A (with the 8th book)—E in fours. With separate titles and dedications to each book and woodcuts.

Cavalarice, Or The English Horseman : Contayning all the Art of Horse-manship, as much as is necessary for any man to vnderstand, . . . Newly imprinted, corrected & augmented, with many worthy secrets not before knowne : By Geruase Markham. [No imprint, but on the separate title of Book 2 occurs:] London, Printed by Edw : Allde for Edward White . . . 1616. 4°, A—3 B in eights. With cuts.

The titles to Books 2-8 are dated 1616 and 1617, and each part has a separate dedication and preface.

The English Arcadia, Alluding his beginning from Sir Philip Sydneys ending. By Iaruis Markham. London. Printed by Edward Allde, and are to bee solde by Henrie Rocket, at his shop vnder Saint Mildreds Church in the Poultrie 1607. 4°. Title and to the Reader, 2 leaves : B—T in fours, T 4 blank.

In the preface Markham refers to Sydney as "the most excellēt creature that first taught vs the sound of excellent writing." "Yet," adds he, "hath it likewise beene vsed by others in sundrie pamphlets."— Sothebys, March 27, 1884, No. 190.

The Country-mans Recreation, or the Art of Planting, Grafting, and Gardening, in three Bookes. . . . Whereunto is added, The Expert Gardener, containing divers necessary and rare Secrets belonging to the Art, . . . London. Printed by B. Alsop and T. Fawcet for Michael Young, . . . 1640. 4°, A—S in fours : *The Expert Gardener,* A—G in fours.

The latter portion purports to be taken from French and Dutch authors.

The Perfect Horse-man. Or, The Expe-rienced Secrets of Mr Markham's Fifty Years Practice. . . . Published by Lancelot Thetford . . . The last Edition Corrected. London, Printed by J. D. for Richard Chiswel, . . . 1680. 8°, A—M in eights. With a frontispiece containing in the lower centre a portrait of Markham.

The Art of Angling. Wherein are discovered many rare Secrets, very necessary to be knowne by all that delight in that Recreation. London, Printed in the Yeare 1653. 4°. Title, 1 leaf : A, 3 leaves (A 2 wrongly in fact marked A): B, 4 : D, 2 : no C. In prose.

This generally forms part of the *Countryman's Recreations,* 4°, 1654.

A Way to Get Wealth Containing Six Principall Vocations, ... The Twelfth time Corrected, and Augmented by the Author. London, Printed by John Streater, for George Sawbridge, . . . 1668. 4°. With separate titles, &c., to each part.

MARNETTE, MONSIEUR.

The Perfect Cook : Being the most exact Directions for the making all kinds of Pastes, with the perfect way teaching how to Raise, Season, and make all sorts of Pies, . . . As also The Perfect English Cook, . . . To which is added, The way of dressing all manner of Flesh, . . . London, Printed for Obadiah Blagrave, . . . 1686. 12°. A, 6 leaves : B—K in twelves, besides the title and frontispiece.

MARRIAGE.

Matrimonii Pensitatio : Or, No Joynture but the Hugg-Rural. London, Printed for the Author, and are to be sold by Norman Nelson, . . . M.DC.LXXIX. 4°, A—B in fours. In verse.

A Satyr against Marriage. *O Demens ! Ita servus homo est.* Juve. Sat. 6. London, Printed in the Year, 1700. Folio, A—D, 2 leaves each. In verse.

The Pleasures of a Single Life, Or, The Miseries of Matrimony. Occasionally writ upon the many Divorces lately Granted by Parliament. The Second Edition. London, Printed, . . . 1700. Folio, A—C, 2 leaves each. In verse.

The Pleasures of a Single Life, Or, The Miseries of Matrimony. Occasionally Writ upon the many Divorces lately Granted by Parliament. With the Choice, Or, The Pleasures of a Country-Life. Dedicated to the Beaus against the next Vacation. London : Printed and Sold by H. Hills . . . [1710.] 8°, 8 leaves. In verse.

A Short Survey of the Difficulties & Inconveniences that may attend a Married Life. With some Observations thereon By John Thomson's Man. . . . Printed [at Edinburgh] in the Year 1710. 8°, A—C 4 in eights.

MARSHALL, STEPHEN.
The Godly Man's Legacy to the Saints upon Earth, Exhibited in the Life of . . . M' Stephen Marshal, Sometime Minister of the Gospel at Finchingfield in Essex. Written by way of Letter to a Friend. *Si populus vult decipi*—— London, Printed in the Year, 1680. 4°, A—E 2 in fours.
A satirical publication.

MARSHALL, WILLIAM.
[The maner of subuention of poore people. This is the running title, and at the end occurs:] Printed at London by Thomas Godfray. Cū priuilegio Regali. 8°, black letter, A—F 3 in eights.
Puttick, July, 1883, wanting the title and first leaf of dedication by W. Marshall to the Queen (Ann Boleyn).

MARTIN, GREGORY, *Licentiate in Divinity.*
A Treatise of Schisme. Shewing that al Catholikes ought in any wise to abstaine altogether from heretical Conuenticles, to witt, their prayers, sermons, &c. deuided into foure Chapters . . . Dvaci. Apud Ioannem Foulerum. 1578. 8°, A—L 2 in eights, and the title-page.

MARTIN, M.
A Description of the Western Islands of Scotland. Containing A Full Account of their Situation, Extent, Soils, Product, Harbours, Bays, Tides, Anchoring Places, and Fisheries. . . . By M. Martin, Gent. London, Printed for Andrew Bell, . . . 1673. 8°. a, 8 leaves: A—Bb 4 in eights. With a map and a plan of a Heathen Temple. Dedicated to Prince George of Denmark, Lord High Admiral.

MARTIN, WILLIAM.
The Historie and Lives, of the Kings of England : From William the Conqueror, vnto the end of the Raigne of King Henry the Eighth. With other vsefull Obseruations. By William Martyn Esquire, Recorder of the Honourable Citie of Exeter. *Frustra fit per plura, qui fieri potest per posteriora.* London, Printed for Iames Boler. M.DC.XXVIII. Folio. a, 4: b, 6: A—3 B in fours. Dedicated to the Gentry of England. With complimentary verses by the author's three sons and his son-in-law, Peter Bevis.

MARTIN MARPRELATE.
A Sacred Decretall, Or Hue and Cry, From his superlative Holinesse, Sir Symon Synod, for the Apprehension of Reverend Young Martin Mar-Priest. Wherein are displaid many witty Synodian Conceits, both pleasant and Commodious. Europe, Printed by Martin Claw-Clergy, Printer to the Reverend Assembly of Divines . . . . 1645. 4°, B—D in fours, and the title, on which there is a large cut.

Martin's Eccho : Or A Remonstrance from His Holinesse reverend Young Martin Mar-Priest, responsorie to the late Sacred Synoddicall Decretall, . . . [About 1645.] 4°, A—C 2 in fours.

MARTINIUS, HENRICUS.
A Bloody Almanack and Prognostication for the year, 1662. Being the second after Besextile or Leap-year. Predicting several strange Revolutions and Interpositions of the Heavens : With the prodigious effects, Rapines, Murders, Plunderings and Blood-shed . . . Also Astrological Observations on the 12 Months, . . . By Henricus Martinius, Philomath. . . . London, Printed for Robert Mottibee. 1662. 4°, 4 leaves.

MARTINIUS, MARTIN.
Bellum Tartaricum, Or The Conquest of the Great and most renowned Empire of China, By the Invasion of the Tartars, who in these last seven years, have wholy subdued that vast Empire. Together with a Map of the Provinces, and chief Cities of the Countries, for the better understanding of the Story . . . . . faithfully Translated into English. London, Printed for John Crook, . . . 1654. 8°. A, 4 leaves, A 1 with a frontispiece of the Tartar emperor : B—Q in eights, besides the map.

MARVELL, ANDREW.
An Account of the Growth of Popery, And Arbitrary Government in England : more Particularly from the Long Prorogation of November, 1675. . . . Amsterdam, Printed in the Year 1677. 4°, A—U 2 in fours.

MARY, THE VIRGIN.
Hore beatissime virginis Marie ad legitimū Eboracensis ecclesie ritum diligētissime accuratissimecȝ impressa cū multis orationibȝ pulcherrimis et īdulgentiis iā vltimo de nouo adiectis. In conspectu altissimi immaculata permansi. Venūdātur Rothomagi . . . . [Col.] . . . ipensis & sumptibus Guillermi bernard et Jacobi

cousin ciuiũ Rothomagen. . . . Anno dñi M. CCCCC. XVII. die vero XXVI. mensis Januarii. Laus deo. 4°, A—B in eights: C, 6: A (repeated)—Y in eights. With Calendar and woodcuts.

Officium B. Mariæ Virg. Nuper reformatum . . . Londini Typis Henrici Hills. [1688.] 8°. Title, 1 leaf: * and ** in eights: c—pp 2 in eights.

MARY [TUDOR], *Queen of England.*
The History of the Life, Bloody Reign and Death of Queen Mary, Eldest Daughter to Hen. 8. . . . Faithfully Collected and seasonably published for a Caution against popery. Illustrated with Pictures of the most considerable passages. Engraven on Copper plates. London, Printed for D. Brown . . . and T. Benskin . . . 1682. 12°, A—I 6 in twelves, besides 4 leaves of engravings.

MARY [STUART], *Queen of Scots.*
Vera, e Compita Relazione del Svccesso della Morte della Christianissima Regina di Scotia con la dichiarazione del essequie fatte in Parigi dal Christianissimo Re suo Cognato e nome de' personaggi interuenntiui. Ad Instanzia di Francesco Dini da Colle. [1588.] 4°, 4 leaves. With a woodcut on title, representing the Queen praying.

Martyre de la Royne D'Escosse Douairiere de France. Contenant le vray discours des traisons à elle faictes à la suscitation d'Elizabet Angloise, par lequel les mensonges, calvmnies & faulses accusations dressees contre ceste tresvertueuse, trescatholique & tresillustre Princesse sont esclaircies & son innocence aueree . . . En Anvers, Chez Gaspar Fleysben. M.D.LXXXVIII. 8°. a, 4: A—Tt in eights, Tt 8 blank.

La Mort de la Royne D'Escosse, Douairiere de France . . . M.D.LXXXIX. 12°. A, 4: A—O 6 in eights, the last leaf with the colophon: Acheué d'imprimer ce dernier iour de Decembre, Mil cinq cens quatre vingtz & huict. With folded plates at pp. 12, 18, 28, and 112.

Histoire et Martyre de la Royne d'Escosse, Douairiere de France, proche heritiere de la Royne d'Angleterre. . . . A Paris, Chez Guillaume Bichon, . . . M.D.LXXXIX. 12°. ã, 4: A—Ll 4 in eights.

Marie Stvard Reyne D'Escosse. Nouuelle Historique. Premiere [Deuxieme et Troisieme] Partie. A Paris, Chez Claude Barbin, . . . M.DC.LXXIV. 12°. Part 1, A—E 5 in twelves: Part 2, A and E in

eights, E 8 blank, B—D in twelves: Part 3, A, 4 leaves: B—E in twelves.

Marie Stvart, Reyne d'Escosse. Nouuelle Historique. Premiere [Deuxieme et Troisieme] Partie. A Paris, . . . M.DC.LXXV. . . . 12°. 3 vols.

A Brief History of the Life of Mary Queen of Scots, and The Occasions that brought Her, and Thomas Duke of Norfolk, to their Tragical Ends. . . . From the Papers of a Secretary of Sir Francis Walsingham. Now Published by a Person of Quality. London: Printed for Tho. Cockerill, . . . 1681. Folio, A—S, 2 leaves each.

MARY OF MODENA, *Consort of James II.*
Remarks upon the Dream of the late Abdicated Queen of England, And upon that of Madam the Dutchess of La Valiere, Late Mistress to the French King, and now Nun of the Order of Bare-Footed-Carmelites at Paris. By the Author of the Harmony of Prophesies, &c. Being the Paper the Publisher whereof was Condemned last Month to be Broken alive on the Wheel, by the Parliament of Roan. Done from the French Copy Printed at Amsterdam. London: Printed for Tho. Salusbury, . . . 1690. 4°, A—D in fours, including a half-title.

MARYLAND.
The Acts of Dr. Bray's Visitation, Held at Annapolis in Mary-Land, May 23, 24, 25. Anno 1700. London, Printed by William Downing . . . 1700. Folio, A—C, 2 leaves each: D, 3.

MASCAL, WILLIAM, *late of Clare Hall, Cambridge.*
A New and True Mercurius: Or, Mercvrivs Metricvs. A true Relation in Meeter (on the behalf of Scepter and Miter) comprising sundry of the most sad and bad Transactions, Occurrences and Passages in England, Scotland and Ireland, for the space of twelve years last past . . . For the true information and reformation of the People. . . . To which is added the Authors Twelve years extream Melancholy, . . . London, Printed for the Author. 1661. 4°, A—D in fours. In verse.

MASON, HENRY.
The New Art of Lying, . . . London, Printed for John Clark, and are to be sold at his shop under S. Peters Church in Cornhill. 1634. 12°, A—R in twelves, R 10 with *Errata*, last two leaves blank.

Dedicated to the Archbishop of Canterbury.

MASON, JOHN, *M.A.*
The Tyrke. A Worthie Tragedie. As it hath bene diuers times acted by the Children of his Maiesties Reuels. Written by Iohn Mason Maister of Artes. *Sume superbiam quesitam meritis.* Horat. London. Printed by E. A. for John Busbie . . . 1610. 4°, B—K 3 in fours, besides title and following leaf with Prologue and Epilogue. *B. M.*

MASON, JOHN, *Governor of Newfoundland.*
A Briefe Discovrse of the New-found-land, with the situation, temperature, and commodities thereof, inciting our Nation to goe forward in that hopefull plantation begunne. *Scire tuum nihil est, nisi te scire hoc sciat alter.* Edinbvrgh, Printed by Andro Hart. 1620. 4°, A—B in fours. Dedicated to Sir John Scott of Scots-Tarvet, Knight. *B. M.*

MASON, JOHN, *of Fordham, Cambridge-shire.*
Mentis Humanæ Metamorphosis; sive Conversio. The History of the Young Converted Gallant. Or Directions to the Readers of that Divine Poem, Written by Benjamin Keach; Intituled Warre with the Devil. . . . Compiled in a Poem by J. Mason Gent. of Fordham in Cambridge-shire. London, Printed by F. L. for B. Harris . . . 1676. 8°, A—L 4 in eights, besides the frontispiece.

Spiritual Songs Or Songs of Praise. . . . The Second Edition, Corrected, with an Addition of a Sacred Poem on Dives and Lazarus. London, Printed for Richard Northcott, . . . 1685. 8°. A, 4 leaves: B—M 4 in eights.

The Remains of M' John Mason, Minister of the Gospel, Author of the Songs of Praise. London, Printed for T. Parkhurst, . . . 1698. 8°, A—E in eights: F, 2.

MASON, ROBERT.
Reasons Monarchic. Set forth by Robert Mason of Lincolnes Inne Gent. [Quot. from Cicero.] London Printed by Valentine Sims, . . . 1602. 8°, A—K 6 in eights, A 1 blank. Dedicated to Sir John Popham, Lord Chief Justice of England. In verse and prose. *B. M.*

MASON, W., *M.A.*
A Handfvl of Essaies. Or Imperfect Offers. . . . London Printed by Aug. Matthewes for Iohn Grismand, . . . 1621. 12°, A—F 8 in twelves. *B. M.*

MASSACHUSETTS.
The General Laws and Liberties of the Massachusets Colony: Revised & Reprinted, by order of the General Court Holden at Boston May 15ᵗʰ, 1672. Cambridge [New England], Printed by Samuel Green, for John Usher of Boston, 1672. Folio. Title, 1 leaf + pp. 1–170. "A Summary of the Laws foregoing Alphabetically digested," 14 leaves unpaged. "Several Laws and Orders made at the General Court holden at Boston, the 15th of May, 1672, 3 leaves. "Several Laws and Orders made, &c., the 8th October, 1672. As also several Laws made, &c., at Boston, 7th of May and 17th of October, 1673," 5 leaves.

"This code of laws gives a life-like picture of the manners and habits of life of the Early English Colonists of America. The laws regarding the observance of Sunday and attending Churches are most rigid, and the enactments against 'the cursed sect of Quakers' are indeed remarkable, being made by people who had themselves left their homes and friends to avoid religious persecution. To be whipped through three towns and banished upon pain of death are among the cruelties ordered to be inflicted on the unfortunate Quakers. Among the laws on marriage is one strictly forbidding the marriage of a widower with his late wife's sister. A copy of this book with the additional leaves and in such perfect condition as the present is of the rarest occurrence."—*Ellis's Catalogue, whence this article is borrowed, as I just missed seeing it.*

The General Laws and Liberties of the Massachusets Colony in New-England Revised and Reprinted, By Order of the General Court holden at Boston, May 25ᵗʰ, 1672 . . . Cambridge in New-England, Printed by Samuel Green, for John Usher of Boston, and are to be sold by Richard Chiswel, at the Rose and Crown in St. Paul's Church-yard, London, 1675. Folio. Title, 1 leaf: B—C, 2 ll. each: D—G in fours: H—Qq, 2 ll. each: Rr, 3 ll.: Summary, A—G, 2 ll. each: Laws made at Boston, 15 May 1672, A in fours, A 4 blank.

Acts and Laws, passed by the Great and General Court or Assembly of His Majesties Province of the Massachusetts-Bay, in New-England. Begun and Held at Boston on Wednesday, the Twenty-fifth of May, 1698. . . . Boston, Printed by Bartholomew Green, and John Allen, Printers to the Governour and Council. 1698. Folio, A—N, 2 leaves each.

Acts and Laws, Passed by the Great and General Court or Assembly of the Province of the Massachusetts-Bay in New-England, From 1692, to 1719. To which is Prefix'd, The Charter, . . . A.D. 1691. . . . London, Printed by John Baskett, . . . MDCCXXIV. Folio, a—d, 2 ll. each : A—4 X, 2 ll. each:

Two Addresses from the Governour, Council, and Convention of the Massachusets Colony Assembled at Boston in New-England, Presented to His Majesty at Hampton-Court. August 7. 1689. By Sir Henry Ashurst Baronet. [Col.] London : Printed for Richard Baldwin, in the Old-Bailey. 1689. Folio, 2 leaves.

MASTERSON, GEORGE, *Preacher of the Gospel at Shoreditch, near London.*
The Triumph stain'd. Being an Answer to Trvths Trivmph, i.e. a Pamphlet so called, and lately set forth by Mr John Wildman, a pretended Gentleman of the Life-guard to his Excellency Sir Tho: Fairfax. . . . London, Printed by John Field. 1647. 4°, A—D 2 in fours, D 2 having the *Imprimatur.*

MATHER, COTTON.
A Family Well-Ordered. Or An Essay to render Parents and Children Happy in one another. . . . By Cotton Mather . . . Boston, Printed by B. Green, & J. Allen, . . . 1699. 12°, A—G in sixes.

MATHER, INCREASE.[1]
A Further Account of the Tryals of the New-England Witches. With the Observations of a Person who was upon the Place several Days when the suspected Witches were first taken into Examination. To which is added, Cases of Conscience concerning Witchcrafts and Evil Spirits personating Men. Written at the Request of the Ministers of New-England. By Increase Mather, President of Harvard Colledge. . . . London : Printed for J. Dunton, at the Raven in the Poultrey. 1693. 4°, A—C, 2 leaves each : *Cases of Conscience*, a—g 2 in fours.

MATHEW, FRANCIS.
To his Highness, Oliver, Lord Protector . . . Is Humbly presented A Mediterranean Passage by Water Betwene the two Sea Towns Lynn & Yarmovth, Upon the Two Rivers The Little Owse, and Waveney. With farther Results. Producing the Passage from Yarmouth to York. London : Printed by Gertrude Dawson, 1656. 4°, A—B in fours. Dedicated by Mathew to the Protector.

MATHEWS, RICHARD.
The Unlearned Alchymist His Antidote : Or A more full and ample Explanation

of the Use, Virtue, and Benefit of my Pill . . . By Richard Mathews, and are to be sold at his house by the Lyons Den at the Tower, next Gate to the By-ward. London, Printed for Joseph Leigh, . . . 1663. 8°, A—O 6 in eights, besides (*) 2 leaves between A and B and a—c in eights between L and M. A 1 is blank, and A 2 has a list of Receipts in the book.

MAUPAS, CHARLES, *of Blois.*
A French Grammar and Syntaxe, Contayning most Exact and certaine Rules, for the Pronunciation, Orthography, Construction, and Vse of the French Language . . . . Translated into English, with many Additions and Explications, peculiarly usefull to us English. Together with a Preface and an Introduction, By W. A. . . . London Printed by B. A. and T. F. for Rich: Mynne, . . . 1634. 8°. A, 4 leaves : *, 8 leaves : B—Ff in eights, Ff 8 blank. Dedicated by W. Aufield to the Duke of Buckingham.

MAY, THOMAS.
The History of the Parliament of England : Which began November the third, M. DC. XL. With a short and necessary view of some precedent yeares. Written by Thomas May Esquire, Secretary for the Parliament. Published by Authority.

Tempora mutantur.
Mutantur Homines.
Veritas eadem manet.

Imprinted at London by Moses Bell, for George Thomason, at the Signe of the Rose and Crown in St. Pauls Church Yard, M.DC.XL.VII. Folio, A—Nn in fours : Oo, 6 leaves. A 1 has the *Imprimatur.*

MAYER, JOHN, *B.D.*
A Patterne for Women : Setting forth the most Christian life, & most comfortable death of Mrs Lvcy late wife to the worshipfull Roger Thornton Esquire, of Little Wratting in Suffolke. Whereunto is annexed a most pithy and perswasive discourse of that most learned & holy Father Ierom, being the last speech before his death, . . . And finally, the last most heauenly prayer of the sayd Ierom, . . . London, Printed by Edw. Griffin for Iohn Marriot, . . . 1619. 12°, A—G in twelves. Dedicated to Roger Thornton Esquire, "my very good Friend and Patron," by the author.

MAYER, MICHAEL, *M.D.*
Lvsvs Serivs : Or, Serious Passe-time. A Philosphicall Discourse concerning the

Inferiority of Creatures under Man. Written By Michael Mayerus. M.D. London, Printed for Humphrey Moseley, ... and Tho. Heath . . . 1654. 12°. A, 4: B—F in twelves: G, 10. Dedicated by J. de la Salle to Cary Dillon, son of the Earl of Roscommon.

MAYNE, JASPER.
Ochlomachia. Or The Peoples War, Examined According to the Principles of Scripture & Reason, In Two of the most Plausible Pretences of it. In Answer to a Letter sent by a Person of Quality, who desired satisfaction. By Jasper Mayne D.D. one of the Students of Ch. Ch. Oxon. . . . Printed in the Yeare, 1647. 4°, A—E in fours.

MEAD, ROBERT.
The Combat of Love and Friendship, A Comedy, As it hath formerly been presented by the Gentlemen of Ch. Ch. in Oxford. By Robert Mead, sometimes of the same Colledge. London, Printed for M. M. G. Bedell, and T. Collins, . . . 1654. 4°. A, 2: B—K in fours: L, 2.

MEAGER, LEONARD, *thirty years Practitioner in the Art*.
The English Gardener: Or, A Sure Guide to young Planters and Gardeners In Three Parts. . . . London, Printed for P. Parker . . . 1670. 4°, A—E 2 in fours, no pp. 29—40: F—L in fours: no pp. 89-160: Aa—Mm 2 in fours, besides 24 leaves of designs and plans. Dedicated to Master Philip Hollman of Warkworth, co. Northampton. *B. M.*

There are later editions, with additions.

MEG OF WESTMINSTER.
[The Life and Pranks of Long Meg of Westminster.] Imprinted at London for Abraham Veale, dwellinge in Pauls church yeard at the signe of the Lambe. [Col.] Imprinted at London by William How, for Abraham Veale, dwelling in Pauls churchyearde at the signe of the Lambe. 1582. 8°, black letter, A—B 4 in eights. *B. M.* (imperfect.)

The title given above between brackets is taken from the head-line. The only other copy known appears to be that which sold at Jolley's Sale in 1844 for £7, 7s. This impression is said to vary considerably from the later; but I have not had any opportunity of comparing them. As an allusion is made in one of the chapters to Bishop Bonner, who died in 1569, as living and in office, there were probably much earlier issues of this popular and amusing piece.

MELANCTHON, PHILIP.
A Godly treatyse of Prayer, translated into Englishe, By John Bradford . . . [Col.] Imprinted at London in Paules Church yearde, at the sygne of the Rose, By John Wight. 8°, black letter, A—I 6 in eights, A 8 blank.

MELLIS, JOHN, *Schoolmaster*.
A Brief Instruction and maner how to keepe bookes of Accompts after the order of Debitor and Creditor & aswell for proper Accompts partible, &c. . . . Imprinted at London by Iohn Windet, . . . 1581. 8°. A—S 4 in eights. [Col.] At London Printed by Iohn Windet, for Hugh Singleton, . . . 1588. *B. M.*

MELVIN, A.
Principis Scoto-Britannorvm Natalia: Hagæ-Comitis, Ex Officina Alberti Henrici D. Ordinum Hollandiæ Typographi. CIↃ.IↃ.XCIV. 4°, 4 leaves.

MENTET DE SALMONET, ROBERT.
Histoire des Trovbles de la Grand Bretagne, Contenant ce qvi s'est passé depvis l'année six cens trente trois, iusques a l'année mille six cens quarante six . . . A Paris, . . . M.DC.LXI. Folio. à, 6 leaves, à 1 blank: ê, 4: A— in fours (copy described ending imperfectly on Vv 4): Tome Second, with a new title—title and preface, 2 leaves: A—EEe in fours : *Errata*, 1 leaf: Relation des veritable cavses et des Conionctvres Favorables qvi ont contribve av Restablissement dv Roy . . . Title and dedication by Riordan de Musery to the Minister Fouquet, 2 leaves: a—f in fours, f 4 blank. With a portrait by Lochon after Mignard.

MERCURIUS.
Mercurius Politicus. Comprising the Summe of all Intelligence, with the Affairs, and Designs now on foot, in the three Nations of England, Ireland, and Scotland. In defence of the Commonwealth, and for Information of the People. From Thursday June 6 [1650, to Thursday, January 10, 1655.] 4°, 291 Numbers. [Col. at end of No. 291:] London, Printed by Tho. Newcomb, . . . 1655.

Crossley, part 2, No. 1766.

MERITON, GEORGE.
The Praise of York-shire Ale Wherein is enumerated several Sorts of Drink, with a Discription of the Humors of most sorts of Drunckards. . . . The Third Edition. With the Addition of some Observations of the Dialect and Pronunciation of Words in the East Ryding of York-shire. Together with a Collection of significant and usefull Proverbs. By G. M. Gent. York, Printed by J. White, for Francis Hildyard

at the Signe of the Bible in Stone Gate, 1697. 8°, A—H in eights.

MERLIN.

Catastrophe Mundi: Or, Merlin Reviv'd, In a Discourse of Prophecies & Predictions, And their Remarkable Accomplishment. With M⟨r⟩ Lilly's Hieroglyphicks Exactly Cut. And Notes and Observations thereon. As also A Collection of all the Antient (Reputed) Prophecies, that are Extant, Touching the Grand Revolutions like to happen in these Latter Ages. By a Learned Pen. London: Printed and are to be sold by John How . . . and Thomas Malthus. . . . 1683. 8°, A—G in eights, H, 9 leaves. With woodcuts.

MERRETT, CHRISTOPHER, *M.D.*, *F.R.S.*

A Collection of Acts of Parliament, Charters, Trials at Law, and Judges Opinions Concerning Those Grants to the Colledge of Physicians London, taken from the Originals, Law-Books, and Annals. Commanded by Sir Edward Alston K⟨t⟩. President, and the Elects and Censors. Made by Christopher Merrett, Fellow and Censor. Anno Dom. 1660. 4°. Title and Contents, 2 leaves: A—R in fours.

A Short View of the Frauds, and Abuses Committed by Apothecaries; As well in Relation to Patients, as Physicians: And of the only Remedy thereof by Physicians making their own Medicines. . . . London, Printed for James Allestry, . . . 1669. 4°, A—G in fours, A 1 and G 4 blank.

MERRIMENT.

Political Merriment: Or, Truths told to some Tune. Faithfully Translated from the Original French . . . By a Lover of his Country. London . . . . 1714. Small 8°, pp. 255.

METHOD.

A True Method, I. For Raising of Souldiers. II. For bringing those Seamen that are in the Land, into the Navy. III. For the Increase of Seamen. IV. For Employing of Seamen in time of Peace. V. For the Improvement of Seamen. . . . London. Printed for John Nutt. . . . 1703. 4°, A—C in fours, besides a plate.

MEXIA, PEDRO.

The Rarities of the World. Containing, Rules and Observations touching the beginning of Kingdoms and Common-Wealths, the Divisions of the Ages, . . . With Excellent discourses of Creatures bred in the Sea, to the likenesse of Man; and others on Earth. . . . First written in Spanish by Don Petrus Messie, afterward translated into French, and now into English, By J. B. Gent. London, Printed by B. A. 1651. 4°, A—S in fours, S 4 with the colophon dated 1650. Dedicated by Joshua Baildon, the translator, to his friend and kinsman Paul Holdenby, Esq.

MIDDLESEX.

Answers to the Reasons against passing the Earl of Clevelands Bill as to the Mannors of Stepney and Hackney in the County of Middlesex. A broadside.

MIDDLETON, THOMAS.

The Roaring Girle. Or Moll Cut-Purse. As it hath lately beene Acted on the Fortune-stage by the Prince his Players. Written by T. Middleton and T. Dekker. Printed at London for Thomas Archer, . . . 1611. 4°, A—M in fours, A 1 and M 4 blank. With a cut on the title purporting to represent Moll Cut-Purse.

Dedicated thus: "To the Comicke, Play-readers, Venery, and Laughter."

MIEGE, GUY.

The Great French Dictionary. In Two Parts. The First, French and English; The Second, English and French; According to the Ancient and Modern Orthography . . . . By Guy Miege, Gent. London, Printed by J. Redmayne, for T. Basset, . . . MDCLXXXVIII. Folio. Title and Preface, 2 leaves: a—f, 2 leaves each, f 2 with the title to the First Portion: A—4 C 2 in fours: The French-English, of which the title is on 4 C 2, A (in a new alphabet)—4 L in fours.

To each part is prefixed a grammar.

MILITIA.

A Necessary Abstract of the Laws Relating to the Militia. Reduced into a Practical Method. To which is added, Instructions for exercising the Trained Bands. London; Printed for Robert Vincent . . . 1691. 8°, A—D and a—b in eights. With a frontispiece.

MILTON, JOHN.

Poems upon Several Occasions. Compos'd at several times . . . The Third Edition. London: Printed for Jacob Tonson . . . 1695. Folio, A—Q, 2 leaves each. In two columns.

This edition was doubtless intended to accompany the folio edition of the *Paradise Lost*, &c.

The Tenure of Kings and Magistrates: Proving, That it is Lawfull, and hath been held so through all Ages, for any, who have the Power, to call to account a Tyrant, or wicked King, . . . And that

they, who of late so much blamed Deposing, are the Men that did it themselves.
The Author, J. M. London, Printed by
Matthew Simmons, . . . 1649. 4⁰, A—F 2
in fours.

Joannis Miltoni Angli Pro Populo Ang-
licano Defensio Contra Claudii Anonymi,
alias Salmasii, Defensionem Regiam.
Editio emendatior. Londini, Typis Du-
Gardianis, Anno Domini 1651. Folio.
Title and preceding leaf with note as to
Errata: B—Ll in fours.

Claudii Salmasii Defensio Regia, . . .
Et Joannis Miltoni Defensio pro Populo
Anglicano, . . . Apud viduam Mathv-
rini Dv Pviss, . . . M.DC.LII. 4⁰. *, 4
leaves: ä and ë, 4 leaves each: A—Pp in
fours, Pp 4 blank: Milton's portion, with
a fresh title, A—P in fours.

    A Dutch reissue of the copies of Salma-
    sius and Milton, the former printed at Paris,
    1650, the latter at London, 1651.

Paradise Lost . . . The Sixth Edition,
with Sculptures. To which is added,
Explanatory Notes upon each Book, and
a Table to the Poem, never before Printed.
London, Printed by Tho. Hodgkin, for
Jacob Tonson, . . . MDCXCV. Folio.
Title and *The Verse,* 2 leaves : B, 2 leaves:
C—Yy 2 in fours. With a portrait by R.
White and illustrations to each book de-
tached from the text.

    The Notes were written by Patrick Hume.

Paradise Regain'd . . . . London, Printed
by R. E. and are to be sold by Randal
Taylor . . . MDCLXXXVIII. Folio, A—R,
2 leaves each.

    Uniform with the *Paradise Lost.*

Samson Agonistes . . . London, Printed,
and are to be sold by Randal Taylor . . . .
MDCLXXXVIII. Folio, A—H in fours.

Accedence Commenc't Grammar, Supply'd with sufficient Rules, For the use of
such (Younger or Elder) as are desirous,
without more trouble than needs to attain
the Latin Tongue. The Elder sort especially, with little Teaching, and their own
Industry. By John Milton. London,
Printed for S. S. and are to be sold by
John Starkey . . . 1669. 12⁰, A—C 10
in twelves. *B. M.*

A Brief History of Moscovia : And of other
less-known Countries lying eastward of
Russia as far as Cathay. Gathered from
the Writings of several Eye-witnesses.
By John Milton. London, Printed by
M. Flesher, for Brabazon Aylmer . . .
1682. 8⁰, A—H in eights, H 8 blank.

Miscellanea. I. A Survey of the Constitutions and Interests of the Empire,
Sueden, Denmark, Spain, Holland, France,
and Flanders, with their Relation to England, in the Year 1671. II. An Essay
upon the Original and Nature of Government. III. An Essay upon the Advancement of Trade in Ireland. . . . By a
Person of Honour. London : Printed by
A. M. and R. R. for Edw. Gellibrand,
. . . 1680. 8⁰. A, 4 leaves : B—Q in
eights.

    Following the title is "The Author's
    Letter to the Stationer, upon occasion of
    the following Papers."

Letters of State, Written by Mr. John
Milton, To most of the Sovereign Princes
and Republicks of Europe. From the
Year 1649. Till the Year 1659. To
which is added, An Account of his Life.
Together with several of his Poems ; And
a Catalogue of his Works, never before
Printed. London : Printed in the Year,
1694. 12⁰. A, 12 leaves : a—b 6 in
twelves : B—P in twelves.

MISERERE.

Miserere mei Domine. A Thought upon
the Latter Day. . . . Five Hymnes. London : Printed by R. Y. for Ph. Nevill . . .
1638. 12⁰, A—C in twelves, first and
last leaves blank. With separate titles to
the two portions. *B. M.*

MISSALE.

Missale secundum vsum insignis Ecclesie
Sarum. [Col.] In laudem sanctissime
trinitatis totiusq ; milicie celestis ad ho-
norē et decorē scō ecclesie Sarū angli-
cane eiusq ; deuotissimi cleri : hoc missale
diuinorum officiorum vigilanti studio
emendatum Jussu et impēsis p̄stantissimi
viri Winkin de Worde. Impressum London. apud Westmonasteriū per Julianum
notaire et Johanem barbier felici numine
explicitu; est Anno dñi. M.cccc.lxxxviij.
xx. die mensis. Decembris. Folio. Title
and Calendar, 9 leaves : *Benedictio Panis,*
1 leaf : a—z in eights, followed by 20
leaves, folioed 203-222 : A—II in eights.
Printed in two columns in red and black
inks. With a large cut on a i.

Sothebys, July 9, 1886, No. 1097, imperfect.

Missale Secundū vsum insignis ecclesie
Sar [The rest of the title is occupied by
a large woodcut. Colophon on fol. 244:]
Anno incarnationis dominice quingentesimo octauo supra millesimum . die vero
xxvii. mensis maii arte et industria Magistri Martini morin impressoris Rothomagi iuxta insignē prioratū sancti Laudi

L *

cōmorañ / Impensa vero Johannis richardi mercatoris . . .] Folio, printed in two columns in red and black, with woodcuts and music. a, 8 leaves: A—X in eights: a—i in eights: the *Accentuarium,* A—B in sixes.

Sothebys, July 9, 1886, No. 1098, imperfect.

Missale ad vsum insignis ac preclare ecclesie Sar. . . . Anno domini, 1533. [Col.] Missale ad vsũ ecclesie Sarisburiẽsis optimis formulis (vt res ipsa indicat) diligẽtissime reuisum ac Correctũ / cũ multis annotatiũculis / ac litteris alphabeticis Euangelior. atq; epistolarũ originẽ ĩdicantibꝰ. Impressũ Parisiis sũptibꝰ Francisci regnault alme vniuersitatis parisien. librariũ iuratũ. Anno dñi Millesimo quingẽtessimo trigesimo tertio. Die vero. xxvij. May. 4", printed in red and black, with numerous woodcuts. Title and Calendar, 8 leaves: a—p in eights: q, 6 leaves: r, 7 leaves: s, 6 leaves: A—F in eights: G, 4.

The *Canon Missæ* is (as usual) printed on vellum.

Missale ad vsum ecclesie Eboracẽ. tam in catũ q̃ in litera recognitũ / cõgruẽtibus historijs adornatum / marginalibꝰ quotationibꝰ prosisq; ac varijs additamentis locupletatum sumptibus Frãcisci Regnault parisiis morã tenentis. Anno domini. M. ccccc. xxxiii. Venũdatur in vice sãcti Jacobi / e regione porticus maturinorũ. Ad signum Elephantis. 4". Title, Calendar, &c., 8 leaves: a—z in eights, followed by two sheets of 8 and 10.

Printed in red and black in two columns.

MISSON, F. M.

The New Voyage to Italy : . . . . Done out of French. The Second Edition, Enlarg'd above one Third, and enrich'd with several New Figures. By Maximilian Misson, Gent. In Two Volumes. London, ... 1699. 8°. With frontispiece and plates, including a large folding one of the *Heidelberg Tun* and (at p. 148 of vol. 2) an engraving of the Barberini or Portland Vase—the earliest representation of it, perhaps, in any book.

Some of the first volume is taken up with other countries, and a portion of the second with *Instructions to a Traveller.*

MOLESWORTH.

An Account of Denmark, As it was in the Year 1692. *Pauci prudentiâ,* . . . Tacit. lib. 4". Ann. . . . London : Printed in the Year 1694. 8". A, 2 leaves: a—c in eights: B—S in eights.

MOLL, HERMAN.

A System of Geography : Or, A New & Accurate Description of the Earth in all its Empires, . . . Illustrated with History and Topography, And Maps of every Country. Fairly Engraven on Copper, . . . By Herman Moll . . . London : Printed for Timothy Childe . . . MDCCI. Folio. Two titles and frontispiece, 3 leaves : B—Gg in fours : Hh—Nn, 2 leaves each : Oo, 1 leaf. With the maps on the letterpress.

MONEY.

The Miracles Perform'd by Money ; A Poem. By the Author of the Humours of a Coffee-house. . . . London : Printed, ... 1692. 4°. E 2 in fours.

Dedicated to Sir Martin Mony-less by *Tom of Ten Thousand.*

Reflections upon a Scandalous Libel, Entituled, *An Account of the Proceedings* . . . in relation to the Re-coyning the Clipp'd Money, and falling the price of Guinea's . . . London, Printed . . . MDCXCVII. 8°, A—F in fours.

MONIPENNIE, JOHN.

The Abridgement Or Svmmarie of the Scots Chronicles, . . . Latelie corrected and augmented. Edinbvrgh, Printed by I. W. for Iohn Wood. 1633. 8°, A—R 6 in eights.

MONK.

The Monk's Hood Pull'd off ; Or, The Capvchin Fryar Described. In two Parts. Translated out of French. London, Printed for James Collins, at the Sign of the Kings Arms in Ludgate street. MDCLXXI. 8°, A—Dd 2 in eights, besides the frontispiece. Dedicated by the nameless translator to Anthony, Lord Ashley.

MONK, GEORGE, *Duke of Albemarle.*

A Copie of a Letter from General Monck, in answer to a Letter sent from hence by Col. Jones and others. For the Commander in chief of the Forces in Ireland, to be communicated to the rest of the Officers of the Army there. Dublin, Printed by William Bladen, by special Order Anno Domini 1659. A broad-side.

Three Letters from the Lord General Monck, Commander in Chief of the Forces in Scotland, and one of the Commissioners by Act of Parliament for the Government of the Army of this Commonwealth, Viz. To M' Speaker, To the Lord Fleetwood, To the Lord Lambert. Edinbvrgh, Printed by Christopher Higgins, in Harts Close, over against the Trone Church, Anno Dom. 1659. 4", 4 leaves.

To the Right Honorable Major General Sir Hardress Waller, and the rest of the

of Officers of the Army in Ire-
Dublin. [A Letter from General
lated Coldstream, 28 Dec. 1659.]
lside.

idezvouz of General Monck, upon
lines of England ; And the Sei-
of the Parliaments Standard on
: Hills : . . . York : Printed for
Foster living in the Minster Yard;
e-printed in London for publick
ion. [1659.] 4", 4 leaves.

to his Excellency The L.d General
at Skinners-Hall on Wednesday
l. 1660. At which time he was
ned by that honourable Company.
: Printed for William Anderson,
'ear, 1660. A broadside in verse.

tertainment of the Lady Monk,
bers-Folly. Together with an
e made to her by a Member of the
: of Bedlam at her visiting those
ques [About 1660.] A broad-
/erse.

UTHSHIRE.

t Discovery of a Damnable Plot
and Castle in Monmoth-shire in
Related in the High Court of
ent by Iohn Davis, November
1641. The chiefe Actor being
rle of Worcester. . . . London
by Bernard Alsop, MDCXLJ. 4",

: from the Marquesse of Worcester
immittee of Parliament sitting in
ity of Monmouth, Concerning His
ding with Irish Forces : and the
tees Answer thereunto. . . . Lon-
inted for Edw. Husband, . . .
1646. 4", 4 leaves.

GU, HENRY, *Earl of Manchester.*
ster Al Mondo . . . The former
iot intended for the Presse, haue
the publishing of these. Im-
at London by Robert Barker, . . .
.2", A—I 6 in twelves, I 6 with
tle.

ster Al Mondo. Contemplatio
Et Immortalitatis. . . . The Sixth
ion much enlarged, with the
Sentences rendred into English.
Printed by T. R. and E. M. for
Thrale, . . . 1635. 12", A—K in
besides the engraved title and

ster Al Mondo. . . . The fourth
on much inlarged. London,
by John Haviland, for Francis

Constable, . . . 1638. 12", A—I in
twelves, 1 11-12 blank, besides the engraved title and portrait, both dated 1639.

This work, originally designed for private
circulation, according to the statement on
the title of the second edition, was reprinted in 1642, 1655, 1661, 1667, 1676, 1688.

MONTANUS, ARNOLDUS.

Atlas Chinensis : Being a Second Part of
A Relation of Remarkable Passages in
Two Embassies from the East-India Company of the United Provinces, to the
Vice-Roy Singlamong and General Tai-
sing Lipovi, and to Konchi, Emperor of
China and East-Tartary. With a Relation
of the Netherlanders assisting the Tartar
against Coxinga, and the Chinese Fleet,
who till then were Masters of the Sea.
. . . Collected out of their several Writings and Journals, by Arnoldus Montanus.
English'd, and Adorn'd with a hundred
several Sculptures, By John Ogilby, Esq;
. . . London, Printed by Tho. Johnson
for the Author, . . . M.DC.LXXI. Folio.
Frontispiece, printed title, and dedication
to Charles II., 3 leaves : B—4 Z 2 in
fours. With numerous engravings on the
text, and others detached, of which there
is a printed list on the back of the dedication.

The frontispiece reads : The Second &
Third Embassie to y Empire of Taysing or
China. with Priviledge A°. 1672. This
volume gives a very copious account of
China.

MONTGOMERY, ALEXANDER.

The Flyting betwixt Montgomerie and
Polwart. Newly corrected and amended.
Edinburgh, Printed Anno Dom. 1666.
Sm. 8", A—B 4 in eights.

Collier's Sale, August 1884, No. 510.

MOORE, SIR JONAS.

England's Interest : Or, The Gentleman
and Farmer's Friend. . . . By Sir J. Moore.
London, Printed for A. Bettesworth, . . .
1721. 12", A—H in twelves.

A tolerably comprehensive manual on
wine and cyder-making, cookery, medicine,
&c. There are directions how to catch and
cook fish, with terms of carving.

MORE, GEORGE.

A true Discourse concerning the certaine
possession and dispossessio of 7 persons in
one familie in Lancashire, which also may
serve as part of an Answere to a fayned
and false Discouerie which speaketh very
much evill aswell of this, as of the rest
of those great and mightie workes of God
which be of the like excellent nature. By
George More, Minister and Preacher . . .
1600. 8", A—F 4 in eights, F 4 blank.

At the end it is stated that the MS. was ready in December last (1599), but was delayed in the press.

MORE, HENRY.

A Collection of Aphorisms. In Two Parts. Written by the late Reverend and Learned D' Henry More, Fellow of Christ's College in Cambridge. London, Printed by J. Downing . . . 1704. 8°, B—E in eights, besides the title and Preface.

MORE, RICHARD, of Lintey. Esquire.

A True Relation of the Murders committed in the Parish of Clunne in the County of Salop by Enoch ap Evan upon the Bodies of his Mother and Brother, with the Causes moving him thereunto. Wherein is examined, and refuted a certaine Booke written upon the same Subject by P. Studley, Entituled the Looking-glasse of Schisme. Also an Appendix in further defence of this Relation. . . . Printed by order of a Committee of the Honourable House of Commons . . . London, Printed by T. B. for P. Stephens & C. Meredith . . . 1641. 12°, A—H 6 in twelves, A 1 blank. *B. M.*

MORE, SIR THOMAS.

Utopia, &c. Basileæ, December. 1518.

The *Utopia* is dated in the colophon to that portion *November* 1518; but the signatures are continuous, and the whole was doubtless intended to sell together.

The supplycacyon of soulys. Made by syr Thomas More knight councellour to our soueravn lorde the Kynge and chauncellour of hys Duchy of Lancaster. ꝃ Agaynst the supplycacyon of beggars. [London, W. Rastell, 1530 ?] Folio, black letter. Title with Errata on the back : a. 2 leaves : b—l in fours : m, 2 leaves. At the end occurs only : Cum priuilegio.

A dialoge of comfort against tribulacion, made by Syr Thomas More Knyght, and set foorth by the name of an Hũgarie, not before this time imprinted. Londini in aedibus Richardi Totteli. Cum Priuilegio . . . [Col.] Imprinted at London in Fletestrete within Temple barre at the signe of the hand & starre by Richarde Tottel y^e . xviii. day of Nouēbre in ye yere of our lord. 1553. Cum priuilegio . . . 4°, black letter. Title and Table, 3 leaves : A—U in eights : X, 4. The title is within a very curious allegorical compartment.

Sothebys, June 29, 1885, No. 792.

The Life of The Great Picus Prince of Mirandula. Taken from the Workes of Sir Thomas More Knight. Printed in

the Year 1720. 8°. Title and dedication by Edward Jesup to William Law Junior, 4 leaves : A—F in sixes.

The Life and Death of S' Thomas Moore, Who was Lord Chancelor of England to King Henry the Eight. Printed for N. V. 1642. 4°. A—3 H in fours, 3 H 4 blank, and the title.

MORETTI. TOMMASO, of Brescia.

A Treatise of Artillery : Or, Great Ordnance. . . . Translated into English, with Notes thereupon, and some Additions out of French for Sea-Gunners, By Jonas Moore, junior. London. Printed by William Godbid, . . . 1673. 8°, A—I in eights. With 6 folded plates. Dedicated to Captain George Wharton, treasurer of the Artillery.

MORGAN, SYLVANUS.

Armilogia Sive Ars Chromocritica. The Language of Arms by the Colours and Metals : Being Analogically handled according to the Nature of Things, and fitted with apt motto's to the Heroical Science of Herauldry in the Symbolical World. . . . A Work of this Nature never yet extant. By Sylvanus Morgan Arms-Painter. *Est aliquid prodire tenus, si non datur ultra.* London, Printed by T. Hewer for Nathaniel Brook . . . 1666. 4°, A—Mm in fours. With numerous cuts of arms. Dedicated to Edward, Earl of Manchester.

MORRELL, WILLIAM.

New-England. Or A Briefe Enarration of the Ayre, Earth, Water. Fish and Fowles of that Country. With A Description of the Natures. Orders, Habits, and Religion of the Natiues : In Latin and English verse. *Sat breuè, si sat benè.* London, Imprinted by I. D. 1625. 4°, A—D in fours. Dedicated by the author to the Lords. Knights, and Gentlemen Adventurers for New England. *B. M.*

MORRELL, WILLIAM.

The Notorious Impostor, Or the History of the Life of William Morrell, Alias Bowyer, Sometime of Banbury, Chirurgeon. Who lately personated Humphrey Wickham of Swackly, in the County of Oxon. Esquire, at a Bakers House in the Strand, where he Died the third of Jan. 169½. Together with an Authentick Copy of his Will, . . . London. Printed for Abel Roper . . . 1692. 4°, A—G 2 in fours. *B. M.*

MORTIMER, MARGARET, Widow.

Proposals Tender'd for an Addition to

the late Act of Parliament for Collecting Charity on Briefs by Letters Patents . . . London : Printed in the Year 1707. 4°, A—B 2 in fours.

Proposals for a Supplement to the late Act of Parliament . . . [London, 1707.] 4°, 4 leaves. Without a regular title.

MORTON, NATHANIEL, *Secretary to the Court for the Jurisdiction of New Plymouth.*
New-Englands Memorial : Or, A brief Relation of the most Memorable and Remarkable Passages of the Providence of God, manifested to the Planters of New-England in America : With special Reference to the first Colony thereof, Called New-Plimouth. . . . Cambridge : Printed by S. G. and M. J. for John Usher of Boston. 1669. 4°, A—Dd in fours, and a, 2 leaves. Dedicated to Thomas Prince Esq'. Governor, and the Magistrates, of New Plymouth.

> The author was nephew of William Bradford, of whose papers, as well as those of Edward Winslow, he had the use.

MOUNDEFORD, THOMAS.
Vir Bonvs.
Q. Vir Bonus est quis?
R. *Qui consulta Patrum, qui leges Iuraque seruat.*
Temperantiae, Prvdentiae, Ivstitiae, Fortitudinis. . . . . Authore Tho. Moundeford, Cantabrigiense alumno, Collegiorum Regalium Canta. & Ætone : nunc Socio Coll. Med. Lond. Impressum Londini per F. Kingstonvm. 1622. 8°. A, 3 leaves with title and dedication to James I. ; ¶, 8 leaves : B—Q in eights, Q 8 blank. *B. M.*

IOUNTAGU, RICHARD, *afterwards successively Bishop of Chichester and Norwich.*
Appello Cæsarem. A Ivst Appeale from Two Vniust Informers. London, Printed by H. L. for Mathew Lownes. M.DC.XXV. 4°. a, 4 leaves : *. 4 leaves : A—Ss in fours, and a leaf of Tt.
> The author was summoned to the bar of the House of Commons in the first Parliament of Charles I. for this work.

IOUNTFORT, WILLIAM.
The Successfull Straingers. A Tragi-Comedy : Acted by their Majesties Servants, at the Theatre Royal . . . London. Printed for James Blackwell, at Bernards-Inn-Gate, Holbourn ; . . . 1690. 4°, A—I 2 in fours ; and a, 2 leaves. Dedicated to Thomas Wharton. Comptroller of the Household, and of the Privy Council.

MOXON, JOSEPH, *late F.R.S. and Hydrographer to K. Charles II.*
Mechanick Dvalling : Teaching any Man, though of an Ordinary Capacity, and unlearned in the Mathematicks, to draw a True Sun-Dyal on any Given Plane, . . . By Joseph Moxon, Hydrographer to the Kings most Excellent Majesty. London. Printed for Joseph Moxon on Ludgate-hill, at the Sign of Atlas. MDCLXVIII. 4°, A—G in fours.

A Brief Discourse of a Passage by the North-Pole to Japan, China, &c. Pleaded by Three Experiments : . . . With a Map of all the Discovered Lands neerest to the Pole. By Joseph Moxon . . . London. Printed for Joseph Moxon, . . . 1674. 4°, 4 leaves and the map.

Mechanick Exercises : Or, The Doctrine of Handy-Works. Applied to the Art of Smithing in General . . . The Second Edition with Additions. London, Printed and Sold by J. Moxon, at the Atlas in Warwick-Lane, 1693. 4°. A—I in fours, including the plates : Title and frontispiece to Numb. II., 2 leaves : K—L in fours : Title and Preface to Numb. III., 2 leaves : M—Ll in fours, with the plates sometimes counting in the sheets, and sometimes (with the separate titles) not. In R, T, Aa and Ii are two plates besides the separate title. Some of the titles are dated 1694.

MUGGLETON, LODOVICK.
The Interpretation of the Witch of Endor . . . By Lodowick Muggleton. London, Printed in the Year, 1669. 4°, A—P, 2 leaves each, P 2 blank.

MULCASTER, RICHARD, *first Head Master of Merchant Taylors' School.*
The Translation of certaine latine verses written vppon her Maiesties death, called A Comforting Complaint. This onely way I could declare my thankefull mind. Printed at London for Edward Aggas dwelling in long lane at the signe of the Oken tree. Anno Dom. 1603. 4°, A—B 2 in fours. *B. M.*

MULLINS, JAMES.
Some Observations Made upon the Cylonian Plant. Shewing its Admirable Virtues against Deafness. Written by a Physitian to the Honourable Esq; Boyle. London, Printed in the Year 1695. 4°, 4 leaves.

MUNDAY, ANTHONY.
The Admirable Deliverance of 266. Christians by Iohn Reynard Englishman from the captiuitie of the Turkes, who had

beene Gally slanes many yeares in Alexandria. . . . London Printed by Thomas Dawson, and are to be sold at the little shop at the Exchange. 1608. 4°, black letter. A—C in fours. *B. M.*

Licensed to T. Dawson and Stephen Peele, 23d July 1579.

The true reporte of the prosperous successe which God gaue vnto our English Souldiours against the forraine bands of our Romaine enemies, lately arined (but soone inough to theyr cost) in Ireland, in the yeare 1580. Gathered out of the Letters of moste credit and circumstance, that haue beene sent ouer, and more at large then in the former printed Copie . . . . Imprinted at London for Edward White. . . . [1581.] 4°, 4 leaves. With a cut on the title.

The English Romayne Lyfe. Discouering: The lines of the Englishmen at Roome: the orders of the English Seminarie: the dissention betweene the Englishmen and the welchmen: . . . . There vnto is added, the cruell tirranny. vsed on an English man at Rome, his Christian suffering, and notable Martirdome, for the Gospel of Iesus Christ, In Anno 1581. . . . Imprinted at London, by Iohn Charlwoode, for Nicholas Ling: dwelling in Paules Church-yarde. Anno. 1590. 4°, A—I in fours, besides the folded woodcut representing the execution of Richard Atkins at Rome.

Compare *Bibl. Coll.*, 1st Series, p. 15. Munday was doubtless the writer of the tract giving a separate account of the execution of Atkins, purporting to be sent in a letter from an English gentleman beyond the seas to his friend in London, 8°, 1581.

MUÑOZ, LUIS.

Vida Y Virtvdes de la Venerable Virgen Dõna Lvisa de Carvaial y Mendoça. Su jornada a Inglaterra, y successos en aquel Reyno. . . . En Madrid . . . Año M.DC.XXXII. 4°. Title, &c., 6 leaves: A—Ff in eights. With an engraved portrait of Dõna Luisa and poetry at the end.

MUNSTER, SEBASTIAN.

A treatyse of the newe India, with other new founde landes and Ilandes aswell eastwarde as westwarde, as they are knowen and found in these oure dayes, after the description of Sebastian Munster in his boke of vniuersall Cosmographie: wherin the diligent reader may see the good successe and rewarde of noble and honest enterpryses, . . . Translated out of Latin into Englishe. By Rycharde Eden. *Prater spem sub spe.* [Col.] . . . 1553. Imprinted

at London, in Lombarde strete, by Edward Sutton. 8°, aa, 8 leaves, and A—M 6 in eights. Dedicated by Eden to the Duke of Northumberland.

MURET, M.

Rites of Funeral Ancient and Modern, in Use through the Known World. Written originally in French by the Ingenious Monsieur Mvret. And Translated into English by P. Lorrain. London, Printed for Rich. Royston, . . . 1683. 8°. A, 6 leaves: B—T in eights: U, 2. Dedicated to the Honourable Samuel Pepys, Esq.

Inside the cover of this copy is the bookplate of the Earl of Oxford and Mortimer with *Henrietta Cavendish Holles. Given me by my Lord July.* 1732 added.

MURIELL, CHRISTOPHER, *the Elder.*

An Answer vnto the Catholiques Svpplication, Presented vnto the Kings Maiestie, . . . Wherein is contained a confutation of their vnreasonable petitions, . . . Written by Christopher Muriell tho elder. Imprinted at London by R. R. for Francis Burton, . . . 1603. 4°, A—D in fours, A 1 blank.

MURRELL, JOHN.

Mvrrels Two Books of Cookerie and Carving. The fifth time printed with new Additions. London, Printed by M. F. for Iohn Marriot, . . . 1638. 8°, black letter, A—N in eights. *B. M.*

Murrels Two Bookes of Cookerie and Carving. The seventh time printed, with new additions. London, Printed by Ja, Fl. for Rich. Marriot, . . . 1650. 8°, A—N in eights. *Patent Office.*

The dedication dated July 20, 1630, is still retained.

MUSÆ.

Musarum Anglicanarum Analecta. . . . Editio secunda priore multó Emendatior. Oxon. . . . M.DC.XCIX. 8°. 2 vols.

MUSGRAVE, CHRISTOPHER.

Mvsgraves Motives, and Reasons, For his Secession and Disseuering from the Chvrch of Rome and her Doctrine, after that hee had for 20. yeeres liued a Carthusian Monke, returning at Easter last into England. . . . At London, Imprinted by F. K. for Richard Moore, . . . 1621. 4°, A—F in fours, A 1 and F 4 blank. *B. M.*

MUSIC.

Certaine notes set forth in foure and three parts to be song at the morning Communion, and euening praier, very necessarie for the church of Christe to be frequented and vsed: & vnto them added diuers godly praiers & Psalmes in the like forme to the honor & praise of God. Imprinted at London ouer Aldersgate beneath S. Martins by John Day. 1560. Cum gratia . . . Folio. With the music.

The copy here used (Sothebys, July 1886, No. 1363, Simes Sale) was made up from the two issues of 1560 and 1565. *Collation :—Bassus*, A—T, 2 leaves each, A 2 misprinted A 3: *Medius, Tenor*, and *Contratenor*, the same.

Musicks Hand-maide Presenting New and Pleasant Lessons for the Virginals or Harpsycon. London, Printed for John Playford at his Shop in the Temple. 1663. Obl. 4". A—G in fours, besides the title with a beautiful engraving by Vaughan and the preface by Playford.

G 4 has only a list of books sold by Playford.

Musicks Recreation on the Viol, Lyraway. Being a new Collection of Lessons Lyra-way. To which is added a Preface, Containing some Brief Rules and Instructions for young Practitioners. London, Printed by W. Godbid, for John Playford, . . . 1669. 4", A—Q in fours. Obl. With a preface by Playford and a cut on the title.

Musicks Recreation . . . London, Printed by A. G. and J. P. for J. Playford, . . . 1682. 4", A—M in fours. With a cut on the title.

Musick: Or A Parley of Instruments. The First Part. London, Printed in the Year 1676. 4", A—B in fours, and a leaf to the Reader with a curious notice as to the piece. *B. M.*

N.

N. A.
Londons Improvement and the Builder's Security Asserted, By the Apparent Advantages that will attend their Easie Charge, in Raising such a Joint-Stock, as may assure a Re-building of those Houses, which shall hereafter be destroyed by the Calamities of Fire. As it was Presented on New-Years-Day last, 1679. to the Right Honourable, Sir Robert Clayton, Kt. the present Lord-Mayor. *Multorum manibus grande levatur Onus.* London, Printed for the Author, by Thomas Milbourn, in Jewen-Street, 1680. Folio, A—B, 2 leaves each.

N. C.
The Unfortunate Politique, First written in French By C. N. Englished by G. P. Oxford, Printed by L. Lichfield for Ioseph Godwin An. Dom. 1639. 8". †, 4 leaves: A—O 6 in eights.

I have seen this ascribed to N. Caussin.

N. E.
A Manval of Prayers newly gathered ovt of many and diuers famous Authours aswell auncient as of the time present. . . . More, certaine Litanies. Also The Iesvs Psalter with the Goulden Litanie. With a corrected Calendar. . . . Cvm Privilegio 1617. Small 8". ă and ŏ, 8 leaves each: A—Y 4 in eights: the *Jesus Psalter*, with a new title, dated 1618, A—E 4 in eights: Ee—Gg in eights.

At folio 75 back is a prayer by Sir Thomas More.

N. J.
A Perfect Catalogue of all the Knights of the Most Noble Order of the Garter. From the first Institution of it, untill this present April, Anno 1661. Whereunto is prefixed A short Discourse touching the Institution of the Order, the Patron, Habit and Solemnities of it, with many other Particulars which concern the same. Collected and continued by J. N. London: Printed for Anne Seile, . . . 1661. 4", A—E in fours.

The compiler states in the preface that the materials were lent to him by an abler hand.

N. N.
The Scarlet Gown, Or the History of all the present Cardinals of Rome. Wherein is set forth the Life, Birth, Interest, Possibility, rich Offices, Dignities, and charges of every Cardinal now living. . . . Written originally in Italian, and translated into English by H. C. Gent. London, Printed for Humphrey Moseley, . . . 1653. 8", A—M 4 in eights. Dedicated by Henry Cogan, the translator, to the Earl of Rutland.

N. N., *Gent.*
America: Or An exact Description of the West-Indies : More especially of those Provinces which are under the Dominion of the King of Spain. Faithfully repre-

sented by N. N. Gent. London, printed by Ric. Hodgkinsonne for Edw. Dod, ... 1655. 8°, A—Ii 3 in eights. Dedicated by the author to Mr. John Robinson, merchant of London. With a folded map.

N. R.

The Christians Manna. Or A Treatise of the most Blessed and Reuerend Sacrament of the Eucharist. Deuided into two Tracts. Written by a Catholike Deuine, ... Imprinted with Licence, Anno 1613. 4°. *—4 * in fours: A—Hh 2 in fours. Dedicated to James I. *B. M.*

N. S. D.

Lettre de Consolation a la Reine d'Angleterre, svr la mort dv Roy son Mary. Et ses dernieres paroles. A Paris, ... M.DC.XXXXIX. 4", 4 leaves subscribed *S. D. N.*

N. T.

The Disposition or Garnishments of the Sovle to receiue worthily the blessed Sacrament, deuided into Three discourses. ... At Antwerpe. Imprinted by Ioachim Trognesius. 1596. 8", A—Y 4 in eights, and y, 8 leaves between X and Y.

NAPIER, JOHN, *Lord Napier of Merchistoun.*

Rabdologiæ, Sev Nvmerationis per Virgulas Libri Dvo: Cum Appendice de expeditissimo Mvltiplicationis Promptvario. Quibus accessit & Arithmeticæ localis Liber vnvs. Authore, & inventore, Ioanne Nepero, Baronis Merchistoni, &c. Scoto. Edinbvrgi, Excudebat Andreas Hart, 1617. 12°. ¶, 6 leaves: A—G 6 in twelves. Dedicated to Alexander, Earl of Dunfermline.

NARRATION.

An Apologeticall Narration of Some Ministers Formerly Exiles in the Netherlands : Now Members of the Assembly of Divines ... London, Printed for Robert Dawlman. M.DC.XLIII. 4°, B—E in fours, besides title and a curious sort of imprimatur by Charles Herle.

> The ministers were T. Goodwin, Philip Nye, W. Bridge, J. Burroughs, and Sidrach Simpson.

NAUDE, GABRIEL.

The History of Magick By way of Apology, For all the Wise Men who haue unjustly been reputed Magicians, from the Creation, to the present Age. Written in French by G. Naudæus, Late Library-keeper to Cardinal Mazarin. ... Englished by J. Davies. Printed for John Streater, and are to be sold by the Booksellers of London, 1657. 8", A—X 2 in

eights. Dedicated by Davies to Sir Richard Combes, Kt.

NAVY.

A True Relation of the Very Good Service Done by the Antilope And some other ships, under the Earl of Warwicks Command at Barwicke, Newcastle, and the Holy Island, the latter end of May, and beginning of Iune last 1643. Faithfully expressed in a Letter from a Gentleman of Quality, who was in the Service, to a friend of his in London. London : July 4. Printed by Elizabeth Purslow, 1643. 4°, black letter, 4 leaves.

The Answer of the Commissioners of the Navie, To a scandalous Pamphlet, published by Mr Andrewes Burrell. Printed by Will. Bentley, Anno Dom. MDCXLVI. 4°, A—D in fours, and a leaf of E.

> In the commencement of this Reply it is said that the Narrative itself had only come to the notice of the Government "some days since ;" the Council of State, to which Burrell had dedicated his tract, or rather White's, was not in existence till 1649 ; and therefore it is to be presumed that the present Answer is misdated for 1649.

A Declaration of the Representations of the Officers of the Navy, Concerning the Suspected Members of Parliament, Transported beyond the Seas. With a Charge against some Officers, who had Commissions to raise Forces to disturbe the peace of the Kingdome. Also the Kings Majesties Protestation, Sent by Colonell Whaley. Printed at London by Robert Ibbitson, 1647. 4°, 4 leaves.

An Act of the Commons Assembled in Parliament Touching the Regulating of the Officers of the Navy & Customs, ... London, Printed for Edward Husband, ... Jan. 18. 1648. 4°, A—B in fours, B 4 blank.

A List of His Majesties Navy Royal, Hitherto designed in the present Expedition against the Dutch, with the Commanders names, number of Men and Guns, April 30. 1672. London, Printed by E. Crowch, for Thomas Vere ... 1672. A broadside.

Gloria Britannica : Or, The Boast of the Brittish Seas. Containing A True and Full Account of the Royal Navy of England, Shewing where each Ship was built, by whom, ... Together, with every Man's Pay ... London : Printed for Thomas Hawkins, ... 1689, ... 4°, 12 leaves, including a frontispiece.

The State of the Navy Consider'd in relation to the Victualling, Particularly in the Straits, and the West-Indies. With some Thoughts on the Mismanagements of the Admiralty for several years past ; and a Proposal to prevent the like for the future. Humbly offer'd to the Honourable House of Commons, by an English Sailor. London, Printed for A. Baldwin in Warwicklane, 1699. 4°, A—B in fours.

NEALE, THOMAS, *of Warneford, co. Southampton, Esquire.*

A Treatise of Direction, How to travell safely, and profitably into Forraigne Countries. [Quotation from Petronius.] London, Printed for Humphrey Robinson. 1643. 12°, A—H in twelves, A 1-2 and H 12 blank. Dedicated to his brother Mr. William Neale at Tours in France or elsewhere. With a portrait by Marshall.

NEEDHAM, MARCHAMONT.

A Discourse concerning Schools and School-Masters. Offered to Publick Consideration. By M. N. London, Printed for H. H. Anno Dom. 1663. 4°, A—B in fours, and a leaf of C.

The Excellencie of a Free State. London Printed for A. Millar and T. Cadell in the Strand . . . MDCCLXVII. 8°. Title and preface by Richard Baron, 2 leaves : a, 8 : b, 4 : pp. 1-176.

Putticks (Gosford), April 28, 1884, No. 2193, the Hollis copy.

NEEDLE.

A Schole-Hovse for the Needle : Teaching by sundry sortes of patterns and examples of different kindes, how to compose many faire workes ; with an addition, newly invented ; placed in the beginning of the second booke, which being set in order and form, according to the skill & vnderstanding of the work woman, will no doubt yeeld profit vnto such as liue by the Needle, and gine good content to adorne the worthy. London Printed in Sho-lane at the Faulcon, by Richard Shorleyker. 1624. Obl. 4°, A—Q in fours, besides a duplicate and varying title.

The second book on Cut-Works begins on K 3 with a separate title.

The Needles Excellency A New Booke wherin are diuers Admirable Workes wrought with the Needle Newly inuented and cut in Copper for the pleasure and profit of the Industrious. Printed for Iames Boler and are to be sold at the Signe of the Marigold in Paules Church-

yard. The 10th Edition inlarged wth diuers newe workes in needleworkes purles & others neuer before printed. 1634. Obl. 4°. Engraved title, 1 leaf : The Praise of the Needle, by John Taylor the water-poet, in verse, 4 leaves : 31 plates irregularly numbered.

The verses by Taylor consist of a series of poems celebrating the proficiency in this art of several noble ladies. Sothebys, March 2, 1886, No. 2007.
The work is introduced by a "Dialogue, betweene Diligence and Sloth," in verse, occupying five pages.

NEGESCHIUS, PETRUS.

Comparatio inter Clavdivm Tiberivm Principem, et Olivarivm Cromwellivm Protectorem. Excusa Typis Anno M. DC. LVII. A—D 2 in fours.

NELSON, THOMAS.

The Device of the Pageant : Set forth by the Worshipfull Companie of the Fishmongers, for the right honorable Iohn Allot : established Lord Maire of London, and Maire of the Staple for this present yeere of our Lord 1590. By T. Nelson. London, 1590. 4°, 4 leaves. Black letter. *B. M.*

Puttick & Simpson, December 18, 1885, No. 447, the same copy. There is no clue to the printer, and the tract appears almost to have been privately issued.

NERI, ANTONIO.

The Art of Glass, Wherein are shown the wayes to make and colour Glass, Pastes, Enamels, Inkes, and other Curiosities . . . Translated into English [by C. M.], with some Observations on the Author. Whereunto is added an account of the Glass Drops, made by the Royal Society, meeting at Gresham College. London, Printed by A. W. for Octavian Pulleyn, . . . MDCLXII. 8°. *Imprimatur*, title, and author's dedication, dated Florence, 6 Jan. 1611, 4 leaves : A—Aa in eights, Aa 8 blank.

Reprinted at Middle-Hill, folio, 1826.

NESBIT, E.

Caesars Dialogve or A Familiar Communication containing the first Institution of a subiect, in allegiance to his Soueraigne. Matth. 22. 21. *Giue therefore to Cæsar, the things which are Cæsars.* At London Printed by Thomas Purfoot. 1601. 8°, A—H in eights.

NESS, CHRISTOPHER.

The Signs of the Times : Or, Wonderful Signs of Wonderful times. Being A Faithful Collection and Impartial Relation of several Signs and Wonders, call'd properly Prodigies . . . By C. N. London, Printed for the Author. And Published by Langley Curtiss, . . . 1681. 4°, B—M 2 in fours, besides title and preface. With cuts on the back of the title.

NETHERLANDS.

A declaration and publication of the most worthy Prince of Orange, contaynyng the cause of his necessary defence against the Duke of Alba. Translated out of French into English, and cōpared by other copies in diuers languages . . . Imprinted at London by Iohn Day, beneath S. Martins ouer Aldersgate. [1568.] 8°, A—B 3 in eights. *B. M.*

A Defence and true declaration of the thinges lately done in the lowe countrey, whereby may easily be seen in whom all the beginning and cause of the late troubles and calamities is to be imputed. And therewith also the sclaunders wherewith tho adversaries do burden the Churches of the lowe countrey are plainly confuted . . . At London. Printed by Iohn Daye. [About 1575.] 8°, A—H in eights, besides 10 leaves with the preface directed to Lord Cheyne by Elias Newcomen. *B. M.*

A Treatise of the peace made and concluded between the states of the lowe Countries, assembled within the Citie of Brvxels, and the Prince of Orange, the States of Holland and Zeland, with the associates, published the viij. day of Nouember. 1576. With the agreement and confirmatiō of the kings maiestie, as followeth. Translated out of a dutch copy printed in Brvxels by the Kings Printer, with the said Kings Priuiledge. Imprinted at London by William Broome. [1577.] 8°, A—E in fours. *B. M.*

The miserie of Antwerpe : With the Troubles that are (at this instant) in Flaunders, and many other Townes in the Lowe Countries, by meanes of the Prince of Parmas power : who by violent force seekes to oppresse and depriue the Inhabitants there, both of life and goodes. Herein is also described the maner of the Bridge and Fortresses . . . Written by an English Gentleman in Flaunders, to a friend of his in England, as appeareth by his Letter hereunto annexed : Dated the 21. of Iuly last. Anno Domini. 1585. 4°, black letter, 4 leaves. With a cut on the title.

> Dedicated "To my approued good friend Maister Iames Iennings Citizen of London." There is no printer's name.

Newes sent to the Ladie Princesse of

Orange. Translated out of French into English by I. E. London Printed by Iohn Wolfe. 1589. 4°, 4 leaves. *B. M.*

The Second Admonition, Sent by the subdued Prouinces to Holland, thereby to entice them by faire-seeming means, groundlesse threates, and vnlike examples to make peace with the Spaniards. With the Hollanders answere to the same. Translated out of Dutch into English by H. W. London Imprinted by Iohn Wolfe, . . . 1598. 4°, black letter, A—D in fours. *B. M.*

A True Report of all the proceedinges of Grave Mavris before the Towne of Bercke : With all the accidentes that happened in the besiedge of the same, since the .12. day of Iune last. 1601. and lastly, the yeelding vp of the Towne on the 30. of Iuly following, with the conditions . . . Translated out the Dutch Coppie printed at Amsterdam. Imprinted at London for William Iones, dwelling at Holborne Conduit, at the signe of the Gunne. 1601. 4°, A—C 2 in fours.

A Proclamation or Edict. Touching the Opening and restoring of the Traffique, and Commerce of Spain, with these Countries : Although they haue seuered themselues from the obeisance of the Illustrious Arch-Duke, As also with all Vassals and Subiects of Princes and Common-weales, being their friends, or Neutrals. Faithfully Translated out of the Nether-landish tongue according to [a] printed Copy. Imprinted at Brussels. Imprinted at London for Thomas Archer . . . 1603. 4°, black letter, A—C in fours.

The Trve Historie of the Memorable Siege of Ostend, and what passed on either side, from the beginning of the Siege, vnto the yeelding vp of the Towne. Conteining the Assaults, Alarums, Defences, Inuentions of water, Mines, . . . And also what passed in the Ile of Cadsant, and at the siege of Sluice, after the comming of Count Maurice. Translated out of French into English, By Edward Grimeston. At London Printed for Edward Blount. 1604. 4°, A—Gg 3 in fours (A repeated) and a plan of the siege works. Dedicated to the Earl of Devonshire.

Articles of Agreement, concerning the cessation of Warre, betweene the Archduke and the States of the vnited Prouinces. Procured by a Fryar, called Iohn of Nees, Confessour to the Arch-duke and the Infanta. Wherunto is annexed the state of other things happened about the same time. With Warres Testament, or his last Will, made at his departure out of the said Netherlands [in 6-line stanzas.] Translated out of the Dutch. Imprinted at London for Thomas Archer, . . . 1607. 4°, A—C in fours. *B. M.*

Articles, Of A Treatie of Tryce Made and concluded in the Towne and Citie of Antwerp, the 9. of April 1609, betweene the Commissioners of the most excellent Princes, Arch-dukes Albert and Isabella Clara Eugenia . . . together with the Commissioners and Deputies of the renowmed Lords, the Estates Generall of the Vnited Prouinces of the Low-countryes . . . . London Printed for George Potter and Nicholas Browne . . . . 1609. 4°, A—C in fours, A 1 and C 4 blank.

A translation from the Dutch.

An Edict or Proclamation, published by the States generall of the vnited Prouinces, touching an order by them prescribed, how all Jesuits, Priests and Monkes of the Popish, or Romish. Religion (that are within or hereafter shall come into the said vnited Prouinces) shall behaue themselues. Withall, prohibiting all their Subiects from binding themselues by Oath or otherwise, to maintaine and vphold the power and authoritie of the Pope of Rome, . . . Giuen at the Hage the 27. of March Anno. 1612. London Printed by E. A. for Thomas Archer . . . . 1612. 4°, A—B in fours. Black letter. *B. M.*

Newes of the Netherlands. Relating the Whole State of those Countries at this present. At London, Imprinted by Felix Kyngston, for Edward Marchant. 1615. 4°, A—D 2 in fours. *B. M.* (imperfect.)

A Description of the Prosperitie, Strength, and Wise Government of the vnited Prouinces of the Netherlands. Signified by the Batavian Virgin, in her seat of vnitie. Wherein is related the whole state of those countries at this present time. At London, Imprinted by Felix Kyngston, for Edward Marchant. 1615. 4°, A—D 2 in fours, A 1 blank. With some curious verses at the end.

A Vision or Dreame Conteyning the whole State of the Netherland warres, as it appeared to a louer of the Netherlands lying in his bed, vpon the 7. of Nouember, betweene 3. and 4. of the clocke of the morning, wherein was represented vnto him a goodly Country, and therein a fayre comely Horse well brideled and

sadled, whereat being much amazed, he sayde, Behold the Horse, but where is the Rider ? . . . Imprinted at London for Edward Marchant. 1615. 4°, A—F in fours. In prose and verse. English and Dutch. *B. M.*

On E is a new title : " A Short and faithfull Narration from certaine Citizens of note of the Towne of Goch, concerning the abhominable and wicked Treasons attempted and concluded by eighteene persons to haue beene executed vpon the Townes of Goch, Cleef, Emmeryck, and Rees, Discouered by Gods prouidence the last of Februarie. 1615. At London Printed 1615 ; " and on F a third title with the same narrative in Dutch. The volume concludes with the Ten Commandments given by Paul V. to the Marquis Spinola in English and Dutch verse.

Newes out of Holland : Concerning Barnevelt and his fellow-Prisoners their Conspiracy against their Natiue Country, with the Enemies thereof : . . . Wherevnto is adioyned a Discourse, wherein the Duke D'Espernons revolt and pernicious deseignes are truely displayed, and reprehended by one of his Friends. London : Printed by T. S. for Nathanael Newbery, . . . 1619. 4°, A—D 2 in fours. *B. M.*

The Arraignment of John van Olden Barneuelt late Aduocate of Holland and West-Friesland. Containing the Articles alleadged against him, and the reasons of his execution, being performed vpon the 13. of May Anno 1619. *Stilo Nouo.* In the inner Court of the Grauen Hage in Holland. Together with a Letter written by the Generall States, vnto the particular Vnited Prouinces, concerning the foresaid action. . . . London, Printed by Edward Griffin for Ralph Rounthwait . . . 1619. 4°, A—F in fours, A 1 and F 4 blank. *B. M.*

An Oration Made at the Hage, before the Prince of Orange, and the Assembly of the High and Mighty Lords, the States Generall of the Vnited Prouinces. By the Reuerend Father in God, the Lord Bishop of Landaff, one of the Commissioners sent by the Kings most Excellent Maiesty to the Synod of Dort. London, Printed by G. P. for Ralph Rounthwaite, . . . 1619. 4°, A—B in fours, title on A 2.

The Ivdgement of the Synode Holden at Dort, Concerning the fiue Articles : As also their sentence touching Conradvs Vorstivs. . . . London Printed by Iohn Bill. M.DC.XIX. 4°. Title and following leaf : B—Q in fours.

A translation from the Latin.

Orders and Articles Granted by the High and Mighty Lords the States General of the Vnited Provinces. Concerning the erecting of a West India Companie : Together with the priuiledges and rights giuen vnto the same. Printed Anno Dom. M.DC.XXI. 4°, A—B in fours, and a leaf of C. *B. M.*

A Relation of some speciall points concerning the State of Holland. Or The Provident Counsellour's Companion. By many reasons shewing, why for the good and security of the Netherland vnited Prouinces warre is much better then peace. . . . Printed at the Hage by Aert Muris Booke-seller, in the Pape-streat at the signe of the Bible. 1621. 4°, A—C in fours. *B. M.*

Observations Concerning the Present Affaires of Holland and the Vnited Provinces, Made by an English Gentleman there lately resident, & since written by himselfe from Paris, to his friend in England. Printed Anno M.DC.XXI. 8°, A—I 2 in eights. *B. M.*

Observations . . . The second Edition. Augmented with diuers new Chapters, and in some few places also corrected, By the Author of the first Edition. Printed Anno M.DC.XXII. 8°, 8 prel. leaves and A—O 4 in eights. *B. M.*

More Excellent Observations of the Estate and Affaires of Holland. In a discourse, shewing how necessarie and conuenient it is for their neighbouring Countries, as well as the Netherland Prouinces, to trade into the West Indies. . . . Faithfully Translated out of the Dutch Copie. Printed at London by E. A. for Nicholas Bourne and Thomas Archer, . . . 1622. 4°, A—E in fours. *B. M.*

The Hollanders Declaration of the affaires of the East Indies. Or A Trve Relation of that which passed in the Hands of Banda, in the East Indies : In the yeare of our Lord God, 1621. and before. Faithfully translated according to the Dutch Copie. Printed at Amsterdam. 1622. 4°, A—B in fours, A 1 blank.

> I suspect this to be the *News out of Holland*, licensed 24th June 1622. Compare *Bibl. Coll. and Notes*, 2d Series, p. 418.

An Answere to the Hollanders Declaration, concerning the Occurrents of the East-India. The First Part. Written by certaine Marriners, lately returned from thence into England. Printed 1622. 4°, A—D in fours. *B. M.*

A Iovrnall or Daily Register of all those warlike Atchieuements which happened in the Siege of Berghen-vp-Zoome in the Low-countries, betweene the Armies of the Marquesse Spinola Asseylante, and the Prince of Orange, Defendants, of the said Towne, together with the raising of the Siege, . . . All faithfully translated out of the originall Low-Dutch Copie. London, Printed for Nathaniel Butter, Bartholomew Downes, and Thomas Archer. 1622. 4°, A—E in fours. *B. M.*

A Ioynt Attestation, Avowing that the Discipline of the Church of England was not impeached by the Synode of Dort. London, Printed by M. Flesher for R. Mylbourne, . . . 1626. 4°, A—D in fours, first and last leaves blank.

Three Severall Treatises Concerning the Trvce at this present propounded. . . . All truly and faithfully Translated out of the Low-Dutch Copie. London Printed for Nathaniel Butter and Nicholas Bourne. 1630. 4°, A—D in fours, A 1 blank.

Lawes and Ordinances touching military discipline. Set downe and established the 13. of August. 1590. Translated into English by I. D. Imprinted at the Haghe by the widowe & heires of the deceased Hillebrand Iacobs van Wouw, . . . 1631. 4°, A—B in fours, B 4 blank. *B. M.*

Observations upon the Prince of Orange and the States of Holland. [London, about 1641.] 4", A—B in fours.

A Remonstrance presented to the High and Mighty Lords the States of Zealand by the Deputies of the foure Classes of Zealand. Concerning the Welfare of the Church of England. Sent over by Walter Strickland Esquire, now in Holland, Imployed for the Affaires of the Parliament. . . . May 29. London, Printed by R. Oulton, Anno Dom. 1643. 4°, 4 leaves.

A Discourse of a true English-man, Free from Selfe-interest, concerning the interest England hath in the Siege of Graveling. Printed at London for Thomas Walkley. 1644. 4°, 4 leaves.

Severall Apparitions Scene in the Ayre, at the Hague in Holland, upon the $\frac{3}{13}$ day of May last past 1646, about one of the clocke of the Afternoone. . . . London, Printed by T. Forcet, . . . 1646. 4°, 4 leaves.

A Seasonable Expostulation with the Netherlands Declaring their Ingratitude to, and the Necessity of their Agreement with the Commonwealth of England. London, Printed by James Moxon, 1652. 4°, A—B in fours.

A Particular Relation Sent from Sluys in the Low-Countries, touching a Monster there lately born, attested by persons of quality and learning. London, Printed for Tho. Newcomb living in Thames-street, near Baynards Castle. [1658.] A 4° leaf. *B. M.*

A Memorial Delivered to His Majesty (July ³¹⁄₃₁ 1664) from the Lord Vangogh, Ambassador from the States General of the United Provinces. Translated into English. With the Answer which His Sacred Majesty returned thereunto. London, Printed by J. G. for R. Royston, ... 1664. 4", A—B in fours.

> The ambassador's memorial is dated from Chelsea.

The Dutch Remonstrance concerning the Proceedings and Practices of John De Witt Pensionary, and Rywaert van Pythen his Brother, with others of that faction. Drawn up by a Person of Eminency there, and Printed at the Hague. And Translated out of Dutch, August the 30ᵗʰ 1672. London Printed by S. and B. G. and are to be sold by R. O.... [1672.] 4°, A—E 2 in fours.

The Interest of these United Provinces. Being A Defence of the Zeelanders Choice. ... Together with Severall Remarkes upon the present, and Conjectures on the future State of Affaires in Europe, especially as relating to this Republick. By a wellwisher to the Reformed Religion, and the welfare of these Countries. Middelburg, Printed by Thomas Berry, ... 1673. 4°, A—Q 2 in fours, but 2 leaves only in A.

Two Royal Achrostichs on the Dutch in the Ditch. A broadside in verse.

The Answer of the States Generall of the United Provinces of the Low Countreys, to the Declaration of Warr of the King of Great Brittain. Published by Your Lordships order. Hague Anno 1674. 4°, A—E in fours.

Hogan-Moganides: Or, The Dutch Hudibras

Hor. Ser. 1.
——Ridentum [*sic*] dicere verum
Quis vetat?—
London, Printed for William Cademan, ... 1674. 8", A—H in eights.

A Declaration of War of the States General of the United Provinces against the King of Sweden. Translated out of Dutch.

In the Savoy: Printed by Tho. Newcomb. 1675. Folio, 4 leaves.

A Letter from an Eminent Merchant in Ostend, Containing an Account of a Strange and Monstrous Birth hapned there, A Woman being brought to Bed of two Children, which are joined together by the Crowns of their Heads. He being an Eye-Witness thereof. London, Printed for J. Staus, and sold by R. Janeway, 1680. A folio leaf with an engraving separate. *B. M.*

An Extract of the Registers of the Resolutions of the High and Mighty Lords, the States General of the United Provinces of the Netherlands. Thursday the 14ᵗʰ October. 1688. A folio leaf.

A Letter to the Author of the Dutch Design, Anatomized. Written by a Citizen of London, for the Promoting of His Majesties Service. [November the 8ᵗʰ, 1688.] Folio, 2 leaves.

An Account of the Reasons which Induced Charles II. King of England to declare War against the States-General of the United Provinces in 1672. And of the Private league which he entred into at the same Time with the French King to carry it on. And to Establish Popery in England, Scotland, & Ireland. ... London, Printed for Richard Baldwin, ... MDCLXXXIX. Folio, A—E, 2 leaves each, including *Imprimatur.*

An Account of the Passages in the Assembly of the States of Holland and West-Friezeland. Concerning the Earl of Portland's Exclusion from, or Admission into that Assembly. Translated out of Dutch, ... London: Printed, and are to be Sold by Richard Baldwin. ... MDCXC. 4", A—C 2 in fours.

The Delights of Holland: Or, A Three Months Travel about that and the other Provinces. With Observations and Reflections on their Trade ... Together with a Catalogue of the Rarities in the Anatomical School at Leyden. By William Mountague, Esq; London, Printed for John Sturton, ... and A. Bosvile, ... 1696. 8°. A, 4 leaves: B—Q in eights.

The True Interest and Political Maxims of the Republick of Holland and West-Friesland. In Three Parts. ... Written by John De Witt, and other Great Men in Holland. Published by the Authority of the States. London, Printed in the Year MDCCII. 8". A, 8 leaves, title on A 2: a—c 4 in eights:

B—Ii 6 in eights. With a portrait of John de Witt, the back of which has the half-title.

An Exact Relation of the Strange and Vncommon Sleepy Distemper of Dirk Klasz Bakker of Stolwyk, not far from Rotterdam, who slept from the Thirteenth of July, 1706, to the Eleventh of January, 1707, without any Intermission, . . . [Col.] London, Printed : And Sold by John Morphew . . . 1707. (Price 1d.) 4°, 4 leaves. *B. M.*

NEW ENGLAND.

A Proportion of Provisions needfvll for svch as intend to plant themselves in New-England, for one whole yeare. Collected by the Adventurers, with the Advice of the Planters. Printed at London for Fvlke Cliftou. 1630. A broadside. *B. M.*

A Platform of Church-Discipline : Gathered out of the Word of God, and agreed upon by the Elders and Messengers of the Church assembled in the Synod at Cambridge in New-England : . . . Reprinted in London for Peter Cole . . . 1655. 4°. Title and Edw. Winslow's dedication, 2 leaves: B—F in fours.

The Secret Workes of a Cruel People made manifest ; whose little finger is become heavier then their Persecutors the bishops Loyns, who have set up an Image amongst them in New-England, ... London, Printed in the Year 1659. 4°, A—C in fours, besides the title.

A True Account of the Most Considerable Occurrences that have hapned in the Warre between the English and the Indians in New-England, from the Fifth of May, 1676, to the Fourth August last ; as also of the Successes it hath pleased God to give the English against them : As it hath been communicated by Letters to a Friend in London. The most Exact Account yet Printed. . . . London, Printed for Benjamin Billingsley at the Printing-Press in Cornhill, 1676. Folio, A—C, 2 leaves each.

A New and Further Narrative of the State of New-England, Being A Continued Account of the Bloudy Indian-War, from March till August, 1676. Giving a Perfect Relation of the Several Devastations, Engagements, and Transactions there ; . . . Together with a Catalogue of the Losses in the whole, sustained on either side, since the said War began, . . . London, Printed by J. B. for Dorman New-

man . . . 1676. Folio, A—D, 2 leaves each.

NEWFOUNDLAND.

Considerations on the Trade to Newfoundland. [Col.] London : Printed for Andrew Bell, at the Cross-Keys and Bible in Cornhill. Price 2d. [About 1695.] Folio, 2 leaves.

NEWMARKET.

A Tragi-Comedy, called New-Market-Fayre. Or A Parliament Out-Cry of State-Commodities, Set to Sale. The Prologue sung by the Cryer . . . Printed as you may goe look. 1649. 4°, 4 leaves.

NEWS.

Newes lately come on the last day of Februarie 1591. from diuers partes of France, Sauoy, and Tripoli in Soria. Truely translated out of the French Italian Copies, as they were sent to right Honourable persons. London Printed by Iohn Wolfe, ... 1591. 4°, black letter, 4 leaves. With a cut of St. George and the Dragon on the back of the title.

True newes from Mecare and also Out of Worcestershire. Printed at London for William Barley. [1598.] 4°, 4 leaves. Black letter, with a cut occupying nearly the whole title-page.

The date on the title has probably been cut off in the copy used.

The 23. of May. Weekely Newes from Italy, Germania, Hvngaria, Bohemia, the Palatinate, France, and the Low Countries. Translated out of the Low Dutch Copie. London, Printed by I. D. for Nicholas Bourne and Thomas Archer. . . . 1622. 4°, 4 leaves. *B. M.*

The 30. of May. Weekly Newes from Italy, Germanie, Hvngaria, . . . Translated out of the Low Dutch Copie. London : Printed by E. A. for Nicholas Bourne and Thomas Archer. . . . 1622. 4°, 4 leaves. *B. M.*

The 18. of Iune. Weekely Newes from Italy, Germanie, . . . with a strange accident hapning about and in the City of Z tta in Lusatia. Translated out of the High Dutch Copie. London Printed by I. D. for Nathaniel Newbery and William Sheffard, . . . 1622. 4°, 4 leaves. *B. M.*

The Safe Arrivall of Christian Dvke of Brvnswick vnto the King of Bohemia, and the Vniting of their Forces. With a Particvlar Rehersall of Divers Notable Passages and Accidents, as well after as before the Battaile betwixt the aforesaid Dvke and the Imperiall . . . Printed this third of Iuly. London, Printed by I. D. for Nicholas Bourne and Thomas Archer, . . . 1622. 4°, A—C in fours, A 1 and C 4 blank. *B. M.*

The Svrprisall of Two Imperiall Townes by Covnt Mansfield, and the Dvke of Brvnswicke, since the arrivall of Count Mansfeild ; vntill this present the nineteenth of Iuly 1622. Likewise Relating the conragions Sally, and great slaughter made by the English Garrisons in Bergen op Zoone, vpon Spinolas New come English Gallants, having newly layd Siege to the same, . . . London Printed by I. D. for Nicholas Bourne and Thomas Archer, . . . 1622. 4°, A—C in fours, A 1 and C 4 blank. *B. M.*

The Ninth of September. 1622. Covnt Mansfields Proceedings since the last Battaile, with the Great Misfortune which hath lately hapned to the Duke of Brunswicke. With the Great Victory obtained by the Protestants in France, by those of the Towne of Mompeliers against the Kings Forces, . . . Also Relating another Skirmish, which happened betweene Covnt Mansfield and Dom Cordua in the Prouince of Henego [and various other items of current intelligence relating to the struggle in North and South Germany.] London Printed by E. A. for Nicholas Bourne and Thomas Archer . . . 1622. 4°, A—C in fours. *B. M.*

The 27. of September. A Relation of Letters, and other aduertisements of Newes, sent hither vnto such as correspond with friends beyond the Sea. From Rome, Italy, Spaine, France, the Palatinate, and diuers other places. . . . With the lamentable Massacre committed in the Valtoline. Vnto which is added, A Letter from an English Gentleman at Frankford, concerning the render of Heidlebergh to the Enemie. London, Printed for Nathaniel Butter, and Thomas Archer. 1622. 4°, A—C in fours, C 4 blank. *B. M.*

The 25. of September. Newes from Most Parts of Christendome. Especially from Rome, Italy, Spaine, France, the Palatinate, the Low Countries, and diuers other places. . . . With the lamentable losse of the City of Heidlebergh, . . . London, Printed for Nathaniel Butter, and William Sheffard. 1622. 4°, A—C in fours, A 1 and C 4 blank. *B. M.*

The 4. of Octob: 1622. A Trve Relation of the Affaires of Europe, especially, France, Flanders, and the Palatinate . . .

Together with a second ouerthrow giuen the French Kings forces at Mompelier, . . . Last of all, the remoue of the famous siedge before Bergen, vpon the 22. of September last, with the retreat of Spinola to Antwerp, . . . London, Printed for Nathaniel Butter, and Nicholas Bourne. 1622. 4°, A—E in fours, E 4 blank, and the title. *B. M.*

October 15. 1622. Numb. 1. A Relation of the late Occurrents which haue happened in Christendome, especially at Rome, Venice, Spaine, France, and the vpper Germanie. . . . London, Printed by B. A. for Nathaniel Butter, and Nicholas Bourne. 1622. 4°, A—C in fours, A 1 blank. *B. M.*

October 15. 1622. N° 2. A Continvation of the Affaires of the Low-Countries, and the Palatinate, wherein you shall see what hath beene done since the siege of Bergen. The Oration which his Excellencie the Prince of Orange made to the Gouernors, Colonels, and Captaines of Bergen-vpzon, vpon the remoue of the siege. . . . London, Printed for Nathaniel Butter, and Barth. Downes. 1622. 4°, A—C in fours. *B. M.*

October 30. 1622. N° 4. A Continvation of the Weekly Newes from Bohemia, Austria, the Palatinate, Italy, Spaine, France, the Low-Countries, and the East-Indies. . . . As also the true and last Newes of the present Estate of Manheim, and the Generall Veere. . . . London, Printed for Nathaniel Butter, and Barth. Downes. 1622. 4°, A—C in fours. *B. M.*

November 5. 1622. Numb. 5. A Continvation of the Newes . . . The Trve Copie of the Proclamation of the peace in France, translated into English. The preparations of the German Princes to meete the Emperour at the Dyet of Regenspurg: The present estate of Manhem and Frankendale. The discontents of the Grisons. Count Mansfeilds march vp towards Westphalia . . . London, Printed for Bartholomew Downes, and Thomas Archer. 1622. 4°, A—C in fours. *B. M.*

Nouem. 7. 1622. Numb. 6. A Coranto. Relating Divers Particvlars concerning the Newes ovt of Italy, Spaine, Turkey, Persia, Bohemia, Sweden, Poland, Austria, the Pallatinate, the Grisons, and diuers places of the Higher and Lower Germanie. Printed for Nathaniel Butter, Nicholas Bourne, and William Sheffard. 1622. 4°, A—C in fours. *B. M.*

Nouemb. 16. 1622. Numb. 7. A Continvation of the Newes of this present Weeke. Wherein are fully related, the going of the Emperour and the Princes of Germany, to the Dyet of Regenspurgh, with the Imperiall Gists. The Embassage of Bethlem Gabor, . . . Together with the Articles granted to Generall Veere, vpon yeelding vp of Manheim Castle. And a particular Iournall of Count Mansfields proceedings in the Bishopricke of Munster, with some other Occurrences. London, Printed for Nathaniel Butter, Nicholas Bourne, and William Sheffard. 1622. 4°, A—C in fours. *B. M.*

Nouemb. 21. 1622. Numb. 8. A Continuation of the former Newes. Wherein is related the discontents of the Duke of Saxony, for the ill vsage of the Protestant Ministers, in Bohemia, Morauia, Silesia, &c. With the present troubles of the Churches of those Countries. Together with a large story of the present distresse of the Grisons, . . . As also the names of those English Captains and Lieutenants, which came out from Manheim, . . . London, Printed for Nathaniel Butter, . . . 1622. 4°, A—C in fours. *B. M.*

Nouemb. 28. Numb. 9. Briefe Abstracts ovt of Diverse Letters of Trvst. Relating the Newes of this present Weeke, out of Persia, Egypt, Babylon, Barbary, Turkey, Italy, Spaine, Germanie, Silesia, France, and the Low Countries, with diuers passages from Sea. . . . London, Printed by B. A. for Nathaniel Butter, . . . 1622. 4°, A—C in fours, A 1 and C 4 blank. *B. M.*

> This series of News-Letters forms part of the Burney Collection in the British Museum; there are several others similar, of later as well as earlier date, describing periodically the affairs of Europe. This particular volume appears to have been formed by John Robinson, whose autograph is on the titles of most of the pieces, at the time; he is well known as having been formerly the owner of some of the rarest volumes in Early English Literature.

Strange and Lamentable News from Dullidg-Wells: Or, The Cruel and Barbarous Father . . . Together with an Account of Another Sad Accident that lately happened at Bromly by Bow, . . . London: Printed for D. M. 1678. 4°, 4 leaves.

> The first case relates to a man who cried Dulwich water in the streets of London, and who killed his own son.

NEWSMONGER.
The Compleat News-Monger: Being I. True News from the Church, but little in it. II. Sad News from the Court, but nothing in it. III. Strange News from the Bed, and there's something in it . . . London: Printed by Edward Midwinter, at the Star in Pye-Corner, near West-Smithfield. 4°, 4 leaves.

NEWTON, ROBERT.
The Covntesse of Movntgomeries Ersebia: Expressing briefly, The Sovles Praying Robes. Printed at London by George Purslow, for A. G. 1620. 12°, A—G 6 in twelves, G 6 blank. Dedicated to Mary, Countess of Pembroke, &c. *B. M.* (the Bliss copy.)

NEW YORK.
The Laws & Acts of the General Assembly for their Majesties Province of New-York, As they were enacted in divers Sessions, the first of which began April, the 9th, Annoq; Domini. 1691. At New-York, Printed and Sold by William Bradford, Printer to their Majesties, King William & Queen Mary, 1694. Folio, A—X, 2 leaves each, besides the title and Table: *Catalogue of Fees*, dated 1693, A—C, 2 leaves each.

Acts of Assembly, Passed in the Province of New-York, from 1691, to 1718. London, Printed by John Baskett, . . . MDCCXIX. Folio. a—d, 2 leaves each: A—4 D, 2 leaves each.

By His Excellency Richard Earl of Bellomont, Captain General and Governour in Chief of His Majesties Province of New-York, and Territories depending thereon in America, and Vice-Admiral of the same, &c. Printed by W. Bradford, Printer to the King's most excellent Majesty in New-York, 1699. A broadside.

His Excellency, The Earl of Bellomont His Speech to the Representatives of his Majesties Province of New-York, the 21th of March, 1699. [Col.] Printed and Sold by William Bradford, Printer to the King's most Excellent Majesty, in the City of New-York, 1699. Folio, 2 leaves.

NICLAES, HENDRICK.
The Prophetie of the Spirit of Love. Setfourth by H. N. And by him perused a-new / and most distinctlie declared. Translated out of Base-almayne into English. [Quotations.] Anno. 1574. 8°, A—E in eights, E 8 with an emblematical cut and verses only.

> This and the next were probably printed in Holland.

A Publishing of the Peace vpon Earth / and of the gratious Tyme and acceptable yeere of our Lorde / which is now in the last tyme & out of the Peace of Iesu Christ / and out of his holie Spirit of Loue ; published by H. N. on the Earth. . . . Translated out of Base-almayne into English . . . Anno 1574. 8°, 8 leaves.

NICODEMUS.

Nychodemus gospell. [This title is over a woodcut in a border of pieces with the printer's initials at the foot of the page. At the end occurs :] Thus endeth Nychodemus gospell / Imprynted at London in saynt Leonardes parysshe in Foster Lane by me Iohñ Skot. 4°. A, 6 leaves : B—F in fours. With the last page occupied by the printer's device. With woodcuts.

Sothebys, June 27, 1885, No. 825, Heber's copy, bought by him at Forster's Sale in 1806 for £2, 12s. 6d. It had been Herbert's ; yet the latter has not described it in his edition of *Ames*, though it may be this undated one indicated at p. 318.

Nicodemvs His Gospel. Imprinted, 1646. 8°, A—E in eights.

NICOLS, THOMAS.

Gemmarivs Fidelis, Or The Faithful Lapidary, Experimentally describing the richest Treasures of Nature in an Historical Narration of the severall Natures, Vertues and Qualities of all Pretious Stones. With an Accurate discovery of such as are Adulterate and Counterfeit. By T. N. of J. C. in Cambridge . . . London, Printed for Henry Marsh, . . . 1659. 4°.

A new title to the stock of 1652.

NILE.

A short Relation of the River Nile, Of its Sourse and Current. Of its Overflowing the Campagnia of Ægypt, till it runs into the Mediterranean : And of other Curiosities : Written by an Eye-witnesse, who lived many years in the chief Kingdoms of the Abyssine Empire. London. Printed for John Martyn, . . . 1669. 8°, A—G in eights, besides 2 leaves with dedication by Sir Peter Wyche, at whose desire it was translated out of a Portuguese MS., to Henry, Lord Arlington.

NIXON, ANTHONY.

A True Relation of the Trauels of M. Bush a gentleman : who with his owne handes without any other mans helpe made a Pynace, in which hee past by Ayr, Land, and Water : from Lamborne, a place in Bark-shire, to the Custom house Key in London. 1607. London printed by T. P. for Nathaniel Butter. 1608. 4°, black letter, A, 2 leaves : B—

E in fours. With the preface signed by A[nthony] N[ixon.]

Osterley Park Sale, 1885, No. 321.

NOAH.

An Historical Treatise of the Travels of Noah into Europe : Containing the first inhabitation and peopling thereof. As also a briefe recapitulation of the Kings, Governors, and Rulers commanding in the same, . . . Done into English by Richard Lynche, Gent. *Tempo è figliuola di verita.* London Printed by Adam Islip. 1601. 4°, A—O 2 in fours, A 1 blank. Dedicated to Peter Manwood in affectionate terms by the translator.

NOBLENESS.

The Boke of Noblenes. That sheweth how many sortes & kindes there is. And specially to those whiche do folowe and vse the trayne and estate of warre. translated out of laten into Englisshe, by me John Larke. [London, Robert Wyer, about 1550.] 8°, A—H in eights, H 8 presumedly with the colophon. Woodcut on title.

The present was Herbert's copy, and appears to want only the last leaf.

NONCONFORMIST.

The True Non-Conformist In Answere to the Modest and free Conference betwixt a Conformist and a Non-Conformist, about the present Distempers of Scotland. By a Lover of Truth, And Published by its Order. . . . Printed [abroad] in the Year 1672. 8°. *, 8 leaves : A—Ii in eights, Ii 7-8 blank.

NORTH, FRANCIS DUDLEY, *Third Lord North of Kirtling.*

A Forest of Varieties . . . 1645.

On an examination of Park's copy of this book, afterward in the Bindley, Heber, and Currer Collections, I find that it contains, immediately after the title, a dedication to Elizabeth of Bohemia, and two leaves at the end described in the Currer Catalogue as cancelled. On one of these latter occurs : " A Register of Mournful Verses on a Melting Beauty." That copy resembled another before me in having MSS. notes in a coeval hand, probably the author's, and on the title, under the word *Varieties*, " Or rather a Wildernesse." The copy which I am using has on the title also FRA. NORTH, written, I conclude, by the same person. But I am of opinion that the book was printed for friends, and that Lord North made corrections, and even wrote his name, in several copies ; so that it is one of those cases in which it is almost impossible to arrive at knowing which was the author's own copy.

NORTH, DUDLEY, *Lord North.*

The City of London's Loyal Plea : Or, A

M *

Rational stating the Case concerning the Election of Sheriffs for the City of London and County of Middlesex. Read seriously, judge not rashly. London, Printed for Randal Taylor near Stationers Hall. 1682. Folio, 4 leaves.

Light in the Way to Paradise: With other Occasionals. . . . By Dvdley the 2ᵈ late Lᵈ North. London, Printed for William Rogers. . . . 1682. 8°. A, 4 leaves: B—K 4 in eights.

Discourses upon Trade ; Principally Directed to the Cases of the Interest, Coynage, Clipping, Increase of Money. [By Sir Dudley North.] London : Printed for Tho. Bassett, at the George in Fleet-street. 1691. 4°, A—E in fours.

NORTHAMPTONSHIRE.

The Humble Petition of the Inhabitants of the Soake of Peterborow, within the County of Northampton, containing about forty Townes and Villages, against the Undertakers there: with exceptions to their Act : . . . May 28. 1650. 4°, A—B in fours.

A True and Faithful Relation of the late Dreadful Fire at Northampton, ... London, Printed for J. Coniers in Duck-Lane. [? 1680.] 4°, 4 leaves. *B. M.*

Catalogus Librorum Bibliothecæ Joannis Humphry, Nuper de Rowell in Comitatu Northamptoniensi, Cum aliis Eruditorum Virorum Libris. Horum Auctio habebitur Londini 4ᵗⁱˢ die Decembris, 1682. Ædibus Jonathanis Miles, vulgo dicto Jonathan's Coffee-House in Exchange-Alley Cornhill, . . . With French and Italian Books. By William Cooper. . . . London, Printed MDCLXXXII. 4°, A—Q in fours, Q 4 blank, and the title.

NORTHLEIGH, JOHN, *LL.B., Author of the "Parallel."*

The Triumph of our Monarchy, over the Plots and Principles of our Rebels and Republicans, Being Remarks on their most Eminent Libels . . . London, Printed for Benj. Tooke . . . 1685. 8", A—3 D in eights, A 8 and 3 D 8 blank. With a frontispiece. Dedicated to James II.

    Puttick & Simpson, August 8, 1883, No. 413, the King's own copy.

NORTHUMBERLAND.

The Northumberland Monster : Or a true and perfect Relation How one Jane Paterson, Wife to one James Paterson of Dodington in the County of Northumberland was brought to bed of a strange Monster, . . . London, Printed for Roger Vaughan . . . 1674. 4°, 4 leaves. *B. M.*

NORTON, ROBERT.

A Mathematicall Apendix, Containing many Propositions and Conclusions mathematicall : with necessary obseruations both for Mariners at Sea, and for Cherographers and Surueyors of Land. . . . Written by R. N. Gent. London, Printed by R. B. for Roger Jackson, . . . 1604. 4°, A—G in fours. Dedicated to the Earl of Hertford by Robert Norton. With diagrams, of which one at p. 20 is detached from the text. *B. M.*

NORTON, THOMAS, *of Sharpenhoe, Bedfordshire.*

A warnyng agaynst the dangerous practises of Papistes, and specially the parteners of the late Rebellion. ¶ Gathered out of the common feare and speche of good subiectes. Vox populi Dei, vox Dei est. [Col.] ¶ God saue our Queene Elizabeth, and confound her enemies. [London, John Day, 1569.] 8°, black letter, A—O in fours. *B. M.*

    First edition, issued without any place and printer's name. The reverse of the title is blank.

A warnyng against the dangerous practises of Papistes, and specially the parteners of the late Rebellion. ¶ Gathered out of the common feare and speche of good subiectes. *Vox populi Dei, vox Dei est.* Sene and allowed. [Col.] God saue our Quene Elizabeth, and confound her enemies. Imprinted at London by Iohn Daye, dwelling ouer Aldersgate. These Bookes are to be solde in Paules church-yarde at the signe of the Crane. [1570.] 8", A—O in fours. *B. M.*

¶ A warning agaynst the dangerous practises . . . ¶ Gathered . . . Written by Thomas Norton, and newly perused and encreased. Vox populi . . . Seen and allowed, according to the order of the Queenes Iniunctions. [Col.] God saue our Queene . . . Imprinted at London by Iohn Daye, dwelling ouer Aldersgate. [1570.] 8", A—O in fours, and the title. *B. M.*

    On the back of the title occurs : " ¶ The summe of all this Booke. We can not well spare our Queene Elizabeth ;" beneath which is a deprecation of any intentional personalities on the part of the author. A 4 is misprinted B 4.

NOSCE TEIPSUM.

Nosce Teipsum : Or, A Leading-Step to the Knowledge of our Selves, . . . To which is added A Poem, treating of Humane Reason, . . . written nigh One Hundred Years since, by Sir John Davies, . . . London Printed, and are to be sold

by Edward Brewster, ... MDCLXXXIX.
Folio. A, 2 leaves: B, 3: [b]—[c], 2
leaves each: a leaf unsigned commencing
the first portion: C—O, 2 leaves each:
Davies's *Nosce Teipsum*, with a new title
dated 1688, title and dedication, 2 leaves:
Bb—Pp, 2 leaves each.

> The author of the first piece, in verse and
> prose, does not appear.

NOWELL, ALEXANDER.
Catechismvs, seu prima Institutio, Dis-
ciplinaq; pietatis Christianæ, Græcè &
Latinè explicata. Londini. Anno Domini
1573. [Col.] Excusum Londini apud
Reginaldum Wolfium. Anno Domini
1573. 8°. *, 4 leaves: A—Tt 4 in eights.

NUISANCE.
A Briefe Declaration for what manner of
speciall Nusance concerning private dwelling Houses, a man may have his remedy
by Assise, or other Action as the Case re-
quires ... Whereunto is added, The Iustices of Assise their opinion, concerning
Statute Law for Parishes; ... London,

Printed by Tho. Cotes, for William Cooke.
... 1639. 4°, A—G in fours.

NUN.
The Nunns Complaint against the Fryars.
Being the Charge given in to the Court
of France, by the Nunns of St. Katherine
near Provins, against the Fathers Corde-
liers their Confessours. Several Times
Printed in French, and now Faithfully
done into English. London, Printed by
E. H. for Robert Pawlett, ... 1676. 8°.
A, 8 leaves: a, 8: B—O 4 in eights, O
2-4 with Advertisements. With a frontispiece. Dedicated by *Lælio* to *Bellalmo.*

NUTT. THOMAS.
The Nut-Cracker Crackt by the Nutt,
And the Backers cake starke Dow:
Being the Vindication of honest men,
from the scandalous aspersions of Thomas
B[a]kewell the Baker in hanging-sword
Court neere Fleetstreet Conduite. ...
London: Printed, in the Yeare, MDCXLIV.
4°, 4 leaves.

O.

ODALY, FRATER DOMINICUS DE ROSÁRIO.
Initivm, Incrementa, Et Exitvs Familiæ
Geraldinorvm Desmoniæ Comitum, Pala-
tinorum Kyerriæ in Hybernia, ac perse-
cutionis hæreticorum descriptio. Ex
nonnullis fragmentis collecta, ac Latinitati donata. Per Fratrem Dominicvm de
Rosario O Daly ... Vlyssipone: ...
Anno 1655. 8°, a—e in eights: A—Dd 4
in eights.

OECOLAMPADIUS, JOHANNES.
A Sarmon, of Jhon Oecolampadius, to
yong men, and maydens. [Col.] Imprinted at London by me Humfrey
Powell, dwellyng aboue Holburne conduit. And are to be sonld by Hugh
Syngleton, dwellyng at the sygne of
Saynt Augustine, in Poules churchyarde.
8°, black letter, A—C in eights. *B. M.*

OGILBY, JOHN.
England Exactly Described Or a Guide
to Travellers In a Compleat Sett of Most
correct Mapps of Counties in England;
being a Map for each County, Wherein
every Towne and Village is Particularly
Express'd ..... According to Mr
Ogilby's Survey. Very Usefull for Gentlemen and Traveilers being made fit for
the Pockett. Printed Coloured and Sold
by Tho. Bakewell Next y Horn Tavern

in Fleetstreet where are Sold all Sorts of
Mapps and fine French Dutch and Italian
Prints. [About 1670.] Oblong 8°. Title
and table, 5 leaves: the 43 maps on as
many leaves.

OLDMIXON, JOHN.
Poems on Several Occasions, Written in
imitation of the manner of Anacreon,
With Other Poems, Letters, and Transla-
tions. *Cum Thebæ* ... Ovid. Eleg.
London: Printed for R. Parker at the
Unicorn, under the Piazza of the Royal
Exchange, in Cornhill. 1696. 8°. A, 8
leaves: a, 4 leaves, including *Errata* and
half-title: B—H in eights. Dedicated to
Lord Ashley. *B. M.*

> "The author of this volume of poems was
> a laborious historian, but, in his political
> opinions, so violent an opponent of the
> Stuart family, and attacked the best writers
> of his time with such virulence, as to obtain
> from Pope a conspicuous place in the *Dun-
> ciad.*"—*B. A. Poetica.*

Amores Britannici. Epistles Historical
and Gallant, In English Heroic Verse:
From several of the most Illustrious Personages of their Times. In Imitation of
the Heroidum Epistolæ of Ovid. With
Notes. ... London: Printed, ... 1703.
8°. A, 8 leaves, including a frontispiece:
(a), 4 leaves: B—M in eights: Aa—K[k]
3 in eights.

[OLDSWORTH, MICHAEL.]
Gradus Simeonis: Or, The First-Frvits of Philip, Earle of Pembroke and Montgomery, &c. [Sometimes] Knight of the Garter°: And [Now] Knight of Berk-Shire. Presented in a learned Speech upon the Day of his Ascending downe into the Lower House of Commons. In the first yeare of the Lords Freedome. 4°, 4 leaves.

It seems to me likely that this, as well as the other facetious productions printed under the name of Lord Pembroke, was actually penned by Michael Oldsworth.

A Thanks-Giving for the Recovery of Philip, Earl of Pembroke and Montgomery. Who being lately admitted into the Supreame Authority of the Nation a Knight for Berkshire, was unfortunately jeared into a Pestilent-Feaver, . . . Taken verbatim from his own mouth, By Michael Oldsworth . . . Printed in the happy yeer of the Lords Liberty. 1649. 4°, 4 leaves.

The Last Will and Testament of the Earl of Pembroke. [London, reprinted about 1680.] Folio, 2 leaves.

OLIVER, JOHN.
A Present to be given to Teeming Women. By their Husbands or Friends ; Containing Scripture-Directions for Women with child. London ; Printed by A. Maxwell, for Tho. Parkhurst, . . . 1669. 8°. A, 8 leaves, A 1 blank: (a) 8 leaves, a 8 blank: B—M in eights, M 8 blank.

ORGAN.
The Organs Fvnerall Or the Quiristers Lamentation for the Abolishment of Superstition and Superstitious Ceremonies. In a Dialogicall Discourse between a Quirister and an Organist, An. Dom. 1642. London, printed for George Kirby. 4°, 4 leaves.

OSBORN, T., *Schoolmaster.*
A Rational Way of Teaching. Whereby Children. and others, may be instructed in True Reading, Pronouncing and Writing of the English Tongue ; . . . . London, Printed for Thomas Hawkins . . . 1688. 8°, A—I 3 in eights, besides a frontispiece and three leaves at end of engraved specimens.

OSBORNE, SIR THOMAS, *Earl of Danby.*
The Answer of the Right Honourable the Earl of Danby to a Late Pamphlet, Entituled *An Examination of the Impartial State of the Case of the Earl of Danby.* London, Printed by E. B. to be Sold by Randal Taylor . . . 1680. Folio, B—E, 2 leaves each, and the title.

OSORIUS, HIERONIMUS.
Les Graves et Sainctes Remonstrances de l'Empereur Ferdinād . . . Plus, vne bien longue & docte Epistre, escrite par certain personnage Portugallois, homme de grandes lettres, & enuoyée a Ma-Dame Elizabeth Royne d'Angleterre, . . . A Paris, . . . 1563 . . . 8°, A—L in eights.

OUGHTRED, WILLIAM.
Arithmeticæ In Nvmeris et Speciebvs Institvtis: Qvæ tvm Logisticæ, Tvm Analyticæ, atqve adeo totivs Mathematicæ, qvasi Clavis est . . . Londini. Apud Thomam Harpervm. M.DC XXXI. 8°. A, 4 leaves: B—F in eights: G, 4. Dedicated to William Howard, Earl of Arundel and Surrey, Earl Marshal, from his lordship's house on the banks of the Thames. *B. M.*

The Circles of Proportion and the Horizontall Instrvment. Both invented, and the vses of both Written in Latine by Mr W. O. Translated into English and set forth for the publique benefit by William Forster. London Printed for Eiias Allen maker of these and all other Mathematicall Instruments, and are to be sold at his shop ouer against St. Clements church with out Temple-barr. 1632. 4°, A—X in fours, A 4 occupied by a page-diagram and a second between p. 130 and p. 131: *An Addition*, &c., dated 1633, with a separate title, A—K 2 in fours.

Mathematicall Recreations. Or a Collection of sundrie Problemes, extracted out of the Ancient and Moderne Philosophers, as secrets in nature, and experiments in Arithmeticke, . . . Most of which were written first in Greeke and Latine, lately compiled in French, by Henry Van Etten Gent. And now delivered in the English tongue, With the Examinations, Corrections, and Augmentations [of W. Oughtred.] Printed at London by T. Cotes, for Richard Hawkins, . . . 1633. 8°, A—V 5 in eights, besides *, 8 leaves, and **, 4 leaves. With woodcuts and diagrams. *B. M.* (Farmer's copy.)

OVERBURY, SIR THOMAS.
Sr Thomas Ouerbury His Wife . . . . The tenth impression augmented. London, Printed by Edward Griffin for Laurence L'isle, . . . 1618. 8°. ¶ and ¶¶, 8 leaves each, ¶ 1 blank: A—R 4 in eights, R 4 blank.

OVERTON, RICHARD.
Articles of High Treason Exhibited

against Cheap-Side Crosse. With The last Will and Testament of the said Crosse. And certaine Epitaphs vpon her Tombe. By R. Overton. Newly Printed, and newly come forth, with his Holinesse Priviledge, to prevent false Copies. London, Printed for R. Overton, 1642. 4°, 4 leaves.

> On the back of the title occurs : *The Author to his Muse,* in verse, and the Epitaphs are also metrical.

)VIDIUS NASO, PUBLIUS.
Ouids Metamorphosis Translated Grammatically, and also according to the propriety of our English tongue, so farre as Grammar and the verse will well beare. Written chiefly for the good of Schooles. to be vsed according to the directions in the Preface to the painefull Schoole-master, and more fully in the booke called Ludus Literarius. or the Grammar-schoole, Chap. 8. London, Printed by Humfrey Lownes, for Thomas Man, . . . 1618. 4°. ¶, 4 leaves : A, 2 leaves : B—N in fours, N 4 blank. Dedicated to Edward, Lord Denny, Baron of Waltham.

The Passion of Byblis, Made English. From Ovid. Metam. Lib. 9. By M'' Dennis. London, Printed for Rich. Parker at the Unicorn under the Piazza of the Royal Exchange, 1692. 4°, A—L, 2 leaves each. In verse. *B. M.*

Ovids Tristia Containinge fiue Bookes of mournfull Elegies. . . . London Printed for Fra: Groue . . . 1637. 12°. A, 6 leaves : B—I 2 in eights. The title is engraved.

Salmacis and Hermaphroditvs. Salmacida spolia sine sanguine & sudore. Imprinted at London for Iohn Hodgats : And are to be sold at his shop in Fleete-street, at the signe of the Flower de Luce, neere Fetter-lane. 1602. 4°, A—E in fours. In verse. *Bodleian.*

> Dedicated "To the true patronesse of all Poetrie, Caliope." With verses *In laudem Authoris* by W. B., and "To the Authour," by I. B., "To the Author," by A. F., and "The Author to the Reader." The poem begins on B.

Ovid De Arte Amandi, And the Remedy of Love Englished. As also the Loves of Hero & Leander. . . . London, Printed in the Year, 1677. 12°, A—G 6 in twelves, including a portrait of Ovid as a frontispiece.

Ovid's Art of Love. In Three Books. Together with his Remedy of Love. Translated into English Verse by Several Eminent Hands. To which are added,

The Court of Love, A Tale from Chaucer. And the History of Love. Adorn'd with Cuts. London : Printed for Jacob Tonson . . . 1709. 8°.

P. Ovid. Nas. In Ibin. Ovid's Invective Against Ibis. . . . The Second Edition. Oxford, Printed by Hen. Hall Printer to the University, for Ric: Davis, 1667. 8°. †—††† in eights : A—L 4 in eights, with a second title on A 1.

OVINGTON, JOHN.
A Voyage to Suratt, in the Year, 1689. Giving a large Account of that City, and its Inhabitants, and of the English Factory there. . . . To which is added an Appendix, containing 1. The History of a late Revolution in the Kingdom of Golconda. . . . By J. Ovington, M.A. Chaplain to his Majesty. . . . London, Printed for Jacob Tonson, . . . 1696. 8°, A—Qq 7 in eights, A 1 with half-title, and Qq 7 followed by two leaves of coins current in Hindostan, &c. With a folded plate between pp. 146-7. Dedicated to the Earl of Dorset and Middlesex.

OXFORD, CITY OF.
Oxfords Latin Rimes tvrned into English Reason. Or Horrid Blasphemy made excellent Divinitie, . . . [1643.] 4°, 5 leaves.

Newes from Smith the Oxford Jaylor. With the Arraignment of Mercurius Aulicus, who is sentenced to stand in the Pillory three Market dayes, for his notorious Libelling against State and Kingdome. London, Printed for J. B. 1645. 4°, 4 leaves. With a cut on the title.

> This refers to William Smith, Provost-Marshal of the King's Army at Oxford. It is attributed to Sir John Birkenhead.

A Dialogue at Oxford between A Tutor and a Gentleman, Formerly his Pupil, Concerning Government. London, Printed for Rich. Janeway, . . . 1681. 4°, A—C in fours.

OXFORD, UNIVERSITY OF.
Discovrs Veritable Dv Martyre de Devx Prebstres & deux Laycx, aduenu l'an mil cinq cens quatre vingts neuf, à Oxfort Vniuersité d'Angleterre. Qui pourra seruir aux Catholicqves de la France par l'exéple d'autruy d'en auoir compassion. Traduict d'Italien en François, selon l'exemplaire imprimé à Romme 1590. A Paris, . . . M.D.XC. 8°, A—C in fours.

The Answere of the vicechancelovr, the Doctors, . . . in the Vniuersitie of Oxford . . . to the humble Petition of the Ministers of the Church of England, desiring Reformation of certaine Ceremonies and Abuses of the Church. . . . At Oxford, Printed by Ioseph Barnes, . . . 1603. 4°. ¶ and ¶¶, 4 leaves each: A—D in fours. ¶¶ 4 is blank.

An Ordinance of the Lords and Commons Assembled in Parliament. For the Visitation and Reformation of the Universitie of Oxford And the severall Colledges and Halls therein. With the names of the Committee and Visitors for the better regulating of the same . . . London Printed for John Wright [May] . . . 1647. 4°, 4 leaves.

The Priviledges of the University of Oxford, In point of Visitation: Clearly evidenced by Letter to an Honourable Personage Together with The Vniversities Answer to the Summons of the Visitors. Printed for Richard Royston. 1647. 4°, A—B 2 in fours.

An English Catalogue of the Trees and Plants in the Physicke Garden of the Vniversitie of Oxford. With the Latine names added thereunto. Oxford Printed by H. Hall . . . 1648. 8°, A—D 3 in eights. *B. M.*

Catologus [sic] Plantarum Horti Medici Oxoniensis . . . Excudebat Henricus Hall . . . 1648. 8°. A, 2 leaves: B—E 4 in eights, E 4 blank. *B. M.*

The Foundation of the Universitie of Oxford, With a Catalogue of the principall Founders and speciall Benefactors . . . And how the Revennes thereof are and have been increased . . . . London, Printed by M. S. for Thomas Jenner . . . 1651. 4°, A—C 2 in fours.

Academiæ Oxoniensis Notitia. Oxoniæ. Typis W. H. Impensis R. Davis. M.DC.LXV. 4°, A—H in fours, title on A 2.

A Sermon Taken out of an Oxford Scholar's Pocket, Who was found Dead in Bishop's Wood, near High-Gate, on Monday, Feb. 15. 168¾. Together with A True Relation of the Manner of his being Discovered there . . . London: Printed for Tho. Fabian, . . . 1688. 4°, A—E in fours.

Friendly Advice to the Directour of the English Press at Oxford concerning the English Orthographie. London, Printed for Robert Clavell . . . 1682. Folio, A—C, 2 leaves each.

An Impartial Relation of the whole Proceedings against St. Mary Magdalen College in Oxon, In the Year of our Lord 1687. Containing only Matters of Fact as they occurred. Printed in the Year 1688. 4°, A—F in fours.

An Account of Mr Parkinson's Expulsion from the University of Oxford in the late Times. In Vindication of him from the False Aspersions cast on him in a late Pamphlet, Entituled, *The History of Passive Obedience.* London: Printed for . . . Richard Baldwin, . . . 1689. 4°, A—C in fours, C 4 blank.

OXFORD, WENDY.

A prospective for Kings and Subjects. Or A schort discovery of some treacheries acted against Charles the I. and Charles the II. Kings of England, Scotland, and Ireland. with some few advertisements to the people in the 3. Nations concerning the cruel, exorbitant, and most Tyrannical Slavery they are now under . . . Written by Wendy Oxford once an honourer of them and there pretences . . . Printed to Leyden by Iohn Pricton in the Ieare 1652. 4°, A—D in fours. Dedicated to Charles II.

OXFORDSHIRE.

Good News from Banbury in Oxfordshire: Relating how two Troops of Horse, under the command of my Lord Says two sons, pursued divers Cavalleers as they fled from Oxford toward Worcester, . . . Also a great skirmish betweene the men of Coventry and the Kings party; . . . Whereunto is added, The Examination of Joshua Hill, and Augustine Harper, taken at Northampton, . . . London, Printed for J. Wright . 20 . Septemb. 1642. 4°, 4 leaves.

The Proceedings at Banbury since the Ordnance went down for the Lord Brooke to fortifie Warwick Castle, And how they came to be delivered to the Earle of Northampton and his Company. Also the Copie of a Letter from Warwick-shire. [1642.] 4°, 4 leaves.

By the King. A Proclamation for the ease of the Citty of Oxford, and Suburbs, of the County of Oxford, of unnecessary Persons lodging or abiding there. [Jan. 20, 1642-3.] A broadside.

Fair Warning to Murderers of Infants: Being an Account of the Tryal, Condemnation and Execution of Mary Goodenough at the Assizes held in Oxon, in February, 169½. Together with the Advice sent by her to her Children . . . London: Printed for Jonathan Robinson, . . . 1692. 4°, A—C 2 in fours.

P.

P. E.

A Brief Discourse of Friendship. To which are added, A few things in Verse of Various Subject. By E. P. London: Printed in the Year 1695. 4°, A—B in fours.

P. E. N.

To the King, On His Peaceable Return, And Magnificent Entry into London. By E. N. P. ——*Quod Divum.* ... Virg. London, Printed for Elizabeth Whitlock ... MDCXCVIII. Folio, A—C, 2 leaves each.

P. H.

The Generall Junto, Or The Covncell of Union, Chosen equally out of England, Scotland and Ireland, for the better compacting of three Nations into one Monarchy, &c. —*Trojagenis Paries* ... Printed, Anno Dom. 1642. Folio. Title and two following leaves: B—H, 2 leaves each: I, 1 leaf.

<small>Gosford, April 26, 1884 (Putticks), No. 1755. Another copy in Hamilton Sale, May 1884, No. 1996. The writer states that the tract was printed with a wide margin for corrections or remarks. The Gosford was the copy presented to the Solicitor-General.</small>

P. T.

The Accomplish'd Lady's Delight ... The Eighth Edition Inlarged. London, Printed and Sold by Benj. Harris, ... 1701. Small 8°, A—H 10 in twelves, besides the frontispiece and portrait.

PACE, RICHARD.

Oratio Richardi Pacei in pace nuperrime cōposita & foedere percusso : inter inuitissimum Angliæ regem. & Francorum regem christianissimum in æde diui Pauli Londini habita. Venit in ædibus Ioannis Gormontij ad insigne Geminarum Cipparum ... [1518.] 4°, A—B in fours.

<small>On the first page this is headed *Oratio Nuptialis.*</small>

PAGE, JOHN, *Master in Chancery, D.C.L.*

Jus Fratrum, The Law of Brethren. Touching the power of Parents, to dispose of their Estates to their Children, ... London, Printed by I. M. for Henry Fletcher, ... 1658. 8°, A—H 6 in eights. In two parts, with a separate title to Part 2, dated by mistake 1518.

PAGET, BRIDGET.

[Meditations of Death. This is the headline. At the end occurs:] Printed at Dort. By Henry Ash. MDCXXXIX. 12°. *, 6 leaves: A—S in twelves. Dedicated to Elizabeth, Queen of Bohemia,

<small>The copy I have used wanted the title. There is a Preface by R. Paget, who calls himself the publisher.</small>

PAINTERS.

The True Effigies of the most Eminent Painters and other Famous Artists that have flourished in Europe. Curiously Engraven on Copper-Plates. Together with an Account of the Time when they Lived, ... Very useful for all such Gentlemen as are lovers of Art and Ingenuity. Printed in the Year, MDCXCIV. Folio. Engraved and printed titles, 2 leaves: *Lives*, A—D, 2 ll. each: E, 1 leaf: then the title and plates of *Illvstrivm quos Belgivm habvit Pictorvm Effigies*, and Meissens' Series, with a fresh title, altogether 123 leaves.

PALATINATE.

Newes from the Palatinate. A true and comfortable Relation of the wonderfull proceedings of Count Mansfield, from his first comming into the Palatinate, vnto this present Moneth. ... Likewise relating the true and admirable manner of raising of the siege of Franckendale by Sir Horatio Vere, with the rest of his proceedings, vntill this present. Faithfully Translated and extracted out of a Dutch Letter ... Printed at the Hage. 1622. 4°, A—D in fours. *B. M.*

More Newes from the Palatinate, the second time imprinted Iune the 5. Containing the true Copies of certaine Letters of great import written from Manheim, ... As also what befell the Duke of Brunswicke in his passage to ioyne with the King of Bohemia. Together with the true and present estate of Count Mansfield, ... And many other considerable things concerning the affaires of Germanie and the Low Countries. London, Printed by W. Iones for N. Butter and W. Sheffard, ... 1622. 4°, A—C in fours, A 1 blank. *B. M.*

A Trve and Ample Relation of all svch Occvrrences as have happened in the

Palatinate since the first of Iune. 1622. *Stilo Antiquo.* Truely Related in a Letter, received from Doctor Welles the tenth of Iune. 1622. And now Printed the 13. of Iune. 1622. London, Printed by I. D. for Iohn Bartlet, and are to be sold at his Shop, at the gilt Cup in Cheap-side, in the Gold-smiths Row. 1622. 4°, A—C in fours, A 1 and C 4 blank. *B. M.*

A true Relation of all Such Battailes as haue beene fought in the Palatinate, since the Kings arrinall there, vntill this present the 14. of May. . . . Likewise the notable Victory woone by Christian Duke of Brunswicke against the Bauarians, . . . With the famous Victorie obtained by the King of Bohemia against Leopoldvs, before Hagenaw, . . . Lastly, the Victory of the Graue Henrick Van Nassaw in Brabant, . . . London: Printed by E. A. for Nicholas Bourne and Thomas Archer, . . . 1622. 4°, A—C in fours, A 1 blank. *B. M.*

The Trve Copies of two Especiall Letters Verbatim sent from the Palatinate by Sir F. N. Relating the dangerous incounter which hapened betwixt the Duke Christian of Brunswicke, and Monsieur Tillies passing ouer the bridge lying vpon the river Mayne about Ausbourge. With the vniting of his forces with the King of Bohemia, . . . With the late proceedings in the Low Countries, . . . London, Printed by William Iones for Nicholas Bourne and Thomas Archer . . . 1622. 4°, A—C in fours, A 1 and C 4 blank. *B. M.*

His Maiesties Manifestation, Concerning the Palatine Cause. Printed in the Yeare, 1641. 4°, A—B in fours, B 4 blank.

Motives and Reasons, Concerning His Highnesse the Prince Elector Palatines comming into England. . . . With two Letters that were formerly sent from Hagve. London, Printed by Jane Coe. 1644. 4°, 4 leaves.

PALLADIO, ANDREA.
The First Book of Architecture, By Andrea Palladio. Translated out of Italian : With an Appendix touching Doors and Windows, By P^r Le Muet. Translated out of French, by G. R. To which are added Designes of Floors lately made at Somerset-House ; And the Framing of Houses after the best manner of English Buildings, with their Proportions and Scantlings. London, Printed by J. M. and sold by G. Richards, . . . and by Simon Miller, . . . 1663. 4°, A—Ff in

fours, besides 2 leaves of plates between C 3 and 4.

> Dedicated by Godfrey Richards, the translator of the latter portion, to his friend Daniel Colwal, Esq. The plates, except the two noticed, count in the sheets.

PALMER, BARBARA, *Duchess of Cleveland.*
The Gracious Answer of the most Illustrious Lady of Pleasure, the Comtes of Castlem[aine] To the Poor-Whores Petition. [1668.] A broadside.

PALMER, CHRISTOPHER.
Evropae Gavdivm De Felicissimis Nvptiis Serenissimorum Cosmi Medycis, & Mariae Austriacae Principum. Auctore Christophoro Palmerio Anglo Philosophorum, ac Medic^m vtriusq ; Vniuersitatis in almo Bonon. Gymn-Consiliario, & Collegij Nobilium Præfecto. Bononiæ, Apud Io. Bapt. Bellag. 1608. 4°, A—F in fours.

PALMER, ROGER, *Earl of Castlemaine.*
An Account of the Present War between the Venetians & Tvrk ; With the State of Candie : (In a Letter to the King, from Venice.) By the Earl of Castlemaine. London, Printed by J. M. for H. Herringman. . . . 1666. Small 8°. A, 8 leaves, the first blank : a, 2 leaves : B—G in eights, G 8 blank. With a portrait of the writer by W. Faithorne, and a map and a plan of Candia.

A short and true Account of the Material Passages in the late War between the English and Dutch. Written by the Right Honourable the Earl of Castlemain, And now published by Thomas Price Gent. In the Savoy, Printed for H. Herringman . . . 1671. 8°. A—H 4 in eights.

PALMERIN OF ENGLAND.
Le Premier [et le second] Livre dv Prevx Vaillant et Tresvictorievx Chevalier Palmerin d'Angleterre, Filz dv Roy Dom. Edoard. Auquel seront recitees ses grandes proësses & semblablement la chenalereuse bonté de Florian du desert, son frere, auec celle du Prince Florendos, fi.z de Primaleon. Tradvit de Castillan en François par maistre Iaques Vincent, du Crest Arnauld en Dauphiné. Auec ample Indice des singulieres & principales matieres. *Mon Heur viendra.* A Lyon Par Thibavld Payen. M.D.LIII. Auec Priuilege pour dix ans. Folio. *, 4 leaves, with title and Table : a—z in fours : A—P 2 in fours : *Second Livre,* *, 4 leaves : a—z in fours : A—I 3 in fours.

Originally written in Spanish, and printed at Toledo in 1548, it was subsequently translated into Portuguese, and for some time that version was supposed to be the original, whence the French had been really derived.

The Famous History of the Noble and Valiant Prince Palmerin of England : . . . London, Printed by R. I. for S. S. to bee sold by Charles Tyus . . . 1664. 4°, black letter. Part First. A—Dd in eights, A 1 and Dd 8 blank : Part Second, A—3 F in fours, 3 F 4 blank.

PARACELSUS, PHILIPPUS AUREO-
LUS THEOPHRASTUS.
A hundred and foureteene Experiments and Cures . . . translated out of the Germane tongue into the Latin. Where-unto is added certaine excellent and pro-fitable Workes by B. G. a Portu Aqui-tano. Also certaine Secrets of Isacke Hollandus concerning the Vegetall and Animall worke. Also the Spagericke Antidotarie for Gunne-shot of Iosephus Quirsemanus. Collected by Iohn Hester. London Printed by Valentine Sims . . . 1596. 4°, A—M in fours. Dedicated by Hester " To the right Worshipfull, Walter Raleigh Esquier."

PARKER, HENRY.
Of a Free Trade. A Discourse Seriously Recommending to our Nation the won-derfull benefits of Trade, especially of a rightly Governed, and Ordered Trade . . . Written by Henry Parker Esquire . . . London : Printed by Fr. Neile for Robert Bostock . . . 1648. 4°, A—F 2 in fours.

The Trve Portraitvre of the Kings of England ; Drawn from their Titles, Suc-cessions, Raigns and Ends . . . London, Printed by R. W. for Francis Tyton . . . 1650. 4°, A—F in fours, and a leaf of G.

PARKINSON, JOHN.
Paradisi in Sole Paradisvs Terrestris . . . . The second Impression Corrected and Enlarged. London, Printed by R. N. and are to be sold by Richard Thrale . . . 1656. Folio. *, 6 leaves: A—3 E in sixes : 3 F, 8 leaves.

PARLIAMENT.
The Names of the Knights, Citizens, Bvrgesses for the Borovghs, and Barons for the Ports for the Honourable Assembly of the House of Commons . . . . 18. day of Iune, in the First yeere of . . . . Charles . . . 1625. And also the Names of those that were of the precedent Par-liament, held 1624, and likewise of the former held 1620 . . . London Printed .

1625. 4°, A—C 3 in fours : A, 2 : B—C in fours.

The Copies of two Speeches in Parlia-ment. The one by Iohn Glanvill Esquire. The other by Sir Henry Martin Knight. At a generall Committee of both Houses, the 22. of May. 1628. No place, &c. 4°, A—B in fours, B 4 blank, and A or a repeated.

A Briefe Discovrse, Concerning the Power of the Peeres and Commons of Parlia-ment, in point of Judicature. Written by a Learned Antiqvarie, at the request of a Peere of the Realm. Printed in the Yeare, 1640. 4°, A—B in fours, A 1 and B 4 blank.

A Damnable Treason, By a Contagious Plague-Sore : Wrapt-up in a Letter, and sent in to Mʳ Pym : Wherein is discovered a Divellish, and Unchristian Plot against the High Court of Parliament. October 25 . 1641 . . . Printed for W. B. Anno Dom. 1641. 4°, 4 leaves. With a woodcut portrait of Pym on title and a second cut on back.

The Lord Finch His Speech in the House of Commons, the 21. of December, 1641. Hee being then Lord-Keeper. Printed in the Yeere, 1641. 4°, A—B in fours, A 1 blank.

The Hellish Parliament Being a Counter-Parliament to this in England, containing the Demonstrative Speeches and Statutes of that Court. Together with the perfect league made between the two Hellish Factions the Papists and the Brownists. Printed in the yeare, 1641. 4°, 4 leaves. With a large cut on the title.

Articles of Accusation . . . Against Sʳ John Bramston Knight . . . Printed for I. H. 1641. 4°, A—G 2 in fours.

An Anti-Remonstrance, to the Late Hvmble Remonstrance [by Joseph Hall] to the High Covrt of Parliament. Printed Anno 1641. 4°, 6 leaves, or A—B 2 in fours, A 1 blank.

A Dreame : Or Newes from Hell. With a Relation of the great God Pluto, sud-denly falling sicke by reason of this pre-sent Parliament. Printed in Sicilia on the back-side of the Cyclopean Moun-taines. 1641. 4°, A—B in fours. With a large cut on title.

The Order of Assistance given to the Committees of both Houses, concerning their going to Hull. Aprill. 28. 1642. Imprinted at London by Robert Barker . . . 1642. A broadside.

A Declaration by the Lords and Commons in Parliament declaring that none shall aprehend, or arest any of his Maiesties Subiects or Servants that obeyeth the ordinance of Parliament, under pretence of his Maiesties warrant. Mercurii 12. July 1642. London Printed for Francis Leach. A broadside.

The Declaration of the Lords and Commons ... concerning the Earl of Stamford and others his Assistants, whom the King Proclaimed Traytors for executing the Ordinance of the Militia. [23 July 1642.] A broadside.

An Ordinance of the Lords and Commons for the better Observing and Keeping a Monethly Fast, within the Kingdom of England, and Dominion of Wales. [London, August 1642.] A large broadside in black letter.

The Parliaments Instructions to the Earl of Essex, Lord Generall of the Army ... September the 17. Likewise the Resolution of his Excellencie, to advance his Forces from Northampton, and march towards the Kings most Excellent Majesty; ... Also, the Resolution of the Earl of Cumberland, the Earl of New-Castle, and the Lord Strange, to joyn their Forces together in a full Body, and meet the Earl of Essex, with Sir Iohn Hothams Determination concerning the same. London: Printed for H. Blund. Septemb. 20. 1642. 4°, 4 leaves. With a woodcut portrait of Essex at the end.

Two speciall Orders made by the House of Commons . . . : The One: Prohibiting that no Carriers, or Waggoners whatsoever shall be permitted hereafter to go to Oxford or elsewhere without speciall License from the Parliament. The Other That if any Agent, or Servant to any person that bear Arms against the Parliament, shall presume to come to Westminster, or reside about London, shall be forthwith apprehended as a Spy, and proceeded against accordingly. London, Printed for John Frank, and are to be sold at his shop the next door to the Kings head Tavern in Fleet-street. Januar. 17. 1642. A broadside.

The Humble Desires and Propositions of the Lords and Commons . . . Presented to the Kings most Excellent Majesty at Oxford, by foure Lords, and eight Members of the House of Commons, February 3. 1642. With His Majesties Answer thereunto, and six Propositions propounded by him to both Houses, to be debated upon, with the rest, at the Treaty. . . . Feb. 8. Printed for Iohn Wright in the Old-Bailey. 1642. 4°, 4 leaves.

A Declaration of the Lords and Commons . . . Shewing the Reasons why they cannot consent to the keeping of Easter Teerme at Oxford, but in the usuall places : . . . London. Aprill 19 Printed for John Wright, . . . 1643. 4°, 4 leaves.

An Ordinance of the Lords and Commons . . . For the speedy raising and levying of Money for the maintenance of the Army raised by the Parliament, and other great Affaires of the Common-wealth By a Weekly Assessment upon the Cities of London and Westminster, and every County and City of the Kingdom of England, and Dominion of Wales. . . . London, Printed for Edw. Husband, . . . 1643. 4°, A—D in fours.

An Ordinance of the Lords and Commons . . . For the speedy Raising and Levying of Moneyes, by way of Excise or New-Impost, upon several Commodities in the Kingdome of England, and Dominion of Wales. Which is for the maintenance of the Forces Raised for the Defence of King and Parliament, both by Sea and Land, and towards the Payment of the Debts of the Common-wealth, for which the Publique Faith is, or shall be given. . . . London, Printed for John Wright in the Old Baily. Iuly 27. 1643. 4°, A—D 2 in fours.

Sober Sadnes : Or Historicall Observations vpon the Proceedings, Pretences, & Designs of a prevailing party in both Houses of Parliament. . . . Printed for W. Webb Bookseller, neer Queens Colledge. M.DC.XLIII. 4°, A—F in fours.

God appearing for the Parliament. In sundry late victories bestowed upon their Forces. Which command and call for great Praise and Thanksgiving both from Parliament and People. . . . Printed at London for Edward Husband. March 10. 1644. 4°, A—C in fours.

This is just what Buonaparte used to say, that God was always on the side of the strongest battalions.

The Answer of the Commons Assembled in Parliament, To the Scots Commissioners Papers of the 20th, and their Letter of the 24th of October last. . . . London, Printed for Edward Husband, . . . December 4. 1646. 4°. A—I 2 in fours.

Hells Trienniall Parliament, Summoned five yeeres since, by King Lucifer. With their severall Acts, Orders, Votes, and

Ordinances, Also, Iack Presbyters enterteynment into the Kingdome of Darknesse, . . . Printed in the Yeere, 1647. 4°, 4 leaves.

A New Remonstrance of the Eleven Impeached Members, Declaring the true reasons, why some of them have now chosen to goe into Forraigne Kingdomes, and others to obscure themselves in this. Also the cleereing of themselves from the severall Accusations . . . Printed in the yeere 1647. 4°, 4 leaves.

A List of Divers Persons whose Names are to be presented to the Kings Majestie, to dye without Mercy. Also A Declaration of the Kingdoms of England and Scotland for the Vindication and defence of their Religion, Liberties, and Laws. By the Honourable Houses of the Parliament of England, and the Honourable Convention of the Estates of the Kingdome of Scotland. London printed for V. V. and are to be sold at the Exchange, Anno Dom. MDCXLVII. 4°, 4 leaves. *B. M.*

> Among the persons to be capitally condemned are Prince Rupert, Maurice, Count Palatine of the Rhine, the Marquis of Winchester, the Marquis of Huntley, the Earls of Derby, Bristol, Worcester, Montrose, &c. There are 71 names.

Desires Propounded to the Honourable House of Commons from Denzill Holles Esq; Sir John Clotworthy, Sir William Waller, Sir John Maynard, Knight, Major Generall Massey, John Glynne Esquire, Recorder of London, Walter Long, Esq; Col. Edward Harley, and Anthony Nicoll, Esq; Members of the Honourable House of Commons. Who stand Impeached by his Excellency Sir Tho. Fairfax, and the Army under his Command. Also Their Demurrer to the Charge: And the Votes of the House, giving them leave to goe beyond the Seas, and to absent themselves for six Moneths: And Mr Speaker to grant them Passes. Printed at London by Robert Ibbitson 1647. 4°, 4 leaves.

The Parliaments Petition to the Divell. To the most high and mighty Emperour of Darkenesse, Don sel de Lucifer, King of Acheron, . . . Printed in the Yeare 1648. 4°, 4 leaves.

Mistris Parliament Presented in her Bed, after the sore travaile and hard labour which she endured last weeke, in the Birth of her Monstrous Offspring, the Childe of Deformation. . . . By Mercurius Melancholicus. Printed in the Yeer of the Saints fear. 1648. 4°, 4 leaves.

The Parliament Arraigned, Convicted;

Wants nothing but Execvtion. Wherein you may evidently discerne all the blessed fruit of their seven yeers session . . . Written in the Yeer of wonders, . . . By Tom. Tyranno-Mastix, alias, Mercurius Melancholicus, . . . Printed for the Publick view of all His Majesties faithfull Subjects, and are to be sold at the old signe of YOU MAY GOE LOOK. Anno Dom. 1648. 4°, A—C 2 in fours.

· A Narration of the most material Parliamentary Proceedings of this present Parliament, and their Armies, in their Civil and Martial Affairs. Which Parliament began the third of November, 1640. and the remarkable Transactions are continued until this Yeer. . . . London, Printed for Th. Jenner, at the Southentrance of the Royal Exchange. MDCLI. 4°, A—D in fours. With cuts.

To the Parliament of the Common-wealth of England, The humble Petition of Elizabeth Dutchesse (dowager) of Hamilton, and her Foure Orphan Daughters. [1651.] A broadside. *B. M.*

> This document embraces the Petition itself, the Parliament's Declaration, and the Duchess's Case in rejoinder.

A True Narrative of the Cause and Manner of the Dissolution of the late Parliament, vpon the 12. of Decemb. 1653. By a Member of the House then present at that Transaction. London, Printed in the Year, 1653. 4°, 4 leaves.

A Declaration of the Parliament of the Commonwealth of England. [Col.] London, Printed by John Field, 1653. Folio, A in fours. Black letter.

A Second Narrative of the Late Parliament (so called.) Wherein, after a brief Reciting some Remarkable Passages in the former Narrative, is given an Account of their Second Meeting, and Things transacted by them; As also, how the Protector (so called) came Swearing by the living God, and dissolved them, after two or three Weeks Sitting. · . Printed in the Fifth Year of Englands Slavery under its New Monarchy, 1658. 4°, A—C in fours and A—I in fours.

By the Parliament. [A Proclamation declaring Randolph Egerton, Robert Verden, Sir George Booth, Sir Thomas Middleton, and their Adherents, Traitors, for endeavouring to bring in Charles Stuart, and possessing themselves of Chester.] London, Printed by John Field, Printer to the Parliament. . . . 1659. A broadside.

A Declaration of the Parliament Assembled at Westminster, January 23, 1659 [-60], London, Printed by John Streater and John Macock, . . . 1659. 4°, A—B in fours.

An important tract.

The Petition of M[r] Praise-God Barebone, and several others, to the Parliament. Presented on Thursday the 9th of February, 1659. London, Printed in the Year, 1659. A broadside. *B. M.*

To the Right Honourable The Knights, Cittizens, and Burgesses Assembled in Parliament. The Humble Petition of the Merchants Trading to the Dominions of the King of Spain. [1659.] A broadside. *B. M.*

To the Honourable the Knights, Citizens, and Burgesses in this present Parliament assembled. The humble Petition of Clement Walker, and William Prynne, Esquires. [1659 60.] A broadside. *B. M.*

A Perfect List of the Names of the Knights, Citizens, and Burgesses, and Barons of the Cinque Ports of England and Wales : For the Parliament begun at Westminster the 25th day of Aprill in the year 1660. As they were returned into the Crown Office. London Printed for Robert Pawley, . . . 1660. 4°, 4 leaves.

To the Right Honorable, The High Court of Parliament, sitting at Westminster: The Illegal and Immodest Petition of Praise-God Barbone, Anabaptist and Leather-seller of London. London, Printed by Hen. Mason, in the year of Restauration. 1660. A broadside. *B. M.*

A Perfect List of the Names of the Knights, Burgesses, and Barons of the Cinque Ports of England and Wales, for the Parliament begun at Westminster the eighth day of May. . . . 1661. . . . London, Printed from the Crown Office for Samuel Brooke, . . . [1661.] 4°, 4 leaves.

A Catalogue of the Names of all such who were Summon'd to any Parliament, (or Reputed Parliament) from the Year 1640 . . . London, Printed for Robert Pawley, . . . 1661. 8°, A—E in eights.

A Catalogue of the Names of the Lords Spiritual, Lords Temporal, and Commons Assembled in Parliament Begun at Westminster the 8th of May (13 Caroli Regis) and continued to . . . the 20th of November 1661 . . . London, Printed for Robert Pauley, . . . 1661. 4°, A—B

2 in fours, besides 2 leaves between A and A 2.

The Grand Question concerning the Judicature of the House of Peers, Stated and Argued. And the Case of Thomas Skinner Merchant, complaining of the East India Company, with the proceedings thereupon, which gave occasion to that Question, faithfully related. By a true Well-wisher to the Peace and good Government of the Kingdom. . . . London, Printed for Richard Chiswell, . . . 1669. 8°. B—E in eights : F—Aa in fours : Bb, 2 leaves, and the title.

By the King. A Proclamation for further Proroguing the Parliament [25 Sept. 1678.] London, Printed by John Bill. . . . 1678. A broadside.

A Coppy of the Journal-Book of the House of Commons for the Sessions of Parliament Begun at Westminster the 21. day of October, 1678. and continued until the 30. day of December next following, . . . London, Printed MDCLXXX. 8°, B—P 4 in eights, besides 2 leaves with title and Preface.

The Debates in the House of Commons Assembled at Oxford The Twenty first of March, 1680. The Three first days being spent in choosing their Speaker, the Confirming of him, and taking the Oaths. . . . [Col.] London, Printed for R. Baldwin, 1681. Folio, A—E, 2 leaves each.

Some Proposals Offered to Publick Consideration, Before the Opening of Parliament : May 19. 1685. [Col.] London, Printed by F. Leach, for Luke Meredith, . . . MDCLXXXV. Folio, 2 leaves.

The Address of the Lords Spiritual and Temporal. And Commons Assembled in Parliament, to the King's Most Excellent Majesty. Presented by the Right Honourable the Lord Marquess of Halifax, Lord Privy Seal, and Speaker to the House of Lords. In the Banqueting-House at White-hall, the Eighth of March, 168⁵⁄₆. With His Majesty's Most Gracious Answer thereunto. London, Printed by James Partridge, Matthew Gillilower, and Samuel Heyrick, Printers to the House of Lords. 168⁵⁄₆. Folio, B C, 2 leaves each, besides title and *Imprimatur.*

A New Song on the Calling of a Free Parliament. January 15th 168⁵⁄₆. An engraved sheet.

A Letter to a Member of Parliament on the Account of some present Transactions.

[Col.] London, Printed for F. Leach in Grey-Friers, 1689. A folio leaf.

Memorials of the Method and Manner of Proceedings in Parliament in passing Bills . . . from the time of Edward VI. London, Printed for R. Baldwin. 1689. 8°, A—H 4 in eights.

The Faithful Register ; Or, The Debates of the House of Commons In Four several Parliaments [1680-5.] . . . London. Printed [1690.] 8°, B—Z in eights and the title : the Debates, May 1685, A—C in eights : the same, November 1685, A—C in eights, C 8 blank : D, 4 leaves; D 4 with an Index of names.

The Journals of all the Parliaments [1558-1601] during the Reign of Queen Elizabeth, both of the House of Lords and House of Commons. Collected by Sir Simonds D'Ewes of Stow-Hall in the County of Suffolk, Knight and Baronet. Revised and Published by Paul Bowes, of the Middle-Temple London, Esq; London, Printed for John Starkey . . . 1682. Folio. Frontispiece of *Queen Elizabeth in Parliament*, 1 leaf : printed title, 1 leaf : dedication by Bowes to Sir Willoughby D'Ewes, 1 leaf : the work, A—4 X 2 in fours.

The Debate at Large, between the House of Lords and House of Commons, at the Free Conference held in the Painted Chamber . . . Anno 1688. Relating to the Word, Abdicated and the Vacancy of the Throne, . . . Printed for J. Wickins, . . . 1695. 8°, A—B in fours : C—F in eights : G—Q in fours.

A Short History of the Last Parliament. London : Printed for Jacob Tonson. . . . 1699. 4°, A—H in fours.

The Proceedings in the House of Commons, Touching the Impeachment of Edward Late Earl of Clarendon . . . Anno 1667 . . . The Second Edition carefully Corrected. Printed in the Year 1700. 8°. A, 4 leaves : B—L in eights : M, 4.

Private Debates in the House of Commons, In the Year 1677. In Relation to a War with France, and an Alliance with Holland, &c. . . . Together with Speeches by King Charles II. to the Lords and Commons. . . . London, Printed . . . 1702. 8°, A—H 4 in eights, including a half-title, and a, 4 leaves.

PARSONS, ROBERT.

A Booke of Christian exercise, apperteining to Resolvtion, that is, shewing how that we should resolue our selues to be-

come Christians in deed : by R. P. Perused, and accompanied now with a Treatise tending to Pacification : by Edmvnd Bvnny. . . At Oxford, Printed by Ioseph Barnes . . . 1585. 8°, A Cc in eights, Cc 8 blank.

> In the Epistle to Edwin, Archbishop of York, Bunny refers to " that little book of Kempicius " called *The Imitation of Christ.*

PARTRIDGE, JOHN.

The Treasury of commodious Conceits, and hidden Secretes. Commonly called The good Huswynes Closet of prouision for the health of her housholde. Meete and necessary for the profitable vse of all estates. Gathered out of sundrye experyments, lately practised by men of great knowledge : and now amplified and inlarged with diuers necessary and new additions. At London. Printed for Henrye Car. Anno. 1586. 8°, black letter, A—F 4 in eights. Dedicated " To the worshipfull Master Richard Wistow, gentleman." *B. M.*

> On the back of the title occur some verses by the printer " to all that couet the practise of good Huswynerie, as well wyues as maydes," from which it appears that the little book was published at 4d. ; and on the third leaf come the lines by Partridge headed : " The Author to this Booke concerning his freende, whose importunate hire procured him to publish the same."

The Treasvrie of Hidden Secrets, ... London, Printed by Richard Oulton, dwelling neere Christs-church. 1637. 4°, black letter, A—I in fours. *Patent Office.*

The Treasury of Hidden Secrets, . . . London, Printed by Jane Bell, . . . 1653. 4°, A—I in fours. Black letter.

PARTRIDGE, JOHN, *Astrologer.*

Mene, Mene, Tekel, Upharsin. The Second Part of Mene Tekel. Treating of the Year MDCLXXXIX. . . . By John Partridge . . . London, Printed, and Sold by Richard Baldwin . . . MDCLXXXIX. 4°, A—E in fours.

PASCALIUS, CAROLUS.

False Complaints. Or The Censure of an vnthankfull mind, the labour of Carolus Pascalius translated into English by W. C. . . . At London. Printed by Humfrey Lownes, and are to be sold at the West-dore of Paules. 1605. 4°, A—Ii in fours. Dedicated to Prince Henry.

PASQUIER, ETIENNE.

The Iesuites Catechisme. Or Examination of their doctrine. Published in French this present yeere 1602. and nowe translated into English . . . Printed Anno Domini . 1602. 4°. ¶ and ¶¶, 4 leaves each : A—Pp in fours.

PASQUIN OR PASQUIL.
Pasquin risen from the Dead : Or, His own Relation of a late Voyage he made to the other World, in a Discourse with his Friend Marforio. London : Printed by J. C. for N. C. 1674. 8°. A, 4 leaves, title on A 2 : B—R 3 in eights.

PASTORAL.
An Essay upon Pastoral ; Together with some Briefe Reflexions on Eclogue verse. Written by a Gentleman of Quality. . . . London : Printed for Benj. Bragg, . . . 1708. 4°. A², B⁴, C⁴, D⁴, E².

> At the foot of the present copy occurs : "A. Coventry, 1710."

PATERNOSTER.
Here begynneth a ryght profytable treatyse cōpendiously drawen out of many & dyuers wrytynges of holy men / to dyspose men to be vertuously occupyed in theyr myndes & prayers. And declared the Pater noster. Aue. & Credo, in our moder tonge with many other deuoute prayers in lyke wyse medefull to religyous people as to the laye people with many other moost holsomest Instruccyons / as here after it shall folowe. [No imprint but with the mark of Wynkyn de Worde on the *recto* of last leaf and a woodcut of the Crucifixion on the *verso*. The first leaf has cuts on either side, that of the Crucifixion at the end being repeated here. 4°, a—c in sixes.

> One of the instructions in this tract are "to keep your books clean." Fuller Russell, June 1885, No. 109. Lowndes ascribes the tract to Thomas Betton, the Russell Sale catalogue to Thomas Betson ; but it can only be viewed as a translation.

The Pater noster. ӯ Crede. & the cōmaundementes of god in englysh. With many other godly lessons / ryght necessary for iunctions gyuen by thauctoritie of the youth & al other to lerne & knowe : accordyng to the commaūdement & Inkynges hyghnes through this his realme. [Col.] Imprynted at London in Flete strete, at the sygne of ӯ sonne, by me Johan Byddell. Anno dñi. 1537. Cum priuilegio. 8°, A—K in fours. Black letter.

PATERSON, NINIAN.
The Fanatick Indulgence Granted, Anno 1679.

> *Si natura negat, facit indignatio versum Qualem cunque potest.—Juvenal. Sat. I.*

By Mr Ninian Paterson. Edinburgh,

Printed by David Lindsay and his Partners at the foot of Heriot's-Bridge, 1683. 4°, A—C 2 in fours. In verse. Dedicated to James, Duke of Albany. *B. M.*

PATHWAY.
The Pathway to the pleasant Pasture of delitesome and eternall Paradyse . . . Scene and allowed . . . Imprinted at London by Henry Bynneman. 8°, black letter, A—E in eights.

> This work was licensed to John Judson in 1569-70, and probably either assigned to Bynneman or printed by him for Judson.

PAYNELL, THOMAS.
The Piththy and most notable sayinges of al Scripture, gathered by Thomas Paynell : after the manner of common places ; very necessary for al those that delite in the consolations of the Scriptures. 1550. [Col.] Imprinted at London at Fleetebridge by Thomas Gaultier, at the costes & charges of Robert Toye, dwelling in Paules churcheyard at the signe of the Bel. 8°, black letter. Title and dedication to the Lady Mary, 3 leaves : B—aa in eights, aa 8 blank.

> Sothebys, March 1884, Bedford Sale, No. 1078.

PEDANTIUS.
Pedantivs. Comœdia, Olim Cantabrig. Acta in Coll. Trin. Nunquàm antehac Typis evulgata. Londini. Excudebat W. S. Impensis Roberti Mylbourn . . . 1631. 12°. Title and following leaf, 2 leaves : B—H in twelves. With portraits of Dromodotus and Pedantius, the former on the back of the title, the latter on A 2.

PEEBLES.
The thrie Tailes of the thrie Priests of Peblis. Contayning manie notabill examples and sentences, and (that the paper sould not be voide) supplyit with sundrie merie tailes verie pleasant to the reader, and mair exactlie corrected than the former Impression. Ovid, Expectanda dies . . . Imprinted at Edinbvrgh be Robert Charteris. 1603. Cvm Privilegio Regali. 4°, A—E in fours. Black letter.

> Puttick & Simpson, Dec. 10, 1884, No. 232. At the end the printer tells us that he had license to print sundry other delectable discourses, viz., David Lyndsay's Play, Philotus, the Freres of Berwick, and Bilbo, "Quhilk," says he, "are to be sauld in his Buith at the west side of Auld Prouosts close-head on the North side of the Gate, ane lytill aboue the Salt-trone." The "Merry Tales" occupy the margin, and are a selection from the old English book so called, and from other sources.

PEELE, GEORGE.
The Tale of Troy : By G. Peele M. of Arts in Oxford. Printed by A. H. 1604. [Col.] London. Printed by Arnold Hatfield, dwelling in Eliots court in the Little old Baylie : And are to be sold by Nicholas Ling. 1604. A—Q 6 in eights, A blank.

A thumb-book, having two lines on a page. Sothebys, April 8, 1884. No. 829, original vellum wrapper with strings.

PEELE, JAMES.
The maner and fourme how to kepe a perfecte reconyng, after the order of the moste worthie accompts, of Debitour and Creditour, set foorthe in certain tables, with a declaracion therunto belongyng, verie easie to be learned, and also profitable, not onely vnto suche that trade in the facte of Marchauudise, but also vnto any other estate, that will learne the same. 1553. Imprinted at London, by Richard Grafton, printer to the kinges Maiestie . . . Folio. Dedicated to Sir William Densell, Knight, Treasurer of the Queen's Woods, and Governor of the Company of Merchants Adventurers. With eight 4-line stanzas by the author, containing an Exhortation to learn sciences, "especially of the Accompt in the trade of marchaudize." *B. M.*

This copy is imperfect, and contains A, 6 leaves : B, 5, followed by a series of tables, &c., occupying 18 leaves, some numbered.

PELIGROMIUS, SIMON.
Synonymorvm Sylva olim a Simone Pelegromio Collecta. & Alphabeto Flandrico ab eodem authore illustrata : nunc autem è Belgarum sermone in Anglicanum transfusa, & in Alphabeticum ordinem redacta per H. F. . . . Londini, Ex officina Nortoniana. 1606. 8°. ¶, 8 leaves : A—Hh in eights, last leaf blank. Dedicated to Sir F. Walsingham.

This is an enlarged edition of a volume originally printed in 1580.

PELL, DANIEL, *Preacher.*
Pelagos. Nec inter vivos, Nec inter Mortuos. Neither Amongst the living, nor amongst the Dead. Or, An Improvement of the Sea . . . London, Printed for L. C. . . . 1659. 8°. a—d in eights : B—Vv 4 in eights, Vv 4 blank, and A 1 with label. Dedicated to Lord Desborough and others.

PELLEGRINO.
Il Pellegrino Inglese. Ne 'l quale si difende l'innocente, & la Sincera vita de'l pio, & Religioso Re d'Inghilterra Henrico ottauo, bugiandiamente calóniato da Clemēte vii. & da gl' altri adulatori de la Sedia Antichristiana. . . . [Col.] Fine

M. D. LII. 8°, roman letter, A—I in eights.

PEMBLE, WILLIAM.
The Period of the Persian Monarchie. Wherein sundry places of Ezra, Nehemiah and Daniel are cleered . . . by the late learned and godly Man William Pemble, . . . Published and enlarged since his death by his friend, Richard Capel. . . . London Printed by R. Y. for Iohn Bartlet . . . 1631. 4°. A, 2 : B—M in fours.

PEMBROKESHIRE.
A True Relation of the late Successe of the King, And Parliaments Forces in Pembroke-Shire : Wherein the great Victory against the Kings Forces in Wales by Major Generall Lavghorne is fully Related. London, Printed for Edward Husband, . . . Aug. 25. 1645. 4°, 4 leaves.

To the Right Honorable the Parliament of the Common-wealth of England. The humble Petition of Iohn Elliot, of the County of Pembrook Esquire, With Sundry Observations by the Registers to the Committee of Parliament, for the Army, thereupon. A broadside. *B. M.*

PENITEAS.
Peniteas cito libellus iste nuncupatur tractans compendiose de penitentia et eius circumstantijs / ac vitam peccatis depranatam emendare cupientibus multum vtilis et neccessarius. [Col.] Finis opusculi de modo penitendi et confitendi. Londini impressi per Wynadundum de Worde . . . 4°. A, 8 : B, 6. With cuts on both sides of the title. *B. M.*

Peniteas cito . . . [Col.] Finis opusculi . . . Lōdoñ. impressi per winandū de worde . . . 4°, A, 8 : B, 6. *B. M.*

PENN, WILLIAM.
England's Present Interest Discover'd with Honour to the Prince, and Safety to the People. . . . Presented and Submitted to the Consideration of Superiours. . . . Printed in the Year 1675. 4°. A, 4 : a—d in fours : B—E 2 in fours, E 2 blank.

A Treatise of Oaths, Containing Several Weighty Reasons Why the People call'd Quakers refuse to Swear ; . . . Presented to the King and Great Council of England, Assembled in Parliament. . . . Printed Anno 1675. 4°, A—X in fours, X 4 with the *Errata*, and a, 4 leaves.

On the flyleaf of the present copy occurs : " For the Duke of Yorke. W. P."

A Letter from William Penn Proprietary and Governour of Pennsylvania in America, to the Committee of the Free Society of Traders of that Province, residing in London. Containing a General Description of the said Province, . . . Of the first Planters, the Dutch, &c. To which is added, An Account of the City of Philadelphia Newly laid out. . . . With a Portraiture or Plat-form thereof, . . . Printed and Sold by Andrew Sowle, at the Crooked-Billet in Holloway-Lane in Shoreditch, . . . 1683. Folio, pp. 1–14, besides the plan, p. 3 misnumbered p. 1. A—B, 2 leaves each, a leaf unmarked, another marked D, and a final one repaired in the copy used, so as to make it impossible to say if it is properly marked or not.

The last four pages are devoted to a list of localities, residents, &c., in Philadelphia.

A Further Account of the Province of Pennsylvania. And its Improvements. For the Satisfaction of those that are Adventurers, and enclined to be so. [London, 1683-4.] 4", A—C 2 in fours. Directed by Penn from Worminghurst-Place, 12ᵇ of the 10ᵗʰ month, 1683.

The Man of Honour, Occasion'd by the Postscript of Pen's Letter. 4°, 2 leaves. In verse.

PENNINGTON, ISAAC.
The Fundamental Right, Safety and Liberty of the People . . . Briefly Asserted. . . . By Isaac Pennington (junior) Esq; London, Printed by John Macock, . . . 1651. 4°, A—G in fours, G 4 blank.

PENNY, JOHN.
Epigrammata Religiosa, Officiosa, Iocosa. Anglo-latina, Latina, Anglica. Quibus miscentur Anagrammata eiusdem varietatis. In castam Senerioris Musæ Recreationem. Propriorum Amicorum Iussu Publici Iuris facta. . . . [No place, &c. About 1625.] 4°, A—I 2 in fours.

Osterley Park Sale, 1885, No. 1293, with the name of *Edward Gwynn* in gold on cover. Among the poems are some to Sir Edwin Sandys, Mistress Hester Sandys before her marriage, Sir Henry Rainsford, Queen Henrietta Maria, and Charles I. (on his expedition into Spain in 1623). At the end occur verses by W. Neub[urgh] on *I Pen Hony*, anagram of the author's name, *John Peny;* the letters between brackets are supplied on the strength of the name of G. Neuburgh in the body of the volume.

PENOTUS, BERNARDUS.
The Alchymists Enchiridion. In Two Parts. . . . The whole written in Latin long since by the Famous Helvetian Bernardus Penotus a Portu Sancta Maria Aquitani, and now faithfully Englished and Claused By B. P. Philalethes. Lon-

don, Printed for John Wyat, . . . 1692. 8". A, 4 leaves : B—G in eights.

PENRI, JOHN.
An exhortation vnto the gouernours, and people of his Maiesties countrie of Wales, to labour earnestly, to haue the preaching of the Gospell planted among them. There is in the ende something that was not in the former impression. . . . 1588. 8", A—I 2 in fours. Dedicated to the Earl of Pembroke.

A Treatise Wherein is manifestlie proved, that Reformation and those that sincerely fauor the same, are vniustly charged to be enemies, vnto hir Maiestie, and the state. Written both for the clearing of those that stande in that cause : and the stopping of the sclaunderovs mouthes of all the enemies thereof . . . 1590. 4°. *, 4 leaves : ¶, 2 leaves : B—I 2 in fours.

A defence of that which hath bin written in the questions of the ignorant ministerie, and the communicating with them. By Iohn Penri. 8°, B—I in fours, or pp. 64. Without a title and sign. A. *B. M.*

PENTON, STEPHEN, *Principal of St. Edmund Hall, Oxford.*
A Horn Book, or A. B. C. for Children. [About 1670.]

Mentioned by Knight in his *Life of Colet,* ed. 1823, p. 129, as by Penton; who also, it seems, wrote *The Guardian's Instruction,* 8°, 1688.

PERCIVAL, THOMAS.
The Rye-house Travestie. Or, A True Account and Declaration of the Horrid and Execrable Conspiracy against His Majesty King William and the Government. Collected out of Original Papers. . . . In a Letter to . . . Thomas Sprat, Lord Bishop of Rochester . . . London, Printed for A. Bell at the Cross-Keys in the Poultry. 1696. 4°, B—L in fours, and the title.

PERCY, JAMES, *Claimant of the Earldom of Northumberland.*
A Narrative of the Proceedings of the Petitioner, Since, His Petitions were Dismissed by the Right Honorable, the House of Lords, and his Case left to the Law. [About 1688.] Folio. A—D, 2 leaves each, besides an extra leaf between C and D, or pp. 18.

The British Museum copy (ª,ᵛ̣ K. 21) contains some other Petitions in this case.

James Percy claimed to be cousin and next heir of Jocelin, Earl of Northumberland, who died s. p. m. in 1668.

PERCY, WILLIAM, *Gentleman.*
The Compleat Swimmer : Or, The Art of Swimming ; Demonstrating the Rules

and Practice thereof, in an Exact, Plain and Easie Method . . . London : Printed by J. C. for Henry Fletcher, . . . 1658. 8⁰. A, 4 : B—G 2 in eights, besides the title and frontispiece.

PEREGRIN, JAMES [? *pseud.*]
The Letters Patents of the Presbyterie : With the Plea and Frvits of the Prelacie Manifested out of the Scriptures, . . . By Iames Peregrin. . . . Printed, MDCXXXII. 4⁰, A—H 2 in fours.

PERICLES OF GREECE.
The Most Renowned History of . . . Pericles of Greece . . . Printed for the Booksellers of London and Westminster. 12⁰, A—H 6 in twelves, including a woodcut frontispiece. With rough cuts.

PERKINS, WILLIAM.
A Discovrse of the Damned Art of Witchcraft ; . . . Printed by Cantrel Legge, . . . 1610. 8⁰. ¶, 8 leaves : A—Q in eights : ¶¶, 4.

PERLIN, ETIENNE.
Description Des Royavlmes d'Angleterre et d'Escosse. Composé par Maistre Estienne Perlin. A Paris, Chez François Trepeau, . . . 1558. 8⁰, A—E 5 in eights. Dedicated by Perlin to the Duchesse de Berri, only sister of Henri de Valois, king of France, "futur monarque & Empereur de tout le monde." *B. M.*

PERRAULT, FRANÇOIS.
The Devill of Mascon. Or, A true Relation of the chiefe things which an Vncleane Spirit did, and said at Mascon in Burgundy, in the House of Mʳ Francis Perreand Minister of the Reformed Church in the same Towne. Published in French lately by Himselfe ; And now made English by one that hath a particular knowledge of the truth of this Story. Oxford, Printed by Hen : Hall, . . . for Rich : Davis, 1658. 8⁰, A—D in eights. With a very interesting preface to the translator P. Du Moulin by Robert Boyle, and Du Moulin's reply.

PERRINCHIEF, RICHARD.
Nvutivs A Mortvis, Hoc est Stvpendvm Ivxta ac Tremendû Colloquiû . . . Inter Manes Henrici VIII. & Caroli I. . . . Londini, Sumptibus R. P. Et veneunt, Parisiis. . . . M.DC.LVII. 4⁰, A—C in fours, besides an extra leaf with verses by the author.

A Messenger from the Dead, Or, Conference Full of Stupendious horrour, . . .

Between the Ghosts of Henry the 8. and Charles the First of England, in Windsore-Chappel, where they were both Buried . . . London, Printed for Tho. Vere, and W. Gilbertson . . . 1658 4⁰, A—C in fours, A 1 with a frontispiece and C 4 blank.

The Syracusan Tyrant : Or, The Life of Agathocles. With some Reflexions on the practices of our Modern Usurpers. [Quotations.] London, Printed by T. F. for R. Royston, . . . MDCLXI. 8⁰. A, 8 : (a), 8 : B—S 4 in eights. Dedicated in a very adulatory strain to Thomas, Earl of Southampton.

> This was, of course, written just after the Restoration, to throw odium on Cromwell and the Republic.

The Sicilian Tyrant : Or, The Life of Agathocles. London, Printed by J. Grover for R. Royston . . . 1676. 8⁰, A—T 4 in eights, besides a folded plate representing Tyrannus (Cromwell) crowned by Perfidy and Cruelty. With a portrait of Agathocles and an engraved title, both included in the sheets.

PERROT, LUCE.
An Account of Several Observable Speeches of Mʳˢ Luce Perrot The Late Wife of Mʳ Robert Perrot of London, Minister. Spoken by her chiefly in the time of her sickness, and a little before her Death ; . . . . London, Printed for R. P. 1679. 4", A—E 2 in fours, the last two leaves with "Some Breathings upon the Death of Mʳˢ Luce Perrot, December 14, 1678," and the Epitaph, both in verse.

PERSIUS FLACCUS, AULUS.
Aulus Persius Flaccus His Satyres : Translated into English, By Barten Holyday, . . . And now newly by him reviewed and augmented. . . . London Printed by W. Stansby for W. Arundell, . . . 1617. 8⁰, A—G 4 in eights, A 1 and G 4 blank. *B. M.*

PETER À VALCAREN, JOHN.
A Relation or Diary of the Siege of Vienna. Written by John Peter a Valcaren, Judge-Advocate of the Imperial Army. Drawn from the Original by His Majestie's Command. London, Printed for William Nott . . . and George Wells . . . 1684. 4⁰, B—P in fours, the title and two plans, one of Vienna, the other of the Turkish Camp, accompanied by description, 2 leaves more.

PETERS, HUGH.
Milke for Babes, And Meat for Men. Or, Principles necessary to be knowne, and

N

learned, of such as would know Christ here, to be knowne of him hereafter. . . . London Printed by E. P. for J. W. 1641. 8°, A - C 4 in eights, C 4 blank.

The History of the Life and Death of Hugh Peters that Arch-traytor, from his Cradell to the Gallowes. With a Map of his prophane Jests, cruell Actions, and wicked Counsels. Published as a Warning piece to all Traytors. . . . London, Printed for Fr. Coles, at the Lambe in the Old-Baily, 1661. 4°, A—B in fours, with a large cut on the title, repeated at the end.

PETRE, FATHER.

A Man in Favour, Or, The way to Preferment. To the Tune of, Would you be a Man of Fashion. Printed for J. H. 1688. A broadside, containing 6 stanzas of 8 lines. With the music.

Father Peter's Policy Discovered : Or, the Prince of Wales Prov'd a Popish Perkin. London, Printed for P. M. A leaf of verses.

PETRIE, ALEXANDER, *Minister of the Scots Congregation at Rotterdam.*

A Compendious History of the Catholick Church, From the Year 600 untill the Year 1600. Shewing Her Deformation and Reformation. Together with the Rise, Reign, Rage, and Begin-Fall of the Roman Antichrist . . . Hague : Printed by Adrian Vlack. M. DC. LXII. Folio. a—e, 2 leaves each : A—7 1, 2 leaves each : (A)—7 (K), 2 leaves each. Dedicated to William, Prince of Orange.

PETT, SIR PETER.

The Happy Future State of England : Or, A Discourse by way of Letter to the late Earl of Anglesey, Vindicating Him from the Reflections of an Affidavit Published by the House of Commons, A° 1680. by occasion whereof Observations are made concerning infamous Witnesses. . . . Before the Discourse, is a large Preface, giving an Account of the whole Work. . . . London, Printed MDCLXXXVIII. Folio. Title and following leaf : (a)—(b), 2 leaves each : A*—S*, 2 leaves each : [a]—[d], 2 leaves each : [e], 1 leaf : A - 4 Z, 2 leaves each : *Errata,* 1 leaf : *Part Second,* with a new title, A—Oo, 2 leaves each : *Errata,* 1 leaf. *B. M.*

The first portion is inscribed to the Earl of Sunderland ; the second, treating of the Dispensative Power, to the Earl of Melfort, by the author.

PETTIT, EDWARD, *M.A.*

The Vision of Purgatory, Anno 1680. In which The Errors and Practices of the Church and Court of Rome are Discover'd. . . . Written by Heraclito Democritus . . . London Printed by T. N. for Henry Brome . . . 1680. 8°. A, 5, besides a frontispiece : B—L in eights.

The Visions of the Reformation : Or, A Discovery of the Follies and Villanies that have been Practis'd in Popish and Fanatical Thorough Reformations, since the Reformation of the Church of England. . . . By Edward Pettit, M.A. the Authour of *The Visions of Purgatory.* . . . London, Printed for Joanna Brome. 1683. 8°, A—Q 4 in eights, including a frontispiece.

PETTO, SAMUEL, *of Sudbury, Suffolk.*

A Faithful Narrative of the Wonderful and Extraordinary Fits which Mr Tho. Spatchet (Late of Dunwich and Cookly) was under by Witchcraft : Or, A Mysterious Providence in his even Unparallel'd Fits. . . . The whole drawn up and written by Samuel Petto, Minister of the Gospel at Sudbury in Suffolk, who was an Eye-witness of a great part. With a Necessary Preface. . . . London, Printed for John Harris . . . 1693. Price 6d. 4°. A, 2 : B—E in fours.

PETTY, SIR WILLIAM, *F.R.S.*

The Discourse Made before the Royal Society The 26. of November 1674. Concerning the Use of Duplicate Proportion . . . London : Printed for John Martyn, . . . 1674. 12°, A—F in twelves : G, 8, and (a), 4 leaves. A 1 has the *Imprimatur.*

Political Arithmetick . . . London, Printed for Robert Clavel . . . 1691. 8°. A, 4 leaves : B—H in eights : I, 4 : and a, between A and B, 8.

From the *Imprimatur* it appears that this book was written long before it was published.

The Political Anatomy of Ireland. With the Establishment for that Kingdom when the late Duke of Ormond was Lord Lieutenant. Taken from the Records. To which is added Verbum Sapienti, or an Account of the Wealth and Expences of England. . . . By Sir William Petty . . . Surveyor-General of the Kingdom of Ireland. London : Printed for D. Brown, and W. Rogers, . . . 1691. 8°, A—Q 4 in eights. Dedicated by N. Tate to the Duke of Ormond.

PEYTON, THOMAS, *of Lincoln's-Inn.*

The Glasse of Time In the two first Ages. Divinely handled. By Thomas Peyton of Lincolnes-Inne. London, Printed by B. A. & T. F. 4°, A—Z in fours, the leaf after the engraved title marked A, but only two other leaves in that signature.

> A reissue of the copies of 1623 with a new imprint and the second title cancelled, leaving a gap between L 3 and M 2. Sothebys, June 30, 1885, No. 881, the Heber copy.

PHAER, THOMAS, *M.D.*

The regiment of life, Wherevnto is added a treatise of the pestilence, with the Booke of children, newly corrected and enlarged by Thomas Phaire. [Col.] Imprinted at London by Edwarde Whitchurche, in the yeare of oure Lorde God M.D.LX. Cum priuilegio . . . 8°, A—X in eights.

The Regiment of Lyfe, Whereunto is added a treatise of the pestilence . . . newly corrected & enlarged by Thomas Faier An. 1567. 8°, black letter.

> Puttick & Simpson, Dec. 10, 1884, No. 189, imperfect. The *Book of Children* is included.

The Regiment of Life . . . Imprinted at London by Edward Allde 1596. 4°, black letter, A—Y in fours.

PHILANACTODEMUS.

Quæres, Seasonable to be humbly presented to King Charles, at Holmby, and others, for his Parliament at Westminster: With a few to be taken to heart, by the Common people of England, to be communicated. Whereunto is added a Prologue and an Epilogue, for the better Illustration of the thing to the different Reader. Printed in the Yeare 1647. 4°, A—D 2 in fours.

PHILANDER ANTIPHILOINOS.

Bacchus Conculcatus, Or, Sober Reflections upon Drinking. An Essay. . . . By Philander Antiphiloinos, A Probationer. Printed in the Year MDCXCI. 4°, 4 leaves. In verse.

PHILANDER MISIATRUS.

The Honour of the Gout: Or, A Rational Discourse, demonstrating that the Gout is one of the greatest Blessings which can befal Mortal Man ; that all Gentlemen who are weary of it, are their own Enemies ; that those Practitioners who offer at the Cure, are the vainest and most mischievous Cheats of Nature. By way of Letter to an Eminent Citizen, Wrote in the heart of a violent Paroxysm, and now Published for the Common Good. London, Printed for A. Baldwin, in Warwick-Lane. MDCXCIX. 8°, A—F in sixes.

PHILANGLUS, JOHANNES.

England's Alarm : Or, A most Humble Declaration, Address, and Fervent Petition, to Charles the Second, . . . and . . . the Parliament . . . As also to the City of London, and the whole Nation in general. Concerning the great Overtures, . . . about to inundate and pour in upon us, . . . London : Printed for Thomas Pasham in Fleet-lane. 1679. Folio, A—C, 2 leaves each.

PHILEROY, E. [*? pseud.*]

A Satyrical Vision, Or, Tragy-Comedy as it was lately Acted in the City of Bristol, Discovered in a Dream. [Here follow some verses.] By E : Phileroy. London, Printed by G. Croom, for the Author. 1684. 4°, A—C in fours, C 4 blank. In verse.

PHILIPS, FATHER.

The Coppy of a Letter of Father Philips, the Queenes Confessor, which was thought to be sent into France to Mr Mountagues ; discovered and produced . . . . Lamentably complaining of the times and present state of things, and this was written presently after Piercy and Jermyn fled. Printed in the yeare, 1641. 4°, 4 leaves.

PHILIPS, JOHN.

Don Jvan Lamberto : . . . London, Printed by J. Brudenell, for Henry Marsh . . . 1661. 4°, black letter, A—G in fours, besides the title and a woodcut frontispiece representing Richard Cromwell led by Desborough and Lambert. Without cuts.

Don Jvan Lamberto : Or, A Comical History of the Late Times. The First Part. By Montelion, Knight of the Oracle, &c. The second Edition Corrected. London : Printed by J. Brudenell for Henry Marsh . . . 1661. 4°, black letter, A—O in fours, and the title. With some coarse ballad cuts.

Don Juan Lamberto : Or, A Comical History of Our Late Times . . . In Two Parts. By Montelion Knight of the Oracle, &c. The Third Edition Corrected. London, Printed for Henry Marsh . . . 1664. 4°, black letter, A—O in fours. With a portrait of Richard Cromwell led by Desborough and Lambert.

> The second part, dated 1661, commences on H 2, preceded by a frontispiece of the *Giant Husonio* [Lord Hewson]. G 4 is apparently a blank. It purports to be " Printed by T. Leach for Henry Marsh," and has a few rough cuts.

Don Juan Lamberto: .. In Two Parts. By Montelion Knight of the Oracle, &c. The Third Edition Corrected. London, Printed for Henry Marsh, . . . 1665. 4°, B— in fours, and the title-page. Black letter.

The copy used ended imperfectly on E 3 with the commencement of Part 2, and had no frontispiece.

The English Fortune-Tellers : Containing several Necessary Questions Resolved by the Ablest Antient Philosophers, and Modern Astrologers. Gathered from their Writings and Manuscripts, By J. P. Student in Astrology. . . . Licensed and Entred, according to Order. London, Printed for E. Brooksby, . . . B. Deacon . . . 1703. Large 4°, A—U 2 in fours, including a frontispiece. With diagrams and other cuts. In verse.

A satire on the astrologers and fortunetellers. Sothebys, June 30, 1885, No. 883, the B.A.P. copy.

PHILLIPS, FABIAN.

The Speech without Doore. Delivered July 9. 1644. In the absence of the Speaker, and in the hearing of above 200003 persons then present ; who unanimously consented to all propositions therein contained, . . . [London, 1644.] 4°, A—B in fours, B 4 blank.

The copy employed is subscribed at the end *Fab: Phillips,* apparently in the autograph of Phillips.

The Antiquity, Legality, Reason, Duty and Necessity of Præ-emption and Pourveyance for the King : Or, Compositions for his Pourveyance : . . . . By Fabian Philipps . . . London, Printed by Richard Hodgkinson, for the Author, and are to be sold by Henry Marsh . . . 1663. 4°, A—3 R in fours, *Errata,* 1 leaf, and a—b in fours. Dedicated to Christopher, Lord Hatton.

There are copies on large paper.

The Established Religion of England, Vindicated from All Popular and Republican Principles and Mistakes : With a Respect to the Laws of God, Man, Nature and Nations. By Fab. Philipps of the Middle Temple, Esquire. London, Printed for the Author, MDCLXXXVII. Folio. Title and dedication to James II., 3 leaves : (a)—(d), 2 leaves each : (a) repeated—(b), 2 leaves each : B—7 G 2 in fours.

PHILLIPS, R.

The Victory of Cupid over the Gods and Goddesses : Display'd in Several Poetical Stories. . . . London, Printed for Tho. Simmons . . . 1683. 4°, A—H in fours,

H 4 blank, besides the title and a leaf of dedication to the Duchess of Somerset.

PHILO-BRITAN.

The Defence of the Scots Settlement at Darien, Answer'd, Paragraph by Paragraph. By Philo-Britan. London, Printed, and Sold by the Booksellers . . . 1699. 8°, B—N 2 in fours.

PHILOMELA.

Poems on Several Occasions. Written by Philomela. London : Printed for John Dunton at the Raven in Jewen-street. 1696. 8°. Title and Preface, 8 leaves under A or a : a, 4 leaves : A—E 4 in eights : Aa—Ee in eights, Ee 4-8 with Advertisements.

The Preface, written by Elizabeth Johnson, from Harding's Rents, May 10, 1696, states that the book was written by a young lady, whose modesty prevented her from putting her name. At the end we are told that, as the young lady resided far from London, she was in no way responsible for misprints.

PHILOMUSUS.

The Academy of Complements. . . . The last Edition, with two Tables, . . . London, Printed for Humphrey Moseley, . . . 1654. 12°. Frontispiece by W. Marshall, dated 1650, 1 leaf : A, 12 leaves : a, 4 leaves : B—P in twelves.

The Academy of Complements. . . . The last Edition, with two Tables, . . . London, Printed by Tho. Leach, and Tho. Child, 1663. 12°. *, 12 leaves, including a frontispiece, and B—P in twelves ; no A.

The Academy of Complements, . . . The last Edition, with two Tables, . . . London, Printed for A. Mosely, at the Princes Arms in St. Pauls Church-yard. 1664. 12°, A—P in twelves.

PHYSICIANS.

An Historical Account of Proceedings, betwixt the College of Physicians and Surgeons, since their Incorporation. Folio, 4 leaves.

PIEDMONT.

A short and faithfull Account of the late Commotions in the Valleys of Piedmont, Within the Dominions of the Duke of Savoy. With some Reflections on Mʳ Stouppe's collected Papers touching the same businesse. Printed for W. P. and G. L. 1655. 4°, 4 leaves.

A Rare, True, and Wonderful Relation of a Town in the Principality of Piedmont, within these few Weeks sunk under

Ground, so as nothing of it appears, only two of the Inhabitants survive in safety. . . . London, Printed for T. Simmons. 1679. 4°, 4 leaves.

An Account of the Late Persecution of the Protestants in the Vallys of Piemont; By the Duke of Savoy and the French King, In the Year 1686. Never before Publisht. Oxford, Printed at the Theatre for John Crosley, 1688. 4°. Imprimatur, title, and preface, 3 leaves : A—1 2 in fours.

PIERS PLOUGHMAN.
Piers plowmans exhortation vnto the lordes knightes and burgoysses of the Parlyamenthouse. Imprinted At London by Anthony Scoloker Dwelling in the Sauoy rentes. Without Tempelbarre. Cum priuilegio . . . 8°, A—B 4 in eights. *B. M.*

PIGGE.
Pigges Corantoe, Or Newes from the North. London, Printed for L. C. and M. W. 1642. 4°, 4 leaves. In prose.

PIRATES.
An Exact Narrative of the Tryals of the Pirates : And all the Proceedings at the late Goal-Delivery of the Admiralty, held in the Old-Bayly, on Thursday & Saturday, the 7th and 9th of Jan. 167¾. . . . . For Taking and Robbing a Ship called the Palm-Tree, neer Harwich. As likewise the Fineing of an Ostend Captain £400 and Two of his Officers £50 a Piece, for not Strikeing Sail to the Woolwich, one of his Maiesties Frigates . . . Printed in the Year. 1675. 4°, 4 leaves.

An Exact Narrative of the Tryals of the Pyrats : And all the Proceedings at the late Goal-Delivery of the Admiralty, Held in the Old-Bayly, on Thursday and Saturday, the 7th and 9th of Jan. 167¾. . . . For taking and Robbing Two Ships, viz. the *Robert*, near the Fly : and the *Anne* on the Dogger-Sands ; With several others. And many other Circumstances there very Remarkable : The like Court having not been held for many years before. Printed in the Year, 1675. 4°, 4 leaves.

PLAGUE.
A short fourme of thankesgeuyng to God for ceassing the contagious sicknes of the plague, to be vsed in Common prayer, on Sundayes, Wednesdayes, and Frydayes, in steade of the Comon prayers, used in the time of mortalitie. Set forth by the Byshop of London, . . . [Col.]

Imprinted at London in Powles Church yarde, by Richard Jugge and John Cawood, Printers to the Quenes Maiestie. 22 Iannarii. 1563. Cum priuilegio . . . 4°, 4 leaves.

Orders, Thovght Meete by her Maiestie, and her priuie Counsell, . . . Also, an aduise set downe vpon her Maiesties expresse commaundement, . . . Imprinted at London by the Deputies of Christopher Barker, . . . An. Do. 1592. 4°, A—B in fours. Black letter.

The Families best Guide, or a Looking-glass in time of Plague and Pestilence . . . London : Printed for F. Clifton in the Old-Bailey. [1636.] A broadside. With four cuts.

PLAGUES.
The Fifteen Plagues of A Lawyer, A Quack Doctor, A Recruiting Captain, A Fleetstreet Madam, A Pawn-Broker, A Tally-man, ... To which is added, The Fifteen Plagues of a Foot-man, Butler, Cook-maid, Chamber-maid, and Nursery-maid. London, Printed by H. Goodwin, in the Strand. [About 1700.] 8", 4 leaves. In verse.

PLANTATIONS.
The Groans of the Plantations : Or A True Account of their Grievous and Extreme Sufferings by the Heavy Impositions upon Sugar, and other Hardships. Relating more particularly to the Island of Barbados. By a Merchant. London, Printed by M. Clark in the Year MDCLXXXIX. 4°, A—E 2 in fours.

PLATT, SIR HUGH.
Delights for Ladies, . . . London, Printed by R. Y. and are to bee sold by Iames Boler. 1632. 12°, A—H in twelves, H 12 blank.

Delights for Ladies, ... London, Printed by Robert Young. 1636. 12", A—H in twelves, H 12 blank. Printed within borders.

PLAYFORD, JOHN.
A Brief Introduction to the Skill of Music : . . . London, Printed by William Godbid for John Playford, . . . 1666. 8°, A—L 4 in eights, besides the title and portrait.

PLEUNUS, HENRY.
A New, Plain, Methodical and Compleat Italian Grammar, whereby you may very soon attain to the perfection of the Italian Tongue. Dedicated to the Worthy English Gentlemen, Merchants at Legorne . . . By Henry Pleunus Master of the

Latin, French, Italian, German, and English Tongue. In Livorno . . . . [Circâ 1700.] 8°. Title, &c., 4 leaves: A—R in eights. *B. M.*

A New, Plain, And Compleat Italian Grammar . . . . Legorne M.D.CCII. 8°. *, 4 leaves: A—V 6 in eights, R 8 blank. *B. M.*

Nuova, E Perfetta Grammatica Inglese, Che contiene con metodo tutta la Teorica, e Pratica di questa Lingua ; . . . Da Arrigo Pleunus, Maestro di Lingue. . . . In Livorno, . . . M.DCC.I. 8°. *, 4 leaves: A—R 7 in eights. Dedicated to Cosmo III., Grand Duke of Tuscany. *B. M.*

PLINIUS SECUNDUS, CAIUS.

A Summarie of the Antiquities, and wonders of the Worlde, abstracted out of the sixtene first bookes of the excellent Historiographer Plinie, wherein may be seene the wonderfull workes of God to his creatures, translated out of French into Englishe by I. A. Imprinted at London by Henry Denham, for Thomas Hacket, and are to be solde at his shop in Lumbert streate. [1566.] 8vo, black letter, A—H in eights. *B. M.*

Pliny's Panegyrick Upon the Emperor Trajan, Faithfully Rendred into English from the Original. By George Smith of North Nibley in the County of Glocester, Esq ; . . . London ; Printed . . . MDCCII. 8°, A—L in eights.

PLOT, ROBERT, *Keeper of the Ashmolean Museum, and Sec. R. S.*

De Origine Fontium, Tentamen Philosophicum . . . Per Rob. Plot, L.L.D. . . . Oxonii . . . . M.DC.LXXXV. 8°. Frontispiece: a—c 2 in fours: A—Aa 2 in fours. Dedicated to Elias Ashmole.

On the title of the copy employed occurs : "E Libris Edm. Halley ex dono Authoris."

PLUTARCH.

The Philosophy. Commonly Called, The Morals . . . . Newly Revised and Corrected. London, Printed by S. G. and are to be sold by George Sawbridge . . . 1657. Folio. A, 4 leaves with title, &c., and A (repeated)—5 E in sixes.

POEMS.

Poems on Several Occasions : Together with some Odes in Imitation of M' Cowley's Stile and Manner. *Solus sapiens scit amare.* London, Printed for Luke Stokoe, . . . and George Harris, . . . 1703. 8°, A—H in eights, including a half-title.

Poems on the Four Last Things : Viz. I.

Death. II. Judgment. III. Hell. IV. Heaven. *Learn to live well,* . . . Sir J. Denham. London : Printed and Sold by A. Betsworth, at the Red-Lyon on London-Bridge. 1706. 12°. Title, the *Author to his Book,* in imitation of Ovid, in verse, and Table, 3 leaves : B—H in eights : I, 5.

POETÆ.

Poetæ Britannici. A Poem, Satyrical and Panegyrical. [Quot. from Horace.] London, Printed for A. Roper . . . and R. Basset, . . . MDCC. Folio. A—G, 2 leaves each.

POLAND.

Newes from Poland. Wherein is Trvly inlarged the Occasion, Progression, and Interception of the Turks formidable threatning of Europe. And particularly the inuading of the Kingdome of Poland. . . . At London, Imprinted by F. K. for B. D. and William Lee, . . . 1621. 4°, A—D in fours, A 1 blank. *B. M.*

POLICIES.

Modern Policies, taken from Machiavel, Borgia, and other choise Authors, by an eye-witnesse. . . . London, Printed for Thomas Dring . . . 1652. 12°, A—G in twelves. Dedicated "To my very good Lord My Lord R. B, E."

The writer does not disclose himself.

POLLANUS, V.

Vera Expositio Dispvtationis institvtæ mandato D. Mariae Reginae Angl. Franc. & Hibern. &c. in Synodo Ecclesiastica, Londini in Comitijs regni ad 18. Octob. Anno 1553. . . . 1554. [Col.] Impressvm Romae Coram castro S. Angeli ad signum S. Petri. Anno 1554. 8°, A in eights and a—d in eights.

Probably printed at London.

POLLEXFEN.

A Discourse of Trade, Coyn, and Paper Credit : And of Ways and Means to Gain, and Retain Riches. To which is added the Argument of a Learned Counsel, upon an Action of the Case brought by the East-India-Company against M' Sands an Interloper. London, Printed for Brabazon Aylmer . . . 1697. 8°. Title, &c., 4 leaves : B—M 4 in eights : The Argument, A—E in eights.

England and East-India Inconsistent in their Manufactures. Being An Answer to a Treatise, Intituled, An Essay on the East-India Trade. By the Author of, The Essay of Wayes and Means. [By M' Pollexfen, one of the Com" for Trade.]

London, Printed in the Year, 1697. 8°, A—D in eights, D 7-8 blank.

The authorship is noted on the title in a coeval hand.

Discourses on the Publick Revenues, and on the Trade of England. In Two Parts. . . . By the Author of the Essay on Ways and Means. . . . London : Printed for James Knapton, . . . 1698. 8°. 2 vols.

[A Vindication of some Assertions Relating to Coin and Trade, From the Reflections made by the Author of the Essay on Ways and Means . . . London, Printed for Geo. Grafton, . . . 1699. 8°. A, 3 leaves : B—M in eights : N, 1.]

POLSTED, EZEKIEL.
The Excise-Man. Shewing the Excellency of his Profession, how and in what it precedes all others ; the Felicity he enjoys, the Pleasures as well as Qualifications that inevitably attend him, notwithstanding the opprobrious Calumnies of the most inveterate Detractor : Discovering his Knowledge in the Arts, Men and Laws. In an Essay . . . London, Printed and Sold by John Mayor, at the Golden Cross in Thames-Street near Queenhithe. 1697. 12°, A—Q in fours, and (a), 4 leaves. Dedicated to the Commissioners of the Excise.

POLTER, RICHARD.
The Pathway to perfect Sayling. Being a deliuerie in as breefe manner as may bee, of the sixe principall pointes or groundes, concerning Nauigation : Written by Richard Polter, one of the late principall Maisters of the Nauie Royall. . . . London Printed by Edward Allde for Iohn Tappe, . . . 1605. 4°, black letter, A—F 2 in fours.

POPERY.
The Popes Proclamation : Together with the Lawes and Ordinances established by him and his Shavelings, concerning his adherents and rights which hee claimeth in England. Whereunto is added Six Articles exhibited against Cheapside Crosse, . . . Printed in the yeare 1641. 4°, 4 leaves.

Plots, Conspiracies and Attempts of Domestick and Forraigne Enemies, of the Romish Religion. Against the Princes, and Kingdomes of England, Scotland and Ireland . . . Briefly collected by G. B. C. . . . London, Printed by G. M. for Ralph Rounthwait, 1642. 4°, A—F in fours.

By the King. A Proclamation for banishing all Popish Priests and Jesuits, and putting the Laws in speedy and due Execution against Popish Recusants. In the Savoy, Printed by the Assigns of John Bill and Christopher Barker, . . . 1666. A broadside.

A Poem on that Execrable Treason Plotted by the Papists on the 5th of November, Anno 1605. . . . Cambridge, Printed by John Hayes, . . . 1670. 4°, A—B in fours.

Trap ad Crucem ; Or, The Papists Watchword. Being an Impartial Account of some late Informations taken before several of his Majesties Justices of the Peace in and about the City of London. Also a Relation of the several Fires that of late have hapened in and about the said City . . . London, Printed in the Year, 1670. 4°, A—C in fours.

The Last Speech, and Confession of the Whore of Babylon, at her place of Execution, on the Fifth of November last. Whereunto is added, The Famous Story of the Bell, used by the Irish Papists, taken out of the Bishop of Down and Conner's Epistle to his Persuasive against Popery. . . . London, Printed for K. B. in Little Britain. MDCLXXIII. 4°, 4 leaves.

A Present for a Papist : Or The Life and Death of Pope Joan, Plainly Proving out of the Printed Copies, and Manuscripts of Popish Writers and others, that a Woman called Joan, was really Pope of Rome, And was there Deliver'd of a Bastard Son in the open Street, as She went in Solemn Procession. By a Lover of Truth, denying Roman Infallibility. London, Printed for T. D. and are to be sold at the Ship in St. Mary Axe, and by most Booksellers, 1675. 8°. A, 3 leaves besides a frontispiece : B—M 3 in eights.

The Character of A Turbulent, Pragmatical Jesuit and Factious Romish Priest. London : Printed for Langley Curtis, . . . 1678. 4°, 4 leaves.

The Pope's Advice to His Sons. A Conference in the Castle St. Angelo, Between the Pope, the Emperour, and the King of Spain. Printed from an Ancient Manuscript. London, Printed for J. S. at the Grate in Little Britain. 1679. 4°, A—B 2 in fours. In verse.

A Passionate Satyr upon a Devillish Great He-Whore that lives yonder at Rome. [1679.] A broadside in verse.

A Ballad upon the Popish Plot. Written by a Lady of Quality . . . To the Tune of *Packington's Pound.* A broadside. [1679.]

The Whore of Babylon's Pockey Priest ; Or, a True Narrative of the Apprehension of William Geldon alias Bacon, a Secular Priest of the Church of Rome now Prisoner in Newgate . . . London, Printed for Thomas Fox Bookseller in Westminster-Hall. 167⁹⁄₈₀. Folio, A—E, 2 leaves each.

The Papists Bloody Oath of Secrecy, And Letany of Intercession for the Carrying on of the present Plot. . . . Together, with some further Information, relative to the Plot, and Murther of Sir Edmundbury Godfrey. . . . London, Printed for Randal Taylor, . . . 1680. Folio, A—F, 2 leaves each.

An Amicable Accommodation of the Difference between the Representer and the Answerer. In Return to the Last Reply against The Papist Protesting against Protestant Popery. Permissu Superiorum. London, Printed by H. Hills, . . . 1686. 4°, A—F 2 in fours.

The Muses Farewel to Popery and Slavery, Or, A Collection of Miscellany Poems, Satyrs, Songs, &c. Made by the most Eminent Wits of the Nation, as the Plans, Intreagues, and Plots of Priests and Jesuits gave occasion. *Suis & ipsa Roma viribus ruit.* Hor. London, Printed for N. R. H. F. and J. K. . . . 1689. 8°. Part 1, B—K in eights, besides 3 leaves with title, preface, and contents. Supplement, B—G in eights, besides title and contents.

The Intrigues of the Conclave, Set forth in a Relation of what passed therein at the Election of Sixtus V. & Clement VIII. With an Historical Account of the Election of Popes in Former Ages : . . . London, Printed for J. C. near Fleetbridge. 1690. 4°, B—E in fours, a leaf after E 4, and the title.

A Tragedy, Called The Popish Plot, Reviv'd : Detecting the Secret League between the late King James and the French King; . . . Dedicated to Sir Roger L'Estrange . . . By a sincere Lover of his Country. London, Printed for the Author, 1696. 4°, A—G in fours.

PORDAGE, SAMUEL.

Mundorum Explicatio ; Wherein are couched the Mysteries of the External, Internal, and Eternal Worlds ; Also, The Explanation of an Hieroglyphical Figure. A Sacred Poem, by S. P. Armig. . . . London, Printed for Lodowick Lloyd, . . . 1663. 8°. A, 3 leaves, with the title, dedication to the Saviour, and first

leaf of Preface : (a)—(b) in eights : B—Y in eights, Y 7–8 with Advertisements. With a plate of the Figure.

PORTIFORIUM.

Portiforiū seu Breuiarium ad vsum ecclesie Sarisburiēsis castigatum / suppletum / marginalibus quotationibus adornatū / ac nunc primum ad verissimum ordinalis exemplar in suum ordinem a peritissimis viris redactum. Pars Estivalis. [Col.] Pars estiualis tam de tēpore / q̄ de sanctis portiforii ad vsuȝ insignis ecclesie Sar. optimȩ formulȩ (vt res ipsa īdicat) diligentissime reuisum et correctū . . . impressa p̄ franciscū regnault. Anno domini Millesimo quingentesimo trigesimo quinto. Large 4°. Printed in red and black, in two columns, with numerous woodcuts, including one occupying nearly the whole of the title. Title, Calendar, and *Extracta de Compoto*, 8 leaves : Aa—Ff 6 in eights : *Psalterium*, with a separate title, a—p 6 in eights : *Propriū sanctor.*, with a separate title, aa—oo in eights.

Cc 2 is unmarked, and Cc 8 is wrongly so marked.

PORTUGAL.

The Explanation. Of the Trve and Lawfvll Right and Tytle, of the Moste Excellent Prince, Anthonie the first of that name, King of Portugall, concerning his warres, againste Phillip King of Castile, and against his subiectes and adherents, for the recoucrie of his kingdome. Together with a Briefe Historye of all that hath passed aboute that matter, vntill the yeare of our Lord. 1583. Translated into English and conferred with the Latine Copie. By the commaundement and order of the Superiors. At Leyden In the Printing house of Christopher Plantyn. 1585. 4°, A—G in fours, besides the title and folded table.

Don Sebastian King of Portugall. An Historical Novel. In Four Parts. Done out of French by Mr Ferrand Spence. London, Printed for R. Bentley and S. Magnes. 1683. 12°. A, 6 leaves, A 1 blank : B—G in twelves : H, 6. Dedicated by Spence to the Countess of Stanford [*sic*].

Grammatica Anglo-Lusitanica : Or a Short and Compendious System of an English and Portugueze Grammar. . . . Lisboa. . . . Anno de 1705. 8°, A—Ii in fours, besides the title and preface, 3 leaves.

This includes a vocabulary.

POTTER, WILLIAM.

The Key of Wealth : Or, A new Way, for

Improving of Trade : Lawfull, Easie, Safe and Effectuall : Shewing how a few Tradesmen agreeing together, may both double their Stocks, and the increase thereof, . . . London, Printed by R. A. and are to be sold by Giles Calvert . . . 1650. Folio. A, 3 leaves : B 2, &c., 5 leaves : B (repeated]—Y, 2 leaves each.

POWELL, GABRIEL.

A Consideration of the Papists Reasons of State and Religion, for toleration of Poperie in England. Intimated in their Supplication vnto the Kings Maiestie, & the States of the Present Parliament. . . . At Oxford, Printed by Ioseph Barnes, . . . 1604. 4°, A—R 2 in fours.

POWELL, NATHANIEL, *Esquire.*

A Remonstrance of Some Decrees, and other Proceedings, of the Commissioners of Sewers, for the Vpper Levels, in the Counties of Kent and Svssex ; touching the Proportioning of Water-Scots vpon the said Levels. . . . London, Printed by Thomas Mabb for the Authour. 1659. 4°, B—F in fours, and the title.

POWELL, VAVASOR.

Vavasoris Examen, & Purgamen : Or, Mr Vavasor Powell's Impartiall Triall : Who being apprehended upon the late Hue and Cry, raised after him, hath appealed to God and his Country, and is found Not Guilty. Or, The Thanks of the Welsh Itinerants for their pretious New-years-gift, . . . London, Printed for Thomas Brewster and Livewell Chapman . . . 1656. 4°, A—G in fours, G 4 blank.

PRANCE, MILES.

L Estrange a Papist, Proved by the De-positions upon Oath of Miles Prance, Mr Lawr. Mowbray, Mrs Jane Curtis, . . . London, Printed for Richard Baldwin, . . . MDCLXXXI. Folio, A—I, 2 leaves each.

PRAYER.

A fourme of Prayer, with thankes genyng, to be vsed euery yeere, the 17. of Nouember, beyng the day of the Queenes Maiesties entrie to her reigne. . . . . [Col.] Imprinted at London by Richard Iugge, Printer to the Queenes Maiestie. Cum priuilegio . . . 4°. A, 8 leaves : B, 2, the last leaf having only the colophon.

A necessarie and godly Prayer appoynted by the right reuerend Father in God Iohn, Bishop of London, to be vsed throughout all his Dioces vpon Sondayes and Frydayes, for the turning away of Gods Wrath . . . 1585. No printer's name. 4°, 4 leaves.

An Order for Prayer and Thankes-giuing (necessary to be vsed in these dangerous times) for the safetie and preseruation of her Majesty and this realme. Set forth by Authoritie. London, Printed by the Deputies of Christopher Barker, . . . 1594. 4°, A—C in fours.

An order . . . . renewed with some alterations vpon the present occasion. Imprinted at London by the deputies of Christopher Barker . . . 1598. 4°, A—D in fours.

A Forme of Praier to be vsed in London, and elsewhere in this time of Drought. Set forth by Authoritie. Imprinted at London by Robert Barker, . . . 1611. 4°, A—B in fours, A 1 and B 4 blank.

A Forme of Prayer to be publikely vsed in Churches, during this vnseasonable Weather, and abvndance of Raine. Set forth by Authoritie . . . Imprinted at London by Robert Barker . . . 1613. 4°, A—B in fours.

A Forme of Prayer, Necessary to bee vsed in these dangerous times, of Warre and Pestilence, for the safety and preseruation of his Majesty and his Realmes. Set forth by Authoritie. London Printed by Bonham Norton, and Iohn Bill, . . . 1626. 4°, A—L in fours, A 1 and L 4 blank.

The pomander of prayer. [This is the whole title over a cut of the Passion occupying the rest of the page, with the verses at the foot :

The greatest comfort in al temptacyon
Is the remembraunce of crystes passyon.

At the end :] Imprynted at London in Fletestrete at the sygne of the sonne by Wynkyn de Worde / the yere of our lorde. M.CCCC.xxxii. 4°. Title and *an exhortacion to the reder by a brother of Syon*, &c., 4 leaves : A—G in fours.

Pulpit Sparks Or Choice Forms of Prayer, By Several Reverend and Godly Divines Used by them, both before and after Sermon. With other Prayers, for extraordinary occasions, Together with Dr Hewitt's last Prayer . . . . London, Printed for W. Gilbertson at the Bible in Giltspurstreet, 1659. 12°, B—V in twelves, and the title. With a Preface by T. Reeve.

Private Forms of Prayer, Fit for these Sad Times. Also a Collection of all the Prayers Printed since these Troubles began. Oxford, Printed by Leonard Lichfield, . . . 1645. 8°, A—E 4 in eights.

Private Forms of Prayer, Fitted for the late Sad-Times. Particularly, A Form of Prayer for the Thirtieth of January, Morning and Evening. With Additions, &c. London, Printed by Tho. Mabb, and to be sold by William Not, . . . 1660. 8", Aa 4 in eights, Aa 4 blank.

PRAYERS.

Prayers of Holy fathers / Patriarches / Prophetes / Judges / Kynges / men and women of holy conuersacyon of the Apostles also of eyther testament. [This is a head-line in the middle of A 3, the volume being introduced by a head-line : The testament of Moyses . Deuteronomii the xxxii. chapter. At the end occurs:] Imprynted at London in Fletestrete by me Robert Redman. Cum gratia et priuilegio Regali. [About 1530.] Small 8°, black letter, A—I 4 in eights.

A selection made from Wycliff's version.

Certaine prayers and other godly exercises for the seuenteenth of Nouember: Wherein we solemnize the blessed reigne of our gracious Soueraigne Lady Elizabeth, . . . Imprinted at London by Christopher Barker, . . . 1585. 4°. A, 2 leaves: B—E in fours, besides the folded Table. With a preface by Edmund Bunny.

The tract concludes with an anthem.

Certain Prayers set foorth by Authoritie, to be vsed for the prosperous successe of her Maiesties Forces and Nauy. Imprinted at London, by the Deputies of Christopher Barker, . . . 1597. 4°, A, 2 leaves : B—C in fours. *B. M.*

A different edition from the Lambeth copy.

A Booke of Christian Prayers, . . . At London. Printed by Richard Yardley, and Peter Short, for the assignes of Richard Day. 1590. 4°. ¶, 4 leaves : A—Oo in fours.

A Booke of the Forme of common prayers, administration of the Sacraments, &c. agreeable to Gods Worde, and the vse of the reformed Churches. To this fourth editiō is added the maner of ordination and admission of a Pastor to his charge, . . . Middelbvrgh, Imprinted by Richard Schilders, . . . 1602. Cum priuilegio. 8", A—F in eights, F 8 blank.

A Manval of Godly Prayers, and Litanies, newly Annexed, Taken ovt of many famous Authonrs . . . To Antworpe . . . 1650. 12°, A—Xx 3 in twelves, Xx 3 with the colophon.

PRECEPTS.

Certaine Precepts, Or Directions, for the Well ordering and carriage of a mans life : as also œconomicall Displine, for the gouernement of his house : with a Platforme to a good foundation therof, in the aduised choice of a wife : Left by a Father to his sonne at his death, who was sometimes of eminent Note and Place in this Kingdome. And Published from a more perfect Copy, then ordinary those pocket Manuscripts goe warranted by. With some other Precepts and Sentences of the same nature added : taken from a person of like place and quality. London, Printed by T. C. and B. A. for Rich. Meighen, and Thom. Iones, and are to be sold at S. Clemens Church without Temple-Barre. 1616. 8°, A—C 7 in eights.

Sothebys, July 17, 1883, No. 156.

PRECHAC, M.

The Heroine Musqueteer: Or, The Female Warrier. A True History : Very delightful, and full of Pleasant Adventures in the Campagnes of 1676, & 1677. Translated out of French. London : Printed for Richard Magnes, and Richard Bentley . . . 1678. 12°. A, 4 leaves : B—F in twelves : G, 4 leaves, G 4 with advertisements. Dedicated by the author to the Count de Louvigny, Governor of Navarre and Bearn.

The translator is unnamed.

PREMPART, JAMES, *Engineer to the King of Sweden.*

A Historicall Relation of the famous Siege of the Citie Called the Bysse. Herevnto is added a generall Mappe of the Whole Campe and Siege, with particular Mappes of all the seuerall Approches in euery Quarter. Compyled togeather and designed according to the iust measure and rule of Geometrie. At Amsterdam. For Henrico Hondio. M.DC.XXX. [Col.] Printed at Amsterdam, By Ian Fredericksz Stam. M.DC.XXX. Folio, A—H, 2 leaves each, besides a List of English Volunteers, &c., at the Siege, and the plates.

Among the names is Ensign Quarles. *Boswell Lord Peelding* has been corrected in a coeval hand to *Bazill Lord Feilding.*

PRESBYTERY.

The Trojan Horse of the Presbyteriall Government Unbowelled. Printed in the Year 1646. 4°, A—C in fours.

The last Will and Testament of Sir Iohn Presbyter, Who dyed of a new Diseas called The particular Charge of the Army. With divers Admonitions and Legacies left to his deare Children of the Presbyterian Commons . . . With his Life, Death, Buriall, and Epitaph . . . Printed in the yeare of Jubilee, 1647. 4°, 4 leaves.

The Ghost of Sr. John Presbjter, Wherein he desireth that the rest of that faction may desist, and prosecute no further that Monster of Presbytery. Also, his advertisement to one of his deare children, whom he left out of his Will, by reason of his great rage of his sicknes. Printed in the yeare, of the Presbyterian feare, 1647. 4°, 4 leaves.

The Elders Dreame. With the Armies Message or Declaration to both Houses Parliament. Printed in the Yeare. 1647. 4°, 4 leaves. In verse. *B. M.*

PRESTON, JOHN, *Minister at East Ogwell.*

A Sermon Preached at the Fvnerall of Mr Iosiah Reynel Esquire, the 13. of August 1614. in East-Ogwell in Devon. London Printed by Nicholas Okes, for Richard Boulton, and are to be sold at his shop in Chancery-lane. 1615. 4°, A—D in fours, first and last leaves blank.

> Dedicated to "The Right Worshipfvl Sir Thomas Reynel. Sir George Reynel, Sir Carew Reynel. Knights : Mr Richard Reynel Esquire." On the title of the copy used occurs the autograph of Ralph Thoresby.

PRIDEAUX, MATHIAS, *M.A., of Exeter College, Oxford.*

Tabvlæ ad Grammatica Græca Introductoria. . . . Oxoniæ, Excudebat Iohannes Lichfield, & væneunt apud Eliam Pearse. An. D. 1629. 4°, A—D in fours, and a leaf of E.

Tyrocinivm ad Syllogismvm Legitimum contexendum, ... Oxoniæ, Excudebat Iohannes Lichfield, . . . An. D. 1629. 4°. A, 3 : B—C 2 in fours.

An Easy and Compendious Introdvction for Reading all sorts of Histories : In a more facil way then heretofore hath been published, out of the Papers of Mathias Prideaux . . . Oxford, Printed for Leonard Lichfield, Printer to the University ; M.DC.XLVIII. 4°, A—Xx 2 in fours, besides title and 3 other introductory leaves.

> Dedicated "To the Right Worshipfull Sr Thomas Reynell And the Virtuous Lady Katharine His Wife : For the Vse of Their Towardly young Sonnes Mr Thomas and Mr Henry Reynell."

PRIMATT, STEPHEN, *of Clifford's Inn.* The City & Covntry Purchaser & Builder. Composed by S. P. Gent. London. Printed for S. Speed. Sold by T. Rookes . . . [1668.] 8°, A—M 4 in eights, besides the frontispiece and a folding plate at p. 150. With diagrams.

PRIMER.

This prymer of sarysbury vse set out a lōg vvout any serchyng vvith many prayers and goodly pyctures in e kalēder in the matyns of our lady / in the houres of the crosse / in th. vii. psalmes ād ī the dyryge. And be newly imprynted at Parys. Venūdātur Parisiis apud Frāciscū Regnault / in vico scti Jacobi / ad signū Elephātis. [Col.] Explicīūt Hore . . . Impresse Parisiis in edibus Francisci regnault . . . Anno domini millesimo quingētesimo trigesimo primo. Die vltima Junii. 8°, A—D in eights : a—bb 4 in eights, besides two sheets of eight between z and aa. With numerous woodcuts.

This prymer of Salysbury vse is set out a long wout ony serchyng / with many prayers. And be newly emprynted at Rouen 1537. [Col.] Explicīunt hore . . . cum orationibʒ beate Brigite ac multis aliis orationibus Impresse pro Francisco Regnault . . . 1537. 8°, A—R 6 in eights : aa—II in eights : KK, 10 leaves. Printed within borders, with woodcuts.

Sothebys, June 30, 1885, No. 910.

The Prymer in Englysshe, and Latyn wyth the Epystles and Gospelles : of euerye Sonday, & holye daye in the yere, and also the exposycion vpon Miserere mei deus. wyth many other prayers Prynted in London by Roberte Toye. Cum priuilegio . . . 1542. 4°, printed in red and black, with a few woodcuts : the *Primer*, A—T 4 in eights : the *Epistles and Gospels*, with a new title, A—F 4 in eights.

This prymer of Salysbury use is set out a longe without anye searchynge with many prayers. Imprynted at London the xxv. day of Novēbre M.D.XLV. [Col.] Explicīunt hore beatissime virginis marie secūdum usum Sarum. Excusum Londini in cemiterio divi Pauli per Thomam Petit. Año. M.D.XLV. Sm. 8°, A—Y in eights.

> On the reverse of B 1 is the following declaration :—"The kynges hyghnes greatelye tenderynge the welth of his realme hath suffered heretofore the paternoster, Ave, Crede, and ten commaundementes of God to be hadde in the Englishe tongue,

but his grace perceyvynge now the great diversite of the translacyons hath wylled them all to be taken up, and in stede of theym hath caused an uniforme translation of the sayde Paternoster, Ave, credo and the ten commaundementes to be set forth," &c.

The Primer, Set Fvrth by the Kinges maiestie & his Clergie, to be taught lerned, and red : & none other to be vsed thorowout all his dominions. Imprinted at London within the precinct of the late dissolued house of the graye Fryers by Richard Grafton Printer to the Princes grace, the xvii. day of August, the yeare of our lorde M.D.XLVI. Cum priuilegio ... 4°. Title and Calendar, 4 leaves : *An Injunction*, &c., 4 .leaves : A—U in fours : Aa—Hb in fours, the last leaf with Grafton's device.

The Primer, in Englishe & Latin, set forth by the kynges maiestie & his Clergie to be taught learned, and read : and none other to be vsed th[r]oughout all his dominions. 1546. [Col.] Imprinted at London, in Fletestrete at the signe of the Sunne, ouer against the conduyte, by Edward Whitchurche the ix day of Iannari. M.D.XLVI. Cum priuilegio ... 8°. Title and Calendar, 8 leaves : Preface, 4 leaves : *An Iniunction*, 2 leaves : Graces, 2 leaves : A—v in eights, v 8 blank. With the Latin in the margin in roman letter.

The Primer, Or Office of the Blessed Virgin Marie, in Latin and English: According to the reformed Latin : And with lyke graces Priuiledged Printed at Antwerp by Arnold Conings. Anno M. DC. IIII. 8°, A—Gg in eights, Gg 8 occupied by a notice respecting the errors in some copies. With a short Preface by R[ichard] V[erstegan.]

PRINCE, THOMAS.

The Silken Independents Snare Broken. By Thomas Prince, close Prisoner in the Tower. Turning the mischief intended upon him, in Walwyns Wyles, upon the Seven Independent Authors thereof, viz. William Kiffin, David Lordell, John Price, Richard Arnald, Edmund Roster, Henry Foster, Henry Barnet. . . . London Printed by H. H. for W. L. . . . 1649. 4°, A—B in fours, B 4 blank.

PRISONERS.

A List of the Prisoners of War, who are Officers in Commission, in Custody of the Marshal-General . . . London : Printed by John Field, . . . 1651. 4°, 4 leaves.

A List of all the Prisoners in the Upper Bench Prison, remaining in Custody the

third of May, 1653. Delivered in by Sir John Lenthall to the Committee appointed by the Councell of State, for examining of the state of the said Prison . . . London, Printed for Livewell Chapman, . . . 1653. 4°, A—D 2 in fours.

The humble Petition of the poor distressed Prisoners in Ludgate. Being above an hundred and fourscore poor persons in number. Against this time of the Birth of our blessed Lord and Saviour Jesus Christ. 1664. A small broadside.

The Confession and Execution of the Five Prisoners That suffered on the new Gallows at Tyburn on Friday the 6th of September, 1678. . . . London : Printed for R. G. 1678. 4°, 4 leaves.

The Behaviour, Confession, And Execution of the Twelve Prisoners That Suffer'd on Wednesday the 22 of Jan. 167$\frac{8}{9}$ . . . Printed for C. I. 167$\frac{8}{9}$. 4°, 4 leaves.

The Behaviour, last Speeches, Confession, And Execution of the Prisoners that Suffer'd at Tyburn on Fryday the 7th of March 167$\frac{8}{9}$ . . . London : Printed for L. C. 167$\frac{8}{9}$. 4°, 4 leaves.

PRIZES.

Reasons Humbly Offer'd for allowing the Merchants, &c. of New-England, New-York, and Carolina, Relief upon the Dutys paid on Prize-Goods, as those who have Bonded the same in other Colonies. A broadside.

PROCESSIONALE.

Processionale ad vsum ecclesie Sarisburiesis. M.d.xxx. Venñdatur Parisiis in edibus Francisci Regnault / in vico sancti Jacobi / ad signum Elephantis. [Col.] Explicit Processionale ad vsum ecltie Sarisburiesis pluribus in locis tam in cantu q̄ in litera recognitum. Impressum Parisijs in edib₉ Fracisci regnault. 4°, A—X in eights, and Y, 6. With the device of the Elephant on the last page. Finely printed in red and black, with the musical notation.

Processionale ad vsum insignis ecclesie Sarisbu. observandos accommodum presertim in iis que in habendis processionibus ac ceremoniarum splendorem faciunt . . . . Impressum Lond. 1555. [Col.] Explicit Processionabile [sic] . . . Londini. Anno domini. 1555. 4°, A—T in eights, T 8 blank.

PROCTOR, THOMAS.

Of the knowledge and conducte of warres, two bookes, latelye wrytten and set foorth, profitable for suche as delight in Hystoryes, or martyall affayres, and necessarye for this present tyme.

¶ Virtuti pariter cunctis contendite neruis : Ignaua (vt scopulos) otia diffugite.

Seeke vertue, noble youth betymes,
Which breadeth honour true :
Base idlenesse, and all her baytes,
Euen as a rocke eschue.

¶ In ædibus Richardi Tottelli. vij. die Iunij. Anno Domini. 1578. Cum priuilegio . . . . 4°. ¶, 4 leaves: A—M in fours.

On ¶ 2 recto occur the author's arms, and on the reverse some verses to the book signed with the initials T. P.

The Righteous Man's Way. Wherein are given Certaine Directions, how man may profitably meditate upon the Commandements of God : . . . . Printed in the yeare 1621. 4°, A—K 2 in fours.

The Epistle to the Reader is signed " Yours in the Lord Thomas Proctor."

PROTESTANTS.
A Christian Letter of certaine English Protestants, vnfained fauourers of the present state of Religion, authorised and professed in England : vnto that Reuerend and learned man, M' R. Hoo. requiring resolution in certaine matters of doctrine : . . . 1599. 4°, A—F in fours.

Occasioned by the publication of the Ecclesiasticul Polity.

The Confession and publike recantation of thirteene learned personages, lately conuerted in France, Germanie, and the Lowe-Countreys, from Poperie to the Churche reformed : . . . Translated out of the French and Dutch Printed copies, by 1. M. Imprinted at London for G. P. and are to be solde at the signe of the Bible in Paules Church-yard. 1602. 4°, ¶—3 ¶ in fours: A—M in fours, M 4 blank.

An Epistle Dedicated to an Honovrable Person. In the which, are discouered a Dozen bad spirits, who from the beginning haue much haunted, & grieuously tormented the Protestant Congregation : so that euery one may perceaue, if he be not too to partiall, and ouermuch carryed away with affection, that such an Assembly cannot be the true Church of God. Imprinted, M.DC.XXII. 4", A—E 2 in fours.

The Old Protestants Letanie : Against all Sectaries, and their Defendants, Both Presbyterians and Independants. Composed by a Lover of God, and King Charles. Printed in the yeare of Hope.

1647. [Sept. 1.] 4°, 4 leaves. In verse. B. M.

The Case of the Persecuted and Oppressed Protestants in some Parts of Germany and Hungary : Laid open in a Memorial, which was lately presented at Vienna to His Imperial Majesty, By His Majesty the King of Sweden's Ambassadour Extraordinary, the Count of Oxenstierne. In the Savoy, Printed by Tho. Newcomb, 167⅔. Folio, 4 leaves.

Raree show Or the true Protestant Procession. A new Ballad to the Tune of the Northumberland man. Printed for A. B. 1681. A leaf of verses.

The Protestant-Flayl : An Excellent New Song. To the Tune of Lacy's Maggot ; Or, the Hobby-Horse. London : Printed for A. Banks, MDCLXXXII. A broadside.

The Way to Peace amongst all Protestants : Being a Letter of Reconciliation sent by Bp. Ridley to Bp. Hooper. With some Observations upon it. London : Printed for Richard Baldwin, 1688. 4°, 6 leaves, including one of Advertisements.

[An Account of the mode in which the money collected for the distressed French Protestants was distributed. London, about 1689.] Folio, 2 leaves. Without any title and imprint.

The Providences of God, Observed through Several Ages, towards this Nation, in introducing the True Religion : . . . London, Printed for R. Baldwin . . . 1691. 4°. A, 2 leaves : B—I 2 in fours.

The Groans of the Oppressed. Or : An Account of the cruel, inhumane, and bloody persecutions of the Protestants in France and Savoy by the Papists ; . . . [Col.] Glasgow, Printed in the Year, 1700. 8°, 4 leaves.

PRYNNE, WILLIAM, of Lincoln's-Inn.
The Perpetvitie of a Regenerate Mans Estate. Wherein it is manifestly proued by sundry arguments, . . . That such as are once truly regenerated and ingrafted into Christ by a liuely faith, can neither finally nor totally fall from grace. . . . By William Prynne Gent : Lincolniensis. . . . London, Printed by William Iones dwelling in Redcrosse-streete. 1626. 4°. ¶, 4 leaves : ¶¶, 4 leaves : *, 4 leaves : **, 4 leaves : a, 4 leaves : A—3 F 2 in fours.

Newes from Ipswich : Discovering certaine late detestable practises of some domineering Lordly Prelates, to undermine the established doctrine and discipline of our Church, . . . Printed at Ipswich. [1636.] 4°, A—B 2 in fours.

Written under the name of *Matthew White.*

Newes from Ipswich . . . Printed at Ipswich, An. 1636. 4°, 4 leaves, marked ¶.

This appears to be a London reprint, with Ipswich fictitiously retained, of the genuine first issue.

PSALMS.

The Whole Booke of Psalmes : With their Wonted Tunes, as they are song in Churches, composed into foure parts : All which are so placed that foure may sing, ech one a seuerall part in this booke. Compiled by Sondry Avthors, who haue so laboured herein, that the vnskilfull with small practice may attaine to sing that part, which is fittest for their voice. Imprinted at London by Thomas Est, the assigne of William Byrd, dwelling in Aldersgate streete at the signe of the black Horse, and are there to be sold. 1592. 8°. Title and dedication by the printer to Sir John Puckering, Keeper of the Great Seal, whose arms are on the back of the former, 2 leaves : B—V 4 in eights. With the music.

The four parts are Cantus, Altus, Tenor, Bassus. The composers are John Farmer, W. Cobbold, E. Blanckes, G. Kirby, E. Hooper, John Douland, Richard Allison, E. Johnson, Michael Cavendish, and G. Farnaby.

PUCKLE, JAMES.

England's Interest : Or, A Brief Discourse of the Royal Fishery. In a Letter to a Friend. The Second Edition. London : Printed by J. Southby, at the Harrow in Cornhill. 1696. 8°, A—E in fours.

PULESTON, HAMLET, *M.A. of Jesus College, Oxford.*

Epitome Monarchiæ Britanicæ. Or, A Brief Cronology of the British Kings, . . .

to the Happy Restauration of King Charles the Second. . . . London, Printed, for Philemon Stephens the Younger, Stationer, . . . [1663.] 4°. Title and Errata, 2 leaves : B—I 2 in fours.

PURCELL, HENRY.

The Songs in the Indian Queen : As it is now Compos'd into an Opera. By Mr Henry Purcell, Composer in Ordinary to his Majesty. And one of the Organists of his Majesty's Chapel-Royal. London, Printed by J. Heptinstall, . . . 1695. Folio. Title with address on the back to Purcell by the publishers, J. May and J. Hudgebutt, 1 leaf : B—D, 2 leaves each : E, 1 leaf.

PURCHAS, SAMUEL.

Pvrchas his Pilgrim. Microcosmvs, Or the Historie of Man. Relating the Wonders of his Generation, ... By Samvel Pvrchas, Parson of S. Martins neere Ludgate, London . . . London Printed by W. S. for Henry Fetherstone. 1619. 8°. ¶, 6 leaves : A—3 G 2 in eights, last leaf blank.

PURITANS.

A Pack of Pvritans, Maintayning the Vnlawfvlnesse, Or Vnexpediencie or Both. Of Pluralities and Nonresidency . . . As also a defence of the authority of Princes and Parliaments to intermeddle with matters of Religion, . . . London, Printed for William Sheeres. 1641. 4°, A—H in fours, A 1 blank.

A Discourse concerning Puritans. Tending to a Vindication of those who unjustly Suffer by the mistake, abuse, and misapplication of that Name. . . . The second Edition, much inlarged, augmented and corrected by the Authors. London, Printed for Robert Bostock, 1641. 4°, A—I in fours, besides title and following leaf.

Q.

QUAKERS.

The Quakers Ballad : Or, An Hymn of Triumph and Exaltation for their Victories, at the two late great Disputes by them held with the Baptist. . . . 1674. To an excellent new Tune, called, *The Zealous Atheist.* London, Printed for James Naylor. A broadside on two sheets, with three cuts. Black letter.

The Quakers Art of Courtship : . . . London : Printed, . . . 1737. Price Bound, One Shilling. 12°, A—G 6 in twelves, title on A 2.

QUARLES, FRANCIS.

Emblemes . . . London Printed for J. Williams . . . 1676. 8°, A—Bb 3 in eights.

Emblemes . . . London Printed for I. Williams at the Crowne in St. Pauls Churchyard & sould by Wᵐ Grantham at yᵉ Crown and Pearl oner agst Exeter Change in yᵉ Strand 1684. 8º, A—Bb 4 in eights, Bb 4 blank.

Emblems, . . . London : Printed for D. Midwinter [and Others] 1736. 12º, A—P in twelves, Q, 13 leaves. The Frontispiece makes A 1.

QUARLES, JOHN.

Fons Lachrymarum ; . . . London, Printed for Nathaniel Brooks . . . 1655. 8º. A, 6 leaves, besides the portrait and engraved title : B—K 2 in eights.

QUICK, JOHN.

A Serious Inquiry into that Weighty Case of Conscience, Whether a Man may Lawfully Marry his Deceased Wife's Sister : . . . By John Quick Minister of the Gospel. London, Printed for J. Lawrence. . . . and R. Parker . . . 1702. 4º, A—F in fours, including half-title. Dedicated to Sir Samuel Blewett of Walthamstow in Essex.

QUILIBET.

Let Qvilibet beware of Qvodlibet. [This is a half-title. No place, &c. Printed abroad, 1600-1.] 8º, 6 leaves.

R.

R. E., *Gent.*
The Experienc'd Farrier : Or, A Compleat Treatise of Horsemanship. In Two Books. Physical and Chyrurgical . . . The Second Edition much Enlarged, . . . London, Printed for W. Whitwood . . . 169½. 4º, A—3 M in fours, A repeated.

R. F. D.
Le Discours de la guerre ei Descente qve les Anglois & Flamans se sont efforcez faire en Bretaigne. Et de la resistence qui leur a esté faicte par les gentilshommes & commune du pays. A Paris, . . . 1558. 8º, a—b in fours.
At the end occur the initials *F. D. R.*

R. J.
A Paire of Spectacles for Sir Hvmfrey Linde to see his way withall. Or An Answeare to his booke called, *Via Tuta* . . . Permissv Svperiorvm. 1631. 8º. ã—õ 4 in eights : A—Ll 4 in eights.

R. M., *Gent.*
The Pilgrims Pass to the New Jerusalem : Or, The serious Christian his Enquiries after Heaven. . . . London, Printed by R. W. for the Author, . . . 1659. 12º, A—L 7 in twelves, A 1 blank. With a portrait of the author.

R. R.
An Account of Spain : Being A New Description of that Country and People ; And of the Sea Ports along the Mediterranean : . . . Written by a French Gentleman, who was in disguise Aboard the English Fleet. With an Account of the most Remarkable Transactions of the Fleet. To which is added, A Large Preface, concerning the Establishment of the Spanish Crown, on the Duke of Anjou. London, Printed for Joseph White, at the Elephant at Charing-Cross. 1700. 8º. A, 4 leaves : a—c in fours : B—N in eights. Dedicated by E. L., the translator, to Henry, Duke of Norfolk.

R. J., *A.M. Oxon.*
Lux Occidentalis : Or Providence Display'd, In the Coronation of King William and Queen Mary ; and their Happy Accession to the Crown of England : With other Remarks . . . London, Printed, and are to be sold by Randal Taylor, . . . MDCLXXXIX. 4º, A—E 2 in fours. Chiefly in verse.

RAKE.
The Rake : Or, The Libertine's Religion. A Poem. . . . London, Printed for R. Taylor . . . 1693. 4º. A, 2 : B—C in fours : D—E, 2 each.

RALEIGH, SIR WALTER.
An Abridgment of Sir Walter Raleigh's History of the World, In Five Books . . . To which is Added, His Premonition to Princes. London, Printed for Matthew Gelliflower, . . . 1698. 8º. A, 4 leaves, including a portrait : a—c in eights : B—Dd in eights.
¡The abridger was Laurence Eachard.

Tvbvs Historicvs : An Historicall Perspective ; Discovering all the Empires and Kingdomes of the World, as they flourisht respectively under the foure Imperial Monarchies . . . By the late famous and learned Knight Sir Walter Raleigh. . . . London, Printed by Thomas Harper, for Benjamin Fisher, 1636. 4°. A, 2 leaves : B—D in fours, D 4 blank.

Three Discourses of Sr Walter Ralegh. 1. Of a War with Spain, and our Protecting the Netherlands. Written by the Command of King James I. in the First Year of his Reign, 1602. II. Of the Original, and Fundamental Cause of Natural, Arbitrary, and Civil War. III. Of Ecclesiastical Power. Published by Phillip Ralegh, Esq ; *Sapiens uno minor est Jove.* Horat. London, Printed for Benjamin Barker, . . . 1702. 8°. A, 4 leaves, including the portrait : B—M in eights, M 8 blank.

RAMSAY, WILLIAM. *M.D.*
Elminthologia, Or, Some Physical Considerations of the Matter, Origination, and several Species of Wormes, Macerating and Direfully Cruciating every part of the Bodies of Mankind, ... By William Ramesey, Doctor of Physick, and Physitian in Ordinary to His Majesty Charles the II. . . . London, Printed by John Streater, for George Sawbridge, . . . 1668. 8°. *, 7 leaves, title on * 2 : A—Aa 4 in eights, last leaf with an Advertisement. With an anonymous but very fine portrait of the Author, anno æt. 42. Dedicated to Sir Roger Burgoyne of Sutton, co. Bedford. There is a folded leaf in A.

A Præmonition is dated from Plymouth, 1st December 1667.

RANTERS.
The Ranters Reasons Resolved to nothing, Or, The fustification instead of the justification of the Mad Crew : wherein the people called the Gods of Godmanchester may, as in a Glasse, behold that they are a deluded and defiled people, if not incarnate Devils . . . London, Printed by R. L. for Nathanael Webbe, and William Grantham . . . . 1651. 4°, A—D 2 in fours, D 2 with the *Imprimatur.*

An answer to A Justification of the Ranters.

A Looking-Glasse for the Ranters. In two Short Treatises. The 1. Being some Glimpses of the Good-Old-Way. 2. A Treatise of Virginity . . . London Printed by T. M. for Richard Moon, . . . 1653. 4°, A—C in fours, C 4 blank, and the title-page.

RASTELL, WILLIAM.
A Table collected of the yeares of our Lord God, . . . Written by William Rastal, . . . At London Printed by W. I. for Thomas Adams, . . . 1607. 8°, A—M in eights.

The date in the colophon is 1606.

RATES.
The Rates of Merchandise, That is to say, The Subsidy of Tonnage, Subsidy of Poundage, And the Subsidy of Woollen Clothes or Old Drapery. As they are Rated and Agreed on by the Commons House of Parliament . . . . London, Printed by Edward Husband and Thomas Newcomb, . . . 1660. Folio, A—P, 2 leaves each.

RAVENHILL, WILLIAM.
The Case of the Company of Grocers Stated. And their Condition in their Present Circumstances Truly Represented. Together with a short Accompt of their Original ; How Eminent they have been in the City, and also of some of their Ancient Priviledges and Usages. Designed for Information and Satisfaction of the Members, and Vindication of the Company. London, Printed for the Company of Grocers, An. Dom. 1682. Folio, A—D, 2 leaves each.

RAWLINS, JOHN.
The Famous and Wonderfull Recoverie of a Ship of Bristoll, called the Exchange, from the Turkish Pirates of Argier. With the Vnmatchable attempts and good successe of John Rawlins, Pilot in her, and other slaues : who in the end with the slaughter of about 40 of the Turks and Moores, brought the ship into Plimouth, the 13. of February last ; . . . London, Printed for Nathaniel Butter, dwelling at the Pide Bull at saint Austins Gate. 1622. 4°. A—E in fours. *Bodleian.*

Reprinted in Arber's *Garner,* iv. The tract is dedicated by Rawlins to the Marquis of Buckingham.

RAY, JOHN. *F.R.S.*
Catalogus Plantarum Angliæ, Et Insularum Adjacentium : Tum Indigenas, tum in agris passim cultas complectens. . . . Opera Joannis Raii . . . Londini, Typis E. C. & A. C. . . . MDCLXX. 8°, A—Z in eights, and A[a], 4 leaves, besides 3 leaves with title, &c.

Historia Plantarum species hactenus editas aliasque insuper multas noviter inventas & descriptas amplectens. . . . Auctore Joanne Raio . . . Londini . . . Typis Mariæ Clark : . . . 1686[-1704.] Folio. 3 vols. A, 6 : (a), 8 : B—4 O in sixes. Dedicated to Sir Charles Hatton, son of Lord Hatton.

> The Sunderland copy was on large thick paper.

Stirpium Europæarum Extra Britannias Nascentium Sylloge. Quas Partim observavit ipse, partim . . . collegit Joannes Raius. . . . Londini : . . . . MDCXCIV. 8⁰, A—Bb in eights : *Stirpes Orientales*, A—C in eights. With a portrait.

Joannis Raii Synopsis Methodica Stirpium Britannicarum, . . . Editio Secunda : . . . Londini : . . . MDCXCVI. 8⁰. A, 4 : (a) and (b) in eights : B—Aa in eights : *De Plantarum Methodis*, A in eights : (a*)—(e*) in eights : *Ricini Epistola ad Joan. Raium*, A—D 4 in eights. Dedicated to Sir Thomas Willoughby, Bart.

REA, JOHN.

Flora : Seu, De Florum Cultura. Or, A Complete Florilege, Furnished with all Requisites belonging to a Florist. In III. Bookes. By John Rea, Gent. London, Printed by J. G. for Richard Marriot, . . . 1665. Folio. Frontispiece, 1 leaf : title and dedication to Lord Gerard of Gerard's Bromley, co. Stafford, and Sir Thomas Hanmer, 4 leaves : Verses by Rea to Lady Gerard and Lady Warner, 2 leaves : b, 4 leaves : ∴, 1 leaf : C—K [k] 2 in fours.

Flora : Seu, De Florum Cultura. Or, A Compleat Florilege, Furnished with all Requisites belonging to A Florist. The second Impression Corrected, With many Additions, and several new Plates. In III. Books. By John Rea, Gent. London, Printed by T. N. for George Marriott, . . . 1676. Folio. Mind of the Frontispiece, 1 leaf : a, 4 leaves, including the same frontispiece as in 1st edition : B, 4 : c. 4 : Designs for gardens, 8 leaves : C—Hh in fours : Ii—Ll, 2 leaves each. *B. M.*

> There was a third edition in 1702. A copy is in the British Museum.

RECKONING.

The iust reckenyng or accompt of the whole number of the yeares, from the beginnyng of the world vnto this presente yere of. 1547. A certaine and sure declaracion that the worlde is at an ende. Translated out of the Germaine tonge into Englishe by Anthony Scoloker the . 6. daye of July . Anno Dñi . 1547. . . . 8⁰, black letter, A [—B 4 *l*] in eights.

> Sothebys, July 9, 1886, No. 1006, imperfect at end.

RECORDE, ROBERT, *M.D.*

Records Arithmetick, Or, The Ground

of Arts . . . enlarged . . . By John Mellis. . . . London, Printed by James Flesher, . . . 1658. 8⁰, A—Mm in eights. With a postscript by Thomas Williams.

REEVE, EDMUND, *B.D.*

An Introduction into the Greeke Tongue, in most plaine manner, delivering the principall matters of the Grammar thereof, so farre forth as may helpe toward the understanding of the Greeke Text of the Holy Gospel. . . . Printed in London, Anno 1650. 4⁰, A—F in fours.

REFORMATION.

Proposals for a National Reformation of Manners, Humbly offered to the Consideration of our Magistrates & Clergy. As also, The Black Roll. Containing the Names and Games of several hundreds Persons, who have been prosecuted by the Society, for Whoring, Drunkenness, Sabbath-breaking, &c. Published by the Society for Reformation. . . . London. Printed for John Dunton . . . MDCXCIV. 4⁰, A—E in fours.

REGICIDES.

The Cry of Royal Innocent Blood, Heard and Answered : Being a True and Impartial Account of Gods extraordinary and Signal Judgments upon Regicides. . . . London, Printed for Daniel Brown . . . 1683. 8⁰, A—I in eights, I 8 blank, besides A, 4 leaves with title, &c., and a frontispiece of portraits.

REGIMEN SALERNI.

Regimen Sanitatis Salerni. This boke teachinge all people to gouerne them in helthe . is translated out of the Latyne tonge in to englyshe by Thomas Paynel. Wheche boke is amended, augmented, and diligently imprinted. [Col.] Londini in Ædibvs Tho. Bertheleti Typis impres. . . . Anno. M.D.XLI 4⁰. A, 6 leaves : B—Y in fours : a—i in fours, i 4 with the colophon. With a Preface directed to John, Earl of Oxford, by Paynell.

Regimen Sanitatis Salerni. . . . [Col.] Imprinted at London, in Paules churcheyarde at the sygne of the Lambe by Abraham Vele. Anno Domini . MD.LVII. 8⁰, black letter. *, 8 leaves : †, 8 leaves : A, 4 leaves, A 4 blank : B—Z 4 in eights, Z 3 with the colophon and Z 4 blank.

REGISTRY.

Reasons for a Registry : Shewing briefly the great Benefits and Advantages that may accrew to this Nation thereby. And likewise Reconciling those mistaken In-

O

conveniences which many have conceived thereof. By a Well-wisher to the Publick Interest of the Nation . . . London: Printed for Charles Harper . . . 1678. 4°, A—D in fours, A 1 and D 4 blank.

A Treatise, Shewing how Usefull, Safe, Reasonable and Beneficial, the Inrolling & Registring of all Conveyances of Lands, may be to the Inhabitants of this Kingdom. By a Person of Great Learning and Judgment. London, Printed for Mat. Wotton, . . . 1694. 4°, B—D in fours, a leaf of E, and the title.

REID, JOHN.
The Scots Gard'ner In Two Parts. With an Appendix, shewing how to use the Fruits of the Garden . . . The Second Edition Corrected, with Additions. Edinburgh, Printed by John Moncur, and Sold at his Printing-House, opposite to the Head of Foster's Wynd, at the Scots Arms ; . . . MDCCXXI. 8°, A—O in eights: The Calendar, A—D in eights: *The Florists Vade Mecum,* with a head-line only, A—B 4 in eights, followed by three plates.

> There is an enlarged and improved edition, Edinburgh, 1766, 12°.

RELATION.
A Briefe Relation of some affaires and transactions, Civill and Military, both Forraigne and Domestique. Licensed by Gualter Frost Esquire, Secretary to the Councell of State . . . [October 2, 1649—October 22, 1650.] 4°, A—5 X in fours.

> The colophon to the last part is : London, Printed by William Du-Gard Printer to the Council of State. Anno Dom. 1650.
> Crossley, part 2, No. 333, very imperfect.

RELIGION.
An Enquiry after Religion : Or, A View of the Idolatry, Superstition, Bigotry and Hipocrisie of all Churches and Sects throughout the World. Also some Thoughts of a late Ingenious Gentleman of the Royal Society concerning Religion. . . . . London, Printed for Richard Baldwin . . . 1691. 4°, A—F, 2 leaves each. In verse.

REMARKS.
Short Dull Remarks upon the Long Dull Essay upon Poetry. London : Printed by J. Grantham, for J. Walthoe, 1683. 4°, 4 leaves. In verse.

REMNANT, RICHARD.
A Discourse Or Historie of Beer. Shewing their Nature and usage, and the great profit of them. Whereunto is added the causes, and cure of blasted wheat. And some remedies for blasted Hops, and Rie. and Fruit. Together with the causes of smutty Wheat : . . . London, Printed by Robert Young for Thomas Slater, . . . 1637. 4°, A—G in fours. *B. M.*

REMY [NANNINI] OF FLORENCE.
Civill Considerations vpon many and syndrie Histories, as well Ancient as Moderne, and principallie vpon those of Guicciardin . . . . done into French by Gabriel Chappuys, Tourangeau, and out of French into English, by W. T. At London, Imprinted by F. K. for Matthew Lownes, . . . 1601. Folio. A, 6 leaves : B, 4 : C—Aa in sixes, last leaf blank.

RENWICK. JAMES.
Antipas, Or The Dying Testimony of Mr James Renwick, Minister of the Gospel, who suffered at the Grass-Market of Edinburgh, Feb. 17, 1688. [Edinburgh, 1688.] 4°, 4 leaves.

REPREHENSION.
A Just and Seasonable Reprehension of Naked Breasts and Shoulders. Written by a Grave and Learned Papist. Translated by Edward Cooke, Esquire. With a Preface by Mr Richard Baxter. London, Printed for Jonathan Edwin . . . 1678. 8°, A—L in eights.

REYNARD THE FOX.
The Most delectable History of Reynard the Fox. Newly Corrected and purged . . . London, Printed by Elizabeth All-de, dwelling neere Christ-Church. 1629. 4°, black letter, A—V in fours. With cuts. *B. M.*

REYNER, EDWARD.
Considerations Concerning Marriage, The

{ Honour, Duties, Benefits, Troubles, } of it. Whereto are added,

I. Directions in two Particulars. 1. How they that have wives may be as if they had none. 2. How to prepare for parting with a dear yoke-fellow by death, or otherwise. 2. Resolution of this Case of Conscience. Whether a man may lawfully marry his Wives Sister ? London, Printed by J. T. for Thomas Newbery, . . . MDCLVII. 8°. A, 8 leaves, including *Errata :* B—E in eights : F, 4 : G, 8. With a Preface by Simeon Ashe.

RICHARD OF SAINT VICTOR.
Here foloweth a veray deuoute treatyse (named Benyamyn) of the myghtes and vertues of mannes soule / & of the Way to true contemplacyon / compyled by a noble & famous doctoure a mã of grete

holynes & denocyon / named Rycharde
of saynt Vyctor. [Col.] Imprynted at
London in Poules chyrchyarde at the
sygne of the Trynyte / by Henry Pep-
well. In the yere of our lorde god.
M. CCCCC. xxi. the xvi. daye of Nouembre.
4⁰, black letter, with woodcuts. A, 4 :
B, 6 : C, 4 : D, 6 : E, 6 : F, 3, but F i
wanting : [a new title, making perhaps
F 4 :] Here foloweth a denoute treatyse
compyled by mayster Walter Hylton of
the songe of aungelles, 1 leaf : G, 4 : H, 6 :
I, 4 : K, 6.

Sothebys, June 30, 1885, No. 1022.

RIDLEY, SIR THOMAS, *D.C.L.*

A View of the Civile and Ecclesiastical
Law, and wherein the practise of them is
streitned, and may be relieued within
this Land. Written by Thomas Ridley
Doctor of the Ciuile Law. . . . London,
Printed for the Company of Stationers
Anno. 1607. 4⁰, A—Gg in fours, Gg 4
blank, besides title and dedication to the
King. Black letter.

A View of the Civile and Ecclesiasticall
Law : . . . The Third Edition, by J. G.
Mʳ of Arts. Oxford Printed by W. Hall
for Edw. Forrest 1662. 8⁰, A—Dd in
eights, Dd 8 with the Label.

[RIDPATH, G.]

An Enquiry into the Causes of the Mis-
carriage of the Scots Colony at Darien.
Or An Answer to a Libel Entituled A
Defence of the Scots Abdicating Darien.
Submitted to the Consideration of the
Good People of England. . . . Glasgow.
1700. 8⁰. A, 4 : B—G in eights : H—I
in fours.

RIVE, EDMUND.

Heptaglottologie, That is, A Treatise
Concerning Seven Langvages, Wherein,
The excellencie and the necessitie of the
knowledge of them is plainely and breifely
declared : By Edmund Rine, Minister of
the word of God, and Teacher of the
Hebrew, &c. in London . . . London,
Printed by William Iones and are to
be sold by Mathew Lownes. 1618. 8⁰.
a, 6 leaves, 6th blank : A—E in eights.

RIVETUS, ANDREAS, *Junior.*

Mʳ Smirke. Or, The Divine in Mode :
Being Certain Annotations, upon the
Animadversions of the Naked Truth.
Together with a Short Historical Essay,
concerning General Councils, Creeds, and
Impositions, in matters of Religion.
Nuda, sed Magna est Veritas, & prævale-
bit. By Andreas Rivetus, *Junior,* Anagr.
Res Nvda Veritas. Printed Anno Do-

mini MDCLXXVI. 4⁰. Title and *To the*
Captious Reader, 2 leaves : B—K in fours,
I repeated, and between F and G, g, 3
leaves.

At sign. g 2 of this curious piece is an
allusion to the King of Virginia.

RIZZIO, DAVID.

A Relation of the Death of David Rizzi.
Chief Favorite to Mary Stuart Queen of
Scotland, Who was killed in the Apart-
ment of the said Queen on the 9ᵗʰ of
March 1565. Written by the Lord Rvth-
ven, one of the principal Persons con-
cerned in that Action. Published from
the Original Manuscript. . . . London,
Printed for A. Baldwin . . . 1699. 8⁰,
A—D 2 in eights.

An account of Rizzio from Buchanan is
also given.

ROBERTS, JOHN, *of Weston, near Bath*

Great Yarmovths Exercise. In a very
compleat and martiall manner performed
by their Artillery men, upon the twenty
second of May last, to the great commen-
dations and applause of the whole Town,
according to the modern Discipline of
this our Age. 1638. *Non solum nobis,*
sed patriæ. Written by Iohn Roberts, of
Weston, neere Bathe, Gent. London,
Printed by Thomas Harper, and are to
be sold by Ellis Morgan, at his shop in
Little Brittain. 1638. 4⁰, A—B in fours,
and a leaf of C. Dedicated to Henry
Davie, President of the Artillery Yard ;
John Robins, Esquire, both Bailiffs of
Yarmouth, and to the Aldermen thereof.
B. M.

The Compleat Cannoniere : Or, The
Gunners Guide. Wherein are set forth
exactly the Chiefe grounds and principals
of the whole Art, in a very briefe and
compendious forme, never by any set
forth in the like nature before . . . London : Printed by J. Okes, and are to be
sold by George Hurlock at his shop in
Thames-street neere S. Magnus Church.
1639. 4⁰, A—I in fours, including a
woodcut frontispiece. Dedicated to Charles
I. *B. M.*

ROBIN.

Poor Robin's Jests : Or, The Compleat
Jester. Being A Collection of several
Jests not heretofore published. Now
newly composed and written By Poor
Robin, Knight of the burnt Island, and
well-willer to the Mathematicks. Together with the true and lively Effigies
of the said Author. Licensed Feb. 2.
1666. Roger L'Estrange. London : Prin-

ted for Francis Kirkman and Richard Head. 8°, A—I 4 in eights.

> Inserted is a fine portrait of William Winstanley, 1667, with verses beneath it by F. K[irkman.]

The Path-Way to Knowledge, According to those undeniable Grounds and Actions delivered by the Ancient Philosophers and Astronomers, ... Experienced by the 21 Years Study and Practice of Poor Robin, a well-wisher to the Mathematicks. The Second Edition, with many Additions. London Printed, and are to be sold by Joseph Collier at the Bible upon London-Bridge, 1685. 8°. Title and frontispiece, 2 leaves : B—L 4 in eights. With cuts.

ROBINSON, HENRY.

Certaine Proposals in order to a new Modelling of the Lawes, and Law-Proceedings. For a more Speedy, Cheap, and Equall Distribution of Justice throughout the Common-Wealth . . . By Henry Robinson. London : Printed by M. Simmons . . . 1653. 4°, A—E 1 in fours, and a, 4 leaves, and b, 1 leaf, between A and B.

> This tract also contains remarks on trade and navigation.

ROBINSON, JOHN, *Pilgrim father.*

New Essayes Or Observations Divine and Morall. Collected out of the holy Scriptures, ... By Iohn Robinson . . . Printed Anno MDCXXVIII. 4°. A, 2 leaves : B—Tt in fours, Tt 4 blank.

ROBINSON, THOMAS, *Rector of Ousey, Cumberland.*

New Observations on the Natural History of the World of Matter, and this World of Life : In Two Parts. . . . London : Printed for John Newton . . . 1696. 8°. A, 8 leaves : b, 4 : a folded leaf : B—P in eights, besides a folded leaf in G. Dedicated to Mr. William Nicholson, Archdeacon of Carlisle, after which comes a second epistle "To the Gentlemen Miners."

ROCHEFORT, HENRY.

An almanack and pronosticatiō for this year of our Lorde God M.DLX. Practised in London for the comone good of all men. Made by Henry Rogeforde. Imprinted at London by Owen Rogers dwelling betwixt both sainct Barthelmewes at the signe of the spredde Egle. All the faires in England. 8°. The *Almanac*, A—B in eights, B 8 blank : the *Prognostication*, A—B in eights, B 6—8 blank. *B. M.*

ROE, J., *M.A., Chaplain to the Earl of Burlington.*

The Certainty of a Future State : Or, An Occasional Letter concerning Apparitions. . . . London, Printed for Joseph Wild, . . . MDCXCVIII. 4°, A—G 2 in fours, besides 3 leaves with title and dedication.

ROE, SIR THOMAS.

Sir Thomas Roe His Speech in Parliament. Wherein He sheweth the cause of the decay of Coyne and Trade in this Land, especially of Merchants Trade. And also propoundeth a Way to the House, how they may be increased. Printed in the yeare, 1641. 4°, 6 leaves.

Sir Thomas Rowe His Speech at the Councell-Table touching Brasse-Money, or against Brasse-Money, with many notable observations thereupon, Iuly, 1640. Printed Anno 1641. 4°, A in fours, and the title-page.

ROESSLIN, EUCHARIUS.

The byrth of Mankynde / newly translated out of Laten into Englysshe. In the which is entreated of all suche thynges the which chaunce to women in theyr labor, and all suche infyrmitees whiche happen vnto the Infantes after they be delyuered. . . . Cum priuilegio Regali, ad imprimendum solum. [Col.] Imprynted at London by T. R. Anno Domini. M.CCCCC.XL. 4°, A—Y in fours, but A—B making only one sheet of four. With two leaves of engravings on copper between F and G. Dedicated to Queen Katherine by Richard Jonas the translator.

The byrth of mankynde, other Wyse named the Womans booke. Newly set furth, corrected and augmented . . . By Thomas Raynold phisition. Anno. M.D.XLV. [Col.] Imprynted at London by Tho. Ray[nalde.] 4°, black letter. A, 4 leaves : B—I in eights : Hh, 8 : Hhh, 6 : three plates : K—Y in eights. With two other anatomical engravings between L and M.

The Birth of Man-kinde ; Otherwise Named The Womans Booke . . . London, Printed for I. H. and are to be sold by Iames Boler. 1626. 4°. A, 4 leaves : B—O in eights. Black letter. With cuts counted in the sheets.

ROGERS, DANIEL, *B.D.*

Matrimoniall Honovr : Or, The mutuall Crowne and comfort of godly, loyall, and chaste Marriage. . . . London, Printed by Th. Harper for Philip Nevil, . . . MDCXLII. 4°, A—3 F 2 in fours, and a,

4 ll. Dedicated to Robert, Earl of Warwick.

ROPE.

A Rope for a Parret, Or, A Cure for a Rebell past Cure. Being An Appendix or Rejoynder, to *A Caveat to all People of the Kingdome,* in Answer to Mercurio Cælico Mastix, . . . by George Naworth, . . . London, Printed for John Partridge. 1653. March. 7. 4°, 4 leaves.

ROPER, WILLIAM.

The Mirrovr of Vertve in Worldly Greatnes. Or The Life of Syr Thomas More Knight, sometime Lo. Chancellour of England. At Paris. M.DC.XXVI. 12°. Title (engraved), containing three-quarter portrait of More, 1 leaf : *, 4 leaves, with dedication by T. P. to the Countess of Barnbury : A—G in twelves.

> T. P., in the Epistle to Lady Banbury, acknowledges himself to be merely the Editor.

ROSE, GILES, *one of the Master-Cooks in His Majesty's Kitchen.*

A perfect School of Instructions for the Officers of the Mouth : Shewing the Whole Art of A Master of the Houshold, a Master Carver, a Master Butler, a Master Confectioner, a Master Cook, a Master Pastryman. . . . Adorned with Pictures curiously Ingraven, displaying the whole Arts. London, Printed for R. Bentley and M. Magnes, . . . 1682. 12°, A—Bb 6 in twelves. Dedicated to Sir Stephen Fox, one of the Commissioners of the Treasury, and Chief Clerk of the Board of Green Cloth, and to his honoured Lady, from Langly Park, June 24, 1681. With woodcuts.

ROSE, JOHN, *Gardener.*

The English Vineyard Vindicated, By John Rose Gard'ner to His Majesty at his Royal Garden in St. James's. Formerly Gard'ner to her Grace the Dutchess of Somerset. With an Address, Where the best Plants may be had at easie Rates. London, Printed by John Grismond for John Crook, . . . 1666. 8°. A—D in eights, A 1 and D 8 blank. With a plate of a Vineyard and a preface by Philocepos [John Evelyn.]

ROSS, JOHN, *Gentleman, an Eye-witness.*

Tangers Rescue ; Or a Relation of the late Memorable Passages at Tanger ; Giving a full and true account of the several Skirmishes of His Majesties Forces there against the Mores, . . . Together with a Description of the said City . . . London Printed for Hen. Hills 1681. 4°. A, 2

leaves : B—F 2 in fours. With a leaf of verses at the end.

ROSSE, ALEXANDER, *of Aberdeen, Preacher at St. Mary's, near Southampton, and one of His Majesty's Chaplains.*

The First and Second Books of Qvestions and Answers vpon the Booke of Genesis . . . London, Printed by Iohn Legatt, for Francis Constable, . . . 1622. 8°, A—I 2 in eights, besides a leaf of Argument : A—O 4 in eights, besides 4 leaves of prefixes under ¶. *B. M.*

> The first Book is dedicated to Bacon.

ROSWORM, COLONEL JOHN.

Good Service Hitherto ill rewarded. Or, An Historicall Relation of eight yeers Services for King and Parliament done in and about Manchester and those parts. By Lien: Col. John Rosworm. London : Printed in the Yeer, 1649. 8°, A—C in eights.

ROUNDHEADS.

The Rovnd-Head Vncovered. Being a moderate triall of his spirit. With a distinction betwixt the Round-heads and such as Papists call Puritans. London, Printed for George Lindsey, 1642. 4°, 4 leaves.

The Sovndheads Description of the Rovndhead. Or The Rovndhead Exactly Anatomised in his Integralls and Excrementalls, by the vntwisting a threefold Knott. . . . London Printed in the year 1642 for I. B. 4°, A—B 2 in fours.

The Resolution of the Round-Heads : Being A Zealovs Declaration of the Grievances wherewith their little Wits are consumed to destrvction. And what things they (in their Wisedome yet left them) conceiue fit to be reformed. London, Printed, Anno Domini, 1642. 4°, 4 leaves.

The Resolution of the Rovnd-Heads to pull down Cheap-side Crosse. Being a Zealovs Declaration of the Grievances wherewith their little Wits are consumed to destruction. And what things they (in their Wisdome yet left them) conceive fit to be reformed Imprinted in the yeare, 1642. 4°, 4 leaves.

A Sad Warning to all Prophane, Malignent Spirits, who reproach True Protestants with the name of Round-Heads. Wherein is declared five sad examples of Gods fearfull and just Judgements upon them. London, Printed for H. U. 1642. 4°, 4 leaves.

A Short, Compendious, and True Description of the Round-Heads, and the Long-Heads, Shag-polls, briefly declared, with the true discovery both of the time and place of both their Originall beginnings, ... Or, An Answer to a most ridiculous, absurd, and beyond comparison most foolish Baffle, sent into the world by a stinking Locust, and Intituled, *The Devil Turn'd Round-Head.* . . . Printed in the yeer. 1642. 4°, A—B 2 in fours. With a few verses at the end.

A New Anatomie, Or Character of a Christian, or Round-head. Expressing His Description, Excellencie, Happiness, and Innocencie . . . London, Printed for Robert Leybourne . . . 1645. 8°, A in eights.

The Riddle of the Roundhead. An Excellent New Ballad. To the Tune of, *Now at last the Riddle is Expounded.* London: Printed by N. Thompson. 1681. A leaf of verses.

ROUS, FRANCIS, *Provost of Eton.*

Testis Veritatis. The Doctrine of King Iames our late Soueraigne of famous Memory. Of the Chvrch of England. Of the Catholicke Chvrch. Plainely shewed to bee One in the points of Praedestination, Free-will, Certaintie of saluation. With a discouery of the Grounds both Naturall and Politicke of Arminianisme. By F. Rovs. Printed at London, by W. I. 1626. 4°, A—O in fours.

The Onely Remedy, That can cvre a People, when all other Remedies faile. By F. Rovs. . . . London, Printed for Iames Boler . . . 1627. 12°. A, 6, but title on A 3: B—L in twelves: M, 4. Dedicated to his Country.

Archæologiæ Atticæ Libri Septem. Seven Bookes of the Attick Antiquities. Containing The description of The Citties Giory, . . . With an Addition of their Customes in Marriages, Burials, . . . The Fifth Edition . . . Oxford, . . . 1658. 4°. *, 4 leaves : A Bbb in fours.

ROUSE, J.

Rouse His Case, Truly Stated and Written with his own Hand in Newgate, Two Days before his Execution, to prevent any false Reports. . . . To which is Annexed a Letter to his Wife, from Newgate. London : Printed by J. Grantham, by the Order of the Widdow Rouse. 1683. Folio, B—E, 2 leaves each, and the title.

ROWLANDS, SAMUEL.

The Famous History of Guy Earle of Warwick. By Samuel Rowlands. Im-

printed at London by Edw: All-de . . . [1608.] 4°, A—Q 2 in fours, A 1 blank. Woodcut on title and others in the volume.

> This is the earliest edition known, and is probably that which was printed pursuant to the registration of the book by W. Ferbrand, June 23, 1608. Ferbrand, who was not a printer, may have employed Allde to execute it for him ; in the only copy at present known, the imprint, which perhaps contained Ferbrand's name as the seller, is imperfect.

Well met Gossip : Or, Tis merrie when Gossips meet : Newly Enlarged with diuers merrie Songs. London, Printed by I. W. for Iohn Deane, and are to be sold at his Shop iust vnder Temple-barre. 1619. 4°, A—D 2 in fours. With cut on title.

ROWLANDSON, MARY

A True History of the Captivity & Restoration of Mrs. Mary Rowlandson, A Minister's Wife in New-England. Wherein is set forth, The Cruel and Inhumane Usage she underwent amongst the Heathens for Eleven Weeks time : And her Deliverance from them. Written by her own Hand, for her Private Use . . . Printed first at New-England : And Reprinted at London, and sold by Joseph Poole at the Blue Bowl in the Long-Walk, by Christes-Church Hospital. 1682. 4°, A—E in fours. With a sermon annexed by the writer's husband, Mr. Joseph Rowlandson.

> The collation given does not include the *Sermon*, which was deficient in the Hamilton copy here used.

ROWZEE, LODWICK, *M.D., of Ashford, Kent.*

The Qveenes Welles. That is, A Treatise of the nature and vertues of Tunbridge Water. Together, With an enumeration of the chiefest diseases, which it is good for, and against which it may be used, and the manner and order of taking it. London, Imprinted by Iohn Dawson. 1632. 8°. A, 4 leaves : B—F in eights. Dedicated to Edward, Viscount Conway. *B. M.*

ROYALISTS.

The Royall and the Royallists Plea. . . . Corrected and Enlarged by the Author. An°. Dom¹. 1647. 4°, A—D in fours, A 1 occupied by quotations.

A New Message to the Royalists of the two Kingdoms of England & Scotland ; Communicating the great and potent proceedings, of the victorious and renowned English heroes, against the great Duke of

Scotland, and his disloyall Army. As also, A further Character, and discovery of their present proceedings and Atchivements, against the Royal Navy at Sea, the Northern Army, the Welch, Cornish, & Scottish Forces. Likewise, A Caveat to the Army, . . . London, Printed for J. J. 1648. 4°, 4 leaves. In verse.

RUDDIERD, SIR BENJAMIN.
Two Speeches By Sir Beniamin Rudyard, Concerning the Palatinate. London, Printed for Francis Constable, 1641. 4°, 4 leaves.

RUDIARD, EDMUND.
The Thvnderbolt of Gods Wrath against Hard-Hearted and Stiffe-necked sinners, or an Abridgement of the Theater of Gods fearefull iudgements executed vpon notorious sinners. [Three quotations.] London, Printed by W. I. by the Assignement of Adam Islip, for Thomas Pauier 1618. 4°, A—N in fours.

> Dedicated to Sir Vincent Corbet and other gentlemen, and to their religious ladies, from Utoxeter, Sept. 10, 1615. At p. 29 occurs the account of " Marlin, a Cambridge Scholler, who was a Poet, and a filthy Play-maker."

RUMP.
The Private Debates, Conferences and Resolutions of the Rump: Imparted to publick view, as soon as they could be gotten together. *Risum teneatis Amici?* London, Printed in the year, 1660. 4°, A—D in fours, and a leaf of E.

The Character of the Rump. London, Printed in the Year 1660. 4°, 4 leaves.

The Rump Held forth last first-day in a Brotherly Exercise, at the Bull and Mouth at Aldersgate. Rump-*atur quisquis* Rump-*itur cc merito.* London, Printed, 1660. 4°, A—B 3 in fours.

A Mirror; Wherein the Rumpers and Fanaticks (Especially those, who even yet desire to continue Religious Rebells, . . .) may see their Deformity, and abhor both themselves and their Actions. Sent in a Letter by a Friend, to a Votary and Follower of that Faction. Occasioned by a Seditious Sermon lately Preached . . . London, Printed for Robert Pawley . . . 1660. 4°, A—B in fours.

The Qualifications of Persons, declared Capable by the Rump, Parliament to Elect, to be Elected, Members to supply their House. Printed in the year 1660. 4°, A—B in fours.

The Acts and Monuments of the Late Rump, From the time of their Last Ses-

sions, Untill the coming in of the Secluded Members. London; Printed in the Yeare, 1660. 4°, 4 leaves.

A Seasonable Speech, Made by Alderman Atkins in the Rump Parliament. Printed in the Year, 1660. 4°, 4 leaves.

The Rump, Or A Collection of Songs and Ballads, made upon those who would be a Parliament, and were but the Rump of an House of Commons, five times dissolv'd. London, Printed for H. Brome, and H. Marsh, at the Gun in Ivy-Lane, and the Princes Arms in Chancery-Lane near Fleetstreet 1660. 8°. Title and frontispiece, 2 leaves: To the Reader, 2 leaves: B—M in eights.

The Petition of the Rump to the Honourable City of London. [1660.] A broadside. *B. M.*

RUMSEY, W., *of Gray's Inn.*
Organon Salutis. An Instrument to cleanse the Stomach, As also divers new Experiments of the virtue of Tobacco and Coffee. How much they conduce to preserve humane health. By W. R. of Grays Inne, Esq. *Experto credo.* London, Printed by R. Hodgkinsonne, for D. Pakeman, . . . 1657. 8°. a, 8 leaves: b, 4 leaves: B—E 4 in eights, no A. Dedicated to the Marquis of Dorchester, and (in a second Epistle) to his friend Sir Henry Blount. *B. M.*

Organon Salutis. An Instrvment to cleanse the Stomach. As also divers new Experiments of the virtue of Tobacco and Coffee : How much they conduce to preserve humane health. By W. R. of Gray's Inne. Esquire. The second Edition, with new Additions. *Experto credo.* London, Printed for D. Pakeman, . . . 1659. 8°. A—F in eights, first and last leaves blank. Dedicated to Henry, Marquis of Dorchester. With a letter from Rumsey to Sir Henry Blount, and Blount's Answer.

RUPERT, PRINCE.
His Highnesse Prince Ruperts late Beating up the Rebels Qvarters at Post-Combe & Chinner in Oxford-shire. And his Victory in Chalgrove Field, on Sunday morning Iune 18. 1643. Whereunto is added Sʳ Iohn Urries Expedition to West-Wickham the Sunday after: Iune 25. 1643. Printed at Oxford by Leonard Lichfield, . . . 1643. 4°, A—C 2 in fours.

RUSDEN, MOSES, *Apothecary, and Bee-Master to the King.*
A Further Discovery of Bees. Treating

of the Nature, Government, Generation & Preservation of the Bee. . . . London, Printed for the Author, and are to be sold at his house next the Sign of the King's Arms in the Bowling-Alley, near the Abby in Westminster ; . . . 1679. 8°, A—K in eights, and a, 4 leaves, besides a frontispiece and plates at pp. 2, 66, and 82. Dedicated to the King.

RUSE, HENRY, *Engineer, and Captain of a Foot-Company belonging to the City of Amsterdam.*
The Strengthening of Strong-Holds : Invented on several Occasions, and practised during the late Wars, as well in the Vnited Provinces as in France, Germany, Italy, Dalmatia, Albania, and the Neighbouring Countries. Translated out of the Low-Dutch-Copy, by His Majesties Command. In the Savoy, Printed by the Assigns of John Bill and Christopher Barker. . . . 1668. Folio, B—P, 2 leaves each : Q, 1 leaf, besides the English title and Dutch frontispiece and dedication, 3 leaves more, and eight folded plates.

RUSSELL, LORD WILLIAM.
Considerations upon a Printed Sheet, Entituled the Speech of the Late Lord Russell . . . London, Printed by T. B. for Joanna Brome . . . MDCLXXXIII. 4°, A —G 2 in fours.

RUSSHE, ANTHONY, *D.D.*
A President for a Prince. Wherein is to be scene by the testimonie of auncient Writers, the ductie of Kings, Princes, and Gouernours. . . . [Col.] Imprinted at London by H. Denham. Anno. 1566. 4°. A—N, 2 leaves each, besides a leaf at end with four lines of Latin verse. Dedicated to the Queen. *B. M.*

RUSSIA.
A Relation Concerning the Particulars of the Rebellion Lately raised in Muscovy by Stenko Razin ; Its Rise, Progress, and Stop ; together with the maner of taking that Rebel, the Sentence of Death passed upon him, and the Execution of the same. Published by Authority. In the Savoy:

Printed by Tho. Newcomb. 1672. 4°, A—D in fours, D 4 blank. With a folded frontispiece, having a portrait of Razin in the top left-hand corner, and containing a representation of the prisoner riding to execution.

RUTHVEN, PATRICK, LORD.
The Ladies Cabinet Enlarged and Opened : Containing many Rare Secrets and Rich Ornaments, of several Kindes, and different uses . . . Whereunto is added, Sundry Experiments and choice Extractions of Waters, Oyls, &c. Collected and practised ; By the late Right Honorable and Learned Chymist the Lord Ruthuen. The second Edit. with Additions ; . . . London, Printed by T. M. for G. Bedell and T. Collins, . . . 1655. 12°. Title, &c., 4 leaves : B—N 8 in twelves, the last 10 pages occupied by advertisements.
The Stationers' address to the Reader is dated the 18th September 1645, and seems to imply that this is in fact the third impression.

RYCAUT, SIR PAUL.
The Present State of the Ottoman Empire. . . . In Three Books. By Paul Rycaut Esq ; . . . London, Printed for John Starkey and Henry Brome, . . . 1668. Folio. Frontispiece with portrait of Sultan Mahomet 1666, 1 leaf : A, 4 leaves : (a), 2 leaves : B—Gg 2 in fours, Gg 2 blank. With engravings accompanying the text. Dedicated to Lord Arlington.

RYMER, THOMAS.
Edgar, Or The English Monarch ; An Heroick Tragedy. By Thomas Rymer of Grays-Inn Esq ; . . . London, Printed for Richard Tonson . . . MDCLXXVIII. 4°, A—l in fours, A 1 blank.

RYVES, BRUNO.
Englands Iliads in a Nvt-Shell. Or, A briefe Chronologie of the Battails, Sieges, Conflicts, and other most remarkable passages from the beginning of this Rebellion, to the 25. of March, 1645. . . . Oxford, Printed in the Yeare, 1645. 8°, A, 2 leaves : B—C in eights : D, 6.

S.

S. G.
Anglorum Speculum, Or The Worthies of England, In Church and State. Alphabetically digested into the several Shires and Counties therein contained ; . . . London, Printed for Thomas Passinger . . . William Thackaray . . . and John Wright . . . 1684. 8⁰. A, 3 leaves : B —3 Q in eights.
An abridgment of Fuller with Additions.

S. I.
The Vnerring and Vnerrable Chvrch Or An answer to a Sermon preached by Mᵣ Andrew Sall, formerly a Iesuit, and now a Minister of the Protestant Church. Written by I. S. and Dedicated To His Excellency The most honorable Arthur Earl of Essex Lord Lieutenant of Ireland. Anno 1675. 8⁰. ꭓ, 8 : č, 2 : A—V 3 in eights.

S. J.
The Second Spira : Being a fearful Example of an Atheist, who had Apostatized from the Christian Religion, and dyed in Despair at Westminster, Decemb. 8. 1692. . . . By J. S. a Minister of the Church of England, . . . The Second Edition, well Attested. London, Printed for John Dunton, . . . 1693, 12⁰, A—F in sixes, A 1 with *Imprimatur.*

S. J.
Virtue and Science. Pindarick Poems. Dedicated to the Most Illustrious Princess, Anne, Dutchess of Richmond and Lenox, and to her Sister, The Right Honourable, Frances, Countess of Newburgh. London, Printed in the Year, 1695. Folio, B—E, 2 leaves each, besides title and Preface, and B repeated.

S. J.
The Principles of the Cyprianic Age, with Regard to Episcopal Power and Jurisdiction : . . By which it is made evident, that the Vindicator of the Kirk of Scotland is obliged by his own Concessions to acknowledge, that *he and his associates* are Schismaticks. In a Letter to a Friend. By J. S. London, Printed for Walter Kettilby . . . MDCXCV. 4⁰. A, 2 leaves : B—N in fours.

S. M.
Crvm's of Comfort and Godly Prayers . . . Printed for Henry Brome. 12⁰, A—P in twelves. With two folding plates.

S. M.
The Great Birth of Man. Or, The Excellency of Man's Creation and Endowments above the Original of Woman. A Poem. The Second Edition. By M. S. London : Printed for J. M. and Sold by John Taylor . . . 1688. 4⁰.
I have so far only seen the title-page.

S. M.
Enchiridion Geographicum. Or, A Manual of Geography. Being A Description of all the Empires, Kingdoms, and Dominions of the Earth . . . Edinburgh, Printed in the Year, M.DCCIV. 8⁰, A—M in fours and twos.

S. R.
Late Newes out of Barbary. In a Letter written of late from a Merchant there, to a Gentl. not long since imployed [*sic*] into that countrie from his Maiestie. Containing some strange particulars, of this new Sainted Kings proceedings : as they haue been very credibly related from such as were eye-witnesses. Imprinted at London for Arthur Ionson. 1613. 4⁰, A—C in fours, A 1 blank. *B. M.*
A second letter at the end is subscribed *G. B.*

S. R.
Ludus Ludi Literarii ; Or, School-Boys Exercises and Divertisements in XLVII Speeches : Some of them Latine, but most English. Spoken (and prepared to be spoken) in a Private School about London, at Several Breakings up, in the Year 1671. London, Printed by W. R. for Tho. Parkhurst, . . . 1672. 8⁰, A—I in eights : K, 9. *B. M.*

S. R.
[A Letter of news about Ostend, &c. to a friend, dated from Dunkirk, November 19, 1688.] A folio leaf.

S. T.
A Letter to his Excellency The Lord General Monck. London, Printed in the Year, 1659. A broadside.

S. T.
Youths Tragedy A Poem : Drawn up by way of Dialogue . . . For the Caution, and Direction, of the Younger Sort. . . . London, Printed for John Starkey . . . and Francis Smith . . . 1671. 4⁰, A—C in fours.

Youth Undone : A Tragick Poem . . . .
London : Printed by T. Hive for Jonathan Robinson. . . . 1709. 4°. A, 2
leaves : B—D in fours.

Youth's Tragedy under a new title.

S. T., *Weaver in London.*

Reasons Humbly offered for the Passing
a Bill for the hindering the Home Consumption of East-India Silks, Bengals
&c. And an Answer to the Author of
several Objections against the said Bill,
in a Book, Entituled, An Essay on the
East-India Trade. . . . With a Postscript,
containing the French King's Decree concerning India Manufactures. London,
Printed by J. Bradford . . . 1697. 8°,
A—C 2 in eights.

S. W.

The Poems of Ben. Johnson Junior.
Being A Miscelanie of Seriousness, Wit,
Mirth, and Mysterie. In Vulpone. The
Dream. Iter Bevoreale. Songs, &c.
Composed by W. S. Gent. *Parce—valem-*
sceleris damnare—— London, Printed for
Tho. Passenger . . . 1672. 8°. A, 4
leaves : B—H in eights.

SACHEVERELL, WILLIAM, *late Governor of Man.*

An Account of the Isle of Man, Its Inhabitants, Language, Soil, remarkable Curiosities, the Succession of its Kings and
Bishops, down to the present Time. By
way of Essay. With a Voyage to I. Columb-kill. To which is added, A Dissertation about the *Mona* of Cæsar and
Tacitus, . . . By Mr Thomas Brown. . . .
London : Printed for J. Hartley, . . . and
Tho. Hodgson . . . 1702. 8°. Title, dedication to his kinsman Robert Sacheverell of Barton in Nottinghamshire, and
preface, 4 leaves : B—N in eights.

SADEUR, JACQUES.

A New Discovery of Terra Incognita
Australis, Or The Southern World. By
James Sadeur a French-man. Who Being cast there by a Shipwrack, lived 35
years in that Country, . . . London,
Printed for John Dunton, . . . 1693. 12°.
A, 4 leaves : B—F 6 in twelves : Aa—
Dd in twelves. There are no pp. 89-96.

It is stated that these Memoirs were kept
for many years secret, and only printed
after the author's death.

SAINT.

The Saint turn'd Curtezan : Or, A New
Plot discover'd by a precious Zealot, of
an Assault and Battery design'd upon the
Body of a Sanctify'd Sister, &c. . . . To
the Tune of the *Quakers Ballad :* or, *All*

in the Land of Essex. Printed for the use
of the Protestant-Cobler in Pall-Mall.
[A.D. : 168?.] A broadside in ——e.

SALES.

Innoqui Sales. A Collection of —w Epigrams. Vol. I. With a Prefate Essay
on Epigrammatic Poetry. Epigrammatidis omnium Scenarum Hoc London,
Printed by T. Hodgkin ; —t are to
be sold by Matth. Gillyflower, Westminster Hall. 1694. 8°, 64 leaves.

No more is known.

SALMON, WILLIAM, *M.D.*

Seplasivm. The Compleat Eng—h Physitian : Or, The Druggist's Shop opened.
Explicating all the Particulars which
Medicines at this day are composed and
made. . . . In X. Books. By Wiam Salmon, Professor of Physick, ne Holbourn-Bridge, London. London, rinted
for Matthew Gillifl wer . . . at —eorge
Sawbridge . . . 1693. 8°. A, 8. cluding half-title ; a, 3 leaves : (a—f), 4
leaves each : B—— in eights. Dicated
to the Queen.

Pharmacopœia Bateana : Or, Bate Dispensary. Translated from the —cond
Edition of the Latin Copy, Published
by Mr James Shipton. Containg His
Choice and Secret Recipes, . . The
Arcana Goddardiana, . . . To weh are
Added in this English edition, Goard's
Drops, Russel's Powder, and the Eplastrum Febrifugium : . . . London : —inted
for S. Smith and B. Walford, . . 1694.
8°, A—3 P in eights : qqq, 4 leav : 3 q
(repeated)—3 r in fours.

SALT.

A draught of the Contract about St, on
the behalf of Nicholas Murford, so a
Proposition made by Thomas orth
Merchant, an l others owners of Sa-Pans
at South, and North-Shields, and other
Petition on the behalf of the own
of great Yarmouth . . . The con ieration
whereof is humbly presented the
most honourable houses of Parliment.
[1638-9.] A broadside. *B. M.*

SALUSTE, GUILLAUME, *Seignor du Bartas.*

Divine Weeks and Works . . . translated
by J. Sylvester . . . 1605-6-7. 4

I annex the collation of Dr. Bliss copy,
the most complete which I ha yet
seen :—
A, 8 leaves, the first marked A on. and
the anonymous engraved title : B— 4, 4
leaves : sonnets by Jonson, Daniel, Daes of
Hereford, &c., 5 leaves : printed title *The*
First Weeke. Or Birth of the World. 605,

eaf : C—Kk 6 in eights : [A new title :]
Posthumus Bartas. The Third Day of
.is Second Weeke ; Containing 1. The Vo-
.tion. 2. The Fathers. 3. The Lawe. 4.
:e Captaines. . . . 1606.——Title and
:nnet Dedicatorie, 2 leaves : Ll *—Kr * 1 in
vars : [a fresh title :] Fragments, and other
..all Workes of Bartas. With other Trans-
.ions, By Iosvah Sylvester. 1605. With
.dication on *verso* to the wife of William
:sex of Lamborne—title and following
.af, 2 leaves : Ll—3 A in eights, besides 4
.plicate signatures, XX—XX 4, XX 4
:nk : Rr* 2 – Ggg 2 in fours, last leaf
.nk : [fresh title :] II. Posthumus Bartas.
:e Fore-noone of the fourth Day of his
:cond Week : Containing 1. The Tropheis.
The Magnificence. [3 and 4 are left blank]
. Imprinted at London by. Humfrey
:wnes. 1607.——Aaa—Eee in eights, be-
des title and dedications, 2 leaves.
The Second Week opens with a separate
tle having the imprint, At London Printed
r Humfrey Lownes. . . . 1605. On Yy
:curs a title : *Tetastrika. Or The Qua-
:rins of Guy de Faur, Lord of Pibrac.*
:anslated by Iosvah Sylvester. At London
rinted by Humfrey Lownes. 1605.
Dedicated by Sylvester to James I. in
rench and Italian, after which come the
iscriptio and the *Corona Dedicatoria* (6 ll.),
.llowed by *A Catalogue of the Order of the
ookes,* which, as it does not mention Weeks
hird and Fourth or the Quadrains of Pib-
:c, seems to shew that these were pub-
-shed afterward. Throughout the volume
.a series of dedications to contemporary
.lebrities.
Complete copies of this 4° of 1605-7 are
.rtainly uncommon.

L'ranie Ov Mvse Celeste G. de Saluste
Scneur du Bartas. Vrania Sive Mvsa
. . Londini Excudebat Iohannes Wolfius.
1 :. 4°, A—D in fours. Dedicated by
Ro rt Ashley, the translator from French
im Latin, to Sir Henry Unton. Fr. and
L.. *B. M.*

T Second Weeke or Childhood of the
Wrld, of the noble, learned and diuine
Sustius, Lord of Bartas : translated by
Iouah Svluester. At London, Printed
b. P. S. dwelling on Bredstreet hill at
tl -igne of the Starre. 1598. 8°, A—F
ii ights, F 8 blank. Dedicated to the
E . of Essex.

T. Colonies of Bartas. With the Com-
n:taries of S. G. S. in diuerse places cor-
r. ed and enlarged by the Translatour.

.ores hominum multorum narrat & vrbes.

L.lon, Printed by R. F. for Thomas
Ma. 1598. 4°. A, 2 leaves : B—G 2 in
f:rs. Dedicated by Guilielmus de In-
:-:. (William Lisle) to Charles, Earl of
N tingham, in two epistles, one Latin
v:e, the other English verse and pro-e.

In the dedication Lisle speaks of himself
as a lawyer, who merely engaged in literature at leisure intervals. He also refers
to the *Babilon,* previously translated and
published by him.

The Third Dayes Creation. By that
most excellent, learned and diuine Poet,
William, Lord Bartas. Done verse for
verse out of the originall French by
Thomas Winter, Maister of Arts. At
sacri vates . . . Ouid. Amorum, lib. 3,
Eleg. 8. London, Printed for Thomas
Clerke. 1604. 4", A—F in fours. Dedicated to Prince Henry. *B. M.*

With commendatory verses by John San-
ford, John Dunster, Thomas Mason, Nathanael Tomkins, and Henry Ashwood.
The translation itself ends on F 2 *verso,* and
the rest of the volume is occupied by a son-
net to the translator by Thomas Mason
Suffolciensis and others by the translator to
Sir Thomas Chaloner, Sir George Somers,
Sir Thomas Lucy, and Dr. James, Justice
of Peace and Quorum for Somersetshire.

Fovre Bookes of Du Bartas : I. The Arke,
II. Babylon, III. The Colonnyes, IIII.
The Colvmnes or Pillars : In French and
English for the Instrvction and Pleasvre
of svch as delight in both langvages.
By William L'Isle . . . Together with a
Large Commentary by S. G. S. London
Printed by T. Paine, for Francis Egils-
fielde, . . . 1637. 4°. ¶ and ¶¶, 4 leaves
each : A—Ll in fours : Mm, 1 leaf.

A reissue of the edition of 1625.

SANSON, M., *Missionary from the French
King.*
The Present State of Persia : With a
Faithful Account of the Manners, Reli-
gion, and Government of that People
. . . Adorn'd with Figures. Done into
English. London : Printed for M. Gilli-
flower, . . . 1695. 12°. A, 6 leaves :
B—l in twelves : K, 6 : L, 2. Dedicated
to Sir Charles Barrington in a long ad-
dress by John Savage the translator.
With plates at pp. 1, 38, 46, 56, 62, and
66.

SARPI, PAOLO.
The Historie of the Covncel of Trent.
Conteining eight Bookes. In which (besides the ordinarie Actes of the Councell)
are declared many notable occurrences,
which happened in Christendome, . . .
Written in Italian by Pietro Soaue Po-
lano, and faithfully translated into English by Nathanael Brent. London Printed
by Robert Barker, and Iohn Bill . . .
Anno Dom. M.DC.XX. Folio. ¶, 6 leaves,
first blank : A—3 Z in sixes : 4 A—B in
fours, 4 B 3 with colophon and 4 B 4 blank.
Dedicated to the King.

A Fvll and Satisfactorie Answer to the Late Vnadvised Bull, thundred by Pope Paul the Fift, against the renowned State of Venice : Being modestly entitled by the learned Author, Considerations Vpon the Censvre of Pope Pavl the Fift, against the Common-Wealth of Venice : By Father Pavl of Venice, a Frier of the Order of Servi. Translated out of Italian. Psal. 108. . . . London Printed for Iohn Bill. 1606. 4°. A—K in fours, K 4 blank. *B. M.*

A Discovrse vpon the Reasons of the Resolvtion taken in the Valteline against the tyranny of the Grisons and Heretiqves. To the most Mighty Catholique King of Spaine, D. Phillip the Third . . . Faithfully translated into English. With the Translators Epistle to the Commons House of Parliament. London, Printed for William Lee, . . . 1628. 4°, A—N in fours.

A contemporary hand ascribes the translation to Sir Thomas Rowe, then ambassador at Constantinople.

SARATE or ZARATE, AUGUSTINE.
The Discoverie and Conqvest of the Provinces of Peru, and the Navigation in the South Sea, along the Coast. And also of the ritche Mines of Potosi. Imprinted at London by Richard Ihones. Febru. 6. 1581. 4°, black letter. With cuts. Two title-pages varying: dedication by Thomas Nicholas the translator to Thomas Wilson, LL.D., 3 leaves: To the Reader, two addresses, 4 leaves: verses by S. Gosson, 1 leaf: B—Aa in fours.

SATIRES.
A Ternary of Satyrs. Containing,
1. A Satyr against Man.
2. A Satyr against Woman.
3. A Satyr against the Popish-Clergy. Composed in French by an Exquisit Pen, And now done into English. London, Printed for W. Leach, at the Crown in Cornhill, 1679. 4°, A—F in fours.

SAUTERIUS, DANIEL.
The Practise of the Banckrvpts of these Times. . . . . A worke now very necessary . . . London, Printed by Iohn Norton, for William Garret, Anno M.DC.XL. 8°, A—H in eights, H 8 blank.

SAVAGE, ELIZABETH.
A Narrative of the Late Extraordinary Cure Wrought in an Instant vpon M'' Eliz. Savage, (Lame from her Birth) without the using of any Natural Means. With the Affidavits . . . With an Appendix, attempting to prove, That Miracles are not ceas'd. London, Printed for John Dunton at the Raven, and John Harris at the Harrow in the Poultry. MDCXCIV. Price 6ᵈ. 8°, A—F in fours.

Elizabeth Savage was the daughter of Mr. William Morton of Hitchington, Bucks, and the wife of a schoolmaster living in Horse-Shoe Alley, Little Moorfields.

SAVOY.
The Oracle of Savoy : Containing the predictions made for truth to the Duke of Savoy, as concerning the Estate of Fraunce, in the month of August, Anno 1600. With a discourse worthy note, vpon the same subiect. According to the Coppy Printed in French, both at Lyons and Paris. London, Printed for William Ferbrand, and are to be solde at his shop at the signe of the Crowne neere Guild-hall gate. 1600. 4°. 4 leaves, black letter, except the Prognostication in verse, which occupies the last leaf.

A Relation of the now present Warres, betweene the illustrious L. Charles Emanvel, D. of Savoy, Piedmont, &c. and the L. Cardinal of Mantua, D. of Montferrat, seconded by the King of Spaine. The Emperors Decree, and the Duke of Savoy his Letter to the Emperor, wherein the whole occasion of the Warres is briefly declared. Translated out of the Latin Copie. London, Printed by W. Stansby for Nathaniel Butter, . . . 1615. 4°, A—D 2 in fours, A 1 blank.

A Relation Or Remonstrance of what was negotiated by the Remonstrant, in the name of this Common-wealth, at the Court of Savoy. [1652.] 4°, A—D in fours, D 4 blank.

A Collection of the Several Papers sent to his Highness the Lord Protector . . . Concerning the Bloody and Barbarous Massacres, Murthers, and other Cruelties, committed on many thousands of Reformed, or Protestants dwelling in the Vallies of Piedmont by the Duke of Savoy's Forces, joyned therein with the French Army and severall Irish Regiments. Published by Command of his Highness. Printed for H. Robinson, at the three Pigeons in St. Paul's Church Yard, 1658. 4°. *, 4 leaves: A—G 2 in fours.

Edited by J. B. Stouppe, and dedicated by him to Cromwell.

The Barbarous & Inhumane Proceedings against the Professors of the Reformed Religion within the Dominion of the Duke of Savoy. Aprill the 27ᵗʰ, 1655. As also, A True Relation of the Bloody

Massacres . . . in Ireland . . . And the
Lamentable and Miserable Condition of
Germany, . . . Illustrated with Pictures,
that the eye may affect the heart. London : Printed by M. S. for Tho. Jenner
. . . 1655. 4°, A—G in fours.
Compare PIEDMONT, *supra.*

SCARRON, PAUL.
The Whole Comical Works of Mons. Scarron. . . . The Second Edition, Revised
and Corrected. London : Printed for S.
and J. Sprint [and others.] 1703. 8°. A,
4 leaves, besides a frontispiece, portrait of
Scarron, and a plate of *A Company of
Stage Players:* B—Nn in eights. With a
plate at p. 82.
This version purports to have been executed by Mr. Thomas Brown, Mr. Savage,
and others.

SCHEFFER, JOHN, *Professor of Law and
Rhetoric at Upsala in Sweden.*
The History of Lapland Wherein are
shewed the Original, Manners, Habits,
Marriages, Conjurations, &c. of that
People. At the Theater in Oxford.
M.DC.LXXIV. And are to be sold by George
West and Amos Caurtein. Folio, A—Oo,
2 leaves each, besides the frontispiece,
title, Preface, and Map, 4 leaves more.
With woodcuts.
In the Preface it is mentioned that the
author was assisted in his labours by the
Chancellor of Sweden, who had commanded
him to undertake it ; but the translator's
name does not present itself.

The History of Lapland : . . . To which
are added, The Travels of the King of
Sweden's Mathematicians into Lapland :
The History of Livonia, and the Wars
there : Also a Journey into Lapland, Fin-
land, &c. written by Dr. Olofs Rudbeck
in the Year 1701. London : Printed for
Tho. Newborough, . . . 1704. 8°. A, 4
leaves : B—Ff 3 in eights. With a frontispiece, folded map, and plates at pp.
134, 144, and 304, besides those which
count in the sheets.

SCINTILLA [? MICHAEL SPARKE].
Scintilla, Or A Light Broken into darke
Warehouses. With Observations vpon
the Monopolists of Seauen severall Patents, and Two Charters. Practised and
performed, By a Mistery of some Printers,
Sleeping Stationers, and Combining Booksellers. Anatomised and layd open in a
Breviat, in which is only a touch of their
fore-stalling and ingrossing of Books in
Pattents, and Raysing them to excessive
prices. Left to the Consideration of the
High and Honourable House of Parliament now assembled. *Let not one Brother*

*oppress another. Doe as you would be done
unto.* At London, Printed, not for profit,
but for the Common Weles good : and
nowhere to be sold, but some where to be
be given. 1641. 4°, 4 leaves.

SCIOPPIUS, GASPARUS.
Gasp. Scioppii Collyrivm Regivm Sere-
nissimo D. Jacobo Magnæ Britanniæ
Regi. Graviter ex oculis labor ante Omnium Catholicorum nomine gratiæ volun-
tatis causa muneri missum. . . . Anno
cɪɔ. ɪɔ. cxɪ. 8°, a—e in eights : A—P 4
in eights.

Is. Casavboni [G. Scioppii] Corona Regia.
Id est Panegyrici Cvivsdam vere Avrei,
Quem Iacobo 1. Magnæ Britanniæ, &c.
Regi, Fidei defensor delinearat. . . .
M.DC.XV. Pro Officina Regia Io Bill.
Londini. 12°. A—E in twelves : F, 4.
A satire on Henry VIII. and Elizabeth
published under Casaubon's name.

SCLATER, WILLIAM, *D.D.*
Civil Magistracy by Divine Authority,
. . . London, Printed by T. M. for George
Treagle at Taunton : . . . 1653. 4°, A—
G 2 in fours.
Probably the earliest notice of a stationer
at Taunton. This is merely a sermon
preached at the Winchester Assizes, and
afterward at Taunton.

SCOT, ALEXANDER, *Scotus, I.V.D.*
Vniversa Grammatica Græca . . . : Lvg-
dvni, . . . M.D.XCIII. 8°. *, 8 leaves :
a—z in eights ; Aa—Ss 2 in eights, and
the Index, followed by 3 pp. of verses.

SCOT, PHILIP.
A Treatise of the Schism of England.
Wherein particularly Mr Hales and Mr
Hobbs are modestly accosted. By Philip
Scot. Permissu Superiorum. Amster-
dam. Printed Anno Dom. 1650. 12°.
A, 6 : B—M in twelves : N, 6.

SCOT, REGINALD.
Scot's Discovery of Witchcraft : . . .
London, Printed by E. Cotes, and are to
be sold by Thomas Williams . . . 1654.
4°. Title, 1 leaf : A, 4 leaves : a, 4 : B—
3 E in fours.

The Discovery of Witchcraft : . . .
Whereunto is added An excellent Discourse of the Nature and Substance of
Devils and Spirits, In Two Books : The
First by the aforesaid Author : The Second now added in this Third Edition,
as Succedaneous to the former . . . With
Nine Chapters at the beginning of the
Fifteenth Book of the Discovery. London : Printed for A. Clark, and are to be
sold by Dixy Page . . 1665. Folio. Label,

1 leaf : Title, 1 leaf : (a)—(b) in fours : B—3 F in sixes : 3 G, 2.

SCOT, WALTER.

A True History of several Honourable Families of the Right Honourable Name of Scot, In the Shires of Roxburgh and Selkirk, and others adjacent. Gathered out of Ancient Chronicles, Histories, and Traditions of our Fathers. By Capt. Walter Scot, An old Souldier, and no Scholler,

And one that can Write nane,
But just the Letters of his Name.

Edinburgh, Printed by the Heir of Andrew Anderson, . . . 1688. 4°, A—Y in fours. Dedicated to John, Lord Yester, Appearand Earl of Tweddale. In verse.

SCOTLAND.

Reasons for a Generall Assemblie. . . . Printed in the year of God, 1638. 4°, A—B 2 in fours.

Quæres Concerning The state of the Church of Scotland. . . . Reprinted in the yeare 1638. 8°, 8 leaves.

Against the apple of the left eye of antichrist, or the masse book of lurking darknesse, making way for the apple of the right eye of antichrist, the compleat masse book of palpable darknesse . . . Printed, Anno 1638. 8°, A—E in eights, and Answers to the Censure, 2 leaves.

A Remonstrance concerning the present Troubles from the Meeting of the Estates of the Kingdome of Scotland, Aprill 16. unto the Parliament of England. Printed in the Year of God, 1640. 4°. A, 6 : B, 2 : C, 4 : D, 2.

Eight Articles of the Scots Demands, Lately put into the Parliament by the Scots Commissioners. 1° July. 1641. Printed in the Yeare, 1641. 4°, 4 leaves.

A Great Discoverie of a Plot in Scotland. By a Miraculous meanes. Two great Actors in the same being so taken with the sweet disposition of those Worthies, against whom they Plotted ; that their troubled Consciences would not permit them to proceed . . . With the Copy of a letter sent to the Papists in London. London, Printed by Bernard Alsop, MDCXLI. 4°, 4 leaves.

Certaine Instrvctions given by the L. Montrose, L. Nappier, Laerd of Keer and Blackhall. With A Trve Report of the Committe for this New Treason, that they had a three-fold Designe. London, Printed in the yeare 1641. 4°, 4 leaves.

A Discovrse concerning the Svccesse of Former Parliaments. Imprinted at London : MDCXLII. 4°, A—B in fours, B 4 blank.

A Necessary Warning to the Ministerie of the Kirk of Scotland, From the Meeting of the Commissioners of the Generall Assembly at Edinburgh 4. Jan. 1643 . . . Edinburgh, Printed by Evan Tyler, . . . 1643. 4°, A—B in fours.

A Declaration against the Crosse Petition : Wherein Some secret letts of the intended Reformation are discovered. The Danger of Division prevented. And The Unitie of this Hand in Religion urged. By the Commissioners of the Generall Assembly. Edinburgh, Printed by Evan Tyler, . . . 1643. 4°, A—C 2 in fours.

The Proceedings of the Commissioners Appointed by the Kings Majestie and Parliament of Scotland, for conserving the Articles of the Treaty and Peace betwixt the Kingdomes of Scotland and England. With Two Letters sent to His Majestie, by the Lords of His Privie Councel. . . . Printed by Evan Tyler, . . . 1643 . . . 4°, A—D in fours.

Two Speeches delivered before the subscribing of the Covenant, the 25. of September, at St Margarets in Westminster. The One By Mr Philip Naye. The other By Mr Alexander Henderson. Published by speciall Order of the House of Commons. Edinburgh, printed by Robert Bryson. 1643. 4°, A—C in fours.

The Humble Petition of the Commissioners of the Generall Assembly to the Kings Majesty. Their Declaration sent to the Parliament of England. Their Letter to some Brethren of the Ministerv there. And their Commission to their Brother Master Alexander Henderson, January 1643. Edinburgh, Printed by Evan Tyler, . . . 1643. 4°, A—B in fours.

The Kings Majesties Declaration to all His loving Subjects of His Kingdome of Scotland. With An Act of the Lords of His Majesties Privie Councell for the printing and publishing thereof. Edinburgh, Printed by Evan Tyler, . . . 1643, 4°, C—B 2 in fours.

The Solemne League and Covenant, For Reformation and defence of Religion, the honour and happinesse of the King, and the peace and safety of the three Kingdomes of Scotland, England, and Ireland. [Edinburgh, 1643.] Folio, 2 leaves.

A Declaration of the Lords and Commons . . . with the advice and concurrence of the Commissioners of Scotland, to publish their proceedings upon His Majesties Letter, touching a Treaty of Peace . . . London, Printed for Edward Husbands, March 30. 1644. 4°, A—E in fours.

A more perfect and particular Relation of the Late great Victorie in Scotland Obtained over Montrosse and the Rebels there, by the Forces under the Command of Lieutenant-Generall David Lesley, . . . To which is likewise added a Letter written from Master Balsame Minister at Berwick, . . . concerning the said Victory. London, Printed by M. B. for Robert Bostock . . . 25 Sep. 1645. 4°, A—B 2 in fours.

A Declaration from the Commission of the Generall Assembly. Wherein the stumbling blocks laid before the people of God by their enemies are removed ; Complyance with these enemies is reprehended ; And Courage and constancy in the Cause of God against them, seriously recommended and enjoyned. Imprinted at London for Robert Bostock, . . . 1646. 4°, A—B in fours.

A Declaration Against A late dangerous and seditious Band, under the name of An humble Remonstrance, &c. Wherein the Plots and Projects of the Contrivers . . . are discovered by the Commission of the Generall Assembly. Printed at Edinburgh by Evan Tyler, . . . 1646. 4°, A—C 2 in fours.

Treason and Rebellion against their Native Country justly rewarded upon severall Traitors and Rebels lately executed in Scotland. . . . Together with a Declaration of the Generall Assembly of the Church of Scotland. Published by Authority. London, Printed for Robert Bostocke, . . . 1646. 4°, 6 leaves.

His Majesties Proclamation, against a Traiterous Band contrived in the North. Printed at Edinburgh by Evan Tyler, . . . 1646. A broadside.

The Lord Marques of Argyles Speech to a Grand Committee of Both Houses of Parliament, The 25th of this instant June, 1646. Together with some Papers of the Commissioners for the Kingdom of Scotland. . . . Published by Authority. London : Printed for Laurence Chapman. June 27. 1646. 4°, A—B in fours.

Manifest Truths, Or an Inversion of Truths Manifest. Containing a Narration of the Proceedings of the Scottish Army, and a Vindication of the Parliament and Kingdome of England from the false and injurious aspersions cast on them by the Author of the said Manifest. . . . Published by Authoritie. London Printed by M. S. for Henry Overton, . . . and Giles Calvert . . . 1646. 4°, A—K in fours, and a leaf of L.

A Declaration or Remonstrance from the Kingdome of Scotland, to their Well beloved Brethren in England. . . . London : Printed for G. Horton, . . . 1647. 4°, 4 leaves.

The People and Sovldiers Observations on the Scotch Message to the Parliament, Concerning the King ; 5. of November 1647. 4°, A—B in fours.

A Letter of the Parliament of Scotland to Both Houses of the Parliament of England. Together with the Declaration of the Parliament of Scotland, concerning His Majestie : Their Desires, and the Answer of the Parliament of England. Printed at Edinburgh by Evan Tyler . . . [1647.] 4°, A—B in fours, B 4 blank.

A Declaration from the Lords and Commons assembled at Edinburgh, To the Right Honourable, the Lord Mayor, . . . concerning the Report of the Commissioners touching the said City [of London] and Army. . . . Together with their Protestation to defend and maintain the Kings Majesties Royal Person, Honour, and Estate, according to the Nationall League and Covenant. . . . London, Printed for R. W. 1648. 4°, 4 leaves.

A Declaration from the Generall Assemblie of the Kingdome of Scotland In Answer to a Declaration sent by the Parliament of England, concerning the King and Kingdome. . . . London, Printed for R. W. 1648. 4°, 4 leaves.

The Answer of the Parliament of Scotland to the Petitions presented from the Synode and Presbyteries. Edinburgh, Printed by Evan Tyler, . . . 1648. A broadside.

The Declaration of the Commission of the General Assembly, To this whole Kirk and Kingdome of Scotland of the fifth of May : Concerning the present publike proceedings . . . London, Printed for T. R. and E. M. 1648. 4°, A—I in fours, I 3 with a woodcut of the Royal Arms, and I 4 blank.

The Explanation of a former Act of the

Sixth of October, 1648. For Renewing of the Solemn League and Covenant. Edinburgh, Printed by Evan Tyler, . . . 1648. 4°, 4 leaves.

A Solemn Testimony against Toleration and the present Proceedings of Sectaries and their Abettors in England, In Reference to Religion & Government. . . . Edinburgh, Printed by Evan Tyler, . . . 1649. 4°, A—C 2 in fours, and A in fours, with a repetition of the title, augmented with *a Paper of the 5th of July*, and the three following leaves occupied with this Paper only, though the whole of the tract might be expected.

Two Letters. The One to his Excellency the Lord Fairfax. The other to Lieutenant General Cromwell, From the Commissioners of the Kingdom of Scotland now residing in London. Edinbvrgh, Printed by Evan Tyler, . . . 1649. A broadside.

God Save the King. [A Proclamation of the Parliament of Scotland in favour of Charles II.] Edinbvrgh, Printed by Evan Tyler, . . . 1649. A broadside.

A Letter of Protestation Given in by the Commissioners of Scotland, to the Speaker of the House of Commons. Printed by Evan Tyler, . . . 1649. A broadside.

Severall Letters and Passages Between his Excellency the Lord Generall Cromwell, and the Governour of Edinburgh Castle, And the Ministers there ; Since his Excellencies Entrance into Edinburgh. Edinburgh, Printed in the yeare 1650. 4°, A—B in fours.

A Letter of an Independent, To his Honoured Friend in London. [1650-1.] 4°, 4 leaves.

A Word of Advertisement & Advice to the Godly in Scotland. By a Scotch Man, and a Cordial Wel-wisher to the Interest of the Godly in Scotland, both in Civils and Spirituals. . . . Edinburgh, Printed by Evan Tyler, 1651. 4°, A—C in fours, C 4 blank.

Protesters no Subverters, And Presbyterie no Papacie ; Or, A Vindication of the Protesting Brethren and of the Government of the Kirk of Scotland from the Aspersions unjustly cast upon them, in a late Pamphlet of some of the Resolution-Party, Entituled, *A Declaration*, &c. . . . Edinburgh, Printed Anno Domini, 1658. 8°, A—H 4 in eights.

A Lively Character of some Pretending Grandees of Scotland to the good old cause. London, Printed in the Year, 1659. 4°, 4 leaves.

A Letter of the Officers of the Army in Scotland, under the Commander in Chief there, To the Officers of the Army in England. [Col.] Edinburgh, Printed by Christopher Higgins, . . . And Re-printed at London, 1659. 4°, 4 leaves. Without a regular title.

The Last Discourse of the Right Honble the Lord Waresbonne, As he delivered it upon the Scaffold at the Mercat-Cross of Edinburgh, July 22. 1663, being immediately before his Death. . . . By a Favourer of the Covenant and Work of Reformation. . . . Printed in the Year, 1664. 4°, A—C 2 in fours.

A true Account of the Rising of the Rebels in the West of Scotland. Together with their Declaration on the 29th of May last. London : Printed in the Year 1679. 4°, 4 leaves.

An Exact Relation of the Defeat of the Rebels at Bothwell-Bridge. Published by Authority. In the Savoy : Printed by Tho. Newcomb, 1679. Folio, 4 leaves.

A further and more particular Account of the Rebels in Scotland ; . . . A Letter from Edinburgh, June 24, At Midnight. [1679.] 2 leaves.

A True Relation of the Inhuman Cruelties Lately Acted by the Rebels in Scotland. With the manner of their taking of Glascough, . . . Being the substance of a Letter sent to a Person of Quality. London : Printed by A. M. and R. R. 1679. 4°, 4 leaves.

The Loyal Scot. An Excellent New Song. To an Excellent New Scotch Tune. [About 1680.] A leaf of verses, with the music.
The imprint in the copy used has been cut off.

The Spirit of Popery Speaking out of the Mouths of Phanaticall-Protestants, Or the Last Speeches of Mr John Kid and Mr John King, Two Presbyterian Ministers, Who were Executed for High-Treason and Rebellion, at Edinburgh, August the 14th 1679. . . . London, Printed by H. Hills, and are to be sold by Walter Kittelby, . . . 1680. Folio, A—X, 2 leaves each, besides * and **, 2 leaves each after the leaf, which follows the title.

The Proceedings of the Convention of Estates in Scotland. [Col.] London : Printed for Ric. Chiswell. . . . 1689. Folio. [? 13 Numbers, 1 leaf each, March —April, 1689.]

An Account of the Proceedings of the Meeting of the Estates in Scotland. With the Letters of King William, And the late King James, to the said Estates. London : Printed for Richard Chiswell, .. MDCLXXXIX. Folio, A—D, 2 leaves each.

The Preliminaries to the Crown of Scotland, As Proposed by the Grand Committee. [Col.] London : Printed for Richard Baldwin, in the Old Baily. MDCLXXXIX. A folio leaf.

A Letter to a Member of the Convention. Col.] Re-printed in the Year, 1689. 4°, 2 leaves.

The Pastor and the Prelate, Or Reformation and Conformity shortly compared by the Word of God . . . Edinburgh. Printed for Alexander Henderson, . . . 1692. 4°, A—F in fours.

A Proper Project for Scotland. To startle Fools, and frighten Knaves, but to make Wise Men Happy. Being a Safe and Easy Remedy to cure our Fears, and ease our Minds. With the Undoubted Causes of God's Wrath, and of the present National Calamities. By a Person neither unreasonably Cameronian, nor Excessively Laodicean, and Idolizer of Moderation, but, *entre deus*, avoiding Extreams, . . Printed in a Land where Sell's Cry'd up, and Zeal's Cry'd down : and therefore in a time of Spiritual Plagues and Temporal Judgments. 1699. 4°, A—U, 2 leaves each.

The Sighs and Groans, of a Sinking Kingdom, In an Humble Address to His Grace the Duke of Queensberry, His Maiesties High Commissioner and the Honourable Members of the Parliament of Scotland. [1699.] 4°. A—D, 2 leaves each, and a leaf of E. Without any regular title.

Some Thoughts concerning the Affairs of his Session of Parliament, 1700. . . . . Printed in the Year M.DCC. 8°, A—D in fours, D 4 blank.

Scotland's Lament for their Misfortunes. February, 1700.] A broadside in verse and in two columns.

This partly refers to the fire in Edinburgh, Feb. 3, 1700.

A Letter from A Member of the Parliament of Scotland, To his Electors, the Gentlemen of the Shire of —— Containing his Reasons for withdrawing from the Assembly, . . . Printed in the Year 702. 4°, A—D in fours.

A Speech in Parliament, of the Lord Belhaven ; Upon the Act for Security of the Kingdom, in case of the Queens Death. Edinburgh, . . . 1703. 4°, A—B in fours, and the title.

The Last and Heavenly Speech and Glorious Departure of John Viscount Kenmuir. Edinburgh, Printed by the Heirs and Successors of Andrew Anderson, . . . 1703. 8°, A—B in eights.

An Essay, Shewing, That there is no Probability of there being so much French Interest, as it's certain there's English Influence in our present Parliament of Scotland. Printed in the Year 1704. 4°, 4 leaves.

A Pill for Pork-Eaters : Or, A Scots Lancet for an English Swelling. . . . Edinburgh, Printed by James Watson, in Craigs Closs, 1705. 4°, A—B 2 in fours. In verse.

Lawful Prejudices against an Incorporating Union with England ; Or, Some Modest Considerations on the sinfulness of this Union, and the Danger flowing from it to the Church of Scotland. . . . Edinburgh, printed in the year 1707. 4°, A—B in fours.

Eschol Grapes, Or, Some of the Ancient Boundaries, and Covenanted March Stones, set up by Kirk and State, in the Days when they Acted for the Lord, . . . betwixt the years 1638 and 1649. . . . Printed in the Year MDCCVIII. 8°, A—O in fours, besides title and following leaf.

Memoirs of North Britain ; Taken from Authentick Writings, aswell Manuscript as Printed. In which is Prov'd, That the Scots Nation have Always been Zealous in the defence of the Protestant Religion and Liberty. . . . London : Printed for J. Baker . . . and J. Graves . . . MDCCXV. 8°, A—U in eights.

This volume contains a section on the Darien scheme.

The New Actis and Constitvtionis of Parliament maid be the rycht excellint Prince Iames the Fift Kyng of Scottis. 1540. [The remainder of the title-page is occupied by the Royal Arms. At the end occurs :] Imprentit in Edinburgh, be Thomas Dauidson, dwelling aboue the nether bow, on the northsyde of the gait, the aucht day of Februarii. The zeir of god. 1541. zeris. Folio, A—B in sixes : C. 4 : D, 6 : E, 6, the last leaf blank. With a few small cuts.

Compare Herbert's *Ames*, p. 1474. Sothebys (Wodhull), Jan. 15, 1886, printed on vellum, russia, by Roger Payne, £151. This cost Mr. W. £1, 8s. 6d.

P

The Actis of the Parliament of the Maist Hie, maist Excellent and Michtie Prince . . . Iames the sext . . . begune and haldin at Edinburgh, the xv. day of december. The zeir of God ane thousand fine hundreth lxvij. zeiris . . . Imprentit at Edinburgh be Iohne Ros. M.D.LXXV. Folio, A—F in fours.

In the Parliament . . . begune at Striniling, the . xxviii. day of August, the zeir of God ane thousand fine hundreth thre scoir and elleuin zeiris . . . Imprentit at Edinburgh be Iohne Ros. M.D.LXXV. . . . Folio, A—D in fours.

In the Parliament Haldin at Striviling the xxv. day of Iulij, the zeir of God, ane thousand, fyue hundreth, three scoir and auchtene zeiris . . . Imprentit at Edinburgh be Iohne Ros. Anno Do. 1579. . . . Folio, A—F in fours, G—H, 2 leaves each, H 2 with colophon.

Regiam Majestatam. The Avld Lawes and Constitvtions of Scotland, Faithfvllie Collected fvrth of the Register, and other avld authentick bukes, fra the dayes of King Malcolme the second, vntill the time of King James the first, of gude memorie : . . . Qvherevnto are adjoined twa Treatises, the ane, anent the Order of proces, . . . the other of Crimes, . . . At Edinbvrgh. Printed by Thomas Finlason, . . . 1609. . . . Folio. Title, &c., 6 leaves : A, 4 : B—Gg in sixes : Hh, 4.

Regiam Maiestatam Scotiæ, . . . Londini, Apud Ioannem Billivm, Anno Domini. 1613. . . . Folio. Title, 1 leaf : dedication by Sir John Skene to the King, 3 leaves: to the Reader, 2 leaves : a blank : Verses, 4 leaves : A—T in sixes, T 6 with the *Errata*.

The Acts made in the Second Parliament of . . . Charles . . . Edinburgh. Printed by Robert Young and Evan Tyler, . . . 1641 . . . Folio, A—P in sixes.

Canons and Constitvtions Ecclesiasticall Gathered and put in forme, for the Government of the Church of Scotland. Ratified and approved by His Majesties Royall Warrand. . . . Aberdene, Imprinted by Edward Raban, . . . 1636. With Royall Priviledge. 4º, A—F 2 in fours, A 1 blank.

A Seasonable Admonition and Exhortation to some who separate themselves from the Communion of the Church of Scotland. . . . Edinburgh, Printed by George Mosman, Anno M. DC. XCIX. 4º, A—D 2 in fours.

SCOTT, EDMUND.

An Exact Discovrse of the Subtilties, Fashions, Policies, Religion, and Ceremonies of the East Indians. as well Chyneses as Iauans, there abyding and dweling. Together with the manner of trading with those people, aswell by the English, as by the Hollanders : as also what hath happened to the English Nation at Bantan in the East Indies, since the 2. of February 1602. vntill the 6. of October 1605. Whereunto is added a briefe Description of Iaua Maior. Written by Edmund Scott, resident there, and in other places adioyn[in]g, the space of three yeares, and a halfe. At London, Printed by W. W. for Walter Burre. 1606. 4", A—N in fours. Dedicated to Sir W. Romney, Governor of the East India Company and Alderman of London. *B. M.*

SCOTT, ROBERT, *Bookseller.*

Catalogus Librorum Roberti Scott, Bibliopolæ Regii Londinensis . . . Quorum Auctio habenda est Londini, ad Insigne Ursi in Vico(vulgo dicto) Ave-Mary-Lane, . . . Decimo Tertio Die Februarii, 168⅞. Per Benjaminum Walford, Bibliopolam Londinensem. London, . . . 1687-8. 4º, A—Aa 2 in fours, and the title.

SCOTT, THOMAS, *of Utrecht.*

Robert Earle of Essex His Ghost, Sent from Elizian : [sic] To the Nobility, Gentry, and Commvnaltie of England. *Virtutum Comes Inuidia.* Printed in Paradise. 1624. 4º, A—E 2 in fours.

SCRIPTURE.

Hereafter folowe. X. certayne Places of Scrypture, by whome it is proued, that the doctrynes and tradyceyons of men, ought to be auoyded. [Col.] Imprynted be me Robert Wyer / dwellynge in saynt Martyns parysshe besyde charynge Crosse. Cum priuilegio. 8º, black letter, b—f in fours, besides title and following leaf.

Sothebys, June 30, 1885, No. 1055.

A Compendious olde treatyse / shewynge / howe that we ought to haue yᵉ scripture in Englysshe. [Col.] Imprinted at Marlborow in the läde of Hessen / be me Hans Luft / in the yere of oure lorde MCCCCC. and . XXX. 8º, 8 leaves. With a cut on the title of the Graces and Truth coming up out of a well.

SCUTE, CORNELYS.

A pronostication for the yere of our Lord God M.CCCCC.xliiii. Practysed by the right expert Doctour in Astronomy and phisicke Maister Cornelys Scute resydent in

Bridges in the Wolfe strete. [Col.] Imprinted at London in the Olde Bayly in Sayntpoulchres parysh by Rychard Lant/ for Rychard Grafton. Cū priuilegio ad imprimendū solū. This Pronostication is to be sold at ȳ west dore of Paules by Wyllyam Telotson. 8°, A—F in fours, A 1 and F 4 blank. *L. M.* (imperfect.)

SEA.

A Fight at Sea, Famously fought by the Dolphin of London against fiue of the Turkes Men of Warre, and a Satty the 12. of Iannuary last 1616. being all vessells of great Burthen, and strongly mand. Wherein is shewed the noble Worth and braue Resolution of our English Nation. Written and set forth by one of the same Voyage, that was then present and an eye witnes to all the proceedings. Printed at London for Henry Gosson, dwelling vpon London Bridge. 1617. 4°, A—B in fours. With cuts. *B. M.*

A notable and wonderfull Sea-Fight, betweene Two great and well-mounted Spanish Shipps, And a Small not very well provyded English Shipp. Who par force was constrayned to enter into this conflict. At Amsterdam. Printed by George Meseler / Anno 1621. 4°, black letter, 4 leaves. *B. M.*

A Trve Relation of a Wonderfvll Sea Fight betweene two great and well appointed Spanish ships or Men of Warre. And A small and not very well prouided English Ship, . . . The Margaret and Iohn, or the Black Hodge. London Printed for N. B. 1621. 4°, A—C in fours, A 1 blank. With two cuts. *B. M.*

A different narrative of the same affair.

The Trve Relation of that Worthy Sea Fight, which two of the East India Shipps, had with 4. Portingals, of great force, and burthen, in the Persian Gulph. With the Lamentable Death of Captaine Andrew Shilling. With other Memorable Accidents in that Voiage. Printed this 2. of Iuly. London Printed by I. D. for Nathaniel Newbery and William Sheffard. . . . 1622. 4°, A—D in fours. *B. M.*

Two Famovs Sea-Fights. Lately made, Betwixt the Fleetes of the King of Spaine, and the Fleetes of the Hollanders. The one in the West-Indies : The other, The Eight of this present Moneth of February, betwixt Callis and Gravelin. . . . Two Relations not vnfit for these Times to animate Noble Spirits to attempt and accomplish braue Actions. London, Printed for Nath: Bytter and Nic: Bovrne.

With Priviledge. 1639. 4°, A—B in fours.

A Trve Relation of a late very famous Sea-fight, made betwixt the Spaniard and the Hollander in Brasil, for many dayes together : Wherein the oddes was very great, which made the successe doubtfull, but at last the Hollander got the Victory. . . . London, Printed for Nathaniel Butter, Iune 12. 1640. With Privilege. 4°, 8 leaves. [Col.] London, Printed for Nath: Butter.

A part of some larger publication.

A Terrible Sea-fight: Related in the Copie of a Letter sent to I. M. Councellour, Pensioner, and Bailiffe to the Citie of Batavia. Concerning the great fight betweene nine East India ships of the Hollanders, and three great Gallions which happened about Goas Bare in the East Indies, the 20. 30. of September, 1639. London, Printed by Thomas Harper, for Nathaniel Butter. 1640. With privilege. 4° A, 2 : B, 1 : C, 4.

A True Relation of the late Great Sea Fight As it was sent in a Letter to his Excellency the Lord-General Cromwell, From Gen. Blake and Gen. Monck. Wherein is a List of what Dutch Ships were taken and Sunk, . . . London, Printed by Henry Hills, . . . and by Thomas Brewster . . . 1653. 4°, 4 leaves.

To His Highness the Lord Protector : The Humble Petition of the Sea-men, belonging to the Ships of the Commonwealth of England. [With the Report. 1659.] A broadside. *B. M.*

To the Right Honourable The Knights, Cittizens, and Burgesses Assembled in Parliament. The Humble Petition of the Captains, Commanders, and Owners of English Shipping, and other Sea-faring Men of this Nation. London, Printed by Joseph Moxon : . . . 1659. A broadside. *B. M.*

Under the press-mark, 190. g. 12, there is a thick folio volume of Petitions of all kinds addressed to Parliament between 1638 and 1675.

SECTS.

A Discoverie of 29 Sects here in London, all of which, except the first [Protestants], are most Devillish and damnable, being these which follow. [The list is beneath.] Printed, Anno 1641. 4°, 4 leaves.

SECURIS, JOHN.

A Prognosticacion [and · Almanac] for the Yere since the birthe of our Lorde

Iesus Christ, 1562, which is the yere frō the beginnyng of the worlde 5524. Wherin is declared the dispo-icion of the whole yere, as touchyng the weather, victuals, disea-es, &c. Practi-ed in Salisburie in the Newe strete. By Maister Jhon Securis. professour of Phisicke. 1562. Imprinted at London, by Ihon Waley. 8°, A—B in eights; the *Almanac* (apparently), A—C in eights. With cuts. *B. M.* (George Steevens's copy.)

The *Almanac* seems to want the title only ; the leaves are misplaced.

SEDDON, JOHN, *Writing-Master.*

The Pen-mans Paradise both Pleasant & Profitable Or Examples of all yᵉ usuall Hands of this Kingdom . . . Invented and Performd by John Seddon. Sold by Wᵐ Court at yᵉ Mariner & Anchor on little Tower-hill London. [About 1700.] Obl. 4", 34 leaves, all engraved, including the title and dedication to Major John Ayres and Mr. Richard Alleine.

SEDLEY, SIR CHARLES.

The Miscellaneous Works of the Honourable Sir Charles Sedley, Bar! Containing Satyrs, Epigrams, Court-Characters, Translations, Essays, and Speeches in Parliament. Collected into one Volume. To which is added, The Death of Marc Antony : A Tragedy never before Printed. Published from the Original Manuscripts, by Capt. Ayloffe. London : Printed, and sold by J. Nutt, . . . 1702. 8°, A—Q in eights : Aa—Dd in eights.

The Mulberry-Garden, A Comedy. As it is Acted by His Majesties Servants at the Theatre-Royal. Written by the Honourable Sir Charles Sidley. London, Printed for H. Herringman, . . . 1675. 4". A, 3 leaves, with title, dedication to the Duchess of Richmond and Lenox, and *dramatis personæ :* B—L 2 in fours.

Bellamira, Or The Mistress, A Comedy : As it is Acted by Their Majesties Servants. Written by the Honourable Sir Charles Sedley Baronet. . . . London : Printed by D. Mallet, for L. C. and Timothy Goodwin, . . . 1687. 4", A—I in fours, A 4 with an Advertisement.

The Happy Pair : Or, A Poem on Matrimony. By the Honourable Sir Charles Sidley, Baronet. London : Printed for John Nutt, . . . MDCCII. Folio, A—D, 2 leaves each.

SELDEN, JOHN.

Analecton Anglo-Britannicvm Libri Dvo. . . . Opere et Indvstria Ioannis Selden

Terringensis... Francoforti. . . . cɪɔɔcxv. 4". ¶, 4 leaves : A—S in fours, S 4 blank. Dedicated " Illvstriss. Foeliciss. Angliæ Patriæ."

Mare Clavsvm ; The Right and Dominion of the Sea in Two Books. . . . Written at first in Latin by that late Famous and Learned Antiquary John Selden, Esquire. Formerly Translated into English, and now perfected and restored by J. H. Gent. ——*Pontus quoque serviet* ILLI. London. Printed for Andrew Kembe and Edward Thomas, . . . MDCLXIII. Folio. Title and frontispiece of Royal arms, 2 leaves : a. 2 leaves : (e) —(k), 2 leaves each : B—4 F in fours.

Of the Dominion, Or, Ownership of the Sea Two Books. . . . Translated into English ; and set forth with some Additional Evidences and Discourses, By Marchamont Nedham. Published by special Command. London, Printed by William Du-Gard, by the appointment of the Council of State : . . . 1652. Folio. Verses headed *Neptune to the Common-Wealth of England,* 1 leaf : frontispiece and title, 2 leaves : Dedication to the Supreme Authority of the Nation, the Parliament, 9 leaves : Author's Preface and Table, (e)—(k), 2 leaves each : B— Rrr 3 in fours : Aaaa—Ffff in fours.

I do not understand what Malone means (*Maloniana* apud Prior's *Life of Malone,* 1860, p. 424), where he tells us that " it is not generally known that the translation of Bacon's *Essays* into Latin, which was published in 1619, was done by the famous John Selden." I do not think that any such book appeared in that year. But Malone quotes a letter from *N. N.* to Camden, and explains the initials as *John Selden N.,*—on what authority he omits to state.

SENAULT, JEAN FRANÇOIS.

The Use of Passions. Written in French by J. F. Senault. And put into English by Henry Earl of Monmouth. An. Dom. 1649. London, Printed for J. L. and Humphrey Moseley, . . . 1649. 8°. Frontispiece and engraved title by W. Marshall, the latter containing a bust of the translator, 2 leaves : The author's dedication to Jesus Christ, 11 leaves : the Translator upon the Book, in verse, 1 leaf : Translator to Reader, 2 leaves : Author's Preface, 6 leaves : Table, 2 leaves : the Work, B—Kk in eights.

Man become Guilty, Or The Corruption of Natvre by Sinne, According to St. Augustines sense. Written originally in French, By Iohn-Francis Senault. And put into English By the Right Honᵇˡᵉ

Henry Earle of Monmouth. London, Printed for William Leake, . . . 1650. 4°, A—3 D in fours, 3 D 4 with *Errata*, and B repeated. Dedicated to the Countess of Rutland.

SENECA, LUCIUS ANNÆUS.

The Tragedies of L. Annæus Seneca the Philosopher ; Viz. Medea, Phædra and Hippolytus, Troades, or the Royal Captives, And the Rape of Helen, out of the Greek of Coluthus ; Translated into English Verse ; with Annotations. . . . Adorn'd with Sculptures representing each History. By Sir Edward Sherburne, Knight. *Nec in Turbam, nec Turba—*Manil. Astr. l 2. London : . . . 1702. 8°. Frontispiece containing bust of Seneca, title, dedication to Richard Francis Sherburne, Esq., son and heir-apparent to Sir Nicholas Sherburne of Stony Hurst, co. Lancaster, &c., 8 leaves : [a]—[c] in eights : B—Cc in eights.

I have seen a presentation copy dated 1701.

Seneca moralissmus philosophus de quatuor virtutibus cardinalibus. optimo commento illustratus. [Col.] Explicit . . . Impressus Lōdoñ. per me winādū de worde . . . Anno. M. cccccc. xvi. 4°. A, 8 : B, 6. *B. M.*

The woorke of the excellent Philosopher Lucius Annæus Seneca concerning Benefyting, that is too say the dooing, receyuing, and requyting of good Turnes. Translated out of Latin by Arthur Golding. Imprinted at London by John Day, dwelling ouer Aldersgate. 1578. 4°. *, 3 leaves : A—Gg 4 in fours, Gg 4 blank. Dedicated to Sir C. Hatton by the translator from his house in the parish of All Hallows in the Wall, 17 March 1577-8.

SERMONES.

Quatuor Sermones [This begins with a head-line only. At the end is :] Finitum westmonasterii Per Julianum Notarii. Anno dñi. M. cccc. lxxxxix. 4°, A—E in sixes : F, 8.

> This work usually occurs bound up with the *Festival* of the same date and printer. Osterley Park Sale, May 1885, No. 662, with the *Festival*.

SERPENT.

The Serpent Salve, Or, A Remedie for the Biting of an Aspe : Wherein, The Observators Grounds are discussed and plainly discovered to be unsound, Seditious, nor warranted by the Laws of God, . . . For the reducing of such of His Majesties well-meaning Subjects into the right Way who have been mis-led by that

Ignis fatuus. Printed in the year 1643. 4°, A—Ll 2 in fours, and the title.

Some Observations Made upon the Serpent Stones, Imported from the Indies : Shewing their Admirable Virtues in Curing Malignant Spotted Feavers. Written by a Countrey Physitian to Dr Burwell, President of the Colledge of Physitians in London. London, Printed in the Year 1694. 4°, 4 leaves.

SETTLE, ELKANAH, *of Trinity Colleye, Oxford.*

The Life and Death of Major Clancie, The Grandest Cheat of this Age. Wherein is set forth many of his Villanous Projects (Real matter of Fact) both in England, Ireland, France, Spain and Italy ; at last was Executed at Tyburn, the Reading of which will give the Reader great satisfaction. Published by Authority. London, Printed by D. Mallet, and are to be sold at his House in Half-Moon Court adjoining to Ludgate. 1680. 8°. A, 4 leaves : B—L 3 in eights. With a dedicatory epistle to an unnamed Lady by E. S., some verses by him to the Ladies of the Court, and a notice to the Reader.

Insignia Bataviæ : Or, The Dutch Trophies Display'd ; Being Exact Relations of the Unjust, Horrid, and most Barbarous Proceedings of the Dutch against the English in the East-Indies. . . . By Elkanah Settle. Published with Allowance. London, Printed for Thomas Pyke in Pall-Mall ; . . . 1688. 4°. A, 2 : B—D in fours. With a frontispiece.

The Compleat Memoirs of the Life of that Notorious Impostor Will. Morrell, alias Bowyer, alias Wickham, &c., who died at Mr Cullen's the Bakers in the Strand, Jan. 3. 169½. With Considerable Additions never before Published. . . . London : Printed for Abel Roper and E. Wilkinson . . . 1699. 8°. A, 4 leaves : B—F in eights : G, 4. Dedicated by E. Settle to Gabriel Balam, Esq.

Minerva Triumphans. The Muses Essay, To the Honour of the Generous Foundation the Cotton Library at Westminster, As it is now given to the Publick. Confirm'd by Act of Parliament. *Majora Canamus.* By E. Settle. London, Printed for J. Nut, near Stationers-Hall, 1701. Folio.

Eusebia Triumphans. The Hannover Succession to the Imperial Crown of England, An Heroick Poem. *Pro aris & focis.* London, Printed for John Nutt, . . . MDCCII. Folio, A—X, 2 leaves each, Lat. and Engl.

Carmen Irenicum. The Happy Union

of the Two East India Companies. An
Heroick Poem. By E. Settle. *Vis unita
fortior*. London : Printed for John Nutt
near Stationers Hall. 1702. Folio, A—C,
2 leaves each.

Carmen Irenicum. The Union of the
Imperial Crowns of Great Britain. An
Heroick Poem. London, Printed for the
Author, M DCC VII. Folio, A—L, 2 leaves
each, E repeated, A—B not marked.
Lat. and Engl.

SEWELL, WILLIAM.
A New Dictionary English and Dutch,
Wherein the Words are rightly inter-
preted, and their various significations
exactly noted. Enriched with many
elegant Phrases and select Proverbs.
Whereunto is added a small Treatise concerning the Dutch Pronunciation ; and
the right use of the Dutch Particles De,
Die, Derze, and Het, Dat, Dit . . . Door
Wᵐ Sewel. t' Amsterdam, By de Weduwe
van Steven Swart, . . . 1691, 4⁰, A—4 Y
in fours, besides the frontispiece, and
+, 4 leaves : the Dutch and Engl. with
a new title, *—* * *, 4 leaves each : a—3 h
in fours : Beknopt Vertoog der Engelsche
Spraak-Konst, A—I in fours.

SFORZA, ISABELLA.
The Heauen of the Mynde, or the Myndes
Heauen A moste excellent, learned and
religious Treatise, declaring the way and
rediest manner how to Attayne the True
Peace and Quiet of the Mynde. Written
in the Italiane tongue by the right honourable Ladie, Madonna Isabella Sforza,
sister to the Great Duke of Mylane ; and
translated into English by A. M. [1602.]
4⁰, 53 leaves.

> MS. on paper, described as above from the
> original, then in a collection at Colchester,
> in *Current Notes* for September 1854. Not
> known to have been printed : but it was
> licensed for the press, 7 Feb. 1603.
> Dedicated by Anthony Munday to Alder-
> man Swinnerton, under date of 22 Dec.
> 1602 ; it appears hence as if he was now
> contemplating employment as a writer of
> the city pageants, of several of which we
> know that he became the author.

SHADWELL, THOMAS, *of Caius College,
Cambridge, and of the Middle Temple.*
The Works of Tho. Shadwell, Esq ; Late
Poet Laureat, and Historiographer Royal.
Containing in One Volume, in the Method
they were first published, [Here follow
the names of the 17 plays.] London,
Printed for James Knapton, at the Crown
in St. Pauls Church-yard, 1693. 4⁰.

> Each piece is separately signatured, and
> was intended to be sold separately, if de-
> sired.

The Libertine : A Tragedy. Acted by
His Royal Highness's Servants. Written
by Tho. Shadwell. London, Printed by
T. N. for Henry Herringman, . . . 1676.
4⁰, A—M in fours, and b, 2 leaves. Dedicated to the Duke of Newcastle.

The Woman-Captain : A Comedy Acted
by His Royal Highnesses Servants.
Written by Tho. Shadwell. London,
Printed for Samuel Carr, . . . 1680. 4⁰,
A—K in fours. Dedicated to Henry, Lord
Ogle, son to the Duke of Newcastle.

The Squire of Alsatia. A Comedy, As it
is Acted by Their Majesty's Servants.
Written by Tho. Shadwell. *Creditur, ex
medio* . . . Hor. Ep. ad Aug. i. lib. 2.
London, Printed for James Knapton, . . .
1688. 4⁰, A—I in fours, I 4 blank.

Bury-Fair. A Comedy, As it is Acted by
His Majesty's Servants. Written by Tho.
Shadwell, Servant to His Majesty. London, Printed for James Knapton . . .
1689. 4⁰, A—I in fours, I 4 with Advertisements. Dedicated to Charles, Earl of
Dorset and Middlesex.

The Amorous Bigotte : With the Second
Part of Tegue O Divelly. A Comedy,
Acted by their Majesty's Servants.
Written by Tho. Shadwell, . . . London :
Printed for James Knapton, . . . 1690.
4⁰, A—H 2 in fours. Dedicated by the
Author to Charles, Earl of Shrewsbury,
May 5, 1690.

The Scowrers. A Comedy, Acted by
Their Majesties Servants. . . . London :
Printed for James Knapton, . . . 1691.
4⁰. A, 2 leaves : B—H in fours.

The Volunteers, Or The Stock-Jobbers.
A Comedy, As it is Acted by Their Ma-
jesties Servants, at the Theatre Royal.
Written by Tho. Shadwell, Esq ; Late
Poet-Laureate, and Historiographer Royal.
Being his last Play. London, Printed for
James Knapton, . . . 1693. . . . 4⁰, A—
H in fours. Dedicated to the Queen by
Anne Shadwell, the writer's widow.

SHAKESPEAR, WILLIAM.
The Historie of Henry the Fourth : . . .
Newly corrected, by William Shakespeare. London, Printed by John Norton,
and are to bee sold by William Sheares,
. . . 1632. 4⁰, A—K in fours.

The Tragedy of Hamlet Prince of Denmark. As it is now Acted at his Highness
the Duke of York's Theatre. By William
Shakespeare. London : Printed for H.
Heringham and R. Bentley, . . . 1683.

4°, B—M in fours, besides title, to the Reader, and *Dramatis Personæ.*

This is the play as altered by Betterton, who took the principal part.

SHARPHAM, EDWARD, *of the Middle Temple.*

Cvpids Whirligig. As it hath bene sundry times Acted by the Children of the Kings Majesties Reuels. London, Imprinted by E. Allde, and are to bee solde by Arthur Iohnson at the signe of the white Horse, nere the great North doore of Saint Paules Church. 1607. 4°. A, 2 leaves: B—L in fours, L 4 blank. Dedicated to Master Robert Hayman.

The Fleire. As it hath beene often played in the Blacke-Fryers by the children of the Reuels. Written by Edward Sharpham, of the Middle Temple, Gentleman. At London, Printed and are to be solde by F[rancis] B[urton] in Paules Churchyard, at the signe of the Flower de Luce and the Crowne. 1607. 4°. A, 2 leaves: B—H in fours.

SHAW, SAMUEL.

The Voice of One Crying in the Wilderness. Or, The business of a Christian, . . . By S. S. a Servant of God in the Gospel of his Son. . . . London, Printed by Robert White, for Henry Mortlock, . . . 1674. 8°, A—M 6 in twelves. With some verses at the end.

SHELTON, THOMAS.

A Centvrie of Similies. Psal. 78. 2. *I will open my mouth in a parable.* London, Printed by Iohn Dawson. 1640. 8°. A, 4 leaves: B—E in eights: F, 4.

Zeiglographia. Or A New Art of Short-writing never before published. . . . By Thomas Shelton Author and teacher of y° said art. . . . London Printed by M. S. and are sold at the Authors house in Bore's-head Court by Cripple-Gate. 1659. 8°.

The Crossley copy ended imperfectly on E 3.

SHEPHERDS.

Here begynneth the Kalender of Shepherdes. [Col.] Imprinted in Powles chyrchyarde at the sygne of the thre Kynges by Julyan Notary the yere of our lorde a. m. ccccc. x. Folio, black letter. With woodcuts, including one which occupies the greater part of the title. A—N in eights.

Sothebys (Fuller Russell), July 1, 1885, No. 1078. This copy was in Thorpe's Catalogue for 1836, according to a MS. note on the fly-leaf, at £12, 12s.; and though the two last leaves were in facsimile by Harris, was pronounced to be the most perfect copy known. I give the particulars as I find

them; but whence the end leaves were facsimiled, I have yet to learn.

SHEPPARD, SAMUEL.

The Fallacy of Infants Baptisme Discovered. Or, Five Arguments, to prove that Infants ought not to be baptized. Delivered in private by Captain Hobson, . . . London, Printed in the yeer of Discoveries. 1645. 4°, A—C in fours.

The Preface is subscribed *S. S.*

The False Alarum Or, An Answer to a Libell lately published, entituled, An Alarum to the House of Lords . . . Written by S. Shepheard. London, Printed for Iohn Hardesty, . . . 1646. 4°, A—B in fours.

SHIRLEY, JOHN.

The Illustrious History of Women, Or A Compendium of the Many Virtues that adorn the Fair Sex. . . . The whole Work enrich'd and intermix'd with Curious Poetry and Delicate Fancie, suitable to so Charming a Subject. London, Printed for John Harris . . . 1686. Price Bound One Shilling. 12°, A—H in twelves, besides a frontispiece.

The Accomplished Ladies Rich Closet of Rarities: Or, The Ingenious Gentlewoman and Servant Maids Delightfull Companion. Containing many Excellent Things for the Accomplishment of the Female Sex, after the exactest Manner and Method. . . . To which is added a Second Part, Containing Directions for the Guidance of a Young Gentlewoman as to her Behaviour & seemly Deportment, &c. The Second Edition, with many Additions. London, Printed by W. W. for Nicholas Boddington . . . and Josiah Blare . . . 1687. 12°, A—K in twelves, including a frontispiece.

The Preface is signed by John Shirley.

The Accomplish'd Lady's Rich Closet of Rarities . . . The Fourth Edition, with large Additions, Corrected and Amended. London, Printed by W. Wilde, for N. Boddington . . . and J. Blare . . . 169 . [?]. 12°. A, 6 leaves: B—I in twelves: K, 6, besides a frontispiece.

SHROPSHIRE.

A Copy of A Letter sent from Sir Tho. Middleton, to the Honorable, William Lenthall Esq; . . . Concerning the raising of the Siege at Oswestree, Iuly 3. 1644. By the Forces Commanded by the Earl of Denbigh, Sir Tho. Middleton, and Sir Will. Brereton . . . London, Printed for Edward Husbands. Iuly 10. 1644. 4°, 4 leaves.

A true and perfect Relation of the Tryal and Condemnation, Execution and last Speech of that unfortunate Gentleman M͏ʳ Robert Foulks Late Minister of a Parish near Ludlow in Shropshire, who Received Sentence of Death in London for Murder and Adultery, and accordingly was carried privately in a Coach to the place of execution, on Fryday the last of January, 1678. Also his behaviour in Prison, . . . Likewise The Tryal, Condemnation and Execution of two grand Traytors, Will. Ireland and John Grove, both Jesuits, . . . Printed for L White in White-cross street. [1679.] 4°, 4 leaves. *B. M.*

A True Relation of the Most Horrible Murther : Committed by Thomas White of Lane Green in the Parish of Aulfley in the County of Salop Gent. upon the Body of his Wife M͏ᵐ Dorothy White in the Town of Kederminster in the County of Worcester, the 10ᵗʰ day of this instant May 1682. . . . [London, 1682.] 4°, 4 leaves. *B. M.*

The imprint in this copy is cut off.

SHUTE, JOHN, *Painter and Architect.*
The First and Chief Grovnds of Architectvre vsed in all the auncient and famous monymentes : with a farther & more ample discourse vppon the same, than hitherto hath been set out by any other. Published by Ihon Shute, Paynter and Archytecte. Imprinted at London in Fletestrete nere to Sainct Dunstanschurche by Thomas Marshe. 1563. Folio, A—F 2 in fours. With woodcuts and plates separate from the letterpress at B 3, C 1, C 3, and D 2. The large wood-engraving representing the composite style is worked with the text. Dedicated to Queen Elizabeth.

Shute mentions that he had been servant to the Duke of Northumberland in 1550, and that the Duke was at the expense of his pursuit of architectural studies in Italy, and had shown his drawings or sketches made there to Edward VI., who was much pleased with them.

SIAM.
A Full and True Relation of the Great and Wonderful Revolution that hapned lately in the Kingdom of Siam in the East-Indies, Giving a particular Account of the Seizing and Death of the Late King, . . . London, Printed for Randal Taylor . . . 1690. 4°. A, 5 leaves, including *Imprimatur* : a, 1 leaf : B—D in fours, D 4 blank.

In the Sunderland Catalogue, part 5, No. 13,836, this tract was misdated 1620.

SIBBALD, SIR ROBERT, *M.D.*
Scotia Illustrata Sive Prodromus Historiæ Naturalis in quo Regionis natura, Incolarum Ingenia & Mores, Morbi iisque medendi Methodus, & Medicina Indigena accurate explicantur. . . . Cum Figuris Æneis. Opus Viginti Annorum . . . Edinburgi, Ex Officinâ Typographicâ Jacobi Kinblo . . . Sumptibus Auctoris. Anno Domini M.DC.LXXXIV. Folio. First title, dedication to the King (at whose command the book is said to have been prepared), Ordo Operis, &c., 4 leaves : A—E, 2 leaves each : dedication to the Duke of York, &c., 7 leaves : A 2—Ee, 2 leaves each : Ff, 1 leaf : Index, 3 leaves : Part 2, title, dedication, and index, 3 leaves : A, 1 leaf : B—O, 2 leaves each : P, 1 leaf : index and list of plates, 2 leaves : the plates (22).

SICILY.
An Account of the Late Terrible Earthquake in Sicily ; With most of its Particulars. Done from the Italian Copy Printed at Rome. London : Printed for Richard Baldwin . . . 1693. 4°, A, 2 : B—E in fours.

SIDNEY, ALGERNON, *M.P.*
Discourses Concerning Government, . . . The Second Edition carefully corrected. To which is Added, The Paper He deliver'd to the Sheriffs immediately before his Death. And an Alphabetical Table. London, Printed by J. Darby in Bartholomew-Close. MDCCIV. Folio. With a portrait. Title and preface, 2 leaves : a, 2 leaves : B—3 G in fours : [3 H], 2 leaves : Iii—Ttt, 2 leaves each.

A Just and Modest Vindication of the proceedings of the Two last Parliaments. 4°, A—F in fours.

Written and printed in 1681.

SIDNEY, SIR PHILIP.
Arcadia. . . . R. Waldegrave, Edinburgh, 1599. Folio.

It appears (Collier's *Bibl. Cat.* ii. 350) that Waldegrave printed this edition for John Harison the younger of London, a circumstance of which there does not seem to be any other example.

SIKES, GEORGE.
Evangelical Essayes, Towards the discovery of a gospel-state. The first part. By Geo: Sikes. Printed in the yeer, 1666. 4°, A—Bb 2 in fours, besides the title and following leaf with a Table.

SILVER, RICHARD, *of Exeter, M.D.*
De Præstigiis et Incantationibvs Dæmonvm et Necromanticorvm Liber Singu-

laris nunquam ante hac editus. Basilææ [*sic.*] 1568, 8°, A—O 4 in eights, and the index, 11 leaves.

SINCLAIR, D.
De Avspicatissima Inavgvratione Iacobi Primi Omnivm Britanniarvm Regis. Concilinm deorum . . . Auctore D. Sanclaro, Profess. R. Mathematico. Parisiis, Apud Danielem Gvillemot, Typographum. M.D.C.III. 4°. Title, dedication to the King, and a blank before the title, 4 leaves : B—G, 2 leaves each : Concilii Deorvm Apothevsma, and Errata, 1 leaf. *B. M.*

> On G 2 is the King's horoscope. The Bright copy was probably described in error as large paper. The tract is a large 4° or small folio.

SINCLAIR, GEORGE.
G. Sinclari P. Professoris, Hydrostatica. Edinburgi. Ann. Dom. 1672. [The printed title follows :] Natural Philosophy Improved by New Experiments. Touching the Mercurial Weather-Glass, the Hygroscope, Eclipsis, Conjunctions of Saturn and Jupiter. By New Experiments, Touching the Pressure of Fluids, the Diving-Bell, and all the Curiosities thereof. . . . Together with a true Relation of an Evil Spirit, which troubled a Man's Family for many days. Lastly, There is a large Discourse anent Coal, Coal-fields, Dipps, Risings, and Streeks of Coal, Levels, Running of Mines, . . . By G. S. *Ars longa, vita brevis.* Printed in the Year, 1683. And are to be Sold by Gideon Schaw Bookseller, at the Sign of the Bible, in the Parliament-Close in Edinburgh. 4°. Engraved title, printed title, dedication to the Provost and Council, 4 leaves : B, 2 leaves : ¶¶, 4 leaves : ¶¶¶, 2 leaves : A—Rr in fours, Pp 4 with the label *Sinclar on the Hydrosticks*, and plates at pp. 1, 9, 32, 80, 116, 144, 178.

> As the dedication is dated from Leith in January 1683, the discrepancy between the engraved and printed titles as to date is probably due to the employment of a plate which had been used for some earlier work.

SKEFFINGTON, SIR JOHN.
The Heroe of Lorenzo, Or The way to Eminence and Perfection. A piece of serious Spanish wit Originally in that language written, and in English. By Sir John Skeffington, Kt. and Barronet. London, Printed for John Martin and James Allestry . . . 1652. 12°. A, 6 : B—G in twelves : H, 6.

SKELTON, JOHN.
A ballade of the scottysshe kynge. [This is over a rough romance cut, under which the text begins. At the end occurs :] Amen / for saynt charite And god saue noble. Kynge / Henry / The. viij. [London, Richard Fawkes, 1513-14.] 4°, 2 leaves. *B. M.*

> This ballad, perhaps the oldest printed one of its kind in the English language, was recovered from the wooden covers of an edition of *Huon de Bordeaux*, folio, Le Noir, 1513, in which occurred also the piece of the prose tract on Flodden wanted to complete the Britwell copy. The *Huon de Bordeaux* appears to have been bound by or for Fawkes, and his binder no doubt employed shop-waste for the end papers or pasteboard.
> This is a first draught of what Skelton subsequently rewrote or considerably altered in his verses against the Scots printed with his Works. At the time this was written the news of the Scotish king's death had not been received in London, and Skelton merely echoes the then general belief when he speaks of him as a prisoner of war.
> I cannot quite make up my mind whether this ballad does not form part of a larger tract—not of the prose tract, I think, because that was written on later and fuller information ; yet it just completes the sheet of four, and the publisher would not be particular as to historical consistency.

SKENE, SIR JOHN.
De verborum significatione. The Exposition of the Termes and Difficile Wordes . . . London. Printed by E. G. 1641. 4°, A—Y in fours.

SKIPPON, PHILIP.
The Christian Centurians Observations, Advices, and Resolutions Concerning Matters Divine and Morall. Collected according to his owne experience, By Philip Skippon, Serjeant-major-generall, &c. . . . London printed by T. B. for Samuel Enderby . . . 1645. 12°. A, 4 leaves : B—R in twelves.

SLEZER, JOHN, *Captain of Artillery Co., and Surveyor of Stores and Magazines.*
Theatrum Scotiæ. Containing the Prospects of Their Majesties Castles and Palaces : Together with those of the most considerable Towns and Colleges ; The Ruins of many Ancient Abbeys, Churches, Monasteries and Convents, Within the said Kingdom. All Curiously Engraven on Copper Plates. With a Short Description of each Place. London, Printed by John Leake for Abel Swalle, . . . MDCXCIII. Folio. Title, dedication, and Privilege, 3 leaves : To the Reader and Contents, 2 leaves : B—S, 2 leaves each : S 2 with

"The End of the Prospects" only:
58 numbered plates preceded by a half
title, "The Prospects."

SMEETON, THOMAS, *Principal of Glas-
gow University.*
Ad virvlentvm Archibaldi Hamiltonii
Apostatæ Dialogvm, De Confusione Cal-
uinianæ sectæ apud Scotos, impiè con-
scriptum orthodoxa responsio. . . . Edin-
bvrgi, Apud Johannem Rosseum Pro
Henrico Charteris. Anno Do. 1579.
Cvm Privilegio Regali. 4". ¶, 4 leaves:
A—Q 2 in fours. Dedicated to James
VI.

SMITH, CAPTAIN JOHN, *Governor of
Virginia.*
A Trve Relation of such occurrences and
accidents of noate as hath hapned in Virginia since the first planting of that
Collony, which is now resident in the
South part thereof, till the last returne
from thence. Written by Captaine Smith
one of the said Collony, to a wor-ship-
full friend of his in England. London
Printed for Iohn Tappe, and are to bee
solde at the Grey-hound in Paules Church-
yard, by W. W. 1608. 4°, A—E in
fours, first leaf (marked A) blank.
> In this copy there is no mention of Wat-
> son on the title-page. Sothebys, April 5,
> 1882, No. 1535.

SMITH, CAPTAIN JOHN.
The Trade & Fishing of Great-Britain
Displayed : With a Description of the
Islands of Orkney and Shotland. By
Captain John Smith. London, Printed
by William Godbid, . . . M. DC. LXII.
4°, A—C 2 in fours.

SMITH, SIMON, *Agent for the Royal
Fishery.*
A True Narration of the Royall Fishings
of Great Britaine and Ireland. Instituted
Anno 1632, and prosecuted by the Right
Honourable, Philip, Earle of Pembrook
and Montgomery, and his Associats, un-
till Anno 1640, from the River of Thames.
Whereunto is added a Discovery of new
Trades, for the employing of all the poore
people and Vagrants in the Kingdome.
London, Printed by E. P. for Nicholas
Bourne, . . . 1641. 4", A—B 2 in fours.

The Herring-Bvsse Trade : Expressed in
Svndry Particulars, both for the building
of Busses, making of deepe Sea-Nets, and
other appurtenances, . . . Written by
Simon Smith, . . . London, Printed by
E. P. for Nicholas Bourne, . . . 1641. 4°,
A—F in fours.
> This tract deals with the herring-trade,
> &c.

SMITH, SIR THOMAS, *of Queen's College, Cambridge, and of Hilhall, Essex.*
De Repvblica et Administratione Anglorvm Libri Tres : . . . . Nunc primûm
Ioannis Buddeni, Legvm Doctoris, fide
optimâ diligentiâq ; . . . in Latinum con-
versi. Pro Officina Nortoniana Londini.
[*Circâ* 1620.] 8", A— L 4 in eights, L 4
blank.
> The original writer states that his book
> represented the state of England in 1565,
> and was written by him when he had com-
> pleted his fifty-first year. It is to be pre-
> sumed, perhaps, that it was composed about
> the period to which it applies, though the
> author does not quite clearly say so. The
> first edition was in 1583, so that the MS.
> must have lain aside for seventeen years.

SOLDIER.
The Souldiers Pocket Bible : Containing
the most (if not all) those places contained in holy Scripture, which doe shew
the qualifications of his inner man, that
is a fit Souldier to fight the Lords Battels,
both before the fight, in the fight, and
after the fight. . . . Printed at London by
G. B. and R. W. for G. C. 1643. [Aug.
3.] 8°, A in eights, A 8 blank B. M.

SOLOMON.
The bokes of Salomon namely
    Prouerbia
    Ecclesiastes
    Cantica canticorum
    Sapientia
    Ecclesiasticus or Jesus
      the sonne of Syrach.
Anno do. M. D. L. I. Mensis Aprill. [Col.]
Imprinted at London in the Flete-strete
at the sygne of the Rose Garland, by
Wyllyam Copland. 8°, black letter, A—
Z in eights, and a—h 4 in eights.

SOMERSETSHIRE.
The crying Murther : Contayning the
cruell and most horrible Butcher[y] of
Mr Trat, Curate of olde Cleane, who was
first murthered as he trauailed vpon the
high way, . . . For this fact by the Iudgement of my Lord chiefe Baron Tanfield,
young Stephen Smethwicke, Andrew Baker, Cyrill Austen, and Alice Walker
was executed this last Summer Assizes,
the 24. of July, at Stone Gallowes, neere
Taunton in Summerset-shire. At London :
Printed by Edw: Allde for Nathaniell
Butter. 1624. 4", A—C in fours. Woodcut on title. Dedicated by C. W. to the
Chief Baron. B. M.

A Brief Relation of the taking of Bridgewater by the Parliaments Forces under
the command of Sir Tho: Fairfax, and

therein, all the Lord Gorings Train, . . .
Together with A Letter concerning the
delivering up of Pontefract Castle . . .
London, Printed for Edw: Husband, . . .
Iuly 25. 1645   4°, 4 leaves.

A Fuller Relation from Bridgewater Since
the last Fight : Wherein is declared the
fierce and terrible storming of the Town,
Sent . . . by a worthy Gentleman in Sir
Tho: Fairfax his Army. . . London,
Printed for Edw: Husband, . . . Iuly 26.
1645.   4°, 4 leaves.

SOMNER, WILLIAM, and CHARLES
   DU FRESNE.
Julii Cæsaris Portus Iccius Illustratus:
Sive 1. Gulielmi Somneri ad Chiffleti
Librum de Portu Iccio, responsio : . . .
2. Caroli Du Fresne Dissertatio de Portu
Iccio. . . . Oxonii, E Theatro . . . MDCXCIV.
8°. Title, 1 leaf : dedication by Edmund
Gibson to White Kennett, 3 leaves : a—c
4 in eights, A—Il in eights. With a por-
trait of Somner and plan.

SOREL, C.
The Extravagant Shepherd : Or, The
History of the Shepherd Lysis. An Anti-
Romance. . . . Now made English and
published the Second time. London,
Printed for Thomas Bassett. . . . 1660.
Folio. With the same plates as in the
two former issues of 1653-4, and the same
collation. An engraving from Benlowes
is also worked on e 2 *verso.*

SOUTHWELL, ROBERT.
An Hvmble Svpplication to Her Maiestie.
Printed, Anno Do. 1595.   8°, A—F 4 in
eights.

An Epistle of Comfort : To the Reverend
Priests, and to the Honourable Worshipfull, and other of the lay sort, restrayned
in durance for the Catholike Faith. . . .
Printed with Licence. 1605.   8°, A—Dd
3 in eights. *Bodleian.*

SOUTHWICK, C.
Fames Genius. Or, A Panegyrick Vpon
His Excellency the Lord General Monck.
At Vintners-Hall, Thursday the 12ᵗʰ of
April 1660.   C. Southwick. London,
Printed for J. Jones, . . . 1660. A broad-
side in verse.

SPAIN.
The True Copie of an Edict, made by the
King of Spaine, concerning the new
Christians Dwelling in Portugall, and of
their departure out of his saide Realmes
& Dominions, freely without Molestation
or losse of their goodes, . . . Translated
out of the Portugall language, into

English. 1602.   At London, Printed by
R. B. for Thomas Panier, . . . [1603.]
4°, 4 leaves, black letter.
The imprint in this copy is mutilated.

A Briefe Declaration of the Proceedings
of the Peace that is now intreating of betweene the King of Spaine, the Archduke,
and the Generall States of the Vnited
Prouinces : Together with an Abstract of
diuers weightie Reasons and Arguments
alleged by the Netherlanders, to proue
that the generall States ought not by any
meanes to grant vnto the discontinuance
of their trade and trafficke into the East-
Indies. Translated out of Dutch into
English. London Printed for Philip
Harison, and are to be solde at the little
shop at the Exchange, ouer against the
Conduit. 1608.   4°, black letter, A—B
in fours, A 1 blank. *B. M.*

Newes from Spaine. The King of Spaines
Edict, for the expulsion & banishment
of more then nine hundred thousand
Moores out of his Kingdome, which con-
spired and plotted to bring the Kingdome
of Spaine vnder the power and subiection
of the Turkes and Saracens. Translated
out of Spanish into English by W. S.
Imprinted at London for Nathaniel
Butter, . . . 1611.   4°, A—B in fours,
A 1 blank. *B. M.*

Remonstrances made by the Kings Maiesties Ambassadovr, vnto the French King
and the Queene his Mother, Iune last
past, 1615. Concerning the marriages
with Spaine ; As also certayne Diabolicall
opinions maintayned by Cardinall Perron,
about the deposing and murthering of
Kings. Together with the French Kings
Letter to the Prince of Conde, Dated the
26. of Iuly last, 1615. and the Prince his
Answere thereunto. Translated according
to the French Copie. London, Printed
by William Stansby for Nathaniel Butter,
. . . 1615.   4°, A—D in fours. *B. M.*
(imperfect.)

A Trve Relation of that which lately
hapned to the great Spanish Fleet and
Galeons of Terra-Firma in America.
With many strange Deliueries of Captaines, and Souldiers in the tempest, and
other remarkable Accidents, worthy the
Obseruation . . . Faithfully translated
out of the Spanish Originall, . . . London, Printed for Nathaniel Butter, . . .
1623.   4°, A—D in fours, D 4 blank.
B. M.

Extraordinary Newes from the Court of

Spaine : Declaring the late Solemnities that were performed in the highest way of magnificence, at the Reception of the Young Queen, the Emperors Daughter . . . Some Passages also of the English Ambassadors in that Court. Sent in a large Letter to a Person of quality in the Kingdom, from Madrid. London, Printed for Richard Lowndes, . . . 1650. 4°, A—B in fours.

The Spanish History : Or, A Relation of the Differences that happened in the Court of Spain, between Don John of Austria, and Cardinal Nitard ; With other Transactions of that Kingdom. . . . London : Printed for Will. Cademan, and Simon Neale, . . . 1678. 8°, B—Ll in eights, Mm, 6 leaves, and the title.

A Journal of the Siege of San Matheo, Capital of the Mastership of the Military Order of Montesa, in the Kingdom of Valencia. . . . Translated into English from the Original [Spanish.] London : Printed, and Sold by Benj. Bragge . . . 1707. 4°. A, 2 : B—D in fours : E, 2.

SPANHEMIUS, FREDERICUS, *Professor of Divinity in the University of Leyden.*

Englands Warning by Germanies Woe: Or, An Historicall Narration, of the Originall, Progresse, Tenets, Names, and severall Sects of the Anabaptists, in Germany, and the Low Countries : . . . London, Printed by John Dover & Robert Ibbitson, for John Bellamie, . . . 1646. 4°, A—G in fours, G 3–4 blank.

Ad Augustissimum Magnae Britanniæ, Franciæ, Hiberniæque Regem Guilielmum Una cum Maria Aug. Consecratum ˣⁱⁱ ˣˣ April. Æ. Vulg cɪɔɪɔcLXXXIX. Adlocutio. Londini, Typis S. R. . . . MDCLXXXIX. Folio, A—D, 2 leaves each : E, 1 leaf.

In this tract the author is described as the principal professor in Leyden University.

SPECULUM.

Concavvm Cappo-Cloacorum ; Or, A View in Little of the Great Wit and Honesty contain'd under a Brace of Caps, and wrap'd up in the Querpo-Cloak of a Phanatick. In some Reflections on the Second Part of a late Pamphlet, intituled, Speevlvm Crape-Gownvrum, Being A Dialogue between True-man and Cappo-cloak-man. By an Honest Gent. and a true Lover of all such. London, Printed for Benj. Tooke, . . . MDCLXXXII. 4°, A—I in fours.

SPEECH.

An Introdvction of the Eyght Partes of speche, and the Construction of the same, compiled and sette forthe by the commaûdement of our most gracious souerayne lorde the king. Anno. MD.XLII. [Col.] Londini In Officina Thomæ Bertheleti typis impress. Cum prinilegio . . . M. D. XLII. 4°, A—H in fours, I, 6 leaves, the last blank. With the printer's device of Lucretia on I 5 *verso*. *B. M.* (on vellum.)

This was apparently intended to sell alone, or with the *Institutio Compendiaria* of the same date.

SPEECHES.

The several speeches of Duke Hamilton Earl of Cambridge. Henry Earl of Holland, and Arthur Lord Capel. Spoken upon the Scaffold immediately before their Execution, on Friday the ninth of March, 1649. [London. T. Jenner, 1650.] 4°, A—D in fours. With cuts, including one between B 4 and E 1 printed separate from the letterpress, the space left for it on C 1 being apparently insufficient.

SPELLING.

A New Booke of Spelling with Syllables: Or An Alphabet and plaine pathway to the facultie of reading the English, Romane, Italian, and Secretarie hands, with severall Copies of the same. Deuised chiefly for Children, that hereby with the lesse losse of their time, they may be able to passe from Reading to the Latine Tongue. . . . At London Imprinted for the Companie of Stationers. 1610. 4°, A—D 2 in fours, partly black letter. Without any prefixes. *B. M.*

SPELMAN, SIR HENRY.

De Sepultura. By Sʳ Henry Spelman, Knight. London, Printed by Robert Young, . . . Anno 1641. 4°, A—E in fours, and a leaf of F.

SPENCE, FERRAND.

Miscellanea : Or Various Discourses upon
1. Tragedy,
2. Comedy,
3. The Italian
4. The English Comedy
5. And Operas,
to his Grace the D. of Buckingham. Together with Epicurus his Morals. Written Originally By the Sieur de Saint Euvremont And made English By Ferrand Spence. . . . London, Printed for Sam. Holford . . . 1686. 12°. A, 12 : a—c,

12 each : d, 6 : B—G in twelves : II, 6 ; I, 12.

> Dedicated "To My Honour'd Friend Thomas Milton Esquire."

SPENCER, BENJAMIN, *Minister at Bromley.*
A Dvmb Speech. Or, A Sermon made, but no Sermon preached, at the Funerall of the Right Vertuous, Mrs Mary Overman, Wife of Mr Thomas Overman, the younger. Of the Parish, formerly called, Saint Saviour, or vulgarly Mary Overis, in Southwarke. . . . London, Printed for John Clark, . . . 1646. 8°, A—F 6 in eights, including the Appendix, besides the title and following leaf. Dedicated to Mr. Thomas Overman. *B. M.*

SPENCER, JOHN, *B. D., of Corpus College, Cambridge.*
A Discourse Concerning Prodigies : Wherein The Vanity of Presages by them is reprehended, and their true and proper Ends asserted and vindicated. By John Spencer, B.D. . . . Printed by John Field for Will. Graves Bookseller, . . . Cambridge. 1663. 4°, A—P in fours, and a leaf of Q.

SPENCER, ROBERT, *Earl of Sunderland* (1643–1702).
The Earl of Sunderland's Letter to a Friend in London. Plainly discovering the Designs of the Romish Party, and others, for the Subverting of the Protestant Religion, and the Laws of the Kingdom. [Col.] London, Printed by J. Partridge at Charing-Cross, and M. Gilliflower in Westminster - Hall. 1689. A folio leaf.

SPENCER, WILLIAM, *Grandson of the Poet.*
The Case of William Spencer of Kilcolman in the County of Cork in the Kingdom of Ireland, Esq ; Grandson and Heir to Edmond Spencer, the Poet. [*Circâ* 1700.] A folio leaf.

SPHINX.
Sphinx Lvgdvno-Genevensis Sive Reformator Proteus. Containing the True Character of Sanctified Legion : Together with His Relations, Associates, and Retinue ; Viz. Jealousies, Fears, Scruples, Qualms, Liberty, Property, Sack-Possets, Caudles, Guns, Pikes, Trumpets, Drums, . . . London, Printed for R. Sellers. MDCLXXXIII. 4". A, 2 leaves : B—D in fours, D 4 blank.

SPORT.
Sport upon Sport or Youth's Delight.

Printed & Sold by Willm & Cluer Dicey in Bow Church Yard London. [About 1720.] A sheet of engravings in compartments.

> Collier's Sale, August 1884, No. 1025.

SPRAT, THOMAS, *Bishop of Rochester.*
A Letter from the Bishop of Rochester, To the Right Honourable The Earl of Dorset and Middlesex, Lord-Chamberlain of His Majesties Houshold. Concerning his Sitting on the Late Ecclesiastical Commission. In the Savoy : Printed by Edw: Jones. MDCLXXXVIII. 4°, A—C 2 in fours.

A Relation of the late Wicked Contrivance of Stephen Blackhead and Robert Young, against the Lives of several Persons by Forging an Affidavit under their Hands. Written by the Bishop of Rochester In Two Parts. . . . In the Savoy : Printed by Edward Jones. MDCXCII. 4°. Part 1, A—K 2 in fours, A 1 with *Imprimatur :* Part 2, A—Y 2 in fours.

ST. CLAIR, ROBERT, *M.D.*
The Abyssinian Philosophy Confuted : Or, Vellvro's Theoria Neither Sacred, nor agreeable to Reason. Being, for the most part, a Translation of Petrus Ramazzini, Of the Wonderful Springs of Modena. Illustrated with many Curious Remarks and Experiments by the Author and Translator. . . . London, Printed for the Author, and Sold by W. Newton, . . . 1697. 12", A—I in twelves, and a 2—c 12 in twelves. With two folded plates. Dedicated to the truly Honourable Sophronius Philalethes.

STAFFORD, ANTHONY.
Staffords Heauenly Dogge : Or The life, and death of that great Cynicke Diogenes, whom Laertius stiles *Canem Cœlestem,* the Heauenly Dogge, By reason of the Heauenly precepts he gaue. Taken out of the best Authors, . . . London, Printed by George Purslowe, for Iohn Budge, . . . 1615. 12°, A—F 9 in twelves, A 1 blank, A 2 with a frontispiece, and F 9 blank. Dedicated in terms of strong friendship to Sir John Wentworth, Bart.

STAFFORD, WILLIAM, *Viscount Stafford.*
Stafford's Memoires : Or, A Brief and Impartial Account of the Birth and Quality, Imprisonment, Tryal, Principles, . . . of William late Lord Viscount Stafford, . . . Published for Rectifying all Mistakes upon this Subject. . . . Hereunto is also annexed a short Appendix concerning some Passages in Stephen

Colledge's Trial. Printed in the Year, MDCLXXXI. Folio, B—V, 2 leaves each, and the title.

STAFFORDSHIRE.

A more Exact and Perfect Relation of the Treachery, Apprehension, Conviction, Condemnation, Confession, and Execution of Francis Pitt, Aged 65. Who was Executed in Smithfield on Saturday, October the 12. 1644. for endeavouring to betray the Garrison of Rvshall-Hall in the County of Stafford, to the Enemy. . . . London, Printed for John Field. Octob. 18. 1644. 4", A—B in fours,

The Substance of the Information of Richard Perkin of Shutborrow, in the County of Stafford ; Taken upon Oath at Stafford Assizes 1679 . . . London, Printed for Richard Baldwin . . . 1681. Folio, 4 leaves.

STALBRIDGE, HENRY.

The Epistel Exhortatorye of an Inglyshe Chrystian vnto his derely beloued coûtrey of Ingland / agaynst the pompouse popysh Bisshops therof, as yet the true members of theyre fylthye Father the great Antischryst of Rome. Made by Henry Stalbrydge. [Quot. from Jeremiah. Printed abroad, about 1550.] 8", A—E 4 in eights. Black letter.

A discourse wherin is debated whether it be expedient that the scripture should be in English for al men to reade that wyll. Fyrst reade this booke with an indifferent eye, and then approve or condempne, as God shall moue your heart. . . . . Exevsvm Londini in ædibus Roberti Caly, Typographi: Mense Decembris. Anno. 1554. Cum priuilegio. 8", black letter, A—L 4 in eights, L 4 with *Errata.*

STANBRIDGE, JOHN, *Grammarian, and first Usher of Magdalen College School, Oxford.*

Vulgaria quædam . . . . collecta / et in Anglicanam lin]guam traducta . . . . præcedit vulgare. [Col.] Imprynted at London in Flete strete at the sygne of the Sône by me Wynkyn de Worde. The yere of our lord god. M. D. &. xxix. 𝕵. iii. day of August. 8", A—D 4 in eights.

Sothebys, July 1, 1885, No. 1247, title mutilated.

Cocabula magistri stâbrigi primũ iam edita sua saltem editiõe. [This title is on a ribbon over the common cut of a schoolmaster. At the end occurs:] Enprynted by Wynkyn de Worde dwellÿge at London in the flete strete at ÿ sygne of the sonne. 4". A, 6 : B, 4 : C, 6 : D, 4 = 20 leaves.

Vocabvla Magistri Stanbrigii . . . . studio & industria Thomæ Newtoni . . . Edinburgi, Excudebat Iacobus Lindesius Sumptibus Ioannis Thriepland. Anno Dom. 1644. 8", A—C in eights.

STANLEY, JAMES, *Earl of Derby.*

The True Speech Delivered on the Scaffold By Iames Earl of Derby, In the Market-place at Boulton in Lancashire, on wednesday last, being the 15. of this instant October, 1651. With the manner of his deportment and Carrage on the Scaffold : . . . . Likewise, how the King of Scots took shipping at Gravesend, . . . London, Printed for Robert Eles, for general satisfaction to the People. [1651.] 4", 4 leaves.

STANLEY, THOMAS.

The History of Philosophy, In Eight Parts. By Thomas Stanley. London, Printed for Humphrey Moseley, and Thomas Dring ; . . . 1656. Folio. With a portrait of the author by Faithorne and plates of some of the Philosophers. Dedicated to the author's uncle, John Marsham, Esq.

Each part has a separate title and signatures.

The History of Philosophy, The Third and Last Volume, In Five Parts. By Thomas Stanley. London, Printed for Humphrey Moseley and Thomas Dring, . . . 1660[-2]. Folio. With a portrait of Stanley by Faithorne and plates of Pythagoras, Archytas, Empedocles, Heraclitus, Xenophanes, Pyrrho and Epicurus. General title, title to Part 1, and extract from Bacon, 3 leaves : B—5 X 2 in twos: *the Chaldaic Philosophy,* title, dedication by Stanley to Sir John Marsham, Kt., and preface, 3 leaves : A—M 2 in fours : Aa, 2 leaves : Bb—Nn 2 in fours.

STAR CHAMBER.

A Briefe Relation of certain speciall and most materiall passages, and speeches in the Starre-Chamber, occasioned and delivered Iune the 14th. 1637. at the censure of those three worthy Gentlemen, Dr Bastwicke, Mr Byrton, and Mr Prynne, as it hath beene truely and faithfully gathered from their owne mouthes by one present at the sayd Censure. Printed in the Yeere 1637. 4", A—D in fours.

STARKEY, STANLEY.

Upon the Death of the Honourable and truly Worthy Gentleman Sr Edward Massie, One of His Majesties most Honourable Privy Council. Who dyed the

23. of May, 1674. Dublin, Printed for the Authour. 1674. A broadside in verse. *B. M.*

STARKEY, THOMAS.
[An Exhortation to the people, instruc-tynge theym to Unitie and Obedience. Col.] Londini in AEdibvs Thomae Ber-theleti Regii Impressoris Excvsa. Cvm Privilegio. 4°. a, 4 leaves: A—Y in fours: Z, 6.

> Sothebys, July 1, 1885, No. 1120. The copy used had no title, and the matter be-tween brackets is taken from the head-line on C 4.

STATHAM, NICHOLAS.
[Abridgment of the Law. Norman French, without any title-page. Rouen, W. Le Tailleur for R. Pynson, about 1495.] Folio, a—x in eights, besides two leaves at the beginning with the Table: z, 6 leaves, and another sheet of six. With Le Tailleur's device and monogram on the last page. *B. M.*

> At the end of the Table occurs: *Per me R. pynson*, which has been inserted in a different character from the rest of the book, perhaps after the delivery of the quire stock in London. An imperfect copy of this book was sold at Sothebys, July 8, 1886, No. 1298, as an edition of Lyttelton's *Tenures.*

STATIONERS.
A Beacon Set on Fire: Or The Humble Information of certain Stationers, Citizens of London, to the Parliament and Com-monwealth of England. Concerning the Vigilancy of Jesuits, Papists, . . . By Writing and Publishing many Popish Books, (Printed in England in the Eng-glish Tongue within these three last Years, . . .) London, Printed for the Sub-scribers hereof. 1652. 4°, A—B in fours.

A Second Beacon Fired by Scintilla [? Michael Sparke]: With His Humble Information and Joint Attestation for the Truth of his Brethrens former Declaration & Catalogue . . . London, Printed for the Author, 1652. 4°, A—B 2 in fours.

> This sequel purports to embrace an expo-sition of the misery of the whole Company of Stationers.

The Orders, Rules and Ordinances, Or-dained, Devised and Made by the Master and Keepers or Wardens and Comminalty of the Mystery or Art of Stationers of the City of London, for the well Governing of that Society. London, Printed for the Company of Stationers, 1678. 4°, A—D in fours, D 4 blank. Black letter.

STATUTES.
The Statutes at Large in Paragraphs, From Magna Charta Until this Time, . . . By John Keble of Grays-Inne, Esquire. London, Printed . . . MDCLXXVI. Large folio.

A Collection of certaine Statutes in force With full and ready notes in the Margent, . . . Published for the better caution of such as are inclinable to Delinquency . . . London printed by Robert White, . . . MDCXLIV. 4°, A—F in fours.

> These statutes refer to unlawful pastimes, cursing and swearing, &c.

An Exact Abridgment of Publick Acts and Ordinances of Parliament, Made from the year 1640, to the year 1656 . . . By William Hughes of Grays Inne Esq; . . . London, Printed by T. R. for H. Twyford . . . 1657. 4°, B—4 I 2 in fours, and Table, 4 leaves, besides the title.

The effect of certaine branches of the Statute made in Anno. XXXIII. Henrici viij. and confirmed by the Kings most excellent Maiestie, touching the mainte-nance of Artillery, and the punishment of such as vse vnlawfull games, now to be put in execution. Cum priuilegio Regiae Maiestatis. [About 1604.] A folio broad-side.

STAYLEY, WILLIAM.
The Behaviour of Mr Will. Stayley in Newgate, . . . With the Substance of his last Speech and Discourses at the usual place of Execution. . . . London: Printed for R. G. 1678. 4°, 4 leaves.

STEDMAN, FABIAN.
Campanalogia: Or The Art of Ringing Improved. With plain and easie Rules to guide the Practitioner in the Ringing all Kinds of Changes. To which is added, great Variety of New Peals. London, Printed by W. Godbid, for W. S. . . . 1677. 8°. A, 4 leaves: B—Q 4 in eights. Dedicated to the Society of College Youths (i.e. the College of Bell-Ringers). *B. M.*

STEED, CAPTAIN J.
Fortification and Military Discipline In Two Parts. The First shews the Prin-ciples and Practice of all manner of For-tifications, . . . The Second Part treats of the Rules for the Exercise of Horse and Foot, . . . All Illustrated with 54 Copper Plates. Improved and Designed by Capt. J. S. Published and Sold by Robert Morden . . . London. 1688. 8°. Title and preface by publisher, 3 leaves: B—K 4 in eights: Part 2, title, preface, and

contents, 4 leaves : B—II in eights, and the 54 plates.

STELLA.

Stella clericorum. [London,] Richard Pynson. 4°. A⁶, B⁴, C⁶. With Pynson's device on the last page.

On the back of the title are 16 Latin lines unsigned, " in laudem libelli."
Sothebys, July 1, 1885, No. 1123.

STEPHENS, EDWARD, *of Cherington, co. Gloucester.*

Important Questions of State, Law, Justice and Prudence, Both Civil and Religious, Upon the late Revolutions and Present State of these Nations. . . . By Socrates Christianus. London, Printed in the Year, 1689. 4°, A—B in fours.

STEPHENS, JOHN, *the Younger, of Lincoln's Inn.*

Essayes and Characters Ironicall, and Instrvctive. The second impression. With a new Satyre in defence of Common Law and Lawyers : Mixt with reproofe against their common Enemy. With many new Characters, & diuers other things added ; & euery thing amended . . . By Iohn Stephens the yonger, of Lincolnes Inne. Gent. London, Printed by E: Allde for Phillip Knight, . . . 1615. 8°, A—Ee 4 in eights. Dedicated by the author to his honoured friend Thomas Turnor, Esq. With complimentary verses by Anthony Croftes, &c.

STEVENS, CHARLES.

Maison Rustique, Or The Covntrey Farme : . . . London Printed by Arnold Hatfield for Iohn Norton and Iohn Bill. 1606. 4°. A, 8, the first leaf blank : b, 8 : B— 3 N in eights.

STEVENSON, MATTHEW.

The Wits Paraphras'd : Or, Paraphrase upon Paraphrase. In a Burlesque on the Several late Translations of Ovids Epistles. Juven. Sat. 10. *Et facilis* . . . London : Printed for Will. Cademan, . . . 1680. 8°. A, 4 leaves : Dedication by M. T. to his friend Mr. Julian, 4 leaves in verse : B—M 2 in eights. In verse.

The Wits : Or, Poems & Songs on Various Occasions. Made Publick for the Delight of the Ingenious. By a Lover of the Muses. London, Printed for Dorman Newman, at the Kings Armes in the Poultrey, 1685. 8°. A, 4 leaves : B—I in eights, last leaf blank. Dedicated to Mrs. Mary Hunt, of Sharington Hall in Norfolk, and to Thomas Brown, Esq., of Elsing Hall in the same county.

STEWART, JAMES.

James Steuarts Answer to a Letter Writ by Mijn Heer Fagel Pensioner to the States of Holland, and West-Frisland, Concerning the Repeal of the Penal Laws and Tests. London Printed, and Re-Printed in Edinburgh, by John Reid, 1688. 8°, A—E in fours.

STEWART, RICHARD.

The English Case, Exactly set down by Hezekiah's Reformation, in a Court Sermon at Paris. By D⁷ Steward, Then Dean of Westminster . . . London, Printed for T. Garthwait . . . 1659. 12°. A, 4 leaves : B—D in twelves.

STOCKWOOD, JOHN.

A bryefe and necessary Catechisme or Instruction. Very needefull to be knowne of al Housholders. Wherby they may the better teach and instructe theyr Families, in such pointes of Christian Religion as is most meete. . . . Imprinted at London by John Charlwood. 1577. 8°, A—C in eights.

ST. OLON, M.

The Present State of the Empire of Morocco. With a Faithful Account of the Manners, Religion, and Government of that People. By Monsieur de St. Olon, Ambassador there in the Year 1693. Adorn'd with Figures. London : Printed for R. Bently, . . . 1695. 12°, A—L 6 in twelves. Dedicated by Peter Motteux, the translator, to Sir William Trumbull, one of the Commissioners of the Treasury. With plates at pp. 86, 90 (4), 93, 94 (3), and 130 (plan of Larache [El Araish]), besides a frontispiece.

STOREHOUSE.

A Storehovse of Physicall and Philosophicall Secrets. Teaching to distill all manner of Oyles from Gummes, Spices, Seedes, Rootes, Hearbs, and Mineralls, &c. With their severall vertues, out of sundry approved Authors. The first Part. London, Printed by Thomas Harper, M.DC.XXXIII. 4°, A—D in eights.

STORY, GEORGE.

A True and Impartial History of the Most Material Occurences in the Kingdom of Ireland during the Two Last Years. With the Present State of Both Armies. . . . Written by an Eye-witness to the most Remarkable Passages. London : Printed for Ric. Chiswell, . . . MDCXCI. 4°, A—Y in fours, A 1 with the half-title. With folding leaves at pp. 8 and 124.

An Impartial History of the Wars of Ireland, With a Continuation thereof. In Two Parts . . . Illustrated with Copper Sculptures describing the most Important Places of Action. Together with some Remarks . . . . By George Story Chaplain to the Regiment formerly Sir Tho. Gower's, now the Earl of Drogheda's ; an Eye-witness . . . London : Printed for Ric. Chiswell, ... MDCXCIII. 4°, A—Y in fours: the Continuation, A—U in fours, and a, 4 leaves. The first part is dedicated to Lord Morpeth, the second to the King. The former has no plates. In the latter they occur at pp. 4, 8, 10, 16, 22, 38, 46, 88, 124, 134, 172, 206, and 224.

The testimony of Story as an eyewitness is peculiarly valuable ; and he has inserted many curious accounts of the manners and traditions of the localities affected by the war.

STORY, JOHN.
A declaration of the lyfe and Death of Iohn Story, Late a Romish Canonicall Doctor. by professyon. 1571. Imprinted at London, by Thomas Colwell. 8°, black letter, A—D in fours. St. John's College, Cambridge.

STOW, JOHN.
The Svrvay of London : Containing, The Originall, Antiquitie, Encrease, and more Moderne Estate of the sayd Famous Citie . . . . Written in the yeere 1598. by Iohn Stow, Citizen of London. Since then, continued, corrected and much enlarged, with many rare and worthy Notes, both of Venerable Antiquity, and later memorie ; such as were neuer published before this present yeere 1618. London, Printed by George Purslowe, dwelling at the East end of Christs Church. 1618. 4°. Dedicated by Anthony Munday the Editor to the Mayor and Corporation of London. Title and dedication, 4 leaves : A, with a second inscription to Bp. King, 2 leaves : B—3 R 4 in eights, besides 2 extra leaves between C 2 and C 3 with an account of the New River.

STRINGER, MOSES.
Variety of Surprising Experiments Made of Two incomparable Medicines : Elixir Febrifugum Martis, and Salt of Lymons. Shewing Their Vertues, Use and Operations : Being the Peculiar Secrets and Aquisitions of the Author. Moses Stringer, Chymist and Physitian, at his Laboratory in Hugh's-Court, Black-Fryers near Ludgate . . . London : Printed for the Author, 1703. 8°. A, 8 : B, 2.

STRYPE, JOHN, M.A.
The Life of the Learned Sir Thomas Smith K[t] Doctor of the Civil Law ; Principal Secretary of State to King Edward the Sixth and Queen Elizabeth. . . . With an Appendix, wherein are contained some Works of his, never before published. London, Printed for A. Roper . . . MDCXCVIII. 8°, A—Q in eights, besides a, 4 leaves : Aa—Ii in eights : Contents of Appendix, 2 leaves. Dedicated by J[ohn] S[trype] to Sir Edward Smith of Hilhal, in Essex, Baronet. With a portrait of Sir T. Smith.

STUART, HENRY, Duke of Gloucester.
Epicedia Academiæ Oxoniensis, in Obitum Celsissimi Principis Henrici Ducis Glocestrensis. Oxoniæ, Typis Lichfieldianis, M DC LX. 4°. A—H in fours, and d, 4 leaves between C and D.

STUBBE, HENRY.
Clamor, Rixa, Joci, Mendacia, Furta, Cachini, Or, A Severe Enquiry into the late Oneirocritica published by John Wallis, Grammar-Reader in Oxon . . . London, [no printer,] 1657. 4°, A—H in fours : Aa—Ee in fours, Ee 4 blank.

In the preface there is a curious allusion by Stubbe to Pasquil's Jests and Mother Bunch, to which he suggests that the English writings of Wallis may hereafter serve as appendices.
In Quaritch's Catalogue of MSS. 1886, No. 35,843, occurs : An Account of the Life of Mahomet, by Henry Stubbe, MS. in 4°, 1671-2, with eight autograph letters addressed to Gideon Harvey, giving an account of the author's life and the progress of this work. The volume was from the libraries of Lord Verney and John Disney.

[A Letter to M[r] Henry Stubs concerning His Censure upon certain passages contained in the History of the Royal Society. London, Printed for Octavian Pullen, . . . 1670. 4°, A—C in fours.]

STUBBES, PHILIP.
A Christall Glasse for Christian Women. . . . Imprinted at London for Edward White, . . . 1600. 4°, black letter, A—C in fours.
Collier's Sale, August 1884, No. 891.

A Christal Glasse for Christian Women. . . . London. Printed by W. I. for Thomas Panier and Iohn Wright. 1621. 4°, A—C in fours, black letter.
Collier's Sale, August 1884, No. 982.

A Christal Glasse for Christian Women. . . . London, Printed by W. I. for Thomas Panier and Iohn Wright. 1623. 4°, black letter, A—C in fours.

A Christal Glasse for Christian Women. . . . London, Printed for Iohn Wright,

. . . 1626. 4°, black letter, A—C in fours.

A Chrystall Glasse for Christian Women. . . . London, Printed for Iohn Wright, . . . 1641. 4°, black letter, A—C in fours, C 4 blank.

STUBBS, JOHN.

For the King and both Houses of Parliament, who are desired to read over this following Treatise, and in the Fear and Wisdom of the pure holy God to consider, and lay to heart what is contained therein. . . . Written by John Stubbs. . . . Printed in the Year, 1670. 4°, A—C 2 in fours, C 2 with a Postscript.

SUFFOLK.

The Woefull and Lamentable wast and spoile done by a suddaine Fire in S. Edmonds-bury in Suffolke. on Munday, the tenth of Aprill. 1608. London Printed for Henrie Gosson, and are to be solde in Pater-noster rowe, at the Signe of the Sunne. 1608. 4°, A—B in fours, B 4 blank. With a cut on title. *B. M.*

Reprinted at Ipswich, 4°, 1845.

A Magazine of Scandall. Or, A heape of wickednesse of two infamous Ministers, consorts, one named Thomas Fowkes of Earle Soham in Suffolk, convicted by Law for killing a man, and the other named Iohn Lowes of Brandeston, who hath beene arraigned for witchcraft. . . . Printed at London for R. H. 1642. 4°, 8 leaves.

Newes from Dennington Castle Or A true Copy of Major William Rives his Letter, in Vindication of himselfe and others. . . . Printed for Henry Twyford, . . . Aprill the first 1646. 4°, 4 leaves.

SUGAR-BAKERS.

An Answer to the Sugar-Bakers or Sugar-Refiners Paper. [Col.] London, Printed and are to be sold by E. Whitlock. 1695. Folio, 2 leaves.

SULPITIUS, JOHANNES, *Grammarian.*

Qñita Recognitio Atq; Additio ad Gramaticen Sulpitianam Cum textu Ascensiano in plurimis locis presertim de syllabarū quātitate & de figuris & preceptis orthographie, illustrato emuncto atq; aucto : nullo prorsus vtili detracto. [The device of W. de Worde.] Venundantur Lōdonijs a magistro Wynnando de worde / in vico: vulgariter nūcupato fletestrete sub intersignio solis aurei. [Col.] Impressum est iam quinto loco: exacteq; recognitū & rursus auctum hoc opus aureum : Accuratione Ioannis bar-

bier Impressoris necnõ librarij Iurati alme vniuersitatis Parisiēsis Sūptibus vero wynnādi de worde librarij Lōdoñ cōmorantis zephiris felicibus suū sortitur terminū Anno. dñi Millessimo . ccccc. xj. iiij Nonas Aprilis. 4°, Title and prel., 4 leaves : A, 6 leaves ; a—b in eights : g, 6 leaves : h—n in eights : o, 6 : p, 8 : q, 6 : r, 8 : s, 6 : t, 6 : v, 6 : x, 8 : no y : z, 6 : *Vocabulorum Interpretatio*, 8 leaves. Altogether, 181 leaves. *B. M.*

This edition seems to differ from any described by Herbert and others.

SURREY.

An Exact Relation of the Bloody and Barbarous Murder, committed by Miles Lewis, and his Wife, a Pinmaker upon their Prentice, dwelling in Barnsby-street in Southwark. . . . London, Printed for J. C. Novemb. 30. 1646. 4°, 4 leaves.

The Sad and Bloody Fight at Westminster betwene the Souldiers of the Parliaments guard and the Club-men of Svrrey. . . . London, Printed for H. Becke, . . . 1648. 4°, 4 leaves.

Merry Newes from Epsom-Wells : Being a witty and notable Relation, of a Lawyers lying with a London Goldsmiths Wife, at Epsom, Whilest the kind Cuckold went for Water : And the manner of the beating up of their Quarters one morning early by the Lawyers wife, as they lay embracing each other in Bed together. With the Goldsmith's loving speech in Vindication of his Wife, . . . London, Printed for G. Kendal, and are to be sold near the Old-Bayley, 1663. 4°, 4 leaves. In prose and verse.

Sothebys, March 31, 1882, No. 495.

A true Narrative of the Great and Terrible Fire in Southwark, on Fryday the 26th of May, 1676 . . . London : Printed for D. M. 4°, 4 leaves.

This disaster involved the Counter, the Meal-Market, about 500 dwellings, and the following "eminent Inns :"—The Queen's Head, the Talbot, the George, the White Hart, the King's Head, and the Green Dragon.

A Caution to Married Couples : Being a true Relation how a Man in Nightingale-lane Having beat and abused his Wife, Murthered a Tub-man that endeavoured to stop him from Killing her with a Half-pike. . . . London : Printed for D. M. 1677. 4°, 4 leaves.

The Proceedings at the Assizes in Southwark, For the County of Surry. Begun on Thursday the 20th of March, and not ended till Tuesday the 26 of the same month, 1678. . . . London : Printed for D. M. 1678. 4°, 4 leaves.

The Last Words and Sayings of the True-Protestant Elm-Board, which lately suffer'd Martyrdom in Smithfield, and now in Southwark : . . . London : Printed for F. Shepherd. 1682. A broadside.

An Argument in Defence of the Hospitaller of St. Thomas Southwark and of His Fellow-Servants and Friends in the same House. London, Printed in the Year, MDCLXXXIX. Folio, A—G 2 in fours, besides the title and John Turner's dedication to the Lord Mayor and Aldermen.

Queries upon a Clause in a Statute of the 25ᵗʰ H. 8. c. 21. Relating to the Present Controversies in the Hospital of S. Thomas, Southwark. [1690.] A single leaf.

A Full and True Relation how one Jane Hancock, Alias Parry, sold herself to the Devil to turn Witch at Farnum in the County of Surrey. . . . London, Printed for D. Brown . . . 1705. 8°, 4 leaves.

SUSSEX.
A Defence of the Profession which the Right Reverend Father in God, John, Late Lord Bishop of Chichester, made upon his Death-Bed ; Concerning Passive Obedience, and the New Oaths. Together with an Account of some Passages of His Lordships Life. London : Printed in the Year MDCXC. 4°, A—I 2 in fours.

SWEDEN.
A True Relation of the Reasons which necessitated His Majesty of Sweden to continue the War with Denmark. . . . London, Printed for T. Pierrepont at the Sun in Pauls Church-yard. 1658. 4°, A—E in fours.

SWETNAM, JOSEPH.
The Araignment of Lewd, Idle, Froward, and vnconstant women : . . . . London : Printed for Thomas Archer, . . . 1616. 4°, A—I in fours. Woodcut on title.

The Araignment of Lewde, idle, froward, and vnconstant women : Or the vanitie of them, choose you whether. With a commendation of wise, vertuous, and honest Woman. Pleasant for married Men, profitable for young Men, and hurt-full to none. Edinbvrgh Printed by Iohn Wreittoun. 1629. 8°, A—E in eights, E 8 blank. B. M.

The Dedication, "Neither to the best, nor yet to the worst, but to the common sort of Women," is signed Thomas Tel-trouth.

SYLVIA.
Sylvia's Complaint, of her Sexes Unhappiness : A Poem. Being the Second Part of Sylvia's Revenge, . . . London, Printed, and are to be sold by Richard Baldwin . . . 1692. 4°. Title and Preface, 2 leaves : B—D in fours, D 4 blank.

SYMONDS, WILLIAM, Preacher at St. Saviour's, Southwark.
Virginia. A Sermon Preached at White-Chappel, in the presence of many, Honourable and Worshipfull, the Adventurers and Planters in Virginia . 25. April. 1609. Pvblished for the Benefit and Vse of the Colony, Planted, and to bee Planted there, . . . London Printed by I. Windet, for Eleazar Edgar, . . . 1609. 4°, A—H in fours, H 4 blank. Dedicated to the Adventurers to Virginia. B. M.

SYMONDS, WILLIAM, of Milton, near Gravesend.
A New-Years-Gift to the Parliament Or, Eng'and's Golden Fleece Preserv'd, in Proposals Humbly laid before this Present Parliament. London, Printed in the Year 1702. 4°, A—F in fours, F 4 blank.

SYMS, CHRISTOPHER.
An Introdvction to the Art of Teaching, the Latine Speach. Which by this method may easily bee taught to any boy howsoever dul of capacity within the space of four years. . . . Invented, practised, and proved by the author Christofer Syms. Experientia artium fundamen. Dvblin, Printed by the Society of Stationers, 1634. Cum privilegio. 4°, A—L 2 in fours. Dedicated to Charles I. B. M.

SYMSON, PATRICK.
A Short Compend of the Historie of the First Ten Persecvtions moved against Christians, . . . Edinbvrgh, Printed by Andro Hart, . . . 1613. 4°, A—P in eights, Q, 2. Dedicated by P. Symson to Mary, Countess of Mar.

T.

T. G.

Roger the Canterburian, That cannot say Grace for his Meat, with a low-crowned Hat before his Face. Or The Character of a Prelaticall Man affecting great Heighths. Newly written, by G. T. London, Printed for William Larmar, 1642. 4⁰, 4 leaves.

T. H., M.A., of St. John's College, Cambridge.

Meditations Divine & Morall. . . London Printed for Robert Gibbs at the Signe of yᵉ Golden Ball in Chancery Lane near Serjants Inn 1650. 12⁰, B—I in twelves, last leaf blank, and the engraved title.

T. R.

The Opinion of Witchcraft Vindicated. In an Answer to a Book Intituled the Question of Witchcraft Debated. Being a Letter to a Friend. By R. T. London, Printed by E. O. for Francis Haley, . . . 1670. 8⁰, B—F 4 in eights, and the title.

TABLES.

Wryting Tables, with a necessarie Calender for xxv. [yea]res, with all the principall Fayres in Englande, with the beginning and the ending of the Termes, with the Festinall holydayes for all the yeare : and the hie wayes from one notable towne in Englande to another : with a rule to knowe the change, full, and quarters of the moone for euer, with certaine prayers. Made at London, [by] Franke Adams Bookebynder, dwelling in the Greene Arbour without Newgate. [1577.] Square 12⁰. With two leaves of vellum for tablets.

> Sothebys, July 1886, No. 1515 (Simes), very mutilated. The Calendar for twenty-five years begins with 1577. This is the book referred to in *Hamlet*.

Writing Tables with a Kalender for xxiiij yeres, with other necessary rules, the Contentes therof you shall finde on the other side of this Leafe. Made at London, by Franke Adams, Stationer, or Bookebinder, dwelling in Thames Street, at the Signe of yᵉ black Rauen, nere Londō Bridge, & are there to be sold : or els at the Royal Exchange, at the signe of the halfe Rose, and halfe Sun, next to the north doore, by Thomas Frethen. 1581. 8⁰, A—D in eights, besides the Tables or Tablets on parchment or vellum. With woodcuts of coins.

> Sothebys, April 11, 1885, No. 562.

Writing Tables with a Kalendar for xxiiii. veeres, with sundry necessarie rules. The Tables made by Robert Triplet. London Imprinted for the Companie of Stationers. 1604. Square 12⁰. A—B in eights : plates of coins, 3 leaves : C 4 —D 8 in eights. *B. M.*

Writing Tables with a Kalender for xxiiii. veeres, with sundry necessarie rules. The Tables made by Robert Triplet. London Imprinted for the Companie of Stationers. 1611. Small square 8⁰, A—D in eights. Black letter. *B. M.*

> The *Tablet* or *Tablets* for writing memoranda are on vellum, and are not, of course, included in the collation. Triplet was probably a manufacturer of these commodities, and the number inserted in copies varies. In the present one they are interleaved with paper.

TAFILETTA.

A Short and Strange Relation of some part of the Life of [Muley Arxid, King of] Tafiletta, The Great Conqueror and Emperor of Barbary. By one that hath lately been in his Majesties Service in that Country. London : Printed by T. N. for Samuel Lowndes, . . . 1669. 4⁰, A—D in fours, title on A 2. With a portrait of Tafiletta.

Compare FREJUS, p. 88.

TAILORS.

The Lamentation of Seven Journey men Taylors, Being Sent up in a Letter from York-Shire, and written in verse by a wit. Giving a true account of a Wench, who being with Child, laid it to seven Journey-men Taylors, . . . To the Tune of, *I am the Duke of Norfolk*. Printed for J. Deacon, . . . A broadside in black letter, with four cuts.

The Trappand Taylor Or, A Warning to all Taylors to beware how they Marry. . . . To the Tune of, How many Crowns and pounds have I spent, &c. . . . Printed for F. Coles, T. Vere, J. Wright, and J. Clarke. A broadside with two cuts, one of "Tom the taler & his Wife Ione." Black letter.

The Taylor's Wanton Wife of Wapping : Or, A Hue-and-Cry after a Lac'd Petticoat, flow'r'd Gown, and rich Cornet, with other Apparel, which was lost in the Chamber of Love. To the Tune of, *What shall I do to show how much I love her*. . . . Printed for P. Brooksby, I. Deacon, J. Blare, and J. Back. A broadside in black letter, with two cuts.

Poor Tom the Taylor His Lamentation. Giving an Account how he pickt up a Miss near the Maypole in the Strand, and also how he handed her to the Fair, . . . To the Tune of *Daniel Cooper.* Printed for I. Deacon, at the Angel in Guilt-spur-street, without Newgat. A broadside with two cuts. Black letter.

TALBOT, ELIZABETH, *Countess of Kent.*
A Choice Manuall, Or Rare and Select Secrets: Collected, and practised by the Right Honourable, the Countess of Kent, late deceased. . . . The Thirteen[th] Edition. London. Printed, by Gartrude Dawson, and are to be sold by William Sheares, . . . 1661. Small 12⁰. A, 9 leaves: B—S 6 in twelves.
On L 11 occurs *A True Gentlewomans Delight* with a new title.

TANGIER.
The Present Interest of Tangier. Folio, 2 leaves.

A Particular Narrative of a Great Engagement between the Garison of Tangier, and the Moors. And of the Signal Victory which His Majesties Forces obtained against them on the 27ᵗʰ of October last. Published by Authority. In the Savoy: Printed by Thomas Newcombe. 1680. Folio, 4 leaves.

TAPPE, JOHN.
The Seamans Kalender, Or An Ephemerides of the Sun, Moon, and certaine of the most notable fixed Starres. Together with many most needfull and necessary matters, to the behoofe and furtherance principally of Marriners and Seamen. . . . The Tables being for the most part calculated from the yeere 1601. to the yeere 1624. By I. T. London. Printed by E. Allde for Iohn Tappe, . . . 1602. 4⁰, A— N 2 in fours. Dedicated by Tappe to Sir John Paieton, Lieutenant of the Tower. *B. M.*

TASSO, ERCOLE AND TORQUATO.
The Housholders Philosophie. Wherein is perfectly and properly described, the true Oeconomia and Forme of House-keeping With a Table added thereunto of all the notable thinges therein contained. First written in Italian by that excellent Orator and Poet Signior Torquato Tasso, and now translated by T. K. Whereunto is anexed a dairie Booke for all good huswiues. At London Printed by J. C. for Thomas Hacket, . . .

M.D.LXXXVIII. 4⁰, A—G 3 in fours, besides the title, verses by T. K. to Thomas Reade, Esquire, and the Table, 6 leaves. *B. M.* (title imperfect.)
This copy, like Lord Jersey's (Osterley Park Sale, 1885, No. 1699), does not contain the *Dairy Book,* which was licensed conditionally to Hacket on the 9th July 1588, nor does the Table refer to such a tract as actual part of the volume. The work itself is a translation of the *Padre di Famiglia.*

TATE, NAHUM.
The Ingratitude of a Common-Wealth : Or, The Fall of Caius Martius Coriolanus. As it is Acted at the Theatre-Royal. By N. Tate. . . . London, Printed by L. M. for Joseph Hindmarsh, . . . 1682. 4⁰, A—I in fours. Dedicated to Charles, Lord Herbert, son of the Marquis of Worcester.

A Present for the Ladies : Being an Historical Vindication of the Female Sex. To which is added, The Character of an Accomplish'd Virgin, Wife, and Widow, In Verse. London, Printed for Francis Saunders, . . . 1692. 8⁰, A—I in eights, 1 8 blank.

The Anniversary Ode for the Fourth of December, 1697. His Majesty's Birth-Day. Another for New-Year's Day, 1697. Both Set to Musick, and Perform'd at Kensington ; The Words by N. Tate Servant to His Majesty. London : Printed for Richard Baldwin . . . MDCXCVIII. 4⁰, A—B 2 in fours.

Panacea : A Poem upon Tea : In Two Canto's. By N. Tate, Servant to His Majesty. . . . London : Printed by and for J. Roberts. 1700. 8⁰, A—D 4 in eights. Dedicated to Charles Montague Esq.

TAYLOR, JOHN, *the Water-Poet.*
Three Weekes, three daies, and three houres Observations and Travel, from London to Hambvrgh in Germanie : Amongst Jewes and Gentiles, with Descriptions of Townes and Towers, Castles and Cittadels, artificiall Gallowses, Naturall Hangmen : And Dedicated for the present, to the absent Oldcombian Knight Errant, Sʳ Thomas Coriat, Great Brittaines Error, and the worlds Mirror. By Iohn Taylor. London, Printed by Edward Griffin, and are to be sold by George Gybbs . . . 1617. 4⁰, A—F 2 in fours, A 1 blank. In prose.

An Arrant Thiefe, Whom
　　　　Euery Man may Trust :
　　　　In Word and Deed,
　　　　Exceeding true and iust.

With a Comparison betweene a Thiefe and a Booke. Written by Iohn Taylor: London. Printed for Henry Gosson, and are to be sold at Christ Church Gate. 1625. 8°, A—C in eights, first and last leaves blank.

The Fearefvll Svmmer: Or Londons Calamity, the countries courtesy, and both their misery. By Iohn Taylor. Oxford, Printed by Iohn Lichfield and William Turner, Printers to the famous Vniversity. 1625. 8°, A—B in eights, B 8 blank. *B. M.*

> The *Fearful Summer* ends on B 2, and on B 3 begins the tract *Against Swearing*, promised in the first Oxford edition. But, instead of forming it into a separate publication, Taylor added it to the second impression of his *Fearful Summer*. It appears likely, from being printed of a larger size than the rest, that the body of the piece against swearing is merely a broadside reissued in book form, with a leaf of preface, and a concluding one with " My farewell to the famous Vniuersity of Oxford." The latter is omitted in the reprint among the Works in 1630. Perhaps Taylor's hospitable reception at Oxford prompted him to change the tone of his allusion to the country in this reprint of the tract on the Plague.
> Crossley, part 2, No. 2575, in a volume with the Dudley arms on either side, having possibly belonged to Sir Robert Dudley, son of Robert, Earl of Leicester.

A Warning for Swearers and Blasphemers. Shewing Gods fearfull Iudgements against diuers for profaning his holy name by swearing. Necessary to be set vp and read in euery house, for the auoiding of Oaths. Printed at London for Francis Couls, . . . 1626. A large broadside in two columns, subscribed I. T. In verse.

Collier's Sale, August 1884, No. 1045.

A Meditation on the Passion. Printed at London by Thomas Harper. 1630. A broadside subscribed *Io. Tailor*. In verse.

Collier's Sale, August 1884, No. 1045.

A Iuniper Lecture. With the description of all sorts of women, good, and bad ; From the modest to the maddest, from the most Civil, to the scold Rampant, their praise and dispraise compendiously related. The second Impression, with many new Additions. . . . London: Printed by I. O. for William Ley, . . . 1639. 12°. A—K in twelves, including a frontispiece.

The Devil Turn'd Round-Head : Or. Plvto become a Brownist. Being a just comparison, how the Devil is become a Round-

Head ? In what manner, and how zealously (like them) he is affected with the moving of the Spirit. With the holy Sisters desire of Copulation (if he would seem Holy, Sincere, and Pure) were it with the Devill himself. As also, the Amsterdammian Definition of a Familist. [1641.] 4°, 4 leaves. With a strange cut on the title.

The Bible [This is a half-title followed by the title:] Verbum Sempiternum. Aberdene, Printed by John Forbes. 1670. a—h in eights. A thumb-book.

Sothebys, July 7, 1885, No. 134.

TAYLOR, SILAS, *Gentleman.*
The History of Gavel-Kind, With the Etymology thereof; Containing also an Assertion that our English Laws are for the most part Those that were used by the Antient Brytains, . . . To which is added a short History of William the Conquerour, Written in Latin by an Anonymous Author, in the time of Henry the First . . . London, Printed for John Starkey, . . . 1663. 4°. A, 4: a—b in fours: B—Ee in fours, Ee 4 a folded leaf. Dedicated to Sir Edward Harley.

TAYLOR, ZACHARY.
Popery, Superstition, Ignorance, and Knavery, Very Unjustly by a Letter in the General pretended ; But as far as was Charg'd, very fully proved upon the Dissenters that were concerned in the Surry Imposture. By Zach. Taylor. London : Printed for John Jones, at the Dolphin and Crown in St. Paul's Church-yard ; and Ephraim Johnson, Bookseller in Manchester, MDCXCVIII. 4°, A—D 2 in fours.

Popery, Superstition, Ignorance, and Knavery, Confess'd and fully Proved on the Surey Dissenters, From the Second Letter of an Apostate Friend, to Zach. Taylor. To which is added, A Refutation of Mr T. Jollie's Vindication of the Devil in Dugdale ; or, The Surey Demoniack. London, Printed for W. Reblewhite at the White Swan, and J. Jones, at the Dolphin and Crown in St. Paul's Church-yard, 1699. 4°. A, 3 leaves: B—E in fours: the *Refutation of Jolley*, with a new title, F—H 2 in fours.

TEMPLE, SIR WILLIAM, *Baronet.*
Miscellanea. The First Part . . . The Fourth Edition. London : Printed for Jacob Tonson . . . and Awnsham and John Churchill . . . 1705. . . . . Miscellanea. The Second Part. . . . The Fifth Edition. London : Printed for Ri.

Simpson, at the Three Trouts, and Ra. Simpson at the Harp in St Paul's Church-Yard. 1705. 8°. Title and the Stationer to the Reader, 2 leaves : B—Q 4 in eights : *Second Part*, title, *Temple's inscription to Cambridge University*, and 4 following leaves : B—Aa 2 in eights.

In the Preface by the stationer to the first portion, it is stated that the author, in consequence of the publication of certain books under his name since the appearance of the first edition, had accorded him leave to put his name on the title-page of this issue. The paper on Gardening, the second of the Second Part, is very interesting ; it presents us with a view of gardening in England in 1685, particularly in relation to the writer's historical grounds at Sheen.

TESTAMENT.

The Newe Testament yet once agayne corrected by Willyam Tindale : Where vnto is added a necessarye Table : Wherin easely and lightelye may be foûde any storye contaynd in the foure Euangelistes / and in the Actes of the Apostles . . . [Quotation from Mark xvi.] Prynted in the yere of oure Lorde God. M.D. and . xxxvij. Folio. Title, to the Reader, &c., 4 leaves : a—z in eights : A—H in eights : I, 10 : +, with the Table, 8 leaves.

THEODORET, *Bishop of Cyrus.*

The Ecclesiasticall History . . . Deuided into fiue Bookes. Written in Greeke aboue twelue hundred yeares agoe : And now translated into our English tongue, for the benefite of our Nation . . . Imprinted with Licence, Anno M.DC.XII. 4°. *—*** in fours : A—Ee in fours.

THEODULUS or THEODOLUS, *of Athens.*

Liber theodoli cum cōmento incipit feliciter. [This title is over a common cut. At the end :] Sanctissima explanatio Theodoli finit feliciter. With Richard Pynson's device below. [London, about 1506.] 4°, A—G in sixes : II, 8. *B. M.*

A second copy, wanting two leaves, is in the Grenville Collection.

Liber Theodoli cum commento Nouiter impressus Londonijs per Winandum de Worde hac ĩ vrbe in parrochia sãcte brigide ĩ the fletestrete ad signũ solis cōmorañ. [Col.] Sanctissima explanatio Theodoli finit feliciter. Impensis honesti viri Winandi de Worde Londonijs in vico vulgariter nuncupato (the fletestrete) co[m]morantis. Anno dñi Millesimo quingentesimo nono. Die vero . xxviij. mẽsis Aprilis. 4°. A, 8 : B, 4 : C, 8 : D, 4 : E, 8 : F, 6, with the printer's device on F 6 *verso. B. M.*

Liber Theodoli cum commento nouiter Londoniis impressus. [This title is over the common cut of the master and pupils. At the end we find :] Sanctissima explanatio Theodoli finit feliciter. Impensis honesti viri wynandi de worde Londoniis in vico vulgariter nuncupato (the fletezstrete) sub intersignio solio cōmorantis. Anno Millesimo quingētesimo decimo quīto. Die vero . x. mensis Martij. 4°, A—F in eights and fours, except that F has only six leaves. The printer's device is on F 6 *verso. B. M.* (Baynton's copy.)

I merely give the editions printed in London of this performance.

THEOPHANIA.

Theophania : Or Severall Modern Histories Represented by way of Romance : And Politically Discours'd upon ; By An English Person of Quality. . . . London, Printed by Thomas Newcomb for Thomas Heath, . . . 1655. 4°, A—Ff 2 in fours, A 1 blank. With a preface by the publisher.

THEOPHILUS.

Divine and Politike Observations Newly translated out of the Dutch language, wherein they were lately divulged. Upon Some Lines in the speech of the Arch. B. of Canterbury, pronounced in the Starre-Chamber upon 14. June, 1637. . . . Printed in the yeare of our Lord MDCXXXVIII. 4°, A—H in fours, besides title and Preface, 3 leaves.

The Preface, headed The Translator's Dedicatory Epistle, is subscribed *Theophilus,* who appears to have altered *Translators* with his pen into *Authors.*

THOMAS, DALBY.

An Historical Account of the Rise and Growth of the West-India Collonies, And of the Great Advantages they are to England, in respect to Trade. Licensed according to Order. London, Printed for Jo. Hindmarsh . . . 1690. 4°, A—H in fours, H 4 blank, and the title.

THOMPSON, JOHN, *of Bingley, co. York.*

A Glass, or Brief Description of two Great Errors, or Main Causes of all our Confusions in Church and Common-wealth ; the one in Teaching, and the other in Practice. [London, 1651-2.] 4°, A—D 2 in fours, besides a leaf of dedication to Cromwell, on the blank side of which is an autograph inscription by the author to the Lord General. Without a regular title.

Sothebys, June 11, 1884, No. 1236.

THOMPSON, ROBERT, *LL.D.*

Sponsa nondum Uxor : Or The Marriage between the Lady Katharine Fitz-Gerald and Edward Villiers Esq; Asserted by Robert Thompson LL.D. Being an Answer to a Treatise, intituled, Digamias Adikia, &c. Published under the name of Dudley Loftus . . . . London : Printed for Benjamin Tooke, . . . M.DC.LXXVII. 4°. A, 3 : B—D in fours : E, 6. Dedicated to Viscount Grandison.

THOMPSON, THOMAS.
Midsummer-Moon : Or, The Livery-Man's Complaint. By Tho. Thompson. London : Printed for E. Harris, 1680. 4°, A—C 2 in fours. In verse.

Toms-Son his Repetition to His Wife ; Bewailing his present state. To the Tune of, Young Jemmy. Printed for J. Deacon. . . . A broadside with music.

TILLINGHAST, JOHN.
Knowledge of the Times, Or, The resolution of the Question, how long it shall be unto the end of Wonders. . . . Printed at London by R. I. for L. Chapman, . . . 1654. 8°. A, 8 leaves, A 1 with the label : a, 8 leaves : B—Aa in eights. *B. M.*
The Museum possesses several other works of a similar character by this honest enthusiast.

TILLINGHAST, MARY.
Rare and Excellent Receipts. Experienced, and Taught by M⁰ˢ Mary Tillinghast. And now Printed for the Use of her Scholars only. London, Printed in the Year, 1678. 8°, A—B in eights. *B. M.*
Reprinted, 8°, 1690.

TITUS.
Titvs, Or The Palme of Christian Covrage : To be exhibited by the Schollars of the Society of Iesvs, at Kilkenny, Anno Domini 1644. . . . Printed at Waterford by Thomas Bourke, M. DC. XLIV. 4°, 2 leaves.
Sothebys, March 15, 1883, No. 1519. This dramatic piece is said in the Argument to relate the history of Titus, a noble Christian, whom the King of Bungo tried to convert, and the plot is taken from the Ecclesiastical History of Japan by Father Francis Solier, 1620.

TITUS, COLONEL SILAS.
Killing no Murder : . . . Reprinted in the Year 1689. 4°. A, 2 leaves : B—E 2 in fours.

TOBACCO.
An Ordinance of the Lords and Commons . . . Concerning the Excise of Tobacco. [Saturday, Dec. 23, 1643.] London, Printed by Richard Cotes and Joh. Raworth, 1643. 4°, 4 leaves.

An Ordinance . . . London, Printed by Richard Cotes and John Raworth. [1644.] 4°, 4 leaves.

TOKENS.
Here beginneth a lytel treatyse the whiche speketh of the xv. tokens the whiche shullen bee shewed afore ȳ drefull daye of Iugement. And who that oure lorde shalle aske rekenyng of euery body of his wordis workis and thoughtes. And who oure lorde wyll shewe vs other xv. tokens. of his passion vnto theym that been depeth in dedely synne. [Printed at Antwerp by John of Doesborch.] 4°, black letter, with woodcuts.
Sothebys, July 1, 1885, No. 1188, Heber's copy, A—D in sixes, but ending imperfectly. No other seems to be known.

[A Treatise of the xv. Tokens. On d 4 *recto* occurs :] Here endeth the lytill treatyse that whiche is called the xv tokens which been late translated oute of frenshe into Englishe. [And on d 5 *recto* we have :] Emprinted by me Iohan fro doesborch / dwellige at Anverpe by the Iron ballaunce. 4°. With woodcuts. *M. B.*
∴ This is complete with a—d in sixes, the last page being occupied by a Fleming in the costume, and with the appointments, of the time, who represents probably the Angel blowing the Last Trumpet. In his other hand he holds a sword. This copy wants a ii, c i-ii and vi, and d 5.

TOM HICKATHRIFT.
The most Pleasant and Delightful History of Thomas Hickathrift. Part the First. Printed and Sold at the Printing-Office in Bow-Church-Yard. 8°. With woodcuts. In two parts, and making 12 leaves.

TONGE, EZREEL.
Popish Mercy and Justice. Being An Account, not of those (more than an hundred Thousand) massacred in France by the Papists formerly, but of some later Persecutions of the French Protestants. Set forth in their Petition to the French King. Translated for the Information of English Protestants. By Ezreel Tonge, the first Discoverer of this most horrid Plot to His Majesty . . . London, Printed by Th. Dawks, . . . 1679. 4°, A—C 2 in fours.

TOOKE, GEORGE.
The Deplorable Tragedy of Floris The Fifth of that Name, Earle of Holland, Zealand, And Lord of Frisland. As it hath been Sojunctly left us by a Learned Netherlander : And is now digested into this entire piece. By G. T. Esq ; London, Printed for Charles Webb at the Bore's Head in St. Paul's Churchyard. 1659. 4°, A—F in fours, title on A 2. Dedicated to "My honorable friend Mr. Charles Fairfax."

TOOKER, WILLIAM.

Charisma Sive Donvm Sanationis. . . .
Londini Excudebat Iohannes Windet.
1597. 4°. *, 4 leaves : ¶, 4 leaves :
A—R 3 in fours. Dedicated to the
Queen.

This is said to be the earliest publication
on the Healing by touch.

TORTELLO, FR. ARCANGELO.

The Pope's Cabinet Unlocked : Or, A
Catalogue of all the Popes Indulgences
Belonging to the Order of S. Mary. With
a List of all the Indulgences . . . Translated into English by John Sidway . . .
Vicar of Selling in Kent. . . . Whereunto
is added an Appendix by the Translator,
. . . London, Printed for Isaac Cleve . . .
1680. 4°, A—S in fours. Dedicated to
the Earl of Shaftesbury.

TORY.

The Tory - Poets : A Satyr. ——*Nun-
quamne reponam* . . . Juven. Sat. 1. London, Printed by R. Johnson. MDCLXXXII.
4°, A—C 2 in fours. In verse.

TRADE.

A Discourse about Trade, Wherein the
Reduction of Interest of Money to £4 per
Centum, is Recommended. Methods for
the Employment and Maintenance of the
Poor are proposed. . . . Never before
Printed. Printed by A. Sowle, at the
Crooked-Billet in Holloway-Lane : . . .
1690. 8°. A, 4 leaves : B, 8 leaves : (A)—
(E) in eights, and (d) 4 leaves between (C)
and (D) : A (repeated)—P in eights, P 8
blank.

TRAHERON, BARTHOLOMEW.

An Exposition of the 4. Chapter of S.
Johns Reuelation, made by Bar. Tra-
heron, in sundry Readings before his
countrimen in Germany. Wherein the
Prouidence of God is treated, with an
answere made to the obiection of a gentle
aduersarie. Imprinted at London by
Henry Bynneman for Humfrey Toy.
Anno. 1573. Small 8°, black letter, G 4
in eights, G 4 blank. Dedicated "To
master Ro. Parker, and to maistres Anne
his Godly wife, exiles for Christes cause."

TRAITORS.

The Oglio of Traytors ; Including the
Illegal Tryall of his late Maiesty. With
a Catalogue of their names that sat as
Judges and consented to the Judgment: . . .
With the whole proceedings against Colo-
nel J. Penruddock of Compton in Wilts.
. . . . As also, the speech of that resolved
Gentleman, Mr Hugh Grove of Chissen-
bury Esquire. London, Printed by T. M.

for William Shears . . . [1660.] 8°. Title,
&c., 6 leaves : B—M in eights.

The proceedings in the Penruddock case
have a new title dated 1660.

TRANSPROSER.

The Transproser Rehears'd : Or the Fifth
Act of Mr Bayes's Play. Being a Postscript to the Animadversions on the Preface to Bishop Bramhall's Vindication, &c.
. . . Oxford, Printed for the Assignes of
Hugo Grotius, and Jacob Van Harmine,
on the North-side of the Lake-Lemane.
1673. 8°, B—L 3 in eights and the title.

TRAVELS.

A Collection of Curious Travels & Voyages. In Two Tomes. The First containing Dr Leonhart Rauwolff's Itinerary
into the Eastern Countries, as Syria, . . .
Translated from the High Dutch by
Nicholas Staphorst. The Second taking
in many parts of Greece. . . . from the
Observations of Mons. Belon, . . . To
which are added. Three Catalogues of
such Trees, Shrubs, and Herbs as grow in
the Levant. By John Ray, Fell. of the
Royal Society. London, Printed for S.
Smith and B. Walford, . . . 1693. 8°.
A, 8. including half-title : a, 8 : B—Nn 4
in eights ; the Catalogues, A—C 4 in
eights, A 1 with half-title. Dedicated to
the Royal Society.

TREASURE.

Here begynneth a good booke of mede-
cines called the Treasure of pore men.
[Col.] Here endeth this boke of Mede-
cynes called the Treasure of pore me.
Imprynted at London in Fletestrete by
wyllyam Myddylton / dwellynge at the
signe of the George nexte to saynt Dunstons churche. The yere of our Lorde.
M. CCCCC. XLIIII. The XIII. daye of December. 8°. A, 4 leaves : B—K in eights.

TREATISE.

A Treatise : Wherein is declared the sufficiencie of English Medicines, for cure of
all diseases, cured with Medicine. At
London, Printed by Henrie Middleton,
for Thomas Man. Anno. 1580. 4°, A—
F in fours. Dedicated to Lord Zouch.

A Treatise of the Execution of Justice,
wherein is clearly proved, that the Execution of Judgement and Justice, is as
well the Peoples as the Magistrates Duty ;
And that if Magistrates pervert Judgement, the People are bound by the Law
of God to execute Judgement without
them, and upon them. [*Circâ* 1650.] 4°,
A—D in fours.

Without any title-page.

TRIBULATION.

The . xii. profytes of tribulacyon. [This title is on a ribbon over a woodcut of the crucifixion. At the end occurs :] Thus endeth this treatyse / shewyng the . xii. pfytes of tribulacyon. Imprinted at London in Fletestrete at the sygne of the sonne by Wynkyn de Worde. The yere of our lord. M.CCCCC.XXX. the . xxviii. day of Maye. 4⁰. A, 6 : B, 4 : C, 6 : D, 4.

TRYE, JOHN, *of Gray's-Inn, Esquire.*

Jus Filizarii : Or, The Filacer's Office in the Court of King's - Bench. Setting forth the Practice by Original Writ, . . . London, Printed, by the Assigns of R. and E. Atkyns, Esquires, for Richard Tonson . . . 1684. 8⁰. A, 4 leaves : B—S in eights : T, 4 : U, 2. Dedicated to Lord Keeper Guilford.

The present copy has the armorial book-plate of "The Right Honble William Earl of Portland Viscount Woodstock and Baron of Cirencester Knight of the Most Noble Order of the Garter 1704."

TRYE, M.

Medicatrix, Or the Woman Physician : Vindicating Thomas O Dowde, a Chymicall Physician, and Royall Licentiate, and Chymistry, against the Calumnies and abusive Reflections of Henry Stubbe a Physician at Warwick. Stubbe in nomination with Cicero. . . . The Life of M^r O Dowde ; . . . The Second Part. The Authors opinion of Learning ; . . . A Revival of M^r O Dowds Medicines ; . . . Written by M. Trye the Daughter of M^r O Dowde . . . London, Printed by T. R. & N. T. and Sold by Henry Broome . . . 1675. 8⁰. A, 4 leaves : B—K 4 in eights. Dedicated to Lady Fisher, wife of Sir Clement Fisher, of Packington Hall, co. Warwick.

TRYON, THOMAS.

Friendly Advice to the Gentlemen-Planters of the East and West Indies. In Three Parts. . . . By Philotheos Physiologus. Printed by Andrew Sowle, in the Year 1684. 8⁰, B—P in eights, P 8 blank, and the title. Without prefixes.

TURKEY.

The Great Tvrkes Defiance : Or his Letter Denvntiatorie to Sigismund the Third, now King of Polonia, as it hath beene truly aduertised out of Germany, this present yeere, 1613. With the King of Poland his replie, Englished according to the French Copie. By M. S. London, Printed by Melchisedech Bradwood, for William Aspley. 1613. 4⁰, A—C in fours, A 1 and C 4 blank. *B. M.*

Ottoman Gallantries : Or The Life of Bassa of Buda. Done out of French. London : Printed for R. Bentley and S. Magnes . . . 1687. 12⁰. Title and dedication to William, Lord Cavendish, by B. Berenclow, the translator, 2 leaves : B—M in twelves : N, 4.

TURNER, JOHN, *M.A.*

A Discourse on Fornication : Shewing the Greatness of that Sin ; And Examining the Excuses pleaded for it, . . . By J. Turner, M.A. Lecturer of Christ-Church, London. . . . London : Printed for John Wyat, at the Rose in St. Paul's Church-Yard. MDCXCVIII. 4⁰, B—I in fours, besides title and contents, 2 leaves.

TURNER, WILLIAM, *M.A.*

The History of all Religions in the World : From the Creation down to the Present Time. In Two Parts . . . With Various Instances upon Every Head. To which is added, A Table of Heresies : As Also A Geographical Map, shewing in what Countrey Each Religion is Practised. . . . By William Turner, M.A. and Vicar of Walberton in Sussex. . . . London, Printed for John Dunton . . . 1695. 8⁰, A—Xx in eights. Dedicated to Robert, Bishop of Chichester.

TURNER, WILLIAM, *M.D.*

Libellus de Re Herbaria Novvs, in quo herbarum aliquot nomina, græca, latina, & Anglica habes, vna cum nominibus officinarum, in gratiam studiose inuentutis nunc primum in lucem ædibus. [Col.] Londini Apvd Ioannem Byddellum. Anno dñi 1538. 4⁰, A—C 2 in fours. *B. M.*

Turner's earliest publication. The only introductory matter is a Latin address by the author to the Reader on the back of the title-page. which is enclosed in a broad engraved border.

The hunting of the Fox and the Wolfe, because they make hauocke of the sheepe of Christ Iesus. Take heede of false prophetes, . . . [About 1569.] 8⁰, black letter, A—E 4 in eights.

Sothebys, July 1, 1885. No. 1211. Heber's copy, formerly Rawlinson's and Forster's, with a note by Heber, shewing that it is a reprint of the *Hunting of the Romish Wolf* under a new title. and printed about, but before, 1569, as Bishop Bonner is mentioned as living. On B the head-line is : A Dialogue betweene the Foster, the Hunter, and the Deane. A preface by Knox occupies in this republication the place of the dedication and poem *The Romyshe Foxe lately returned,* &c.

TWYN, JOHN, *Stationer.*

An Exact Narrative of the Tryal and

Condemnation of John Twyn, for printing and dispersing of a Treasonable Book, With the Tryals of Thomas Brewster, Bookseller, Simon Dover, Printer, Nathan Brooke, Bookbinder; For Printing, Publishing, and Uttering of Seditious, Scandalous, and Malitious Pamphlets. At Justice-Hall in the Old-Bayly London, the 20ᵗʰ and 22ᵗʰ of February 166¾. Published by Authority. London, Printed by Thomas Mabb for Henry Brome . . . 1664. 4°, A—L in fours.

TWYNE, THOMAS.

A View of certain wonderful effects, of late dayes come to passe: and now newly conferred with the presignyfications of the Comete, or blasing Star, which appered in the Southwest vpō the . x. day of Nouem. the yere last past. 1577. Written by T. T. this . 28. of Nouember. 1578. [Col.] Imprinted at London by Richarde Jhones, and are to be sould ouer against Saint Sepulchres Church without Newgate. 1. Decem. 1578. 4°, black letter, A—C in fours. With a large cut of the Blazing Star on the title. *B. M.* (Bright's copy.)

Dedicated by Twyne to Master Giles Lambert.

TYMME, THOMAS.

A Dialogve Philosophicall. Wherein Natvres Secret Closet is opened, and the Cavse of all Motion in Natvre shewed ovt of Matter and Forme, . . . Together with the wittie inuention of an Artificiall perpetuall motion, presented to the Kings most excellent Maiestie. All which are discoursed betweene two speakers, Philadelph, and Theophrast, brought together by Thomas Tymme, Professour of Diuinitic . . . London, Printed by T. S. for Clement Knight, . . . 1612. 4°, A—K in eights. Dedicated to Sir Edward Coke.

TYNDALE, WILLIAM.

An Exposicion vpon the . v. vi. vii. chapters of Mathew, which thre chapters are ỹ keye & the dore of the scripture, and the restoring agayne of Moyses lawe, . . . [Col.] Imprynted At London, at the signe of the Hyll, at the west dore of Paules, By Wyllyam Hill. And there to be sold. 8°, A—N in eights.

U.

JNIVERSITY.

The Pollution of Vniuersitie-Learning, Or, Sciences (Falsely so called) Whereby most of the youth are so infected, . . . that when they come to age, they prove either unprofitable or hurtfull Members to the Common-wealth, . . . London, Printed in the yeare, Anno Dom. 1642. 4°, 8 leaves.

JRINES.

Hereafter foloweth the Judgemēt of all Urynes: And for to knowe the mānes from the womannes / and beastes both from the mānes & womans / with the coloure of euerye Uryne. Exercysed & Practysed with dynerse other by Doctor Smyth and other at Mountpyller. [Col.] Here endeth the boke of Seyng of Waters. Imprynted by me Robert Wyer: . . . 8°, black letter. A—I in fours, I 4 verso with the device. *B. M.*

Here begynneth the seynge of Vrynes of all the coloures that Vrynes be of / with the medicynes annexed to euery Vryne,

and euery Vryne his Vrynall muche profytable for euery man to knowe. [Col.] . . . Imprinted at London in Fletestrete at the sygne of the George neare to saynct Dunstons churche by Wyllyam Powel. In the yere of our Lorde. MD.XLVIII. The . XVI . day of September. 8°, A—F in eights.

URSULA, ST.

The confraternyte of seynt Vrsula in seynt Laurence in the Jury. [These words are printed at top and bottom of a woodcut of the Saint standing with a javelin in her right hand with figures at her feet. Below is a seated figure of her on a square white-grounded block enclosed in a circular border with the inscription: *Sancta vrsula cum sodalibus tuis ora pro nobis.*] A small broadside, possibly forming part of some other publication. *B. M.*

USURY.

Vsvrie Araigned and Condemned. Or A Discouerie of the infinite Iniuries this Kingdome endureth by the vnlawfull trade of Vsvrie. London, Printed by W. S. for Iohn Smethwicke, . . . 1625. 4", A—D in fours, A 1 blank. *B. M.*

The Death of Vsvry, Or, The Disgrace of Vsvrers. Compiled more pithily then hitherto hath beene published in English. . . . London, Printed by I. L. for Robert Allot . . . 1634. 4", A—F in fours, A 1 blank.

A Discourse of Usury: Or Lending Money for Increase. (Occasioned by Mr David Jones's late Farewel Sermon). . . London: Printed for Samuel Cronch . . . 1692. 4". A, 2 leaves: B—F 2 in fours.

V.

V. P.
Narratio Historica Vicissitvdinis Rervm, que in inclyto Britanniæ Regno acciderunt, Anno Domini 1553 Mense Iulio. 1553. 8", A—B in eights. B 6 with a Genealogical Table of the Tudors, and B 7-8 blank.

VALENTINE AND ORSON.
Valentine and Orson, . . . London, Printed by A. Purslow for T. Passinger. . . . 4", black letter, A—Gg in fours, A 1 with the frontispiece. With cuts.

VALENTINE, BASIL.
The Last Will and Testament of Basil Valentine, Monke of the Order of St. Bennet. Which being alone, He hid under a Table of Marble, behind the High-Altar of the Cathedral Church, in the Imperial City of Erford, . . . To which is added Two Treatises . . . Never before published in English. London, Printed by S. G. and B. G. for Edward Brewster . . . 1671. 8", A—Nn in eights, and b, 4 leaves. With cuts and a folded diagram.

Basil Valentine His Triumphant Chariot of Antimony, With Annotations of Theodore Kirkringius, M.D. With the True Booke of the Learned Synesius a Greek Abbot taken out of the Emperour's Library, concerning the Philosopher's Stone. London Printed for Dorman Newman . . . 1678. 8°, A - M in eights. With plates at pp. 82, 96, 101, 128, and 133, that at 82 repeated in the copy before me as a frontispiece.

VALERA, CIPRIANO.
Two Treatises: The first, Of the Lives of the Popes, and their Doctrine. The Second, Of the Masse : . . . The second edition in Spanish augmented by the Author himselfe, M. Cyprian Valera, and translated into English by Iohn Golburn. 1600. Printed at London by Iohn Harison, . . . 1600. 4". A. 6 : B, 8 : C- Ee in fours : Ff, 6 leaves. Dedicated to Sir Thomas Egerton, Lord Keeper.

VANBRUGH, SIR JOHN.
A Defence of Dramatick Poetry : Being A Review of Mr Collier's View of the Immorality and Profaneness of the Stage. London : Printed for Eliz. Whitlock, . . . 1698. 8°. First Part, B—I 3 in eights, besides title and Preface dated from Lincoln's Inn, May 26, 1698. Part 2, B—F 4 in eights, besides half-title and Preface.

VANE, SIR HENRY.
A pilgrimage into the land of promise, By the light of the vision of Jacobs ladder and faith ; . . . Written in the year 1662, by Henry Vane, Knight, towards the latter end of his prison-state ; by himself reviewed and perfected, . . . Printed in the yeare 1664. 4°, A—O in fours, and the title.

VAN SLOETTEN, CORNELYS.
The Isle of Pines, Or, A late Discovery of a fourth Island near Terra Australis Incognita By Henry Cornelius Van Sloetten. Wherein is contained, A True Relation of certain English persons, who in Queen Elizabeths time, making a Voyage to the East Indies were cast away, and wracked near to the Coast of Terra Australis Incognita and all drowned, except one Man and four women. And now lately Anno Dom. 1667, a Dutch Ship making a Voyage to the East Indies, driven by bad weather there, by chance have found their Posterity.(speaking good English) to amount (as they suppose) to ten or twelve thousand persons. The whole Relation (written and left by the

Man himself a little before his death, and delivered to the Dutch by his Grandchild) is here annexed with the Longitude and Latitude of the Island, the scituation and felicity thereof, with other matter observable. . . . London, Printed for Allen Banks and Charles Harper, next door to the three Squerrills in Fleetstreet, over against St. Dunstons Church, 1668. 4", A—Ee in fours, A 1 blank.

" A rather dull mystification by a tolerably obscure writer. The island is supposed to be inhabited by the descendants of an Englishman, George Pines, amounting in the fourth generation to about ten thousand persons. The details are necessarily of a coarse and indecent character. " The author of *American Nuggets* included the book in his list of Americana."— *Quaritch*, 1882.

VAN VEEN OR VÆNIUS, OTTO, *of Leyden.*
Amorvm Emblemata, Figvris Æneis Incisa Stvdio Ottonis Væni Batavo-Lvgdvnensis. Emblemes of Loue. With verses in Latin, English, and Italian. Antwerpiæ, Venalia apud Auctorem. M. DC. IIX. [1608.] Oblong 4". Title and dedication to William, Earl of Pembroke, and Philip, Earl of Montgomery, by Van Veen from Antwerp, Aug. 20, 1608, 2 leaves : verses by Heinsius, Verstegan, &c., 6 leaves : A—Hb in fours.

VAUGHAN, RICE, *of Gray's Inn.*
Practica Walliæ ; Or the Proceedings in the Great Sessions of Wales : Containing the Method and Practice of an Attorney there, . . . Whereunto is added, The Old Statuts of Wales at large ; . . . By Rice Vaughan, late of Grays-Inne Esquire. London, Printed for Henry Twyford, . . . 1672 . . . 12". A, 6 leaves : B—K in twelves.

A posthumous publication, dedicated by J. M. to Sir Job Charleton, Chief Justice of Chester, and three other gentlemen.

A Discourse of Coin and Coinage : The first Invention, Use, Matter, Forms, Proportions, and Differences, ancient and modern . . . Together with a short Account of our Common Law therein. As also Tables of the Value of all sorts of Pearls, . . . London, Printed by Th. Dawks, for Th. Basset, . . . 1675. 12". A, 6 : B—L in twelves : M, 6. Dedicated by the author's near kinsman, Henry Vaughan, to the Earl of Clarendon.

VAUGHAN, ROBERT, *Esquire, of Hengwrt.*
British Antiquities revived : Or A friendly Contest touching the soveraignty of the three Princes of Wales in ancient times, managed with certain arguments, Whereunto answers are applyed. To which is added the Pedigree of the right Honourable the Earl of Carbery, Lord President of Wales : with A Short account of the five Royall Tribes of Cambria, by the same Author. . . . Oxford, Printed by Hen: Hall, Printer to the University, for Thomas Robinson. 1662. 4", A—G 2 in fours. Dedicated to Sir Richard Wynne of Gwedir.

VAUGHAN, SIR WILLIAM, *of Rûg.*
Natvrall and Artificial Directions for health, derived from the best Philosophers, as well moderne, as auncient. By William Vaughan, Master of Artes, and student in the Ciuill law. London Printed by Richard Bradocke. 1600. 8", A—F in eights, first and last leaves blank. Dedicated to his sister, Lady Margaret Vaughan, from Jesus College, Oxford, April 1, 1600. *B. M.*

Directions for Health, . . . The seventh Edition reviewed by the Author. Whereunto is annexed Two Treatises of approved Medicines [by Dr. Baily and others.] London : Printed by Thomas Harper for Iohn Harison. 1633. 4", A—Ee in fours.

VAVASOR, FRANCIS.
Francisi Vavassoris Societ. Jesu De Epigrammate Liber et Epigrammatum Libri Tres. Editio auctior. Parisiis. . . . M.DC.LXXXII. . . . 8", A—Qq 3 and A—T 4, in fours, the second part having a separate half-title.

VENICE.
A True Copie of the Sentence of the high Councell of tenne Judges in the State of Venice, Against Ridolfo Poma, Michael Viti Priest, Alessandro Parrasio, John of Florence, the sonne of Paul and Pasquall of Bitonto ; who of late most trayterously attempted a bloudy and horrible Murder vpon the person of the reuerend Father Dr Paolo Servite, . . . Faithfully translated out of Italian. At London, Printed by Hunifrey Lownes, for Samuel Macham, . . . 1608. 4", A—D in fours, D 4 blank.

On D 1 occurs : *Farther Intelligence from Venice*, 1 leaf, which is followed by two copies of Latin verses, *In Innocentiam* and *In Meretricem dolosam.*

The History of the Qvarrels of Pope Pavl V. with the State of Venice. In Seven Books. Faithfully translated out of the Italian, and compared with the Printed Copie. London, Printed by John Bill. . . . M.DC.XXVI. 4". ¶, 2 leaves : ¶¶,

4 : A—3 K 2 in fours. Dedicated by C. P. to Sir Thomas Coventry, Keeper of the Great Seal, whom the translator calls his "sincerely and thankefully devoted."

Dominium Maris : Or, The Dominion of the Sea. Expressing the Title, which the Venetians pretend unto the sole dominion, and absolute Sovereigntie of the Adriatick Sea, commonly called The Gulph of Venice. Manifested in a Pleading, or Argument, betwixt the Republick of Venice and the Emperor Ferdinand. . . . Translated out of Italian. London, Printed by William Du-Gard. An. Dom. 1650. 4°, A—D in fours.

The Preface is subscribed *Clareamontos.*

A Journal of the Venetian Campaign, A.D. 1687. Under the Conduct of the Capt. General Morosini, General Coningsmark, Providitor Gen. Cornaro, General Venieri, &c. Translated from the Italian Original, sent from Venice. . . . London : Printed by H. C. and Sold by R. Taylor . . . 1688. 4°, A—G 2 in fours. With a map.

The Pleasant Intrigues and Surprizing Adventures of an English Nobleman at the Last Carnival at Venice. By a Person of Quality. London, Printed for J. How, . . . and M. Hotham, . . . 1707. 12°, A—G 6 in twelves.

VENN, THOMAS, AND OTHERS.
Military & Maritine [*sic*] Discipline In Three Books. Book I. Military Observations or Tacticks put into Practice for the Exercise of Horse and Foot ; . . . By Captain Thomas Venn. Book II. An Exact Method of Military Architecture, . . . Rendered into English by John Lacey, out of the Works of . . . Andrew Tacquet. . . . Book III. The Compleat Gunner, . . . Translated out of Casimir, . . . London, Printed by E. Tyler and R. Holt for Rob. Pawlet . . . 1672. Folio. General title, 1 leaf : A, 2 leaves : a—c, 2 leaves each : B—3 G in twos : the *Architecture*, title and dedication, 2 leaves : Bb—Pp, 2 leaves each : the *Gunner*, 3 B —3 Z, 2 leaves each, besides title and preface, 2 leaves : the third part of the *Gunner*, 4 A 2—4 T, 2 leaves each. With folded plates in part 2 of the *Gunner* at pp. 70 and 72, and in part 3 at page 1 (2), and at the end (8).

VERGIL, POLYDORE, *of Urbino.*
An Abridgemēt of the notable worke of Polidore Vergile conteygnyng the denisers and first finders out aswell of Actes, Ministeries, Feastes, cinill ordinaunces, as of Rites, & Ceremonies, commonly vsed in the churche and the originall beginnyng of the same. Compendiousely gathered by Thomas Langley. Imprinted at London within the precincte of the late dissolued house of the grey Friers, by Richarde Grafton . . . M. D. XLVI. . . . [In the colophon is added :] xxv. daie of Ianuarie. 8°, black letter. A, 8 leaves : a—x in eights, x 7 with colophon and x 8 blank.

An abridgement of the notable worke of Polidore Vergile . . . 1551. Mense Iulij. [Col.] Imprinted at London, by Richard Grafton, Printer to the Kynges Maiestie. Anno. 1551. Cum priuilegio. . . . 8°. A, 7 leaves (A 8 hauing probably been blank) : a—v 6 in eights. *B. M.*

A Pleasant and Compendious History of the first Inventers and Instituters of the most Famous Arts, Misteries . . . in the whole World. . . . To which is Added, Several Curious Inventions, peculierly Attributed to England & English-men. . . . London, Printed for John Harris, . . . 1686. 12°. A, 6 : B—H in twelves : I, 6.

The Preface is signed with the initials of the publisher.

VERNON, CHRISTOPHER, *of the Exchequer.*
Considerations for regulating the Exchequer, in the more timely answering, better husbanding, and more orderly and due conduct of the Revenues of the Crown into his Majesties Coffers, as hath been heretofore used by Sheriffes. . . . Printed by Tho. Harper, . . . 1642. 8°. A, 4 leaves : B—H in eights : I, 4. Dedicated to Sir John Culpeper, Knight, Chancellor and Under-Treasurer of the Exchequer.

VERNON, SAMUEL.
News from Hell : Or, The Devils Court in an Uproar. His Devilships falling Sick, upon the News of the Pope and Poperies likely Downfall. His Last Will and Testament. His Legacies to the Pope and Jesuits ; and to other Sinners in particular. Written by S. V. London, Printed for R. G. MDCLXXIII. 4°, 4 leaves.

VERON, JOHN.
A Dictionarie in Latine and English, heretofore set forth by Master Iohn Veron, and now newlie corrected and enlarged. For the vtilitie and profit of all young students, . . . by R. W. Imprinted at London by Rafe Newberie and Henrie

Denham . . . 1584. 4°, A—Vv in eights, Vv 8 blank. In two columns.

VICARY, THOMAS, *Esquire.*

A profitable Treatise of the Anatomie of mans body : Compyled by that excellent Chirurgion, M. Thomas Vicary Esquire, Seriaunt Chirurgion to King Henry the eyght, to King Edward th . vj. to Queene Mary, and to our most gracious Soueraigne Lady Queene Elizabeth, and also chiefe Chirurgion to S. Bartholomewes Hospital. Which work is newly reuyued, correcred, and published by the Chirurgions of the same Hospital now beeing. 1577. Imprinted at London, by Henry Bamforde, 8°. ¶, 8 leaves : A—N 4 in eights. *B. M.*

> The book is published or edited by William Bremer.

The Englishe-mans Treasure : With the true Anatomie of Mans bodie : . . . Also the rare treasure of the English Bathes, written by William Turner, Doctor in Phisicke . . . At London, Imprinted by George Robinson for Iohn Perin, . . . 1587. 4°, A—P in fours. Dedicated to the President, Masters, &c., of Bartholomew's Hospital.

The English Mans Treasure : . . . London Printed by Thomas Creede. 1596. 4°, black letter, A—P in fours.

VIGO, GIOVANNI.

The most excellent workes of Chirurgerye, made and set forth by maister John Vigon, heed Chirurgiã of our tyme in Italie, translated into english. Whereunto is added an exposition of straunge termes and vnknowen symples, belonging to the arte. Imprynted by Edwarde Whytchurch, wyth the kynges moste gratious priuelege for seuen yeares. . . . 1543. Folio, black letter, in two columns. ✠, 6 leaves : A—Zz in sixes, followed by 10 leaves, the last blank.

> Dedicated by Bartholomew Traheron, the translator, to the truest favourer of all good and godly learning, Master Richard Tracy, at whose request he had undertaken the work.

VILLIERS, GEORGE, *Second Duke of Buckingham.*

A Reply to His Grace the Duke of Buckinghams Letter to the Author of a Paper, Entituled, *An Answer to His Graces Discourse* . . . London, Printed by W. D. for Thomas Graves, 1685. Folio, 2 leaves.

VINDEX.

Vindex Anglievs : Or, The Perfections of the English Langvage. Defended, and asserted. Printed, Anno Dom. 1644. 4°, 4 leaves.

VINTNERS.

An Ordinance . . . for Freeing and discharging the Vintners, From any Demand for, or concerning any Delinquencies, concerning the Imposition of 40s. per Tunne on Wines or any thing concerning the same, Except the persons herein excepted. Printed by T. W. for Ed. Husband, May the 12. 1645. 4°, 4 leaves.

VIOLET, THOMAS.

A True Discovery to the Commons of England, How they have been Cheated of almost all the Gold and Silver Coyn of this Nation, . . . By Thomas Violet . . . London, Printed by W. B. and are to be sold by W. Sheares . . . 1650. 12°, A—D in twelves.

Proposals Humbly Presented to his Highness Oliver Lord Protector of England, &c. and to the High Court of Parliament, now assembled ; For the calling to a true and just Accompt all Committee-men, Sequestrators, Treasurers, . . . With Several Reasons for the doing thereof . . . . Also, For the Regulating of the Manufacture of Gold and Silver Thread and Wyer, and for the Passing an Act against Transporting Gold and Silver, and against Melting down the Currant Silver Monies of the Nation. Likewise, A Narrative of the Proceedings in the Court of Admiraltie against the Silver - Ships, Sampson, Salvador, and George. By Tho. Violet of London Goldsmith. . . . London, Printed Anno Domini M.DC.LVI. Folio. Frontispiece and title, 2 leaves : B—O, 2 leaves each : a—ee, 2 leaves each : G—Ce, 2 leaves each.

VIRGILIUS MARO, PUBLIUS.

[Bucolica cum commento. At the end :] Publii Maronis buccolica carmina vtcunmq; exposita. Impressa per Wynandum de Worde Londonijs commorantem in vico anglice nuncupato (the Flete strete) in signo solis aurei. Anno dñi. M.CCCCC [xij.] Die vero. viij. Aprilis. 4°, (presumably) A—F in eights and fours, F 4 with the device. *B. M.*

> This copy commences on D 1, and is mutilated and cropped.

Virgiliana Poesis . . . R. Pynson. 8°.

> See Herbert, p. 288. He speaks of it being in the collection of Mr. Wodall [Wodhull]; but I do not observe any such book in the Wodhull Catalogue, 1886, when that library was dispersed by auction.

The Works of Publius Virgilius Maro.

Translated by John Ogilby . . . London. Printed by Thomas Maxey for Andrew Crooke, . . . 1650. 8°, A—Dd 4 in eights. With a portrait of Ogilby and a frontispiece by W. Marshall.

An Essay Vpon two of Virgil's Eclogues, and Two Books of His Æneis (If this be not enough) Towards the Translation of the whole. By James Harrington. *Ce ne sont pas nos folies qui me font rire, Ce sont nos sagesses.*—Montaigne. London, Printed by T. C. for Thomas Brewster. 1658. 8°, A—D in eights, D 8 blank.

Didos death. Translated out of the best of Latine Poets, into the best of vulgar Languages. (***) By one that hath no name [? Robert Stapylton.] London : Printed by N. O. for Walter Burre. 1622. Small 12°, A and B in twelves, C in four. A 1 and C 4 blank. *Bodleian.*

> This book was licensed to Walter Burre, Dec. 11, 1621, as "A booke called *Deus nobis hæc otia fecit,* or Dedo's death, extracted out of the best of Latin poets to English. To be printed in Latine and English together."

The Fourth Booke of Æneis. Translated by Robert Stapylton. London [privately printed, ? 1634]. Small 8°, A—D in eights. Dedicated to Lady Twisleton.

> Licensed to William Cooke. Nov. 11, 1634. This appears to be the same work as that of 1622 ; but I have had no opportunity of comparing them.

VIRGINIA.

A Trve and Sincere declaration of the purpose and ends of the Plantation begun in Virginia, of the degrees which it hath receiued ; and meanes by which it hath beene aduanced : and the resolution and conclusion of His Maiesties Councel of that Colony, . . . Set forth by the authority of the Gouernors and Councellors established for that Plantation. . . . At London. Printed for I. Stepney, and are to be sold at the signe of the Crane in Paules Churchyard. 1610. 4°, A—D in fours, first and last leaves blank.

> A curious list of the persons required as Colonists occurs at the end.

A Declaration of the State of the Colonie and Affaires in Virginia : With The Names of the Aduenturers, and Summes aduentured in that Action. By his Maiesties Counsell for Virginia. 22 Iunij. 1620. London : Printed by T. S. 1620. 4°, A—B in fours : Notes of the Shipping, &c., 4 leaves : C—F in fours, A 1 and F 4 blank : Names of Aduenturers, 2 leaves : Orders and Constitutions, A—E in fours (without a regular title) : A Briefe Declaration of the present state of things in Virginia, A in fours, with a head-line only.

A Short Collection of the Most Remarkable Passages from the originall to the dissolution of the Virginia Company. London, Printed by Richard Cotes for Edward Husband, . . . 1651. 4°, A—C in fours.

A New Map of Virginia and Mary-Land And the Improved Parts of Penn-Sylvania & New-Jersey. Sold by Christopher Browne at the Globe near the West end of St. Pauls Church London. A sheet.

> Sothebys, Nov. 1885, No. 2046.

The Fair Traders Objections, Against the Bill, Entituled, A Bill for preventing Clandestine Trading, as it relates to the Plantations of Virginia and Maryland. A broadside.

VIRTUE.

A Pindarique Ode, Describing the Excellency of true Virtue, with Reflections on the Satyr against Virtue. . . . London, Printed in the Year 1679. 4°, 4 leaves.

VIRVESIUS, F. ALFONSUS.

F. Alfonsi Virvesii Vlmetani theologi, Canariensis episcopi, de matrimonio regis Angliæ, Tractatus . . . Impressvm recens, Anno M.D.LXI. 4°, A—I in fours. Roman letter.

VIVES, JOHANNES LUDOVICUS.

A very frutefull and pleasant boke called the Instructiõ of a Christẽ womã / made fyrst in Laten / and dedicated vnto the quenes good grace by the right famous clerke mayster Lewes Vines / and turned out of Laten into Englysshe by Rycharde Hyrd. . . . [Col.] Imprinted at London in Fletestrete / in the house of Thomas Berthelet nere to the Cundite / at the sygne of Lucrece. Cum priuilegio a rege indulto. 4°. A, 3 leaves, with title in a border of boys and elephants, and dedication to Queen Katherine : B—Y in fours : a—r in fours : s, 6 leaves. *B. M.*

> Following the dedication of Hyrd to the Queen, comes the original Preface of Vives, addressed to the same lady, and dated from Bruges, April 5, 1523. The present copy, formerly Mr. Grenville's, bears on the title the autograph, " Roger Twysden, 1637."

A Very Frvtefvl and Pleasant boke callyd the Instrvction of a Christen woman, . . . [Col.] Impress. Londini in ædibus Thomæ Berth. regij impressoris Cvm priuilegio ad imprimendum solum. Anno M.D.XLI. 4°. A, 6 leaves : B—Z in fours : a—n in fours. *B. M.* (Herbert's and Tasker's copy.)

In this edition Hyrd's dedication to the Queen is withdrawn.

VOKINS, JOAN.
God's Mighty Power Magnified: As Manifested and Revealed in his Faithful Handmaid Joan Vokins, who departed this Life the 22ᵈ of the 9ᵗʰ Month, 1690, ... London: Printed for Thomas Northcott, . . . 1691. 8°. A, 4 leaves: a, 8: B—K 2 in eights.

VOLCANOES.
The Vulcano's: Or, Burning and Fire-vomiting Mountains, Famous in the World: With their Remarkables. Collected for the most part out of Kircher's Subterraneous World; And expos'd to more general view in English, . . . London, Printed by J. Darby, for John Allen; . . . 1669. 4°, A—K 2 in fours, and the frontispiece.

VOWELL, JOHN, *alias* **HOOKER,** *of Exeter.*
Orders enacted for Orphans and for their portions within the Citie of Excester, with Sundry other instructions incident to the same. Collected and set foorth by Iohn Vowell alias Hooker gentleman and Chamberlaine of the same Citie. [Quot. from Psalm 82, *Doo right to the poore* . . .] Imprinted at London by Iohn Allde. 4°,

A—F in fours: *The Charter* [of Elizabeth] *for the order for the Orphans* . . . A—B in fours: *Act of Parliament* [of the same], E (no C—D)—H in fours, besides the *Errata*, 1 leaf, and G 1 repeated. Dedicated to the Mayor and Senators of Exeter in a long Epistle dated from Exeter, July, 1575.

VOYAGE.
A voyage round the World: or, a Pocket-Library. Divided into several volumes. The first of which contains the Rare Adventures of Don Kainophilus from his Cradle to his 15ᵗʰ year. The like Discoveries in such a Method never made by any Rambler before. The whole work intermixt with Essays Historical Moral and Divine, and all other kinds of Learning. Done into English by a Lover of Travels. Recommended by the Wits of both Universities.

——All may have,
If they dare try, a glorious Life or Grave.
Herb. Ch. Por.

London Printed for Richard Newcombe. [1691.] 12°. 3 vols. Vol. 1, A—K in eights: Vol. 2, A—H in eights, I, 4 leaves: Vol. 3, Title and dedication, 3 leaves: B, 7 leaves: C—E in eights: F, 2 leaves: Aa—Dd in eights.

Vols. 2 and 3 have separate titles, dated 1691. The translation or editorship is attributed to John Dunton.

W.

V. A.
A Booke of Cookerie. Verie necessarie for all such as delight therein. Gathered by A. W. And nowe newly enlarged, . . . At London, Printed by Edward Allde. Anno. Dom. 1594. 8° A—E in eights. *B. M.*

V. B., *of Derby.*
To the Faithfull and True-Hearted Covenanters, which are the Noble Philadelphians. A Diurnall of the Desires and Indeavours of one that earnestly desires the advancement of the Cause of Christ. Reade all or none. London Printed. 1644. 4°, A—B in fours.

V. C.
Common-Prayer-Book Devotions Episcopal Delusions; Or, The Second Death

of the Service-Book. . . . Printed in the Year, 1666. 4°, A—K in fours, A 1 and K 4 blank.

W. E., *an Eye and Ear-Witness of his Sayings and Doings.*
The Life and Death of William Lawd, late Archbishop of Canterburie: . . . London: Printed for Iohn Hancock, . . . 1645. 4°, A—F 2 in fours, besides 2 leaves *to the Reader.*

W. F.
Warm Beer . . . . London: Printed for J. Wilford, at the Three Flower De Luces in Little-Britain. 1724. 8°. A—E in fours, A repeated: F, 8 leaves, F 5–8 with advertisements.

A reprint of the Cambridge edition of 1641.

W. J.
Romæ Ruina Finalis, Anno Dom. 1666.
. . . Sive, Literæ ad Anglos Romæ versantes datæ, . . . Londini, Excudebat T. C. . . . 1655. 4°. Title and three following ll. : A—H in fours.

W. J., *Gent.*
A Speedie Poste, With certaine New Letters. Or, The first fruits of new Conceits, neuer yet disclo-ed. Now published for the helpe of such as are desirous to learne to write Letters. Printed at London by M. F. for William Sheares, and are to be sold at his shop at the Signe of the Bucke in . . . [1625.] 4°, black letter, A—H in fours, A 1 and H 4 blank. With a cut of a Post on the title. *B. M.*
The imprint is mutilated, and the date is cut away. But this was the work licensed to Sheares, 15th January 1624-5.

W. N., *a Friend to the Commonwealth.*
A Discourse concerning the Engagement : Or, The Northern Subscribers Plea opposed to their dissenting Neighbors importune Animosities. . . . London, Printed for Francis Tyton, . . . 1650. 4°, A—C in fours.

W. T.
A Succinct Philosophicall declaration of the nature of Clymactericall yeeres, occasioned by the death of Queene Elizabeth. Written by T: W: London Printed for Thomas Thorpe, and are to be sold in Paules Church-yard at the signe of the Crane, by Walter Burre. 1604. 4°, A—C 3 in fours. Without prefixes.

W. T.
The Pleasant Companion ; Or, Tryal of Wits : Being a choice Collection of most excellent Stories, gathered from the Latin, French, Italian, and Spanish Authors: . . . London. Printed by J. Grantham, for D. Brown, . . . and T. Goodwin, . . . 1684. 8". A, 4 : B—G 7 in eights. Dedicated by T. W. to the Honourable Charles Townshend, Esq.

W. T.
A Letter to a Dissenter, Upon occasion of His Majesties Late Gracious Declaration of Indulgence. London : Printed for G. H. 1687. 4°, A—C 2 in fours.

W. W.
The New Help to Discourse, . . . By W. W. Gent. The Ninth Edition with many new Additions. . . . London : Printed for J. Marshall . . . 1733. 12°, A—G in twelves.

WAGSTAFF, JOHN, *M.A., O.C.*
Historical Reflections on the Bishop of

Rome : Chiefly Discovering those Events of Humane Affaires which most advanced the Papal Vsurpation. Oxford, Printed by Hen: Hall for Ric. Davis, . . . 1660. 4°. A, 2 leaves : B—F in fours.

WAITE, J., *Minister of the Word.*
The Parents Primer And the Mothers Looking-Glasse Or Counsel for Parents in the Education of Children . . . in a Dialogue between a Minister and a Father . . . London, Printed by J. A. for the Author. and are to be sold by N. Ponder . . . 1681. 8", A—T 2 in eights.

WALES.
Certain seasonable Considerations and Reasons Humbly Offered, Against Reviving the Act, Intituled, An Act for the better Propagation and Preaching of the Gospel in Wales, and redresse of some Grievances there . . . [1652-3.] 4°, 4 leaves.

WALKER, GEORGE.
A True Account of the Siege of London-Derry. By the Reverend Mr George Walker, Rector of Donoghmoore in the County of Tirone and late Governour of Derry in Ireland. London, Printed for Robert Clavel, and Ralph Simpson, in St. Paul's Church-yard. MDCLXXXIX. Also published, A new and exact Map of *London-derry*, and *Culmore Fort*, drawn with great Exactness, by Captain Macullach, who was there during the Siege. Price 6d. Sold by Robert Clavel, and Ralph Simpson. 4°. Title and dedication to K. William and Q. Mary, 3 leaves: B—I 2 in fours.

A True Account of the Siege of London-Derry . . . The Third Edition Corrected. London, Printed for Robert Clavel, . . MDCLXXXIX. 4", A—I 2 in fours.

A Vindication of the True Account of the Siege of Derry in Ireland. By Mr George Walker, &c. Published by Authority. London : Printed for Robert Clavel, at the Peacock, at the West-End of St. Pauls. 1689. 4°, B—E in fours, E 4 blank, and the title.

WALKER, OBADIAH.
The Greek and Roman History Illustrated by Coins & Medals. . . . In Two Parts. Necessary for the Introduction of Youth into all the useful Knowledge of Antiquity. By Ob: W—. London, Printed by G. Croom, for William Miller . . . and Christopher Wilkinson . . . 1697. 8°, A—Aa 4 in eights. Dedicated to William Charleton of the Middle Temple.

WALKER, WILLIAM.
A Treatise of English Particles : . . .
London, Printed for T. Garthwait, . . .
1663. 8º. A, 4 leaves: a, 8 leaves: B—Kk
in eights.

WALLACE, JAMES.
An Account of the Islands of Orkney.
By James Wallace, M.D. and Fellow of
the Royal Society : To which is Added,
An Essay concerning the Thule of the
Ancients. London, Printed for Jacob
Tonson . . . 1700. 8º. A, 5 leaves :
B—N 3 in eights.

> Second edition, published by the author's
> son, without any suggestion as to the actual
> writer.

WALLER, EDMOND.
Poems, &c. Written upon several Occasions, And to several Persons. By Edmond
Waller, Esq ; . . . The Fifth Edition.
with several Additions Never before
Printed. *Non ego morduci* . . . Printed
for H. Herringman and are to be sold by
J. Knight and F. Saunders . . . 1686.
8º. Title and *To the Reader*, 3 leaves :
B—T in eights : V, 9 leaves. With a
portrait having no engraver's name, but
with the motto below, *Sed Carmina major
Imago.*

The Second Part of Mr Wallers Poems.
Containing His Alteration of the Maids
Tragedy, And whatever of his is yet
unprinted : Together with some other
Poems, Speeches, &c. that were Printed
severally, and never put into the First
Collection of his Poems.
——Siquis tamen . . .
London, Printed for Tho. Bennet, . . .
MDCXC. 8º. A, 8 leaves, A with *Impri-
matur :* a, 4 leaves : B—H in eights, H
8 blank.

Mr Wallers Speech in the House of Commons, on Tuesday the fourth of July,
1643. Being brought to the Barre, and
having leave given him by the Speaker,
to say what he could for himselfe, before
they proceeded to expell him the Hovse.
London, Printed by G. Dexter, Anno
Dom. 1643. 4º, 4 leaves.

Further Advice to a Painter. Or, Directions to draw the Late Engagement Aug.
11ᵗʰ 1673. Hor. de arte Poet. *Pictoribus*
. . . London. Printed for R. Vaughan
in the Little Old Baily, 1673. 4º, 4 leaves.
In verse.

WALLIS, JOHN.
Due Correction for Mr Hobbes. Or School
Discipline, for not saying his Lessons
right. In Answer to his Six Lessons,

. . . By the Professor of Geometry [J.
Wallis.] . . . Oxford, Printed by Leonard
Lichfield, . . . 1656. 8º. A, 6 leaves :
B—K 2 in eights, K 2 with *Errata.* With
a folded leaf of diagrams. Dedicated to
the Marquis of Dorchester.

Hobbius Heauton-timorumenos. Or A
Consideration of Mr Hobbes his Dialogves.
In an Epistolary Discourse, Addressed to
the Honourable Robert Boyle, Esq. By
John Wallis, D.D. Professor of Geometry
in Oxford. Oxford. Printed by A. & L.
Lichfield, for Samuel Thomson, . . . Lon.
1662. 8º, A—K in eights, besides the
title and Contents, 2 leaves.

> See Quaritch's Catalogue of MSS., 1886,
> Nos. 35,858-61, for an account of some un-
> published MSS. by Wallis, and papers rela-
> ting to him and his works, and to Edmund
> Elis and Mr. [Laurence ?] Maidwell, his
> contemporaries.

WALLIS, RICHARD.
Londons Armory Accuratly delineated in
a Graphical display of all the Arms Crests
Supporters Mantles & Mottos of every
distinct Company and Corporate Societie
in the Honourable City of London as
they truly bear them faithfully collected
from their severall Patents which have
been approved and Confirmed by Divers
Kings at Arms in their visitations. A
work never till now exactly perfected or
truly Published by any and will rectify
many essentiall Mistakes and manifest
Absurdities Committed in Painting &
Carving. London Printed for the Author
Rich Wallis Citizen & Arms painter of
London & are to be sold by him at his
Shop against ȳ Royall Exchange. 1677.
Folio, 33 engraved leaves, except that the
patent of Charles II., the dedication to
the Lord Mayor Davies, and the preface,
are printed.

WALSH, PETER.
A Prospect of the State of Ireland, From
the Year of the World 1756. to the Year
of Christ 1652. Written by P. W.
Printed for Johanna Brome at the Gun
in St. Pauls Church-yard, 1682. 8º. A,
8 leaves : (a)—(c) in eights : A (repeated)
—Ii in eights. Dedicated to the King,
and introduced by a long Preface.

WALSINGHAM, FRANCIS.
A Search made into Matters of Religion,
By Francis Walsingham Deacon of the
Protestants Church, before his change to
the Catholicke . . . Dedicated to the
Kings most Excellent Maiesty . . . Per-
missu Superiorum, Anno M.DC.IX. 4º,
*—3 *, 4 leaves each : A—3 T in fours.

WALSINGHAM, THOMAS.
Histoire Tragiqve et Memorable de Pierre de Gaveston Gentil-homme gascon, iadis le mignon d'Edouard 2, Roy d'Angleterre, tirée des Chroniques de Thomas Walsingham, & tournée de Latin en François. . . . M.D.LXXXVIII. 8°, A—E in fours.
Published to suit the political circumstances in France at this time, and dedicated to the Duc d'Espernon.

WALWYN, WILLIAM.
Walwins Wiles : Or The Manifestators Manifested Viz. Liev. Col. John Lilburn, M' Will. Walwin, M' Richard Overton, and M' Tho. Prince. Discovering themselves to be Englands new Chains and Irelands back Friends. Or The hunting of the old Fox with his Cubs And the Picture of the Picturers of the Counsel of State. London, Printed for H. C. and L. L. [1649.] 4°, A—D in fours, and (a) 4 leaves, (a 4) blank.

Walwyns Jvst Defence against the Aspertions Cast upon-Him, In A late un-christian Pamphlet entituled, Walwyns Wiles. By William Walwyn, Merchant . . . London, Printed by H. Hils, for W. Larnar, ... M.DC.XLIX. 4°, A—E 2 in fours.

The Fountain of Slaunder Discovered. By William Walwyn, Merchant. With some Passages concerning his present Imprisonment in the Tower of London . . . London, Printed by H. Hils, . . . M.DC.XLIX. 4°, A—D 2 in fours.

WANSLEBEN, J. M.
A Brief Account of the Rebellions and Bloodshed Occasioned by the Anti-Christian Practices of the Jesuits and other Popish Emissaries in the Empire of Ethiopia. Collected out of a Manuscript History Written in Latin by Jo. Michael Wansleben, a Learned Papist. London, Printed, and are to be Sold by Jonathan Edwin, . . . 1679. 4°, A—F² 2 in fours.

WARD, EDWARD.
A Journey to H——: Or, A Visit paid to, &c. A Poem. Part II. Both Parts by the Author of the London-Spy. London, Printed, . . . 1700. Folio, A—G, 2 leaves each.

WARD, JOHN.
The Christians Incovragement Earnestly to contend
For Christ his gospell & for all
Our Christian liberties in thrall
Which who refuseth let him bee
For aye Accursed——
Written by J. Ward Gent.
Reade } and { Iudge
Consider } { Censure

To which is added Irelands Grievances. London Printed for Io : Hancock 1643. 4", A—C 2 in fours.
A re-issue of the former edition, with a new title, entirely engraved, with six portraits : A Bishop, a Judge, a Cavalier, on one side, and Burton, Prynne, and Bastwick on the other. The three first, Laud being the Bishop, are said to pray, plead, and fight for Desolation, the other three for Reformation.

WARD, NATHANIEL.
Mercurius Anti-mechanicus. Or The Simple Coblers Boy. With his Lap-full of Caveats (or Take-heeds) Documents, Advertisements and Præmonitions to all his honest-fellow-tradesmen-Preachers, but more especially a dozen of men, in or about the City of London. [Here follow some verses.] By Theodore de la Guarden. London, Printed for John Walker, . . . 1648. 4°, A—H 2 in fours.

WARDEN.
The Speech of a Warden to the Fellowes of his Companie : Touching the great affaires of the Kingdome. . . . Published by Antibrownistus Puritanomastix. Printed for N. V. 1642. 4°, 4 leaves.

WARE, SIR JAMES.
The Antiqvities and History of Ireland, By the Right Honourable Sir James Ware, Knt. Containing 1. his Inquiries into the Antiquities of Ireland, Illustrated with Copper Cutts : . . . . 2. His Annals of Ireland . . . 3. His Commentaries of the Prelates of Ireland . . . 4. His two Books of the Writers of Ireland . . . 5. . . . that Discourse of Sir John Davis, ... Now first Published in one Volume in England ; and the Life of Sir James Ware prefixed. London : Printed for Awnsham and John Churchill . . . . MDCCV. Folio. Title, 1 leaf : dedication to the Duke of Ormonde, 1 leaf : Preface, 2 leaves : Life of Ware, 1 leaf : Contents of the Antiquities, 2 leaves : Testimonials from the City of Dublin, 1 leaf : Rules and Orders, 2 leaves : List of promoters and Calendar, 1 leaf : the *Antiquities*, A—Yy, 2 leaves each, Zz, 1 leaf : Aaa—Bbb, 2 leaves each : Ccc, 1 leaf : The *Annals*, A—T, 2 leaves each, besides the title and preface, 2 leaves : the Annals, Henry VII., B—X in fours, Y, 2 leaves : Annals, Eliz., A*—Q*, 2 leaves each : Aa*—Ee*, 2 leaves : Ff*, 1 leaf : *Prelates of Ireland*, title, preface, and arms of the four Archbishops, 3 leaves : A—R, 2 leaves each : S, 1 leaf : *Bishops*, Aa—Ff, 2 leaves each : *Archbishops of Tuam*, &c., 4 A—4 G, 2 leaves each : *Writers of Ireland*, B—N, 2

leaves each, a leaf of O, and the title and dedication, 2 leaves: A—P, 2 leaves, reckoning title, &c., as A: An *Abstract*, &c., 5 leaves. With plates at pp. 24, 52, 96, and 152 of the Antiquities.

This volume was printed at two or three presses.

WARING, ROBERT.
Amoris Effigies : Sive, *Quid sit Amor ?* ... Hinc quartæ editioni præfigitur ejusdem Autoris Carmen Lapidarium Memoriæ Vatum Principis, Ben. Jonsoni, sacratum. Londini Excudebat J. Redmayne, 1668. 12°. a, 12 leaves: A—F in twelves. Dedicated by William Griffiths to Sir John Birkenhead.

Amoris Effigies . . . Londini, Excudebat J. Redmayne, 1671. 12°, a in twelves, and A—F in twelves. Dedicated as before.

This seems to be a re-issue of the former.

WARRIN, JOHN, *Priest.*
Vita Jesu Christi. Vitā Diū nostri Iesv Christi Gloriosissima ex scripturis. sanctorū euāgelistarū ex[c]erpta . . . Que quidē hystoria iam vltimo collecta est, industria Iohānis warrin presbiterorū minimi : finaliter cōpleta mense martij, āno salutis nostre et gratie : M.D.LXVIII. Folio. In two columns.

An unpublished MS. on sale by Parsons of Knightsbridge in November 1882, Cat. 175, No. 414.

WATERHOUSE, EDWARD, *Esquire.*
An humble Apologie for Learning and Learned Men. By Edward Waterhous, Esq. [Quotations.] London, Printed by T. M. for M. M. G. Bedell, and T. Collins, . . . 1653. 8°. A, 4 leaves : B—S 4 in eights.

A Modest Discourse, of the Piety, Charity & Policy of Elder Times and Christians . . . By Edward Waterhouse Esq ; . . . London, Printed by A. M. for Simon Miller, . . . 1655. 8°. A, 2 leaves : B—S in eights. Dedicated to " My most Dear and Indulgent Father, Francis Waterhouse of Grenford in the County of Middlesex, Esq."

A Short Narrative of the late Dreadful Fire in London : Together with certain Considerations Remarkable therein, and deducible therefrom ; Not unseasonable for the Perusal of this Age. Written by way of Letter to a Person of Honour and Virtue. London, Printed by W. G. for Rich. Thrale . . . and James Thrale . . . 1667. 8°, A—M in eights.

This volume is addressed by Edward Waterhouse to his affectionate kinsman, Sir Edward Turnor, Speaker of the House of Commons.

WATERHOUSE, WILLIAM, *Esquire.*
One Tale is good, until another is told. Or, Some Sober Reflections upon the Act for Chimney-money. Drawn up for the use of some Neighbors, . . . London, Printed by R. Norton, 1662. 4°, B—E in fours, preceded by title and another leaf.

WATSON, RICHARD.
The Royal Votarie laying down Sword and Shield to take up Prayer and Patience. . . . Printed for the Author, and are to be solde at the Brazen Serpent in Saint Pauls Church-yard. 1660. 8°, A—I in fours : Royall Missive to the Prince of Wales, A—C 2 in fours.

A new title only to the Caen edition.

WATSON, RICHARD, *of Pewsey, near Marlborough, Wilts, Chaplain to the Duke of York.*
An Answer to Elymas the Sorcerer. By Dr Watson, Chaplain to His Royal Highness the Duke of York. [Col.] London: Printed for N. Woolfe at the seven stars in Newgate street, 1682. A folio leaf.

A Fuller Answer to Elimas the Sorcerer : or to the most Material Part (of a Feign'd Memoriall) toward the Discovery of the Popish Plot. . . . In a Letter addressed to Mr Thomas Jones. . . . London, Printed by H. Brugis for N. Woolfe. . . . MDCLXXXIII. Folio, A—II, 2 leaves each.

WATSON, WILLIAM.
A Sparing Discoverie of ovr English Iesvits, and of Fa. Parsons proceedings vnder pretence of promoting the Catholike faith in England : For a caueat to all true Catholiks, our very louing brothers and frends, how they embrace such very vncatholike, though Iesuiticall deseignments. . . . Newly Imprinted. 1601. 4°, A—K in fours, A 1 and K 4 blank, and a, 4 leaves.

WEBB, JOHN, *of Butleigh, co. Somerset, Esquire.*
A Vindication of Stone-Heng Restored : In which the Orders and Rules of Architecture Observed by the Ancient Romans, are discussed. Together with the Customs and Manners of several Nations of the World in matters of Building of Greatest Antiquity. As also an Historical Narration of the most memorable Actions of the Danes in England. By John Webb of Butleigh in the County of Somerset

Esquire. London, Printed by R. Davenport for Tho. Basset, ... MDCLXV. Folio. Title and Dedication to Charles II., 3 leaves : B—3 M, 2 leaves each. With plates.

WEBBE, JOSEPH.

A Petition to the High Covrt of Parliament, In the behalfe of anncient and authentique Authors, For the vniversall and perpetuall good of euery man and his posteritie : Presented by Ioseph, Webbe, Dr in Ph. Printed 1623. 4º, A—C in fours, C 4 blank.

WEBSTER, JOHN, *Military Chaplain.*

Academiarum Examen. Or The Examination of Academies. Wherein is discussed and examined the Matter, Method and Customes of Academick and Scholastick Learning, ... By Jo. Webster. ... London, Printed for Giles Calvert, ... MDCLIV. 4º, A—Q in fours, Q 4 blank. Dedicated to Major General Lambert. With a preface by Webster and some commendatory verses.

The Saints Guide, Or, Christ the Rule, and Ruler of Saints. Manifested by way of Positions, Consectaries, and Queries. ... By Iohn Webster late Chaplain in the Army. London, Printed for Giles Calvert ... 1654. 4º, A—F in fours.

WEBSTER, JOHN, *Physician and Surgeon.*

Metallographia: Or, An History of Metals. Wherein is declared the signs of Ores and Minerals both before and after digging, ... Gathered forth of the most approved Authors. ... By John Webster Practitioner in Physick and Chirurgery. ... London, Printed by A. C. for Walter Kettilby. ... M.DCLXXI. 4º, A—3 E in fours. Dedicated to Prince Rupert.

WELLS, E.

Elementa Arithmeticæ Numerosæ et Speciosæ. In Usum Juventutis Academicæ. Oxoniæ, E Theatro ... An. Dom. MDCXCVIII. 8º. Title, 1 leaf : a, 4 leaves : A—Ee 2 in fours. Dedicated to Edmund Feilde of Stanstead - bury, co. Herts, Thomas Bennet of Welby, co. Leicester, and Andrew Fountain of Narford, co. Norfolk.

WELLS, JOHN, *Esquire.*

Sciographia, Or The Art of Shadowes. Plainly demonstrating, out of the Sphere, how to project great and small circles, upon any Plane whatsoever : with a new Conceit of reflecting the Sunne beames upon a Diall, ... All performed, by the doctrine of Triangles, ... By I. W. Esquire. London, Printed by Thomas

Harper, ... 1635. 8º. ¶, 8 leaves : A, 8 leaves : aa, 6 leaves : a leaf of diagrams : B—Ff 2 in eights, besides folding leaves at pp. 74, 82, 98, 116, 126, 136, 143, 148, 174, and 221. With many diagrams on the letterpress, and a Preface by Henry Gellibrand. *B. M.*

WELWOD, WILLIAM.

De Dominio Maris, Ivribvsqve ad Dominivm Praecipve spectantibvs Assertio Brevis et Methodica. Cosmopoli, ... 1615. 4º. Title, dedication by Welwod to Queen Anne of Denmark, and *Lectori Æquiori*, 3 leaves : B—E 2 in fours.

WENTWORTH, SIR THOMAS, *Earl of Strafford.*

The Conclusion of the Earle of Straffords Defence. Printed in the yeare 1641. 4º, 4 leaves.

> In this edition the date of the month does not occur.

A Letter sent from the Earle of Strafford to his Lady in Ireland a little before his death : May 11. 1641. Printed in the yeare 1641. 4º, 4 leaves, the last blank. *B. M.*

WEST, WILLIAM, *of the Inner Temple, Esquire.*

The First Part of Simboleography. Which may be termed the Art, or Description, of Instruments and Presidents. Collected by William West of the Inner Temple Esqvire. And now newly augmented with diuers Presidents touching Marchants affaires. ... London, Printed for the Companie of Stationers. 1605. (ii.) The Second Part ... 1606. 4º. The first part, ¶, 6 leaves : A—Rr 6 in eights : part 2, ¶, 2 leaves, A—Qq in eights, Qq 8 blank.

WESTMORELAND.

The Murthers Reward. Being A True and Exact Account of a most Cruel and Barbarous Murther, committed by a Gentleman in Tredenton in the County of Westmoreland, who inhumanly murthered his own Wife, ... London, Printed by A. M. for W. Tackery, and T. Passinger ... 8º, 4 leaves.

WESTON, ELIZABETH.

Parthenicon Elisabethæ Ioannæ Westoniæ. Virginis nobilissimæ, poetria florentissimæ, linguarum plurimarum peritissimæ. Liber I. operâ ac studio G. Mart. à Baldhoven, Sil. Collectus : & nunc denuò amicis desiderantibus communicatus. Pragæ Typis Pauli Sessii. [1604.] 8º, A—D in eights : *Liber II.*, with a new title, A—C 4 in eights : *Liber III.*, with a new title, A—F in eights.

The Third Book chiefly consists of letters to or from the poetess and verses upon her. This book is inscribed by the author herself to James I., King of Great Britain.

WHALLEY, EDWARD, *M.P.*
A Letter sent from Col Whaley [to Sir Arthur Haselrigg] : Being Commanded by the King to declare His Maiesties great dislike of a late Pamphlet scandalous to his Majesty : Being Intituled, His Majesties Declaration . . . the 27. of August 1647. . . . London : Printed by I. Coe, for Henry Overton in Popes-head Ally, 1647. 4°, 4 leaves, the fourth blank. *B. M.*
Dated from Hampton-Court, Aug. 29, 1647.

WHARTON, GEORGE, *Student in Astronomy.*
No Merline, nor Mercurie ; But A new Almanack after the old fashion, for the year of our Redemption 1647. . . . Printed Anno Dom. 1647. 8°. A, 8 leaves : A (repeated)—B in eights, A 1 of the second gathering opening with a head-line : Wharton . 1647. Merlino-Anglico-Mastix. Or Lilly lasht with his own Rod. *B. M.*

Merlini Anglici Errata. Or, The Errors, Mistakes, and Mis-applications of Master Lillys New Ephemeris for the yeare 1647. Discovered, Refuted, and Corrected. By George Wharton, Student in Astronomy. Printed in the yeare 1647. [Dec. 4, 1646.] 8°, A—D in eights, D 8 blank. *B. M.*

Calendarium Carolinum : . . . For the Year of Christ 1664. Being Bissextile or Leap-year. . . . By George Wharton. London, Printed by J. Grismand, 1664. 8°, A—F in eights. With a portrait by Loggan.

WHETCOMBE, TRISTRAM.
A Sad Relation of the Miseries of the Province of Munster in the Realm of Ireland : Signified by Letters written from thence very lately, by a Gentleman of good credit, to his brother here in London. . . . London, Printed by G. Miller, 1645. 4°, 4 leaves.

WHIG.
The Whig's Exaltation, A Pleasant New Song of '82, To an Old Tune of '41. London, Printed by Nath. Thompson Anno Domini 1682. A broadside in verse, with the music.

WHIP.
A Flaming Whip for Lechery : Or, The Whoremasters Speculum. Containing, A fearful Historical Relation of such unclean Persons, as have been made Publick and Private Examples of God's Divine Vengeance, . . . London : Printed by Eliz. Harris, at the Harrow, in Little-Britain. 1700. 8°. A, 4 leaves : a, 1 leaf : B—X in eights, X 8 blank.

WHIRLIGIG.
The Whirligigge Tvrning to his Points, and Numbers, and pointing at the remarkable Turnes of these uncertaine Times. Or, The varietie of the late, wonderfull alterations in this Kingdome. Printed in the yeare, 1647. 4°, 4 leaves. In prose, except a song at the end. *B. M.*

WHISTON, JAMES.
Englands State-Distempers, Trac'd from their Originals : With Proper Remedies and Means to make her Vertuous and Prosperous. Humbly Presented by James Whiston. . . . The Mismanagement in Trade Discovered, and adapt Methods to Preserve and Improve it . . . with an Appendix shewing the Decrease of Protestants in Europe. 1704. 4°, Part I., A—F 1 in fours : Part II., A, 2 leaves : B—E 2 in fours. [Col.] Published by John Nutt near Stationers-Hall.

WHITBOURNE, RICHARD, *of Exmouth.*
A Discovrse and Discovery of New-Fovnd-Land, With many reasons to prooue how worthy and beneficiall a Plantation may there be made, after a far better manner than now it is. Together with the Laying Open of certaine Enormities and abuses committed by some that trade in that countrey, and the meanes laide downe for reformation thereof. Written by Captaine Richard Whitbourne. . . . Imprinted at London by Felix Kyngston, for William Barret. 1620. 4°, A—N 2 in fours, A 1 and N 2 blank. Dedicated to James I.

WHITE, IGNATIUS.
Mr Ignatius White his Vindication as well from all Imputations concerning Mr Scot (of which Affaire he doth give herein an exact, faithfull, and authentick account) as also from all other Reports. . . . Published for the Author. [1660.] 4°, B—D in fours, D 4 blank, and the title.

WHITE, JOHN.
A Rich Cabinet, With variety of Inventions : . . . Collected by J[ohn] W[hite] a lover of Artificial Conclusions. The Third Edition, with many Additions. London, Printed for William Gilbertson . . . 1658. 8°, A—N in eights, including a frontispiece and *The Authour to his Book* in verse. With woodcuts.

Gainsford's book, under a similar title, seems to differ completely from this.

WHITE, PETER.

A Memorable Sea-Fight Penned and Preserved by Peter White. One of the IIII. Masters of Attendance in Englands Navie. (Never before now,) Published for the good of Englands Common-wealth, By Andrewes Byrrell, Gent. Or, A Narrative of all the Principall Passages which were Trans-acted in the Downes in the Year 1639. Betweene Antonio de Oqvendo, Admirall of the Spanish Armado, And Martin Van Tromp, Admirall for the States of Holland. Wherein (by a Similary Illustration) Englands (present) sluggish Navie is proved to be Unserviceable, and in a like Condition with the Spanish Fleet. . . . London, Printed by T. Forcet, (Septem. 1. 1649.) dwelling in Old Fish-street. 4⁰, A—H 2 in fours, besides a fifth leaf in A. With two copies of verses by Andrewes Burrell at the end, and a dedication by him to the Council of State.

WHITE, RICHARD, *of Basingstoke.*

Ælia Lælia Crespis. Epitaphivm Antiqvvm quod in agro Bononiensi adhuc uidetur, a diuersis hactenus interpretatum uarie : nouissime autem à Ricardo Vito Basintochio, amicorum precibus explicatum. . . . Patavii . . . MDLXVIII. 4⁰, A—G 2 in fours. Dedicated to Christopher Jonson, Master of Winchester School.

Reprinted at Dordrecht, 8⁰, 1618.

WHITE, THOMAS.

A Discoverie of Brownisme : Or, A briefe declaration of some of the errors and abhominations daily practised and increased among the English company of the seperation remayning for the present at Amsterdam in Holland. . . . London, Printed by E. A. for Nathaniell Fosbrooke, . . . 1605. 4⁰, A—E 2 in fours.

WHITE, THOMAS.

A Letter to a Person of Honour : Written by Mʳ Thomas White, In Vindication of Himself and his Doctrine. M. DC. LIX. 8⁰, 12 leaves.

WHITE, THOMAS, *Minister of the Gospel.*

A Little Book for Little Children : Wherein are set down, in a plain and pleasant way, Directions for Spelling, And other remarkable Matters. Adorn'd with Cuts. London, Printed for G. C. and sold at the Ring, in Little-Britain. 12⁰. A, 6 leaves : A (repeated)—D in twelves. *B. M.*

On A in the second alphabet occurs a new title : A Little Book for Little Children : Wherein are set down Several Directions for Little Children. And Several remarkable Stories both Ancient and Modern of Little Children. Divers whereof are of those who are lately Deceased. By Thomas White, Minister of the Gospel. The Twelfth Edition. London : Printed for Tho. Parkhurst, at the Bible and Three Crowns in Cheapside, 1702. On A 3 of the first gathering the head-line is : "Youths Delight : A pleasant Way to teach Children to Read."

WHITE, WILLIAM, *Merchant.*

The Rarities of Russia With the Interest of England in point of Trade with that Country : Which occasioned the magnificent Entertainments of the Russian Ambassadours ; 1. By Queen Elizabeth, Anno 1589. 2. By King James, November 5. 1617. 3. By King Charles the Second, 1662. Which are here described. London, Printed for the Author, 1662. 4⁰, A—D in fours. *B. M.* (imperfect.)

WHITEHALL, JOHN.

Miscellaneous Poems, With some Remarks on the Death of King Charles the II. And the Happy Succession of King James the II. In a Poem to the Magistracy of England . . . London : Printed for T. Salusbury, at the Black-Lion-Post-Office between the two Temple-Gates in Fleet-street, 1685. 4⁰, A—E 2 in fours, A 1 blank.

WHITEHALL, ROBERT.

The Coronation. A Poem. By Ro: Whitehall, Fellow of Merton College, Oxon. *Divisum Imperium cum Jove Cæsar habet.* London, Printed for John Playford, at his Shop in the Temple, near [the Church, 1661.] 4⁰, 4 leaves. *B. M.* (imprint mutilated.)

WHITEHORNE, PETER.

Certain waies for the orderyng of Souldiers in battelray, & settyng of battailes, after diuers fashions, with their maner of marchyng : And also yᵉ figures of certaine new plattes for fortificacion of Townes : And more ouer, howe to make Saltpeter, Gunpoulder, and diuers sortes of Fireworkes or wilde Fyre, with other thynges apertaining to the warres. Gathered and set foorthe by Peter Whitehorne. [Col.] Imprinted at London, By Ihon Kingston : for Nicolas Englande. Anno salutis M. D. LXII. Mense Aprilis. 4⁰, A—N in fours. With numerous woodcuts and diagrams.

This formed in the prior and subsequent editions part of Whitehorne's version of Machiavel's *Art of War ;* but no impression of the latter dated 1562 seems to be known.

WHITTINTON, ROBERT, *of Lichfield, Grammarian.*

Whittintoni primā in Anglia Lauri coronam gestantis de sillabarū quātitate congeries: vtilitatis non parū Heliconis ad fontē tendentibus conferens. [This ends on G 8 *verso,* and on the next leaf *recto* begins with a head-line :] Whittintoni editio cum interpretamento Francisci nigri. [Col.] Explicit Whittintoni editio nuperrime recognitā : Diligētissimeq; nostre salutis anno. M. CCCCC. xix. impressa Londini per wynandū de worde. vii. Idᵉ Mar. 4°. The first tract, A, 8 : B, 4 : C, 8 : D, 4 : E, 8 : F, 6 : G, 8. The second : A, 8 : B, 4 : C, 8.

Sothebys, November 1885, No. 3074.

This impression appears to be the later of two bearing the date 1519, the earlier one having been printed in November 1519, and this in March 1519-20.

Whitintoni Ædítio cum interpretamento Francisci Nigri. Diomedes de accentu in pedestri oratione potius quam soluta observanda. Excussum Londinis in officina Petri Treueris. 4°, 18 leaves.

Roberti Whitintoni Lichfeldiensis de Syllabarum quantitate Editio. Secunda pars grammatices ... [Col.] Finis quātitatis sillabarū. 4°. A, 6 : B, 4 : C, 8 : D, 4 : E, 8 : F, 6 : G, 8. With W. de Worde's name and device on the first page. Then commences : Whittintoni editio cum interpretamēto frācisci nigri Diomedes de accentu in pedestri oratione ... with a head-line, A, 8 : B, 4 : C, 7 : Then another head-line, De Magistratibus ... Col. Anno post virgineū partū . xv. supra Millessimū quingentessimū octauo kalendas Martias, which makes 4 leaves, marked AA.

Sothebys, June 4, 1884, No. 569.

Verborū præterita & supina. Grammaticae Prima Pars ... [Col.] Lōdini in ędibᵘˢ Winādi de Worde . xxix. supra sesquimillessimū nostre redēptioīs anno. Ad Cal. Septemb. 4°. A, 4 : B, 6 : C, 4 : D, 6.

Roberti Whitintoni Lichfeldiensis lucubrationes. [Col.] Londini in ędibus Winandi de Worde, anno domini. M.CCCCC.XXIX. Mense Martio. 4°. A, 8 : B, 4 : C, 8 : D and E. 4 each.

Sothebys, July 26, 1883, No. 440. There is no regular title.

Roberti Whitintoni lichfeldiensis / grāmatices magistri & protonatis Anglie in florentissima Oxoniensi achademia Laureati lucubrationes. [Col.] Expliciunt synonima Lodoū, per wynandum de worde impressa. 4°. A, 8 : B, 4 : C, 8 : D, 6. With the printer's large device on D 6 *verso.*

Sothebys, Jan. 20, 1885, No. 547, the *Synonima* only.

Whittyntoni editio secunda. Opusculum affabre recognitum et ad unguem elimatum. [Col.] Finis opusculū affabre. Impressum London p Wynandū de worde / in vico vulgariter nūcupato (the Fletestrete) ad signū Solis aurei cōmorantē. 4°. A, 8 : B—C, 4 leaves each. With the printer's device and name on the first page. The preface to the reader is on the back of the title.

Sothebys, June 4, 1884, No. 569.

Editio roberti Whittintoni lichfeldiensis grāmatices magistri & ptouatis Anglie ī florētissima Oxonieñ academia laureati. [Col.] Explicit . . . Impressa Londoñ. per wynandū de worde . . . 4°. A, 8 : B, 6.

Sothebys, June 4, 1884, No. 569.

De heteroclitis nōibus. Editio Roberti Whittintoni . . . [Col.] . . . Londini impressa per wynandū de worde . . . 4°, A, 6 : B, 4.

Roberti Whitintoni, alma vniuersitate Oxoniensi laureati, de octo partibus orationis. Impressum diligenterque enucleatum per me Petrum Treueris. 4°, 14 leaves. With the title within a border and the printer's device on the last page.

Syntaxis Roberti Whitintoni Lichfeldiensis in florentissima Oxoniensi achademia laureati opusculum de Syntaxi siue constructione recensitum. 1522. Impressum per me Petrum Treueris. 4°, 36 leaves.

WHORE.

The Poor-Whores Petition. `To the most Splendid, Illustrious, Serene and Eminent Lady of Pleasure, the Countess of Castlemayne, &c. The Humble Petition of the Undone Company of poore distressed Whores, Bawds, Pimps, and Panders, &c. [1668.] A broadside.

WICKLIFFE, JOHN.

Wycklyffes Wycket : whyche he made in kyng Rycards dayes the second in the yere of our lorde God M. CCC. XCII. Ihon the . vi. chapiter. I am the liuynge bread. . . . [Col.] Here endeth the Exposicion of wyllyam Tyndall. Imprynted at Noremburch. 1546. 8°, black letter, A—C 3 in eights.

Wickliff's Wicket concludes on B 3 *recto,* and on the reverse commences the *testament* of *maister wyllium Tracie,* with Tyndale's exposition. Sothebys, July 1, 1885, No. 1288.

Wycklyffes Wycket : whych he made in
Kyng Rychards days the second in the
yere of our lorde God a M. CCC. XCII.
[Col.] Here endeth the Exposicion of
wyllyam Tyndall. Imprynted at Noren-
burch. 1546. 8°, A—C 3 in eights.

Sothebys, July 1, 1885, No. 1289, Heber's
copy. *Tracy's Testament* begins in this
edition as in the other of 1546.

WIFE.
The Stubborn Wifes Warning-Piece : Or,
Good Instructions for A Scolding Wife.
Wherein the Wifes Duty of obeying her
Husband, is proven from Scripture &
Reason. Glasgow, Printed by Robert
Sanders, . . . 1700. 8", 8 leaves. In prose.

WIGAND, JOHN.
De Neutralibus, & Medijs. Grosly Englished, lacke of both sides . . . London :
Printed by G. M. for Edward Blackmore,
. . . 1626. 4°, A—M in fours. *B. M.*

WIGHT.
A Terrible Thunder-Clap from the Isle
of Wyght, to the City of London, Wherein
is discovered. Severall passages of great
importance, . . . Sent in a Letter from
one of His Majesties near friends, to a
Gentleman in London. Printed in the
Year, 1648. 4°, 4 leaves.

WILD, ROBERT.
Moon-shine : Or The Restauration of
Jews-Trumps and Bagpipes. Being an
Answer to Dr R. Wild's Letter &c. and his
Poetica Licentia, &c. London, Printed
for R. C. . . . 1672. 4°, B—F in fours,
and the title.

Dr Wild's Humble Thanks for His Majesties Gracious Declaration for Liberty
of Conscience, March 15. 1672. London,
Printed in the Year, 1672. A broadside
in verse.

WILDMAN, JOHN.
Truths triumph, Or Treachery anatomized
Being An impartiall Discovery of the
false, and treacherous information of W.
Masterson, pretended Minister of Christ
at Shore-ditch, against L. C. I. Lilburne,
and I. Wildman, at the Lords Barre,
January 18. 1647, concerning a meeting
of severall honest men, at East Smithfield,
Ian. 17, &c. In relation to which Information, the said L. C. Lilburn stands committed to the Tower, and J. Wildman
to the Fleet. . . . London Printed for
Ia. Hornish. Feb. 1. 1647. 4°, A—C 2 in
fours. *B. M.*

Putney Projects. Or the Old Serpent in
a new Forme. Presenting to the view of

all the well affected in England, the Ser-
pentine deceit of their pretended friends
in the Armie, indeavouring to introduce
Tyranny and Slavery in a new Method.
Composed by the diligent and impartiall
observation and certain intelligence of
John Lawmind [John Wildman] . . .
London, Printed in the Yeare. 1647. 4°,
A—F in fours. *B. M.*

WILKINS, JOHN, *Bishop of Chester.*
Le Monde dans la Lune. . . . De la Tra-
duction du Sr de la Montagne. . . . A
Rouen, . . . M. DC. LVI. 8°. ã, 4 leaves :
A—Nn in fours. With diagrams.

WILLES, THOMAS, *late Minister at Shadwell.*
A Help for the Poor who are visited with
the Plague : to be communicated to them
by the Rich ; . . . Consisting of Two
Parts. . . . The Second Edition Corrected and Enlarged. London, Printed for
Peter Parker in Popes-head-Alley, 1666.
8°, A—E in eights, besides the frontispiece.

WILLIAM OF NEWBURY.
Rervm Anglicarvm Libri Qvinqve, Recens
ceu è tenebris erecti, & in studiosorum
gratiam in lucem dati : Cum rerum me-
morabilium luculentissimo Indice. Antwerpiæ, Ex officina Gulielmi Silvij. typographi Regij. M.D.LXVII. 8°, A—Mm 6
in eights. Dedicated by the printer to
Queen Elizabeth.

WILLIAM OF ORANGE, *King of Great Britain* (1688–1702).
The Royal Message from the Prince of
Orange to the Peeres and Commons of
England, to advertise them of some dan-
gerous Plots . . . Printed for Tho. Powel.
1641. 4°, 4 leaves.

A Prayer for His Highness the Prince of
Orange. In the Savoy. 1688. A broadside.

The Prince of Orange His Declaration :
Shewing the Reasons why he Invades
England. With A Short Preface. and
some Modest Remarks on it. London :
Published by Randall Taylor, near Stationers-Hall. MDCLXXXVIII. 4°, A—D
in fours.

Compare *Life of Thomas Gent*, 1832, p.
20, *note.*

The Prince of Orange His Third Declaration. [1688.] 4°, 2 leaves.

An Enquiry into the Measures of Submission to the Supream Authority : And of
the Grounds upon which it may be Lawful or necessary for Subjects, to defend

their Religion, Lives and Liberties. [1688.] 4°, 4 leaves.

[Address of the Prince of Orange delivered to divers members of Parliament, Aldermen, &c. who had met him by appointment at St. James's, Dec. 26, 1688. Col.] London, Printed by John Starkey, Awnsham and William Churchill, MDCLXXXVIII. Folio, 2 leaves.

The Minister's Reasons for his not reading the Kings Declaration, Friendly Debated. [Col.] London : Printed by G. Larkin . . . 1688. 4°, A—C in fours.

In Expeditionem Britannicam ab Illvstrissino . . . Guiljelmo III. Fœliciter susceptam, Carmina, Quibus Monachorum Parisiensium Convitiis respondetur. [No place, &c.] 4°, 4 leaves.

A Pastoral, on the Success and Coronation of William and Mary, King and Queen of England. . . . London, Printed for Randal Taylor, 1689. 4°, 4 leaves.

1688. To the Tune of Lilli Bolero, &c. An engraved sheet.

A Brief History of the Succession of the Crown of England, &c. Collected out of the Records, and the most Authentick Historians. Written for the Satisfaction of the Nation. London, Printed, and are to be sold by Richard Janeway . . . 168⁸⁄₉. Folio, A—E, 2 leaves each.

Popish Treaties not to be rely'd on : In a Letter from a Gentleman at York, to his Friend in the Prince of Orange's Camp. Addressed to all Members of the next Parliament. [1690.] Folio, 2 leaves. Without a title-page.

Gallienus Redivivus, Or, Murther will out, &c. Being a True Account of the De-Witting of Glencoe, Gaffney, &c. . . . Printed at Edinburgh in the Year 1695. 4°, A—F, 2 leaves each.

This supplied Macaulay with much of his information on the subject of the massacre of Glencoe.

Mᵣ De Labadie's Letter to his Daughter Mⁿ Delabadie, Nurse to the pretended Prince of Wales. . . . Printed in the Year, 1696. 8°, A—F 3 in fours.

An Account of the Principal Officers, Civil and Military, of England, in the Year 1697. London, Printed for Abel Roper, . . . 1697. A large broadside.

These lists appear to have been printed annually.

Animadversions on a late Factious Book, Entituled, Essays upon, 1. The Ballance

of Power, . . . With a Letter Containing a Censure upon the said Book : . . . London : Printed . . . 1700. 8°, A—L in fours.

The Principles of a Member of the Black List ; Set forth by way of Dialogue. *Non Quis, sed Quid.* . . . London, Printed for George Straban, . . . 1702. 8°, A—Oo in eights, and a, 8, and c, 4 leaves, no b. Dedicated to Robert Harley, Esq.

WILLIAMS, JOHN, *Rector of St. Mildred's, Poultry.*

A Vindication of the History of the Gunpowder Treason, And of the Proceedings and Matters relating thereunto, . . . To which is added, A Parallel betwixt That and the Present Popish Plot. London, Printed by J. D. for Richard Chiswell, . . . 1681. 4°, A—N 2 in fours.

WILLIAMS, JOHN, *Pastor of the Church at Deerfield.*

Warnings to the Unclean : In a Discourse from Rev. xxi. 8. Preacht at Springfield Lecture, August 25ᵗʰ 1698. At the Execution of Sarah Smith. Boston, Printed by B. Green, and J. Allen, . . . 1699. 8°, A—D in eights.

WILLIAMS, ROGER.

A Key into the Language of America : Or, An help to the Language of the Natives in that part of America, called New-England. Together with briefe Observations of the Customes, Manners, and Worships, &c. of the aforesaid Natives, in Peace and Warre, in Life and Death. On all of which are added Spirituall Observations, Generall and Particular by the Author, . . . By Roger Williams of Providence in New-England. London, Printed by Gregory Dexter, 1643. 8°, A—O in eights.

WILLIS, THOMAS, *M.D., of Christ-Church, Oxford.*

Phraseologia Anglo - Latina ; Diu in Scholis desiderata & nunc primùm in lucem edita. In Vsum Scholæ Bristoliensis. [This is a half-title on A.] Proteus Vinctus. Sive Æquivoca Sermonis Anglicani, ordine Alphabetico digesta, & Latinè reddita . . . . [On the back of the half-title :] Anglicisms Latinized. Or, English Proprieties rendered into Proper Latine. Autore T[homa] W[illis] utriusq; Academiæ olim in Artibus Mᵣ. London, Printed by E. Cotes, and are to be sold by Will. London Bookseller in Newcastle, 1655. 8°, A—Ii in eights, including half-title.

Cerebri Anatome : Cui Accessit Nervorvm Descriptio et Usus. Studio Thomæ *

Willis, Ex Aede Christi Oxon. M.D. . . . Londini, Typis Ja. Flesher, . . . MDCLXIV. 4°, A—3 M in fours, and a—d in fours. Dedicated to Archbishop Sheldon. With thirteen numbered copper-plates, besides one at p. 302.

Affectionum quæ dicuntur Hysteriæ & Hypochondriacæ Pathologia . . . . Cui accesserunt . . . 1. De Sanguinis Accensione. 2. De Motu Musculari. Studio Tho. Willis . . . Londini, Apud Jacobum Allestry, ... MDCLXX. 4°. Title and Preface, 3 leaves : B—P in fours. With two folded leaves and a portrait by Loggan.

De Anima Brutorum quæ Hominis Vitalis ac Sensitiva est, Exercitationes Duæ. . . . Studio Thomæ Willis, M.D. . . . . Amstelodami, . . . MDCLXXII. 8°, A—Dd in eights, and a—b in eights between A and B. Dedicated to Gilbert Sheldon, Archbishop of Canterbury, with eight numbered copper-plates.

De Anima Brutorum Quæ Hominis Vitalis ac Sensitiva est, Exercitationes Duæ. . . . Studio Thomæ Willis M.D. . . . Londini, Typis E. F. Impensis Ric. Davis, Oxon. 1672. 8°, A—Dd in eights, and a—b in eights.

WILMOT, JOHN, *Earl of Rochester.*
A Pastoral Dialogue between Alexis and Strephon, Written by the Right Honourable, The Late Earl of Rochester, at the Bath, 1674. London, Printed for Benj. Billingsley, . . . 1683. A folio broadside.

Poems on Several Occasions by the Right Honourable, the E of R—— Printed at Antwerpen. 8°, A—K 4 in eights. With a portrait.

WILSON, JOHN, *of Lincoln's Inn.*
Andronicus Commenius : A Tragedy. By John Wilson. [Quot. from Juvenal, Sat. 13.—Fatebere tandem . . .] London, Printed for John Starkey, . . . 1664. 4°, A—M in fours, A 1 blank. Dedicated to his friend, A. B. *B. M.*

The Projectors. A Comedy. By John Wilson *Ætatem habet, ipse de se loquatur* . . . London, Printed for John Playfere, . . . and William Crook, . . . 1665. 4°. Title and *Persons*, 2 leaves : B—I in fours, I 4 with the Epilogue. *B. M.*

To His Excellency Richard Earle of Arran &c. Lord Deputy of Ireland. A Poem.

———*Nec deficit alter*
Aureus, & simili frondescit virga metallo

Dvblin, Printed at His Majesties Printing-House for Joseph Wild Bookseller in Castle-Street. 1682. Folio, 2 leaves. *B. M.*

In the same volume of tracts follows " On Mr Wilsons Admirable Verses dedicated to his Ex. the Earle of Arran " in MS., 2 folio leaves.

The Cheats. A Comedy : Written in the Year, M.DC.LXII. The Third Edition. . . . London, Printed by James Rawlins for John Wright . . . 1684. 4°, A—I in fours.

A Discourse of Monarchy, More particularly, of the Imperial Crowns of England, Scotland, and Ireland, According to the Ancient, Common, and Statute-Laws of the same. With a Close from the whole, As it relates to the Succession of his Royal Highness, James Duke of York. . . . London : Printed by M. C. for Jos. Hindmarsh, . . . 1684. 8°, A—S in eights, A 8 blank, and *Errata*, 1 leaf. Dedicated to James, Duke of Ormond. *B. M.*

Belphegor : Or The Marriage of the Devil, A Tragi-Comedy. Lately Acted at the Queen's Theatre in Dorset-Garden. By Mr Wilson. —*Prodesse potest, aut delectare*— . . . London : Printed by J. Leake, and are to be sold by Randal Taylor. 1691. 4°, A—I in fours. *B. M.*

A second copy in the Museum reads in the imprint : London : Printed by J. L. for Luke Meredith . . . 1691 ; but it does not seem to vary otherwise.

WILSON, SAMUEL.
An Account of the Province of Carolina in America. Together with an Abstract of the Patent, and several other Necessary and Useful Particulars, . . . London : Printed by G. Larkin for Francis Smith, . . . 1682. 4°, A—D 2 in fours. Dedicated to William, Earl of Craven.

WILSON, THOMAS, *LL.D.*
The rule of Reason, conteinyng the Arte of Logique, set forth in Englishe, by Thomas Wilson. An. M.D.LI. [Col.] Imprinted at London by Richard Grafton, printer to the Kynges Maiestie. Anno. M.D.LI. Cum priuilegio . . . 8°, A—X in eights, A 8 blank, and X 8 with woodcuts only. Dedicated to Edward VI. With a copy of Latin verses by Walter Haddon. *B. M.*

Sothebys, March 14, 1882, Sir Thomas Smith's copy, with his autograph and notes. No other has, I believe, occurred.

The Arte of Rhetorique, for the vse of all suche as are studious of Eloquence, sette forth in English by Thomas Wilson.

Anno Domini. M.D.LIII. Mense Iannarij. [Col.] Richardus Graftonus, typographus Regius excudebat. Cum priuilegio . . . 4°. Title and leaf with verses by N. Udall, &c. 2 leaves : A—Hh in fours, A repeated. Dedicated to John Dudley, Lord Lisle, Earl of Warwick.

WILTSHIRE.
A Faithfull Narrative of the Strange Appearance of the Spirit of Edward Aven, late of Marleborough, to Tho. G. his Son in Law, and his own Son, the 23, 25th, and 26th of November last past. With his Confession of Money he had formerly borrowed of Mʳ E. L. and forsworn, and of a Robbery and Murther by him Committed Thirty Nine Years ago, &c. . . . Printed in the Year, 1674. 4°, 4 leaves. With two rough cuts.

WINDSOR.
The Order of the Ceremonies Used at the Celebration of St. Georges Feast at Windsor, when the Sovereign of the Most Noble Order of the Garter is present. Printed by his Majesties special Command. E. W. Gʳ London : Printed by Andr. Clark, for Sam. Mearne . . . 1674. 4°, A—F in fours.

> Probably drawn up by Garter.

WING, JOHN.
The Best Merchandise Or, A Cleare Discovery of the evident difference, and admirable advantage, betweene our traflike with God, for the true treasure, and with men, for the temporall commodity. . . . Preached at Middleburgh in Zeelande, immediately before the remoovall of the famous fellowship of Merchant Aduenturers of England, from thence, vnto Delft, in Holland. . . . At Flvshing, Printed by Martin Abraham van der Nolck, dwelling at the signe of the Printing house. 1622. 4°, A—S 2 in fours, S 2 with *Errata*. Dedicated to Master Edward Bennet, Deputy, and the rest of the Merchant Adventurers, from his house at Flushing, March 26, 1622. *B. M.*

> Following the dedication is " The summe of the Sermons " in verse, which is followed by "The methode of the whole matter," containing the heads of rules for commercial conduct.

WINNE OR WYNNE, CAPTAIN EDWARD.
A Letetr [*sic*] Written by Captaine Edward Winne, to the Right Honourable, Sir George Caluert, Knight, his Maiesties Principall Secretary : From Feryland in Newfoundland, the 26. of August. 1621.

Imprinted MDCXXI. 8", A—B 4 in eights. *B. M.*

WINSLOW, EDWARD.
Good Newes from New-England : Or A true Relation of things very remarkable at the Plantation of Plimoth in New-England. . . . Together with a Relation of such religious and civill Lawes and Customes, as are in practise amongst the Indians. . . . Written by E. W. who hath borne a part in the fore-named troubles, and there liued since their first Arrivall. London Printed by I. D. for William Bladen and Iohn Bellamie, . . . 1624. 4°, A—K 2 in fours, K 2 with a Postscript. Dedicated " To all Well-Willers and Furtherers of Plantations in New-England."

WINSTANLEY, JERRARD.
The Law of Freedom in a Platform : Or, True Magistracy Restored. Humbly presented to Oliver Cromwel, General of the Common-wealths Army in England . . . And to all English-men my Brethren. Wherein is Declared, What is Kingly Government, and what is Commonwealth's Government. By Jerrard Winstanley. London, Printed for the Author, . . . 1652. 4°, A—M 2 in fours.

> A reasonable plea for Communism and for the title of the people to the land.

WINSTANLEY, WILLIAM.
Histories and Observations Domestick and Foreign. Or, A Miscellany of Historical Rarities, Collected out of approved Authors. With other Remarkable Observations. By William Winstanley, Author of *Englands Worthies.* London, Printed for Will. Whitwood, . . . 1683. 8°, A—U in eights. Dedicated to Sir Thomas Middleton, of Stansted Mountfichet.

WINTER, SALVATOR.
A New Dispensatory of Fourty Physicall Receipts. Most necessary and Profitable for all House-Keepers in their Families. Besides three other pleasant Arts fit for young Gentlemen. Published by Salvator Winter of Naples, An Expert Operator. London, Printed in the Year, 1649. 4°, A—B in fours.

WISE MASTERS.
The History of the Seven Wise Masters of Rome . . . Glasgow, By Robert Sanders, one of their Majesties Printers. 1693. 8°, black letter, A—I in fours. *B. M.*

> Sothebys, January 28, 1884, No. 67.

[WISE, THOMAS.]
Animadversions vpon Lillies Grammar,

Or Lilly scanned. An Extract of Grammaticall Problemes. Gathered out of the Inquiries, and disputes, of the most judicious Grammarians. . . . London Printed by W. Stansby for Richard Hawkins, . . . 1625. 8°, A—K 4 in eights. *B. M.*

WIT.

A Satyr against Wit. London : Printed for Samuel Crouch, . . . 1700. Folio, A—D, 2 leaves each. In verse.

WITHER, GEORGE, *of Lincoln's Inn.*

Parallelogrammaton. An Epistle to the three Nations of England, Scotland, and Ireland ; whereby their Sins being Parallel'd with those of Judah and Israel, they are forewarned, and exhorted to a timely Repentance, lest they incur the like Condemnation . . . Written by Geo. Wither. . . . Imprinted MDCLXII years after the Birth of Christ, to prepare for the year MDCLXVI after his Passion. 8°, A—R in fours, and a leaf of S. In prose, except an Address from Newgate, dated March 8, 1662.

WITCHCRAFT.

A Collection of Modern Relations of Matter of Fact, Concerning Witches & Witchcraft upon the Persons of People. To which is prefixed a Meditation concerning the Mercy of God, in preserving us from the Malice and Power of Evil Angels. Written by the Late Lord Chief Justice Hale, upon Occasion of a Tryal of several Witches before him. Part I. London. Printed for John Harris, . . . MDCXCIII. 4°. A, 4 leaves : *, 4 leaves : B—H in fours.

The principal part of the tract, which is very curious, consists of the Relations. Hale's part seems to have been left unfinished.

WITTIE, ROBERT, *M.D.*

Gout Raptures, . . . Or an Historical Fiction of a War among the Stars : Wherein are mentioned the 7 Planets, . . . Useful for such as apply themselves to the Study of Astronomy, and the Celestial Globe. By Robert Witty, Dʳ in Physick. Cambridge, Printed by John Hayes, . . . 1677, 8°, A—D in eights, A 1 blank, and D 8 with *Errata.*

WOLLEY, EDWARD, *D.D.*

Loyalty amongst Rebels. The True Royalist, or Hushay the Archite. A happy Counsellour in King David's Greatest Danger . . . Written by Edward Wolley D.D. and Chaplain in Ordinary to his Sacred Majesty . . . London, Printed for John Williams, . . . 1662. 8°. *—3 * 4 in eights, including a frontispiece : A—M

4 in eights, M 4 with *Errata.* With portraits of Louis XIV. and Charles II. Dedicated to John Granville, Earl of Bath.

WOLLEY, HANNAH.

The Gentlewoman's Companion . . . 1682.

The print attached to this book is probably fictitious, as the best impressions, according to Walpole, occur with the name of Mrs. Sarah Gilly.

WOLLEY, R.

The Present State of France. Containing A General Description of that Kingdom. Translated from the last Edition of the French, Enriched with Additional Observations and Remarks of the New Compiler, and digested into a Method Conformable to that of The State of England. By R. W. M.A. London : Printed for Gilbert Cownly, . . . 1689. 12°. A, 8 leaves : B—Z in twelves. Dedicated to Richard, Viscount Preston, by R. Wolley.

It appears as if Wolley was the " London Divine " employed by John Dunton to edit or write " The Compleat Library : Or, News for the Ingenious, &c.," 1692. Compare p. 142 *suprà, v.* LIBRARY. The title is worded rather ambiguously, however, and does not quite clearly tell us whether Wolley was responsible for the whole or merely a portion of this monthly publication.

WOMEN.

The deceyte of women, to the instruction and ensample of all men, yonge and olde, newly corrected. [Col.] Imprynted at London in Paules Churche yard at the sygne of the Lambe, by Abraham Vele. 4", black letter, A—K in fours. With cuts. In prose, except a metrical prologue. *B. M.*

This is a singular mixture of ancient and modern examples, Adam and Eve, a proctor of the Arches in London, Lot's daughters, Judith, &c. On a fly-leaf to the volume, which is in the old parchment cover at present, and was acquired from a gentleman at Woolwich recently for the Museum, occurs : "John Hodge, of the Six Clerks Office 1682."

The good Womens Cryes against the Excise of their Commodities. Shewing. As the businesse now stands, they are in no Case able to bear such heavy Pressures, . . . Written by Mary Stiff, Chair-woman, in Vineger Verse. Westminster : Printed at the Signe of the Hornes in Queenstreet, neare my Lord Fairfax's House, and are to be sold at the Dildoe in Distaffe-Lane. 1650. 4°, 4 leaves.

An Essay to Revive the Antient Education of Gentlewomen, In Religion, Manners,

Arts, & Tongues. With An Answer to the Objections against this Way of Education. London, Printed by J. D. to be sold by Tho. Parkhurst, . . . 1673. 4°, A—F 2 in fours. Dedicated by the anonymous writer to Mary, eldest daughter of the Duke of York.

The Woman as good as the Man : Or, The Equallity of Both Sexes. Written Originally in French, and Translated into English by A. L. London : Printed by T. M. for N. Brooks, . . . 1677. 12°, A—I in twelves, A 12 with the *Errata*.

An Answer to the Mantuan, Or, False Character, lately wrote against Womankind. London, Printed in the Yeer 1679. A broadside.

Hæc & Hic ; Or, The Feminine Gender more worthy than the Masculine. Being a Vindication of that Ingenious and Innocent Sex from the Biting Sarcasms, Bitter Satyrs, and Opprobrious Calumnies, wherewith they are daily tho undeservedly Aspers'd by the violent Tongues and Pens of Malevolent Men . . . London, Printed by Jo. Harefinch, for James Norris, . . . 1683. 12°. Title and To the Female Readers, signed *J. N.*, 3 leaves : B—H in twelves, H 12 blank.

> A compilation from various sources, probably by Norris.

The Pleasures of Love and Marriage, A Poem in Praise of the Fair Sex. In Requital for *The Folly of Love* and some other late Satyrs on Women. London : Printed for H. N. and are to be Sold by R. Baldwin . . . 1691. 4°. A, 2 leaves : B—D in fours : E, 2.

A Dialogue Concerning Women, Being a Defence of the Sex. Written to Eugenia. London, Printed for R. Bentley . . . and J. Tonson . . . 1691. 8°. A, 4 leaves : B—K 3 in eights.

> With a preface by John Dryden, in which he speaks of the author as a young acquaintance. He refers in a very interesting manner to Waller ; and the book itself is by no means without merit. Dryden also pays, in the introductory pages, a graceful and deserved compliment to the memory of Waller.

An Essay in Defence of the Female Sex. In which are inserted the Characters of A Pedant, A Squire, A Beau, A Virtuoso, A Poetaster, A City-Critick, &c. In a Letter to a Lady. Written by a Lady . . . London, Printed for A. Roper and E. Wilkinson, . . . 1696. 8°, A, 8 : B, 4, with verses by James Drake to the

anonymous authoress : B (repeated)—L 4 in eights.

The Excellent Woman Described by her True Characters and their Opposites. Being A Just and Instructive Representation of the Vertues and Vices of the Sex. . . . In Two Parts. Done out of French, by T. D[orrington.] London, Printed for John Wyat . . . 1695. 8°, A—X in eights, and a, 8 leaves. Dedicated by the translator to the Lady Mary Walcot.

WOOD, ANTHONY.

Athenæ Oxonienses. An Exact History of all Writers and Bishops who have had their Education in the most ancient and famous University of Oxford, From the Fifteenth Year of King Henry the Seventh, Dom. 1500, to the End of the Year 1690 . . . To which are added, The Fasti or Annals, of the said University, For the same time . . . . *Antiquam exquirite Matrem.* Virgil. London : . . . MDCXCI–II. Folio. 2 vols.

WOOD, WILLIAM.

New Englands Prospect. A true, lively, and experimentall description of that part of America, commonly called New England ; discovering the state of that Countrie, both as it stands to our newcome English Planters, and to the old Native Inhabitants. Laying downe that which may both enrich the knowledge of the mind-travelling Reader, or benefit the future Voyager. By William Wood. Printed at London by Tho. Cotes, for Iohn Bellamie, . . . 1634. 4°, A—O in fours, besides a map of the South Part of New England. Dedicated to the author's honoured friend Sir William Armyne.

WOOL.

An Act for the Burying in Woollen. 1678.

> This inflicted a penalty of £5 on any offender ; but the law was more often transgressed than enforced. In 1730, Mrs. Oldfield the actress was buried in Westminster Abbey in a Holland shift trimmed with lace and a Brussels lace headdress.

WORCESTERSHIRE.

A more full Relation of the great Victory Obtained by our Forces near Worcester,— The taking of the City of Worcester And totall routing of the Scotch Army. . . . London, Printed for Edward Griffin, . . . Septem. 8. 1651. 4°, 4 leaves.

WORLD.

A Geographical Description of the World. With A brief Account of the several Empires, Dominions, and Parts thereof. . . .

Together with a short Direction for Travellers. London, Printed for William Leake, . . . 1671. 12°. A, 6 leaves, A 6 with *Errata*, besides the title : B—Q in twelves. On B is a second title.

WORLIDGE, JOHN.

Systema Agriculturæ ; . . . The Second Edition carefully corrected and Amended, with many large and useful Additions throughout the whole Work : By the Author. . . . London: Printed by J. C. for Thomas Dring, . . . 1675. Folio. A, 2 leaves, besides the frontispiece and metrical explanation of it : no B : C—D in fours : E, 2 leaves : e, 4 leaves : F—Zz in fours.

Systema Agriculturæ ; . . . The Third Edition carefully Corrected and Amended, . . . London, Printed for Tho. Dring, . . . 1681. Folio. Frontispiece with metrical explanation, title and preface, 4 leaves : A, 2 leaves : a—b, 2 ll. each : *, 4 ll.: B—Zz in fours : Aaa, 2 leaves.

Systema Horti-culturæ : Or, The Art of Gardening in Three Books. The I. Treateth of the Excellency, Scituation, Soil, Form, Walks, Arbours, Springs, Fountains, . . . The II. Treateth of all sorts of Trees planted for Ornament or Shade, Winter Greens, Flower Trees, . . . The III. Treateth of the Kitchin Garden, and of the great variety of Plants propagated for food or for any culinary uses : . . . Illustrated with Sculptures, representing the form of Gardens, according to the newest Models. By J. W. Gent. London, Printed for Tho. Burrel, . . . and Will. Hensman, . . . 1677. 8°, A—V in eights, and a, 4 leaves, besides a frontispiece and plates at pp. 17, 18, 53, by Van Hove.

Systema Horti-culturæ : Or, The Art of Gardening. In Three Books. . . . Illustrated with Sculptures. . . . The Second Edition with large Additions. By J. W. Gent. London, Printed for Tho. Dring. . . . 1683. 8°. Frontispiece, 1 leaf : A, 4 leaves : a, 8 leaves : B—X in eights, X 7-8 with advertisements. With plates at pp. 15, 17 and 53 by Van Hove.

Apiarium ; Or A Discourse of Bees : Tending to the best Way of Improving them, and to the Discovery of the Fallacies that are imposed by some, . . . Written by J. W. Gent. London, Printed for and Sold by Thomas Dring Bookseller, . . . MDCLXXXVI. 8°. A, 4 : B—C in eights. With a frontispiece.

The Most Easie Method of making the Best Cyder. By J. W. Gent. . . . London, Printed for George Grafton, at the Mitre in Fleetstreet, near Temple-Bar, 1687. 4°, A—D in fours.

WOTTON, EDWARD, *of Oxford.*

Edoardi Wottoni Oxoniensis De Differentiis Animalivm Libri Decem. Ad Sereniss. Angliae Regem Edoardvm VI. . . . Lvtetiae Parisiorvm . . . M.D.LII. . . . Folio. a, 4 leaves : ā and ē, 4 leaves each : A—Nn in sixes: Oo, 4 leaves : a, 6 leaves : b—c, 4 leaves each, c 4 blank.

WRIOTESLEY OR WORSLEY, E.

Reason and Religion. Or The Certain Rvle of Faith, where the Infallibility of the Roman Catholick Church is asserted, . . . Printed at Antwerp, By Michael Cnobbaert, in the Year 1672. . . . 4°, a—e 2 in fours : a leaf with the contents of the First Discourse : A—4 P in fours : 4 Q, 5.

A Discovrse of Miracles wrought in the Roman Catholick Chvrch, Or, A full refutation of Dr Stillingfleets unjust exceptions against Miracles, . . . By E. W. Antwerp, Printed by Michael Cnobbaert, at the Sign of St. Peter. 1676. Permissu Superiorum. 8°, a—b 4 in eights: A—Bb 4 in eights.

WRIGHT, EDWARD.

A Short Treatise of Dialling : Shewing, The Making of all sorts of Sun-dials, Horizontal, Erect, Direct, Declining, Inclining, Reclining, vpon any flat or plaine superficies, howsoeuer placed, with ruler or compasse onely, without any Arithmeticall calculation. By Edward Wright. London, Printed by Iohn Beale for William Welby. 1614. 4°. Title, contents, and *Errata*, 2 leaves : B—G in fours. With many diagrams.

WRIGHT, PETER.

R. P. Petri Writi Sacerdotis Angli E Societ. Iesv Mors, Qvam ob Fidem Passvs est Londini xxix. Maii M.DC.LI. 12°, A—G 4 in twelves. With a portrait of Wright on A ii.

There is no imprint. Printed abroad, probably in Belgium.

WYNDHAM, ANNE.

Clavstrvm Regale Reseratvm or The Kinges Concealment at Trent published by A. D. . . . London Printed for Will. Nott at the Queens Arms in the Pell-Mell. 1667. 4°, A—E in fours. The title is engraved.

Dedicated to the Queen.

X.

XAVIER, ST. FRANCIS.
An Instruction to performe with fruit the Devotion of Ten Fridays in Honour of S. Francis Xaverius Apostle of the Indies. Much practised in Rome and augmented particularly of late by some most authentick miracles wrought by the intercession of this glorious Saint. . . . Superiorum permissu. 12º, A—E in twelves : F, 2. Dedicated by the translator N. N. "To the Honourable the Lady Mary Caryll Abbesse of the English Benedictin Dames at Dunkerque."

XENOPHON.
The Historie of Xenophon : Containing The Ascent of Cyrvs into the Higher Covntries. Wherein is described The Admirable Iovrney of Ten thousand Grecians from Asia the Lesse into the Territories of Babylon, and their retrait from thence into Greece, notwithstanding the Opposition of all their Enemies. Where-unto is added A Comparison of the Roman manner of Warres with this of our time, out of Ivstvs Lipsivs. Translated by Joh. Bingham. London, Printed by John Haviland for Raphe Mabb. 1623. Folio, A—X in fours, A 1 and X 8 blank. Dedicated to Hugh Hammersley, Alderman and Coronel of London, and President of the Artillery Company.

Xenophons Treatise of Hovsholde. Anno. M. D. LVII. [Col.] Imprinted at London in Paules Churche yarde at the signe of the Lambe by Abraham Vele. 8º, A—H in eights.

With the Preface on the back of the title.

[Xenophons Treatise of Household. Colophon :] Imprinted at London at the long Shop adioyning vnto S. Mildreds Church in the Pultrie, by Iohn Allde. 8º, A—H in eights.

The copy examined wanted the title.

Y.

Y. E.
Parliaments Power, In Lawes for Religion. Or, An Answer to that old and groundles Calumny of the Papists, nicknaming the Religion of the Church of England, by the name of Parliamentary Religion. Sent to a friend, who was troubled at it, and earnestly desired satisfaction in it. Oxford, Printed by Henry Hall . . . 1645. 4º, A—F 2 in fours, A 1 blank.

Dated from Covent Garden, June 29, 1645.

YARRANTON, ANDREW.
England's Improvement . . . 1677-81, 1698.

At the end of Part the First the author furnishes an interesting sketch of his personal history, from which it appears that he was originally a linen-draper's apprentice.

YEARWOOD, RANDOLPH, *Chaplain to the Lord Mayor*.
The Penitent Murderer. Being an Exact Narrative of the Life and Death of Nathaniel Bvtler ; Who (through Grace) became a Convert, after he had most cruelly murdered John Knight. With the several Conferences held with the said Butler in Newgate, . . . London, Printed by T. Newcomb for J. Rothwell . . . and Tho. Matthews . . . 1657. [Sept. 14.] 8º, A—G in eights : *Serious Advice to the Citizens of London*, *, 8 leaves : **, 4 leaves. A 1 has the Lord Mayor's Certificate. *B. M.*

This copy has no frontispiece ; but possibly the print was added afterward.

YONGE, WILLIAM.
Englands Shame : Or the Unmasking of a Politick Atheist : Being a Full and Faithful Relation of the Life and Death of that Grand Impostor Hugh Peters. Wherein is set forth his whole Comportment, Policies, and Principles exercised from the Ingress, in the Progress, and to the Egress of his Unhappy Life. By William Yonge, Dr Med. London, Printed by Da. Maxwel, for Theodore Sadler, next Door to the Golden Dolphin, over against Exeter House in the Strand, 1663. 8º, A—H 4 in eights, besides the frontispiece of Peters preaching. Dedicated to the Queen Mother.

YORK, CHURCH OF.

Sermo exhortatoriȝ cancellarij Ebor. hijs qui ad sacros ordines petunt promoueri. W. de Worde. [about 1525.] 4º, 8 leaves without a regular title.

> There is no imprint; but at the end over the printer's mark is a sort of imprimatur of Dean Colet. Sothebys, June 30, 1885, No. 1058, where the following note occurs : " Dibdin, on the authority of Mr. Utterson's copy (this) and Lowndes assign this sermon to W. Melton, Chancellor of York in 1317; but neither could have read the work, or they would have seen the absurdity of doing so, as on the reverse of signature A 7 printing is mentioned. On the previous page the 'a ludis theatralibus' must allude to the Corpus Christi Plays at York."

YORKSHIRE.

The Declaration and Votes . . . concerning the Magazine at Hull, . . . London Printed for Francis Leach 1642. 4º, 4 leaves.

A Reall Protestation of Many, and Very eminent persons in the County of Yorke, Declaring Their Resolutions concerning the present distractions, some of whose names are subscribed. London, Printed for H. Blunden. 1642. 4º, 4 leaves. With a singular cut on the title.

A Letter from the Right Honovrable Ferdinando Lord Fairfax, Sir Hugh Cholmley, Sir Philip Stapleton, Sir Henry Cholmley. Committees of the Commons house of Parliament residing at Yorke. With a Relation of all the Passages at the great meeting at Yorke, on Thursday the 12. of this instant May . . . London, Printed by A. Norton for Iohn Franke, . . . 1642. 4º, A—B in fours.

To the Kings Most Sacred Majestie. The Humble Petition of Sir Francis Wortley Knight and Baronet, In behalfe of your Majesties Commons of the Covnty of York. [With the reply of the King.] Printed at York by Stephen Bulkley, for Marke Foster, July 23, 1642. A broadside B. M.

The Declaration of the Right Honourable Henry Earle of Cumberland, Together with divers Gentlemen of the County of York, who desire it may be put in print, . . . reprinted at London for Iohn Thomas. Septem. 8. 1642. 4º, 4 leaves.

A Letter from the Speaker of the House of Commons, To the Gentry, Freeholders and Inhabitants of the County of Yorkshire, In Answer to their Protestation. September 8. 1642. London, Printed by L. N. and J. F. for E. Husbands and I.

Franck, . . . 4º, 4 leaves subscribed at end " Your loving Friend, W. L[enthall.]"

A True Relation of the Late Fight Between the Parliament Forces and Prince Rupert, within Four Miles of Yorke . . . London : Printed for Robert White. July 8. 1644. 4º, 4 leaves.

A Letter to a Person of Honour in London, From an Old Cavalier in Yorkshire, concerning the Papists. London, Printed in the Year MDCLXXII. 4º, A—B 2 in fours.

The Narrative of Lawrence Mowbray of Leeds, in the County of York, Gent. concerning the Bloody Popish Conspiracy, . . . London, Printed for Thomas Simmons, . . . and Jacob Sampson, . . . MDCLXXX. Folio, A—I, 2 leaves each.

YOUNG, EDWARD, *Prebendary of Salisbury.*

The Idea of Christian Love. Being a Translation, at the Instance of Mr Waller, of a Latin Sermon upon John xiii. 34, 35. Preach'd by Mr Edward Young, Prebend of Salisbury. With a Large Paraphrase on Mr Waller's Poem of Divine Love. . . . London, Printed for Jonathan Robinson, . . . 1688. 4º, A—H in eights, and a, 8 ll.

> Included are copies of verses by and to Mrs. Wharton.

YOUNG, RICHARD, *of Roxwell, Essex.*

A Christian Library. Or, A Pleasant and Plentiful Paradise of Practical Divinity, in 37. Treatises . . . By R. Yovnge of Roxwel in Essex, Florilegus. London, Printed by M. I. and are to be sold onely by James Crumpe, . . . 1660. 8º. 4 prel. leaves, and the 37 tracts with separate signatures.

YOUTH.

Youths Behaviour, Or Decency in Conversation amongst Men. Composed in French by grave persons for the Use and benefit of their Youth. Now newly turned into English by Francis Hawkins. The fourth Edition, with the Addition of Twenty sixe new Precepts (which are marked thus *) London, Printed by W. Wilson for W. Lee : and are to be sold at the Turks-head neere the Miter Taverne in Fleetstreet. 1646. [Octob. 5th] 8º, A—D in eights, A 1 and D 8 blank. B. M.

Youths Behaviour, Or, Decency in Conversation amongst Men. . . . The sixth Edition . . . London, Printed for W. Lee, . . . 1654. 8º, A—E 4 in eights, A 1 occupied by a portrait of the translator, an. æt. 8. *B. M.*

Youths Behaviour, Or, Decency in Conversation Amongst Men. Composed in French . . . Now newly turned into English, by Francis Hawkins . . . The Tenth Impression. Whereunto is added Lilies Rules, translated out of the Latin into English Verse. There is likewise added the first Entrance of a Youth into the University ; together with English and Latin Proverbs, and a very useful Table for expounding of hard words in the English Tongue, much enlarged. London, Printed by S. G. and B. G. for William Lee, . . . 1672. 8°, A, 4 leaves, including a portrait of the translator an. æt. 6 : B—I 4 in eights, including Advertisements.

On sign. E occurs a separate title : New Additions unto Yovths Behaviovr 1650. Of some Letters. As also A Discourse upon some Innovations of Habits and Dressings. . . . 1672 ; on the back of which are portraits by Cross (after Hollar) of *Virtue* and *Vice*. On the following leaf, however, the Additions are said to have been made in 1663. The Second Part does not seem to have been reprinted.

The work had been licensed to W. Lee, 7th July 1636.

YSBRAND, EVERARD, and ADAM BRAND.

A Journal of the Embassy from Their Majesties John and Peter Alexievitz, Emperors of Muscovy, &c. Over Land into China, . . . By Everard Ysbrand, Their Ambassador in the Years 1693, 1694, and 1695. Written by Adam Brand, Secretary of the Embassy. Translated from the Original in High-Dutch, Printed at Hamburgh, 1698. To which is added, Curious Observations concerning the Products of Russia. By H. W. Ludolf. London : Printed for D. Brown . . . and T. Goodwin . . . 1698. 8°, B—K 4 in eights, and the title. With a portrait of Peter the Great.

Y-WORTH, W., *of Rotterdam.*

A New Art of Making Wine, Brandy, And other Spirits, Compliant to the Act of Parliament, concerning Distillation. Illustrated by the Doctrine of Fermentation, . . . Lastly is subjoyn'd, A General Treatise concerning the Original and Nature of Diseases, . . . By W. Y. Spagyrick Physician in both Medicines, and Philosopher by Fire. London, Printed for T. Salusbury . . . 1691. 12°, A—K 6 in twelves, K 6 blank.

Z.

ZUIS-PENNINCK, JUDITH.
Some Worthy Proverbs Left behind by Judith Zuis-Penninck, To be read in the Congregation of the Saints. Translated into English by . . . W. C. London, Printed for William Warwick. 1663. 4°, A—B 2 in fours.

At the end this tract is dated from Colchester, 2ᵗ of the 6ᵗʰ month, 1663.

ZOUCH, RICHARD.
Descriptio Juris & Judicii Militaris ad

qvam Leges qvæ Rem Militarem, & Ordinem Personarum, Nec Non Juris & Judicii Maritimi . . . referuntur : Autore R. Z. P.R. Oxoniæ. Oxoniæ, Excudebat Leonardus Lichfield. M.DC.XXXX. 4°, A —F 2 in fours : the Maritime Section—title and contents, 2 leaves : a—c in fours: *Errata*, 1 leaf.

At the foot of the first title-page in the copy before me occurs : "Ex Dono Authoris. Arundell & Surrey. June 1640."

ADDITIONS.

[.*. This Appendix has been somewhat extended by the reception of items from the Solly and other sales, and also by the obliging loan to me of about eighty rare and curious tracts by Mr. Henry Gray of Leicester Square. These latter chiefly consisted of pamphlets relating to the Civil War in 1641-8, a series well-nigh interminable, though the pieces belonging to 1642 appear to be the most numerous.

The Earl of Crawford and Balcarres had the kindness to forward me (through Mr. Quaritch) the proof sheets of his privately printed Catalogue of Proclamations from Edward VI. to George II., in case I might wish to insert here such as had not otherwise fallen in my way. His Lordship's Catalogue is highly interesting, both from a historical and bibliographical point of view ; but it proceeds on a different plan from my own.

My old friend, Mr. Halliwell Phillipps, has also afforded me the opportunity of going through his Early English collections, both in London and at Brighton.]

ÆSOP.

The Swearers. Or, Innocence Opprest and Sacrific'd, In Consequence of Indulgence to Perjurious Prostitutes. London, Printed in the Year, 1681. 4°, A—B 2 in fours, B 2 with Advertisements. *B. M.*

The translation by John Ogilby of the 81st Fable, *Of the Dog and the Sheep*, with remarks by an anonymous writer, pointing out its applicability to existing circumstances.

Æsop from Islington. *Secretum divitis ullam . . .* Juven. ——*de te fabula narratur.* Printed in the Year, 1699. 8°, A—D in fours, D 4 blank. In verse.

ALBERTUS, MAGNUS.

Liber Aggregationis . . . *W. de Machlinia.* 4°.

In the forty-ninth volume of *Archæologia,* Professor Ferguson, of Glasgow, has performed a very acceptable service to early English literature and typography by giving a copious account for the first time of the *Liber Aggregationis* and *Secreta Mulierum.* Of the former the Professor was so fortunate as to secure a copy at the Syston Park Sale (December 1884, No. 53), formerly belonging to Herbert, and described by the latter at page 1773 of his well-known work. But at that time the two tracts, which have since been separated, were bound up together. The question as to whether they were originally intended to make one book is difficult to settle, or which was the earlier in order, unless the word *Nœnon* in the colophon to the *Liber Aggregationis* is to be received as a clue. Perhaps the *Secreta Mulierum* would be the likelier subject as a starting venture ; and the absence of an imprint is also favourable to the hypothesis that it really constituted the first of two pieces in a volume, the second alone exhibiting the name of the printer.

ALLIBONE, JOHN, *Master of Magdalen College School Oxford, a native of Buckinghamshire.*

Rustica Academiæ Oxoniensis Nuper Reformatæ Descriptio, In Visitatione Fanatica Octobris sexto, &c. Anno Domini 1648. Cum Comitiis ibidem Anno sequente : Et aliis notatu non Indignis. Londini, Impensis G. Redmayne. Folio, A—E, 2 leaves each. In Latin verse.

The author was at one time Vicar of Bradwell in Gloucestershire. Reprinted, 8°, 1717, and, with notes and a preface, 8°, Oxford, 1834.

ALMANAC.

A spirituall Almanacke, wherin euery Christē man and womā may se what they ought daylve to do, or leaue vndone. Not after the doctrine of the Papistes, nor after the lernynge of Ptolomy, or other Heythen Astronomers, but out of the very true & wholsome doctryne of God our almyghty heuenly father, shewed vnto vs in his worde, by his prophetes Apostles, and specyally by his dere sonne Jesus Christ. And is to be kept not onely this newe yeare, but contynually vnto the daye of the Lordes cōmyng agayne. [Col.] Printed at Londō by Rychard Kele, dwellynge at the longe shoppe in the Poultry vnder saynt Myldreds church Cum priuilegio . . . 8°, D—E 4 in eights, preceded by the title as above and two other consecutive leaves.

Sothebys, July 1886 (Simes), No. 1402, apparently part of some larger book, but complete in itself. I do not notice, however, in Herbert or in the British Museum Catalogue any work from the press of Kele, of which this could have made part.

AMADIS OF GAUL.

The Famous and Delightful History of the Renowned and Valiant Prince Amadis de Gaul. . . . London, Printed for J. Gwillim, over against the Great James tavern in Bishops-gate-street. 1702. 12°, A—H in twelves.

> An abridgment by John Shirley.

ANGEL GUARDIAN.

The Angel-Gvardians Clock Translated out of latin into English. At Rouen of the impression of Nicolas Covrant in the streete of the poterne neer to the Pallace. 12°, A—N in twelves. The title is engraved.

> Translated by Hier. Drex. There is a series of prefatory addresses by the unnamed author and by the translator.

ANSWER.

An Answer to a Paper, called, The Case of the Auditors and Receivers of His Majesty's Revenue. With A Brief Description of the Antient Course of the Exchequer for bringing in the Crown-Revenues. As also, Some Reasons wherefore the Augmentation-Revenues of the Crown may be charged in the Great Roll of the Exchequer, and brought in by the Sheriff's. Humbly offered to Consideration. London, Printed by W. G. 1662. 4°. A, 4 leaves, besides the Table : B, 4 : C, 5.

ARCANDAM.

The Most Excellent, Profitable, and Pleasant Booke of the famous Doctor, and expert Astrologian, Arcandam, or Alcandrin, . . . London, Imprinted by Felix Kingston, 16[02 ?] 8°, A—M 4 in eights, A 1 blank. Black letter, with a few cuts.

> The last two figures of the date are erased. On the title of this copy the book purports to have been newly turned out of French by William Warde. There is no introductory matter.

B. G., Gent.

Love the Leveller : Or, The Pretty Purchase. Acted at the Theatre Royal, in Bridges-Street, Covent-Garden.——Populus me sibilat . . . Hor. Sat. L. 1. London, Printed for E. Rumbal, at the Post-House in Russel-Street, Covent-Garden ; . . . 1704. 4°, A—K 2 in fours.

B. L.

Murther will out. [London, July 18, 1692.] Folio, 4 leaves. Without any title.

> A letter on the subject of the alleged murder of Arthur Capel, Earl of Essex.

B. O.

Qvestions of Profitable and Pleasant Concernings, Talked of by two olde Seniors, the one an ancient retired Gentleman, the other a midling or new vpstart frankeling, vnder an Oake in Kenelworth Parke, where they were met by an accident to defend the partching heate of a hoate day, in grasse or Buck-hunting time, called by the reporter The Display of vaine life, together with a Panacea or suppling plaister to cure if it were possible, the principall diseases wherewith the present time is especially vexed. London Printed by Richard Field, dwelling in the Blackfriers by Ludgate. 1594. 4°, A—K in fours, and a leaf of L. Dedicated by O. B. "To the Right Honorable Robert Devorax, Earle of Essex and Ewe . . . ," after which comes "The Epistle to the Reader." The head-line on A 4 is "The Display of Follie ; " but the running one throughout is "The display of vaine life." B. M., Bodleian and Sion College.

> This piece is of peculiar curiosity as being apparently the only Warwickshire publication of the time of Shakespeare, and indeed the only early piece connected with that county, except Laneham's Letter from Kenilworth, 1575, and Gascoigne's Entertainment, 1576, so that all three productions arise, as it were, from the same vicinity. Moreover, the name in the imprint is of local significance, for Richard Field, the publisher of this little volume and fellow-townsman of the great poet, had brought out the year before the Venus and Adonis, and this year followed up with the Lucrece of Shakespear ; and the Questions of Concernings is of further interest as containing phrases and allusions of a popular character. Not more than four copies of it, one slightly imperfect, appear to be known.

BACON, FRANCIS.

Saggi Morali Del Signore Francesco Bacono, Cavagliere Inglese, Gran Cancelliero D'Inghilterra. Con vn altro suo Trattato Della Sapienza Degli Antichi. Tradotti in Italiano. In Londra Appresso di Giovanni Billio. 1618. 8°. * 8 leaves : A—Q 4 in eights, Q 4 as well as * 8 blank. Dedicated by Sir Toby Matthews to Cosmo de' Medici, Grand Duke of Tuscany.

BAKER, HUMPHREY, Londoner.

Such as are desirous, eyther themselues to learne, or to haue theyr children or seruants instructed in any of these Arts and Faculties heere vnder named : It may please them to repayre vnto the house of Humfry Baker, dwelling on the North side of the Royall Exchange, next adjoyning to the signe of the shippe. Where they shall fynde the Professors of the said Artes, &c. Readie to doe their diligent endevours for a reasonable consideration. Also if any be minded to haue their children boorded at the said house, for the speedier expedition of their learning, they shall be well and reasonably vsed, to theyr contentation. . . . The Arts and Faculties to be taught are these, . . . God saue the Queene. [About 1580.] A broadside. *Soc. of Antiq.*

BALLOT.
The Benefit of the Ballot : With the Nature and Use thereof : Particularly in the Republick of Venice. Folio, 2 leaves.

BARNARD, JOHN, *D.D., Rector of Waddington, near Lincoln.*
Theologo-Historicvs, Or The True Life of the Most Reverend Divine, and Excellent Historian Peter Heylyn D.D. Sub-Dean of Westminster. Written by his Son in Law John Barnard . . . to correct the Errors, supply the Defects, and confute the Calumnies of a late Writer . . . London, Printed by J. S. and are to be Sold by Ed. Eckelston . . . 1683. 8°, A—V in eights, A 8 with *Errata*, A 1 and V 8 blank.

> Dedicated to the Bishop of Durham. This volume includes a confutation of Baxter's attacks on Heylin.

BARNFIELD, RICHARD.
Cynthia . . . 1595.

> The Isham copy appears to be really the same as that at Oxford, the date having been altered with the pen from 1595 to 1596. There is clearly only a single edition. Barnfield's works have been edited by Dr. Grosart for the Roxburghe Club and also by Professor Arber.

BAROZZI, JACOPO, *of Vignola.*
The Rule of the V. orders of Architecture composed by M' Iacob Barozzio of Vignola. Which [*sic*] a New Augmentation of Michael Angelo Buonaroti, and divers other Architects according to the Italian fashion. t'Amstelredam. . . . 1646. Folio. Titles, printed and engraved, 2 leaves : preliminary letterpress, 4 leaves : and 42 numbered plates.

> In the present copy a second part is added, the Dutch bookseller having apparently bought the plates from Venice. I merely notice the book, because the text is in English and four other languages.

BASSET, THOMAS, *Bookseller.*
A Catalogue of the Common and Statute Law-Books of the Realm ; And some Others Relating thereunto. Alphabetically Digested under Proper Heads. . . . Collected by Thomas Basset Bookseller ;

And are to be Sold at his Shop at the George, near St. Dunstans Church in Fleetstreet. 1682. 12°. A, 4 leaves : B—G in twelves.

BEHN, APHRA.
Le Montre : Or The Lover's Watch. By M" A. Behn. London, Printed by R. H. for W. Canning, at his Shop in Vine-Court, Middle-Temple. 1686. 8°. A, 8 leaves, besides the frontispiece, A 1 with *Imprimatur* : a, 2 leaves : B—Q in eights : R, 2. Dedicated to Peter Weston, Esq., of the Inner Temple. With verses by C. Cotton, N. Tate, &c. *B. M.*

BELIANIS OF GREECE.
The Honour of Chivalry : Or, The Renowned and Famous History of Don Bellianis of Greece : . . . London : Printed by W. O. and Sold by the Booksellers of Pye-corner and London-bridge. 4°, A—C in fours. With cuts.

BELLARMINE, ROBERT, *Cardinal.*
A Shorte Catechisme of Card" Bellarmine illustrated with the Images. In Augusta. With Licence of Superiours. 1614. Small 8°, A—H 4 in eights. With the title in a border and engravings on every page.

> The address to the Reader is subscribed *Georgius Mayr.* The last leaf has only the Errata and the colophon. Under the former occurs : Cætera lector Anglus typographo Germano ignoscet.

BELLENDEN, WILLIAM.
Gwilielmi Bellendeni Scoti, Magistri Svpplicvm Libellorvm Avgvst Regis Magnæ Britanniæ, De Tribvs Lvminibvs Romanorvm Libri Sex-Decim. Parisiis, . . . M.DC.XXXIV. Folio. 3 prel. leaves : A—5 Q in fours.

BELLERS, JOHN.
Essays about the Poor, Manufactures, Trade, Plantations, & Immorality, and of the Excellency and Divinity of Inward Light. . . . London, Printed and Sold by T. Sowle, . . . 1699. 4°. A, 3 leaves : B—C in fours : D, 1 leaf : E, 4 leaves. *B. M.*

BELLOT, JACQUES.
Le Jardin de Vertv, et Bonnes Moevrs plain de Plvsievrs Belles Flevrs, & riches sentences auec le sens d'icelles, recueillies de plusieurs autheurs, & mises en lumiere par, J. B. gen. Cadomois. Imprimè a Londres par Thomas Vautrouillier demeurant à Blacke-friers. 1581. 8°. *, 8 leaves : A—E in eights. Fr. and Engl. *B. M.*

> Dedicated to Queen Elizabeth. There is a curious leaf of *Errata* for the French as well as the English slips of the press.

BERNIER, F., *Physician of the Faculty of Montpelier.*

The History of the Late Revolution of the Empire of the Great Mogol : Together with the most considerable Pasages, for 5 years following in that Empire. To which is added, A Letter to the Lord Colbert, touching the Extent of Indostan ; the Circulation of the Gold and Silver of the World, to discharge it self there ; . . . English'd out of French. London, Printed, and Sold by Moses Pitt [and others] . . . 1671. 8°, A—R in eights : S, 1 leaf : Tom. II. with a new title, Aa—Ll in eights : Mm, 1 leaf : Letter to Colbert, Aaa—Ggg 4 in eights.

BERTRANDI, PETRUS.

Vita & processus sancti Thome cantuariensis martyris super libertate ecclesiastica. [Col.] Explicit quis libellus super iurisdictione ecclesiastica factus p dñm petrum bertrādi / & in cōsilio [con]uenientibus platē regni francie . . . recitatu? : Impressus parisij per mgr̄m Johem philippi alemāni : In vico sc̄t iacobi ad intersignium sancte barbare Anno dn̄i millesimo quadrigetesimo nonagesimo quinto sc̄la Aprilis. Folio, a—l in eights : m, 6 : A, 4 leaves with the Table : a new set of signatures with a different work by the author, aa, 8 leaves : bb, 10 leaves. *B. M.*

The printer's device occupies bb 10 *verso.*

BEVIS OF SOUTHAMPTON.

The Gallant History of the Life and Death of that most Noble Knight, Sir Bevis of Southampton. . . . Printed for J. Deacon, at the Angel in Guilt-spurstreet, . . 4°, black letter, A—C in fours. With cuts.

BILLINGSLEY, MARTIN.

The Pens Excellencie or The Secretaries Delighte. Wherein aswell the abuses wᶜʰ are offered vnto yᵉ worthines of yᵉ Pen by vnworthy Pen men are trulie discouered as yᵉ dignity of yᵉ Art it selfe by yᵉ Antiquitie : Excellencie & diuersitie thereof is breifly demonstrated . . . [London, 1618.] Obl. 8°. . . . Portrait of the author, by Holle (?), dated 1618. an. æt. 27, title and dedication to Prince Charles, all probably engraved by Holle, 3 leaves : B—D in fours, with the Preface, dated from the author's house in Bush Lane, near London Stone, Dec. 22, 1618, and the *Directions :* the plates of handwriting, 26 leaves, or with the engraved title and dedication, 28. *B. M.*

A Coppie Booke Containing Varietie of Examples of all the most Curious hands

written . . . M. B. The second editioⁿ 1637. Are to be sold by Thomas Dainty at the three [rest left unsupplied in this copy.] Obl. 8°. Title and 13 numbered leaves, all engraved : *Directions,* 4 leaves.

BISHOPE, GEORGE.

New England Judged, Not by Man's, but the Spirit of the Lord : And The Summe sealed up of New-England's Persecutions. Being a Brief Relation of the Sufferings of the People called Quakers in those Parts of America, . . . In Answer to a Certain Printed Paper, Intituled, *A Declaration of the General Court* of the Massachusets holden at Boston, the 18. October, 1658. . . . London, Printed for Robert Wilson, . . . 1661. 4°, A—Y in fours.

New England Judged. The Second Part. Being A Relation of the cruel and bloody Sufferings of the People called Quakers, in the Jurisdiction chiefly of the Massachusets ; . . . [1661-5.] . . . London, Printed in the Year, 1667. 4°, A—T 2 in fours.

BLUNDEVILE, THOMAS.

The foure chiefest Offices belonging to Horsemanship : That is to say, The office of the Breeder, . . . Imprinted at London by Humfrey Lownes, for the Company of the Stationers. 1609. 4°, A—Gg in eights. With cuts and with separate titles to the several portions.

BOCCACCIO, GIO.

The tragedies gathered by Jhon Bochas. John Wayland. Folio.

This volume has been usually dated 1558 ; but on the title of the Huth copy occurs, in a coeval hand : " this booke was bought in the yere of oʳ Lorde god 1555."

BOILEAU DESPREAUX, NICOLE.

Le Lutrin : An Heroick Poem, Written Originally in French, By Monsieur Boileau : Made English by N. O. London, Printed by J. A. for Benjamin Alsop at the Angel and Bible in the Poultrey, 1682. 4°, A —F 2 in fours.

BOOK.

[The Book of Hawking, . . .] St. Albans, 1486. Folio.

Mr. Popham of Littlecote's copy, with two leaves in facsimile, was sold in March 1882, for £600, just before Sir George Dasent discovered the copy at Powderham Castle. The latter, I understand, is perfect, except the corner of one leaf.

BORLASE, E.

The History of the Execrable Irish Rebellion Trac'd from many preceding Acts, to the Grand Eruption The 23. of October,

1641. And thence pursued to the Act of Settlement, MDCLXII.

> *Spartanos (genus est audax,*
> *Avidumque feræ) nodo cautus*
> *Propriore liga.* Sen. Hippolytus.

London, Printed for Robert Clavel in St. Paul's Churchyard. MDCLXXX. Folio. A, 4 leaves: b—d in fours: *Errata,* 1 leaf: B—Tt in fours: (A*)—(T*) in fours, besides a folded leaf, with statistics of the cost of subduing Ireland in 1641, which he estimates at £22,000,000.

BOUVET, J., *Missionary.*
The Present Condition of the Muscovite Empire, Till the Year 1699. In Two Letters: The First from a Gentleman, who was conversant with the Muscovite Ambassadour in Holland: The Second from a Person of Quality in Vienna, Concerning the late Muscovite Embassy, His present Czarish Majesty, the Russian Empire, and Great-Tartary. With the Life of the present Emperour of China. [Translated] By the Author of the *Antient and Present State of Muscovy.* London, Printed for F. Coggan, in the Inner-Temple-Lane. MDCXCIX. 8°. First title, 1 leaf: Preface, 2 leaves: To the Reader, 4 leaves: B—H 7 in eights: the Account of China, B—H in eights, besides the separate title. *B. M.*

BOXOLL, JOHN, *President of Wickham College.*
Oratio Longe Elegantissima, eademq; doctissima, D. Ioannis Boxolli, wicamensis collegij prope Wintoniam præsidis, viri eruditissimi, et optimi, in cętu episcoporum, et Cleri prouincię, Cantuariensis, in ecclesia cathedrali diui Pauli London. habita. 22. die Octobris. 1555. Excusum Lōdini in ædibus R. Caly. 8°, A—B 4 in eights. Italic letter. *Corpus Christi College Cambridge.*

BOYLE, ROBERT, *F.R.S.*
Medicinal Experiments; Or, A Collection of Choice Remedies, for the most part Simple, and Easily Prepared. By the Honorable R. Boyle, Esq; Fellow of the Royal Society. London: Printed for Sam. Smith at the Princes Arms in St. Paul's Church-Yard, 1692. 12°, A, 6 leaves, A 1 with *Imprimatur:* a, 6 leaves, a 6 with half-title to the Catalogue, which is, however, printed at the end: B—K in sixes, with separate titles to Part 2 of the *Experiments* and to the Catalogue of Boyle's Works.

BOYSE, J.
A Vindication of the Reverend Mr Alex-

ander Osborn, In reference to the Affairs of the North of Ireland: In which Some Mistakes concerning him in the Printed Account of the Siege of Derry: The Observations on it, and Mr Walker's Vindication of it, are rectified. And a brief Relation of those Affairs is given so far as Mr Osborn and other N.C. Ministers in the North, were concern'd in 'em. Written at Mr Osborn's Request by his Friend Mr J. Boyse. . . . London. Printed for Tho. Parkhurst, Tho. Cockerill, John Lawrence, and John Dunton, in Cheapside and the Poultry. 1690. 4°. A, 2 leaves: B—D in fours: E, 1 leaf.

BRENTIUS, JOHANNES.
Newes from Niniue to Englande, brought by the Prophete Jonas: Which newes is plainlye published in the Godly and learned exposition of Maister Iohn Brentius folowing, translated out of Latine into Englishe by Thomas Tymme Minister.

> The silent tongue, the listning eare,
> which harkeneth after newes:
> With staring eye and gaping mouth
> this title makes me vse.

Imprinted at London by Henrie Denham, . . . 1570. 8°, A—L in eights. Dedicated to Lord William Cobham, Lord Warden of the Cinque Ports. With two pages of verse headed The Translator to the Reader. *B. M.*

BRERETON, JOHN.
A Briefe and true Relation of the Discouerie of the North part of Virginia; . . . second impression. 1602.

> *Revised Collation:*—A—C in fours: Inducements to the taking of the voyage, &c., D 1—F 4 in fours.
> Reprinted by Mr. H. Stevens. Of the three copies in the British Museum, one (the Grenville) ends on C 4.

BREWER.
The Brewers Plea. Or, A Vindication of Strong-Beere and Ale. Wherein is declared, The wonderfull bounty and patience of God. The wicked and monstrous unthankfulnesse of man. . . . London, Printed for I. C. [Aug. 30,] 1647. 4°, 4 leaves. *B. M.*

BROOKSOP, JOAN.
The Invitation of Love unto the Seed of God, Throughout the World. With a Word to the Wise in Heart. And A Lamentation for New-England. Given forth from the movings of the Spirit of the Lord, by one who is Known to the World by the Name of Jone Brooksop. London, Printed for Robert Wilson. [1662.] 4°, A—B in fours. *B. M.*

BROUGHTON, HUGH.
A Letter to a Friende [A. T.], Tovching
Mardochai his Age, . . . Imprinted for
G. S. and W. W, 1590. 4º, A—B 2 in
fours. The title is within an engraved
border.

BROWNE, ARTHUR.
Arthur Browne A Seminary Priest, His
Confession after he was Condemned to be
hanged, at the Assizes holden at Dorchester the sixteenth day of August. After
which sentence of death pronounced he
fell upon his knees, asking God for for-
giveness, . . . Humbly praying this
Honourable House to pardon him, and
he would unfold a great part of their
villany which in secret he hath bin sworne
vnto. August 25. Printed at London
for George Tomlinson. 1642. 4º, 4 leaves.

BUCHANAN, GEORGE.
Ane Admonition direct to the trew Lordis
mantenaris of the Kingis Graces Authoritie. M. G. B. Imprinted at London
by Iohn Daye, according to the Scotish
copie Printed at Striuilyng by Robert
Lekpreuik. Anno. Do. M.D.LXXI. 8º,
A—D in fours. *C. C. C. Cambridge.*

> This copy is bound up in a volume of
> tracts of small octavo size, and though it
> has clearly been cut, it can scarcely ever
> have been a quarto.

Georgii Bvchanani Scoti, Poetarum nostri
sæculi facilè principis, Elegiarvm Liber 1.
Sylvarvm Liber 1. Endecasyllabon Lib.
1. Eiusdem Buchanani Tragædia, quæ
inscribitur Baptistes, siue Calumnia.
Lvtetiæ, . . . in officina Roberti Stephani. M.D.LXXIX. Sm. 8º, A—H 6 in
eights. Dedicated from Edinburgh, 24
July, 1566, " Petro Danieli suo."

> The Thuanus copy, with his *early* arms in
> gold and silver, in old red morocco binding,
> sold at the Beckford sale for £54 ! The
> same copy was offered to me in October
> 1886 for £15.

BURLES, EDWARD, *A.M., Schoolmaster
at East-Acton, Middlesex.*
Grammatica Burlesa : Or A New English
Grammar Made Plain and Easie for
Teacher and Scholar, and profitable to
Gentlemen for the recovery of what they
have lost by discontinuance from their
studies . . . Printed for the benefit of the
Grammar-Schools in the Counties of Middlesex and Hartford. . . . London, Printed
by T. N. for Humphrey Moseley, . . .
1652. 12º. A, 12 : (a), 6 : B—S 6 in
twelves. Dedicated to John Clarke, Esq.,
and his son William.

BURNET, GILBERT, *Bishop of Salisbury.*
Some Letters, Containing, An Account of
what seemed most remarkable in Switzer-
land, Italy, &c. Written by G. Burnet,
D.D. to T. H. R. B. At Rotterdam,
Printed by Abraham Acher, Bookseller
by the Exchange. 1686. 12º, A—M in
twelves : N, 6.

BURTON, HENRY.
A Tryall of Private Devotions. Or, A
Diall for the Houres of Prayer. By H.
B. of St. Mathewes Friday-street. . . .
London. Printed for M. S. 1628. 4º,
A—M in fours, besides the title and
dedicatory leaf. *B. M.*

CAMFIELD, BENJAMIN, *Rector of
Aileston, near Leicester.*
Of God Almighty's Providence both in
the Sending and Dissolving Great Snows
& Frosts, And the Improvement, we
ought to make, of it. A Sermon, Occasioned by the Late Extreme Cold Weather,
Preached in It to his Neighbours, And
now thought fit to be made more Public,
for the Common Good. London, Printed
for R. Chiswell. . . . 1684, 4º, A—D in
fours, and a, 2 leaves, with an address to
the Reader. *B. M.*

CANTERBURY, PROVINCE OF.
Articles to be enquired of, in the visita-
tion of the moste Reuerend father in God,
Matthew, by the sufferaunce of God,
Archebyshop of Canterbury, Primate of
all Englande, and Metropolitane. In the
yeare of our Lorde God, M.D.LXIII. Im-
printed at London by Reginalde Wolfe,
Anno Domini. M.D.LXIII. 4º, black letter,
A in sixes.

Articvli, de quibus conuenit inter Archi-
episcopos, & episcopos vtriusq ; prouinciæ,
& clerum vniuersum in synodo, Londini.
An. Dom. 1562. . . . Londini, apud
Iohãnem Dayum Typographum. An.
Domini. 1571. 4º, A—C in fours.

Articuli per Archiepiscopum, Episcopos &
reliquum Clerum Cantuariensis Prouinciæ
in Synodo inchoata Londini, vicessimo
quarto die Mensis Nouembris, Anno
Domini 1584. . . . stabiliti . . . Londini,
In ædibus C. B. 4º, 4 leaves.

Capitvla Sive Constitvtiones Ecclesias-
ticæ per Archiepiscopum, Episcopos, &
reliquum Clerum Cantuariensis Prouinciæ in Synodo inchoata Londini vicessimo
quinto die mensis Octobris. . . . Londini
Excudebant Deputati Christopheri Barker
. . . 1597. 4º, A—D 2 in fours.

> By the royal authority under the Great
> Seal these Constitutions were declared to be
> in force in both Provinces.

CATO, DIONYSIUS, &c.
1. Catonis disticha de Moribus ; . . . 1.
Cato's Distichs concerning Manners ; 2.
Excellent Sayings of the Seven Wise men
of Greece. 3. Publius's Stage-Verses, or
Seneca's Proverbs in Latine and English.
Likewise Cato Construed Grammatically,
with one row Latine and another Eng-
lish. Whereby little Children may under-
standingly learn the Rules of common
Behaviour. By Charles Hoole, M' of
Arts, and teacher of a private Grammar
School in Goldsmiths Alley, London.
London, Printed by R. W. for the Com-
pany of Stationers. 1675. 8°, A—F in
eights. Lat. and Engl.

CAUSTON, PETER, *Merchant of London*.
Tvnbrigialia : Or, The Pleasures of Tun-
bridge. A Poem. In Latin and English
Heroic Verse. Written by Peter Causton
Merc. Lond. Movnt Sion : Printed and
Sold at the End of the Upper Walk, at
Tunbridge-Wells, 1705. 4°, A—C in
fours, including the half-title, marked A.
> Probably the earliest book printed at
> Tunbridge Wells.

CELLIER, ELIZABETH.
Malice Defeated : Or a Brief Relation of
the Accusation and Deliverance of Elizabeth Cellier, Wherein her Proceedings
both before and during her Confinement,
are particularly Related, and the Mystery
of the Meal-Tub fully discovered. . . .
London, Printed for Elizabeth Cellier,
and are to be sold at her House in Arun-
del-street neer St. Clements Church, 1680.
Folio, A—M, 2 leaves each.

CERVANTES SAAVEDRA, MIGUEL.
Don Quixote . . . translated by Charles
Jarvis. 1742.
> The translator was the same person who
> occupies so prominent a place in the *Life of
> Pope*, where he is called Jervas. He was
> a painter, as well as a man of letters, and
> at one time gave Pope lessons.

CHARLES [STUART] THE FIRST,
King of Great Britain (1625-48).
Strange Newes from Yorke, Hull, Bever-
ley, and Manchester. Or A continuation
of the proceedings . . . As also of my
Lord Strange comming in a warlike man-
ner against the Town of Manchester and
slew three of the Inhabitants thereof.
. . . Also The Humble Petition of Sir
Francis Wortley Knight and Baronet, to
the Kings most Excellent Majestie. With
his Majesties Answer thereunto. Edw.
Nicholas. London, printed for John
Thomas. 1642. 4°, 4 leaves.

His Majesties Demands to the honourable

House of Parliament, Also Certaine In-
telligences from Windsore, Marlborough,
Bathe. Touching the execution of the
Militia. . . . London Printed, 1642. 4°,
4 leaves.

The Lord Marquesse of Hertford His
Letter, Sent to the Queen in Holland.
Also a Letter from the Committee in
Sommersetshire, to the Houses of Parlia-
ment, . . . Likewise the Information
that both Houses received from a Mar-
chant in Roterdam, . . . Whereunto is
added, Certain Votes of the Lords and
Commons in Parliament, for the appre-
hending, and bringing up, Sir Ralph
Hopton, Master Thomas Smith, Captain
John Digby ; Members of the House of
Commons. With Sir Ferdinando Gorges,
Sir Francis Dodington, and some others
as Delinquents . . . [London, 1642]. 4°,
8 leaves.
> The imprint is cut off.

The Cavaliers Advice to his Majesty, with
his Majesties Answer to their desires. . . .
With the relation of Oxford Schollers,
shewing how many of them were taken,
and how they were taken, by London
Troopers : . . . Likewise the Resolution
of two hundred Scots landed at Dover
Castle, with their witty inventions used
to the overthrow of many of the Caval-
liers. Printed at London for Thomas
Banks. 1642. 4°, 4 leaves.

The Earle of Essex His Speech in the
Artilrie garden to the Souldiers on
Tuesday Last. With His Majesties Pro-
positions to the Citizens of London.
Likewise Terrible and Blovdy News from
Yorke concerning the great affront, which
was given to the said City, by the Cavi-
leers, . . . July 28. Printed for Thomas
Baley. 1642. 4°, 4 leaves.

A Royall Protestation made by the Kings
most Excellent Majestie, To the Dukes,
Marquesses, Earles, Barons, Gentlemen,
now assembled at Beverley in Yorkshire.
July 23. 1642. . . . London, Printed by
T. F. for I. Horton July 28. 1642. 4°, 4
leaves.
> This piece includes the Parliament's
> counter-protestation.

The Kings Majesties Resolution Concerning the Lord Major of London, now Prisoner in the Tower, . . . Likewise exceeding Joyfull News from Manchester
and Hull, . . . July 28. London, Printed
for I. Smith. [1642.] 4°, 4 leaves.

An Alarum to Arms, Or The Kings Majesties Resolution, to raise Arms against

all those that shall oppose or resist Him, in the suppressing the Ordinances of Parliament concerning the Militia. . . . The last news from Hull, of sixty Cavaliers slain by Sir John Hothams men. London, Printed for George Tomlinson, July 29. 1642. 4°, 4 leaves.

> This tract includes the Parliament's counter-resolution in respect to the Militia.

Two Petitions. The One to the Kings most Excellent Majesty, The humble Petition, of the Grand Jury attending His Majesties service at the Assizes in the County of Southampton. The Other To the Right Worshipfvll the Justices of the Peace now assembled at the Assizes holden at Bury St. Edmonds for the County of Suffolk. The humble Petition of the Chiefe Constables. and Freeholders, Inhabitants in the said County attending the service there. August 15. 1642. London, Printed by E. G. for H. Overton. 4°, 4 leaves.

Propositions from the Kings most Excellent Majesty: Propounded by

The Earle of Devon. ⎫   ⎧ The Earle of Rivers.
The Earle of New- ⎪   ⎪ The Lord Mowbray.
  castle.   [ton. ⎬   ⎨ The Lord Rich.
The E. of Southamp- ⎪   ⎪ The Lord Chapel.
The Earle of Lindsey.⎭   ⎩

Accompanyed with 5000. Horse and Foot for their Guard. To the Lo. Brooks, and the Gentry and Commonalty assembled at Warwick, on Thursday last, August 18. . . . London, Printed for Henry Fowler. 1642. 4°, 4 leaves.

> This comprises Lord Brooke's reply and the Parliament's Resolution in respect thereof.

August 19th. A True and Exact Relation of all the Proceedings of Marquesse Hartford, Lord Pawlet, Lord Seymor, Lord Coventry, Sir Ralph Hopton, and other His Maiesties Commissioners in the publishing of the Commission of Array in his Maiesties County of Somerset. . . . Whereunto is added True Newes from Yorke, Hull, Newcastle and Darbyshire. Also a List of the Horse under the Command of William Earle of Bedford, . . . London Printed, 1642. 4°, 4 leaves.

A True Relation of His Majesties comming to Coventry Upon Saterday last, and how the Citizens of Coventrie shut up the Gates against him, comming with a great Number of Cavaleers, with the number of those forces that came with him thither, and his Majesties Resolution thereupon . . . Likewise the Confession of four Popish Priests before the Com-

mittee, August 23. With the taking of two pieces of Ordnance . . . at one Mr Molleins house neer Grayes Inne, a great Papist, and now with the King . . . Printed for J. Hanson August 24. 1642. 4°, 4 leaves.

Exceeding Joyfull Newes from the Earle of Bedfords Army, brought to London by Captain Johnson, September, 6. . . . With the Resolution of Collonell Lunsford, . . . Likewise the Resolution of the Trayned Band of Devonshire . . . September 7. London Printed for Iohn W[r]ight, 1642. 4°, 4 leaves.

> The Devonshire Trained Band was appointed to march against Lunsford from Dorchester. It consisted of 900 foot, accompanied by 200 horse and many brave gallants.

True and Remarkable Passages from Several places in this Kingdome. From Munday the fifth of September, to Saturday the 10. of September. 1642. Viz. From

Westminster.	Scotland.
Ireland.	Kent.
Yorke.	Portugall.
Norfolke.	Pomfret.
Earle of Warwicke.	Northampton.
Nottingham.	

Printed at London for D. F. 1642. 4°, 4 leaves.

A Remonstrance of all the Proceedings, Passages, or Occurrences at Nottingham, Yorke, and New-Castle, from the 3. of Septem. to the 10. . . . London, Printed for John Thomas, Sept. 13. [1642.] 4°, 4 leaves.

Three Declarations, First, The Declaration of the Lords and Commons . . . With His Majesties Answer thereunto. Secondly, A declaration and Protestation agreed upon by the Grand Iury at the Assizes held in the County of Worcester, the third day of August, 1642. . . . Thirdly, the Declaration of the Isle of Wight to the King and Parliament . . . Reprinted at London, September 17. 1642. 4°, 4 leaves.

Sylloge Variorvm Tractatvvm Anglico quidam idiomate & ab Auctoribus Anglis conscriptorum sed in linguam Latinam translatorum ; . . . Auctore I. V. A. R. Anno Domini ƆƆ IƆC XLIX. 4°. *, 4 leaves: (a)—(f) in fours : A—E in fours: &c., each piece being separately signed.

> A collection of tracts relating to the Civil War period, by John Cooke of Gray's Inn and others.

CHARLES [STUART] THE SECOND,
King of Great Britain (1660–85).
The Reasons & Narrative of Proceedings betwixt the Two Houses : . . . touching the Tryal of the Lords in the Tower. On Monday the 26th of May, 1679. Folio, 2 leaves.

The Naked Truth. The Second Part. In Several Inquiries concerning the Canons and Ecclesiastical Jurisdiction, . . . Also of the Church of England, and Church - Wardens. And the Oath of Church - wardens. And of Sacriledge. . . . London, Printed for Francis Smith, . . . 1681. Folio, B—R, 2 leaves each, and the title-page.

The Great Point of Succession Discussed. With a Full and Particular Answer to a late Pamphlet, Intituled, A Brief History of Succession, &c. London, Printed for H. Rodes, next door to the Bear Tavern near Bride-Lane in Fleetstreet, 1681. Folio, A—K, 2 leaves each.

Two Great Questions Determined by the Principles of Reason & Divinity. I. Whether the Right to Succession, in Hareditary Kingdoms, be Eternal and Unalterable? *Neg.* II. Whether some certain Politick Reasons may not be sufficient Grounds of *Divorce? Affirm.* . . . London, Printed for Richard Janeway, . . . 1681. Folio.

> The copy employed ended imperfectly on the second leaf of sign. I, and contained A—I, 2 leaves each.

The Character of a Popish Successor, And what England may expect from such a One. Part the Second. Or the Dispute of the Succession Moderately discuss'd uponthe Considerations of National Practise, Reason, and the Statutes of the Realm. With some Reflections upon Mr L'Estrange's (and another) Answer to the First Part of the Character, &c. London : Printed, and are to be sold by Richard Janeway. MDCLXXXI. Folio, B—I, 2 leaves each, a leaf of K, and the title.

The Character of a Popish Successour Compleat : In Defence of the First Part, Against Two Answers, One Written by Mr L'Estrange, Called The Papist in Masquerade, &c. And another By an Unknown Hand. London : Printed for J. Graves, . . . 1681. Folio, B—K, 2 leaves each, and 4 leaves with the title, &c.

An Address of Thanks to Father Peters and the Lord Chancellor, From the Protestant Religion and English Liberties. A broadside in verse.

The Fourth Part of the Naked Truth ; Or, the Complaint of the Church to some of Her Sons for breach of her Articles. In a Friendly Dialogue between Titus and Timothy, both Ministers of the Church of England. By a Legal Son, and sincere Conformist to the Church of England, as established by Law. . . . London : Printed for Richard Janeway, . . . 1682. Folio, A—II, 2 leaves each : I, 1 leaf : K—L, 2 leaves each.

Augustissimo et Optimo Regi Carolo Secundo, In Statuam Ei in medio Mercatorum Foro positam. [Col.] Londini, Typis Gulielmi Downing, Typographi in vico Sti Bartholomæi, 1684. Folio, 2 leaves. In Latin verse.

A Defence of the Papers Written by the Late King of Blessed Memory, and Duchess of York, against the Answer made to them. By Command. London, Printed by H. Hills . . . 1686. 4°, A—R 2 in fours.

CHEKE, SIR JOHN.
The hurt of Sedition . . . 1576.

> An almost uncut copy before me bears at the top of the title : " xij shillings stirling," and at the foot : " *Robert Gordone.*" Now, this raises the question, whether Sir Robert Gordon of Gordonstoun gave 12s. of English currency for the volume, or bought it at Stirling, where he purchased other books, for twelve shillings Scots = one shilling of English computation. As it is a small volume, which can scarcely have been published at more than a shilling sterling, 1 am inclined to accept the latter hypothesis.

CHRISTMAS.
Christmas Carols. Wynkyn de Worde, 1521. 4°.

> There are repeated entries in the Account-Book of John Dorne, bookseller at Oxford, for 1520, of " Kesmas corals ;" but whether these were in book or broadsheet form does not appear.

CHRYSOSTOM, ST. JOHN, *Bishop of Constantinople, ob.* A.D. 407.
A Sermon of Saint Chrysostome, wherein besyde that it is furnysshed with heuenly wisedome & teachinge, he wonderfully proueth, that No man is hurted but of hym selfe : translated into Englishe by the floure of lerned menne in his tyme, Thomas Lupsette Londoner. [Col.] Londini in officina Thomæ Bertheleti typis impress. Cum priuilegio ad imprimendū solum. M.D.XLII. 8°, A—D in eights, D 6 with the colophon and device, and D 7–8 blank.

CHURCH.
The Chirche of the Euyll Men and Women.

Translated by Henry Watson. Wynkyn de Worde, 1511. 4".

See Osterley Park Catalogue, 1885, No. 187. I did not see this lot, unfortunately, and it has gone to America. But as I notice an edition printed in the same year by Pynson, that other book was probably identical, as in a few other early cases, with this, the imprint being the only difference. Both the issues in London doubtless followed the original Paris impression described in my *Collections and Notes*, 1876, p. 480.

CICERO, M. T.

The thre bokes of Tullius offyce, bothe in latyn tongue and englysh, late translated and dyligently corrected by Robart Whytynton laureat poete. Prima Pars. Cum priuilegio regali. [Col.] Imprynted at London in Fletestrete at the sygne of the Sunne, by John Byddell. In the yere of our Lorde God. 1540. 8", A—X in eights. With the mark of the printer below the colophon. The title is within a border. *B. M.*

A reimpression, with the preliminaries omitted, of W. de Worde's edition of 1534. The copy employed is in the original binding, probably from the printer's own workshop, with fly-leaves from a book printed by W. Middylton, and is doubtless in the precise state in which it came from the press. It was a constant practice on the part of our old publishers to suppress introductory matter in second or later issues, and the fact of Whittinton being dead in 1540 may have had something to do with it in this case.

The copy mentioned by Herbert seems to have corresponded in title with that here used, and to have had no other. I think that he followed Ames, and that Dibdin followed him.

Tullius de Senectute Both in latyn and Englysshe . . . Cum priuilegio regali. [Col.] Imprynted at London in Fletestrete / at the sygne of the Sonne / by me John Byddell. 8". A—D in eights : E, G : F, 4. With the printer's mark on F 3 *verso*, but a different one from that at the end of the *Offices*, 1540. *B. M.*

Sothebys, Dec. 10, 1886, No. 155. Byddell also printed it with the date of 1540. There is no reason why so popular a work should not have been frequently republished. Compare *Bibl. Coll.* 1882, p. 682.

CLAPHAM, HENOCH.

An Epistle Discoursing vpon the present Pestilence. Teaching what it is, and how the people of God should carrie themselues towards God and their Neighbour therein. London Printed for Iohn Newbery, and are to be sold at his shop in Pauls Church yard, at the signe of the Ball. 1603. 4",

A—B in fours. Dedicated to Sir Baptist Hickes, Knight. *B. M.*

Doctor Andros His Prosopopeia answered, and necessarily directed to his Maiestie, for remouing of Catholike Scandale. 2. Sacred Policie, Directed of dutie to our sweet yong Prince Henry. 3. An Epistle, Directed to such as are troubled in minde about the stirres in our Church. By Henoch Clapham, Prisoner in the Gatehouse at Westminster, adjoyning London. 1605. 4", A—M 2 in fours. Dedicated to the King.

A curious piece, containing some verses at the end, as well as a list of the author's other books, with a notice that if any one intended to reprint any of them, he should give him notice, in order to enable him to make corrections ; which seems to indicate the absence of any law or principle of copyright.

CLARKE, SAMUEL.

The Wicked Life and Wofull Death of Herod the Great, A stranger by Nation, yet by the Romans made King of the Jews . . . London, Printed for William Miller . . . 1664. 4", A—H 2 in fours.

CLEVER, ROBERT.

A Godly Form of Hovseholde Gouernement : for the ordering of priuate Families, according to the direction of Gods word. Wherevnto is adioyned in a more particular manner, The seuerall duties of the Husband towards his wife : and the wiues dutie towards her husband. . . . Imprinted at London by Thomas Creede, for Thomas Man, . . . 1598. 8". A, 7 leaves, title on A 2 : B—Cc 6 in eights. Dedicated by R. C. to Master Robert Burgaine, of Roxall, justice of the peace for Warwickshire, Master John Dive, of Ridlington Park, in the County of Rutland, and Master Edmund Temple, of Temple-Hall, co. Leicester. *B. M.*

A Godly Forme of Hovsehold Government, . . . At London Printed by Thomas Creede, for Thomas Man. 1603. 8", A—Aa in eights. *B. M.*

COCKBURNE, SIR WILLIAM, *of Langtoun, Knight.*

Respvblica de Decimis. Edinbvrgh, Printed by Iohn Wreittoun Anno Domini 1627. 4", A—C 2 in fours, C 2 occupied only by woodcuts. *B. M.*

Dedicated "To the right honourable and my noble parts, My Lords Commissioners appoynted for reformation of diuerse abuses, and first of Tithes." On the title is a woodcut print of James I. with the orb and sceptre.

COFFEE.

A Satyr against Coffee. A folio leaf of verses.

COIN.

The Act for Remedying the ill State of the Coyn of the Kingdom . . . London, Printed for E. Whitlock. . . . MDCXCVI. A folio leaf.

A summary of the contents.

COLET, CLAUDE.

The Famous, Pleasant, and Delightful History of Palladine of England. . . . Translated out of French by A. M. . . . The Second Edition. London : Printed by J. F. and Sold by John Marshall, . . . 8°, A—O in sixes. With a preface signed T. J. and a cut at the end. B. M.

The words " second edition " on the title refer to the text first published in 1664.

COLEMAN, EDWARD.

Le Proces de Sᵗ Edouard Coleman Gentilhomme. . . . Imprimé à Hambourg, Sur la Copie Originale de Londres, . . . 1679. 12°, A—K in twelves.

COLLECTION.

A Choice Collection of Wonderful Miracles, Ghosts, and Visions. [London, 1682.] Folio, 2 leaves. In prose and verse. In two columns.

There is no imprint to this copy ; but it may have been cut off.

COOKERY.

This is the Boke of Cookery. R. Pynson, 1500. 4°.

A MS. copy of this work is in the library of the Earl of Leicester at Holkham, and has been printed with an introduction by Mrs. Napier, 4°, 1882. The Editor was evidently unaware that it had been published before. In the *Antiquitates Culinariæ*, edited by Warner, 1791, there is a much fuller text of the Feast at the Enthronement of Archbishop Nevill, and it is dated 1465 ; this also occurs at the end of Rabisha's *Whole Body of Cookery Dissected*, 8°, 1661.

John Byddell reproduced the *Book of Cookery* about 1550 ; and it was often printed during the sixteenth and seventeenth centuries, but with the omission of the Royal Feasts and with other changes.

A Proper newe Booke of Cokerye, declarynge what maner of meates be beste in season, for all times in the yere, and how they ought to be dressed, and serued at the table, bothe for fleshe dayes, and fyshe dayes. With a newe addition, verye necessarye for all them that delyghteth in Cokerye. [Col.] Imprynted at London, in Crede Lane, by John Kynge, and Thomas Marche. [1558.] 8°, black let-

ter, A—B in eights, B 8 blank. *Corpus Christi College, Cambridge.*

A Booke of Cookerie And the order of Meates to bee serued to the Table, both for Flesh and Fast Dayes. London, Printed by E. A. and are to be sold by F. Grove, dwelling upon Snow Hill. 1629. 8°, black letter, A—G in eights. *Patent Office.*

CORNEILLE, PIERRE.

Pompey the Great . . . 1664.

The translators were Edmond Weller, Lord Buckhurst, Sir C. Sedley, and Mr. Godolphin. Pepys, June 23, 1666, calls it "a mean play."

CORNWALL.

The Humble Petition of the Knights, Ivstices of the Peace, Gentlemen, Ministers, Freeholders and others of the Countie of Cornwall. Being, The true Copie of the agrieuances of the said whole Countie, as it was deliuered April the 22. 1642. (to the House of Commons) by some thereunto appointed . . . London, Printed by R. O. and G. D. for John Bartlet, . . . 1642. 4°, 4 leaves.

COUCH, ROBERT, *sometime Practitioner in Physic and Chirurgery at Boston, N. E.*

Praxis Catholica : Or, The Countrymans Universal Remedy : Wherein is plainly and briefly laid down the Nature, . . . of most Diseases, incident to the Body of Man. . . . Now published, with divers useful Additions (for publick benefit) by Chr. Pack, Operator in Chymistry. . . . London, Printed for Robert Harford, at the Angel in Cornhil ; near the Royal Exchange. 1680. 8°. A in eights : a—b in eights : B—M 4 in eights. Dedicated by Pack to his friend Colonel Francis Willis, which is followed by a Preface to the reader, from his Laboratory, at the sign of the Globe and Chymical Furnaces in the Postern near Moor-gate. B. M.

Willis was a friend of Couch, who had died in Virginia before the publication, and he was the means of securing the MS. for Pack, who had previously perused it, or a copy of it, in the hands of a resident of Carolina, while the latter was staying in London.

In the British Museum is a broadside by Couch, apparently belonging to 1667, entitled " New England's Lamentation for the late Firing of the City of London."

CRADOCK, FRANCIS.

Wealth Discovered : Or, An Essay upon a late Expedient for taking away all Impositions, And Raising a Revenue without Taxes. Published, and presented to his most Excellent Majesty, King Charles the

II. By F. C. a Lover of his Countrey. Whereunto is added his Majesties Gracious Order. London, Printed by E. C. for A. Seile . . . 1661. 4°, A—G 2 in fours. Dedicated to the King and (ii.) to the Duke of Albemarle.

CROFT, RICHARD, *A. M., Vicar of Stratford upon Avon in the County of Warwick.*

The Wise Steward. Being a Sermon Preached the Thursday in Whitsun-week, 1696. In the Parish Church of Feckenham, in the County of Worcester ; Before the Trustees, At the Opening of a Free-School, and Publick Charity, there Founded and liberally endowed by the Honourable Sir Thomas Cookes, Baronet. . . . London : Printed by F. Collins for D. T. 1697. 8°, A—E in eights, E 7–8 blank. Dedicated to John Appletre, Esq., High Sheriff of Worcestershire.

CROMWELL, RICHARD, *Lord Protector* (1658-9).

The Humble Petition of Richard Cromwell, Late Lord Protector of England, . . . to the Councel of Officers at Walingford House. [1660.] A broadside. *B. M.*

A satire on the expressions of loyalty and devotion to him expressed prior to the declaration of Monk and the army for the Stuarts.

It is said that in his house at Cheshunt the ex-Protector kept in a chest copies of all the addresses presented to him on his accession.

CROWNE, JOHN.

Pandion and Amphigenia : Or, The History of the Coy Lady of Thessalia Adorned with Sculptures. By J. Crowne. London, Printed by I. G. for R. Mills, at the sign of the Pestel and Mortar without Temple-Bare, Anno, 1665. 8°, A—V in eights. With a frontispiece and plates at pp. 1, 16, 26, 48, 52, 61, 68, 134, 141, 154, 169, and 195. Dedicated by Crowne to Arthur, Viscount Chichester, Earl of Donegal. *B. M.*

The Married Beau : Or, The Curious Impertinent. A Comedy : Acted at the Theater-Royal, By Their Majesties Servants. London : Printed for Richard Bentley, at the Post-House in Russel-Street in Covent-Garden. 1694. 4°, A—K 2 in fours. Dedicated to the Marquis of Normanby.

CUCKOLDOM.

Cuckoldom no Scandal. Written by a Lady. London, Printed in the Year 1715. Price Two Pence. A broadside in verse.

D

Poems in Burlesque ; With a Dedication in Burlesque to Fleetwood Shepherd, Esquire.

Cui bene ni palpere recalcitrat undiq ; tutus.
Hor.

Printed for the Booksellers of London and Westminster, 1692. 4°, A—D in fours. *B. M.*

DAMPIER, WILLIAM.

A Continuation of a Voyage to New-Holland, &c. In the Year 1699. Wherein are described, The Islands Timor, Rotee and Anabao. A Passage between the Islands Timor and Anabao . . . A Description of the Coast of New-Guinea. . . . The Coast of Java, and Streights of Sunda. Author's Arrival at Batavia . . . Their Inhabitants, Customs, . . . Illustrated with Maps and Draughts : also divers Birds, Fishes, &c. not found in this part of the World. Ingraven on Eighteen Copper-Plates. By Captain William Dampier. London, Printed by W. Botham, for James Knapton, . . . 1709. 8°, A—O in eights. With a chart of the course of the voyage, the 18 plates, and other engravings.

This is the second part of vol. iii.

DANIEL, RICHARD.

Daniels Copy-Book : Or, A Compendium of the most Usual Hands of England, Netherland, France, Spain, and Italy, Hebrew, Samaritan, . . . Together with sundry Portraitures of Men, Beasts, and Birds, in their various Forms and Proportions, naturally Drawn with single Touches, without former Presidents. All very useful for Ingenious Gentlemen, Scholars, Merchants, Travellers, and all sorts of Pen-men. Written and Invented by Rich. Daniel Gent. And Ingraven by Edw. Cocker Philomath. London : Printed for Mathew Collins and Francis Cossinet, and are to be sold at the Three Black-Birds in Cannon-street, and at the Anchor and Mariner in Tower-street, 1664. Obl. 4°. Royal Privilege and title, with verses by D. L. and Edward Cocker on the back, 2 leaves : the work, 67 engraved leaves numbered, the last with verses by the author, beneath which occurs : "*Nothing without Iesvs.* Richard daniel, 1663." *B. M.*

DARCIE, ABRAHAM.

The Honovr of Ladies : Or, A Trve Description of their Noble Perfections. By Ab: Darcie, Gen. London, Printed by T. Snodham. 1622. 8°. Title, 1 leaf : Table, 1 leaf : dedication (in verse) to the

Countesses of Derby, Montgomery and Berkshire, 1 leaf: dedication to the young lady Anne Herbert, 1 leaf: B—I in eights. In prose. *B. M.* (Dr. Bliss's copy.)

This copy wants a leaf. The work is probably a translation from the French, though not stated to be so by Darcy, who describes it, on the contrary, in his epistle to Anne Herbert, as the portraiture of her noble and excellent perfections. He also calls it his maiden literary essay. The title is within a border, and the volume is printed on unusually thick paper. Possibly it was printed for Darcy, as no other copy seems to be known

Honors Trve Arbor ; Or, The Princely Nobilitie of the Howards. Wherein, The Trve Source and Originall of their Mightie Name, with all their seuerall Alliances, with the High and Potent Families of diuers Countries since the first man that was knowne, in England by the Name of Howard is described. . . . Collected and written by Abraham De Ville Adrecie, alias Darcie, . . . this present yeare 1625 . . . [London, 1625.] Folio. Pedigree engraved by Elstracke, 1 leaf : Title, 1 leaf : dedication to the Earls of Arundel, Suffolk, and Nottingham, of the Howard family : 4 leaves with verses and complimentary references in prose to different branches of the Howards : A—D, 2 leaves each. In prose and verse.

Putticks, Dec. 16, 1886, No. 149. At the foot of the pedigree occurs a repetition of the title slightly varied, and in the lower left-hand corner : *Engrauen by R. E. for the said Darcie according to his direction.*

The letterpress portion of the title appears to have been partly filled in by hand at the time, the printer not having any case large enough.

DAVID.
The whole Booke of Psalmes, collected into English meetre by T. Sternehold . . . London, Printed for the Company of Stationers. Anno Dom. 1614. 4°. A, 4 : B—Ee in eights : Ff, 3 leaves. With the music. *B. M.*

DAVIES, JOHN, *of Hereford.*
The Writing Schoolemaster or The Anatomie of Faire Writing Wherein is exactlie expressed each seuerall character, Together with other Rules & Documents, coincident to the Art of Faire & speedy writing. By John Danies of Heref. *Viuit post funera virtus.* London Printed, and are to be sold by P. Stent, At the White Horse in Gilt Spur Street, without New Gate. 1663. Obl. 4". Title

and Directions, 4 leaves, and a series of plates. *B. M.* (imperfect.)

This copy contains 25 plates, some numbered, but one or more leaves appear to be deficient, and it does not possess the portrait mentioned by Lowndes. The whole, except the Directions, is engraved. The specimens comprise alphabets and extracts in various characters and languages.

The Writing School - Master : Or The Anatomy of Fair Writing . . . London, Printed by S. Griffin for John Overton, and sold by him at his House at the Sign of the White Horse in Little Brittain, next the Gate. 1667. . . . Obl. 8°, 4 leaves. *B. M.*

This copy contains only the Directions by David Brown, and appears to want the whole of the plates and the portrait.

DE BLANCOURT, H.
The Art of Glass. Shewing How to make all Sorts of Glass, Crystal and Enamel. Likewise the Making of Pearls, Precious Stones, China and Looking-Glasses. To which is added, The Method of Painting on Glass and Enameling. Also how to Extract the Colours from Minerals, Metals, Herbs and Flowers . . . Illustrated with Proper Sculptures . . . now first Translated into English. With an Appendix, containing Exact Instructions for making Glass Eyes of all Colours. London, Printed for Dan. Brown . . . Tho. Bennet . . . MDCXCIX. 8°, A—Aa in eights, A 1 with half-title. With copperplates at pp. 18, 20, 26, 30, 102, 240, 271, and 306.

DE CAUS, ISAAC.
Hortus Pembrochianus, ou Le jardin de Wilton. 4".

Sothebys, Comerford's Sale, December 1881, No. 597, where the following note occurs :—" This was probably the artist's own copy, as the title is without the publisher's imprint, and the etchings are unfinished proofs. No perfect copy has hitherto appeared for sale. That in the British Museum has the intitulation of large folding plate cut off, and Bindley's, which sold for £56, 10s., was also imperfect, and with all the plates mounted."

DE LA PLACE, PIERRE, *one of the King's Council, and Chief President of the Court of Aids in Paris.*
A Treatise of the Excellencie of a Christian man, and how he may be knowen . . . Wherevnto is adioyned A Briefe description of the life and death of the said Authoure, to the end that euerie one may knowe what he was. Translated into English by L. Tomson. . . . Imprinted at London by Christopher Barkar, dwelling in Powles Churchyard at the

signe of the Tygres head. Anno. 1576. 8⁰. *, 8 leaves, the first blank : ¶, 8 leaves : A—E 4 in eights.

Dedicated by Tomson "To the right worshipfull Mistres Vrsula Walsingham," at whose request he had entered on the undertaking.

DE LA QUINTINYE, M., *Chief Director of all the Gardens of the French King.*

The Compleat Gard'ner ; Or, Directions for Cultivating and Right Ordering of Fruit Gardens and Kitchen-Gardens ; With Divers Reflections on several Parts of Husbandry. In Six Books. To which is added His Treatise of Orange-Trees, with the Raising of Melons, omitted in the French Edition. Made English by John Evelyn Esquire, Illustrated with Copper Plates. London, Printed for Matthew Gillyflower . . . and James Partridge, . . . MDCXCIII. Folio. Title and dedication by the publishers to Lord Capell, 2 leaves : Preface and advertisement, 9 leaves : Latin verses, with an English translation, 4 leaves : Explication of Terms in Gardening, 7 leaves : A folded plan of the Garden at Versailles : B—Bb 2 in fours : Vol. II. part 4, B—Dd in fours : Directions concerning Melons, by Evelyn, 2 leaves : Treatise of Orange-Trees, translated by him, A—K in fours. With vignettes and other plates separate from the text at p. 176 of vol. 1, and pp. 10, 15, 20, 23, 25, 33, and 69 of vol. 2, part 4.

DELLA CASA, GIO.

The Refin'd Courtier, Or A Correction of several Indecencies crept into Civil Conversation. [Quot. from Zeno apud Laert.] London, Printed by J. G. for R. Royston, . . . 1663. 12⁰, A—M in twelves, A 1 occupied by a half-title with a wreath at top.

A free paraphrase of parts of the "Galateo," by N. W., who dedicates it to the Duke of Monmouth.

DERING, EDWARD.

A briefe & necessary Instruction, Verye needefull to bee knowen of all Householders, Whereby they maye the better teach and instruct their Families in such points of Christian Religion as is most meete. . . . Imprinted at London by John Awdely. 1572. 8⁰, black letter, A—B 5 in eights. *C. C. C. Cambridge.*

At the end occurs : " From my Chamber, the . 22. of Aprill. 1572. Thyne in the Lord. E. D."

DESAINLIENS, CLAUDE, *otherwise Hollyband.*

The Frenche Littelton : . . . Set forth by Clavdivs Holly-Band, teaching in

Paules Churchyarde at the signe of the Golden Ball . . . Imprinted at London by Thomas Vautrollier dwelling in the blackefriers. 1581. 8⁰, A—O in eights. *B. M.*

This work, in addition to the Littleton, comprises a series of grammatical exercitations and a *Traicté des Danses.*

DE SAN PEDRO, DIEGO.

The Castell of loue, translated out of Spanyshe into Englysshe, by John Bowrchier, knyght, lorde Bernes, at the instaunce of the Lady Elyzabeth Carewe, late wyfe to syr Nicholas Carewe knyght. The whiche boke treateth of the loue betwene Leriano and Laureola doughter to the kynge of Masedonia. [Col.] Thus endeth this Castell of loue. Imprynted by me Robert Wyer. For Richarde Kele. 8⁰, black letter, A—O in eights. In prose, except a metrical apologue in 8 7-line stanzas by Androwe Spigurnell. The last page has Wyer's device only. *B. M.*

DEVEREUX, ROBERT, *Earl of Essex.*

A Declaration of the Noble Resolution of the Earle of Essex his Excellency. Concerning his intention in going forth with this great Army, consisting of 60000. . . . With an excellent Speech delivered vnto his Honour, immediately before departure, by the Lord Roberts, . . . London, Printed for T. Banks. 1642. 4⁰, 4 leaves. With a rough cut on the back of the title purporting to be an equestrian portrait of Essex.

DEVIL.

A Whip for the Devil ; Or, The Roman Conjurer. Discovering the intolerable Folly, Profaneness, and Superstition of the Papists, in endeavouring to cast the Devil out of the Bodies of Men and Women by Him possest. . . . All faithfully Collected from their own Authors . . . London, Printed for Tho. Malthus . . . 1683. 12⁰, B—H 6 in twelves, besides the title and frontispiece.

DIGBY, SIR KENELM.

The Closet of the Eminently Learned Sir Kenelme Digbie K⁴. Opened : Whereby is Discovered Several ways for making of Methiglin, Sider, Cherry-Wine, &c., Together with Excellent Directions for Cookery : As also for Preserving, Conserving, Candying, &c. Published by his Son's Consent. London, Printed by E. C. for H. Brome, at the Star in Little Britain. 1669. 8⁰, Title and to the Reader, 2 leaves : B—X 2 in eights.

T

With a portrait by Cross, as in the impression of 1668, representing Digby an. æt. 62.

DILLON, WENTWORTH, *Earl of Roscommon.*

An Essay on Translated Verse. By the Earl of Roscommon. [Quot. from Horace and Virgil.] The Second Edition Corrected and Enlarged. London, Printed for Jacob Tonson . . . 1685. 4°. A, 4: (a), 3: B—D in fours, and a leaf after D 4 unsigned. With a preliminary copy of verses by Charles Dryden.

DIVINITY.

Forced Divinity . . . [1640.] 8°.

Bibl. Coll. and Notes, 2nd Series, p. 180. The original of the mock-sermon before thieves appears to be the piece printed in the *Reliquiæ Antiquæ,* ii. 111.

DODDRIDGE, SIR JOHN.

The Lawyers Light : Or, A due direction for the study of the Law, . . . Written by the Reverend and learned professor thereof, I. D. To which is annexed for the affinitie of the Subiect, another Treatise, called The Vse of the Law. [By Francis Bacon.] Imprinted at London for Beniamin Fisher, . . . 1629. 4°. ¶, 4 leaves, the first blank : A—Q in fours, A 4 blank. With commendatory verses by W. T. and I. S : *The Vse of the Law,* A—N in fours, N 4 blank.

DORSETSHIRE.

A True and Joyfull Relation of two Famous Battels fought against the Lord Marquesse of Hartford, The first by the Earle of Pembroke and the Earle of Bedfords Forces, being in Number 800 foot, and 4000 horse, who having vnited their Forces together, marched towards Shereborne castle and assaulted it, . . . Together with the Earl of Pembrokes Proceedings in the County of Wiltshire, . . . The second a Glorious Victory obtained by the Parliaments Forces against the Cavaleeres neer Norwich and Poole, . . . Printed for R. Watkins. August 27. 1642. 4°, 4 leaves.

Propositions Propounded by the Marquesse of Hartford, to the Earle of Bedford, concerning the delivering up of Sherbourne-Castle. Also Declaring how the Earle of Bedford, after his arrivall at Yeavel, within three miles of Sherbourne, surprised Squire Rogers, as he was going to relieve the Marquesse of Hartford, . . . London, Printed for Henry Fowler. September. 17. 1642. 4°, 4 leaves.

DRAYTON, MICHAEL.

Mortimeriados . . . 1596.

The copies with *Humfrey* Lownes in the imprint instead of *Mathew,* as in the Bright one, now in the British Museum, omit the date, and were probably the second issue. I have seen the latter almost uncut; and Heber was clearly mistaken in supposing that the binder had cut away the figures in his. See *Bibl. Heber.,* part 4, DRAYTON.

Englands Heroicall Epistles. Newly Enlarged. With Idea. By Michaell Drayton. At London. Printed by I. R. for N. L. and are to be sold at his shop, at the West doore of Poules. 1599. 8°. A, 3 leaves : B—Q in eights, Q 8 followed by a leaf with an Epistle by the author to Lucy, Countess of Bedford, on the back of which are the *Errata.* Grenv. Coll.

Englands Heroicall Epistles. Newly Corrected. With Idea. By Michaell Draiton. At London, Printed by I. R. for N. L. and are to be sold at his shop in Fleetstreete, neere Saint Dunstones Church. 1602. 8°. A, 4 leaves : B—Q in eights. *B. M.*

DRYDEN, JOHN.

Threnodia Avgvstalis : A Funeral-Pindarique Poem Sacred to the Happy Memory of King Charles II. By John Dryden, Servant to His late Majesty, and to the present King.

Fortunati ambo, si quid mea carmina possunt. Nulla dies unquam memori vos crimet ævo!

London, Printed for Jacob Tonson, at the Judge's Head in Chancery lane, near Fleet-street, 1685. 4°, A—D 2 in fours.

Aureng-Zebe, A Tragedy. Acted at the Royal Theatre. Written by John Dryden, Servant to his Majesty.

—Sed, cum fregit subsellia versu, Esurit, intactam Paridi nisi vendat Agaven. Juv.

London, Printed by J. M. for Henry Herringman, . . . MDCLXXXV. 4°, A—L in fours. Dedicated to the Earl of Mulgrave.

Aurenge-Zebe : Or, The Great Mogvl. A Tragedy. As it is Acted by Her Majesty's Servants. By M'. John Dryden. . . . London, Printed for J. Tonson, and T. Bennet . . . 1704. 4°, A—K in fours. Dedicated to the Earl of Mulgrave.

Annvs Mirabilis . . . Also A Poem on the Happy Restoration . . . Likewise a Panegyric on his Coronation. Together with a Poem to My Lord Chancellor . . . 1662. And an Elegy on the Death of King Charles the Second. By John Dryden, Esq; London, Printed for Henry Herringman, . . . 1688. 4°, B—Q 2 in fours, besides title and eight prel. leaves, with addresses to the City, &c., by the author.

The first collected edition of the Poems.
The several portions have separate titles.

The Medal Revers'd. A Satyre against Persecution. By the Author of Azaria and Hushai. —*Laudatur ab his, Culpatur ab illis.* London : Printed for Charles Lee, Anno 1682. 4°, B—E in fours, no A. In verse.

The Reasons of Mᶜ Bays Changing his Religion. Considered in a Dialogue between Crites, Eugenius, and Mᶜ Bays. [Quot. from Horace and Ovid.] London, Printed for S. T. and are to be Sold by the Booksellers . . . 1688. 4°, A—F 2 in fours.

A Description of Mᶜ D[ryde]n's Funeral. A Poem. London ; Printed for A. Baldwin in Warwick-lane. MDCC. Price 3ᵈ. Folio.

The copy examined was only a fragment.

DU CHESNE, ANDRÉ, *Historiographe de France.*
Histoire D'Angleterre, D'Escosse, et D'Irlande, . . . Novvelle Edition, Reveve . . . Par le Sʳ Dv Verdier, Historiographe de France . . . A Paris, . . . M.DC.LXVI. Folio. 2 vols.

DU FRESNE, M.
The French Cook, Prescribing the way of making ready of all sorts of Meats, Fish and flesh, with the proper Sauces, . . . The Third Edition. With an Addition of some choice Receits grown in Use amongst the Nobility and Gentry, by a prime Artist of our own Nation. Englished by J. D. G. London, Printed for Thomas Dring, . . . and John Leigh, . . . 1673. 8°. A, 8 : (a). 8 : (b), 3 : B—V 4 in eights. Dedicated by the author to John, Earl of Thanet, his very good lord.

Evelyn, in his version of the "French Gardener," 1658, mentions a second work by the same author, called "Les Delices de la Campagne," which he declined to translate, though wishing that it should be done, but not by him that did the *French Cook*, as if he saw cause to be dissatisfied with the execution of the latter. See my "Cookery Books and Ancient Cuisine," 1886, p. 70.

DU PLOICHE, PIERRE.
A Treatise in English and Frenche right necessary and profitable for al young Children (the contentes whereof apere in a table in the ende of this boke) made by Peter du Ploiche teacher of the same dwelling in Trinitie lane at the signe of the Rose. *Ducite me caute.* [Col.] Imprinted by Rycharde Grafton, Printer to the Kinges Maiestie. Cum priuilegio ad imprimendum solum. 4°, A—N 3 in fours. *B. M.*

This volume comprises the Catechism, Litany, Prayers, the A. B. C. and Syntax, and is printed in two columns, the English in black, and the French in italic, letter.

From the mention in the book of the capture of Boulogne in 1544 by Henry VIII. as an event of recent occurrence, the date of Du Ploiche may be guessed to be about 1545.

DURFEY, THOMAS.
Collin's Walk Through London and Westminster, A Poem in Burlesque. Written by T. D. Gent. [Quot. from Horace de Art. Poetica.] . . London, Printed for Iohn Bullord at the Old Black-Bear in St Pauls-Church-Yard, 1690. 8°, A—O in eights. Dedicated to Peregrine, Earl of Danby.

ELIZABETH TUDOR, *Queen of England.*
Aduertisements partly for due order in the publique administration of common p[r]ayers and vsinge the holy Sacramentes, and partly for the apparrell of all persons ecclesiasticall, by vertue of the Queenes maiesties letters commaunding the same, the xxv. day of January, in the seuenth yeare of the reigne of oure Soueraigne Lady Elyzabeth . . . Imprinted at London by Reginalde Wolfe. 4°, black letter, A—B in fours.

De Iezabelis Angliæ Parricidio Varii Generis Poemata Latina et Gallica. 4°, A—I in fours, and a leaf of K. Without name of place and printer, and with the initials *D. C. A. C. R.* at the end.

Sothebys, November 1886, with some few MS. corrections in a coeval hand. Other initials occur to the various poems, some of which relate to Mary, Queen of Scots.

[EMILIE, DIONIS ?]
An answere in action to a Portingale Pearle, called a Pearle for a Prince : Geuen by a Laye man in a Legacie, which Legacie he desireth to se executed before his death. 1570. Hierom. ad Paulam &c. . . . Imprinted at London in Fleetstreete, by William How for Dionis Emilie. 8°, A—B in eights : C, 4 : D, 1. *C. C. C. Cambridge.*

A very curious tract, apparently printed for the author, apparently in opposition to popish practices. The legacy was in connection with St. Giles's, Cripplegate.

ENGLAND.
A Remonstrance of the State of the Kingdome, Agreed on by the Lords and

Commons assembled in Parliament, and published by Order of both Houses. London, Printed for Henry Fowler. Septem. 13. 1642. 4°, 4 leaves.

ERASMUS, DESIDERIUS.
Twenty Two Select Colloquies out of Erasmus Roterodamus ; . . . The Third Impression Corrected and Amended. By Sir Roger L'Estrange, Knight. . . . London : Printed for R. Sare and H. Hindmarsh. . . . 1699. 8°. Title, Preface, and Contents, 3 leaves : B—T 4 in eights. With a portrait.

ETHEREGE, SIR GEORGE.
The Man of Mode, Or, Sr Fopling Flutter. A Comedy. Acted at the Duke's Theatre. By George Etherege, Esq ; . . . London, Printed by J. Macock, for Henry Herringman . . . 1676. 4°, A—N in fours. With a prologue by Sir Car Scroope. Dedicated to the Duchess of York.

EUGENIUS PHILALETHES.
A Brief Natural History Intermixed with variety of Philosophical Discourses, And Observations upon the Burnings of Mount Ætna. With Refutations of such Vulgar Errours as our Modern Authours have omitted. By Eugenius Philalethes. London Printed for Matthew Smith next door to the Castle next Moor-Gate. 1669. 8°, A—I 3 in eights.

EXPOSITIO.
Expositio sequentiarǫ toti� anni se'd'm vsum Sarꝝ diligentissime re[c]ognitarum multisᵊ elucidationibᵊ aucta Impressa p wynandū de worde hac in vrbe in parrochia scte brigide ī vico anglice nūcupato (the fletestrete) ad signū solis [com-]morantē. [At the end is added :] Anno dñi Millesimo quingentesimo duodecimo. Die vero decima mensis Januarij. 4°, AA—HH in eights and fours: H, 5 leaves, but H 6 probably with the device or else blank.
> Putticks, Dec. 14, 1886, No. 171. This was printed, as usual, to accompany the *Expositio Hymnorum.*
> An edition of both portions was executed by the same printer, 4to, 1502.

FILMER, SIR ROBERT.
Quæstio Quodlibetica, Or A Discourse, Whether it may bee Lawfull to take Use for Money. [Quot. from John of Salisbury, Epist. 198. *In omni arduâ . . .*] . . . London, Printed for Humphrey Moseley, . . . 1653. 12°. A, 12 leaves : a, 8 leaves : B—G in twelves : H, 4, the last leaf blank. With a Preface by Sir Roger

Twysden, dated from East-Peckham, Oct. 9, 1652.
A Discourse whether it may be Lawful to take Use for Money. Written by Sir Robert Filmer, And published by Sir Roger Twisden, with his Preface to it. London, Printed for Will. Crook, . . . 1678. 12°, A—G in twelves. *B. M.*
> Twisden's preface is dated, as before, from East Peckham.

FLAMMEL, NICHOLAS.
Nicholas Flammel, His Exposition of the Hieroglyphicall Figures which he caused to bee painted upon the Arch in St. Innocents Church-yard, in Paris. Together with The secret Booke of Artephivs, And the Epistle of Iohn Pontanus : Concerning both the Theoricke and the Practicke of the Philosophers Stone. Faithfully, and (as the Maiesty of the thing requireth) religiously done into English out of the French and Latine Copies. By Eirenæevs Orandvs, qui est, *Vera veris enodans.* [Quot.] Imprinted at London by T. S. for Thomas Walkley, . . . 1624. 12°. A, 6 leaves : B—L in twelves : M, 4.

FLECKNOE, RICHARD.
Epigrams. Of All Sorts, Made at Several Times, on Several Occasions. By Richard Flecknoe. Being rather a New Work, than a New Impression of the Old. *Odi profanum vulgus & arceo.* Hor. London, Printed for the Author, 1671. 8°. Title, 1 leaf : To his Noble Friends the Readers, 1 leaf : The Proemium of Epigrams, and To His Majesty, 2 leaves : the Work (in Five Books), B—G 4 in eights : [a fresh title :] Epigrams Divine and Moral, Dedicated to His Majesty. . . . Printed in the Year 1670. 1 leaf : H, 8 leaves.
> This volume seems to be partly made up from the edition of 1670. But of most of Flecknoe's books scarcely two copies quite agree.

FLEMING, ROBERT, V[erbi] D[ivini] M[inister].
The Blessedness of those who die in the Lord : A Practical Discourse Occasioned by the Death of King William ; Wherein a Character of Him is given. To which is added, A Poetical Essay on his Memory. . . . London, Printed for Andrew Bell . . . 1702. 8°, A, 8 leaves, besides the frontispiece : a, 2 leaves : B—O 4 in eights : A—B in eights, and C, 6 leaves, with the Essay entitled *Fame's Mausoleum,* which has a separate title.

FOLKINGHAM, WILLIAM.
Panala Medica ; vel Sanitatis et Longævitatis Alumna Catholica : The fruitfull

and frugall Nourse of sound Health and long Life. Per Guil. Folkingham Gen: Math. & Med. Studiosum.

Principiis obsta ; seró Medicina paratur, Cum Mala per longas invaluere Moras.

London, Printed by Miles Flesher. 1628. 8º, A—K 4 in eights, A 1 and K 4 blank. With some curious verses at the beginning and end. *B. M.*

This little book is written in an affected and obscure style, but contains some interesting matter.

FORD, EMANUEL.
The History of Parismus, The Valiant Prince of Bohemia . . . London: Printed by T. Norris . . . 4º, A—C in fours. With cuts.

A chapbook.

FORD, THOMAS.
Virtus Rediviva A Panegyrick on our late King Charles the I. &c. of ever blessed Memory. Attended, With severall other Poems from the same Pen. Viz. I. A Theatre of Wits : Being a Collection of Apothegms. II. Fœnestra in Pectore ; or a Century of Familiar Letters. III. Loves Labyrinth : A Tragi-comedy. IV. Fragmenta Poetica: Or Poeticall Diversions. Concluding, with A Panegyrick on His Sacred Majesties most happy Return. By T. F. *Varietas delectat.* London : Printed by R. & W. Leybourn, for William Grantham . . . and Thomas Basset . . . 1661. 8º, A—Cc 4 in eights, besides the general title. With separate titles to each portion.

FRANCE.
An Edict set forth by the French King, for appeasing of Troubles in his kingdome. Proclaymed in the Court of Parliament at Rowen the sixteenth day of August, the yere of our Lord . 1570. Imprinted at London by Henry Bynneman, for Lucas Harrison. 8º, A—F in fours, F 4 blank. Black letter. *C. C. C. Cambridge.*

Eight learned personages lately converted (in the Realme of France) from papistrie, to the Churches reformed : hauing admisedly and holily set downe the reasons that moued them thereunto. [Here follow *The names and degrees of the Conuerts,* all ecclesiastics.] Printed at London, for I. B. and are to be solde at the signe of the Bible in Paules Church-yard. 1600. 4º. The translator to the Reader, 2 leaves : B—N in fours.

A True Relation of the Unjust Accusation of Certain French Gentlemen, (Charged

with a Robbery, of which they were most Innocent) And the Proceedings upon it, . . . Published by Denzill Lord Holles, London, Printed by J. Darby, for Richard Chiswel, . . . 1672. 4º, B—G 2 in fours, and the title.

Merovens A Prince of the Blood-Royal of France, A Novel. London, Printed for R. Bentley, and M. Magnes, . . . 1682. 12º. A, 6 leaves, the first blank : B—F 10 in twelves. Dedicated by F[errand] S[pence] the translator to the Countess of Oxford.

A True Copy of a Project for the Reunion of Both Religions in France. [Col.] London, Printed for Randal Taylor, 1685. Folio, 2 leaves.

FRENCH LANGUAGE.
Here is a good boke to lerne to speke frenche. R. Pynson, [1492-3]. 4º.

This edition by Pynson is the earlier of the two known of the tract above-named, and also one of the most ancient productions of his press. The type is very archaic, and the signatures are on the left-hand side of the leaf. The edition by Wynkyn de Worde, printed at Westminster before 1501, corrects the text here and there, and has a regular title, Pynson's commencing without any attempt at one beyond a sort of headline.
One of the editions of this vocabulary is doubtless the work registered in the MS. account-book of John Dorne, bookseller of Oxford, for 1520, under the title of *frans and englis.*

FULWOOD, WILLIAM.
The Enimie of Idlenesse :. . . At London Printed by Henrie Middleton, dwelling in Fleetstreet, at the signe of the Falcon. Anno 1582. 8º, chiefly black letter, A—X 2 in eights.

GALLOBELGICUS.
Wine, Beer, And Ale, Together by the Eares. A Dialogue, Written first in Dutch by Gallobelgicus, and faithfully translated out of the originall Copie, by Mercurius Brittannicus, for the benefit of his Nation. Horat. *Siccis omnia nam dura Deus proposuit.* London, Printed by A. M. for Iohn Grove, and are to be sold at his Shop, at Furniuals Inne Gate in Holborne. 1629. 4º, A—C in fours, first and last leaues blank. With a preface by the publisher. *B. M.* (the Roxburghe copy.)

In the two later editions of 1630 and 1658, the title is varied, and the names of Gallobelgicus as the author and Mercurius Britannicus as the translator, do not occur. The foreign origin of the tract is, doubtless, a mere fiction.

GOULART, JEAN.
Admirable and Memorable Histories . . .
1607.

This volume contains a series of stories
or relations similar to some found in *Measure for Measure*, &c. But the analogy is
of the least possible moment; and it is a
very dull and foolish publication, of which
only the first volume appeared in English.

GRAHAM, JAMES, *Marquis of Montrose.*
Montrosse Totally Routed at Tividale in
Scotland on Saturday last, By Lieutenant Generall Lesly, Where were taken
and kill'd, Two thousand Foot, Eight
hundred Horse, and Nine Knights;
And all the Kings Papers and Writings
sent to Montrosse are taken. Sent to a
Member of the Honorable House of Commons, and appointed to be forthwith
printed. London, Printed for Edward
Husband, . . . Sept. 18. 1645. 4°, 4 leaves,
the last blank.

The Declaration of His Excellency James
Marquis of Montrosse, Earle of Kilcairn,
Lord Greme, Baron of Mont-Dieu, Lievetenant Governour of Scotland, and Captaine Generall of all His Majesties Forces
by Sea or Land, for that Kingdome.
London ; Printed for Matthew Simmons,
. . . 1650. 4°, A—C in fours.

GRANVILLE, GEORGE.
Heroick Love : A Tragedy. As it is Acted
at the Theatre in Little Lincolns-Inn-
Fields. Written by the Honourable
George Granville, Esq ; *Rectius Iliacum
Carmen deducis in Actus,*—Hor. de Arte
Poetica. . . . London : Printed for F.
Saunders, . . . and B. Tooke, . . . 1698.
4°, A—K in fours, and 2 leaves after K 4
unsigned. With a copy of verses by
Dryden.

GREENE, ROBERT.
Vision . . . 1593.

The Nicholas Sanders of Ewell, to whom
the publisher dedicates this tract, was probably the father of William Sanders of
Ewell, whose daughter Frances married Sir
Henry Spelman's father.

Ciceronis Amor. Tvllies Loue. . . .
London Printed for Iohn Smethwicke,
. . . 1609. 4°, A—K in fours.

GUARNA, ANDREA, *of Salerno.*
Bellum Grammaticale. A discourse of great
war and dissention betwene two worthie
Princes, the Noune and the Verbe, con-
tending for the chefe place or dignitie in
Oration. Very pleasant & profitable.
Turned into English by W. H[ayward.]
Imprinted at London by Henrie Bynne-
man, dwelling in Knightrider strete,
at the signe of the Mermayde. Anno
1569. 8°, A—F in eights. Dedicated by
Hayward to Master Thomas Powle, Es-
quire, one of the six clerks in Chancery.
B. M.

As Hayward describes himself as Powle's
" daily wellwisher," the former was probably connected with him personally or
officially.

GURNAY, EDMUND, *B.D., Pastor of
Harpley, Norfolk.*
Corpvs Christi. London, Printed by H.
L. and R. Y. for I. Boler, . . . 1630.
12°, A—E 10 in twelves, A 1 blank.
Dedicated " to the very worshipfull,
Richard Stvbbe, Esquire."

In the dedication, which appears to be
the only interesting portion of the book
from its local and personal allusions, the
author states that he commends the perusal to Stubbe's two daughters, his cousin
Yelverton and Lady Strange ; to Mr. Robert
Rudde of St. Florence in South Wales, and
Mr. Henry Goodlye of Onehouse in Suffolk,
his tutors ; to his singular friend, Dr.
Porter of Cambridge, and to his friends the
parishioners of Edgfield.

HALE, SIR MATTHEW.
A Treatise, Shewing how Useful, Safe,
Reasonable and Beneficial, the Inrolling
and Registring of all Conveyances of
Land may be to the Inhabitants of this
Kingdom. The Second Edition. Lon-
don, Printed for Mat. Wotton ; . . .
MDCCX. 4°, B—D in fours, a leaf of E,
and the title.

HALL, JOHN.
Select Observations on English Bodies :
Or, Cures both Empericall and Historicall, performed upon very eminent Persons in desperate Diseases. First, written
in Latine by Mr John Hall Physician,
living at Stratford upon Avon in Warwick-shire, where he was very famous, as
also in the Counties adjacent, as appeares
by these Observations drawn out of
severall hundreds of his, as choysest.
Now put into English for common benefit by James Cooke Practitioner in Physick
and Chirurgery. London, Printed for
John Sherley, at the Golden Pelican, in
Little-Britain. 1657. 12°, A—O in
twelves : P, 2. A 1 has the label and A
12 the *Errata.*

HALL, T., *Free Cook of London.*
The Queen's Royal Cookery : Or, Expert
and Ready Way for the Dressing of all
sorts of Flesh, . . . The Third Edition.
London : Printed for S. Bates, . . . and
A. Bettesworth, . . . 1719. 12°, A—H 6
in twelves, including the frontispiece.

HAMMOND, JOHN.

Hammond versus Heamans. Or An Answer to an Audacious Pamphlet, published by an ignorant and ridiculous Fellow, named Roger Heamans, Calling himself Commander of the Ship *Golden Lion* . . . In which is published His Highness's absolute (though neglected) Command to Richard Bennet Esq ; late Governour of Virginia, and all others not to disturbe the Lord Baltamores Plantation in Maryland. By John Hammond, a Sufferer in these Calamities. . . . Printed at London for the use of the Author, and are to be sold at the Royal Exchange in Cornhill. [1655.] 4°, A—C 2 in fours.

HARDOUIN DE PEREFIXE, *Bishop of Rodez.*

A Collection of some Brave Actions and Memorable Sayings of King Henry the Great. Writ in French by the Bishop of Rodez, as a Supplement to the History of that King, formerly publish'd by the same Author. Done into English. London, Printed for Abel Roper. . . . 1688. 12°. A, 6 leaves: B—C in twelves: D, 4.

HARMAR, SAMUEL.

Vox Populi, Or, Glostersheres Desire : With, The Ways and Means to make a Kingdome Happy (by Gods help.) By setting up of Schoole-masters in every Parish throughout the Land generally. . . . Set forth for the Benefit of all the young Children in the Kings Dominions : With Schoole-Lawes and Orders, for every English Schoole-Master, and Family, to have in their Houses. For the training up young Children, both in Godlinesse and Manners, for the good of the Land. . . . London, Printed for Thomas Bates. . . . 1642. 4°, A—B 2 in fours.

HERTFORDSHIRE.

A Perfect Divrnall of the Proceedings in Hartford-shire, From the 15. of August to the 29. . . . Whereunto is added an Information given by Sir Thomas Dakers (a Member of the House of Commons) intimating that he suspected the Earle of Bedfords Troupes should have battell given them by Sir John Watson before they came to Hartford. Printed for W. M. Septemb. 1. 1642. 4°, 4 leaves.

HEYLIN, PETER.

Microcosmos. A Little Description of the Great World. The sixth Edition. . . . Oxford, Printed for William Turner, and Robert Allott. 1633. 4°, ¶—3 ¶ 2 in fours: A—Ff 4 in eights, Ff 4 blank.

HILL, THOMAS.

The Profitable Arte of Gardening . . . 1593.

Revised Collation :—A—X in fours: [a new title :] A profitable instruction of the perfect ordering of Bees . . . 1593 : title and following leaf with dedication to the "worshipfull Maister M. Gentleman," 2 leaves : Y, 2 leaves : Aa—Mm in fours.

HOLY WEEK.

The Office of the Holy Week According to the Missale and Roman Breviary. Translated ovt of French With a new and ample explication taken out of the Holy Fathers, . . . Enricht with many Figvres. Paris, Printed by the Widow Chrestien. M. DC. LXX. 8°. Title and dedication by the translator, W. K. B., "To my most Honovred Dear Mother The Lady M. B.," 3 leaves : A—Qq 4 in eights, including the engravings, which count in the sheets.

HOOLE, CHARLES.

A New Discovery of the old Art of Teaching Schoole, In four small Treatises.

1.	A Petty Schoole	
2.	The Ushers Duty	in a Grammar Schoole.
3.	The Masters Method	
4.	Scholastick Discipline	

(Concerning)

Shewing how Children in their playing years may Grammatically attain to a firm groundedness in and exercise of the Latine, Greek and Hebrew Tongues. Written about Twenty three yeares ago, for the benefit of Rotherham School, where it was first used ; . . . By Charles Hoole Master of Arts, and Teacher of a Private Grammar School in Lothbury Garden, London. London, Printed by J. T. for Andrew Crook at the Green Dragon in Pauls Church-yard, 1660. 12°. First title and prel. leaves, 12 leaves : A—B in twelves, A 1 and B 12 blank : *The Usher's Duty,* &c., A—N in twelves. Dedicated (i.) to Robert Sanderson, D.D., Rector of Boothby-Pagnell, (ii.) to Mr Robert Doughty, head - master of Wakefield School, and (iii.) to all favourers of good learning.

In the first epistle, Hoole acknowledges the great kindness which he had received from Sir William Brownlow.

HORATIUS FLACCUS, QUINTUS.

Horace's Art of Poetry. Made English By the Right Honorable the Earl of Roscommon. London, Printed for Henry Herringman, and Sold by Joseph Knight and Francis Saunders . . . 1684. 4°, A—E in fours.

HUNE, RICHARD.

The enquirie and verdite of the quest

panneld of the death of Rychard Hune ... [1514.] 8°.

> This tract is reprinted by Fox; but it was entirely unknown till I mentioned it in my *Bibliographical Notes,* 1882, p. 297. Stowe (*Annales,* 1615, p. 497) says:—" Richard Hun, a marchant tailor of London, dwelling in ye parish of S. Margaret in Bridge street, who (for denying to giue a mortuary, such as was demaunded by the Parson for his child being buryed) had bin put in ye Lowlards tower about the end of Octo. last before passed, was now the 5. of December, found hanged with his owne girdle of silk, in the said tower, and after he was burned in Smithfield." A second fragment is in the British Museum.

HUTCHINS, EDWARD, *one of the Prebendaries of New Sarum.*

David's Sling against great Goliah. Containing diuers notable Treatises, the names whereof are in the next Page following. Matth. 16. 41. *Watch and pray.* London Printed for the Companie of the Stationers. 1615. 12°, A—O in twelves : P, 10. Printed within borders.

> A collection of prayers, &c., of which Maunsell records an edition by H. Denham, 8vo, 1580.

IGNATIUS.

Ignativs His Prophecie concerning these Times, sent from France where it was prophecied 159 . into England, and found in the Abbey of St. Benedict neere the City of Norwich in Norfolke. . . . London, Printed for Iohn Greensmith, 1642. 4°, 4 leaves.

IMPRISONMENT.

Imprisonment of Mens Bodyes for Debt, as the practice of England now stands, Is 1. Against the Law of God. 2. Against the Law of Man. . . . 3. Against the Law of Conscience. . . . 4. Against the practice of other Countries. 5. Against the Creditors owne profit. 6. To the prejudice of the King and Common-wealth. Printed in the yeare of our Lord, 1641. 4°, A—D in fours.

> A 1 is occupied by a printed leaf, containing the Petition to the King and Parliament of the Prisoners for debt in the various gaols of England and Wales, which are here stated to be about 10,000 in number.

IN AND OUT.

In and Out. And Turn About. A New C[oun]t-Dance. To the Tune of *John Bob'd in, and John Bob'd out : Or, Bob-in Joan : Or, The Miller of Mansfield.* London : Printed by J. Roberts in Shorts-Gardens. A broadside in verse.

IRELAND.

The Present State of Ireland : Together with some Remarques Upon the Antient State thereof. Likewise a Description of the Chief Towns : With a Map of the Kingdome. London, Printed for Chr. Wilkinson . . . and T. Burrell . . . 1673. 12°, A—M in twelves : N, 10, besides the folded map.

An Account of the Sessions of Parliament in Ireland, 1692. London, Printed for J. T. MDCXCIII. 4°, A—D in fours, A 1 blank.

ISEMBRAS OR ISUMBRAS.

Sir Isembras. London, W. Copland. 4°.

> In the account-book of John Dorne, the Oxford bookseller, for 1520, occurs *Syr hisembras,* which sold, with *balets* or ballads, for twopence. This was of course an earlier edition than Copland's, and may have been the same, of which a single leaf, A ii, is preserved among the Douce fragments.

ITALY.

Straunge Newes out of Calabria, 1586.

> " This book appears by Herbert. p. 1344, to have been licensed to John Perrin in 1586.
> ' The next week Master Bird (if his ink-pot have a clear current) he will have at you cap-case full of French occurrences, that is, shape you a mess of news out of the second course of his conceit, as his brother is said ont of the fabulous abundance of his brain to have invented the newes out of Calabria (John Doletas prophecie of flying dragons, comets, earthquakes, and inundations.'—T. Nash's *four letters confuted,* A.D. 1592, sig. F 1 b."—*MS.* note by *Mr. H. Pyne on the fly-leaf of his copy, formerly Bright's, and the only one known.*

The True History of the Tragicke loves of Hipolito and Isabella Neapolitans. The second Edition. London Printed by Thomas Harper 1633. and are to be sold by Richard Meighen at his shopp at 5 Temple gate. 8°. A, 2 leaves, with the engraved title and verses by G. C., as in the edit. of 1628 : B—L 5 in eights.

JACOBUS DE CESSOLIS, *of Rheims, Dominican.*

Game and Play of the Chess. . . . W. Caxton, Folio. First Edition.

> Putticks, Dec. 16, 1886, No. 66, both blanks deficient, printed on very stout paper, but slighty discoloured, £645. A copy is at Wimpole, but whether of this or the second edition, I do not know. Neither copy was known to Blades.

JAMES [STUART] *VII. of Scotland, and II. of Great Britain.*

An Account of what His Majesty said at His First coming to Council. London, Printed by the Assignes of John Bill Deceas'd : And by Henry Hills, and by

Thomas Newcomb. . . . 1684. A broadside.

JESUITS.

Father Whitebreads Walking Ghost which lately appear'd to a Cabal of Jesuits in Drury-Lane. Folio, 2 leaves. In verse.

JOHNSON, RICHARD.

The Most Pleasant History of Tom A Lincoln, The Ever Renowned Soldier, The Red-Rose Knight. Printed by J. W. for B. Beacon at the Angel in Gilt-Spurstreet. 1704. 4°, A—I in fours, including a duplicate undated title. Without cuts, except a large one on the first title.

> This issue, like that of 1703, is called on the second title, which is fuller, the 13th edition.

JOHNSON, SAMUEL, M.A.

The Sentence of Samuel Johnson, at the Kings-Bench-Barr at Westminster, on Tuesday the 16ᵗʰ of November, 1686. Who was Convicted last Term for High-Misdemeanor, in Writing and Publishing Two False, Scandalous, and Seditious Libels, . . . London, Printed by D. Mallet, . . . 1686. A broadside.

A True and Faithful Relation of the Horrid and Barbarous Attempt to Assassinate the Reverend Mʳ Samuel Johnson. Published to prevent false Reports. London, Printed by J. D. for Richard Baldwin, 1692. A broadside.

JONES, J., M.D.

Practical Phonography : Or The New Art of Rightly Spelling and Writing Words by the Sound thereof. And of Rightly sounding and Reading Words By the Sight thereof. Applied to the English Tongue. Designed more especially for the Use and Ease, of the Duke of Glocester : But that we are lamentably disappointed of our Joy and Hope in him. . . . London : Printed for Richard Smith, . . . MDCCI. 4°. A, 3 leaves : B—T in fours.

KENT.

The Charter of Romney Marsh . . . 1543.

> In the Sussex Archæol. Collections will be found a text of this charter from a 14th century MS. (1350)

Newes from Gravesend . . . 1604.

> Nash, in his Have with you to Saffron Walden, 1596, sign. E. speaks of "a whole Gravesend barge full of news."

A perfect Diurnall of the severall passages in our late journey into Kent, from Aug. 19. to Sept. 3. 1642. by the appointment of both Houses of Parliament. Published for the satisfaction of those who desire true information. [London, 1642.] 4°, 4 leaves.

> An unusually interesting pamphlet.

A True and perfect Relation of the seizing the House of one Master William Barnes a Cavalier, and apprehending him neer Wollage in Kent, by Captaine Willoughby and his Company of Volunteers, and of the finding of a Trunk of Plate valued at a thousand pounds, . . . And likewise of the seizing of threescore and fifteene peeces of Ordnance, by the said Captain and his Company in the Woodyard at Wollage, . . . Also the manner of their dressing of one of their Souldiers in the priests garments, which they found with a Book in his hand of popish prayers, and bringing him on foot from Blackwall to the Tower, with torchlight at ten of the clock at night. London, Printed for T. S. September 2, 1642. 4°, 4 leaves.

KING, WILLIAM.

The Art of Cookery, In Imitation of Horace's Art of Poetry. With some Letters to Dr. Lister, and Others : Occasion'd principally by the Title of a Book published by the Doctor, being the Works of Apicius Cœlius, Concerning the Soups and Sauces of the Antients. With an Extract of the greatest Curiosities contain'd in that Book. To which is added, Horace's Art of Poetry, in Latin. By the Author of the Journey to London. Humbly Inscrib'd to the Honourable Beef Steak Club. London : Printed for Bernard Lintott . . . 8°. A, 4 leaves : B—L in eights. A 1 has the half-title.

> On the half-title occurs : " E Libris Henrici Comitis de Berkshire."

L. Jo.

A good help for weak memories . . . 1671.

> This book was suggested to the author, J. or Jo. L., by a foreign one of similar character called Gemma Fabri. At the end of the Preface he signs himself J. L. ; but at the end of the book the initials Jo. L. occur.
>
> Ritson (Bibliographia Poetica, p. 265) seems to be in error in including this work among the poetical productions of the sixteenth century. Its earliest appearance was doubtless in 1671.

A good help for Weak Memories : Or, The Contents of every Chapter in the Bible . . . The Second Edition. London, Printed for Thomas Helder, . . . 1682. 8°, A—H in eights. In verse.

LAMBARDE, W., of Lincoln's Inn.

The Dvties of Constables, Borsholders,

Tythingmen, . . . now enlarged in the yeare 1606. London, Printed for the Companie of Stationers. 1606. Cum Priuilegio. 8°, black letter, A—E in eights, E 8 blank.

LANGHORNE, RICHARD.

An Account of the Deportment and Last Words of Mr Richard Langhorne, who was Drawn, Hang'd and Quarter'd at Tyburn for High-Treason, on Munday, July 14. 1679. London, Printed 1679. Folio, 2 leaves.

LATIMER, HUGH, *Bishop of Worcester.*

Frvitfvll Sermons : . . . newly imprinted with others not heretofore set forth in print, to the edifying of all which will dispose themselves to the reading of the same. . . . Printed at London by Thomas Cotes, for the Companie of Stationers. 1635. Cum Privilegio. 4°. A, 8 leaves : A (repeated)—Tt in eights, besides the title and portrait.

The last of the editions in 4to.

LETTERS.

Two Letters The one being sent to the Lord Bishop of Peterborough. The other sent from the Bishop of Bangor, to the Ministers of his Diocese. Wherein is discovered the readines of the ill-affected Clergy, toward the furnishing of his Majesty with moneys for the mayntaining of Warre against the Parliament . . . London, Printed for Ed. Husbands, and Iohn Francke, . . . 1642. 4°, 4 leaves.

August 6. Two Letters The One from the Lord Digby: . . . . London, Printed by A. N. for Richard Lownds, 1642. 4°, 4 leaves.

Three Letters. [I. A Letter from a Jesuit of Liege, to a Jesuit at Friburg. . . . II. A Letter from the Reverend Father Petre. . . . III. The Answer to the Same. Concluding with, Popish Treatises not to be rely'd on . . . 1688-9.] 4°, A—C in fours. Without a title-page.

LONDON.

The Trve Report of the burnyng of the Steple and Church of Poules in London. ¶ Jeremy, xviii. I wyll speake suddenlye . . . Imprynted at London, at the west ende of Paules Church, at the sygne of the Hedghogge by Wyllyam Seres. Cum priuilegio . . . Anno. 1561. The x. of Iune. 8°, black letter, 8 leaves. *Corpus Christi Colleye, Cambridge.*

The Loyal Apprentices of London. To the Tune of, *London's Loyelty.* London, Printed by Nat. Thompson, 1682. A copy of verses, with the music, on a broadsheet.

London's Lamentation : Or, An Excellent New Song of the Loss of London's Charter. To the Tune of, *Packington's Pound.* Printed by N. T. at the entrance into the Old-Spring-Garden. A copy of verses.

Londons Joy and Triumph, On the Installment of Sir William Pritchard Lord Mayor for the Ensuing Year. To the Tune of, *Tangier March.* London : Printed in the year MDCLXXXII. A broadside in verse.

M. J.

A Christian Almanacke. Needefvll and Trve for all Countryes, Persons and times. Faithfully Calculated by the course of holy Scripture, . . . London Printed for Iohn Budge, . . . 1612. 8°. A, 4 leaves : B—C in eights : D, 5. *B. M.* (Jolley's copy.)

M. W.

The Queens Closet Opened . . . Corrected and Amended, with many New and larg Additions : together with three exact Tables . . . London, Printed by J. W. for Nath. Brooke, . . . 1668. 12°. A, 6 leaves, A 1 blank : C—K in twelves : L, 4 (with the Table): no B : [a new title :] A Queens Delight, Or, The Art of Preserving, Conserving, and Candying. As also, A right Knowledge of making Perfumes, and Distilling the most Excellent Waters. Never before Published. Printed by J. Winter, for Nat. Brook, . . . 1668. A—E 8 in twelves, E 7-8 with the Table : [a third title :] The Compleat Cook : Expressly Prescribing the most ready

Wayes, Whether { Italian, Spanish or French, } For Dressing of Flesh and Fish, ordering of Sauces or making of Pastry. London, Printed by J. Winter, for Nath. Brooke, . . . 1868. A—F 6 in twelves.

Doubtless, the three pieces were published to sell either together or separately at option.

MALL, THOMAS.

The Axe at the Root of Professors Miscarriages. In a Plain Detection of, and a Wholsome Caveat against the Miscarriages opposite to Faith in God. . . . London, Printed for John Weeks, Bookseller in Tiverton, 1668. Sold for 6d. by the Author's Appointment. 4°, A—G in fours.

On the fly-leaf of this copy occurs: "Tho. Johnson. Giuen me by my worthy friend the Authour Mar. 1668." To a second title there is the following imprint : London, Printed for John Weeks Bookseller, in Tiverton, and are there to be sold at his Shop, and by his Assigns, and by no others in all the West Countrey, 1668.'

MAN.

A Satyr against Mankind. Written by a Person of Honour. Folio, 2 leaves. In verse.

MANLOVE, EDWARD.

The Liberties and Customs of the Lead-Mines . . . London, Printed Anno Dom. 1708. 4", 4 leaves.

MANUALE.

Manuale ad vsum insignis eccl'ie Sarū cū multis additionibus ad ecclesie cultum spectantibus. [Col.] Manuale ad vsum insignis ecclesie Sar : . . . Impensis Francisci byrckman in alma Parisiorū academia impressum. 1515. Folio, a—r in eights. Finely printed in red and black, with the music. Long lines.

MARKHAM, GERVASE.

How to chuse, ride, traine, and diet, both Hunting - horses and running Horses. With all the secrets thereto belonging discouered : an Arte neuer here-to-fore written by any Author. Also, a discourse of horsmanship, wherein the breeding, and ryding of horses for seruice, in a breefe manner, is more methodically sette downe then hath beene heeretofore : with a more easie and direct course for the ignorant, to attaine to the said Arte or knowledge. Together with a new addition for the cure of horses diseases, of what kinde or nature soeuer. *Bramo assai, poco spero, nulla chieggio.* At London, Printed by J. R. for Richard Smith, and are to bee solde at his shoppe at the West-doore of Poules. Anno. Dom. 1595. 4°. ¶, 4 leaves, ¶ 1 blank : A—P in fours, P 4 blank. Dedicated " To the Right worshipfull and his singuler good father, Ma. Robert Markham, of Cotham, in the County of Notingham, Esquire."

The Inrichment of the Weald of Kent : . . . reuised, inlarged, and corrected . . . By Geruase Markham. London, Printed by Nicholas Okes for Iohn Harison, . . . 1631. 4°. A, 2 : B, 8 : C, 4.

MARVELL, ANDREW.

The Rehearsal Transpros'd : Or, Animadversions Upon a late Book, Intituled, A Preface shewing what Grounds there are of Fears and Jealousies of Popery. London Printed in the Year, 1672. 8°, B—Y 4 in eights, Y 4 blank, and the title.

The Rehearsal Transpros'd ; . . . The second Impression, with Additions and Amendments. London, Printed by I. D. for the Assigns of John Calvin and Theodore Beza . . . and Sould by N. Ponder in Chancery Lane, 1673. 8", B—Y 4 in eights, Y 4 blank, and the title.

Three editions the same year, the two others of a smaller size.

The Rehearsal Transpros'd : The Second Part. Occasioned by Two Letters : The first Printed, by a nameless Author, Intituled, A Reproof, &c. The Second Letter left for me at a Friends House, Dated Nov. 3. 1673. Subscribed I. G. and concluding with these words ; If thou darest to Print or Publish any Lie or Libel against Doctor Parker, By the Eternal God I will cut thy Throat. Answered by Andrew Marvel. London, Printed for Nathaniel Ponder, . . . 1673. 8°, A—Cc in eights, besides title and a peculiar *Imprimatur.*

Two editions the same year, the other of a smaller size.

S'too him Bayes : Or Some Observations Upon the Humour of Writing Rehearsals Transpros'd. —*& Hanc Veniam petimusque damusque vicissim.* Oxon : Printed in the Year 1673. 8°, A—K 2 in eights, K 2 with *Errata,* and A 1 blank.

A Reproof to the Rehearsal Transprosed, In A Discourse to its Authour. By the Authour of the Ecclesiastical Politie. London, Printed for James Collins at the Kings Arms in Ludgate-street, 1673. 8°. A, 4 leaves : B—Ll in eights.

MARY STUART, *Queen of Scots.*

¶ A discourse touching the pretended match betwene the Duke of Norfolke and the Queene of Scottes. [London, 1572.] 8°. A in eights, A 1 and A 8 blank. *Corpus Christi Colleye, Cambridge.*

The title given above occurs as a headline on Aij ; but the tract was doubtless printed without any clue to the writer and publisher.

MASTERSON, THOMAS.

Mastersons Arithmetick. Shewing the ingenious inventions, and figurative operations, . . . Newly set forth, . . . By Hvmfrey Waynman, M' of the Lady Ramseys Free-Writing-Schoole in Christs Hospitall, London. Nothing without labour : All things with reason. London, Printed by George Miller, dwelling in the Black-Friers. M. DC. XXXIV. 8°. A, 4 leaves : B—X 4 in eights.

This reprint consists only of two Books and an *Explanation of the Rules of Fractions.*

MATHER, INCREASE.

Christianus per Ignem. Or, A Disciple warming of himself and owning of his Lord ; with Devout and Useful Meditations, Fetch'd out of the Fire, By a Christian in a Cold Season, Sitting before it. A Work though never out of Season, yet more Particularly, designed for the Seasonable and profitable Entertainment, of those that would well Employ their Leisure by the Fire-Side. . . . Boston : Printed by B. Green, and J. Allen, for Benjamin Eliot at his Shop. 1702. 8°, A—N 4 in eights. With an introductory copy of verses by Nicholas Noyes.

The Duty of Parents to pray for their Children, Opened & Applyed in a Sermon, Preached May 19. 1703. Which Day was set apart by One of the Churches in Boston, New-England, humbly to seek unto God by Prayer with Fasting for the Rising Generation. . . . Boston : Printed by B. Green, and J. Allen. . . . 1703. 12°, A—F 6 in twelves.

On C 7 occurs a sermon on the Duty of Children toward their parents, who have prayed for them, by Cotton Mather, with a separate title.

MAXEY, EDWARD, *Gentleman.*

A New Instrvction of Plowing and Setting of Corne, Handled in manner of a Dialogve betweene a Ploughman and a Scholler. Wherein is proued plainely that Plowing and Setting, is much more profitable and lesse chargeable, than Plowing and Sowing. *He that withdraweth the Corne,* . . . Prou. 11. 26. Imprinted at London by Felix Kyngston, dwelling in Pater noster-Rowe, ouer against the signe of the Checker. 1601. 4°, A—E in fours, E 4 blank. With a woodcut on title. Dedicated to Sir Richard Marten, Knight, Master of the Mint, Alderman, and twice Lord Mayor of London.

In the dedication Maxey refers in unfavourable terms to a pamphlet previously published, called *God speed the Plough,* and at the same time signifies his own practical experience.

MESSINGHAM, THOMAS, *Sacerdos Hibernus, S.R.E. Protonotarius, nec non Seminarij Hibernorum Parisiis Moderator.*

Florilegivm Insvlæ Sanctorum Sev Vitæ et Acta Sanctorvm Hiberniæ. Quibus accesserunt non vulgaria monumenta Hoc est Sancti Patricii Purgatorium, . . . Parisiis, . . . M.DC.XXIV. Folio. Title, Dedication, and Preface, 4 leaves : a—e 2 in fours : A—3 M in fours. With a cop-

perplate engraving of St. Patrick on e 2 *verso* signed by the author himself.

MIROPSIUS, NICOLAUS, *called* PREPOSITUS, *of Alexandria.*

Prepositas his Practise. A Worke very necessary to be vsed for the better preseruation of the health of Man . . . Translated out of Latin into English by L. M. London Imprinted by Iohn Wolfe for Edward White, . . . 1588. 4°, A—Q in fours, besides the address to the Reader.

This collection of receipts is only in part taken from Prepositus ; many are copied out of later works.

MISCELLANIES.

Miscellanies over Claret, Or, The Friends to the Tavern the Best Friends to Poetry: Being a Collection of Poems, Translations, &c. to be continued Monthly from the Rose-Tavern without Temple-Bar. Numb. 1. . . . London : Printed and Sold by the Booksellers . . . 1697. 4″, A—F, 2 leaves each, besides title and dedication, 2 ll. more.

In the Huth Library is Number 11 of this publication : " Miscellanies over Claret . . . Numb. 11 . . . London : Printed by S. D. 1697." It makes 14 leaves, and commences at p. 21. I am not aware that any more was printed.

MISSALE.

Missale ad cōsuetudinem ecclesie Sarum : nuper vna cum dicti ecclesie institutis consuetudinibusq ; climatissime impressum : additis plurimis commoditatibus que in ceteris desiderantur. [Col.] Impressum Parrhisii in Sole aureo via sancti Jacobi. Per Magistrum Bertholdum Rembolt Anno Millesimo quingētesimo tredecimo. Die vero vigesimaprima Mensis Januarii. Folio, printed in red and black, in two columns, with the title within a border. Title and Table, 1 leaf : Calendar, 6 leaves : *Exorcismus aque,* 1 leaf : A—K in eights : L, 6 : M—T in eights, includ ing the *Canon Missæ,* 2 ll. on vellum : a—i in eights : A—G in eights : H, 4 : *Index Libri,* 1 leaf, reverse blank.

The three divisions of the book are separately folioed.

Missale ad vsum insignis ecclesie Sarisburiensis nunc recens typis elegantioribus exaratum, historijs nouis, varijs ac proprijs insignitum : & a mendis q plurimis (quibus passim scatebat) omni diligentia nuper emendatum. Parisiis Apud Guillelmum Merlin . . . . 1555. Folio. ✠, 8 leaves with title, calendar, and *Benedictio salis et aque:* a—t in eights, including the two leaves of the *Canon Missæ* on vellum : v, 6 : A—I in eights : A—G in

eights: H—K in sixes. In two columns.
With woodcuts.

Missale ad vsum ecclesie Sarisburiensis.
1555. [The rest of the title is occupied
by a woodcut of the Virgin and Child,
&c., and verses *Ad Sacerdotem.* At the
end :] Missale ad vsum Sarisburiensis
explicit, optimis formulis (vt res ipsa
indicat) diligentissime reuisum ad [*sic*]
correctum, cum multis annotatiunculis,
ac litteris alphabeticis Euangeliorum atq;
Epistolarum originem indicātibus. Lōdini impressum. Per Johannem Kyngstō
et Henricum Sutton typographos. 4°,
red and black inks, in two columns.
Title and Calendar, 6 leaves : *Benedictio
salis et aquæ*, 1 leaf : A—Y in eights :
a—r in eights.

MONK.
**The Monk Unvail'd : Or, A Facetious
Dialogue,** Discovering the several Intrigues, and subtil Practises, together with
the lewd and scandalous Lives of Monks,
Fryers, and other pretended Religious
Votaries of the Church of Rome. Written
by an Eminent Papist in French. Faithfully Translated by C. W. Gent. London, Printed for Jonathan Edwin, . . .
1678. 8°. Title and to the Reader, 2
leaves : B—K in eights. With a frontispiece of a chapman, out of whose mouth
is a scroll with *Old Mony Siluer for Coper.*

MONTS DE PIETÉ.
Observations Manifesting the Conveni-
ency and Commodity of Mount-Pietyes,
Or Publick Bancks for Relief of the Poor
. and others in distresse upon Pawns, At a
certain known moderate Interest, and the
inconveniency and great discommodity of
continuing or countenancing the Ordinary Pawn-brokers or Lenders upon
Pawns. London, Printed in the Year,
1661. 4°, 4 leaves.

MORLEY, THOMAS.
The First Booke of Ayres. Or Little
Short Songs, to sing and play to the Lvte,
with the Base Viole. Newly Pvblished
by Thomas Morley Bachiler of Musicke,
and one of the Gent. of her Maiesties
Royall Chappell. Imprinted at London
in litle S. Helens by William Barley,
the assigne of Thomas Morley, and are to
be sold at his house in Gracious streete.
1600. Cum Priuilegio. Folio. Title,
dedication "To the Worthie and vertuovs
Lover of Mvsicke, Ralfe Bosvile, Esqvire,"
Morley's Address to the Reader, Table,
and following leaf, 4 leaves : B—D in
fours, but ending imperfectly on D 4.

This copy, as appears from the Table, is
imperfect, and contains the *Cantus* only.
In the possession of Mr. J. O. Halliwell-
Phillipps. Unseen by Rimbault. It contains the original music to the song,
"It was a lover and his lass," in *As you
like it.*

MOROCCO.
The King of Morocco's Letter by His
Ambassador to the King of England.
Printed for Robert Clavel at the Peacock
at the West End of St. Pauls. 1689.
Folio, 2 leaves.

MURMURERS.
The Murmurers. A Poem.
*O fortunati nimium, bona si sua nôrint
Angligenæ !*
London, Printed for R. Baldwin. MDC-
LXXXIX. Folio, A—E, 2 leaves each.

MUSIC.
The Second Part of Musick's Hand-Maid :
Containing The Newest Lessons, Grounds,
Sarabands, Minuets, and Jiggs, Set for
the Virginals, Harpsichord, and Spinet.
London, Printed on Copper-Plates, for
Henry Playford, at his Shop next the
Temple Church, 1689. Obl. 8°, A—G in
fours, besides the title and H. Playford's
Address to the Reader.

MYSTERY OF INIQUITY.
**The Grand Imposture : Or The Mystery
of Iniquity. A Satyr.** *Tristius haud
illis Monstrum . . .* Virg. Æneid. lib. 3.
London, Printed Anno 1679. Folio, A—
B, 2 leaves each. In verse.

NETHERLANDS.
The Confession of Michael Renichon of
Templeu, Parson of Bossier, in the
County of Namours Concerning, The
bloudy enterprise which by him should
haue bene committed vpon the person of
County Maurice, Prince of Orange, as
also, The sentence denounced against hym
for the deede, in the Haghe on the third
of June 1594. Printed at Vtrecht . . .
now truely translated into english by R.
R. London Imprinted by Iohn Wolfe.
1594. 4°, 4 leaves. *B. M.*

A Breefe Declaration of that which is
happened aswell within as without
Oasteud sithence the vii. of Ianuarie
1602. As also when the Enemy did giue
Foure, Fiue, or more Assaults vpon the
same Towne. Also The names of the
Commaunders of those which haue made
these Assaults vpon the towne of Oastend,
and the names of the said Conductors
which haue bene slaine. Middleborrow
Printed by Richard Schilders. 1602. At

London Printed for Mathew Law. (1602.) 4", 4 leaves. *B. M.*

> It is not quite clear whether the Middleburgh issue was in English or Dutch.

A Iornall of certaine principall passages in and before the Towne of S'hertogenbosh, from the 18. of August till the 1. of September, at which time they fell to capitulation concerning the Rendition of the Towne . . . London, Printed for Nicholas Bourne . . . 1629. [A second part and title :] Articles Agreed upon and concluded betweene the victorious, excellent, high and mighty Prince, Frederick Henry, Prince of Orange, Count of Nassaw, &c. on the one part, and the vanquished Towne of S'hertogenbosh on the other side. And also, How the Towne, and the Pettler-Sconce was delinered, . . . London, Printed for Nicholas Bourne . . . 1629. 4". Part 1, A—C 2 in fours : Part 2, D—E 2 in fours.

> On the last page of the first portion are some verses "To the Reader," probably by the translator, although the tract does not purport to be otherwise than original.

NEWS.

Newes from Gvlick and Cleve. A Trve and faithfull Relation of the late affairs in the Countries of Gulicke, Cleue, and Bergh, and what townes haue certanely been taken aswell by Marquesse Spinola as by Graue Mavrice, and how it stands with them in those parts at this present. Seruing also to confute the false relation lately published in English. Together with Count Henrie of Nassau his very late expedition in the Country of Marck, &c. Faithfully translated out of Dutch by Charles Demetrivs, publike Notarie of London. Published by Authoritie. London, Printed for H. Holland, and G. Gibbs and are to be solde at the Flower de Luce in Paules Churchyard, 1615. 4°, A—D 2 in fours. *B. M.*

> The translator apprises us that the original Dutch copy had been published a few days before at Amsterdam with a beautiful map of all the townes included in the relation.

The last true Newes from Yorke, Nottingham, Coventry, and Warwicke : Or all the speciall Passages and Occurrences in these parts, from the 24. of August, to the 4 of September, 1642 . . . Septemb. 7. London Printed for Iohn Wright. 1642. 4°, 4 leaves.

Newes from the Citie of Norwich : Of Certain Passages which happened there on Monday last, relating the number of Cavaliers which are dispersed in sundry Villages near the Citie. Also shewing the resolution of the Inhabitants of Northampton-shire, being 4000 men ready arm'd, in the opposition of the Cavaliers, . . . Also a Manifestation how the Gentrie and Traine Bands of York-shire do begin to fall away from the King, . . . With the true Relation of the siege of Coventrie, . . . London, Printed for Th. Clapham. Aug. 26. [1642.] 4°, 4 leaves.

N. NICOLAUS, *Anglus.*

Epistola cvivsdam Angli, qva asseritur consensus Veræ religionis doctrinæ & Cæremoniarum in Anglia, contra nanissimos quorundam cauillos, quibus eandem suis ad plebeculam contionibus impugnare conantur. III. Regvm xviii. Vsqueqve claudicatis . . . [Londini] Anno Dom. m.[d.]lxi. 8°, 8 leaves. *Corpus Christi College, Cambridge.*

> This letter is addressed by *Nicolaus N. Anglus* to *Johannes N.* his old friend staying at Paris, and is dated at the end the Nones of April 1561. There is no printer's name.

NORFOLK.

The Declaration of the Gentry, of the County of Norfolk, And of the County and City of Norwich. [January 1659-60.] A broadside.

> A plea advanced for the recal of the secluded Members.

OBSERVATIONS.

Some Observations made upon the Molucco Nutts, Imported from the Indies : Shewing their Admirable Virtues in Curing the Collick, Rupture, and all Distempers proceeding from the Wind. Anno 1672. 4°, 4 leaves.

Some Observations made upon the Root called Nean, or Ninsing, Imported from the East Indies. . . . London, Printed for the Author. [1680.] 4°, 4 leaves.

Some Observations made upon the Angola Seed : Shewing its Admirable Virtue in Curing all Distempers of the Eyes. Written by a Doctor of Physick in the Country to Dr Goddard, one of the Royal Society at London, Anno 1660. London Printed, &c. 1682. 4°, 4 leaves.

Some Observations made upon the Brasillian Root, called Ipecocoanha : Imported from the Indies . . . London Printed, &c. 1682. 4°, 4 leaves.

Some Observations made upon the Virginian Nutts [Locust fruit] Imported from the Indies: Shewing their Admirable Virtue against the Scurvy . . . London Printed, &c. 1682. 4°, 4 leaves.

Some Observations made upon the Root called Casmemar, Imported from the East-Indies : . . . Published by a Doctor of Physick in Glocester-shire. London, Re-printed in the Year 1693. 4°, 4 leaves.

Some Observations made upon the Banellas, Imported from the Indies : . . . London, Printed in the Year 1694. 4°, 4 leaves.

Some Observations made upon the Blatta Bizantina, . . . London, Printed in the Year 1694. 4°, 4 leaves.

Some Observations made upon the Calumba Wood, Otherwise called Calumback : Imported from the Indies : . . . [By Dr. Peche.] London, Printed in the Year 1694. 4°, 4 leaves.

Some Observations made upon the Wood called Lignum Nephriticum, Imported from Hispaniola : . . . Printed in the Year 1694. 4°, 4 leaves.

Some Observations made upon the Malabar Nutt, imported from the Indies : . . . London, Printed in the Year 1694. 4°, 4 leaves.

Some Observations made upon the Maldiva Nutt : . . . Written by a Physitian in the Countrey to Dr. Hinton at London. 1663. London, Printed in the Year 1694. 4°, 4 leaves.

Some Observations Made upon the Herb called Perigua, Imported from the Indies: Shewing its Admirable Virtues in Curing the Diabetes . . . London, Printed in the Year 1694. 4°, 4 leaves.

Some Observations made upon the Russia Seed, . . . Written by a Doctor of Physick in the Countrey to Esq; Boyle at London, 1674. London, Printed in the Year 1694. 4°, 4 leaves.

Some Observations made upon the Root called Serapias, or Salep, Imported from Turkey . . . Printed in the Year 1694. 4°, 4 leaves.

Some Observations Made upon the Bengala Bean, Imported from the Indies : . . . Printed in the Year 1694. 4°, 4 leaves.

Some Observations made upon the Bermudas Berries : Imported from the Indies : Shewing their Admirable Virtues in curing the Green-Sickness. Written by a Doctor of Physick in the Countrey to the Honourable Esq; Boyle. London, Printed in the Year 1694. 4°, 4 leaves.

Some Observations made upon the Herb Cassiny; Imported from Carolina: Shewing its Admirable Virtues in Curing the Small Pox. Written by a Physitian in the Countrey to Esq; Boyle in London. London, Printed in the Year 1695. 4°, 4 leaves.

Some Observations made upon the Mexico Seeds, Imported from the Indies : . . . London, Printed in the Year 1695. 4°, 4 leaves.

The foregoing Series are contained in a volume in old half binding lettered on the back *Marloes Tracts.* As the authorship of most is unknown to me, I thought it better to range them under this general heading.

OLDCASTLE, SIR JOHN, *Lord Cobham.*
The first part of the true and honorable historie . . . 1600.

A second part of this drama was licensed with the first, August 11, 1600, but does not seem to have been printed. *Arber,* iii. 169.

OLDMIXON, JOHN.
A Pastoral Poem on the Victories at Schellenburgh and Blenheim ; . . . With a large Preface, shewing the Antiquity and Dignity of Pastoral Poetry. . . . London, Printed and Sold by A. Baldwin . . . 1704. 4°, A—O, 2 leaves each, besides title and dedication to the Duchess of Marlborough, 3 leaves more, but sign. G omitted.

OSBORNE, THOMAS, *Earl of Danby.*
The Sentiments. A Poem to the Earl of Danby in the Tower. By a Person of Quality. London : Printed for James Vade, at the Cock and Sugar-loaf in Fleet-street. 1679. Folio, A—C, 2 leaves each.

OVERTON, WILLIAM, *D.D.*
A Godlye, and pithie Exhortation, made to the Iudges, and Justices of Sussex, and the whole Countie, assembled together, at the generall Assises . . . Printed by R. Newbery and H. Bynnman. 8°, black letter, A—D in eights, D 8 blank.

OXFORD, UNIVERSITY OF.
.Vniversity Newes. Or, The Vnfortunate proceedings of the Cavaliers in Oxford. Wherein is declared, The severall Misdemeanors and uncivill Behaviour of the two hundred and fifty Troopers which came from his Majesty to assist the Schollers against the Parliament . . . Septemb. 10. London Printed for Iohn Wright. 1642. 4°, 4 leaves.

A Letter sent from the Provost Vice-Chancellour of Oxford, To the Right Honourable the Earle of Pembroke Lord

Chancellour of Oxford. Together with his Lordships Answer to the said Letter. September 13. 1642. London Printed by L. N. for E. Husbands and J. Franck . . . 4°, 4 leaves.

An Ode in Praise of Musick. Composed by M' Charles King, In five Parts, for the Degree of Batchelour of Musick, Perform'd at the Theatre in Oxford, on Friday the 11ᵗʰ of July 1707. A folio leaf.

OXFORDSHIRE.

Schola Thamensis . . . 1575.

> Comerford, December 1881, No. 3979, where it is described as "an extraordinary fine copy, in the original oak boards, covered with elegantly stamped calf, with brass corners, centres and clasps, having the title of the book printed on vellum, protected by a piece of horn enclosed within brass borders on reverse of cover." It is further stated to be "one of the rarest of all works in English Topography, the only other perfect copy known being that of Mr. Grenville in the British Museum. Two other copies, both imperfect, that in the Bodleian containing 33 leaves and that in the possession of the Warden of New College, as patron of the school, wanting all the Appendices, are all that can be traced to be in existence."

P. S., *Esquire.*
The Portugal History : Or, A Relation of the Troubles that happened in the Court of Portugal in the Years 1667 and 1668 : In which is to be seen that great Transaction of the Renunciation of the Crown by Alphonso the Sixth, the Dissolution of his Marriage with the Princess Maria Frances Isabella of Savoy : The Marriage of the same Princess to the Prince Don Pedro Regent of the Realm of Portugal, and the Reasons alledged at Rome for the Dispensation thereof. By S. P. Esq ; London : Printed for Richard Tonson . . . 1677. 8°, B—Z in eights, besides the title and *Imprimatur.*

> With a long historical Introduction, probably by S. P.—initials which are usually explained Samuel Pepys.

P. T.
The Accomplish'd Lady's Delight in Preserving, Physick, Beautifying, and Cookery . . . The Second Edition Enlarged. London, Printed for Nath. Crouch, . . . 1677. 12°, A—Q in twelves, besides the frontispiece.

The Accomplish'd Lady's Delight . . . The Seventh Edition Enlarged. London, Printed by B. Harris, in Maiden-head-Court in Great East-Cheap. 1696. 12°. A, 6 leaves : B—I in twelves : K, 6.

P. W.
The History of Witches and Wizards : Giving a True Account of all the Tryals in England, Scotland, Sweedland, France and New England ; with their Confession and Condemnation . . . London : Printed for C. Hitch and L. Haws, . . . 12°. A, 6 leaves, A 1 with a frontispiece : B—G in twelves. With numerous rough cuts.

PALLADIO, ANDREA.
The First Book of Architecture, ... The Third Edition Corrected and Enlarged. With the new Model of the Cathedral of St. Paules as it's now to be Built. London, Printed for N. Simmons . . . T. Passinger . . . 1676. 4°, A—G, in fours, besides the frontispiece and numerous plates, some folded.

PARLIAMENT.
The Declaration of the Lords and Commons . . . Concerning His Maiesties severall Messages about the Militia. With an Order of the Lords and Commons touching the Militia of the Citie of London. [5 May, 1642.] London, Printed for I. T. 1642. 4°, 4 leaves.

New Votes of Both Houses of Parliament, the 20ᵗʰ of May, 1642. With the Humble Petition of the Lords and Commons, . . . to the Kings most excellent Majestie at Yorke. Also the Lord Stamfords report to the Parliament concerning the danger of Hull, . . . Printed May 24. 1642. 4°, 4 leaves.

An Order made by the House of Commons, Assembled in Parliament, for the Establishing of Preaching Lecturers throughout the Kingdome of England and Dominion of Wales. . . . May 30. London, Printed for I. T. 1642. 4°, 4 leaves.

> This tract includes Considerations, &c., on the Common Prayer-Book and other liturgical matters.

Propositions made by Both Houses of Parliament to the Kings Majestie, for A Reconciliation of the Differences between His Majesty and the said Hovses. [June 2, 1642.] With an Order of the House of Parliament, concerning the Iewels belonging to the Crown. June 3. London, Printed for I. Green, and A. Coe. 1642. 4°, 4 leaves.

A Replication of the Lords and Commons . . . To His Majesties last Answer, sent by the Right Honorable the Earle of Holland . . . Iuly 29. London printed for Iohn Wright, 1642. 4°, 4 leaves.

A Declaration of the Lords and Commons . . . August 3. London Printed for John Wright, 1642. 4°, 4 leaves.

The Parliaments Censvre on Sir Richard Gvrney, Lord Major of the Honourable City of London August 12. 1642. With the Articles of his Impeachment. . . . London : Printed for Iohn Cave. August 13. 1642. 4°, 4 leaves.

A Declaration and Resolvtion of the Lords and Commons in Parliament, Concerning His Majesties late Proclamation for the suppressing of the present Rebellion under the Command of Robert Earl of Essex, London, Printed by L. N. and I. F. for Edward Husband and Iohn Franck, . . . August 15. 1642. 4°, 4 leaves.

August 20. A Remonstrance and Declaration of the Lords and Commons . . . Manifesting that all such Persons as shall upon any pretence whatsoever assist His Majesty in this Warre, with Horse, Armes, Plate or Money, shall be held and accounted Traytors to His Majesty, the Parliament, and the Kingdome. Likewise two Orders of the Lords and Commons . . . for the ordering of the Souldiers under the Earle of Essex. Also a Letter to a Member of the House of Commons, concerning divers passages which hath lately hapned in the County of Hamp-Shire. Printed for George Tomlinson. 1642. 4°, 4 leaves.

A Declaration of the Lords and Commons . . . Whereby the good Subjects of this Kingdome may better discerne their owne danger, and be stirred up with more earnestnesse to assist the Parliament in the maintenance of Religion, the common Iustice and Liberty of the Kingdome, which seemes to be in no lesse hazard, then if wee had an Army of the Irish Rebels in the Bowels of this Land . . . August 22, Printed for Iohn Wright. 1642. 4°, 4 leaves.

Two Declarations of the Lords and Commons . . . The One, Concerning the Releasing of diverse Worthy Ministers; . . . September 9. London Printed for Iohn Wright. 1642. 4°, 4 leaves.

A Relation of the Actions of the Parliaments Forces, Under the command of the Earl of Bedford Generall of the Horse, against those which came from Shirbourn unto Babell-hill here unto Yerrell, upon Wednesday the 7th of this instant September, 1642. . . . Together with The Copy of Captain Aiscoughs Letter to a Friend of his in London . . . London Printed for E. Husbands and J. Franck. Sept. 13. [1642.] 4°, 4 leaves.

PARTRIDGE, JAMES.
Ayme for Finsbvrie Archers. Or an Alphabeticall Table of the names of euery Marke within the same fields, with their true distances according to the dimensuration of the line. Newly gathered and amended by Iames Partridge. London, Printed by G. M. for Iohn Partridge, . . . 1628. Very small 8°, A—K 2 in eights. *B. M.*

PARTRIDGE, IOHN.
The treasurie of commodious Conceites, and hidden Secrets. Commonly called, The good Hus-wiues Closet of prouision, for the health of her houshold. Meete and necessarie for the vse of all estates. Gathered out of sundry Experiments . . . At London, Printed by Richarde Ihones : dwelling at the signe of the Rose and Crowne, neere Holburne Bridge. 1584. 8°, A—F 4 in eights. Dedicated by Partridge to Master Richard Wistow, Gentleman, one of the Assistants of the Company of Barber-Chirurgeons. With some curious verses on the back of the title by the printer. *B. M.*

The Treasurie of hidden Secrets, Commonlie called, The Good-huswiues Closet of prouision, for the health of her Houshold . . . At London, Printed by I. R. for Edward White, . . . 1600. 4°, black letter, A—I in fours. *B. M.*

PARTRIDGE, JOHN, *Astrologer.*
Defectio Genitvrarvm : Being an Essay toward the Reviving and Proving the True Old Principles of Astrology, Hitherto Neglected, Or, at leastwise, not Observed or Understood. In Four Parts . . . By John Partridge . . . London ; Printed for Benj. Tooke . . . MDCXCVII. 4°. A, 4 leaves : a—b in fours : B—Z 2 in fours : Partridge's Answer to George Parker, 10 leaves. Dedicated to Sir Joseph Tily, Knight, M.P. With an address to Partridge by Sir Edward Dering.

PATRICK, ST.
Histoire de la Vie et du Purgatoire de S. Patrice. Archevesque et Primat d'Hybernie. Mise en François par le R. P. François Bouillon de l'Ordre de S. François [sic], & Bachelier en Theologie. Nouvelle Edition . . . A Troyes . . . 12°, pp. 192, including the frontispiece.

A chapman's edition of the 18th century.

PAYNE, NICHOLAS, *of Dover.*

A True Relation of A Brave Exploit performed by Captain Richard Dawks, in taking of the Castle of Dover for the King and Parliament, . . . on the 21. of August, 1642 . . . London, Printed by L. Norton and I. Field for C. A. Sept. 2. 1642. 4°, 4 leaves.

> The tract mentions the appointment of Sir Edward Boyse as Lieutenant of Dover Castle.

PEACHAM, HENRY.

The Worth of a Penny : . . . London. Printed for Samuel Keble, . . . 1686. 4°. Title and dedication, 2 leaves : B—E 2 in fours.

PET, EDMOND.

Lamentable Newes, Shewing the wonderfull deliuerance of Maister Edmond Pet Sayler, and Maister of a Ship, dwelling in Seething Lane in London, neere Barking Church. With other strange things lately hapned concerning these great windes and tempestuous weather, both at Sea and Lande. Imprinted at London by T. C. for William Barley, dwelling ouer against Gr[a]ce-church, neere Algate. 1613. 4°, black letter, 4 leaves. With a cut of a ship on title. *B. M.*

PETTIT, EDWARD, *M.A.*

The Visions of Government, &c. Wherein The Antimonarchical Principles and Practices of all Phanatical Commonwealthmen, and Jesuitical Politicians are discovered, confuted, and exposed . . . The Second Edition. London, Printed by B. W. for Edward Vize, . . . MDCLXXXVI. 8°. Frontispiece, 1 leaf: A, 4 leaves, with title and dedication to the Duke of Ormond : (a)—(c 4) in eights : B—R 4 in eights.

> The first edition was published in 1685 during Monmouth's rebellion.

PLATT, SIR HUGH.

Hvgonis Platti Armig : Manvale, Sententias aliqvot Dininas & Morales complectens : Partim è Sacris Patribus. Partim e Petrarcha philosopho & Poeta celeberrimo decerptas. *Mel ex floribus, non herbis.* Londini Excudebat Petrus Short. 1594. Small 8°. ¶, 8 leaves, title on ¶ 2, and ¶ 3 imprinted ¶ 2 : A—V in eights, A 8 blank. Without any dedicatory or prefatory matter. *B. M.*

> Licensed to Peter Short, 19 November 1594.

POWELL, ROBERT, *of Wells.*

Depopvlation Arraigned, Convicted and Condemned by the Lawes of God and Man : A Treatise necessary in these

Times. By R. P. of Wells, one of the Societie of New Inne. *Regis, Ecclesiæ, reipublicæ, & pauperum ergò.* London, Printed by R. B. and are to bee sold in S. Dunstans Church-yard neere the Church doore, 1636. 8°. A, 4 leaves : B—K in eights, K 8 blank. Dedicated to Sir John Banks, Attorney-General.

PRANCE, MILES.

Mᵣ Prance's Answer to Mⁿ Cellier's Libel and Divers other false Aspersions cast upon him : Containing likewise a Vindication of Sir William Waller from Popish Scandals ; To which is Added the Adventure of the Bloody Bladder : A Tragi-Comical Farce, Acted with much Applause at Newgate by the said Madam Cellier, on Saturday Sept. 18. instant, . . . London, Printed for L. Curtis . . . 1680. Folio, A—E, 2 leaves each.

PRAYER.

[The Pomander of Prayer. At the end occurs :] At London Printed by Iohn Daye, dwellyng ouer Aldersgate. And are to be solde at his long shop, at the West doore of Paules. An. 1578. Cum gratia . . . Small 8°, A—O in eights. Printed within ornamental borders.

> The copy examined wanted the title and perhaps A ii, the text commencing on A iii.

PRESBYTERY.

Spectrum Anti-Monarchicum. Or, The Ghost of Hugh Peters, As He lately Appeared to his Beloved Son, the whole Assembly of Fanatick Presbyters. Folio, 2 leaves. In verse.

PRICE, LAURENCE.

The Famous History of Valentine and Orson. Being The two only Sons of the Emperour of Greece. Deciphering their wonderful Births, their Valiant Achievements, their Heroical Minds, and their Noble Enterprises. Drawn up in a short Volume, on purpose to give the better satisfaction to them that desire to hear and know the truth in few words. Written by Laurence Price.

> This little Book such vertues doth contain,
> Hardly the like in all the World again.

London, Printed for William Whitwood, at the sign of the Bell in Duck Lane. 1673. Sm. 8°, black letter, 12 leaves, including a woodcut frontispiece.

> A popular abridgment of the story.

PROTESTANTS.

No Protestant-Plot : Or The present Pretended Conspiracy of Protestants against the King and Government. Discovered to be a Conspiracy of the Papists against the King and his Protestant Subjects. London: Printed for R. Lett, 1681. 4°, B—F in fours, no A.

The Second Part of No Protestant Plot. By the same Hand. London: Printed for R. Smith. 1682. 4°, B—E in fours, and the title.

PRYNNE, WILLIAM.
The Chvrch of Englands Old Antithesis to New Arminianisme. . . . By William Prynne Gent Hospitij Lincolniensis. . . . London. 1629. 4°. A, 4 leaves: a, 4 eaves: B—c in fours: ¶—3 ¶ in fours: B (repeated)—G in fours: b*—t* 2 in fours. With dedications to the Parliament and the Bishops, and an address to the Christian Reader.

God no Impostor, nor Delvder. [London, 1629 *l*]. 4°, 14 leaves. A, 8 : B, C.

PUGET DE LA SERRE, JEAN.
The Secretary in Fashion: Or, A Compendious and Refined way of Expression in all manner of Letters. Composed in French by P. S' de la Serre, Historiographer of France. And Translated into English, by John Massinger, Gent. London, Printed by J. B. and S. B. for Godfrey Emerson, and are to be sold at his Shop in Little Brittain. 1640. 4°, A—S 2 in fours, A 1 blank, a, 4 leaves, and sign. I in duplicate, the first gathering marked in top right-hand corner a—d. Dedicated by Massinger to Mr. Thomas Berney of Gray's Inn. With a curious Preface by the translator to the Reader.

Reprinted, 8°, 1654 and 1673. The latter purports to be the fifth edition.

RABISHA, WILLIAM.
The whole Body of Cookery Dissected, . . . London, Printed for E. Calvert, . . . 1673. 8°. A, 8: a—b 4 in eights: B—U 4 in eights. Dedicated in this reprint to the Duchess Dowager of Lenox, the Duchess of Buckingham, the Lady Jane Lane, the Lady Mary Tufton, and the Lady Agnes Walker.

RANDOLPH, THOMAS, *of Trinity College, Cambridge.*
The Ex-Ale-tation of Ale. Written by a Learned Pen. London, Printed by J. R. 1668. 8°, A in eights.

This impression does not contain the Latin version by T. C. P.

In a political tract called *A Curse against Parliament Ale*, 1649, there are on the title-page the subjoined lines :—

" Tom Randal did once, in a merry Tale, Write the Commendation of a Pot of Good Ale,"—

under which title the present production was printed in 1642.

I see in the volume described as *Ben Johnson's Jests*, 1761, an anecdote of "one Thomas Randal"—no doubt the poet; but it has the air of being unauthentic.

At an auction in Leicester Square a few years ago, a copy of Chaucer's Works, 1561, folio, occurred with the autograph of *Tho. Randolphe* on the top of the title, and at the foot *Thomas Randolphe to Thomas his Soñe ;* which, according to the cataloguer, was "doubtless the autograph of the author of the *Muses' Looking Glass*, and the friend of Shakespeare." It was, however, no such thing ; nor was even the poet Randolph a friend of Shakespear.

REFLECTIONS.
Some Reflections on M' Asgill's Essay on a Registry for Titles of Lands. *Qui tacet, consentire videtur.* London, Printed in the year 1698. 8°, A—G in fours. *B. M.*

REMEMBRANCER.
The Office of Generall Remembrance. Of Matters of Record, created by his Maiesties Letters Pattents, for ease of his Subiects in their Searches, and auoyding the inconueniences heretofore incident for want of meanes speedily to finde out all incumbrances vpon Record, &c. Is kept in Cursitors Court, right ouer against Lincolnes Inne in Chauncery Lane. . . . At London Printed by G. Eld for the Remembrancers Generall, the Patentees, . . . and are to bee sold at the Shop of Robert Wilson . . . 1617. 4°, A—G in fours, A 1 and G 4 blank.

REYNOLDS, JOHN, *of Exeter, and of the Assay Office at the Tower Mint.*
Tables of Gold and Silver . . . 1651. 8°.
I think it a misapprehension to distinguish between Reynolds of Exeter, compiler of *God's Revenge*, and Reynolds of the Assay Office in the Tower Mint, as there is almost absolute proof that the *God's Revenge* was written by the same person who translated the *Treatise of the Court*, by Refuges, 1622, while the latter was almost certainly from the same hand as prepared these *Tables.* See *Coll. and Notes*, 1st Series, p. 357.

REYNOLDS, JOHN, *of King's Norton.*
A Discourse upon Prodigious Abstinence : Occasioned by the Twelve Moneths Fasting of Martha Taylor, The Famed Derbyshire Damosell: Proving that without any Miracle, the Texture of Humane Bodies may be so altered, that Life may be long Continued without the supplies of Meat & Drink. With an Account of the Heart, and how far it is interressed in the Business of Fermentation. Humbly offered to the Royal Society. London, Printed, by R. W. for Nevill Seymour, at the Sign

of the three Crowns near Holborn-Conduit : and for Dorman Newman, at the Chyrurgeons Arms in Little Brittain. 1669. 4°, A—F 2 in fours. Dedicated to " the Deservedly Famous, and my Honoured friend, Walter Needham, Doctor of Physick . . ."

RIVIUS, JOHANNES.
A Treatise against the folishnesse of men in differringe the reformation of their liuing, and amendment of their maners. Compyled by the godly lerned man John Riuius, and translated into Englishe by John Bankes. [Col.] Imprynted at London in Flete-strete at the signe of the George nexte to Saynte Dunstones Churche by Wyllyam Powell . . . 8°, A—O 4 in eights. Dedicated by the translator to the Marquis Dorset. *B. M.*

> As Henry Grey, last Marquis of Dorset, was created Duke of Suffolk in October 1551, this book was doubtless printed before that date.

Of the foolishnes of men in putting-off the amendement of their liues from daie to daie, A godlie and profitable treatise for the present time ; Written in the Latine tongue by that reuerend and worthie member of Christ his Church in this age, Iohn Riuius. Newlie translated by Thomas Rogers. [The 23. of Februarie. 1581.] . . . Imprinted at London for Andrew Maunsel, . . . [1582.] 8°. A, 4 leaves : B—M in eights, M 8 with the colophon : Imprinted at London by Iohn Charlewood, for Andrewe Maunsel, dwelling in Paules Church-yard, at the signe of the Paret.

> The dedication of Rivius to Maurice, Duke of Saxony, is dated 1547. The year in which the English version was executed by Rogers is stated at the foot of this Epistle. On the back of the title of this copy occurs the old autograph of *Robert Gibbon.*

ROLLE OF HAMPOLE, RICHARD.
[The remedy ayenst the troubles of temptacyons. At the end occurs :] Here endeth a deuonte medytacyon in sayenge denoutly the psalter of our lady With dyuers ensamples Enprynted at London in Fletestrete at the sygne of the sonne. By Wynkyn de worde. Anno domini. M.CCCCC.viii. the fourth daye of February. 4°, black letter, with woodcuts. A C in sixes : D, 8. With the printer's device on D 8 verso. *B. M.*

> This copy is printed on vellum, but is unfortunately incomplete, wanting A i, D 2, and D 5.

S. R.
Affliction of minde maie not be straunge to Gods seruantes. A folio leaf. [About 1620.]

S. T.
The Perplex'd Prince. London : Printed for R. Allen. 12°. A, 6 : B—G 6 in twelves. Dedicated to the Right Honourable William, Lord Russell.

[The Fugitive Statesman, In Requital for the Perplex'd Prince. London, Printed by A. Grover, 1683. 12°. A, 6 leaves, the first blank : B—F in twelves.]

SCOTLAND.
A Remonstrance and Resolvtion of the Kingdom of Scotland. Shewing the lawfulnesse of the second coming into England to take up Arms against all those that shall oppose the Parliament. Published with the advice of the Councell of Scotland . . . Re-Printed at London for G. T. 1642. 4°, 4 leaves.

Exceeding Joyfull Newes from Scotland Brought over by the Lord Mackland, and read in the House of Commons [Aug. 18 1642.] . . . With the Pa[r]liaments Resolution concerning the Yorkshire propositions . . . Likewise The Resolution of the Earle of Rutland, the Earle of Exceter, and the Lord Paget, with divers others that are come from His Majesty, are resolved to come to the House again, if they may be received . . . August 20. Printed for J. Horton. 4°, 4 leaves.

The Scots Resolution Concerning this present Expedition. Expressed in the voluntary service of diverse Scottish Commanders, who profered themselves to the Parliament to serve in this Expedition for the King and Parliament, with the Parliaments acceptation of the same profer. Also The Setting Forth

Of
{ The Lord Brook,
Colonell Hampden,
Colonell Hollis,
Colonell Fines, and
Colonell Goodwyn

to meet the Cavaliers at Warwick, with about six thousand Horse and Foot, who are now in their march towards Whibits. Also the manner of apprehending two Jesuites in Covent Garden, August 22. Printed for Tho. Edwards. August 23. 1642. 4°, 4 leaves.

To the Kings most Excellent Majesty : The humble supplication and desire of the Commissioners of his Majesties Kingdom of Scotland, here now resident . . . Septem. 4. London Printed for Fr. Coules. 1642. 4°, 4 leaves.

The Grievances Represented by the Estates of Scotland, to the Kings Majesty, to be Redressed in Parliament. Together with His Majesties Instructions to his Commissioner for Redressing the same. Published by Authority. In the Savoy: Printed by Edward Jones. MDCLXXXIX. Folio, 4 leaves.

SCOTT, ANNE. *Duchess of Monmouth.*
The Petticoat Plotters, Or The D[uche]ss of M[onmout]h's Club. London Printed by T. Barns in Fleet-street . . . A broadside.

SEA.
A Paper; Concerning the Affairs of Their Majesties Men of War, And Merchant-Men at Sea: Intended for the Use of the Members of the Honourable House of Commons; which hath been delivered to several of them, tho not to them all as a House. A folio leaf.

Ioyfvll Newes from Sea: Or good tidings from my Lord of Warwicke, of his encounters with some Spanish Ships, with the happy successe he obtained thereby. Also herein is declared what store of Ammunition, Money, and other necessaries for War were by our English ships taken from them, . . . Printed at London for Thomas Bankes. 1642. 4°, 4 leaves.

SENECA, L. A.
Seneca's Morals by way of Abstract. To which is added, A Discourse, under the Title of An After-Thought. By Sir Roger L'Estrange, Knt. The Eighth Edition. London, Printed by W. Bowyer, for Jacob Tonson. . . . 1702. 8°. A, 8: a, 8: B—Mm 4 in eights. With a frontispiece.

SETTLE, ELKANAH.
The Conquest of China, By the Tartars. A Tragedy Acted at the Duke's Theatre. Written by Elkanah Settle, Servant to His Majesty. —Multum sudet . . . Hor. London, Printed by T. N. for W. Cademan, . . . 1676. 4°, A—K 2 in fours. Dedicated to the Lord Castle-Rizing.

Distress'd Innocence: Or, The Princess of Persia. A Tragedy. As it is Acted at the Theatre-Royal by Their Majesties Servants. Written by E. Settle. I't *ridentibus arrident,* . . . Horat. de Arte Poeticâ. London, Printed by E. J. for Abel Roper . . . 1691. 4°, A—I 2 in fours. Dedicated to John, Lord Cutts, Baron of Gowran.

The New Athenian Comedy, Containing The Politicks, Œconomicks, Tacticks, Crypticks, Apocalypticks, . . . of that most Learned Society. *Ede, quid illum esse putes* . . . Juv. Sat. 3. London, Printed for Campanella Restio, next Door to the Apollo, near the Temple, 1693. 4°. Title and dedication to Edward Wilson, Esq., 2 leaves: a, 2 leaves: B—H 2 in fours.

The Heir of Morocco, With the Death of Gayland. Acted by Their Majesties Servants. By E. Settle. *Rectius Iliacum carmen* . . . Hor. London, Printed for Tho. Chapman, at the Golden Key, over against the Meuse, near Charing Cross. 1694. 4°, A—G in fours, G 4 blank. Dedicated to Henrietta, Baroness of Nettlested.

Pastor Fido: Or, The Faithful Shepheard. A Pastoral. As it is Acted by Their Majesties Servants. *Sylvestrem resonare doces Amaryllida Sylvas.* Virg. . . . London, Printed for Tho. Chapman, in the Pall-Mall, over-against St. James's-Square. 1694. 4°, A—H in fours. Dedicated to the Lady Elizabeth Delaval.

Eusebia Triumphans. The Hanover Succession to the Imperial Crown of England. An Heroick Poem. *Pro aris & focis.* London, Printed for the Author, MDCCIV. Folio, A—O, 2 leaves each. Engl. and Lat.

SHADWELL, THOMAS.
Epsom-Wells. A Comedy, Acted at the Duke's Theatre. . . . London, Printed by J. M. for Henry Herringman. . . . M.DC.LXXVI. 4°, A—N in fours, and a leaf of O. Dedicated to the Duke of Newcastle.

SHELTON, THOMAS.
Tachygraphy or Short Writing The most Easie Exact and Speedie First Compyled by Thomas Shelton and now by him Newly Corrected & Enlarged. [This is an engraved title. The printed title adds:] . . . Approved by both the Universities. London Printed by Thomas Milbourn, for Dorman Newman, . . . 1691. 8°, A—D 4 in eights.

SHEPHERDS.
The Shepheards Kalender. Here Beginneth the Kalender of Shepheards. Newly augmented and corrected. Printed at London for Thomas Adams, dwelling in Pauls Church-yard at the signe of the Bell. 1618. Folio, A—R 4 in eights. Black letter. With cuts.

SMITH, JOHN, *Governor of Virginia.*
New Englands Trials. Declaring the
successe of 26. Ships employed thither
within these sixe yeares : with the benefit
of that Countrey by sea and land : and
how to build threescore sayle of good
Ships, to make a little Navie Royall.
Written by Captaine Iohn Smith. London, Printed by William Iones. 1620.
4°. Title and dedication to the Master,
Wardens, and Company of the Fishmongers, 2 leaves : B—C in fours. *B. M.*

SOLINUS POLYHISTOR, JULIUS.
The excellent and pleasant worke of
Julius Solinus Polyhistor. Contayning
the noble actions of humaine creatures,
the secretes & prouidence of nature, the
description of Countries, the maners of
the people: with many meruailous things
and strange antiquities, seruing for the
benefit and recreation of all sorts of persons. Translated out of Latin into English, by Arthur Golding. Gent. At
London Printed by I. Charlewoode for
Thomas Hacket. 1587. 4°, A—Gg 2
in fours. Black letter.

> The copy employed possesses a duplicate
> title, varying as follows : The Worthie
> worke of Iulius Solinus Polyhistor. Con-
> tayning many noble actions of humaine
> creatures, with the secretes of nature in
> Beastes, Fyshes, Foules, and Serpents:
> Trees, Plants, and the vertue of precious
> stones : With diuers Countryes, Citties and
> people. Verie pleasant and full of recrea-
> tion for all sorts of people. Translated out
> of Latine into English by Arthur Golding.
> Gent. At London, Printed by I. Charle-
> woode for Thomas Hacket. 1587. Each
> has the same vignette engraving of a King
> crowned, with a sceptre in one hand and a
> sword in the other.

SOLOMON.
Solomon's Song Paraphras'd : A Pindarick
Poem. [By John Lloyd. Quot. from
Ovid. de Trist. Lib. 1. Eleg. 1.] London,
Printed by H. Hills, for Henry Faithorne,
and John Kersey, . . . 1681. 4°, B—E
in fours, a leaf of F, and the title.

SOMERSETSHIRE.
A Relation of all the passages and proceedings in Somersetshire, and Bristoll,
with their valiant Resolution to fight for
the King and Parliament. With a speech
made by his Excellence the Earle of
Essex . . . Also, Certain Reasons written
by a private Gentleman, Shewing the
cause wherefore Arms are raysed by
both houses of Parliament. . . . London,
Printed for W. Gay, 1642. August 13.
4°, 4 leaves.

SOUTHERN, THOMAS.
The Wives Excuse : Or, Cuckolds make

themselves. A Comedy, As it is Acted
at the Theatre-Royal, By Their Majesties
Servants. Written by Tho. Southern.
Nihil est his, . . . Cicero. London,
Printed for Samuel Brisco, over against
Will's Coffee-house, in Russel-Street, in
Covent-Garden. 1692. 4°, A—H in
fours. With a preliminary copy of verses
by Dryden.

SPAGNUOLI MANTUANO, BAT-
TISTA.
Mantuan English'd, and Paraphras'd :
Or, The Character of A Bad Woman.
Mant. Ecl. 3.
Fæmineum seruile genus crudele superbum.
[1679.] Folio, 2 leaves. In verse.

SPARKE, THOMAS, *D.D.*
A Brotherly Perswasion to Vnitie, and
Vniformitie in Iudgement, and Practise
tovching the received and present Ecclesiasticall gouernement, and the authorised
rites and ceremonies of the Church of
England. Written by Thomas Sparke
Doctor in Dininitie. And seene, allowed,
and commended by publike authoritie to
be printed. . . . London, Printed by
Nicholas Okes for Roger Iackson, . . .
1607. 4°, A—N in fours, A 1 and N 4
blank.

> The dedication to the King is dated from
> Bletchley in Buckinghamshire. 1607. The
> Epistle to the Christian Reader is dated
> 1606. Reprinted, 4to, 1617.

ST. FOINE.
St. Foine Improved, A Discourse Shewing the Utility and Benefit which England hath and may receive by the Grasse
called St. Foine, And answering the Objections urged against it. Being useful
for all Ingenious Men. Written by a
Person of Honour lately deceased. London, Printed by S. G. and B. G. for Nath.
Brooke, . . . 1671. 4°, A—C in fours,
C 4 blank.

STANDFAST, RICHARD.
A Dialogue between A Blind Man and
Death. 4°, 4 leaves, subscribed R. S.
In verse. Without title-page and im-
print. *B. M.*

STANLEY, CHARLES, *Earl of Derby.*
The Protestant Religion is A Sure Foundation and Principle of a True Christian,
And a Good Subject, a Great Friend to
Humane Society ; And A Grand Promoter
of all Virtues, both Christian and Moral.
The Second Edition. By Charles Earl
of Derby, Lord of Mann, and the Isles.
London, Printed for William Cademan,
. . . 1671. 4°, A—I in fours, and a leaf
of K. Dedicated to all Supreme Powers,

. . . Emperors, Kings, . . . The first address to the Reader is dated 1668.

The present copy is in the original binding, much dilapidated, with the crowned device of the Eagle and Child in gold on each side of the cover.

STANLEY, JAMES, *Lord Strange.*

An Impeachment of High Treason Exhibited in Parliament. Against James, Lord Strange. Son and Heire apparant of William, Earle of Derby, by the Commons assembled in Parliament, in the name of themselves, and of all the Commons of England. With an Order of the Lords and Commons in Parliament, for the apprehending of the said Lord, to be published in all Churches and Chappels, Markets and Towns, in the County of Lancaster and Chester. Septemb. 17. London Printed for John Wright, 1642. 4°, 4 leaves.

STATUTES.

The greate abbridgement of all ȳ statutes of Englāde, vntyl the . xxxiii. yere of the reygne of our moste drad soueraygne lord king Henry the eyght. To who be all honour, reuerence, & ioyful cōtinuāce of his prosperous reygne to the pleasure of god and weale of this his realme. Amen. Cvm Privilegio ad Imprimendvm Solvm. [Col.] Imprynted at London in Fletestrete at the sygne of the George by me Wyllyam Myddylton. 8°. Title, 1 leaf : Prologue, 1 leaf : Table, 5 leaves : A—Y in eights : AA—SS in eights : TT, 10 leaves : the Abridgment of the 33rd year, A—C in eights : D, 6. *B. M.*

At the end of TT in the second alphabet occurs : Imprynted at London in Fletestrete by me wyllyam Myddylton dwellynge at the sygne of the George nexte to saynte Dunstones churche. In the yere of our Lorde. mcccc.xlii. Cvm Privilegio. . . . The supplementary portion commences with a headline only, and has no date. It is not mentioned by Herbert.

STREETE, THOMAS.

Memorial Verses on the Ecclesiastical and Civil Calender : With an Epitome of the Heavenly Motions. By Thomas Streete, Student in Astronomy and Mathematicks . . . London, Printed by John Darby, and are to be Sold by John Sellers Compass-Maker, at the Signe of the Mariners-Compasse and Sphere, at the Hermitage Staires in Wapping, 1667. 4°, A—C in fours. With some verses on the back of the title by I[ohn] P[artridge ?]. *B. M.*

Some other pieces by the same writer are in the Museum.

STRONG, NATHANIEL, *Schoolmaster in London : At the Hand and Pen on Great-Tower-Hill, in Red-Cross-Alley.*

England's Perfect School-Master. Or, Directions for exact Spelling, Reading, and Writing . . . . . The Ninth Edition, much Enlarged. London, Printed by T. M. for Benjamin Billingsly, . . . 1706. 8°, A—D in fours, besides the frontispiece and two leaves of caligraphy at p. 72.

The *Imprimatur* is dated Feb. 9, 1675-76.

SUFFOLK.

A Signe from Heaven : Or, A Fearefull and Terrible Noise heard in the Ayre at Alborow in the County of Suffolke, on Thursday the 4. day of August at 5. of the clocke in the Afternoone. . . . Whereunto is annexed, A Prophesie of Merlins, concerning Hull in Yorkshire. Aug. 12. London Printed by T. Fawcet, 1642. 4°, 4 leaves.

The Prophecy is in verse.

SYLVESTER, JOSHUA.

Monodia. Imprinted by Peter short. [This is the whole title. On A 2 is a head-line as follows :] Monodia. An Elegie, in commemoration of the Vertuous life, and Godlie Death of the right Worshipfull & most religious Lady, Dame Hellen Branch Widdowe, (late Wife to the right worshipfull Sir Iohn Branch knight, sometimes L. Mayor of this Honorable Citty, and Daughter of Mʳ W. Nicholson sometimes of London Draper) who deceased the 10. of Aprill last, and lieth interred in Saint Mary Abchurch in London, the 29. of the same, 1594. 4°, 4 leaves *B. M.* (the Bright and Corser copy.)

With this copy is bound up an imperfect one of the *Triumph of Faith*, &c. 4°, 1592. Bright, 1845, £7 ; resold Corser, 1871, £18, 10s.

TALBOT, ELIZABETH, *Countess of Kent.*

A True Gentlewomans Delight . . . Published by W. I. Gent. London, Printed by G. D. and are to be sold by William Shears, . . . 1653. Small 12°. Title, Dedication by W. J. to Mistress Anne Pile, &c., 4 leaves : B, 6 leaves : B (repeated), 4 leaves : C—G in twelves : H, 6 ll.

This seems to be a distinct edition from that registered in *Coll. and Notes*, 1st Series, p. 245.

TATE, NAHUM.

The Triumph, Or Warriours Welcome : A Poem on the Glorious Successes of the Last Year. 1705. By Mr Tate, Poet-Laureat to Her Majesty. . . . London : Printed by J. Rawlins for J. Holland . . . 1705. 4⁰. A, 2 leaves : B—E in fours.

TEMPEST.
An Exact Relation of the Late Dreadful Tempest : Or, A Faithful Account of the Most Remarkable Disasters which hapned on that occasion : . . . . Faithfully collected by an Ingenious Hand, to preserve the Memory of so Terrible a Judgment . . . London, Printed for and sold by A. Baldwin . . . 1704. Price 6d. 4⁰, A—F, 2 leaves each. *B. M.*

TEMPLE, SIR PETER.
Mans Master-Piece : Or, The best Improvement of the worst Condition. In the exercise of A Christian Duty. On Six Considerable Actions . . . By P. T. K^t . . . London, Printed for Joseph Barber at the Lamb, and Samuel Speed at the Printing-Press in Saint Pauls Church-yard. 1658. 12⁰. A, 12 leaves : A 12 with *Errata*, A 1 blank : portrait of Lady Eleanor Temple by Gaywood, dated 1658, and verses on it, 2 ll. : B—M 6 in twelves. Dedicated to Lady Temple.

TERENTIUS AFER, PUBLIUS.
Flowres for latine speakinge. Selected and gathered oute of Terence, . . . Newly corrected and imprinted Anno. 1572. Imprinted at London by Thomas Marshe. Cum Priuilegio Regiæ Maiestatis. 8⁰, A—Aa in eights.

THYNNE, THOMAS, *of Longleat.*
Directions to Fame, About an Elegy on the Late Deceased Thomas Thynne, Esq; And An Eulogy on other most Famous English Worthies. By an Unknown Author. —*It Fama per Orbem.* London, Printed by J. S. and are to be sold by Richard Baldwin, in the Old-Baily, 1682. 4⁰. A, 2 leaves : B—D in fours : E, 2 ll. Dedicated anonymously to Lady Ogle, relict of T. Thynne.

TISDALE, ROGER.
Pax Vobis, Or, Wits Changes : Tyned in a Latine Hexameter of Peace. Whereof, the Numerall Letters present the Yeare of our Lord : and the Verse it selfe (consisting only of nine words) admitteth 1623 seuerall Changes or Transpositions, . . . With a Congratulatory Poem thereupon, and some other Chronograms . . . Composed in celebration of this yeares entrance of his Maiestie into the XXI. yeare of his blessed Reigne . . . and of the hopefull Iournall of the thrice Illustrious Prince

Charles into Spaine. By Ro : Tisdale of Graies Inne Gent. *Præsidium, non Ludibrium cano.* London, Printed by G. Eld and M. Flesher. 1623. 4⁰, A—C in fours. *B. M.*

TITHES.
The Decree for tythes to be payed in London. Anno. M.D.XL.VI. [Col.] Imprynted at London in Powles Churchyarde, by John Cawood, Printer to the Quenes Maiestie. [1553-4.] 8⁰, A in eights. Black letter. *B. M.*

The Decree for Tithes, to be payed in London. Anno M.D.LXXX. Imprinted at London for Gabriel Cawood. [Col.] Imprinted at London by Thomas East, for Gabriell Cawood. 1580. 8⁰, A in eights. *B. M.*

TOLAND, JOHN.
T[o]l[a]nd's Invitation to Dismal, to Dine with the Calves-Head Club. Imitated from Horace, Epist 5. Lib. 1. A folio leaf.

TURKEY.
Strange and Miraculous Newes from Tyrkie. Sent to our English Ambassadour resident at Constantinople. Of a Woman which was seene in the Firmament with a Book in her hand at Medina Talnabi where Mahomets Tombe is. Also severall Visions of Armed men . . . London, Printed for Hugh Perrey neere Ivy-Bridge in the Strand, June 13. 1642. 4⁰, 4 leaves. With a large descriptive cut on the title.

TUTCHIN, JOHN.
A Pindarick Ode, in the Praise of Folly and Knavery. By Mr Tutchin. London, Printed and Sold by E. W. near Stationers Hall. 1696. Price 6^d 4⁰. A—E, 2 leaves each. With a copy of verse to the Author by B. Bridgewater.

URQUHART, SIR THOMAS, *of Cromarty.*
Pantochronokanon : Or, A peculiar Promptuary of Time ; Wherein (not one instant being omitted from the beginning of motion) is displayed A most exact Directory for all particular Chronologies, in what Family soever : And that by deducing the true Pedigree and Lineal descent of the most ancient and honorable name of the Vrqhvarts, in the house of Cromartie, since the Creation of the world, until this present year of God 1652. London, Printed for Richard Baddeley, and are to be sold at his Shop, within the Middle-Temple-gate, 1652.

Small 8", A—E in eights, A 1 and E 8 blank.

> Edited by G. P., who states that the MS. was found among the pillage after the battle of Worcester.

VANBRUGH, SIR JOHN.
The Provok'd Wife : A Comedy. As it is Acted at the New Theatre in Little Lincolns - Inn - Fields. . . . London, Printed for Richard Willington . . . MDCXCVIII. 4°. Title, Prologue, &c., 3 leaves : B—K in fours.

VAN HELMONT, JOHANNES BAP-TISTA.
A Ternary of Paradoxes.
The { Magnetick Cure of Wounds. Nativity of Tartar in Wine. Image of God in Man.
Written originally by Joh. Bapt. Van Helmont, and Translated, Illustrated, and Ampliated By Walter Charleton, Doctor in Physick, and Physician to the late King. . . . London, Printed by James Flesher for William Lee, . . . 1650. [On a duplicate title with a curious engraving occurs in coeval MS.: Nou: 20 1649.] 4°. Two title-pages : a—g 2 in fours, with dedication by Charleton to William, Viscount Brouncker, and Prolegomena : B—V 2 in fours. *B. M.*

> The duplicate title to another copy before me adds : The second Impression, more reformed, and enlarged with some Marginal Additions.

VAUGHAN, SIR WILLIAM, of *Riig.*
Directions for Health, Naturall and Artificiall : . . . The sixth Edition reuised by the Author. Whereunto is annexed Two Treatises of approued Medicines. . . . London, Printed by Iohn Beale for Francis Williams, . . . 1626. 4°, A—Ee in fours, A 1 and Ee 4 blank. Dedicated to William, Earl of Pembroke.

> The two treatises are on the eyesight by Dr. Baily, &c.

VERGIL, POLYDORE, of *Urbino.*
Polydori Vergilii Vrbinatis Anglicæ Historiæ Libri Vigintiseptem Ab ipso autore postremum iam recogniti, ad'q; amussim, salua tamen historiæ ueritate, expoliti. . . . Basileæ, Anno M. D. LVI. Folio.

VIOLET, THOMAS.
An Appeal to Cæsar : Wherein Gold and Silver is Proved to be the Kings Majesties Royal Commodity. Which by the Lawes of the Kingdom, no Person of what Degree soever, but the Kings Majestie, and his Privy Councel, can give Licence to transport either Gold or Silver to any

Person, after it is Landed in any part of the Kingdome of England . . . London, Printed in the Year 1660. 4", A—H in fours, H 3-4 blank.

W. J.
Youths Safety : Or, Advice to the Younger Sort, of either Sex. More valuable than Gold. Laying open the Wicked Practices of the Town-Shifts, Sharpers, Sharks, Beau's, Sweeteners, Rakes, Intreaging Town-Jilts, to Cheat, Ruin and Disgrace Gentlemen, Shop-keepers, Apprentices, Gentlewomen, Servant-Maids, &c. By J. W. Sold by E. Whitlock, near Stationers-Hall, 1698. Price 6d. 8". B—H in sixes, and the title-page. *B. M.*

WALKER, WILLIAM, *S.T.B.*
Idiomatologia Anglo-Latina, Sive Dictionarium Idiomaticum Anglo-Latinum : . . . Quinta Editio . . . Londini, Typis W. Horton, Impensis T. Sawbridg, . . . 1690. 12", A—Zz in sixes.

WARD, EDWARD.
On the Death of the Late Lieutenant General Talmach, A Poem. Humbly Dedicated to her Grace the Dutchess of Lauderdale. By E. Ward, Gent. London, Printed for, an'l Sold by James Blackwel, at Bernards-Inn-Gate, Holbourn, 1694. Folio, 2 leaves.

WARE, SIR JAMES.
De Præsulibus Hiberniæ, Commentarius. A Prima Gentis Hiberniæ ad Fidem Christianam Conversione, Ad Nostra usque Tempora . . . Dvblinii, Typis Johannis Crook, . . . MDCLXV. Folio. Title, to the Reader, and Epistle to Ware by Jo. Parry, 6 leaves : A—4 B, 2 leaves each.

WARREN, ALBERTUS, *Gentleman.*
The Royalist Reform'd Or Considerations of Advice,
To { Gentlemen, Divines, Lawyers.
Digested into three Chapters. Wherein their former mistakes are examined, and their duties of obedience, unto the present Authority, succinctly held forth as rational, and necessary. . . . London, Printed by Francis Leach for George Thompson, 1650, . . . 4°. Title and to the Reader, 2 leaves : B—G 2 in fours. *B. M.*

WESTMINSTER.
The Westminster Combat. A broadside in verse.

WHIGS AND WHIGGISM.

A Loyal Satyr against Whiggism. London, Printed for C. B. and are to be sold by W. Davis, 1682. Folio, 2 leaves. In verse.

WHITTINTON, ROBERT, *of Lichfield, Grammarian.*

Roberti Whittintoni lichfeldiensis Editio. [This is on a ribbon over the large device.] Secunda pars grammatices. De sillaba et eius quantitate. De prima media & vltima cognoscenda . . . [Col.] Finis quantitatis sillabarū. 4°. A, 8 : B, 4 : C, 8 : D, 4 : E, 8 : F, 6 : G, 8.

> Putticks, Dec. 15, 1886, No. 426.

WIFE.

A Pleasant / conceited Comedie, where/in is shewed, how a man / may choose a good wife / from a bad. / As it hath beene sundry times / acted by the Earle of Wor-/cesters seruants. / London, / Printed for Mathew Law, and are to be sold at / his shop in Paules Church-yard, neere vnto S. / Augustines gate, at the signe of / the Foxe. / 1608. 4°, A—L 2 in fours.

> The last figure of the date in this copy has been partly erased; but it is clearly an 8.

WILCOCKE, JAMES, *Vicar of Goudhurst in Kent.*

The True English Protestants Apology, Against the blacke-mouth'd Obloquie of Ignorance and Innovation. . . . London, Printed by I. R. 1642. 4°, A—G in fours. Dedicated to his parishioners.

WILLIAM OF ORANGE, *King of Great Britain* (1688-1702).

A Rare a Show : Or, Englands Betrayers Expos'd, In a Catalogue of the several Persons exempted by his Highness the Prince of Orange ; to be brought to Account, before the next ensuing Parliament. Printed in the Year, 1688. A folio leaf.

A Proclamation. [In coeval MS. is added : ỹ 13ᵗʰ February 168⅞.] London : Printed for James Partridge. . . . A broadside.

The Speech of Mʳ Cox, Envoy Extraordinary from the King of Great Britain, To the Representatives of the Swiss Cantons. Licens'd March 14. 16⅗⅘. London : Printed for Richard Baldwin, near the Black Bull in the Old-Bailey. A broadside.

An Historical Romance of the Wars, between the Mighty Giant Gallieno, and the Great Knight Nasonius, and His Associates.

—— *ridentem dicere cerum Quis vetat !*

Doublin : Printed in the Year 1694. 4°, A—L in fours.

The Plot. A Poem. [Col.] London, Printed for E. Whitlock, near Stationers-Hall. 1696. 4°, 2 leaves.

A True Copy of the Papers Delivered by Mʳ Robt. Chernocke, Mʳ Ed. King, Mʳ Th. Key, to the Sheriffs of London and Middlesex, at Tyburn, the Place of Execution, March 18ᵗʰ 169⅔. London : Printed for William Rogers, . . . 1696. A folio leaf.

WILSON, THOMAS, *LL.D.*

A Discovrse vpon vsurie, by waie of Dialogue and oracions, . . . Imprinted at London by Roger Warde, dwelling neere Holborne Conduit, at the signe of the Talbot. 1584. 8°, B—Dd 4 in eights, besides two sheets of eight with the title and preliminaries.

WIND.

The Windie Yeare. Shewing Many strange Accidents that happened, both on the Land, and at Sea, by reason of the winde and weather. With A particular relation of that which happened at Great Chart in Kent. And Also how a Woman was found in the water, with a sucking Child at her brest, with the nipple in it[s] mouth, both drowned ; with many other lamentable things worthy to be read, and remembered. London. Printed by G. Eld for Arthur Iohnson, dwelling at the signe of the white Horse in Pauls Church-yard neere the great North-dore. 1613. 4°, black letter, A—D in fours, A 1 and D 4 blank. *B. M.*

The last terrible Tempestious windes and weather. Truely Relating many Lamentable Ship-wracks, with drowning of many people, on the Coasts of England, Scotland, France and Ireland : with the Iles of Wight, Garsey & Iarsey. Shewing also, many great misfortunes, that haue lately hapned on Land, by reason of the winde and rayne, in other places of this Kingdome. Imprinted at London for Ios : Hunt and are to be sold by Iohn Wright, 1613. 4°, black letter. With a large descriptive cut on the title. Title-page and to the Reader, 2 leaves : A (misprinted B)—D 2 in fours. *B. M.*

The Wonders of this windie winter. By terrible storms and tempests, to the losse of liues and goods of many thousands of men, women and children. The like by Sea and Land, hath not beene seene, nor heard of in this age of the World. London. Imprinted by G. Eld for Iohn Wright, and are to bee sold at his Shop neere Christ-Church-dore. 1613. 4°, black letter, A—C in fours, A 1 and C 4 blank. With a large cut on the title. *B. M.*

> These three pieces, as well as that registered under PET (EDMOND), are very curious in themselves, and also in connection with Shakespear's *Tempest.*

WINDSORE, MILES.

Academiarvm Qvæ aliqvando fvere et hodie sunt in Europa, Catalogus & enumeratio breuis. Londini Excudebant Georgivs Bishop & Radvlphvs Newberie. An. Dom. 1590. 4°, A—H 2 in fours. Dedicated to Sir C. Hatton from Oxford, 15 May, 1590.

> This appears to be an enlargement of the essay published as a broadside in 1586. See *Handbook*, 1867, v. ACADEMIES.
>
> Thorpe's Cat. for 1842, £1, 11s. 6d. The volume ends with a Latin poem, entitled *Chronographia, sive Origo Collegiarum Oxoniensis Academiæ*, chiefly written by T. Neal, of New College.

WITHER, GEORGE.

A Preparation to the Psalter. By George Wyther, Gent. London, Printed by Ni-

cholas Okes. 1619. [Col.] London Imprinted by Nicholas Okes. 1619. Small folio. Title within a woodcut compartment and following blank, 2 leaves : A—N in sixes : o, 2 leaves.

WOMEN.

The vertuous scholehous of vngracious women. A godly dialogue or communication of two Systers, The one a good and vertuous wedowe, oute of the land of Meissen, The other, a curst vngracious, froward and brawlinge woman, oute of the mountaynes. To the honour and prayse of all good women. And to the rebuke and instruccion of suche as be vnpacient. [London, Walter Lynne, about 1550.] 8°, A—N 4 in eights, N 4 having had doubtless the colophon. Black letter. In prose. *B. M.*

> This copy wants N 4. Prefixed is an address by the printer to the reader. On the title and A 3 *verso* is a woodcut of the two sisters, Justina the good woman and Serapia the bad one, conversing.

Love given o're : Or, A Satyr against the Pride, Lust, and Inconstancy, &c. of Woman. London, Printed for R. Bentley, and J. Tonson. 1685. 4°, A—B in fours.

A SELECT LIST

OF

𝕸orks or 𝕰ditions

BY

WILLIAM CAREW HAZLITT

OF THE INNER TEMPLE

CHRONOLOGICALLY ARRANGED

1860—1886.

1. **History of the Venetian Republic**; Its Rise, its Greatness, and its Civilization. With Maps and Illustrations. 4 vols. 8vo. *Smith, Elder & Co.* 1860.
   A new edition, entirely recast, with important additions, in 3 vols. crown 8vo, is in readiness for the press.

2. **Old English Jest-Books, 1525-1639.** Edited with Introductions and Notes. *Facsimiles.* 3 vols. 12mo. 1864.

3. **Remains of the Early Popular Poetry of England.** With Introductions and Notes. 4 vols. 12mo. *Woodcuts.* 1864-66.

4. **Handbook to the Early Popular, Poetical, and Dramatic Literature** of Great Britain. Demy 8vo. 1867. Pp. 714 in two columns.

5. **Bibliographical Collections and Notes.** 1867-76. Medium 8vo. 1876.
   This volume comprises a full description of about 6000 Early English books from the books themselves. It is a sequel and companion to No. 4. See also No. 6 *infrà*.

6. **Bibliographical Collections and Notes.** SECOND SERIES. 1876-82. Medium 8vo. 1882.
   Uniform with First Series. About 10,000 titles on the same principle as before.
   " Mr. W. C. Hazlitt's second series of *Bibliographical Collections and Notes* (Quaritch) is the result of many years' searches among rare books, tracts, ballads, and broadsides by a man whose specialty is bibliography, and who has thus produced a volume of high value. If any one will read through the fifty-four closely printed columns relating to Charles I., or the ten and a-half columns given to ' London ' from 1541 to 1794, and recollect that these are only a supplement to twelve columns in Hazlitt's *Handbook* and five and a-half in his first *Collections*, he will get an idea of the work involved in this book. Other like entries are ' James I.,' ' Ireland,' ' France,' ' England,' ' Elizabeth,' ' Scotland ' (which has twenty-one and a-half columns), and so on. As to the curiosity and rarity of the works that Mr. Hazlitt has catalogued, any one who has been for even twenty or thirty years among old books will acknowledge that the strangers to him are far more numerous than the acquaintances and friends. This second series of *Collections* will add to Mr. Hazlitt's well-earned reputation as a bibliographer, and should be in every real library through the English-speaking world. The only thing we desiderate in it is more of his welcome marks and names, B.M., Britwell, Lambeth, &c., to show where all the books approaching rarity are. The service that these have done in Mr. Hazlitt's former books to editors for the Early-English Text, New Shakspere, Spenser, Hunterian, and other societies, has been so great that we hope he will always say where he has seen the rare books that he makes entries of."—*Academy*, August 26, 1882.

7. **Bibliographical Collections and Notes.** A THIRD AND FINAL SERIES. 1886. 8vo.
   Uniform with the First and Second Series. This volume contains upwards of 3000 articles. All three are now on sale by Mr. Quaritch.

8. **Memoirs of William Hazlitt.** With Portions of his Correspondence. *Portraits after miniatures by John Hazlitt.* 2 vols. 8vo. 1867.
   During the last twenty years the Author has been indefatigable in collecting additional information for the *Life of Hazlitt*, 1867, in correcting errors, and in securing all the unpublished letters which have come into the market, some of great interest, with a view to a new and improved edition.

9. **Inedited Tracts.** Illustrating the Manners, Opinions, and Occupations of Englishmen during the 16th and 17th Centuries. 1586-1618. With an Introduction and Notes. *Facsimiles.* 4to. 1868.

*

10. **The Works of Charles Lamb.** Now first collected, and entirely rearranged. With Notes. 4 vols. 8vo. *E. Moxon & Co.* 1868-69.

11. **Letters of Charles Lamb.** With some Account of the Writer, his Friends and Correspondents, and Explanatory Notes. By the late Sir Thomas Noon Talfourd, D.C.L., one of his Executors. An entirely new edition, carefully revised and greatly enlarged by W. Carew Hazlitt. 2 vols. 1886. Post 8vo.

11a. **Mary and Charles Lamb.** New Facts and Inedited Remains. 8vo. *Woodcuts and Facsimiles.* 1874.
The groundwork of this volume was an Essay by the writer in *Macmillan's Magazine.*

12. **English Proverbs and Proverbial Phrases.** Arranged alphabetically and annotated. Medium 8vo. 1869. Second Edition, corrected and greatly enlarged, crown 8vo. 1882.

13. **Narrative of the Journey of an Irish Gentleman through England** in 1751. From a MS. With Notes. 8vo. 1869.

14. **The English Drama and Stage, under the Tudor and Stuart Princes.** 1547-1664. With an Introduction and Notes. 4to. 1869.
A series of reprinted Documents and Treatises.

15. **Popular Antiquities of Great Britain.** I. The Calendar. II. Customs and Ceremonies. III. Superstitions. 3 vols. Medium 8vo. 1870.
Brand's *Popular Antiquities*, by Ellis, 1813, taken to pieces, recast, and enormously augmented.

16. **Inedited Poetical Miscellanies.** 1584-1700. Thick 8vo. With Notes and Facsimiles. 50 copies privately printed. 1870.

17. **Warton's History of English Poetry.** An entirely new edition, with Notes by Sir F. Madden, T. Wright, F. J. Furnivall, R. Morris, and others, and by the Editor. 4 vols. Medium 8vo. 1871.

18. **The Feudal Period.** Illustrated by a Series of Tales (from Le Grand). 12mo. 1874.

19. **Prefaces, Dedications, and Epistles.** Prefixed to Early English Books. 1540-1701. 8vo. 1874.
50 copies privately printed.

20. **Blount's Jocular Tenures.** Tenures of Land and Customs of Manors. Originally published by Thomas Blount of the Inner Temple in 1679. An entirely new and greatly enlarged edition by W. Carew Hazlitt, of that Ilk. Medium 8vo. 1874.

21. **Dodsley's Select Collection of Old Plays.** A new edition, greatly enlarged, corrected throughout, and entirely rearranged. With a Glossary by Dr. Richard Morris. 15 vols. 8vo. 1874-76.

22. **Fairy Tales, Legends, and Romances.** Illustrating Shakespear and other Early English Writers. 12mo. 1875.

23. **Shakespear's Library:** A Collection of the Novels, Plays, and other Material supposed to have been used by Shakespear. An entirely new edition. 6 vols. 12mo. 1875.

24. **Fugitive Tracts (written in verse) which illustrate the Condition** of Religious and Political Feeling in England, and the State of Society there, during two centuries. 1493-1700. 2 vols. 4to. 50 copies privately printed. 1875.

25. **Poetical Recreations.** By W. C. Hazlitt. 50 copies printed. 12mo. 1877.
A new edition, revised and very greatly enlarged, is in preparation.

26. **The Baron's Daughter.** A Ballad. 75 copies printed. 4to. 1877.

27. **The Essays of Montaigne.** Translated by C. Cotton. An entirely new edition, collated with the best French text. With a Memoir, and all the extant Letters. *Portrait and Illustrations.* 3 vols. 8vo. 1877.
The only library edition.

28. **Catalogue of the Huth Library.** [English portion.] 5 vols. Large 8vo. 1880. 200 copies printed.

29. **Offspring of Thought in Solitude.** Modern Essays. 1884. 8vo, pp. 384.
Some of these Papers were originally contributed to *All the Year Round*, &c.

30. **Old Cookery Books and Ancient Cuisine.** 12mo. 1886.

31. **An Address to the Electors of Mid-Surrey, among whom I live.** In Rejoinder to Mr. Gladstone's Manifesto. 1886. 8vo, pp. 32.
" Who would not grieve, if such a man there be?
Who would not weep, if Atticus were he?"—POPE.